Macworld®
ClarisWorks® Office Bible

Macworld®
ClarisWorks®
Office Bible

Steven A. Schwartz

IDG Books Worldwide, Inc.
An International Data Group Company

Foster City, CA ◆ Chicago, IL ◆ Indianapolis, IN ◆ Southlake, TX

Macworld® ClarisWorks® Office Bible

Published by
IDG Books Worldwide, Inc.
An International Data Group Company
919 E. Hillsdale Blvd., Suite 400
Foster City, CA 94404
www.idgbooks.com (IDG Books Worldwide Web site)

Library of Congress Catalog Card No.: 97-73224

ISBN: 0-7645-4016-5

Printed in the United States of America

10 9 8 7 6 5 4 3 2 1

IDD/QR/RS/ZX/FC

Distributed in the United States by IDG Books Worldwide, Inc.

Distributed by Macmillan Canada for Canada; by Transworld Publishers Limited in the United Kingdom; by IDG Norge Books for Norway; by IDG Sweden Books for Sweden; by Woodslane Pty. Ltd. for Australia; by Woodslane Enterprises Ltd. for New Zealand; by Longman Singapore Publishers Ltd. for Singapore, Malaysia, Thailand, and Indonesia; by Simron Pty. Ltd. for South Africa; by Toppan Company Ltd. for Japan; by Distribuidora Cuspide for Argentina; by Livraria Cultura for Brazil; by Ediciencia S.A. for Ecuador; by Addison-Wesley Publishing Company for Korea; by Ediciones ZETA S.C.R. Ltda. for Peru; by WS Computer Publishing Corporation, Inc., for the Philippines; by Unalis Corporation for Taiwan; by Contemporanea de Ediciones for Venezuela; by Computer Book & Magazine Store for Puerto Rico; by Express Computer Distributors for the Caribbean and West Indies. Authorized Sales Agent: Anthony Rudkin Associates for the Middle East and North Africa.

For general information on IDG Books Worldwide's books in the U.S., please call our Consumer Customer Service department at 800-762-2974. For reseller information, including discounts and premium sales, please call our Reseller Customer Service department at 800-434-3422.

For information on where to purchase IDG Books Worldwide's books outside the U.S., please contact our International Sales department at 415-655-3200 or fax 415-655-3295.

For information on foreign language translations, please contact our Foreign & Subsidiary Rights department at 415-655-3021 or fax 415-655-3281.

For sales inquiries and special prices for bulk quantities, please contact our Sales department at 415-655-3200 or write to the address above.

For information on using IDG Books Worldwide's books in the classroom or for ordering examination copies, please contact our Educational Sales department at 800-434-2086 or fax 817-251-8174.

For press review copies, author interviews, or other publicity information, please contact our Public Relations department at 415-655-3000 or fax 415-655-3299.

For authorization to photocopy items for corporate, personal, or educational use, please contact Copyright Clearance Center, 222 Rosewood Drive, Danvers, MA 01923, or fax 508-750-4470.

ABOUT IDG BOOKS WORLDWIDE

Welcome to the world of IDG Books Worldwide.

IDG Books Worldwide, Inc., is a subsidiary of International Data Group, the world's largest publisher of computer-related information and the leading global provider of information services on information technology. IDG was founded more than 25 years ago and now employs more than 8,500 people worldwide. IDG publishes more than 275 computer publications in over 75 countries (see listing below). More than 60 million people read one or more IDG publications each month.

Launched in 1990, IDG Books Worldwide is today the #1 publisher of best-selling computer books in the United States. We are proud to have received eight awards from the Computer Press Association in recognition of editorial excellence and three from *Computer Currents'* First Annual Readers' Choice Awards. Our best-selling *...For Dummies*® series has more than 30 million copies in print with translations in 30 languages. IDG Books Worldwide, through a joint venture with IDG's Hi-Tech Beijing, became the first U.S. publisher to publish a computer book in the People's Republic of China. In record time, IDG Books Worldwide has become the first choice for millions of readers around the world who want to learn how to better manage their businesses.

Our mission is simple: Every one of our books is designed to bring extra value and skill-building instructions to the reader. Our books are written by experts who understand and care about our readers. The knowledge base of our editorial staff comes from years of experience in publishing, education, and journalism — experience we use to produce books for the '90s. In short, we care about books, so we attract the best people. We devote special attention to details such as audience, interior design, use of icons, and illustrations. And because we use an efficient process of authoring, editing, and desktop publishing our books electronically, we can spend more time ensuring superior content and spend less time on the technicalities of making books.

You can count on our commitment to deliver high-quality books at competitive prices on topics you want to read about. At IDG Books Worldwide, we continue in the IDG tradition of delivering quality for more than 25 years. You'll find no better book on a subject than one from IDG Books Worldwide.

John J. Kilcullen
John Kilcullen
CEO
IDG Books Worldwide, Inc.

Steven Berkowitz
Steven Berkowitz
President and Publisher
IDG Books Worldwide, Inc.

Eighth Annual
Computer Press
Awards ≥1992

Ninth Annual
Computer Press
Awards ≥1993

Tenth Annual
Computer Press
Awards ≥1994

Eleventh Annual
Computer Press
Awards ≥1995

Credits

Acquisitions Editor
Andy Cummings

Development Editor
Amy Thomas

Technical Editor
Dennis Cohen

Copy Editor
Suki Gear

Production Coordinator
Susan Parini

Quality Control Specialist
Mark Schumann

Graphics and Production Specialists
Doris Figgemeier
Jude Levinson
Maureen Moore
Christopher Pimentel
Mark Schumann
Trevor Wilson
Elsie Yim

Cover Design
Murder By Design

Proofreader
Laura L. Bowman

Indexer
James Minkin

About the Author

Dr. Steven Schwartz has been a computer-industry writer for 20 years and has written more than 30 books about popular business software, the Internet, and games. Formerly a technical support director and magazine editor, Steven is an expert at explaining computer techniques in a simple, straightforward manner. He currently writes for *Macworld* magazine.

To Sheldon and Barbara Schwartz, the best parents anyone could wish for

Preface

About This Book

The *Macworld ClarisWorks Office Bible* is a different kind of computer book. First, it's not a manual. Many people don't like computer manuals — perhaps because they feel obligated to read a manual from cover to cover, or perhaps because manuals are designed to explain how features work rather than how to make a program work for you. The *Macworld ClarisWorks Office Bible* is not a book you *have* to read. It's a book you'll *want* to read — because it provides easy-to-find, easy-to-understand explanations of many common tasks for which you bought ClarisWorks in the first place. When you want to know how to use a particular program feature, you can use the table of contents or the index to identify the section of the book you need to read.

Second, unlike many computer books, this one is *task oriented.* Most people don't buy computer books because they want to become experts with a particular piece of software. Instead, most people have a task they want to accomplish. In addition to the step-by-step explanations of normal ClarisWorks procedures, the book also provides many worked-through task examples. Rather than spend your time reinventing the wheel, you can simply follow the numbered steps to accomplish many common business- and home-computing tasks.

Finally, the philosophy of this book — as well as the other books in the *Macworld Bible* series — is that you don't want or need a handful of books on a computer program; one should suffice. The *Macworld ClarisWorks Office Bible* is an all-in-one book. Rarely will you be referred to your manual or ClarisWorks Help. You can find almost anything you want to know about ClarisWorks in this book.

ClarisWorks Office and ClarisWorks 5.0 are the same program. The only difference between ClarisWorks Office and ClarisWorks 5.0 is the former includes several add-on programs — including Claris Home Page Lite, Netscape Navigator, and a series of business templates.

What Is ClarisWorks?

ClarisWorks belongs to a class of programs known as *integrated software*. The idea behind integrated software is that — within a single box — you acquire a core set of programs that fulfill all your basic computing needs. The typical program components, or *modules*, are word processing, spreadsheet, database, graphics, and telecommunications. And the modules function together as a cohesive unit — more or less. I say "more or less" because the early integrated software packages (as well as many of the current ones) were often only a collection of programs. The programs frequently had little in common beyond being in the same box. Often there was no way to share data among the modules, or there were significant differences in the command structure in the different modules. Therefore, learning how to use one module may have taught you nothing about using the other modules.

As a class of software, integrated software was viewed with disdain by computing purists for several reasons. The modules were often stripped down to bare-bones programs in order to squeeze the entire package into a reasonable amount of memory. Big-time features — such as a spelling checker, thesaurus, character and paragraph styles, and advanced searching and sorting — were routinely missing. Thus, many users felt (rightfully so) that the integrated modules couldn't hold a candle to full-featured, stand-alone programs.

Microsoft Works was the first major integrated package for the Macintosh. The Mac's native support for cut-and-paste made it relatively easy to merge data from different types of documents, enabling you to paste a graphic into a word processing file, for example. Although integration was considerably better than in the early programs, each Works module was essentially a stand-alone tool. To create a new spreadsheet for an annual report, you had to work in both the spreadsheet and word processing modules and then cut and paste the spreadsheet into the final document.

Why Choose ClarisWorks?

ClarisWorks has carried the integration concept forward to the next logical step. ClarisWorks has separate components, but you can use features of the different components no matter what type of document you're currently working on. For example, although a word processing document is primarily composed of words, you can add a spreadsheet section to the document simply by selecting the spreadsheet tool and then drawing a frame, as shown in Figure Preface-1.

Spreadsheet frame

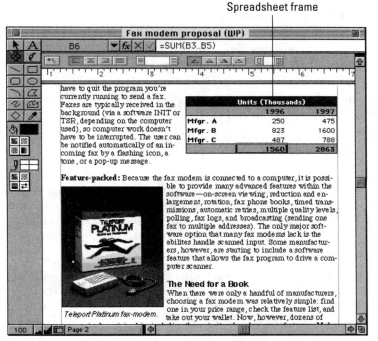

Figure Preface-1: A spreadsheet frame within a word processing document

While you are working in the spreadsheet frame, the menu bar, menu commands, and button bar change and become relevant to spreadsheets. If you click any part of the word processing text, the menus and button bar become appropriate for word processing. This tight integration among components makes ClarisWorks significantly easier and more convenient to use than its competitors. In fact, Claris prefers that the ClarisWorks components be referred to as *environments* — rather than modules — to emphasize the high level of integration among the different parts of the program.

ClarisWorks has also made great strides toward including the "power features" that have traditionally been absent from integrated programs. For example:

+ The word processor includes a spelling checker, thesaurus, and outliner, as well as support for custom text and paragraph styles.

+ The paint environment offers gradients, and the draw environment has advanced drawing tools.

✦ The spreadsheet includes charts, text wrap within cells, cell shading, and variable row heights and column widths, and it supports multiple fonts per worksheet.

✦ The database offers pop-up menu, value list, check box, radio button, and multimedia fields. It also enables you to create multiple custom layouts for each database file.

✦ The communications environment provides standard file transfer protocols and support for the Communications toolbox.

✦ The built-in macro recorder enables you to automate common or repetitive tasks with ease.

ClarisWorks provides solid integration with other programs, too. Numerous import and export filters included with ClarisWorks enable ClarisWorks to exchange data with popular business programs, such as Microsoft Office. And with the System 7 feature called Publish & Subscribe, you can easily embed ClarisWorks documents (or a portion of a document, such as a spreadsheet chart) in documents created in other programs, and vice versa.

Finally, if you use your Mac on the Internet and have (or would like to have) your own home page on the World Wide Web, you'll find the new and enhanced Internet features extremely useful.

Who Should Use This Book

The *Macworld ClarisWorks Office Bible* is for anyone who uses ClarisWorks Office or ClarisWorks 5.0:

✦ If you're a beginning ClarisWorks user, detailed steps help you get up to speed quickly with common (and not-so-common) ClarisWorks features and procedures.

✦ If you're an intermediate or advanced ClarisWorks user — someone who wants only the ClarisWorks essentials but doesn't need much hand holding — the tips and insights in each chapter will help you get the most from ClarisWorks. You'll find Quick Tips sections, sidebars, and icons indicating the newest ClarisWorks features.

How This Book Is Organized

The *Macworld ClarisWorks Office Bible* is made up of parts, chapters, and sections.

The Parts

This book is divided into six parts.

Part I: The Basics

This is a gentle introduction to performing basic ClarisWorks procedures, such as opening and saving documents, printing, and managing windows. This part also lists the major features and enhancements that were introduced in the various releases of ClarisWorks.

Part II: Using the ClarisWorks Environments

This part explains the workings of each of the six major ClarisWorks components (word processing, spreadsheet, database, draw, paint, and communications).

Part III: Integrating the ClarisWorks Environments

This part offers suggestions and examples for using elements of two or more environments in the same document (generating a mail merge and using spreadsheet frames to create word processing tables, for example).

Part IV: Mastering ClarisWorks

This part covers material that helps you make more productive use of ClarisWorks. It isn't essential to learn about these features immediately, but you will want to tackle them after you're comfortable with the ClarisWorks basics.

Part V: Using the ClarisWorks Office Add-Ons

This part discusses the components that are only available to ClarisWorks Office users. (If you purchased the upgrade to ClarisWorks 5.0 rather than the full ClarisWorks Office, the material in this chapter does not apply to you.) Part V explains the purpose of the add-on components, including the use of Claris Home Page Lite for creating Web pages and using Netscape Navigator to browse the World Wide Web.

Part VI: Appendixes

This part includes two appendixes to aid you in your work:

+ *Appendix A* lists the many keyboard shortcuts in ClarisWorks. If you're new to using a mouse or don't want to take your hands off the keyboard, you'll want to check out this appendix.

+ *Appendix B* is a complete reference to the spreadsheet and database functions that are provided in ClarisWorks 5.0.

The Chapters

Each chapter of this book is organized around a major task you're likely to perform in ClarisWorks, such as working with the word processor, setting preferences, recording macros, and so on. When you need to perform a particular ClarisWorks task, scan the table of contents to locate the chapter that addresses your need.

The Sections

Each chapter contains the following sections:

- ✦ *In This Chapter* provides a list of topics covered in the chapter.

- ✦ *Overview* provides an introduction to the chapter.

- ✦ *Steps* appear throughout each chapter. Each Steps section spells out the specific instructions necessary to accomplish a particular task.

- ✦ *Summary* lists the main points covered in the chapter. You can turn to the Summary section of any chapter to see whether it contains the information you need at the moment.

In addition to these sections, many of the chapters include the following:

- ✦ *Quick Tips* give useful tips about additional tasks you can perform in the ClarisWorks environment or the subject being discussed. You can also turn to this section for ideas on how to use the features or the environment better.

- ✦ *Moving On Up* provides you with information on upgrading from a ClarisWorks environment to a more advanced program.

Icons Used in This Book

Four icons are used in this book to highlight important information, new features, and ancillary material that may interest you:

The New to Version 5 icon marks discussions of features that are found only in ClarisWorks Office/5.0 and not in earlier versions of the program (ClarisWorks 1.0–4.0).

The Tip icon offers an insight into the feature or task being discussed, in many cases suggesting better or easier ways to accomplish it.

The Note icon identifies information and issues regarding a feature or topic that might be of interest to you.

The Caution icon warns you about potentially dangerous situations — particularly those in which data may be lost.

How to Use This Book

I won't tell you how to read this book. Reading and learning styles are all very personal. When I get a new computer program, I frequently read the manual from cover to cover before even installing the software. Of course, I'll be flattered if you read the *Macworld ClarisWorks Office Bible* the same way, but I'll be surprised.

This book is written as a reference to "all things ClarisWorks." When you want to learn about the database environment, there's a specific chapter to which you can turn. If you just need to know how to use the spelling checker, you can flip to the table of contents or the index and find the pages where the spelling checker is discussed. Most procedures are explained in a step-by-step fashion, so you can quickly accomplish even the most complex tasks. You can read this book as you would a Stephen King novel (with fewer surprises, and less snappy dialog and bloodletting), read just the chapters that interest you, or use the book as a quick reference for when you need to learn about a particular feature or procedure.

For those who prefer a little more direction than "whatever works for you," I've included some guidelines in the following sections — arranged according to your level of ClarisWorks experience.

I do have one general suggestion: *If at all possible, read this book with ClarisWorks on screen.* Sure, you can read about editing a user dictionary for the spelling checker while relaxing in the tub, but — unless you have exceptional recall — what you read will be more meaningful if you're sitting in front of the computer.

For the New ClarisWorks User

Chapter 1 is a must-read for every ClarisWorks user. Many ClarisWorks tasks, such as arranging windows and printing, are not specific to any one environment. Rather than discuss them again in each of the environment chapters, I have included these procedures and features only in Chapter 1.

From that point on, you should pick a ClarisWorks environment — the word processor is a good place to start — and, with book in hand, work through the appropriate chapter in Part II. Each chapter in Part II explains the fundamentals for a single ClarisWorks environment. The really advanced stuff is in Part III, Part IV, and Part V. Although you'll eventually want to check out the material in those parts, too, you'll note that I've purposely separated the advanced matters from the basics to keep new users from being overwhelmed.

Although this book discusses many of the basic concepts and procedures necessary for the beginning user to start working productively with ClarisWorks, it is not a substitute for the documentation that came with your Mac. As you work on the desktop and begin experimenting with ClarisWorks, you're bound to encounter additional Mac issues. When that happens — and it will — it's time to drag out the manuals for your Macintosh, peripherals (printers, modems, and so on), and system software, and see what you've missed. After you fill in the gaps in your Mac education, you'll feel more confident and comfortable tackling ClarisWorks and any other programs you eventually purchase.

For Those Who Have Upgraded from a Previous Version of ClarisWorks

If you're an experienced ClarisWorks 2.0, 2.1, 3.0, or 4.0 user, the best place for you to start is Chapter 2. This chapter is a quick guide to the new features you need to learn in ClarisWorks Office/5.0, and it directs you to the chapters in which the features are discussed.

Before you jump ahead, however, be sure to skim at least through Chapter 1. Although the basics of using the program haven't changed drastically, you need to be familiar with some new procedures and options.

About System Software Versions

The user interface in System 7.6 and OS 8 has a decidedly different look from that of earlier system software versions (see Figure Preface-2). In OS 8, for example, most elements have a 3D look. And document and folder windows contain a WindowShade box in the upper-right corner that — when clicked — reduces the window to just its title bar.

The majority of the screen shots in this book were created on a Mac running system software 7.5.5. If you are running a later version of system software, your screen may look somewhat different. You should also note that a few features and

operations work differently in OS 8. Where relevant, these differences are
described in the text.

Figure Preface-2: The About This Macintosh window in System 7.5.5 (top)
and About This Computer window in OS 8 (bottom) present the same
information but look very different.

Acknowledgments

I am grateful to the many people who worked so hard and offered their support for this new edition of the book, including Andrew Cummings, Amy Thomas, and Suki Gear, the talented team at IDG Books Worldwide who guided this project from beginning to end; Dennis Cohen, one of the most thorough, conscientious technical editors I know; and my good friend and agent, Matt Wagner of Waterside Productions.

Contents at a Glance

· ·

Contents

Chapter 4: The Spreadsheet Environment 137

Part VI: Appendixes   625

The Basics

ClarisWorks Essentials

Overview

Before you leap into ClarisWorks, you need to get some basics
under your belt. If you're new to the Mac, you'll find this
chapter particularly helpful. Many of the procedures it
describes — such as starting the program, opening and
saving documents, and printing — are applicable to almost
any Mac program. Even if you consider yourself an
experienced Mac user, you can benefit from at least skimming
through this chapter. You may pick up a time-saving tip or
two that improves your productivity with ClarisWorks.

Launching ClarisWorks

As with most Macintosh programs, you can launch
ClarisWorks in several ways. From the desktop, shown in
Figure 1-1, you have two methods from which to choose:

✦ Double-click the ClarisWorks 5.0 program icon.

✦ Click the ClarisWorks 5.0 program icon to select it and
then choose Open from the File menu (or press ⌘-O).

Apple menu   Menus   Window

Application Help menu
Balloon Help menu

Program   Folders   Files   Desktop printer   Disk icons   Trash

The desktop shows icons for all mounted disks (both hard disks and floppy disks), the Trash, windows for open drives and folders, and icons for folders, programs, and data files.

The Balloon Help icon shown in Figure 1-1 is the icon for System 7.5 and 7.6. If you have System 7.0 or System 7.1, this icon is displayed as a cartoon balloon. In Mac OS 8, a separate Help menu is displayed immediately to the right of normal program menus, as shown in Figure 1-1b.

If you want to load a document (or perhaps several) as you launch ClarisWorks, you can use one of the following methods:

✦ Double-click a ClarisWorks document icon.

✦ Select several ClarisWorks document icons (by Shift-clicking the icons or by drawing a selection rectangle around them), and then choose Open from the File menu (or press ⌘-O).

Whether you open documents from the desktop or load them from within ClarisWorks, you can open as many documents as memory allows.

Creating a New Document

Each time you launch ClarisWorks, the program loads, and the New Document dialog box automatically opens so you can create a new document.

This is how the program works when you first install it. If you prefer, you can change ClarisWorks's start-up action so it displays an Open file dialog box (so you can open an existing file) or no dialog box at all. (To change the start-up action, see Chapter 11.)

Steps: Creating a New Document at Start-Up

1. Load ClarisWorks. The New Document dialog box (shown in Figure 1-2) appears. By default, the Create New Document radio button is selected.

If you have changed the *On startup, show* setting in the Preferences dialog box, as described in Chapter 11, you may see the Open file dialog box or no dialog box at all. In that case, you must choose New from the File menu to make the New Document dialog box appear.

2. To start with a blank document from any of the six ClarisWorks environments, select a document type from the scrolling list, and click OK.

Select a document type from this list

Figure 1-2: The New Document dialog box

New documents can also be based on *stationery files* (templates), or they can be created for you by some of the ClarisWorks Assistants.

Steps: Creating a New Document Using a Stationery File or an Assistant

1. Click the Use Assistant or Stationery radio button, as shown in Figure 1-3.

2. Select All Assistants, All Stationery, or a specific class of Assistants or Stationery from the Category pop-up menu.

3. Choose a document from the scrolling list.

4. Click OK.

Select a template or Assistant from this list

```
┌─────────────────────── New Document ───────────────────────┐
│  CLARIS          ClarisWorks 5.0                            │
│                                                             │
│  Category:  [  All Stationery        ▼]                     │
│  ┌─────────────────────────────────┐                       │
│  │ A ClarisWorks 4.0 Stationery Docu▲│                      │
│  │ 🖈 Annual Report                  │  ○ Create New Document │
│  │ 🖈 Border                          │                      │
│  │ 🖈 Business Cards                  │  ◉ Use Assistant or Stationery │
│  │ ▦ Calendar                        │                      │
│  │ 🖈 Certificate A                 ▼│                      │
│  └─────────────────────────────────┘                       │
│  This is a template for a company annual report.            │
│                                                             │
│  [?]                              [ Cancel ]  [   OK   ]     │
└─────────────────────────────────────────────────────────────┘
```

Select a category from this pop-up menu

Figure 1-3: Selecting a ClarisWorks Assistant or a stationery document

For more information on working with stationery documents and Assistants, see Chapter 10.

Note

If you have created a *default stationery document* for an environment (see "Using Stationery to Set New Environment Defaults" in Chapter 10), you see two different documents listed for that environment. For example, a default word processing stationery document is simply listed as Word Processing. On the other hand, the ClarisWorks standard document for that environment is listed as Standard Word Processing. (In ClarisWorks 3.0 and earlier versions, default stationery documents were known as *options stationery documents*.)

Memory Versus Disk Space (Storage Capacity)

New users often confuse a Mac's storage capacity with the amount of memory in the machine. *Storage capacity* refers to a Mac's total disk space, calculated by adding the capacity of all attached hard disks. The Mac's *memory* (also called *RAM* or Random Access Memory) is used to run programs and desk accessories and to manipulate data. Unlike disk storage, the contents of RAM disappears whenever you quit from a program or shut down the Mac. Memory is for temporary storage; disks are for long-term storage. Thus, although you may have free disk space, this has no bearing on the amount of memory available for you to run programs such as ClarisWorks.

If you want to open an existing document instead of creating a new one, click Cancel. Then choose Open from the File menu and select the document (following the steps described in "Opening Existing Documents," later in this chapter).

If you want to create a new document after the program has been running awhile, you can either choose New from the File menu or press ⌘-N. The New Document dialog box appears. Select a document type and click OK.

You can create new documents or open existing documents at any time during a ClarisWorks session. The only limitation on the number of documents you can have open at the same time is the amount of memory available to ClarisWorks. See "Quick Tips" at the end of this chapter for help with changing the memory allocation for ClarisWorks.

New documents are assigned a temporary name that consists of the word *Untitled,* a number that represents the number of documents created thus far in the session, and a pair of letters in parentheses that represents the document type. For example, *Untitled 4 (PT)* indicates the document is a new paint document and is the fourth new document created during the session.

Remember that new documents are not automatically saved to disk. If you neglect to save a new document (see "Saving Documents" later in this chapter), it disappears forever after you click its close box or quit the program. If a document is important to you, be sure to save early and save often. Note that if you attempt to close a new document without saving, ClarisWorks presents an alert box that offers an option to save the document.

Opening Existing Documents

As mentioned earlier in this chapter, you can open existing ClarisWorks documents from the desktop by double-clicking them. Doing so simultaneously launches ClarisWorks and opens the selected document. After the program is running, you can open other ClarisWorks documents as well as documents created in many other programs.

Opening ClarisWorks documents from within the program

To open a ClarisWorks document when the program is running, choose the Open command from the File menu (or press ⌘-O). You see a file dialog box like the one in Figure 1-4. Using the mouse or the arrow keys, select the particular file you want to open and either click Open or double-click the filename.

File selection list
Currently chosen folder

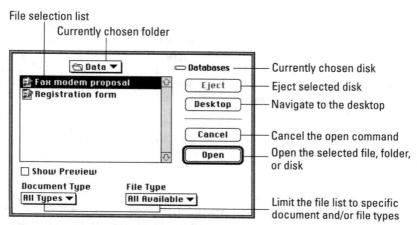

Currently chosen disk
Eject selected disk
Navigate to the desktop

Cancel the open command
Open the selected file, folder, or disk

Limit the file list to specific document and/or file types

Figure 1-4: The Open dialog box

The ClarisWorks Open dialog box has a special pair of pop-up menus at the bottom. You use the Document Type pop-up menu on the left to restrict the documents that appear in the file list to a particular type, such as database files. If you have a large number of files in a particular folder, using the Document Type pop-up menu can make it simpler to find the file you want. If you don't feel like using the menu, you can press a Command-key equivalent to restrict the list to a single document type. Table 1-1 shows the Command-key equivalents.

Note

To enter a Command-key equivalent, hold down the Command key (⌘) and press the number, letter, or character key that should accompany it.

Table 1-1
Document Type Command-Key Equivalents

Document Type	Command-Key Equivalent
All types	⌘-0
Word processing	⌘-1
Drawing	⌘-2
Painting	⌘-3
Spreadsheet	⌘-4
Database	⌘-5
Communications	⌘-6

You use the File Type pop-up menu on the right side of the Open dialog box to restrict the file list to only particular types of documents. You can specify whether you want to see regular ClarisWorks documents (ClarisWorks), ClarisWorks stationery documents (ClarisWorks Stationery), or all document types for which you have Claris translators (All Available). If you want to restrict the file list to just those documents from a particular program, such as Microsoft Word for Windows, you can select that document type in the File Type pop-up menu.

The Open dialog box (shown in Figure 1-5) has a Preview option that enables you to see a thumbnail representation of any graphic document selected in the file list. The Preview option is presented only if Apple's QuickTime system software extension is currently loaded.

By clicking the Show Preview check box, you instruct ClarisWorks to show a preview image for any graphic or movie file that has had a preview saved for it. If no preview is shown for a particular file, you can tell ClarisWorks to construct one by clicking the Create button. (Note that previews are available for some text files, too.)

Finally, if a preview is no longer correct for a file, the Create button changes to Update. Click it to create an updated preview for the file.

Preview of the selected file

Figure 1-5: The modified Open dialog box (with QuickTime active)

Opening non-ClarisWorks documents

Claris programs include a file translation system called the *XTND system*. Depending on which Claris translator files are in the Claris folder within the System Folder, the XTND system can interpret documents that were created by many other programs, such as Microsoft Word, WriteNow, and Microsoft Excel. This capability is particularly useful if you have recently switched from another word processor, spreadsheet, or graphics program or if a friend has given you a document for which you don't have the original program.

New In Version 5

In ClarisWorks 5.0, the XTND system is supplemented by a version of MacLinkPlus that enables other types of files to be translated.

Steps: Opening a Non-ClarisWorks Document from Within ClarisWorks

1. Choose Open from the File menu (or press ⌘-O).

2. *Optional:* In the Open dialog box, click the Document Type pop-up menu and choose the type of file that you want to open (Word Processing, Drawing, Painting, Spreadsheet, Database, or Communications). Similarly, if you want to restrict the file list to a certain type of document (just GIF or MacPaint files, for example), you can choose a program or file type from the File Type pop-up menu.

3. Navigate to the disk and folder where the document files are stored, and select the file you want to open. If the file you want does not appear in the file list, you do not have the translator that is needed to open the file.

4. Click Open, or double-click the filename to load the file and convert it to ClarisWorks format.

After you select the file, the Converting File dialog box appears. A progress thermometer shows how much of the conversion has been completed. You can click Cancel at any time during the conversion if you change your mind about loading the file. Otherwise, after the conversion is finished, ClarisWorks opens the document for you. The file is given a temporary name that consists of its original filename followed by *-Converted* and a pair of letters in parentheses that indicates the document type (such as *DB* for a database document).

Note

The conversion process does nothing to the original file; ClarisWorks simply reads the file and makes a converted copy of it. The file that ClarisWorks creates is not automatically stored on your disk. If you neglect to save the converted file, it disappears at the end of the current session.

When you save a converted file, you have two options:

✦ Save it with a different name from that of the original file.

This option leaves the original file intact and creates a second file that is in ClarisWorks 5.0 format.

✦ Save it with the same name as that of the original file.

This option replaces the original file with the new ClarisWorks-formatted file. Use this option only if you have no further use for the original document.

You also can use the *drag-and-drop* procedure to make ClarisWorks simultaneously launch and open a non-ClarisWorks document. To use drag-and-drop to open a foreign file on the desktop, click once to select the icon for the non-ClarisWorks document you want to open. Drag the icon onto the ClarisWorks program icon.

If ClarisWorks is capable of interpreting the document you've selected, the ClarisWorks icon turns dark, and the program launches and attempts to convert the document — just as it does when you open a foreign document from within ClarisWorks. If the document is not one of the types ClarisWorks can read, the ClarisWorks icon doesn't become dark, and the program doesn't launch.

This drag-and-drop procedure can be used with several files at once — even if the files were created in different programs.

If you are running Mac OS 8 and the foreign files are from a PC, you might need to turn off the Translate Text Files setting of Macintosh Easy Open, thereby avoiding invoking MacLink Plus before the file gets passed to ClarisWorks.

Using the AppleScript named Convert Documents (found in the ClarisWorks Scripts folder inside the ClarisWorks 5.0 folder), you can convert large numbers of files and save them in one step.

To use this or any other AppleScript, you must have the AppleScript 1.1 extension (from Apple Computer) installed and active on your Macintosh. AppleScript is included with System 7.5 and higher, although it can be purchased separately as well.

To use the Convert Documents script to convert foreign files, go to the desktop and Shift-click to select the icons for the non-ClarisWorks documents you want to convert. If you want to convert the contents of an entire folder, simply select the folder instead. Then drag the file icons or folder onto the Convert Documents script icon, shown in Figure 1-6.

The convert documents AppleScript

```
┌──────────────────────────────────────────────────┐
│ ▦▦▦        ClarisWorks Scripts        ▦▦▦          │
├──────────────────────────────────────────────────┤
│ 6 items        235.5 MB in disk    152 MB available│
├──────────────────────────────────────────────────┤
│                      📄                            │
│            ClarisWorks AppleEvents List            │
│                                                    │
│      📄             📄                             │
│  Convert Documents   Print Documents               │
│                                                    │
│      📑             📑             📄              │
│   Mail Merge     Remote Slide Show  About the AppleScripts│
└──────────────────────────────────────────────────┘
```

Figure 1-6: The Convert Documents AppleScript can be found in the ClarisWorks Scripts folder.

Each foreign document is automatically opened in ClarisWorks, converted, and then saved as a new document in the same folder as the original document. A suffix of .cwk is appended to the name of the converted document. (Files that ClarisWorks is unable to convert are simply ignored by Convert Documents.)

For more information about the Convert Documents script, refer to the "About the AppleScripts" document in the ClarisWorks Scripts folder.

Tip

If you use the Convert Documents script often, you'll find it more convenient to make an *alias* of the icon and place it on your desktop. To make an alias, click once to select the Convert Documents icon, choose Make Alias from the Finder's File menu, and then drag the new alias icon onto the desktop. (If you have Mac OS 8, you can quickly create the alias by ⌘-Option dragging the Convert Documents icon onto the desktop.) Because every alias works just like the original document or program that it represents, you can then drag your foreign files onto the alias to activate the Convert Documents script.

Opening documents created with an earlier version of ClarisWorks

One other type of conversion that many users are curious about is the manner in which ClarisWorks 5.0 handles documents created by earlier versions of ClarisWorks. You don't need to worry. When you open a file created with ClarisWorks 1.0, 2.0, 2.1, 3.0, or 4.0, a dialog box appears that states: *This document was created by a previous version of ClarisWorks. A copy will be opened and "[v5.0]" will be added to the filename.* Note that this message says a *copy* will be opened. As with translations of foreign files, the original document is merely read into memory — not replaced on disk. If you want to save a permanent copy of the document in the current version's format, you need to use the Save or Save As command to save a new copy of the file.

ClarisWorks 5.0 documents cannot be read by earlier versions of the program. If some of your colleagues use previous versions of ClarisWorks, you'll be able to read their documents, but they will not be able to read yours. For now, the best solution when preparing a file for them is to use the Save As command to translate the file to a format their version of ClarisWorks can read. A second approach is to save a copy of your word processing documents in ClarisWorks 1.0 Text format. All versions of ClarisWorks except 2.0 can read ClarisWorks 1.0 word processing documents.

Inserting files and graphics

The Insert command in the File menu enables you to place the entire contents of a file into a ClarisWorks document.

If you need to use only part of a file (such as a single paragraph or a graphic), it may be faster to simply open the second file, copy the portion you need, and then paste it into your document. Note that if you have System 7.5 or later, you can also use drag-and-drop to simply drag the selected text from one document to the other.

To insert a file or graphic into a word processing document or frame, position the cursor where you want to place the insert; in other types of frames and documents, click where you want to place the insert. Choose Insert from the File menu. A standard file dialog box appears. If you want to restrict your choices to a particular file type, choose the type from the Show pop-up menu. Navigate to the drive and folder that contain the file. Select the file you want to insert by clicking it and clicking Insert or by double-clicking the name of the file.

Only file types that are supported for the current frame or document environment appear in the Show pop-up menu.

In addition to opening graphic files directly as draw or paint documents, you can use the Library command to insert or drag any of the graphics, text items, or spreadsheet cells from ClarisWorks *libraries* into existing documents. (See Chapter 21 for details about the Library feature.)

Saving Documents

To save a ClarisWorks document to disk, you use either the Save or the Save As command from the File menu. For new Mac owners, determining which command is the correct one to use is often a major source of confusion. This section clears up the confusion once and for all.

Saving existing files

You use the Save command (⌘-S) to save existing files. If the file is already on disk, the Save command merely replaces the old copy of the file with the new copy. No dialog box appears.

Because the Save command automatically replaces the previous copy of the file, at times you may prefer to use the Save As command to save an existing file. The Save As command enables you to assign a new name to the file, as well as to specify a different location on disk in which to store it. You can use the Save As command when you want to keep multiple versions of a file instead of just replacing the old version, or when you want to save a document in a different format.

Steps: Using the Save As Command to Save an Existing File

1. Choose Save As from the File menu. The standard file dialog box appears.

2. Navigate to the disk drive and folder where you want to save the file. If you want to create a new folder in which to store the file, click the New (Folder) button and enter a name for the new folder.

3. Type a name for the file. If you want to save the file as something other than a standard ClarisWorks file, use the Save As pop-up menu to choose a file type.

4. Click a radio button to choose Document or Stationery. Choose Stationery if you want to save the document as a reusable template; otherwise, choose Document.

5. Click the Save button (or press Return or Enter). If you change your mind and decide not to save the file, click Cancel.

If you are saving a file that already exists on disk and you don't change the name from the one suggested, the program asks whether you want to replace the existing file. Click Replace if you want to replace the old file on disk with the new one. Click Cancel if you don't want to replace the old file. You can then specify a new name or location (a different disk or folder), or you can cancel the save altogether. (The Replace dialog box appears whenever you choose the Save As command and try to save a file under its original name or under any other filename that's already in use.)

If you frequently keep or track multiple revisions of important documents, you may find Flashback (a utility program from Aladdin Systems) helpful.

Saving new files

You can save new files by using either the Save or Save As command. After you select either command from the File menu, a standard file dialog box appears and gives you the opportunity to name the new file and specify a location on the disk in which to store it. To avoid overwriting any files that are already on the disk, be sure to enter a name that is different from any existing filenames.

If the file you want to save has never been saved before (that is, it's a new file) and it's empty, ClarisWorks *grays out* the Save command (makes it unselectable). Until at least one character has been typed into the document, the only save option presented is Save As.

ClarisWorks 5.0 enables you to save identifying information with any file by choosing the Document Summary command in the File menu. You can use the Document Summary dialog box to do the following:

✦ Provide a more elaborate title for a document

✦ Identify the author

✦ Specify a version number (to distinguish multiple revisions of a file, for example)

✦ Assign keywords that can be used to help identify the file's contents

✦ Specify a category and enter descriptive text (to classify and explain the purpose of a stationery document when it appears in the New Document dialog box)

An example of a Document Summary is shown in Figure 1-7. Because this information is primarily for your benefit, you can enter as much or as little information as you like. If you later want to change some of the entries, choose the Document Summary command again, make the changes, and then save the document again. (Document Summary information is also discussed in Chapter 10.)

Document Summary	
Title:	Fax Form
Author:	Steven A. Schwartz
Version:	1.0
Keywords:	fax
Category:	Business
Description:	Use this form to create a fax that can be sent from a fax-modem or fax machine.

[?]   [Set Password...]   [Cancel]   [OK]

Figure 1-7: The Document Summary dialog box

Note

For all practical purposes, the Keywords section of the Document Summary dialog box is useless. The Find ClarisWorks Documents Assistant cannot search by keyword — the keywords can only be seen in the Document Summary dialog box. Save yourself some work; don't bother to enter keywords. (For instructions on using the Find ClarisWorks Documents Assistant, see "Locating misplaced ClarisWorks documents" at the end of this chapter.)

Using Save As options

When you use the Save As command to save a file, a Save file dialog box appears, as shown in Figure 1-8. It looks a little different than the Save dialog box used by other programs. Using the radio buttons and the pop-up menu at the bottom of the dialog box, you can do one of the following:

✦ Select from several file formats by clicking the Save As pop-up menu.

✦ Save the file as a document or stationery file by clicking the appropriate radio button.

In most cases, you can leave the Save As pop-up menu alone. The default setting is ClarisWorks, which means the file will be saved as a standard ClarisWorks file.

Depending on the file translators that have been installed, the Save As pop-up menu may have options for saving the document as a non-ClarisWorks file. You may want to save a spreadsheet in Microsoft Excel format, for example, if you plan to give it to a friend who uses Excel rather than ClarisWorks. Or, you may want to save Draw graphic files in PICT format so they can be opened by any draw program. Note that the file format options presented vary, depending on the ClarisWorks environment you're in when you choose Save As. For example, if you're saving a spreadsheet, the Save As pop-up menu lists only spreadsheet formats.

Save the file as a normal document
or a template

Select a file type from this
pop-up menu

Figure 1-8: The ClarisWorks 5.0 Save As dialog box

Tip

When saving a document in a non-ClarisWorks format, it's a smart idea to save a copy of the file in ClarisWorks format, too, so if you ever use the document in ClarisWorks again, you can work on the original rather than a translated copy of the file.

The radio buttons in the lower-right corner of the dialog box enable you to save the file as a normal document or a stationery file. A *stationery file* is a template for frequently used documents, such as fax forms and memos. If you click the Stationery radio button, ClarisWorks automatically navigates to the ClarisWorks Stationery folder within the ClarisWorks 5.0 folder. You can later open any stationery document saved in this folder by clicking the Use Assistant or Stationery radio button in the New Document dialog box. (Choose New from the File menu or press ⌘-N.) See Chapter 10 for additional information on working with stationery files.

Note

The Save As pop-up menu and the radio buttons work together. You must select a file format from the Save As pop-up menu *and* choose a file type by clicking the Document or Stationery radio button.

Password-Protecting Documents

New In
Version 5

In ClarisWorks 5, you can assign a password to any document to protect it from prying eyes. To add a password to a new or existing document, choose Document Summary from the File menu and click the Set Password button in the Document

Summary dialog box that appears. The dialog box shown in Figure 1-9 appears. Type a password you wish to assign to the document, click OK, confirm the password by typing it again, and click OK again. Finally, to record the password, save the document by choosing Save or Save As from the File menu.

Figure 1-9: Assigning a password to a document

If you later wish to change the password for a document, open the document and repeat this procedure. You will be asked to enter the old password before you are allowed to create a new password. To remove an existing password (restoring the document to a "no password" state), leave the password blank when asked to enter and confirm the new password.

Assigning a password to a document does not *encrypt* (scramble) it. Although a password will slow down casual snoopers, password-protected documents can easily be opened and viewed by many Macintosh utility programs. If you want real protection, you have to purchase a security or encryption program, such as FolderBolt-Pro, FileGuard, or PGP (Pretty Good Privacy).

Closing Document Windows

Saving a document copies its contents to a file on disk. It does not close the document window. After you finish using a document, you can close its window by clicking once in its close box (in the upper-left corner of the window, as shown in Figure 1-10), choosing Close from the File menu, or by pressing ⌘-W. If the file has been saved, the window immediately closes. If changes have been made to the file, you are given a chance to save the file before ClarisWorks closes it.

You can close all the document windows at one time by choosing Quit from the File menu (or by pressing ⌘-Q). If you have already saved all the documents, ClarisWorks simply closes all windows and quits. If any documents have not been saved — new files or files you have changed — ClarisWorks gives you an opportunity to save them one by one.

Close box

Figure 1-10: Click the close box to close a window.

Tip

To close all document windows without quitting the program, hold down the Option key and do one of the following:

✦ Click the close box for any window.

✦ Choose the Close command from the File menu.

As usual, if you haven't saved some documents, the program gives you an opportunity to save them or to cancel before their windows are closed. (This tip also works from the desktop and is a fast way to eliminate window clutter.)

Selecting and Using Tools

Along the left side of most document windows is the Tool panel. The tools enable you to create new frames (such as adding paint graphics or a spreadsheet to a word processing document); select drawing and painting tools; and set fill and pen colors, patterns, textures, gradients, and line styles.

If the tools aren't visible, choose Show Tools from the Window menu. Other ways to show and hide the Tool panel are discussed later in this chapter in "Hiding and showing tools."

You can divide the objects in the Tool panel into the following categories, according to their functions: environment tools, drawing tools, painting tools, fill palettes, and pen palettes. The Tool panel has two different states: *basic* and *expanded* (see Figure 1-11). The expanded Tool panel adds painting tools to the basic panel, and it appears only when you are working on a paint document or in a paint frame.

Figure 1-11: The basic and expanded Tool panels

To create a new frame in the current document, click an environment tool: the *A* for a word processing frame, the plus symbol for a spreadsheet frame, or the paintbrush for a paint frame. To add a draw object to the document, click any of the draw icons. To work with colors, patterns, textures, gradients, or line styles, click any of these tool icons at the bottom of the panel and select the option you prefer.

The color, pattern, texture, gradient, line style, and arrow tools are *tear-off* palettes. If you use any of them frequently, you can keep them open and on screen. To tear off a palette, click the palette icon of interest. The panel drops down. While holding down the mouse button, drag the palette away from the Tool panel. Release the mouse button.

After you release the mouse button, the palette appears in its own small window, where it's easily accessible (see Figure 1-12). To close a floating palette of this type, click its close box (in the upper-left corner). To shrink the palette temporarily and cause it to move to the upper-right corner of the document window, click the box in the palette's upper-right corner. To move the palette, click in its title bar and drag it to the desired position.

Click to close palette
Click to drag palette
to a new location
Click to shrink palette or
return it to its normal size

Figure 1-12: Fill Pattern is an example of a tear-off palette.

Option-clicking the close box for any tear-off palette simultaneously closes all open palettes. Similarly, Option-clicking in the grow/shrink box in the upper-right corner of a palette causes all palettes to grow or shrink.

ClarisWorks 5.0 makes extensive use of palettes. For instance, stylesheets are also presented as floating windows with their own miniature title bars, close boxes, and grow/shrink boxes. In other Macintosh programs, such windows are commonly referred to as *windoids*. In this book, the terms *palette* and *windoid* are used interchangeably because every ClarisWorks palette is presented in a windoid.

Using the Button Bar

New In
Version 5

To save you the effort of needlessly pulling down menus to choose commands or memorizing Command-key equivalents, ClarisWorks 5.0 provides button bars that normally appear above each document window (see Figure 1-13). You can issue many common commands by simply clicking a button on the button bar. To make the button bar appear, choose Show Button Bar from the Window menu (or press Shift-⌘-X).

Click to reveal a drop-down menu
of button bar-related commands   Button descriptions are displayed here

Figure 1-13: This button bar appears when working in a spreadsheet or a spreadsheet frame.

The contents of the bar change to match the environment or frame in which you are working. When you are working in a spreadsheet frame, for example, buttons relevant to spreadsheet operations are added to the default button bar.

Note

In previous versions of ClarisWorks, the Shortcuts palette served the same function as the new button bars.

At the left side of the button bar is a drop-down menu with commands that enable you to set options for the current bar, manually switch to a different bar, or create a new bar. You can even customize a button bar by adding and removing buttons or assigning *macros* (user-created ClarisWorks scripts) to buttons. (Chapter 12 discusses customizing the button bars.)

Note

To display button bars above all documents automatically, click the drop-down menu at the left side of any button bar and select the option for Visible at Startup.

Creating and Using Frames

To integrate information from the various ClarisWorks environments, you use *frames*. A frame is a rectangular area within a document that is — in most cases — a different environment than that of the underlying document. For example, Figure 1-14 shows a spreadsheet frame within a word processing document. The three types of frames correspond to the three environment tools in the Tool panel: text, paint, and spreadsheet.

Note

ClarisWorks does not have a separate frame type for draw objects. You can add a draw object to most documents by selecting a draw tool from the Tool panel and then drawing.

To create a frame, select one of the three environment tools (text, spreadsheet, or paint) from the Tool panel. Click the mouse button over the spot where you want to position one of the frame's corners. Drag until the frame is the size and shape you desire. Release the mouse button.

Spreadsheet frame

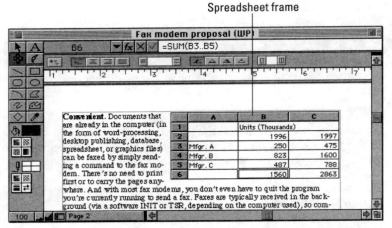

Figure 1-14: A spreadsheet frame in a word processing document

If you've never created a frame before, you might want to try it now. As an example, create a new word processing document or open an existing one, choose Show Tools from the Window menu (if the Tool panel is hidden), select the spreadsheet tool, and then click and drag in the document window. When you release the mouse button, the spreadsheet frame appears.

Note

You can place additional word processing frames into a word processing document or spreadsheet frames into a spreadsheet document by pressing Option as you draw the frame.

After you create a frame, you can immediately begin working in it: entering data in spreadsheet frames, typing in text frames, and creating graphics in paint frames. You may discover, however, that a particular frame is incorrectly positioned, is the wrong size, or is no longer needed.

✦ To move a frame, select the pointer from the Tool panel. Click the frame to select it. A set of black dots (called *handles*) appears around the frame to show it is selected. Click anywhere within the frame and, while holding down the mouse button, drag the frame to the new position.

✦ To resize a frame, select the pointer from the Tool panel. Click the frame to select it. A set of handles appears around the frame to show it is selected. Using the pointer tool, select one of the frame handles, and then drag it to change the size of the frame.

✦ To delete a frame, select the pointer from the Tool panel. Click the frame to select it. A set of handles appears around the frame to show it is selected. Press the Delete key.

See Chapter 14 for additional information about frames.

Using Drag-and-Drop

ClarisWorks 5.0 makes extensive use of a Macintosh system software feature called *drag-and-drop*. In addition to using drag-and-drop to open foreign files in ClarisWorks (as explained in "Opening non-ClarisWorks documents," earlier in this chapter), drag-and-drop can be used to move text and objects from one ClarisWorks document to another, to the desktop (as clipping files), or between other drag-and-drop-enabled programs (such as Adobe Photoshop 4.0).

To copy text or an object (such as a graphic or a spreadsheet frame) between ClarisWorks documents, open both documents, select the text or graphic, and then drag it to the second document. Use the same procedure to copy text or objects between ClarisWorks and any other drag-and-drop-enabled program.

To create a text or graphic clipping file, drag the text or object to your desktop.

Not all versions of System 7 support drag-and-drop.

Changing the Display

In ClarisWorks, you can control what you see on screen in several ways. For example, you can do any of the following:

✦ Show or hide the Tool panel to see more of a partially hidden or wide document.

✦ Switch magnification levels to focus in on important areas or get a bird's-eye view of the document.

✦ Stack or tile windows to make working with several documents at the same time more convenient.

✦ Zoom document windows to switch between two window sizes with a single mouse click.

✦ Split the screen to see two or four parts of a document at the same time.

✦ Create new views of a document to work with two or more copies of the same document.

Hiding and showing tools

Although you usually want to keep the Tool panel handy, sometimes you may want to make it disappear. If you have a small screen or are working on a very wide document, for example, hiding the Tool panel enables you to see more of the document. You can hide or show the tools in one of two ways:

✦ Choose Show Tools or Hide Tools from the Window menu. (The wording for this command changes, depending on whether the Tool panel is presently visible or hidden.) You can also issue this command by pressing ⌘-Shift-T.

✦ Click the Show/Hide Tools control at the bottom of the document (see Figure 1-15).

Figure 1-15: Use the Show/Hide Tools control to view or hide the Tool panel.

Each time you issue the Show/Hide Tools command or click the control, the state of the Tool panel switches. If the Tool panel is currently hidden, it appears. If the panel is visible, it is removed.

Setting the magnification level

Occasionally, you may want to change a document's magnification level. Although this feature is extremely helpful in the paint environment (because it enables you to zoom in to touch up tiny areas), it is also available in the other environments. You can zoom out to get a thumbnail view of the layout for a word processing document without being distracted by the text, for example. You change the magnification with the Zoom Percentage box, the Zoom-Out control, or the Zoom-In control, all of which are located in the bottom-left corner of every document window (see Figure 1-16).

You can change the magnification in two ways:

✦ Click the Zoom Percentage box and drag to select a new percentage. If you select Other, a dialog box appears in which you can type a specific percentage, including percentages that are not listed in the menu.

✦ Click the Zoom-Out or Zoom-In control. Each click reduces or increases the magnification by one step.

Zoom Percentage box
Zoom-Out control
Zoom-In control

Figure 1-16: Use the Zoom Percentage box, the Zoom-Out control, and the Zoom-In control to change a document's magnification.

Resizing windows

Resizable windows, such as ClarisWorks document windows, contain two special boxes: the size box and the zoom box, as shown in Figure 1-17. To change the size of a window, click in the size box and drag until the window is the desired size. Each time you click a window's zoom box, it switches between a full-screen window and the size and position that you last set for the window. (These aren't specifically ClarisWorks features — they work with any Macintosh window that contains zoom and size boxes.)

If you are running System 7.5 or 7.6 and have the WindowShade control panel installed, you can double-click the title bar of any window to display only the window's title bar. In OS 8, double-clicking a title bar or clicking in a window's WindowShade box has the same effect.

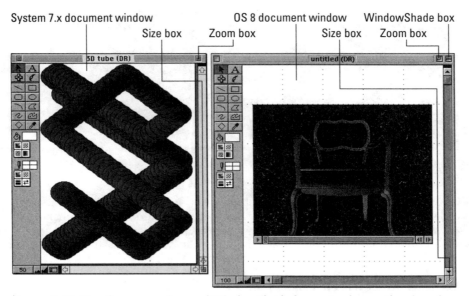

Figure 1-17: Use the zoom, size, and WindowShade boxes to change the size of a window.

Arranging windows

ClarisWorks enables you to open and work with as many documents as available memory permits. Two commands in the Window menu — Tile Windows and Stack Windows — make it easy to juggle several open files.

The Tile Windows command arranges document windows in a vertical stack, one above the other. Documents are full width, but their height is reduced, as shown in Figure 1-18. You can make any document active by simply clicking it.

Figure 1-18: Tiled windows

If you don't need to refer constantly to any of the other open documents, you can expand the current document so it takes over the entire screen by clicking its zoom box (in the right corner of the document's title bar). When you're ready to switch to a different document window, click the current window's zoom box again to make it shrink to its original, tiled position.

The Stack Windows command arranges documents so they cascade from the upper-left corner of the screen to the bottom right. Because a small portion of each document always shows, you can easily switch between documents by clicking the edge of the one you want to bring to the front.

Note

Regardless of how you have your windows arranged, you can bring any window to the front and make it active by clicking in that window or by choosing its name from the Window menu. (All open documents are listed at the bottom of the Window menu.)

Splitting the screen

ClarisWorks enables you to split any document horizontally and/or vertically into two or four panes (see Figure 1-19). In each pane, you can examine or edit a different part of the document. Each pane scrolls independently of other panes, so working on one part of the document while viewing another part is easy to do. Changes you make in any pane are simultaneously recorded in all panes.

Vertical pane control

Dividing line

Horizontal pane control

Top pane

	A	B	C	D	E	F	G	
1	Date	Description	Check	Recpt.	Claim	BilledAmt	CoveredAmt	
26	2/8/97	Medical insurance	Check	√	–	363.28	0.00	
27	3/29/97	Medical insurance	Check	√	–	363.28	0.00	
28	4/25/97	Medical insurance	Check	√	–	363.28	0.00	
29	5/20/97	Medical insurance	Check	√	–	363.28	0.00	
30	6/25/97	Medical insurance	Check	√	–	363.28	0.00	
31	7/25/97	Medical insurance	Check	√	–	363.28	0.00	
32	8/20/97	Medical insurance	Check	√	–	363.28	0.00	
33	9/22/97	Medical insurance	Check	√	–	363.28	0.00	
34	10/25/97	Medical insurance	Check	√	–	363.28	0.00	
35	11/25/97	Medical insurance	Check	√	–	363.28	0.00	
36	12/20/97	Medical insurance	Check	√	–	424.76	0.00	
37		1991 Medical Insurance Summary				$4,420.84	$0.00	
38								
39	1/16/91	West Suburban Radiology		√	√	53.00	0.00	
40	2/5/91	Eye exam (Evan)		√		35.00	0.00	
75								
76		GRAND TOTALS				$12,852.34	$1,521.91	
77								
78								

Title bar: Medical Expenses 1997 (SS)
F37 fx ✕ ✓ =SUM(F25..F36)

Bottom pane

Figure 1-19: A split screen

To split the screen, click the vertical or horizontal pane control and drag it to the spot where you want to divide the document. Release the mouse button. A pair of dividing lines marks the edge of each pane.

To remove a split pane, double-click the dividing line or click the dividing line and drag it to the edge of the document window.

Creating a new view of a document

If you want to open two copies of the same document, choose New View from the Window menu. Any changes you make in one copy are instantly reflected in the other copy. To distinguish between the copies, ClarisWorks appends a number at the end of each name in the title bar. If the original document is called Memo (WP), for example, you end up with two documents on screen: Memo:1 (WP) and Memo:2 (WP).

What's the point of having multiple copies of the same document on screen? Creating multiple views of a document has the following advantages:

✦ It enables you to see a zoomed-out view (the entire document) and a 100% view (the normal view) at the same time. Editing changes are reflected in both views so you can see their effects.

✦ If you have a spreadsheet frame in a word processing or database document, the only way to increase the number of rows and columns in the frame is by creating a new view of the frame (by using the Open Frame command in the Window menu).

✦ In the database environment, you can use two views to look at the document in both Browse and Layout modes at the same time. As you make changes to the layout, you can instantly see how they will affect the formatting of the data.

Printing

The final step for most documents is creating a *printout* — a printed copy of the spreadsheet, memo, graphic image, or database report. To print a document, open or create a ClarisWorks document. Choose Print from the File menu. The Print dialog box appears. Select the print options you want to use for this printout. Click Print to send the print job to the printer.

Note

Some options in the Print dialog box are specific to a particular ClarisWorks environment. When working on a spreadsheet, for example, you can print or omit the row headings, column headings, and the cell grid.

The Print dialog box you see depends on the printer you select in the Chooser and the version of system software that is installed on the Mac. Figure 1-20 shows the Print dialog box for Apple LaserWriters.

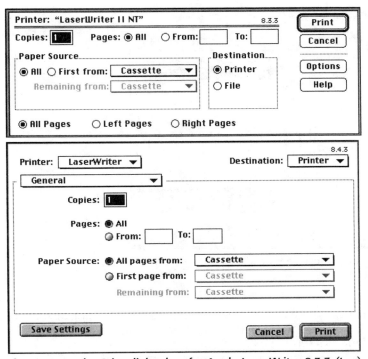

Figure 1-20: The Print dialog box for Apple LaserWriter 8.3.3 (top) and 8.4.3 (bottom)

Note

Be sure you have selected a printer in the Chooser desk accessory, particularly if you have more than one printing device. The printer that is currently selected receives the print job. Whenever you change the printer selection in the Chooser, you should also use the Page Setup command to make sure the options are correct for the newly selected printer.

To select a printer, open the Chooser desk accessory (see Figure 1-21) by selecting it from the Apple menu. Click the appropriate Chooser icon in the left side of the window, and select the printer and other options in the right side of the window. (The printer must be turned on for its name to appear in the right side of the window.)

Chooser icons

Selected printer

Options

Figure 1-21: Use the Chooser desk accessory to select the printer and set other options.

Note

If you have System 7.5 or higher and the Desktop Printer extensions installed, you can specify a default printer by selecting a printer icon on the desktop and choosing Set Default Printer from the Printing menu that appears in the menu bar. You can also print by simply dragging document icons onto the icon of the printer you wish to use.

Using the ClarisWorks Help Features

ClarisWorks 5.0 provides three ways for you to get help. In addition to using QuickHelp (also known as the *ClarisWorks Help System*) for obtaining in-depth help, you can turn on Balloon Help to get assistance in identifying ClarisWorks's tools and controls, or you can view a *FAQ* (a list of frequently asked questions for ClarisWorks 5.0).

Using QuickHelp

In early versions of ClarisWorks, all important program information was located in the manual. Beginning with ClarisWorks 3, major portions of the manual were moved into the online help system. You'll now find that much of the program information is available *only* in QuickHelp, and the manual is more of an annotated index for the Help system.

QuickHelp is a separate program from ClarisWorks. Although you can request help from within ClarisWorks (which launches the QuickHelp program), QuickHelp can also be launched directly from the desktop — whether or not ClarisWorks is running.

When you're running ClarisWorks, you can invoke QuickHelp by doing any of the following:

✦ Choose ClarisWorks Help Contents or ClarisWorks Help Index from the Balloon Help menu in System 7.*x* (see Figure 1-22) or from the Help menu in OS 8.

✦ Press ⌘-? or the Help key (if you have an Apple extended keyboard).

Figure 1-22: The Balloon Help menu

Help summoned from dialog boxes in ClarisWorks 5.0 is context-sensitive. If you click the question mark (?) button in any dialog box, QuickHelp opens to a screen that is relevant to that dialog box.

When you open QuickHelp from the Balloon Help menu, on the other hand, the type of Help information displayed, as well as the particular Help screen shown, can be controlled as follows:

✦ To reach the opening screen of the ClarisWorks Help system (see Figure 1-23), choose ClarisWorks Help Contents from the Balloon Help menu or Help menu, press ⌘-?, or press the Help key (Apple extended keyboards only). If ClarisWorks Help is already open, you can return to the opening screen by clicking the Contents button.

✦ To display an alphabetical list of Help topics, choose ClarisWorks Help Index from the Balloon Help menu or Help menu, or — after you have invoked Help — click the Index button (refer to Figure 1-23).

✦ To view a guided tour of ClarisWorks 5.0, choose Introduction to ClarisWorks from the Balloon Help menu or Help menu, or double-click the Introduction to ClarisWorks icon in the ClarisWorks 5.0 folder.

✦ For general information on using the ClarisWorks Help system, click Getting Help on the opening Help screen.

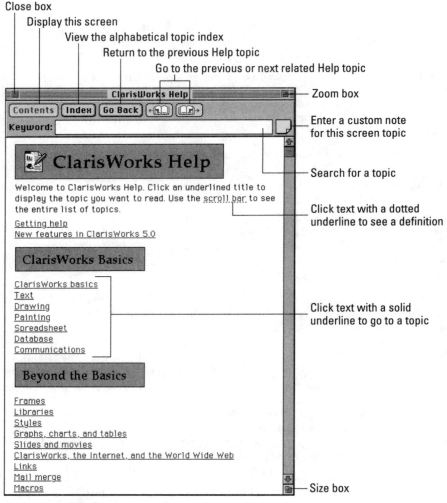

Figure 1-23: The opening Help screen

After QuickHelp opens, you can do any of the following:

✦ Display the opening Help screen by clicking the Contents button.

✦ Display the Help Index by clicking the Index button.

✦ Display the most recent Help screen viewed by clicking the Go Back button.

✦ Go to the next or previous Help screen that is related to the current topic by clicking the book page buttons.

✦ Search for help on a particular topic by typing an entry in the Keyword box. As you type, QuickHelp displays matching topic titles in the Help screen topic list. Press Enter to make QuickHelp display the selected Help topic or index entry.

You can also choose the Global Find (⌘-F) or Global Find Again (⌘-G) commands from the Find menu to perform general searches.

✦ Go directly to any topic of interest by clicking text that contains a solid underline, or by selecting a topic from the Index and clicking Go To Topic. (If you want to view a Help topic chosen with the latter method without closing the Index, click View Topic rather than Go To Topic.)

✦ View glossary definitions by clicking text that contains a dotted underline.

✦ Print the current Help topic or all Help topics by choosing Print or Print All Topics from the File menu.

✦ Copy the current Help topic by choosing Copy Topic Text (for a copy of only the text) or Copy Topic as a Picture (to treat the topic as a graphic) from the Edit menu.

Copy Topic Text displays the entire text of the current topic in a new window. To copy the entire contents of the window to the Clipboard, click Copy All Text. To copy only a portion of the text, highlight the desired text and click the Copy Selected Text button that appears.

Copy Topic as a Picture changes the entire topic to a PICT graphic and transfers it to the Clipboard. This option includes all graphics that are part of the chosen Help topic.

✦ Create bookmarks for Help topics that are important to you.

- To create a bookmark, choose Set Bookmark from the Bookmarks menu and accept the suggested name or enter a new name in the Set Bookmark dialog box. Each bookmark's name is automatically added to the bottom of the Bookmarks menu.

- To assign a Command-key equivalent with which a bookmark can be invoked, choose a number from the ⌘ Key pop-up menu. Up to ten bookmarks can be assigned Command keys.

- To go to a bookmark, you can select it from the Bookmarks menu or press its Command-key equivalent (if one was assigned).

- To edit a bookmark, choose Edit Bookmarks from the Bookmarks menu, select the bookmark from the scrolling list, and click View Topic. (You can also use the Edit Bookmarks command to delete bookmarks.)

✦ Add sticky notes that further explain a Help topic.

- To create a note, drag a note icon from the top of the ClarisWorks Help window into the current topic and begin typing. The note expands as you type. Because word wrap is not supported, however, you must end each line by pressing Return.

- To reposition a note, move the cursor over the note until the cursor changes into a hand. Then drag the note to a new position.

- To delete a note, drag it away from the Help window. When the cursor changes to a trash can, release the mouse button.

- To show or hide all notes, choose Show Notes from the View menu.

One of the fastest ways to find help on a particular subject is to use the Index. The Index, shown in Figure 1-24, is an alphabetical list of all Help topics. Scroll to the topic of interest, select it, and click Go To Topic. You can speed up the process by typing the first letter or two of the topic for which you're searching. The list automatically scrolls to the first topic that begins with the letter or letters you type.

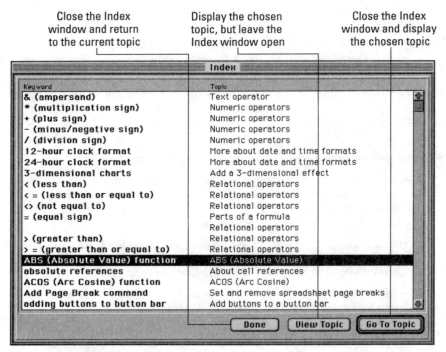

Figure 1-24: The Help Index

Help can remain on screen while you continue to work on ClarisWorks documents. When you are through with QuickHelp, you can dismiss it by selecting Quit from QuickHelp's File menu.

For information on ClarisWorks Assistants (the last command in the Balloon Help menu), refer to Chapter 10.

Using Balloon Help

By choosing Show Balloons from the Balloon Help menu or Help menu, you can get helpful information about ClarisWorks components. Whenever the pointer passes over an object that has a Balloon Help message attached to it, a cartoon-style thought balloon pops up, providing some general information about the object. Resizing controls, icons in the Tool panel, dialog box buttons, and parts of the document window are some of the items within ClarisWorks that have Help balloons. Figure 1-25 shows an example of a Help balloon.

Figure 1-25: A Help balloon that explains a pop-up menu in the button bar

To turn on Balloon Help, choose Show Balloons from the Balloon Help menu or Help menu. Now, whenever you point to a Balloon Help object, a balloon will appear. Because most people find the balloons distracting when they are working, you may want to turn Balloon Help off after you find out what you need to know.

To turn off Balloon Help, choose Hide Balloons from the Balloon Help menu or Help menu.

Help balloons are also available for the buttons in the button bar. Just let the pointer rest on one of the buttons for a few seconds, and a Help balloon will pop up. (See Chapter 12 for more information on the button bars.)

Viewing Frequently Asked Questions

In addition to using QuickHelp, you may also find it useful to examine a list of common questions concerning ClarisWorks 5.0. Using the AppleGuide component

of the system software, Frequently Asked Questions can walk you through many typical ClarisWorks tasks. To use this feature, choose Frequently Asked Questions from the Balloon Help menu or Help menu.

Viewing the On-Screen Tour

New ClarisWorks users can run an on-screen guided tour to get a quick overview of ClarisWorks 5.0's features and capabilities. More experienced users may want to refer to the tour the first time they explore an environment.

You can start the tour from within ClarisWorks 5.0 or run it from the desktop by using one of the following methods:

✦ *From the desktop.* Double-click the Introduction to ClarisWorks icon in your ClarisWorks 5.0 folder.

✦ *When ClarisWorks is running.* Choose Introduction to ClarisWorks from the Balloon Help menu or Help menu.

To move from screen to screen within the tour, click the arrow buttons or choose a new topic from the Menu screen (see Figure 1-26). When you want to leave the tour, click the Exit button.

If you launch the tour from the desktop, you are returned to the desktop after you finish the tour. If you start the tour from within ClarisWorks, after you are done with the tour, you are returned to whatever you were last doing in ClarisWorks.

Quitting the Program

After you finish using ClarisWorks, choose Quit from the File menu (or press ⌘-Q). If you have new documents open that have never been saved or documents with changes that haven't been saved, ClarisWorks gives you an opportunity to save the files before quitting (see Figure 1-27). If a file has never been saved (that is, it's a new file you created in the current session) and you click the Save button in the Save Changes dialog box, ClarisWorks presents the standard Save As file dialog box (as described previously in this chapter in "Saving Documents"). If, on the other hand, the file has been saved before, clicking the Save button simply saves the new version of the file over the older one.

Click to leave the tour
Click to turn music on or off

Click to navigate
from page to page

Click to go to a particular
section of the tour

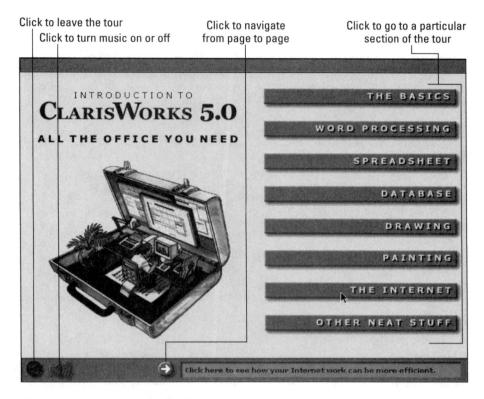

Figure 1-26: Select tour topics from this menu.

Quit without saving the document

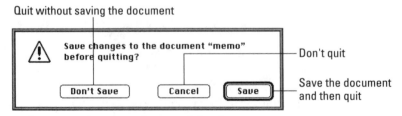

Don't quit

Save the document
and then quit

Figure 1-27: The Save Changes dialog box

A Save Changes dialog box appears for every unsaved open document. If you change your mind about quitting, click the Cancel button. The ClarisWorks session immediately picks up where you left off. Clicking Don't Save tells ClarisWorks to close the document without saving it.

Caution

If you close a document by clicking the Don't Save button (or by pressing ⌘-D), all changes since the most recent save are ignored; that is, they are not recorded on disk. If this is a new document and it has never been saved, the document itself is discarded. Be sure not to click Don't Save by mistake.

Quick Tips

The following tips offer some helpful hints to

- ✦ Ensure you have enough memory for your ClarisWorks sessions
- ✦ Skip the New Document dialog box when you launch ClarisWorks
- ✦ Optimally shrink and expand windows
- ✦ Print from the desktop
- ✦ Compensate for not having a translator for a file you want to open or insert
- ✦ Find misplaced ClarisWorks documents quickly

Changing the memory allocation for ClarisWorks

While running ClarisWorks, you may occasionally receive a message that there is insufficient memory to open a document or that a paint document will be opened in a reduced size. You can increase the memory available to ClarisWorks and your documents by using the following procedure.

Steps: Changing ClarisWorks's Memory Allocation

1. Quit ClarisWorks by choosing Quit from the File menu (or pressing ⌘-Q). If any open documents are new or have been changed, you are given an opportunity to save them. You are then returned to the desktop.

2. Select the ClarisWorks program icon by clicking it and then choose Get Info from the File menu (or press ⌘-I). You see an Info window similar to the one shown in Figure 1-28.

3. Type a larger number into the Preferred Size box. (Increase the Suggested Size by 25 to 50 percent to start. Later, as you determine the amount of memory you require for a typical ClarisWorks session, you can fine-tune the memory allocation.)

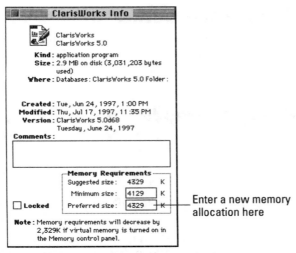

Figure 1-28: The ClarisWorks Info window

4. Click the close box in the upper-left corner of the Info window to save the changes. The next time you run ClarisWorks, the additional memory will be available for your documents.

Using a shareware control panel from Peirce Software called AppSizer, you can change the memory allocation for any application (such as ClarisWorks) as you launch it. To learn more about AppSizer or to download a copy, use your Web browser to visit the following page: http://www.peircesw.com/AppSizer.html.

Skipping the New Document dialog box at start-up

If you want to skip the New Document dialog box that normally accompanies the program start-up, hold down the ⌘ key as you launch ClarisWorks. After the program loads, it immediately presents the Open dialog box, rather than the New Document dialog box.

If you've changed the General Preferences settings to make ClarisWorks present the Open dialog box rather than the New Document dialog box, holding down the Command key as you launch the program makes the New Document dialog box appear instead.

An alternative to tiled and stacked windows

If tiled or stacked windows don't appeal to you, you can take more control over your document window arrangement by shrinking and expanding individual windows.

Steps: Shrinking and Expanding Document Windows

1. Using the size box, shrink each document window to the smallest possible size.

2. Manually arrange the document windows so the title bar of each one is exposed.

3. To make one of the documents active (so you can work with it), click once in its window. (When several windows are on screen, the active window is the one with a series of horizontal lines in its title bar. The title bars for the other windows are blank.)

4. Click the zoom box to expand the document to its full size.

When you're ready to switch to a different document, click the active document's zoom box again; it shrinks back to its reduced size and position. Then repeat Steps 3 and 4 for the next document you want to use.

Printing ClarisWorks files from the desktop

If you aren't currently in ClarisWorks and just want to print an existing document without making changes to it, you can do so by using a special procedure.

Steps: Printing from the Desktop

1. Go to the desktop and select the file or files you want to print.

2. Choose Print from the File menu or press ⌘-P.

   Instead of launching ClarisWorks in the usual way, choosing Print from the desktop loads the selected document(s) into ClarisWorks and immediately presents the Print dialog box.

3. Select print options and then click Print.

   After the document has been printed, ClarisWorks automatically quits and you are returned to the desktop.

You can use this printing procedure with most programs. The only drawback is if you change your mind about printing the document or decide you need to make some changes before printing it, you need to restart the program and reload the documents.

If you are using System 7.5 or higher and have installed Apple's Desktop Printing software, you can also print from the desktop by dragging the files you wish to print onto the appropriate desktop printer icon.

File conversion tips

Although ClarisWorks can understand dozens of foreign file formats, there are formats that ClarisWorks can't read. What do you do if ClarisWorks doesn't have a translator for the foreign file you want to open or insert? One solution is to use the original program to save or export the file into a format that ClarisWorks *does* support.

Suppose, for example, that you have a word processing document that was created in a version of Microsoft Word that ClarisWorks 5.0 doesn't support. All you have to do is open the file in Word and save a new copy of the file in a format that ClarisWorks supports. Alternatively, if you don't have that version of Microsoft Word, see whether you have another program that understands Word files. Then load the file into that particular program and save or export it to a format that ClarisWorks supports.

System 7.5 and higher includes an extensive set of MacLinkPlus translators that — in conjunction with the Macintosh Easy Open control panel — enable you to open a variety of foreign document types. MacLinkPlus is also included as a component of ClarisWorks 5/Office.

In general, when you export a file to be used in ClarisWorks, you should select one of the more specific translators that ClarisWorks supports — that of a particular program, such as Excel, Word, MacWrite, or another popular program of the correct type. When ClarisWorks translates such files, it attempts to retain the proper formatting, margins, styles, formulas, and so on. The next best solution is translating the file to a general format, such as ASCII text or SYLK (spreadsheet). Although much of the original formatting will disappear, at least you can work with the basic text of the document and save some retyping time.

In the case of a word processing document, if you can't find a popular word processing format that's supported, see whether the program can create an *RTF* file (a Microsoft document format that has wide support in the computer industry). Unlike straight ASCII text, you'll find that the majority of the original formatting is retained.

Locating misplaced ClarisWorks documents

You're probably already familiar with the Find menu command that is built into Apple's system software. Simply put, this command enables you to search for files on the hard disk. All you have to know is part of the filename. To make it easy to locate files without leaving ClarisWorks 5.0, an Assistant called Find ClarisWorks Documents is provided.

Choose New from the File menu. In the New Document dialog box that appears, click the Use Assistant or Stationery radio button, choose All Assistants from the Category pop-up menu, choose Find ClarisWorks Documents, and then click OK. The Find Document Assistant dialog box appears (see Figure 1-29). Enter search instructions consisting of any combination of the file's name (or a part of its name), the file date or period you want to consider, and the document type.

Click Start to execute the search. The search progress is displayed in a new dialog box. In the Documents Found box, highlight the file you want to load and click the Open button. If the desired document was not found by the search, click Cancel.

```
┌─────────────────────────────────────────────────────┐
│ 🔍  Find Document Assistant                          │
│                                                       │
│   Find all files that have the following attributes: │
│                                                       │
│   ☒ Name    │Golf                              │     │
│                                                       │
│   ☒ Date    │Within ? d... ▼│  │60│ days             │
│                                                       │
│   ☐ Type    Document Type │All types ▼│              │
│                                                       │
│   ▼ With this Assistant you locate documents by name, the │
│   ⁎  type of document and when you created or edited it.   │
│   Progress                        ┌────────┐ ┌────────┐│
│   [_____]              │ Cancel │ │ Start  ││
│                                   └────────┘ └────────┘│
└─────────────────────────────────────────────────────┘
```

Figure 1-29: Enter search criteria in this dialog box.

The Find Document Assistant searches only the active hard disk — the one from which ClarisWorks is launched. If you have more than one hard disk or the hard disk is partitioned into multiple volumes, the usefulness of this Assistant may be somewhat limited. You may be better off using the Apple Find command or a third-party utility.

If you want to see *every* ClarisWorks document on the active drive, leave all the search criteria blank and unchecked.

Summary

✦ You can launch ClarisWorks in several ways. You can have the program open to a particular document on screen (or several documents), present the New Document dialog box, or present the Open dialog box — depending on your needs for the session.

✦ To make finding a particular document easier, the ClarisWorks Open dialog box contains a Document Type pop-up menu that can restrict document choices to an environment of your choosing.

✦ Using the provided Claris translator filters, ClarisWorks (and other Claris programs) can open or insert many types of non-ClarisWorks files.

✦ You can use the Save command to resave documents that are already stored on disk. You can use the Save As command to save new files and multiple generations or backup copies of existing files.

✦ To keep important documents from being easily viewed by others, you can assign passwords to them.

✦ When you're through with a particular document, you can close its window by clicking its close box or by choosing Close from the File menu. You can simultaneously close all document windows by holding down the Option key while clicking any close box or choosing the Close command.

✦ You can click icons in the Tool panel to add different environment frames to a document, to select drawing tools, and to specify colors, textures, gradients, and patterns for objects. You can hide the Tool panel so you can see larger areas of the document.

✦ The button bar enables you to execute common commands quickly. Its contents change to match the current environment.

✦ You can integrate two or more environments in a single document by using frames.

✦ You can drag selected text from one ClarisWorks document to another, between drag-and-drop enabled programs, and to or from the Macintosh desktop.

✦ You can change the display for any document by hiding or showing tools, resizing the document window, and splitting the screen. If you're working with multiple documents, you can optimize their arrangement with the Tile Windows or Stack Windows commands in the Window menu.

✦ You can print documents from within ClarisWorks or from the desktop.

✦ ClarisWorks offers several forms of program help: the ClarisWorks Help system (QuickHelp), Frequently Asked Questions, a guided tour, and Balloon Help.

✦   ✦   ✦

New Features in ClarisWorks 5.0

Overview

If you have used an earlier version of ClarisWorks and have just upgraded to ClarisWorks 5.0, this chapter will acquaint you with the program's new features and enhancements. The description of each new feature is followed by a reference to the chapter in which it is fully discussed. Thus, this chapter leads you directly to the feature you want to learn about next.

Note If you're still using any version of ClarisWorks prior to 5.0, you can contact Claris Corporation at 800-544-8554 or 408-727-8227 for upgrade information.

ClarisWorks Update History

Although no new environments have been added to ClarisWorks since version 2.0, the program continues to improve — in terms of features, flexibility, and ease of use. You'll see New to Version 5 icons in the margins of this book, which make it easy to identify new features in ClarisWorks 5.0. If you are upgrading from a version earlier than 4.0, however, you may not recognize other features that — although not new in 5.0 — were new in subsequent versions of ClarisWorks (and are new to you). To bring you up to date, the following sections briefly discuss the changes that were introduced in ClarisWorks 2.1, 3.0, and 4.0. The chapter concludes with a list of the new features in ClarisWorks 5.0 and provides references to the chapters in which the features are discussed. If you are upgrading from ClarisWorks 4.0, you can skip directly to this final section.

Note If this is your first version of ClarisWorks, you can skip this entire chapter, because *everything* is new to you!

New in ClarisWorks 2.1

In February 1994, Claris released ClarisWorks 2.1, which included not only a handful of changes that made ClarisWorks easier to use, but also two important new features:

✦ *Hyphenation*. A custom hyphenation dictionary enables you to set automatic hyphenation for any word processing document, database, or text frame. You can also enter discretionary hyphens (which appear only when a word is split across two lines), keep certain words from being hyphenated, and edit the hyphenation dictionary. (Hyphenation is covered in Chapter 3.)

✦ *PowerTalk electronic mail support*. This feature enabled you to add a mailer (an address header) to a ClarisWorks document, making the document a letter you could send to other PowerTalk users. Documents sent via PowerTalk could include enclosures, such as other ClarisWorks documents. Support for PowerTalk messaging has been eliminated in ClarisWorks 5.0.

New in ClarisWorks 3.0

Although the main purpose of ClarisWorks 3.0 was to bring the Windows version of the program up to par with the Macintosh version, a few significant features and enhancements were added to the Mac program:

✦ *Introduction to ClarisWorks*. New users of ClarisWorks will appreciate this guided tour of the program. The feature is still available in ClarisWorks 5.0, and you can run the tour as often as you like by selecting the option from the Balloon Help menu or the Help menu. (The guided tour is discussed in Chapter 1.)

✦ *Welcome screen*. Rather than assume you always want to create a new document, a new Welcome screen enabled you to create a new document, load an existing document, invoke a ClarisWorks Assistant, or view an on-screen tour of ClarisWorks. (The Welcome screen was removed in ClarisWorks 4.0.)

✦ *Assistants*. Assistants are built-in "experts" that make it simple to perform tasks such as formatting footnotes, creating mailing labels and envelopes, and designing newsletters and presentations. (Assistants are discussed in Chapters 1, 3, and 10.)

✦ *Revised Help system*. The Help system was changed dramatically in ClarisWorks 3.0 and is discussed in Chapter 1.

✦ *Document Summary*. You can save identifying information with any file to show a more descriptive title, the name of the person who created the file, a version number, keywords, a category, and a description. (You'll find an explanation of the Document Summary dialog box in Chapter 1.)

✦ *Word count*. This feature provides an accurate count of the number of characters, words, lines, paragraphs, and pages in the current document. Counts in ClarisWorks 3.0, however, were always based on the entire contents of the document. In ClarisWorks 4.0 and higher, this feature can also perform a count on selected text. (See Chapter 3 for more information.)

✦ *Improved Save As and Open dialog boxes.* The new Save As dialog box makes it extremely simple to save any document as a stationery template. With Apple's QuickTime extension, the Open dialog box can show you a thumbnail preview of any graphic image or QuickTime movie before you open the file. (These dialog boxes are discussed in Chapter 1.)

✦ *Automatic macros.* Certain macros can automatically play whenever you launch ClarisWorks, create a new document in a particular environment, or open a document in a particular environment. (See Chapter 13 for a description of automatic macros.)

✦ *Clip art.* To help you create more interesting, attractive documents, ClarisWorks 3.0 included 75 clip-art images. In ClarisWorks 4.0 and higher, clip-art images are organized in libraries (discussed in Chapter 21).

✦ *MacWrite Pro file filter.* ClarisWorks 3.0 added a filter that can translate files created with MacWrite Pro.

New in ClarisWorks 4.0

As in most previous ClarisWorks updates, version 4.0 introduced a few new, big features and a host of small tweaks, enhancements, and changes.

General enhancements

✦ *Stylesheet palette.* ClarisWorks 4.0 introduced a Stylesheet palette you can use to format text, paragraphs, outlines, spreadsheet tables, and graphics quickly. In addition to using the predefined styles, you can also create your own reusable styles. (See Chapter 15 for details.)

✦ *Drag-and-drop support.* Many items that were previously moved via cut-and-paste can now be moved within a document or copied between documents by simply dragging. In version 4.0, ClarisWorks became capable of exchanging text and graphics with other drag-and-drop enabled applications, such as the Scrapbook.

✦ *Libraries.* ClarisWorks 4.0 included 20 ReadyArt libraries of clip art, each organized around a theme, such as education, flags, and foods. Any of the supplied images can be dragged and dropped into your documents. You can also create new libraries to store your own graphics, important text, spreadsheet formulas, and QuickTime movies. (Libraries are discussed in Chapter 21.)

✦ *New Assistants.* ClarisWorks Assistants make it simple to accomplish common personal and business tasks by guiding you through the process via a series of dialog boxes. ClarisWorks 4.0 added new Assistants for home finance, generating mailing labels, and creating certificates. (Assistants are discussed generally in Chapter 10. You'll find additional information about the Mailing

Label Assistant in Chapter 5. Assistants related to word processing tasks are described in Chapter 3.)

✦ *HTML translator and stationery document.* Because people are continually expressing interest in the Internet and the World Wide Web, ClarisWorks 4.0 can be used to create and translate HTML (HyperText Markup Language) documents to present information and graphics on the Web. A stationery document with predefined HTML tag styles was also provided. (For information on viewing, editing, and creating HTML documents, see Chapter 22.)

✦ *Sample AppleScripts.* If you have Apple Computer's AppleScript software installed on your Mac, you can use the sample AppleScripts to print batches of documents, translate groups of non-ClarisWorks documents to ClarisWorks format, run remote slide shows, or use FileMaker Pro data in a mail merge.

Spreadsheet enhancements

✦ *Cell shading.* In previous versions of ClarisWorks, spreadsheet embellishments were largely limited to applying borders, choosing fonts, and adding a background color. ClarisWorks 4.0 enabled you to apply colors and patterns to individual worksheet cells. (See Chapter 4 for more information.)

✦ *Fill Special command.* Spreadsheet users are familiar with the Fill Down and Fill Right commands (enabling you to create mathematical sequences or to number a series of rows, for example). Fill Special is a more powerful version of these two commands, making it easy to create a numerical sequence without having to figure out the formula or label a series of cells with dates, times, month names, days, or quarters. (The Fill Special command is discussed in Chapter 4.)

Database enhancements

✦ *New field types.* ClarisWorks 4.0 introduced seven new field types: name, pop-up menu, radio buttons, check box, serial number, value list, and record info. (See Chapter 5 for a discussion of the new field types and the other changes to the database environment.)

✦ *List mode.* In previous versions of ClarisWorks, all data entry, editing, and record viewing was done in Browse mode. By selecting List mode, any database can now be viewed and worked with in a spreadsheet-like grid.

✦ *Named searches and sorts.* ClarisWorks 4.0 enabled you to save Sort and Find instructions for each database so they could easily be re-executed whenever you liked.

✦ *Report generator.* Report-creation instructions (including the name of the layout to be used, the Sort and Find instructions, and whether or not the report should automatically be printed) can also be saved.

✦ *Mailing Label Assistant.* ClarisWorks 4.0 provided a new Assistant for creating mailing labels.

Word processing enhancements

✦ *Sections*. Complex documents (such as books and reports) can now be divided into logical sections. Each section can have its own title page as well as different headers and footers. Left- and right-facing pages are also supported. (See Chapter 3 for a discussion of the new word processing features.)

✦ *Outlining*. In earlier versions of ClarisWorks, a word processing document could be displayed in normal or outline view. In ClarisWorks 4.0, outlining was fully integrated into the word processing environment — enabling you to create an outline within a regular word processing document.

✦ *Endnotes*. In previous versions of the program, only footnotes could be produced. With the new support for endnotes, users can now move all in-text citations to the end of the current document.

✦ *Selective word count*. In addition to being capable of gathering word count statistics for an entire document, ClarisWorks 4.0 can also create a report based on the current text selection.

✦ *Paragraph Styles menu*. Paragraph and outline formats can be chosen and applied from this pop-up menu in the ruler bar. (In ClarisWorks 5.0, this pop-up menu has been moved to the button bar.)

✦ *New font styles*. ClarisWorks 4.0 added three new font styles: superior, inferior, and double underline.

✦ *On-screen mail merge preview*. When performing a mail merge, users can preview how their documents will look and print using actual merge data.

Drawing enhancements

✦ *Free rotation*. In previous versions of the program, draw objects could only be rotated in 90-degree increments. In ClarisWorks 4.0, objects could be rotated to any angle by using either the Free Rotation or Object Info command (now called the Object Size command in ClarisWorks 5.0). (See Chapter 6 for information on using these commands.)

New in ClarisWorks 5.0

No new environments appear in ClarisWorks 5.0, but the product has acquired a new name and is available in two versions: ClarisWorks 5.0 (the core program) and ClarisWorks Office (ClarisWorks 5.0, plus Internet- and business-related add-on software). ClarisWorks 5.0 is available only to the educational market and as a product upgrade; ClarisWorks Office is the sole retail product.

The most significant features added to the base product are the customizable button bars (replacing the former Shortcuts palette); bookmark, document, and URL links, as well as the new Links palette; and improved support for creating Web pages in ClarisWorks.

ClarisWorks Office enhancements

✦ *Add-ons.* What distinguishes ClarisWorks Office from ClarisWorks 5.0 is a series of add-on programs and templates that are only available as part of ClarisWorks Office. Included are Netscape Navigator (a popular program for browsing the World Wide Web), Claris Home Page Lite (a Web-page design program), and a series of business templates. (For general information about the add-ons and Claris Home Page Lite, see Chapter 23.)

General enhancements

✦ *Button bars.* In previous versions of the program, you could click buttons in the floating Shortcuts palette to perform common and — occasionally — esoteric tasks in any environment. Customizable button bars that are displayed above the current document have taken the place of the Shortcuts palette. (Button bars are covered in Chapter 12.)

✦ *Bookmark, document, and URL links.* Text, objects, and frames can be designated as clickable links in ClarisWorks 5.0 documents. Depending on the type of link, clicking can make the document automatically scroll to a bookmark in the same document, open a different document (including ones created by programs other than ClarisWorks), or launch your Web browser and display a particular page on the World Wide Web. (The new links and the Link palette are discussed in Chapters 19 and 22.)

✦ *Passwords.* To improve security, passwords can be assigned to documents, as explained in Chapter 1.

✦ *Default font.* You can now specify a default font to be used for all text, as explained in Chapter 11.

✦ *Compound styles.* By enabling compound styles, you can apply multiple styles from the current stylesheet to selected text. (Refer to Chapter 15.)

✦ *Business Card Assistant.* This new Assistant enables you to create business cards quickly in several different styles. (For a general discussion of Assistants, see Chapter 10.)

✦ *Context-sensitive help for dialog boxes.* Every major dialog box now has a ? (Help) button that — when clicked — summons help that is relevant to the dialog box. (See Chapter 1 for more information about ClarisHelp.)

✦ *Fonts.* Seven free TrueType fonts are included with ClarisWorks 5.0.

✦ *File translators.* To improve ClarisWorks's file translation capabilities, a special version of the DataViz file translators, control panel, and extensions is provided.

Word processing enhancements

✦ *Ruler guidelines.* When setting margins and tabs in a word processing document, a temporary vertical line extends down the page.

✦ *Equation Editor.* Statisticians and others who work with numbers will be pleased to learn about the new Equation Editor. By selecting options from pop-up menus, you can create extremely complex equations and place them in your documents as resizable graphics.

✦ *Paragraph Sorter.* Using the new Paragraph Sorter Assistant, you can arrange any selected group of paragraphs alphabetically or randomly.

✦ *Descent setting for in-line objects.* In previous versions of ClarisWorks, in-line graphics could be resized but not moved up or down to improve their appearance within the surrounding text. Using the new Descent command, you can raise or lower the placement of any in-line graphic.

Database enhancements

✦ *Multimedia fields.* The new multimedia field type is used to store QuickTime movies, graphics, and sounds in ClarisWorks databases (see Chapter 5). The movies and sounds can be played by clicking the field in which they are stored.

Spreadsheet enhancements

✦ *Named ranges.* To make it simpler to identify key ranges in worksheets, users can now name them and refer to them in formulas by name (Quarterly Sales, for example), rather than by address (C3..C6, for example). Named ranges are discussed in Chapter 4.

Paint enhancements

✦ *New graphic file formats.* Graphic files can now be opened or saved in BMP, GIF, and JPEG formats, improving compatibility with Microsoft Windows and the World Wide Web.

Internet enhancements

✦ *URL links.* Hyperlinks to specific Web pages can be embedded in most ClarisWorks documents. When the hyperlink is clicked, the user's Web browser is launched and the Web page is loaded from the Internet. (URL links are covered in Chapters 19 and 22.)

✦ *Improved HTML translator.* Any standard word processing document can be translated into HTML format — the language of pages on the World Wide Web. To make it even easier to design Web pages, a dozen new stationery templates for personal, business, and student Web pages are provided.

During the process of translating the documents to HTML, embedded graphics are automatically converted to GIF or JPEG format. Support has also been added for tables and page backgrounds. (See Chapter 22 to learn about creating Web pages with ClarisWorks 5.0.)

✦ *Internet button bar.* ClarisWorks 5.0 includes a special Internet button bar that enables you to configure your Macintosh for the Internet, launch a Web browser or e-mail program, add hyperlinks to a document, convert the current document into a Web page, or summon assistance from the Claris Web site. (The Internet button bar is discussed in Chapter 22.)

Using the ClarisWorks Environments

❖   ❖   ❖   ❖

The Word Processing Environment

Overview

Everyone writes. And whether you're working on a letter,
memo, fax, report, or the Great American Novel, a word
processor is the ideal writing tool.

About Word Processors

A word processing program makes it easy for you to edit,
reorganize, and polish your writing. Spelling checkers,
thesauruses, and grammar checkers help you choose the best
(and correct) words. Because you create documents on the
Mac's screen, you can avoid paper waste by not printing until
the document is exactly as you want it. Instead of making
copies of documents for your files, you can simply save them
on disk. If you ever need to refer to the original document
again or want another printed copy, you just open the
document in the word processor. Finally, you can store
frequently used paragraphs on disk and reuse them whenever
you like. You can copy and paste them into the document,
move them from one document to another using drag-and-
drop, or save them as reusable stationery documents (as
described in Chapter 10).

Note

As you read this chapter, keep in mind that almost everything
in it applies to word processing frames as well as documents.
In addition, some of the features you traditionally associate
with word processing, such as the spelling checker and
rulers, are also available in other ClarisWorks environments.
This chapter includes a discussion of these features (because
this is where you'd normally expect to read about them), and
other chapters refer you back to this chapter as necessary.

Word Processing Essentials

The first step in using the word processor is to create a new word processing document. In ClarisWorks, you do this by choosing New from the File menu (or pressing ⌘-N) and selecting Word Processing in the scrolling list box. A blank document opens (see Figure 3-1) with the cursor positioned at the top of the page, ready for you to start entering text.

Text insertion point   I-beam cursor   Ruler   Page guide

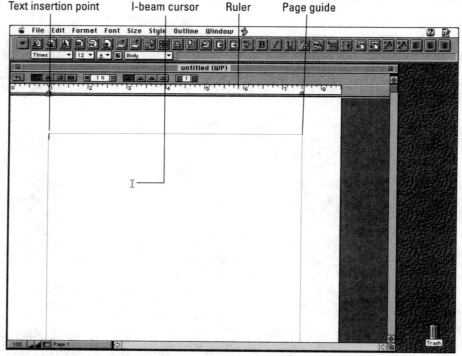

Figure 3-1: A new word processing document

Text you type, paste, or add with the Insert command always appears at the *text insertion point*. The insertion point is marked by a tiny vertical line. You can change the insertion point by moving the mouse and then clicking in a new location anywhere within the existing text. To help you accurately position the text insertion point, ClarisWorks displays an *I-beam cursor* (shown in Figure 3-1) as you move the mouse over the page.

Note

In ClarisWorks 5, you can also add text to a word processing document or frame by simply dragging it from another open ClarisWorks document or from any drag-and-drop-enabled application, such as SimpleText. This same technique can also be used to move text within a document as well as move objects between documents.

As you type, ClarisWorks automatically handles line ends by wrapping extra text to the next line. When you approach the end of a line, the word processor checks whether the word you are typing, plus the other words in the line, exceed the printable page width. If so, the last word is automatically moved or *wrapped* to the next line. Unlike with a typewriter, you don't have to press Return to start a new line in a word processing document. You just keep typing. In fact, the only times you should press Return are to end a paragraph or to insert an extra blank line between paragraphs.

In addition to reformatting lines for you, the word processor features *automatic repagination.* As you insert, delete, or move text in the document, the program automatically adjusts the composition of the pages. Suppose, for example, you add a couple of paragraphs to the middle of a report. If you are using a typewriter, you have to retype all the pages that follow the insertion. In the ClarisWorks word processor, however, any text following the two new paragraphs automatically shifts down, and the program forms new pages as required. Large deletions work the same way. When you delete, the word processor automatically closes up the space and repaginates the document.

Like all current word processing programs, the ClarisWorks word processor is *paragraph-oriented.* Tabs, indents, and text alignment options that you apply always affect an entire paragraph — not just the line where the text insertion point happens to be. When you press Return, a new paragraph is started, which — by default — contains the same settings as the previous paragraph. Because each paragraph is treated as a separate entity, you can change settings on a paragraph-by-paragraph basis.

You also can apply text-formatting options such as fonts, sizes, and styles to entire paragraphs or to selected text strings within a paragraph. You simply select some text and then choose the appropriate text-formatting commands from the Font, Size, and Style menus.

Navigation

ClarisWorks provides several ways to navigate through a document without changing the insertion point. If you're just reading a document on screen or checking what was written on Page 7, for example, you can use the techniques in Table 3-1 to move through the document. Again, when you are using these techniques, the text insertion point does not change.

Table 3-1 Navigational Techniques	
Navigation	*Key or Action*
Move up or down one line of text	Click the up- or down-arrow symbol on the scroll bar.
Move up or down one screenful of text	Press the Page Up or Page Down key (extended keyboard only) or click in the gray area of the vertical scroll bar.
Move up or down to an approximate location	Drag the box in the vertical scroll bar to a new position.
Move to the beginning or end of the document	Press the Home or End key (extended keyboard only) or drag the box in the scroll bar to the top or bottom.
Go to a specific page	Double-click in the page number area at the bottom of the document and type a page number in the dialog box that appears.

Elementary Text Editing

Few of us are blessed with the ability to write precisely what we want the very first time. In fact, depending on the type and complexity of the document, we may actually spend more time editing than doing the initial writing. This section describes some essential techniques for text editing in the word processing environment.

Selecting text

To manipulate text — to cut it, change the font or style, and so on — you first have to select it.

To select text, position the cursor where you want the selection to start and then either Shift-click where you want it to end or drag to complete the selection. In addition to this basic text-selection technique, you can also use these shortcuts:

✦ To select a single word, double-click anywhere within the word.

✦ To select the current line, triple-click anywhere within the line.

✦ To select the current paragraph, quadruple-click anywhere within the paragraph.

✦ To select the entire document, choose Select All from the Edit menu (or press ⌘-A).

Inserting text in a word processing document or frame

Whether you type text, paste it, insert it with the Insert command, or drag it in from another document, it is always entered at the text insertion point (described previously). You can enter new text into a word processing document or a text frame.

Position the cursor over the spot where you want to insert the text and click the mouse button once, or use the arrow keys to move the cursor as described in Table 3-2. Type the text, paste it, or enter it with the Insert command from the File menu.

Table 3-2 Insertion Point Navigational Shortcuts	
Cursor Movement	**Keystroke**
One character left or right	Left- or right-arrow key
One line up or down	Up- or down-arrow key
To the start or end of a line	⌘-left arrow or ⌘-right arrow
One word to the left or right	Option-left arrow or Option-right arrow
To the beginning or end of a paragraph	Option-up arrow or Option-down arrow
To the beginning or end of the document	⌘-up arrow or ⌘-down arrow
Continuous scrolling	Hold down the up- or down-arrow key

When you position the cursor, you need to place it immediately before, after, or within the current text of the document. In a new, blank document, for example, no matter where you click, the insertion point is set at the start of the first page. Similarly, even if you click several inches below the last paragraph in a partially written document, the insertion point is placed immediately following the last character of the document. If you want to start typing well below the current end of the document, you can press Return several times to add the necessary white space so you can position the insertion point where you want it.

When using drag-and-drop to copy or move text, a small vertical insertion bar appears immediately above the cursor, showing exactly where the dragged text will be inserted.

Deleting text from a word processing document or frame

Nobody's perfect. Part of the writing process is deleting text — either character by character or entire text blocks.

To delete a character, position the cursor to the right of the character and press Delete or Backspace. Each key press deletes one character to the left of the cursor. If you have an extended keyboard, you can position the cursor to the left of the character you want to delete and press the Del key. Each press of the Del key deletes one character to the right of the cursor.

To delete a text block, select the text and press Delete, Backspace, Clear, or Del, or choose Clear from the Edit menu. Each of these operations deletes the text selection without copying it to the Macintosh Clipboard. You can also choose Cut from the Edit menu (or press ⌘-X). This method simultaneously deletes the text selection and copies it to the Clipboard. Use this approach when you want to paste the text elsewhere — either in the current document or in another one.

Copying and reusing text

The Copy command comes in handy when you have text strings or phrases you want to use in several places in a document or copy to a different document. To copy text, select the text to be copied, and choose Copy from the Edit menu (or press ⌘-C). A copy of the selected text is transferred to the Clipboard, and the text is immediately available for pasting. Until you copy or cut (⌘-X) something else to the Clipboard, you can paste the copied text repeatedly (⌘-V) in the current document as well as in other documents.

Note

You can also use drag-and-drop to move text within the current document. This works like a cut-and-paste, but does not affect the contents of the Clipboard. When text is dragged from one document to another, the effect is like a copy-and-paste. Again, the Clipboard is unaffected.

Moving text in a word processing document or frame

In ClarisWorks, moving text is usually a two-step process: cut and then paste. You cut selected text from the document and then paste it in another position in the document. To move text by cutting and pasting, select the text to be moved, and choose the Cut command from the Edit menu (or press ⌘-X). The text is deleted and then moved to the Clipboard. Move the text insertion point to the spot where you want to move the text. Choose the Paste command from the Edit menu (or press ⌘-V). The previously cut text is pasted at the text insertion point.

Using the Macintosh Clipboard

Throughout this book, and in many other Macintosh books, magazines, and manuals, you see frequent references to the *Clipboard*. What is the Clipboard, and how does it work?

The Clipboard is a temporary storage area in Macintosh *RAM* (memory). The last object or text selection you copied with the Copy command (⌘-C) or removed with the Cut command (⌘-X) is stored in the Clipboard. Each time you copy or cut a new object or text selection, the new object or text replaces the current contents of the Clipboard.

The beauty of the Clipboard is that whatever it currently contains is available for pasting with the Paste command (⌘-V). And not only can you paste the object or text into the current document, you also can paste it into other documents, even into documents in other programs. You can, for example, copy a name and address from a word processing document and paste it into an address book desk accessory (or vice versa).

The only actions that clear the contents of the Clipboard are cutting or copying a new object or text selection and turning off the Mac. Otherwise, you can quit one program and start another, confident that the Clipboard's contents are still intact. (Note, however, that a few Mac programs create their own Clipboard — separate from the Mac's general Clipboard. Information that is copied or cut to a program-specific Clipboard may not be available for pasting in other programs. See your program manuals for details.)

Tip

ClarisWorks also provides a shortcut for directly moving a text selection to a new location without using the normal cut-and-paste routine or drag-and-drop. To use this method, select the text to be moved and hold down the ⌘ and Option keys while you use the mouse button to click the destination location in the document. The text is transferred from its original location to the destination.

Undoing your actions

While typing or editing a document, you'll probably make errors. You may find you've typed a phrase in the wrong spot — perhaps in the middle of a word — or you've chosen the wrong formatting command. You may be able to correct the damage by using the Undo command.

ClarisWorks keeps track of the last thing you did to change the current document, such as cutting text, typing new text, or applying formatting to text. If ClarisWorks can undo the last action, choosing the Undo command from the Edit menu (or pressing ⌘-Z) puts the document back to the condition it was in immediately before you performed the action. The wording of the Undo command changes to reflect the last action. If, for example, the last change you made was a cut, the command reads *Undo Cut*.

After choosing Undo, you can still change your mind. The Undo menu command now reads Redo *command* (in this case, Redo Cut). Choose the Redo command, and the Undo is undone.

Caution

Undo tracks only the *last* change you made to the document. If you delete some text and then type new text, you cannot undo the deletion. For the Undo command to work, you have to catch the error immediately — before you make any other change to the document. Also, you cannot undo some actions. Saving a new version of a file over an existing file is one example. In those instances, the Undo command is grayed out and reads *Can't Undo.* Think carefully before you make major changes (and be sure to keep current backups).

If you've been experimenting with a document and want to undo all the changes you've made, choose the Revert command from the File menu. Revert replaces the document on screen with a copy of the most recently saved version of the file. It's as though you closed the current document without saving it and then reloaded the original document from disk. Be careful when using Revert — you cannot undo it by using the Undo command. Also note that you can use Revert with any type of ClarisWorks document, not just with word processing files.

Formatting: Word Processing with Style

Formatting is what distinguishes an ordinary document from one with style. Sure, you can just pick a standard font (such as Times or Helvetica) and type the entire document, pausing only to press Return now and then to begin a new paragraph. But the word processor enables you to do much more. You can choose different fonts for headers and body text, apply italic to selected phrases to add emphasis, set left and right indents differently for different paragraphs, create hanging indents to format bullet lists, and use tabs to align items in a list or columns of numbers. You will learn to master these formatting commands, and others, in this section.

Within the word processing environment, there are four classes of formatting:

✦ *Text formatting* is concerned with applying fonts, sizes, and styles to characters, words, phrases, sentences, and paragraphs.

✦ *Paragraph formatting* enables you to set tabs, indents, line spacing, and between-paragraph spacing for paragraphs.

✦ *Section formatting* enables you to divide a document into logical chunks (such as chapters) and specify whether a section begins with a title page, whether left- and right-hand headers and footers are different from each other, and whether page numbering should pick up where the last chapter ended or restart at a particular number. You can also set a different number of columns for text in different sections.

✦ *Document formatting* governs the look of the entire document. It includes setting margins, controlling the on-screen appearance of margins and page guides, setting a starting page number for the document, and specifying whether the document will have footnotes or endnotes.

Note

ClarisWorks has two related features to help you consistently apply text and paragraph styles. They are the Stylesheet palette and the Stylesheet pop-up menu. Both are discussed briefly in this chapter. (For additional information about stylesheets, see Chapter 15.)

Formatting words

Formatting words, as discussed here, refers to applying different fonts, sizes, and styles. Although you can apply these formats to individual characters within a document, you'll usually format words and phrases.

Changing fonts and styles

Most people format correspondence and reports using a single font in a single size. When you want to make some text stand out (for example, by applying italic to emphasize a phrase or by changing the font to differentiate a header from body text), ClarisWorks enables you to apply different fonts, sizes, and styles.

To enter text in a document using a specific font, size, or style, position the text insertion point and choose from the Font, Size, or Style menu before typing. To change existing text, select it and then choose a new font, size, or style from the corresponding menu.

Although each character can have only one font and size combination (Helvetica 12 point, for example), you can assign multiple styles to any text. To apply additional styles, select some text and then choose the Style commands you want to apply to the text.

Styles you can combine include the following:

✦ **Bold** (⌘-B)

✦ *Italic* (⌘-I)

✦ <u>Underline</u> (⌘-U) or <u>Double Underline</u>

✦ ~~Strikethrough~~

✦ Outline

✦ Shadow

In addition, you can do the following:

✦ Apply a color to selected text by choosing a color from the Text Color pop-up menu in the button bar.

✦ Move letters in a text string closer together (Condense) or farther apart (Extend).

✦ Format characters so they appear higher (Superscript, Shift-⌘-+), lower (Subscript, Shift-⌘--), higher in a reduced size (Superior), or lower in a reduced size (Inferior) than the surrounding text.

Note

The following sets of styles are mutually exclusive: Condense and Extend; Underline and Double Underline; and Superscript, Subscript, Superior, and Inferior.

New In Version 5

If the button bar is visible (choose Show Button Bar from the Window menu or press Shift-⌘-X), you can quickly set the font, size, style, and color of text by choosing options from the pop-up menus, as shown in Figure 3-2.

Figure 3-2: The button bar provides pop-up menus for common text-formatting options.

Removing styles

Each command in the Style menu works as a toggle. To remove a single style from a text string, select the text and choose the style command you want to remove (italic, for example). This method of removing styles is particularly useful when a text string has several styles and you want to remove one or some of them but leave the other styles intact. You can instantly remove all styles (except color) from text by selecting the text and then choosing Plain Text (⌘-T) from the Style menu.

Formatting paragraphs

The ClarisWorks word processor treats every paragraph as a distinct entity. If you like, you can give every paragraph different settings for tabs, indents, alignment, and the spacing between lines and between paragraphs. You can set these paragraph formatting options with the ruler or choose the Paragraph and Tabs commands from the Format menu.

Note

When you type new paragraphs, each time you press Return to end one paragraph and begin another, ClarisWorks automatically applies the format of the previous paragraph to the new paragraph. These formatting options remain in effect for additional paragraphs until you specifically change them.

Using the ruler

The word processing ruler serves a greater function than simply showing the page width. By clicking and dragging, you can use the ruler to set most paragraph formatting options, as shown in Figure 3-3.

Choosing and Using Fonts

Regardless of the type of document you're working on, you'll do well to restrict your use of fonts to a small number — perhaps two. (Too many fonts can make a document look like a ransom note.) Within a selected font (Helvetica or Times, for example), you can freely apply other typefaces and styles, such as italic, bold, and so on.

Fonts can be divided into two general types that are referred to as *serif* and *sans serif*. A serif font, such as Times, has angular points and lines (called *serifs*) at the base and top of each character. Serif fonts are designed to be easy on the eyes and are regularly used to format body text. Sans serif fonts, such as Helvetica, are essentially smooth (they have no serifs) and are often used as headings (*sans* means *no* or *without*).

If you're new at selecting and using fonts (as most of us are), try these suggestions as a starting point:

✦ For body text, choose a serif font (such as Times, Palatino, or Adobe Garamond).

✦ For heads, use a sans serif font (such as Helvetica Bold or Franklin Gothic).

Figure 3-3: The ruler and its components

The options you can set with the ruler include:

✦ Outline styles (bullet, check box, or Harvard, for example)

✦ Paragraph alignment (left, center, right, or justified)

✦ Line spacing

✦ Indents (left, right, and first)

✦ Tab stops (left, center, right, or decimal)

✦ Number of columns (described in "Columns," later in this chapter)

When you want to make minor changes to paragraph formatting, this visually guided approach is easy to use. Just change ruler settings until the paragraph looks right. If the ruler isn't visible, choose Show Rulers from the Window menu (or press Shift-⌘-U). To hide the ruler, choose Hide Rulers from the Window menu (or press Shift-⌘-U).

Custom Text Styles

As you work with the word processor, you may find that you frequently use some special text styles (12-point Helvetica Bold, for example). Text styles in the stylesheet are called *basic styles*. You can add custom text styles to the stylesheet, edit existing styles, delete styles, and import or export styles (enabling you to share styles among documents and users). In addition to text styles, the stylesheet can also contain paragraph and outline styles that you can use in word processing documents.

To apply a text style to selected text, display the Stylesheet palette (choose Show Stylesheet from the Window menu or press Shift-⌘-W) and click the name of the style in the Stylesheet palette. Paragraph styles can be selected from the Stylesheet palette or from the Paragraph Styles menu in the ruler bar. (See Chapter 15 for information about using stylesheets in the word processor as well as in other environments.)

New In Version 5

You can now apply multiple text styles to the same text by choosing the Compound Styles command from the stylesheet's Edit menu. When the Compound Styles command is not chosen, each stylesheet text style you set for a particular text block automatically replaces the previously set style.

Although most people prefer a ruler that measures in inches, you can change the measurement units, as well as specify the number of ruler divisions (up to 14). Examples of the different measurement units are shown in Figure 3-4.

Figure 3-4: Text ruler measurement units

Steps: Setting Ruler Measurement Units and Divisions

1. Open an existing word processing document or create a new document.
2. Choose Rulers from the Format menu. The Rulers dialog box appears (see Figure 3-5).

Figure 3-5: The Rulers dialog box

3. Select either the text ruler or the graphics ruler by clicking the appropriate radio button in the Ruler Type box.

The text ruler is a standard horizontal ruler that appears at the top of the page. Selecting the graphics ruler creates a pair of rulers: a horizontal ruler across the top of the page and a vertical ruler down the left side of the page. Graphics rulers, however, are only aids for positioning; they do not contain the same controls that text rulers have. Thus, graphics rulers are not recommended for use with word processing documents — unless you are trying to position a frame or draw object precisely within a page (or something similar).

4. Select a unit of measurement by clicking the appropriate radio button in the Units box.

5. Type a number in the Divisions text-edit box to indicate the number of minor divisions you want in each segment of the ruler. You can specify a maximum of 512 divisions, although ClarisWorks can display only as many as 14 division marks on the ruler.

6. Click OK. A ruler appears with the units and divisions you specified.

ClarisWorks saves the ruler with the document. Note that every document can have a different type of ruler with different divisions.

If you find, for example, that you prefer a ruler with points as the units of measurement rather than inches, you may want to create a blank stationery document that contains that style of ruler. You can also make that style of ruler the default for *all* new word processing documents by including the ruler in a default stationery document. (Chapter 10 includes instructions for creating both types of stationery files.)

Setting indents

Indents are paragraph-specific settings that indicate how far in from the left or right margins the text should be positioned. In ClarisWorks, as in other word processors, you can set a first line indent so the first line is treated differently from other lines in the paragraph. First line indents can be used to create *hanging indents*. Indents are useful for formatting bullet lists, numbered lists, and quotations, as shown in Figure 3-6.

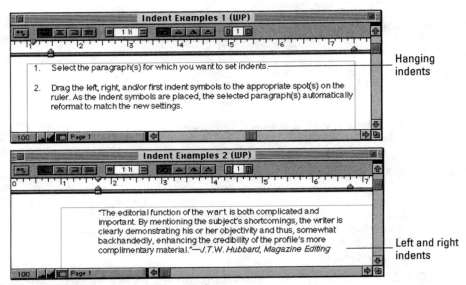

Figure 3-6: Examples of different indents

To set indents with the ruler, select the paragraph or paragraphs for which you want to set the indents and drag the left, right, and/or first indent symbols to the appropriate locations on the ruler. As the indent symbols are placed, the selected paragraphs automatically reformat to match the new settings.

As you drag the indent markers, ClarisWorks 5 extends a dotted line down the page, showing precisely where the new margins or indents will appear.

Hanging indents

Hanging indents are frequently used in documents, particularly for formatting numbered lists and bullet lists. (In a *hanging indent*, the first line begins farther to the left than the remaining lines.) To create a hanging indent, drag the left indent marker (upward-pointing triangle on the left side of the ruler) to the right. Its location marks the spot where the text will begin. Drag the first line marker (the downward-pointing triangle at the top of the ruler) to the desired position. Its location marks the spot where the numbers or bullets will appear. (If you want the numbers or bullets to be flush with the left margin, you don't need to change the position of the first line marker.) Refer to the ruler in the top half of Figure 3-6 for an example of a hanging indent.

New In Version 5

The left indent marker can now be moved with the first line marker or independently from it. To move the left indent marker alone, click and drag the triangular portion of the marker. To move the left indent and first line markers together, click and drag the small rectangle beneath the left indent marker.

To form the hanging indent, start by typing the number or bullet symbol. Then press Tab and type the text of the step or point. If the text is longer than one line, the additional text automatically wraps to the position of the left indent marker.

Tip

ClarisWorks 4.0 and 5.0 contain predefined styles you can use to format paragraphs instantly to show bullets or sequential numbers. Select the paragraphs, and then choose Bullet or Number from the Paragraph Styles menu in the ruler bar or from the Stylesheet palette. Note, however, that you're stuck with the style of bullets or numbers ClarisWorks provides. You cannot change the bullet character (using a Zapf Dingbats character, for example), nor can you change the font or style of the numbers.

Paragraph alignment

Most documents are *left-aligned* (flush with the left margin and with a ragged right margin). For those times when you need it, however, ClarisWorks also provides options for center-aligned, right-aligned, and justified paragraphs. Figure 3-7 shows examples of the four types of paragraph alignment.

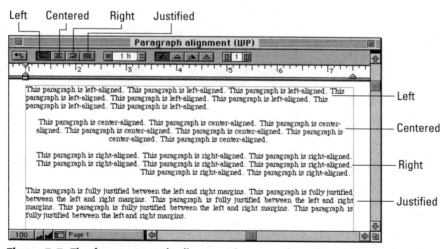

Figure 3-7: The four paragraph alignment icons on the ruler and examples of aligned paragraphs

Making a document title *center-aligned* centers it on the page; you don't need to mess with tabs or the spacebar. You can use the *right-align* setting to position the current date in a letter.

Justified paragraphs are flush with both the left and right margins. ClarisWorks automatically adds extra space between words to make each line edge square with the margins. Magazine articles often have justified paragraphs.

To set paragraph alignment, select the paragraph or paragraphs for which you want to set an alignment and click one of the four paragraph alignment icons in the ruler bar. The chosen alignment is applied to the selected paragraphs.

To be precise, alignment affects the selected paragraph within the current *column*. If you are working in a multicolumn page, a centered title paragraph will be centered within the column rather than across the entire page.

Line spacing

Most documents are printed *single-spaced* (with no blank lines between lines of text). Occasionally, however, you need to alter the between-line spacing. High school and college homework, for example, must often be *double-spaced* (with one blank line between every pair of text lines). Manuscripts submitted to magazines and book publishers must sometimes be double-spaced as well — to make it easier for an editor to edit and write comments on the printed copy.

To set line spacing, select the paragraphs for which you want to set between-line spacing. In the ruler bar, click the line spacing icon on the left to decrease the between-line spacing or click the line spacing icon on the right to increase the between-line spacing. Assuming you have not changed the measurement units from *Lines* (the default setting), line spacing always increases or decreases in half-line increments. The minimum line spacing is 1 line; the maximum is 10 lines. Figure 3-8 shows examples of several of the most common settings for line spacing.

Like other ruler settings, line spacing can be different for every paragraph in a ClarisWorks word processing document. If you want to set line spacing for the entire document, choose Select All from the Edit menu (or press ⌘-A) and then select a line spacing option.

Line spacing also can be set using the Paragraph command (discussed later in this chapter).

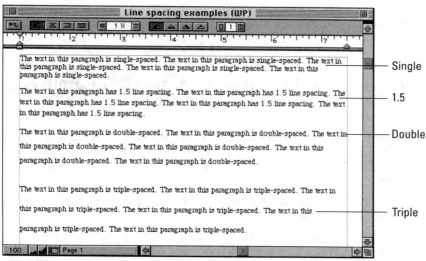

Figure 3-8: Some line spacing examples

Tab stops

If you're familiar with a typewriter (I haven't touched one in more than 20 years), you already know about tabs. Tabs are used to align text in columns, create tables, and position important text strings precisely (enabling you to right-align a page number in a footer, for example). ClarisWorks offers four tab-stop options: left, center, right, and decimal. Figure 3-9 shows examples of the four types of tab stops.

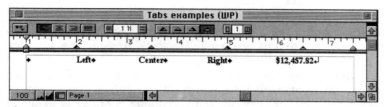

Figure 3-9: Left, center, right, and decimal tabs

Tabs can be set in two ways: by dragging them onto the ruler or by typing their exact locations using the Tab command. After you set a tab, you can reposition it by simply dragging it to a new location on the ruler. You can remove a tab by dragging it off the ruler.

To set tab stops with the ruler, begin by selecting the paragraph or paragraphs for which you want to set tab stops. Click a tab icon and drag it into position on the ruler. As you manually position the tab stop, ClarisWorks 5.0 extends a line down the page to show where the tab will appear.

You can quickly create a new tab stop by clicking the desired tab type (left, center, right, or decimal) and then clicking the spot on the ruler where you want the tab stop to be set.

Steps: Setting Tab Stops with the Tab Command

1. Select the paragraph or paragraphs for which you want to set tab stops.

2. Choose the Tab command from the Format menu. The Tab dialog box appears. (If the Tab dialog box covers any of the paragraphs that will be affected by the command, you can drag the dialog box to a different position.)

   You can quickly summon the Tab dialog box by double-clicking any of the four tab icons on the ruler bar.

3. Choose the settings for the first tab stop you want to set. Click the radio button for the alignment desired, type a number in the Position box, and (optional) click a radio button to select a fill pattern (also called a *leader*).

   A leader is a character, such as a period, that fills the blank space leading up to the tab. Leader characters are particularly useful for formatting entries in a table of contents and separating invoice items from prices (as in, Jello......$0.49).

4. Click Apply to insert the new tab.

5. Repeat Steps 3 and 4 for additional tabs you want to set at this time.

6. Click OK to accept the new tab settings or Cancel to revert to the original tab settings.

The Tab dialog box does not provide a method for removing tab stops. Regardless of how you set tabs, you have to remove them manually by dragging them off the ruler.

The decimal tab (the Align On option) is followed by a text-edit box. Although you normally set such a tab to align on a decimal point (.), you can specify any character you like. You may, for example, want a column of numbers to align on the percent sign (%).

When you are creating a document, such as a résumé, that uses many different indentations, use tabs instead of spaces between items. Although spaces may look as good as tabs on the screen, the printout may look quite different. Tabs are also much easier to adjust than spaces.

Using the Copy Ruler and Apply Ruler commands

After you set formatting options for a paragraph, you may want to reuse these settings in other paragraphs in the document. For example, when writing a report, you may create a paragraph format for long quotations. Manually recreating this format each time you have a new quote is time consuming and prone to error. To simplify the transfer of paragraph formats, ClarisWorks provides the Copy Ruler and Apply Ruler commands.

The stylesheet is also particularly useful for storing and applying paragraph styles. (See Chapter 15 for information about stylesheets.)

Steps: Applying Ruler Settings to a New Paragraph

1. Move the cursor into the paragraph whose ruler settings you want to copy.

2. Choose Copy Ruler from the Format menu (or press Shift-⌘-C).

3. Move the cursor into the target paragraph.

Alternatively, you can use normal text-selection techniques to select several contiguous paragraphs to which you want to apply the ruler settings.

4. Choose Apply Ruler from the Format menu (or press Shift-⌘-V). The ruler settings from the copied ruler are applied to the selected paragraph(s).

Note that the Apply Ruler command remains active even after you paste the settings. You can continue to paste these settings into additional paragraphs until you quit ClarisWorks or issue a new Copy Ruler command.

You also can use the Copy Ruler and Apply Ruler commands to transfer ruler settings between documents. If there are ruler settings you frequently use, you can create a document that contains them all and then copy them to new documents as necessary.

Using the Paragraph command

Although the ruler is handy, you can also use the Paragraph command from the Format menu to set paragraph indents, line spacing, and alignment. The advantages of using the Paragraph command over using the ruler include:

✦ The Paragraph command gives you improved precision in establishing settings.

✦ You can set several options in a single dialog box (as opposed to setting them one by one with the ruler).

✦ You can use any measurement system you like — not just the one shown on the current ruler — for line and paragraph spacing.

✦ You can select outlining label formats for paragraphs — such as diamonds, check boxes, and Roman numerals — and choose a paragraph alignment.

✦ The only way to set spacing above and below a paragraph is with the Paragraph command.

Tip

You can also summon the Paragraph dialog box by double-clicking the line-spacing indicator or the alignment icons on the ruler bar.

Steps: Choosing Paragraph Settings with the Paragraph Command

1. Select the paragraph or paragraphs for which you want to alter paragraph format settings and choose the Paragraph command from the Format menu. The Paragraph dialog box appears, as shown in Figure 3-10.

Choose a format for an outline label

Paragraph		
Left Indent: `0 in`	Line Spacing: `1` `li ▼`	Measurement unit pop-up menus
First Line: `0 in`	Space Before: `0` `li ▼`	
Right Indent: `0 in`	Space After: `0` `li ▼`	
Label: `None ▼`	Alignment: `Left ▼`	Set paragraph alignment
`?`	`Apply` `Cancel` `OK`	

Figure 3-10: The Paragraph dialog box

2. Type numbers in the text-edit boxes and choose options from the pop-up menus for the settings you want to change. Here are some pointers:

- The only measurement settings in the Paragraph dialog box that do not appear on the ruler are Space Before and Space After. Fill in their boxes in the Paragraph dialog box to set the amount of blank space you want to appear before or after the selected paragraphs.

- You can change the measurement system for Line Spacing, Space Before, or Space After by selecting an option from their respective pop-up menus. You can mix and match measurement systems, if you wish.

- You can choose a paragraph alignment from the Alignment pop-up menu.

- If the selected paragraphs are outline topics or subtopics, you can choose a new label format from the Label pop-up menu.

3. Click Apply to apply the new settings to the selected paragraphs. (Apply is a tentative option. You can remove changes made with Apply by clicking Cancel; the formatting instantly reverts to the original settings.)

4. Click OK to accept the paragraph formatting changes or Cancel to revert to the original settings.

Tip

If you routinely want each paragraph to automatically be separated from the next paragraph by one blank line, set Space After to *1 li*. With that setting, you don't have to press Return between paragraphs.

Formatting sections

You can create more complex and varied word processing documents by dividing them into *sections*. Each section of a word processing document can have a different title page, headers and footers, page numbering, and number of columns.

If you are writing a book, for example, you can define each chapter as a separate section and set the following options:

✦ Each chapter begins on a right-hand page and is treated as a title page (with no headers or footers).

✦ Page numbering is chapter-relative (that is, it restarts at 1, but is preceded by the chapter number and a dash, as in 5-1).

✦ The left and right headers and/or footers are different from each other (the book title is in the header of all left pages and the chapter title is in the header of all right pages, for instance).

You must specify section options individually for each section in the document. To create a new section, move the insertion point to where you want the section to begin and choose Insert Section Break from the Format menu (or press Option-Enter).

To set options for a section, place the insertion point anywhere within the section and then choose Section from the Format menu. The Section dialog box appears as shown in Figure 3-11.

```
┌─────────────────────── Section: 2 ───────────────────────┐
│ ┌─ Start Section ──────────┐  ┌─ Columns ──────────────┐ │
│ │  New Page ▼              │  Number Of Columns:  [ 1 ] │
│ │                          │  □ Variable Width Columns  │
│ ┌─ Page Numbers ───────────┐  □ Mirror On Facing Pages  │
│ │ ● Continue From Previous Section                       │
│ │ ○ Restart Page Number:                                 │
│ │                             Settings For Single Column │
│ ┌─ Headers and Footers ────┐                            │
│ │ ● Continue From Previous Section                       │
│ │ ○ Different For This Section  Column Width:  [ 6.5 in ]│
│ │ □ Left & Right Are Different                           │
│ │ □ Title Page                                           │
│                                                          │
│ [?]                          ( Cancel )  ( OK )          │
└──────────────────────────────────────────────────────────┘
```

Figure 3-11: The Section dialog box

The meaning of each option in this dialog box is explained in the following sections. To remove a section break, position the text insertion point at the start of the section that follows the break and press Delete.

Many — perhaps most — documents have only one section. Nevertheless, you can still use the Section dialog box to specify page number, header/footer, and column settings (in this instance, for the entire document).

Start section

Depending on your selection from the Start Section pop-up menu in the Section dialog box, the current section can begin on a New Line, New Page, New Left Page, or New Right Page. (Book chapters often begin on a right-hand page, for example.)

Page numbers

To make page numbering pick up where the previous section left off, click the Continue From Previous Section radio button. If the last section ended on Page 17, for example, this section would start with Page 18.

If you want the page numbering in this section to start with some other number, click the Restart Page Number radio button and enter a page number in the box to the right of this option.

Headers and footers

Click Continue From Previous Section if you want to use the same headers and footers that were used in the previous section; click Different For This Section if you want to specify new headers and/or footers. After making this choice, you can safely edit the headers and footers in the new section without changing the previous section's headers and footers.

If you want to have different headers/footers for left- and right-hand pages, click the Left & Right Are Different check box. This is a common practice in books and in lengthy reports.

When you click the Title Page check box, ClarisWorks treats the first page of the section as a title page. It eliminates the headers and footers for that page only. Normally, you do not want to display page numbers and date stamps (common items for a header or footer) on the first page of a chapter, for example. If the document doesn't have headers or footers, this setting is irrelevant.

Columns

ClarisWorks enables word processing documents and document sections to have multiple columns. Newsletters, magazines, and church bulletins are often formatted with two or more columns, for example.

You can use the ruler bar to specify the number of columns for a section by clicking the Decrease Columns and Increase Columns controls (see Figure 3-12).

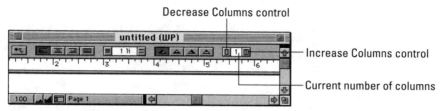

Figure 3-12: Setting the number of columns by using the ruler

You can also manually adjust column widths and the space between columns. To adjust the widths of two adjacent columns manually, move the pointer into the space between a pair of columns and press Option. The pointer changes to a pair of arrows surrounding a hollow box. Press the mouse button and move the pointer to the left or right. As you move the pointer, the widths of the two columns change. Release the mouse button to set the new column widths. Using this procedure, the space between the columns does not change. You are merely allocating the combined widths of the two columns in a new way.

To change the space between two adjacent columns manually, move the pointer so it touches the inside edge of a column and press Option. The pointer changes to a pair of arrows surrounding two vertical lines. Press the mouse button and move the pointer to the left or right. As you move the pointer, the width of the column the pointer is touching and the space between the columns change. Release the mouse button to set the new column width and between-column spacing.

You can also use the Section command to set columns, as described in the following steps.

Steps: Setting Multiple Columns with the Section Command

1. Position the text insertion point within the section you want to format. (If the document contains only one section, position the text insertion point anywhere in the document.)

2. Choose Section from the Format menu. The Section dialog box appears, as shown previously in Figure 3-11.

3. Type a number in the Number of Columns box.

4. If you want all columns to be the same width, leave the Variable Width Columns check box unchecked. The default Column Width and Space Between for that number of columns are shown at the bottom of the dialog box. As long as you don't exceed the page width, you can alter either or both of these numbers.

— or —

If you want the columns to be different widths, click the Variable Width Columns check box. By default, all columns are set to the same width. To change the widths, select a column number (the columns are numbered from left to right) from the Settings for Column pop-up menu, and enter numbers for Space Before, Column Width, and Space After. Repeat this procedure for the remaining columns.

When you set two or more columns, the Columns portion of the Section dialog box changes depending on your choice of variable-width or equal-sized columns (as shown in Figure 3-13).

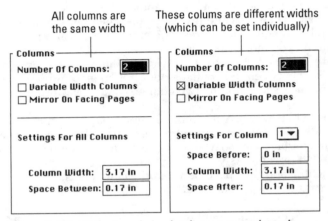

Figure 3-13: When equal-sized columns are selected, Column Width and Space Between are simultaneously set for all columns (left). With variable-width columns, Space Before, Column Width, and Space After can be set individually for each column (right).

5. *Optional*: If the section has multiple, variable-width columns and is to be printed like a book, click the Mirror On Facing Pages check box.

   For example, if the left-hand pages have a two-inch column near the outside margin and a four-inch column beside the inner margin (also called the *gutter*), right-hand pages would be mirrored; that is, the four-inch column would still be beside the gutter and the two-inch column would be near the outer margin. If Mirror On Facing Pages was not checked, the four-inch column would always be on the right.

6. Click OK to use the new column settings or Cancel to revert to the column settings that were in effect before you chose the Columns command. If you click OK, ClarisWorks automatically reformats the text to flow into the columns you created.

Note If you enter an individual column width that is wider than the allowable maximum, the program displays an error message, and you have to enter a new width number. Similarly, if the combined width of all columns and the space between columns exceeds the page width, you are asked to enter new numbers.

Page and column breaks

One feature ClarisWorks lacks is the capability to handle widows and orphans in text. A *widow* is a lone line of text that ends a page or column (the first or only line of a paragraph or a heading). An *orphan* is a lone line of text that starts a page or column (usually the final line of a paragraph). Widows and orphans make a document look unprofessional. To eliminate them, you can manually insert breaks as needed as the final editing step before printing the document.

To insert a page or column break, position the text insertion point at the beginning of the line you want as the first line in the new page or column and choose Insert Page Break or Insert Column Break from the Format menu. The break appears, and the line of text is moved to the next page or column.

Tip ClarisWorks 5.0 also includes a handy way to insert page and column breaks. Simply press the Enter key. If the text-insertion point is in a single-column section, a page break is inserted. If the insertion point is in a multicolumn section, a column break is inserted.

If Show Invisible is on (that is, you have checked it in the Text preferences, have clicked its button on the button bar, or have pressed ⌘-; [semicolon]), a break is indicated by a tiny upward-pointing arrow with three lines on its left side. You can remove a break by selecting the arrow and pressing Delete. If the arrow is invisible, move the text insertion point to the start of the text line that begins the break and then press Delete.

Formatting documents

Document formatting controls the overall appearance of each page — both on screen and when printed. Document options include:

   ✦ Margins (top, bottom, left, and right)

   ✦ Margin and page guides (shown or invisible)

   ✦ On-screen page display (single pages or two pages side by side)

   ✦ Starting page number

   ✦ Footnotes and endnotes

You set document formatting options by choosing Document from the Format menu. The Document dialog box appears, as shown in Figure 3-14. Set options and click OK to put your choices into effect (or click Cancel if you change your mind).

Figure 3-14: The Document dialog box

Note that several of the options (Margins, Footnotes, and Page Numbering) affect the way the document prints. The remaining settings (Page Display) affect only the document's appearance on screen.

Tip

All settings in the Document dialog box affect only the active document. When you create a new document, you have to reset the Document options. Although you can't save these options as preferences, you can avoid the boring, repetitious task of resetting the options. Create a new blank document, set the document preferences, and then save the file as a default stationery document, as described in Chapter 10. New word processing files then use your preferred Document settings automatically. (You can use this same tactic for any ClarisWorks environment you wish to standardize.)

Margins

To change a margin setting in the Document dialog box, simply type a number in the appropriate margin text-edit box.

You'll note that the units of measurement for each margin setting match those of the ruler. If you want to specify a different measurement unit, choose the Rulers command to select the unit, and then choose the Document command.

Note

If you intend to have your document printed double-sided (as you would with a bound book, for example), click the check box for Mirror Facing Pages. The wording for the Left and Right margin settings changes to Inside and Outside.

Number of pages displayed

By default, ClarisWorks is set to display every document one page at a time (One Page Above The Next). If you would rather see pages side by side, click the Facing Pages Side-By-Side radio button in the Document dialog box.

Tip

The Facing Pages Side-By-Side option is particularly useful if you have a monitor that has room to show two complete pages at the same time. Even if you have a small monitor (14 inch, for example), you can choose this option and then zoom the document to 50 percent to check its overall layout and design.

Show Margins and Show Page Guides

The setting for Show Margins determines whether the body text will be separated from the edges of the page by white space (when Show Margins is checked). Checking Show Page Guides causes the work area of the document to be outlined by a faint gray border. Having the page guides visible is particularly useful when you are working with headers and footers.

Start at Page

This option works in conjunction with the automatic page-numbering feature (Insert Page # in the Edit menu). You can specify a starting page number by entering a number in the text-edit box. Although you usually want page numbering to begin with 1 (the default), this feature can be useful. For example, if you are writing a book and you know Chapter 1 ended on Page 26, you can specify a starting page number of 27 for Chapter 2.

Footnotes and endnotes

Important in-text notes can be displayed at the bottom of each page as *footnotes* or grouped together at the end of the document as *endnotes*. If you want footnotes, click the At Bottom of Page radio button; for endnotes, click At End of Document. (Of course, if you don't intend to insert footnotes in the document, your choice is irrelevant.)

When you check the Automatic Numbering check box, ClarisWorks automatically numbers footnotes and endnotes, beginning with the number entered in the Start At box. Leave this option unchecked if you want to number footnotes or endnotes manually or if you want to use characters other than numbers, such as asterisks (*).

Advanced Editing Tools and Techniques

The features and editing techniques discussed in this section are nonessentials. Although you can initially do without them, you'll eventually find many of the following tools and techniques helpful in creating clean, attractive, readable documents:

- ✦ Finding and replacing text
- ✦ Headers and footers
- ✦ Footnotes and endnotes
- ✦ Inserting automatic date, time, and page numbers

✦ Using the spelling checker and thesaurus

✦ Performing a word count

✦ Using the hyphenation feature

✦ Creating outlines

Finding and replacing text

Like other word processing programs, the ClarisWorks word processing environment includes a set of Find/Change commands. Use Find to locate a particular section of a document quickly (where you talked about Social Security, for example). Use the Change option to replace one text string with another. Find/Change enables you to do the following:

✦ Find the next occurrence of a particular text string.

✦ Find subsequent occurrences of the same text string.

✦ Replace a found text string with another text string (or simultaneously replace all instances of one text string with another text string).

✦ Find a text string that matches the currently selected text in the document.

Steps: Finding a Text String

1. Choose Find/Change from the Find/Change submenu of the Edit menu (or press ⌘-F). The Find/Change dialog box shown in Figure 3-15 appears.

Figure 3-15: The Find/Change dialog box

2. In the Find box, type the text string for which you want to search (leave the Change box empty). You can also set these options:

  • *Whole Word.* If you want to search only for complete words, click the Whole Word check box. With Whole Word checked, searching for *and* will find only and — not sand or bandage.

  • *Case Sensitive.* Click the Case Sensitive check box if you want the case of each character in the Find string to be considered during the search. If you check this box, a search for *Young* would not match young or

YOUNG. If you're unsure of the capitalization, don't check Case Sensitive.

3. Click the Find Next button (or press Return or Enter). The search commences downward from the current cursor position. Eventually, the search wraps around so the whole document is searched — including text that is above the initial cursor position.

If the document contains a match, ClarisWorks highlights the first instance of the text string. If no match is found, a message to that effect appears.

4. If the found text is not the instance for which you are searching, click Find Next again. Each click restarts the search from the point of the last found text.

5. When you are finished, click the close box of the Find/Change dialog box.

You can repeat a search by choosing Find Again (⌘-E) from the Find/Change submenu of the Edit menu.

Sometimes the Find/Change dialog box obscures the found text. If necessary, you can move the dialog box to a different location by clicking its title bar, holding down the mouse button, and dragging.

You probably noticed the Find/Change dialog box also contains a Change box. Text you type into this box can replace instances of found text — either one match at a time (with your approval) or globally (automatically replacing all instances without one-by-one approval).

Steps: Finding and Changing Text

1. Choose Find/Change from the Find/Change pop-up menu of the Edit menu (or press ⌘-F). The Find/Change dialog box (previously shown in Figure 3-15) appears.

2. In the Find box, enter the text string to be located, and in the Change box, enter a replacement text string.

3. Set the Whole Word and Case Sensitive settings as desired:

- If you check Whole Word, ClarisWorks will find only whole words that match the Find string.

- If you check Case Sensitive, the program will locate only strings that have capitalization identical to the Find string's capitalization.

4. To change all instances of the Find string to the Change string without prompting from the program, click Change All. A dialog box appears stating: *The Change All feature is not undoable.* Click OK to continue or click Cancel.

— or —

To examine each Find result before you change the text, click Find Next. As text is found, click one of the following:

- Click Change to change only the current instance. Normally, you choose this option when you are ready to end the search (after you have found the single or final instance of text you want to change). If you decide you want to continue the search after you click Change, click Find Next.

- Click Change, Find to change the current instance and then find the next one.

- Click Find Next if the current instance is not one you want to change.

5. When you are finished, click the close box of the Find/Change dialog box.

Note

On subsequent finds in this session, the Find/Change dialog box will contain the last set of Find/Change text strings and settings you used.

Finding special characters

Occasionally, you may want to locate — and optionally replace — some special ClarisWorks characters, such as tabs, paragraph returns (end-of-paragraph markers), or automatic dates. To search for these characters or use them as replacements, enter the symbols shown in Table 3-3 in the Find or Change boxes of the Find/Change dialog box.

Table 3-3
Find/Change Symbols for Special Characters

Search Character	Characters to Type
Space	Spacebar
Nonbreaking space	Option-Spacebar
Tab	\t or ⌘-Tab
Discretionary hyphen	\- or ⌘- - (hyphen)
Paragraph return	\p or ⌘-Return
Line break (soft return)	\n or Shift-⌘-Return
Column break	\c or ⌘-Enter
Page break	\b or Shift-⌘-Enter
Section break	\- Option-6

Search Character	Characters to Type
Automatic date	\d
Fixed date	(Date)
Automatic time	\h
Fixed time	(Time)
Automatic page number	\#
Fixed page number	(Number)
Backslash	\\

Note

Because the backslash character (\) is used to define many of the special characters in the table, you have to type a pair of backslashes (\\) to find a backslash that appears in the text.

Because the need to search for such characters or use them as replacements may not be readily apparent, consider the following examples:

✦ *Removing double spaces*. Modern typesetting conventions frown on double spaces between sentences. (I know you were taught to use double spaces when you learned to type, but double spaces are not necessary when using a computer, a word processing program, and a decent printer.) Use the Find/Change command to substitute a single space for every instance of a double space. In addition to eliminating double spaces between sentences, you'll also get rid of extra spaces between words.

✦ *Substituting spaces for tabs in communications text*. Some information services and bulletin boards aren't prepared to handle tabs in text files. Search for the tab character (\t) and replace each instance with a fixed number of spaces (5 or 8, for example).

✦ *Eliminating extra space at the end of paragraphs*. Some of my publishers are sticklers about this. Search for Space Return (\p) and replace with Return (\p).

✦ *Replacing automatic date and time with a fixed date or time*. Automatic dates or times (which you enter by choosing Insert Date or Insert Time from the Edit menu) change every time you open the document. This is useful if you want to show a new date or time whenever you print the document. If you want to show when a document was written, on the other hand, you can replace the automatic date and time with a fixed date and time.

If you can't remember what to type when you want to execute a search for a particular character or if Table 3-3 isn't handy, you can copy the special characters in your document and then paste them into the Find/Change dialog box.

Steps: Copying and Pasting Special Characters

1. Find an example of the character in your document.

To find characters that are normally hidden, click the Show/Hide Invisibles button in the button bar (Figure 3-16), choose Preferences from the Edit menu and check the Show Invisibles check box in the Text options, or press ⌘-; (semicolon).

 Figure 3-16: The Show/Hide Invisibles button

2. Select the character and choose Copy from the Edit menu (or press ⌘-C).

3. Choose Find/Change from the Find/Change submenu of the Edit menu (or press ⌘-F). The Find/Change dialog box appears.

4. Press ⌘-V to paste the character into the Find or the Change text-edit box, as appropriate. When pasting into a Find/Change text-edit box, ClarisWorks automatically substitutes the correct symbols for the special character.

Creating headers and footers

Headers and footers can contain any text or graphics you want to separate from the body of the document. Because they are printed on the top or bottom of every page, headers and footers are very useful for displaying document-identification text, such as the date, your name, a document filename, or the report title. You also can place logos and other graphics in headers and footers to save yourself the trouble of repeatedly pasting images onto every page of the document. Figure 3-17 shows a header and a footer for a typical letterhead.

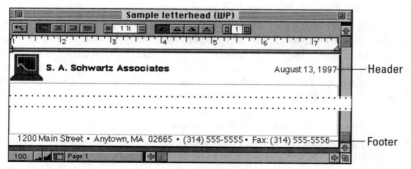

Figure 3-17: Examples of a header and footer

Page numbers are routinely placed in a header or footer. (For page numbers that automatically change to reflect pagination changes in the text, see "Inserting automatic date, time, and page numbers," later in this chapter.)

To create a header or footer, choose Insert Header or Insert Footer from the Format menu. A header or footer appears in the document, and the text insertion point moves into the header or footer area. You can then type the header or footer text.

As with other text, you can format header and footer text with different fonts, styles, sizes, and paragraph/ruler bar settings.

Unless you check the Show Page Guides check box in the Document dialog box (by choosing the Document command in the Format menu), you may have a difficult time distinguishing the header and footer text from the body text. After you check Show Page Guides, faint gray outlines surround the header and footer.

If you later decide you do not need a header or a footer, you can eliminate them by choosing Remove Header or Remove Footer from the Format menu. Doing so instantly deletes all text in the header or footer.

Remember, if a document is divided into sections, you can set different headers and footers for each section, if you like. Refer to "Formatting sections," earlier in this chapter.

Adding footnotes and endnotes

If you're working on a school report or a professional paper, you'll appreciate the ClarisWorks features for managing footnotes.

Steps: Inserting a Footnote

1. Position the text insertion point where you want the footnote to appear.

2. Choose Insert Footnote from the Format menu (or press Shift-⌘-F).

3. If you have checked Automatic Numbering in the Document dialog box (described earlier in this chapter), the next footnote number in sequence appears at the insertion point.

— or —

If you have not checked Auto Number Footnotes, the Mark With dialog box appears, as shown in Figure 3-18. Type the character you want to use to mark the footnote and click OK. The character appears at the insertion point.

Figure 3-18: Use the Mark With dialog box to specify a special footnote character.

After the program inserts the footnote mark, the cursor automatically moves into the footnote area at the bottom of the current page or at the end of the document (depending on whether footnotes or endnotes were chosen in the Document dialog box).

4. Type the footnote or endnote, and then press Enter or click in the body text area to continue working with the document. Figure 3-19 shows an example of a footnote.

Figure 3-19: Footnote example

Tip

If you decide to create your own footnote symbols instead of using a simple numbered sequence, you may want to consider the following characters. (Some of these symbols may appear as an empty square in the Mark With dialog box.)

Character	Keystroke
*	Shift-8
†	Option-T
‡	Shift-Option-7

To remove a footnote or endnote, select the footnote/endnote number or symbol where it appears in the body text and then press Delete or Backspace. The program automatically removes the reference at the bottom of the page or the end of the document and renumbers the remaining footnotes/endnotes if necessary.

Remember, the difference between footnotes and endnotes is simply where they are displayed in the document. Footnotes appear at the bottoms of the pages in which the footnotes are marked; endnotes appear in a single list at the end of the document. For more information about creating footnotes, see "Using the Word Processing Assistants," later in this chapter.

Inserting automatic date, time, and page numbers

Whether for record-keeping purposes or for use in headers and footers, you may want to date stamp or time stamp certain documents to show when you printed or last updated them. To insert the current date or time in a document, position the insertion point. Choose Insert Date or Insert Time from the Edit menu. The program inserts the current date or time for you.

The program takes the date and time from the Mac's clock. If the wrong date or time appears, you can correct it by entering the proper information in the Date & Time control panel.

The format for dates is taken from the setting in ClarisWorks's Text preferences. (For information on setting preferences, see Chapter 11.)

Dates or times you insert in this manner automatically change to reflect the new date and time whenever you reopen the document. To affix the current date or time in the document permanently (so it will not update), press Option as you choose Insert Date or Insert Time.

You use a similar command, Insert Page #, to add page numbers to documents. If you add them inside a header or footer, page numbering automatically carries through to every page in the document.

Steps: Adding Page Numbers to a Document

1. Specify a starting page number in the Document or Section dialog box. (Choose these dialog boxes by choosing Document or Section from the Format menu, as described earlier in this chapter.)

2. If the document already contains a header or footer, skip to Step 3.

— or —

If the document doesn't already contain a header or footer, choose Insert Header or Insert Footer from the Format menu.

3. Position the text insertion point in the header or footer.

4. Choose Insert Page # from the Edit menu.

The Insert Page Number dialog box appears, as shown in Figure 3-20.

Figure 3-20: The Insert Page Number dialog box

5. Select the desired options from the Insert Page Number dialog box, as follows:

   • To insert a page number, click the Page Number radio button.

   • To insert the current section number, click the Section Number radio button.

   • To insert the total number of pages in the current section, click the Section Page Count radio button.

   • To insert the total number of pages in the document, click the Document Page Count radio button.

6. Choose a format for the number from the Representation pop-up menu.

7. Click OK to complete the command or click Cancel if you change your mind. ClarisWorks inserts the current page number and renumbers all pages in the document, beginning with the number specified in the Document or Section dialog box.

   Page numbers inserted in this manner automatically change as the document changes (that is, as you add, delete, or move pages).

Remember, you can add formatting to header and footer text, just as you can to body text. For example, you can right- or center-justify page numbers by clicking the appropriate alignment icon below the ruler or by using tabs. (If the ruler isn't visible, choose Show Rulers from the Window menu.) You also can apply different fonts or styles. After you apply formatting to an element of a header or footer, the program automatically repeats the formatting on every page.

Depending on the type of document you're working on, plain numbers may look odd. You may prefer to precede each number with the word *Page,* for example. To do this, simply type **Page**, followed by a space, in front of where you have inserted or are about to insert the automatic page number.

To create chapter-relative or section-relative page numbers (Page 4-2 or A-1, for example) choose Section Number in the Insert Page Number dialog box. In the

Section dialog box (choose Section from the Format menu), click the Restart Page Number radio button and enter **1** in the text-edit box (for the starting page number). Be sure to choose the same settings for each section in the document.

Using the spelling checker

The inclusion of a built-in spelling checker was one of the first great advancements in word processing. A spelling checker examines every word in a document and compares it to words found in its massive dictionary. The program then flags unknown words and gives you an opportunity to replace them — either by typing the replacement word or by selecting a word from a list of the most likely replacements. Now with only a modicum of effort, every man, woman, and child can produce correctly spelled letters, memos, and reports.

Checking spelling

ClarisWorks provides two spell-checking options: Check the entire document or check only the currently selected text. Spell checking is available for all ClarisWorks documents that contain text except communications documents. (To spell check a communications document, select the text, copy it to the Clipboard [⌘-C], paste it into a word processing document [⌘-V], and then invoke the spell checker.)

You initiate spell checking by choosing the Writing Tools pop-up menu from the Edit menu and choosing either of the following options:

✦ *Check Document Spelling* (⌘-=). Select this option if you want to spell check the entire document. Note that when you choose this command, the position of the cursor doesn't matter. Spell checking automatically starts at the beginning of the document.

✦ *Check Selection Spelling* (Shift-⌘-Y). Select this option if you want to spell check only the currently selected text. Check Selection is particularly useful for checking a single word or just a paragraph or two you've recently edited.

Regardless of which command you use to start the spelling checker, ClarisWorks displays the spelling checker's progress in the Spelling dialog box (see Figure 3-21).

Figure 3-21: The Spelling dialog box

As the spelling checker examines the document or selection, it stops at each word it doesn't find in its dictionary or in the user dictionary you created. For each word, you can do the following:

✦ Correct the spelling by typing the proper word in the Word box and clicking Replace. (After making a manual correction in this fashion, you can click the Check button to make sure the replacement word is spelled correctly.)

✦ Select a replacement by double-clicking any of the words in the list box, by typing its Command-key equivalent (⌘-1, ⌘-2, and so on), or by highlighting the replacement and clicking the Replace button.

✦ Accept the spelling as correct by clicking Skip.

✦ Accept the spelling as correct and add it to the current user dictionary by clicking Learn.

✦ End the spell check by clicking Cancel.

You can click the tiny flag icon in the bottom-right corner of the dialog box to toggle between showing the potentially misspelled word in context and showing only the word itself.

As the spell check continues, ClarisWorks reports the number of words checked, as well as the number of questionable words found. After you deal with each questionable word, the spell checker progresses through the document (or selection) until it finds the next questionable word or until the spell check is completed. When all words have been checked, the top button in the dialog box changes to *Done*. Click Done to end the spell check.

Note

As good as spell checking is, it is not a substitute for proofreading. The ClarisWorks spelling checker does not flag duplicate words (*and and*), grammatical errors, or mistakes in punctuation. Nor will it find words that are spelled correctly but happen to be the wrong words (she *one* the game *to* many times, for example).

Working with dictionaries

At any given moment, you can have two dictionaries available for use with the spelling checker: a main dictionary and a user dictionary (one you've created). When you spell check a document or selection, ClarisWorks automatically uses the words in both dictionaries.

ClarisWorks comes with a 100,000-word dictionary it normally uses as the main dictionary, although replacement dictionaries (most notably for foreign languages) are also available from Claris.

The *user dictionary* contains a list of words you want ClarisWorks to accept as correct, even though they are not in the main dictionary. Whenever you click Learn in the Spelling dialog box, the spell checker adds the current word it is questioning to the active user dictionary. You also can add words manually by using the Edit User Dictionary command from the Writing Tools submenu of the Edit menu. Examples of words you may want to add to a user dictionary include proper nouns (such as product names and company names), technical terms, and current slang.

Tip If you like, you can create several user dictionaries, each for a particular type of writing. If you write about computers, for example, you may want to create a separate user dictionary for computer terminology. If you write many interoffice memos, you may want a second user dictionary that includes the spelling of each employee's name.

When you create multiple user dictionaries, keep in mind that only one of them can be active during a spell check. If the writing in any document covers several dictionary content areas, you will have to check the document in multiple passes — one for each different user dictionary you need. If this situation occurs frequently, you may be better off creating a single, composite user dictionary.

Creating and opening dictionaries

The following instructions tell you how to open a different main, user, or thesaurus dictionary; create a new user dictionary; and how to not use any dictionary at all.

Steps: Choosing a Dictionary

1. Choose Select Dictionaries from the Writing Tools submenu of the Edit menu. The Select Dictionary Type dialog box appears, as shown in Figure 3-22. (ClarisWorks automatically navigates to the Claris folder within the System Folder, where all dictionaries are stored.)

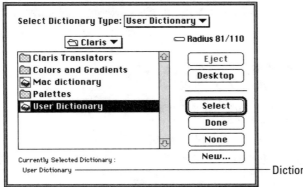

Figure 3-22: The Select Dictionary Type dialog box

2. Choose one of the dictionary types from the pop-up menu at the top of the dialog box (Main Dictionary, User Dictionary, Hyphenation Dictionary, or Thesaurus) to indicate the type of dictionary you want to install. The name of the currently installed dictionary of the selected type appears at the bottom of the dialog box.

3. Select the new dictionary file and click Select.

4. Click Done to close the dialog box. The program now uses the new dictionary.

Note

If you decide not to choose a new dictionary (because you intend to keep using the current one, for example), just click Done without choosing a dictionary. If you don't want to use a user dictionary, select User Dictionary from the pop-up menu at the top of the Select Dictionary dialog box, click None, and then click Done to close the dialog box.

To create a new user dictionary, choose Select Dictionaries from the Writing Tools submenu of the Edit menu. The Select Dictionary dialog box appears, as previously shown in Figure 3-22. Choose User Dictionary from the pop-up menu at the top of the dialog box. The name of the currently installed user dictionary appears at the bottom of the dialog box. Click New. A Save dialog box appears. Type a filename for the new user dictionary. Click Save to create the new dictionary file or Cancel if you change your mind. After you create a new user dictionary in this fashion, ClarisWorks automatically puts it into use.

Dictionary editing

As mentioned earlier, you can add words to the active user dictionary during a spell check by clicking the Learn button. Periodically, however, you may want to examine the contents of the user dictionary to see whether it contains incorrect entries or words you no longer need. You also can add words while editing the dictionary.

Steps: Editing a User Dictionary

1. If the appropriate user dictionary is not already open, choose Select Dictionaries from the Writing Tools submenu of the Edit menu. Select the user dictionary you want to edit and click Open.

2. Choose Edit User Dictionary from the Writing Tools submenu of the Edit menu. The User Dictionary dialog box appears (see Figure 3-23). The name of the current user dictionary is shown at the top of the dialog box.

Click to merge a word list with the current user dictionary

```
┌──────────────────────────────────────────────┐
│ User Dictionary: User Dictionary               │   Name of current user dictionary
│ ┌──────────────────┐┌───┐  ┌──────────┐        │
│ │ AppleWorks       ││▲  │  │   Add    │        │
│ │ ClarisDraw       ││   │  └──────────┘        │
│ │ ClarisImpact     ││   │  ┌──────────┐        │   Click this triangle to hide or reveal
│ │ ClarisWorks      ││   │  │  Remove  │        │   the Import and Export bottons
│ │ FileMaker        ││   │  ┌──────────┐        │
│ │ HTML             ││▼  │  │    OK    │        │
│ └──────────────────┘└───┘  ┌──────────┐        │
│                            │  Cancel  │        │
│ Entry: ┌────────────────┐  Text File ▽          │   Click to save the current user dictionary
│        └────────────────┘                       │   as a text file
│ ┌──────────┐  ┌──────────┐                      │
│ │ Import...│  │ Export...│                      │
│ └──────────┘  └──────────┘                      │
└──────────────────────────────────────────────┘
```

Figure 3-23: The User Dictionary dialog box

3. Add or remove words from the dictionary. To add a new word, type the word in the Entry box and click Add. To remove a word, select the word in the list and click Remove.

4. After you finish editing the dictionary, click OK to save the changes and return to the document (or click Cancel to ignore the changes).

Importing and exporting user dictionaries

The User Dictionary dialog box has two more commands — Import and Export — that make it easy to add entire word lists to a user dictionary or export the current dictionary to a text file. If you've already created a user dictionary in another word processing program, for example, you can import the words into a ClarisWorks dictionary without waiting for them to be individually flagged as questionable during a spelling check.

Steps: Importing Words into a User Dictionary or Exporting a Word List

1. If the appropriate user dictionary is not already open, choose Select Dictionaries from the Writing Tools submenu of the Edit menu. Select the user dictionary and click Open.

2. Choose Edit User Dictionary from the Writing Tools submenu of the Edit menu. The User Dictionary dialog box appears. The name of the current user dictionary is displayed at the top of the dialog box.

3. To reveal the Import and Export buttons in the User Dictionary dialog box, click the small triangle beside Text File. The dialog box expands, as shown previously in Figure 3-23.

4. To import a word list, click Import. Choose a text file in the file dialog box, and then click Open. ClarisWorks compares every word in the document with the words in the current user and main dictionaries and then adds every new word to the user dictionary.

— or —

To export a user dictionary to a text file, click Export. Navigate to the disk and folder where you want the exported text saved, enter a name for the new file, and click Save. ClarisWorks exports the entire contents of the user dictionary as a text file.

Tip

You can use the Import command to import text other than word lists and dictionaries from other programs. Suppose, for example, that you have written a technical paper for work or school. Using the Import command to open the document, you can automatically add all the new technical words to your user dictionary. Other words that are already in the main or current user dictionary are ignored.

Using the thesaurus

When you're stuck for a word or find yourself using the same pet phrase over and over, you can turn to the Word Finder thesaurus for assistance. Because it contains more than 220,000 *synonyms* (words with the same or similar meanings), chances are excellent you can find a new word or phrase that will add a little variety and style to your writing.

Steps: Finding a Synonym

1. Invoke the thesaurus by choosing Thesaurus from the Writing Tools submenu of the Edit menu (or by pressing Shift-⌘-Z).

   If you invoke the thesaurus while a word in the document is selected, the program displays synonyms for that word in the Word Finder Thesaurus dialog box (see Figure 3-24).

   If no word is selected, the dialog box is initially blank. In the Find box, type the word for which you want to display synonyms and click Lookup.

Figure 3-24: The Word Finder Thesaurus dialog box

2. Scroll through the list of synonyms. If you find a word you want to use, select it and click Replace (or double-click the word). The dialog box closes, and the word is inserted at the current cursor position in the document. (If a word was highlighted in the document, that word is replaced by the synonym.)

To exit from the thesaurus without replacing a word, click Cancel.

— or —

If you don't see a synonym you like, but you do see a word with a similar meaning, select it with the cursor. To see synonyms for that word, click Lookup. When you find a word you like, click Replace.

If you want to re-examine other words you've looked at during this thesaurus session, click Last Word. The Last Words dialog box appears. To recheck one of these words, select it and click Lookup. To return to the thesaurus as you left it, click Cancel.

Performing a word count

By selecting Word Count from the Writing Tools submenu of the Edit menu, you can get statistical information about the text in a document, including the number of characters, words, lines, paragraphs, pages, and sections. The Word Count feature is an enormous help to those who must write within a specific length limit (400 words or less, for example), as well as to writers who are paid by the word.

When the Word Count dialog box appears, its statistics are based on the entire contents of the current document. To obtain statistics on part of a document, select the text of interest, choose the Word Count command, and click the Count Selection check box in the Word Count dialog box. The statistics change to reflect only the current selection.

Using hyphenation

Sometimes the traditional "ragged right" formatting used in documents is just too ragged. Hyphenation can work wonders to improve the appearance of documents.

To turn on auto-hyphenation for a document, select Auto Hyphenate from the Writing Tools submenu of the Edit menu or click the Auto Hyphenate button in the button bar, as shown in Figure 3-25.

Figure 3-25: The Auto Hyphenate button

When auto-hyphenation is on, a check mark appears in front of the command. Selecting the command again turns auto-hyphenation off and removes the check mark.

The Auto Hyphenate button is not a standard part of the ClarisWorks 5.0 default button bar. You must add the Auto Hyphenate button manually, as explained in the "Adding Buttons" section in Chapter 12.

After you turn on auto-hyphenation, ClarisWorks automatically examines line ends, consults its hyphenation dictionary, and then determines whether (and how) a word should be hyphenated.

Auto-hyphenation is document-specific; that is, turning on auto-hyphenation affects only the current document. If you want to make auto-hyphenation the default for all new word processing documents, you can do so by creating a default stationery document, as explained in the "Using Stationery Documents to Set New Environment Defaults" section in Chapter 10.

Hyphenating a word your way

Auto-hyphenation is an all-or-nothing affair — that is, it affects the entire document, section, or text frame. If you decide you don't want a particular word hyphenated, or if ClarisWorks fails to hyphenate a word because the word isn't in the hyphenation dictionary, you can edit the hyphenation dictionary.

Only words of five or more letters can be added to the hyphenation dictionary.

Steps: Editing a Hyphenation Dictionary

1. Choose Edit Hyphenation Dictionary from the Writing Tools submenu of the Edit menu. The Hyphenation File dialog box appears.

2. Edit the hyphenation dictionary as desired:

- To specify a word's hyphenation, type the word in the Entry box, inserting the appropriate hyphens. Then click Add.

- To prevent ClarisWorks from hyphenating a particular word, type the word in the Entry box without hyphens. Then click Add.

- To change the hyphenation for a word previously added to the hyphenation file, select the word and make the appropriate changes in the Entry box. Then click Replace.

- To remove a word previously added to the hyphenation file, select it and then click Remove.

3. Click Done to accept the changes to the hyphenation file and return to your document; otherwise, click Cancel.

Even when auto-hyphenation is on, you can adjust a word's hyphenation by manually inserting regular and discretionary hyphens:

Note

✦ To insert a *regular hyphen*, set the text insertion point where you want the hyphen to appear and then press the hyphen key (-).

A hyphen inserted in this manner will always show up at that spot in the word — regardless of where the word appears in the line. As a result, if the text is later edited or reformatted, regular hyphens can show up in the middle of a line. (If you ever see a word like *Mac-intosh* in the middle of a line, someone probably inserted a regular hyphen, edited the surrounding text, and then forgot to proofread the text.) You should insert a regular hyphen only if a word is always hyphenated, as in *money-changer*.

✦ To insert a *discretionary hyphen*, set the text insertion point where you want the hyphen to appear and then press ⌘-hyphen. Unlike regular hyphens, discretionary hyphens appear only when the word must be split between two lines; otherwise, they're invisible.

Installing a different hyphenation dictionary

In the United States, ClarisWorks 5.0 is shipped with a U.S. English hyphenation dictionary. If you work in other languages, you can purchase other language-specific hyphenation dictionaries from Claris. To install a hyphenation dictionary, choose Select Dictionaries from the Writing Tools submenu of the Edit menu. The Select Dictionary Type dialog box appears, as shown previously in Figure 3-22. By default, the dialog box opens to the Claris folder, where the various Claris dictionaries are stored. Click the Select Dictionary pop-up menu and choose Hyphenation Dictionary. Select the hyphenation dictionary you want to use, click Select, and click Done. ClarisWorks installs the new hyphenation dictionary, which will be used for all documents until you choose a different dictionary.

Note

Although most users associate hyphenation with word processing, don't forget you can use it with database fields and text frames that are inserted into other types of documents, such as spreadsheets.

Working with outlines

Think back to your high school or college days. Remember making outlines — those numbered lists you used to help arrange your thoughts for a paper or speech into a coherent, meaningful order? Well, many of us still use outlines, and ClarisWorks 5 makes outlining simple.

The main headings in an outline are called *topics*. Subordinate headings are called *subtopics*. Each subtopic is a point or idea that is related to the topic above it, as shown in Figure 3-26. A ClarisWorks outline can have up to 16 levels of subtopics.

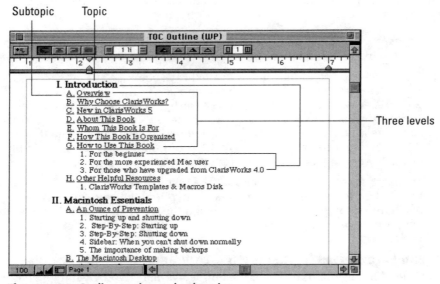

Figure 3-26: Outline topics and subtopics

Note

In versions of ClarisWorks prior to 4.0, the Outline View command worked as a toggle. Each time you chose the command, it toggled between an outline and a normal view of the current document. In ClarisWorks 4.0 and higher, outlining is fully integrated with the word processing environment. An outline can now be a complete word processing document or simply incorporated as part of a word processing document or frame.

What defines a paragraph as being part of an outline — rather than normal word processing text — is that an *outline format* has been applied to it. When working in a word processing document or frame, you can choose from any of three predefined outline formats in the Stylesheet pop-up menu (in the button bar) or the Stylesheet palette (choose Show Styles from the Window menu or press Shift-⌘-W), as shown in Figure 3-27. The predefined outline formats are Diamond, Harvard, and Legal. Each format includes style definitions for between five and twelve outline levels.

Figure 3-27: Outline formats can be chosen from the Stylesheet palette or the Stylesheet pop-up menu in the button bar.

After choosing an outline format, you can immediately type your first topic. As you begin typing, a level-1 label automatically appears to the left. To create a new topic at the same level, press Return. To create a new topic to the left or the right of the current topic, choose New Topic Left or New Topic Right from the Outline menu (or press ⌘-L or ⌘-R).

Note

Each outline should have only one outline format (Diamond, Harvard, or Legal). If you select a topic in the middle of the outline and apply a different outline format to it, ClarisWorks can get confused. It may treat the selected topic as a new outline (resulting in two topics labeled **1** and **I**, for example), or it may change the formatting and labels to something outlandish. To correct this problem, immediately choose Undo from the Edit menu or reapply the original outline style to the affected topics.

Outline formats and topic labels

Every outline has a general format, which you choose from the Stylesheet palette or the Stylesheet pop-up menu. Although you are free to customize individual topics or subtopics (by changing their font or style, for example), an outline format specifies a default style for every new topic and subtopic you create. Thus, you don't need to format individual topics and subtopics; their formatting is handled for you in the outline format definition.

On the other hand, if you want to get fancy, you can create a custom outline format or edit the formatting of the levels of an existing outline format (as explained later in "Custom outline formats").

Note

To change from one outline format to another, select the entire outline and choose a new outline format (Diamond, Harvard, or Legal) from the Stylesheet palette or the Stylesheet pop-up menu.

As you work with outlines, you'll note that each predefined outline format has its own method of assigning *topic labels* (the symbol, letter, or number that precedes each topic and subtopic in the outline), as well as the particular font and style for each level. ClarisWorks has 12 different topic label formats, as shown in Figure 3-28. Although an outline format automatically assigns a topic label to every topic and subtopic, you can change any topic label.

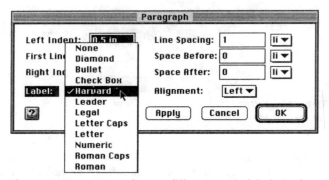

Figure 3-28: You can choose different topic labels in the Paragraph dialog box.

Steps: Changing a Topic Label

1. Select one or more contiguous topics or subtopics in the outline by clicking and dragging through them.

2. Choose Paragraph from the Format menu. The Paragraph dialog box appears.

3. Choose a label style from the Label pop-up menu, as shown in Figure 3-28. The label style is applied to the selected topics and subtopics.

4. Click OK to accept the new topic label style. (If you wish, you can first click Apply to see how the new label looks.)

You can also select topic labels from the Topic Label pop-up menu above the ruler.

When changing topic labels, it's usually best to restrict changes to one level at a time. Remember that the Paragraph command also sets line indents for all selected paragraphs. If you select topics that span two or more levels and then choose a new topic label (as described previously), the indenting of all selected topics is changed to match the new setting.

As you work with outlines, you'll quickly discover you cannot directly edit the topic labels (the numbers, letters, diamonds, and Roman numerals that precede each topic). These labels are governed by the level of each topic and are automatically handled for you by ClarisWorks. In fact, the formatting of each topic label is directly connected to the first character in the topic name. If you change the font, size, color, or style of the first character, the topic label instantly changes to match. Thus, formatting only the first word of a topic as italic, for example, will also change the topic label to italic. Then again, if you change the format of an entire topic — as you would normally do when reformatting a level, for example — you probably want the label to change.

Custom outline formats

For a quick-and-dirty outline, stick with the level definitions that ClarisWorks provides for the outline format you've selected. For presentations or formal papers, on the other hand, you may well want to design your own format for the outline so you can select the topic labels, indents, fonts, styles, and sizes for each level.

Although you can manually alter the appearance of any topic or subtopic in the outline (by selecting the text and changing its font or size, for example), a better way to make the appearance of the levels in the outline consistent is to create a custom format. Regardless of which outline format you've chosen, you can make changes to the level formats, as described in the following steps.

Steps: Creating a Custom Format

1. If the Stylesheet palette isn't visible, choose Show Stylesheet from the Window menu (or press Shift-⌘-W).

2. In the Stylesheet palette, click the Edit button. The palette expands to show a Properties list. The pointer changes to the style-editing pointer — a shadow S.

3. In the left side of the dialog box, click the triangle in front of the particular outline format you want to change. The outline format is selected and expands to show all outline levels.

4. Select the level you want to change. The level's current properties are listed in the Properties window, as shown in Figure 3-29.

Figure 3-29: The expanded Stylesheet palette shows the properties of the selected level.

5. Choose Paragraph from the Format menu. In the Paragraph dialog box that appears, you can change the line indents, line spacing, alignment, and label style of the new level format. (Note that several of these settings can also be selected by merely clicking icons in the ruler bar.)

6. Change any Text settings you want to alter for the level by choosing options from the Font, Size, and Style menus.

7. When you finish making changes for one level, repeat Steps 4 through 6 for each additional level you want to change. Click Done when you've made all necessary changes.

   When you click Done, existing topics and subtopics for any changed levels are instantly updated to match the new styles. Any new topics and subtopics you create for levels you've just modified will have the attributes you specified.

Using different text colors is an excellent way to differentiate levels. In a demonstration, for example, lecture items could all be one color, and points you want to demonstrate could be formatted in another color.

For more information about creating and modifying styles (you may want to define new outline styles rather than edit the existing ones, for example), see Chapter 15.

Creating new topics and subtopics

Now that you know about the components of an outline and how to assign formats and labels to topics, you need to step back and examine the mechanics of entering outline topics and subtopics.

After you type a new topic, you can do the following:

✦ Create a new topic at the same level by pressing ⌘-Return or choosing New Topic from the Outline menu. (These methods apply the default format for the level.)

✦ Create a new topic at the same level with the same formatting as the previous topic by pressing Return.

✦ Create a new topic below and to the right of the current topic (a subtopic) by pressing ⌘-R or choosing New Topic Right from the Outline menu.

✦ Create a new topic below and to the left of the current one (at a higher level) by pressing ⌘-L or choosing New Topic Left from the Outline menu.

Collapsing and expanding an outline

ClarisWorks enables you to expand and collapse the entire outline or just selected topics and subtopics. You may want to collapse the outline to show only one or two levels of topics so you can focus on the main points without the clutter of additional subtopics. Similarly, you may want to collapse only the levels below a particular topic or subtopic. When I'm working with a book outline, I often use this approach to show that a chapter has been completed.

Steps: Collapsing or Expanding the Outline

1. Select the topics and subtopics you want to collapse or expand.

To choose multiple topics, click in the first topic to set the text insertion point and then drag to choose the additional topics. Select all outline topics if you want to collapse or expand the entire outline.

2. Choose Collapse or Expand from the Outline menu. The selected portion of the outline collapses to show only the highest level or expands to show all subordinate levels, respectively.

— or —

Press the Option key as you open the Outline menu, and choose Expand All or Collapse All. For each topic selected, ClarisWorks reveals (Expand All) or conceals (Collapse All) all the subtopics.

— or —

Choose the Expand To command from the Outline menu. The Expand To dialog box appears.

In the text-edit box, type the number of outline levels you want to display and then click OK. The selected portion of the outline changes to show only that number of levels. Enter **1**, for example, to display only the main topics for the selected portion of the outline. Type a larger number (the maximum is 16) to display all levels.

Tips for Expanding and Collapsing

When a topic's subtopics have been collapsed, the topic label is usually underlined. In a diamond-format outline, however, collapsed subtopics are indicated by a gray diamond. Double-click it to reveal the subtopics hidden below.

Although check boxes are excellent for to-do lists, they pose a special problem when you expand or collapse levels. In a normal outline that uses diamond symbols, bullets, or numbers as topic labels, you can expand or collapse levels by double-clicking the label. (Double-clicking is much easier to remember than the keyboard shortcut — Ctrl-Spacebar — and handier than pulling down the Outline menu.) Unfortunately, double-clicking in a check box merely toggles the check mark on and off. The trick to collapsing a check box level is to double-click to the left of the check box, rather than in it.

To collapse or expand a single topic and all associated subtopics, select the topic you want to collapse or expand. Double-click the topic label, choose Collapse or Expand from the Outline menu, or press Ctrl-Spacebar. If a topic cannot be collapsed or expanded, nothing happens. (For example, you cannot collapse the lowest level topic because it has no subtopics.)

Rearranging topics and subtopics

One of the nice things about working with outlines in ClarisWorks is the ease with which you can rearrange topics and subtopics. ClarisWorks provides a variety of features for rearranging topics, including dragging them to different levels and using keyboard or menu commands.

Moving topics

By using the mouse, you can easily move a topic and its subtopics to a new position in the outline.

Steps: Moving a Topic by Using the Mouse

1. Click the topic label to choose the topic and its associated subtopics. (If the topic has a check box label, click to the left of the check box.)

2. Click to the left of the selected topic and press the mouse button. As you drag up or down, the cursor changes to a double-headed arrow, with a tiny horizontal line that separates the arrowheads. A thick horizontal line (called the *insertion marker*) appears, showing where the selected topic will move.

3. When the insertion marker is in the location where you want to move the topic, release the mouse button. The topic and associated subtopics move to the new position, and the outline is re-labeled as necessary.

You can also use the Move Above (Ctrl-up arrow) or Move Below (Ctrl-down arrow) commands from the Outline menu to move a selected topic above or below adjacent topics while retaining the same level in the outline hierarchy.

If you want to move a topic up or down without also moving its subtopics, press the Option key when you choose the Move Above or Move Below command from the Outline menu (or press Option-Ctrl-up arrow or Option-Ctrl-down arrow). This will assign subtopics to the topic.

Raising or lowering topic levels

Although you can use the mouse to move a topic anywhere in the outline, you cannot change a topic's level by moving it with the mouse. If a topic was at level 3 before the move, it will still be at level 3 after the move. To change a topic's level, you need to use the Move Left or Move Right command (or the keyboard equivalents).

Select the topic whose level you want to change by clicking anywhere within its text. Choose Move Left (Shift-⌘-L or Ctrl-left arrow) or Move Right (Shift-⌘-R or Ctrl-right arrow) from the Outline menu. The selected topic and all associated subtopics are promoted or demoted one level in the outline hierarchy. If you want to promote or demote a topic without affecting its subtopics, press Option when you choose the Move Left or Move Right command from the Outline menu (or press Option-Ctrl-left arrow or Option-Ctrl-right arrow).

Note

You can also promote a topic and its associated subtopics by selecting it and then choosing Raise Topic from the Outline menu.

Deleting topics

As you work, you may decide to delete some topics or levels in the outline. The procedure you use to do this depends on whether you want to delete a topic and its subtopics or just delete a single level in the outline without eliminating its subtopics.

To delete a single level, triple-click in the text of the level you want to delete. The entire line of text is selected. If the topic contains more than one line, quadruple-click to select it. You can also drag to select all the text in the level. Press Delete or Backspace. The line is eliminated. If the topic was one of several topics at the same level, the other topics below it move up and are renumbered, as necessary.

To delete a topic and associated subtopics, click the topic label. (If the topic has a check box label, click to the left of the check box.) The topic and all associated subtopics are selected. Press Delete or Backspace. The topic and its subtopics are eliminated. Labels for topics below the deleted topic are automatically renumbered, as necessary.

Concentrate on the Important Outline Commands

Because there are so many different commands for raising and lowering topics, moving topics, and creating new topics, it is unlikely you will remember them all unless you use the commands on a daily basis. Instead, you are better off doing the following:

✦ For reorganizing topics and subtopics, try the visual approach. Select the topics and subtopics and drag them to where they should go.

✦ Expand and collapse topics by double-clicking their labels.

✦ Concentrate on memorizing only the most important keyboard shortcuts, and choose the others from the Outline menu. The commands listed in the following table are the ones you are likely to use most:

Procedure	Keystroke
New topic at the same level	⌘-Return
New topic at the same level with the same formatting	Return
New topic to the left	⌘-L
New topic to the right	⌘-R
Shift topic to the left	Shift-⌘-L
Shift topic to the right	Shift-⌘-R

Outline Ideas

Although the outlines you created in high school or college were usually designed to organize points for a paper or speech, there's no reason you can't write the entire paper or speech with outline formatting. Why use an outline just for notes? After all, a topic doesn't have to be a point — it can just as easily be an entire paragraph.

Outline view is also excellent for creating presentations. You can use the diamond or bullet format to design standard text charts, or you can create a custom format, if you prefer. When you finish the charts, you can use a laser printer to print transparencies or handouts.

Although a word processing document is normally used for outlines, you can also make an outline in a text frame. Insert a text frame into a slide show page, and you can quickly make a bullet list or text chart.

Adding Graphics to Word Processing Documents

The selective use of graphics can go a long way toward enhancing a report or memo. For example, you can add a company logo to letterhead or presentation pages and embed spreadsheet charts in reports. ClarisWorks enables you to add graphics to a word processing document or frame in two ways: as free-floating *objects* or as *in-line graphics* (part of the text).

Because floating objects are not part of the text, you can move them wherever you like. And because they are objects, you can add a new background color, gradient, or bounding lines to them. Finally, you can also specify a text wrap for each object (none, regular, or irregular). Figure 3-30 shows examples of both types of graphics.

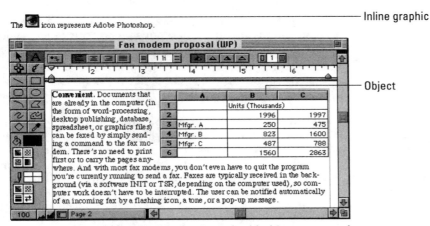

Inline graphic

Object

Figure 3-30: An in-line graphic that is embedded in a paragraph and an object for which regular text wrap has been set

In-line graphics

An in-line graphic in a word processing document is treated exactly the same as text. For all practical purposes, you can think of it as just another character. As a result, if the graphic is in a paragraph by itself, you can use paragraph formatting commands to align the graphic to a tab stop or to center it, for example.

Tip

In most cases, the best place for an in-line graphic is in a paragraph by itself — without any surrounding text. An in-line graphic that is in the same line with text can sometimes cause serious problems with spacing between lines because line height is defined by the largest font or image in the line.

Steps: Adding an In-Line Graphic

1. Set the text insertion point where you want to insert the graphic.

2. To insert a graphic from a file, choose Insert from the File menu and choose a graphic file to insert. The entire contents of the file appear at the text insertion point.

— or —

To insert a graphic from the Clipboard, select and copy the graphic (⌘-C) from a ClarisWorks paint or draw document, from within another graphics program, or from the Scrapbook. In the ClarisWorks document, choose Paste from the Edit menu (or press ⌘-V). The graphic appears at the text insertion point.

If the program or desk accessory supports drag-and-drop, you can drag the graphic into the ClarisWorks document (without using cut-and-paste).

3. *Optional:* Resize the graphic as needed by dragging its handle to a new position. You can maintain the original proportions by pressing Shift as you drag. To resize the graphic by a specific percentage, choose Scale by Percent from the Format menu.

After placing and optionally resizing an in-line graphic, you can use the new Descent command to align the graphic vertically with the surrounding text. Select the in-line graphic and choose Descent from the Format menu (or just double-click the graphic). The Descent dialog box appears. Enter a negative number (in points) to raise the graphic in relation to the text baseline; enter a positive number to lower the graphic.

Graphic objects

You can paste graphic objects into a document, insert them with the Insert command, create them from scratch with the drawing tools, or embed them in a paint frame.

Steps: Pasting a Picture from the Clipboard as a Free-Floating Graphic

1. In the ClarisWorks graphics environment, another graphics program, or in the Scrapbook desk accessory, select the picture.

2. Choose Copy from the Edit menu (or press ⌘-C). A copy of the image is temporarily stored in the Clipboard.

3. Select the pointer tool from the ClarisWorks Tool panel. (If the Tool panel isn't visible, click the Show/Hide Tools control at the bottom of the document window.)

Selecting the pointer tool takes you out of word processing mode and instructs ClarisWorks to treat the graphic to be pasted as a free-floating object rather than as an in-line graphic.

4. Choose Paste from the Edit menu (or press ⌘-V). The picture is pasted as an object that you can resize or move.

After the picture is pasted, it should be surrounded by handles. If the handles are not visible, the picture has probably been pasted as an in-line graphic (part of the text), rather than as an object. Press Delete to remove the picture, and then go back to Step 3.

Steps: Inserting a Picture from a File as a Free-Floating Graphic

1. Select the pointer tool from the ClarisWorks Tool panel. (If the Tool panel isn't visible, click the Show/Hide Tools control at the bottom of the document window.)

Selecting the pointer tool takes you out of word processing mode and instructs ClarisWorks to treat the graphic to be pasted as a free-floating object rather than as an in-line graphic.

2. Choose Insert from the File menu. A standard file dialog box appears.

3. Navigate to the proper drive and folder, and choose the graphics file you want to insert in the document.

4. Click Insert. The program inserts the file in the document as an object that you can resize or move about.

After the picture is pasted, it should be surrounded by handles. If the handles are not visible, the picture has probably been pasted as an in-line graphic (part of the text), rather than as an object. Press Delete once to remove the picture, and then go back to Step 1.

Tip

In ClarisWorks 5, you'll also find it remarkably easy to insert free-floating graphics using drag-and-drop. Begin by selecting the pointer tool in your ClarisWorks word processing document or frame. Then open any drag-and-drop-enabled application or desk accessory (such as the Scrapbook) and drag the graphic onto the word processing document or frame.

Note

ClarisWorks also includes dozens of clip-art images you can place in your documents. To make them easier to work with, the graphics are organized in *libraries*. To insert any of these images into a word processing document, decide whether you want an in-line graphic or a floating graphic (by setting the text insertion point or by choosing the pointer tool), select a ReadyArt library from the Library submenu of the File menu, choose a graphic from the Library palette, and click Use or drag it into your document. (For more information about using, customizing, and creating ClarisWorks libraries, see Chapter 21.)

Chapter 6 discusses the details of creating a picture from scratch. In general, you select drawing tools from the Tool panel and drag to create different shapes.

Wrapping text around graphic objects

If you are going to surround the graphic object with text, you can specify how (or whether) the text should wrap around the object (see Figure 3-31). You can choose from the following text wrap options:

- ✦ *None*. The object obscures any text it is covering. If you move the object to the back, the text appears over the object.

- ✦ *Regular*. An invisible rectangle is drawn around the object, and text wraps to the edges of the rectangle.

- ✦ *Irregular*. Text wraps as closely as possible to the original edges of the object.

New In Version 5

- ✦ *Gutter*. In the Gutter box, enter a number (in points) for the amount of space you want between the object and the surrounding text.

You can also specify a text wrap for other objects, such as spreadsheet frames.

Text wrap can be set for floating objects, but not for in-line graphics. To set text wrap for a floating object or frame, begin by selecting the object with the pointer tool. Choose Text Wrap in the Options menu. In the Text Wrap dialog box that appears, click the icon for None, Regular, or Irregular, depending on the type of wrap you want, and then click OK. The text wraps around the object or frame in the manner you specified.

Tip

When you try to do an irregular text wrap around an imported PICT image, the object often appears to be embedded in a large rectangle — regardless of the actual shape of the image. To get the wrap you want, ungroup the object in ClarisWorks and then group it again (the Ungroup and Group commands are in the Arrange menu). The text should wrap correctly. (Note, however, that if the object really is surrounded by a rectangular box — most scans, for example — this procedure may change nothing.)

This tip will work only if the graphic is a draw object, made up of QuickDraw shapes. If the image is a bitmap, the handles will define the image area. A workaround to this is to insert the bitmap, draw a shape (using the polygon tool) around the text wrap area, assign the appropriate text wrap, and then make the polygon transparent.

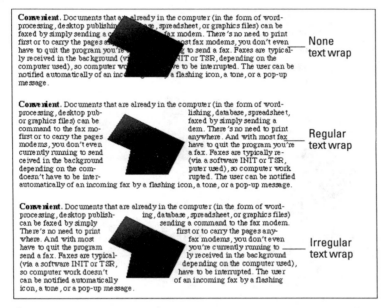

Figure 3-31: Text wraps

Layering pictures and text

Of course, text does not have to be wrapped around graphic objects. You can place a picture behind or in front of text by selecting the picture and choosing the Move Forward, Move to Front, Move Backward, or Move to Back command from the Arrange menu.

With Text Wrap set to None, you can make a graphic float on top of the document, hiding the text beneath it. And by using the Move to Back command, you can make the text print over a graphic. This technique is useful for creating a letterhead watermark or a rubber-stamp effect, as shown in Figure 3-32.

Objects that have been moved to the back of a word processing document usually work best if they are light-colored. Dark objects, or ones with dark areas, may make reading the overlaying text difficult or impossible.

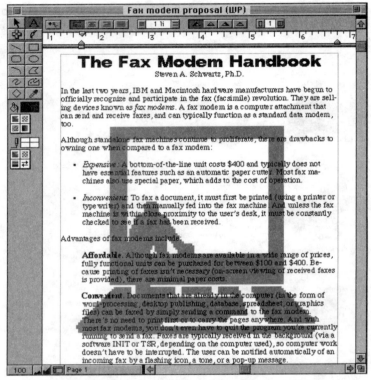

Figure 3-32: A light gray draw or paint graphic can make an interesting background for a word processing document.

Adding Equations to a Word Processing Document

New In
Version 5

Using the new Equation Editor, you can create mathematical and scientific equations and insert them into word processing documents or frames. Figure 3-33 shows two complex equations that were created with the Equation Editor.

Equations are treated as objects — not as text. As such, they can be added as in-line graphics or as floating graphics (discussed previously in this chapter in "Adding Graphics to Word Processing Documents"). Similarly, because they *are* graphics, all changes you wish to make to the equation must be done in the Equation Editor — not in the ClarisWorks document in which the equation is placed.

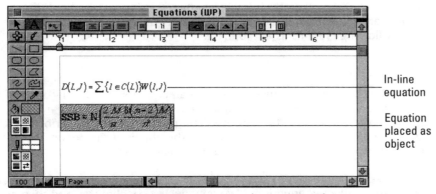

In-line equation

Equation placed as object

Figure 3-33: Two sample equations in a word processing document

Steps: Creating an Equation

1. To create an equation as an in-line graphic, set the text insertion point in the text where you want the equation to appear.

— or —

To create an equation as a floating object, select the pointer tool.

2. Choose Insert Equation from the Edit menu. The Equation Editor launches, as shown in Figure 3-34.

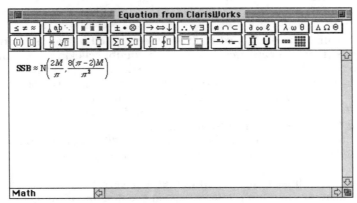

Figure 3-34: The Equation Editor

3. Design the equation by typing and choosing options from the symbol pop-up menus.

4. To complete the equation, click the equation window's close box. The ClarisWorks document is displayed, and the equation is inserted as an in-line or floating graphic, as appropriate.

Like other objects, you can change the size of an equation by clicking and dragging a handle. If you want to embellish an equation by adding a bounding box or a background color, pattern, texture, or gradient, place it as a floating object rather than as an in-line graphic. You can then select the object in the document and set options for it by choosing from the Pen and Fill palettes in the Tool panel.

If you later need to modify an equation, double-click it. The Equation Editor opens and displays the selected equation. Make any necessary changes, and then close the equation window to return to the ClarisWorks document.

You can alter the vertical placement of an in-line equation relative to the surrounding text by choosing the Descent command from the Format menu.

You can change an existing in-line graphic equation to a floating one or vice versa by cutting it, selecting the pointer tool or setting the text insertion point (as appropriate), and then pasting.

Adding Document Links

Using the new Links palette, you can create three types of linked text, images, objects, and frames in ClarisWorks 5.0 documents: book marks, document links, and URL links.

Book marks are place-markers (text strings, objects, paint images, spreadsheet cells, or frames) that you can jump to quickly by double-clicking their names in the Links palette or by clicking an associated document link in a ClarisWorks document. *Document links* are text strings, objects, paint images, spreadsheet cells, or frames in a ClarisWorks document that — when clicked — transport the user to a book mark in the same document or instruct ClarisWorks to open a different document. *URL links* are text strings, objects, paint images, spreadsheet cells, or frames in a ClarisWorks document that — when clicked — connect the user to a particular page on the World Wide Web (a part of the Internet).

By adding document links to a Table of Contents page, you can enable users to click chapter headings and jump to any page in the document. And company memos can contain URL links to related information on the World Wide Web.

To create a link, choose Show Links Palette (Shift-⌘-M) from the Window menu. In the ClarisWorks document, select the text string, object, paint image, spreadsheet cell, or frame that will serve as the link. In the Links palette, choose a link type from the pop-up menu. To create the link, choose the New command (New Book

Mark, New Document Link, or New URL Link), name the link, and set additional options, as necessary.

To learn more about creating, editing, and using links, see Chapter 19.

Using the Word Processing Assistants

When you're working in a word processing document or frame, you can select ClarisWorks Assistants from the Balloon Help menu or Help menu to get assistance with four common tasks: addressing envelopes, inserting and formatting footnotes, sorting paragraphs alphabetically, and creating tables. After you select ClarisWorks Assistants, the Select Assistant dialog box appears, as shown in Figure 3-35.

Figure 3-35: These ClarisWorks Assistants are available in word processing documents.

The following sections explain how to use the four Assistants.

Using the Address Envelope Assistant

The Address Envelope Assistant makes it easy to address and print envelopes from within ClarisWorks. To address an envelope in the document, select (highlight) the address of the individual or company to whom you want to send the letter. (You do not need to copy or cut the address to the Clipboard.) Choose ClarisWorks Assistants from the Balloon Help menu or Help menu. In the Select Assistant dialog box, choose Address Envelope and click OK. The Assistant incorporates the highlighted address into a new word processing document that is formatted as a business envelope. If your envelopes do not include a preprinted return address, you can add one to the document now.

When you are ready to print, choose Page Setup from the File menu and make sure the options are correct (envelopes are printed in landscape mode on most laser printers, for example), insert an envelope into the printer, and choose Print from the File menu (or press ⌘-P). If you have any problems, refer to the printer manual for the special options and procedures necessary for printing envelopes.

Using the Insert Footnote Assistant

Whether you are writing a college term paper, a professional article, or any other work in which you include footnotes, the Insert Footnote Assistant is an enormous help in ensuring that each footnote contains the necessary information. Unlike footnotes you create manually with the Insert Footnote command in the Format menu (Shift-⌘-F), the Insert Footnote Assistant steps you through the process of composing the footnote and then formats it according to the footnote style you've chosen.

Steps: Adding a Footnote with the Insert Footnote Assistant

1. In a word processing document, position the cursor where you want to insert the footnote.

2. Choose ClarisWorks Assistants from the Balloon Help menu or Help menu.

3. In the Select Assistant dialog box, choose Insert Footnote and click OK. The Footnote Assistant dialog box appears, as shown in Figure 3-36.

Figure 3-36: Indicate the type of source you are citing.

4. Click the radio button for the type of source you want to cite and then click Next.

5. Another dialog box appears (such as the one in Figure 3-37), where you fill in the appropriate information for your source. The information requested varies with different types of sources. Any field you leave blank is marked with a placeholder in the footnote, which you can fill in later.

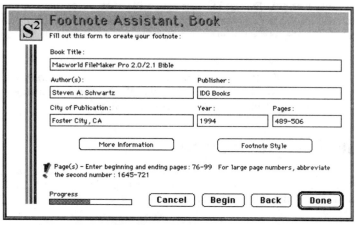

Figure 3-37: Fill in the blanks with your source information.

6. *Optional:* Some source forms include a Footnote Style button you click to select one of two footnote styles: Modern Language Association or *Chicago Manual of Style*. Click OK to continue. If you do not make a style selection, the Modern Language Association style is used.

7. Click Done. The new footnote number is inserted at the cursor position, and the footnote is added to the bottom of the current page, as shown in Figure 3-38.

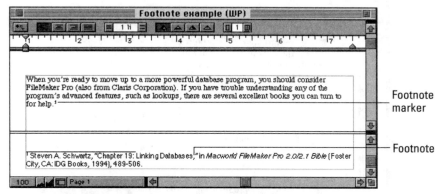

Figure 3-38: After adding a footnote with the Assistant, the footnote automatically appears at the bottom of the current document page.

If you want *endnotes* in the document (notes that are grouped together at the end of the document) rather than *footnotes* (notes that appear at the bottom of the pages on which they are referenced), choose the Document command from the

Format menu, click the At End of Document radio button (in the Footnotes section of the Document dialog box), and click OK. All footnotes — including those created by the Insert Footnote Assistant — are moved to the last page of the document.

Although the Insert Footnote Assistant is also listed in the Select Assistant dialog box when you invoke this dialog box from a word processing *frame*, you can use this Assistant only in a word processing *document*. (An error message appears if you select the Assistant from a word processing frame.)

Using the Paragraph Sorter

The new Paragraph Sorter Assistant enables you to sort selected word processing paragraphs alphabetically — the perfect tool for organizing item lists, for example. To sort paragraphs, follow this procedure:

Steps: Sorting Word Processing Paragraphs

1. In a word processing document or frame, select the paragraphs you want to sort.

2. Choose ClarisWorks Assistants from the Balloon Help menu or Help menu.

3. In the Select Assistant dialog box, choose Paragraph Sorter and click OK. The Paragraph Sorter Assistant appears (see Figure 3-39).

Figure 3-39: The Paragraph Sorter Assistant

4. Select one of the following sort methods:

    • Click the Ascending radio button to sort the paragraphs alphabetically (from A to Z).

- Click the Descending radio button to sort the paragraphs in reverse alphabetical order (from Z to A).
- Click the Randomize radio button to arrange the paragraphs in random order.

5. *Optional:* If some of the paragraphs are preceded by numbers you wish to use in setting the sort order, click the Leading Numbers check box.

With this option checked, the numbers 1, 5, and 12, for example, are sorted numerically. If the option is not checked, an ascending sort results in this order: 1, 12, and 5.

Using the Make Table Assistant

As shown in the "Down to Business" example at the end of this chapter, one of the easiest ways to add a table to a word processing document is to insert a spreadsheet frame. By taking advantage of the Make Table Assistant, you can reduce much of the work required in designing a table.

Steps: Adding a Spreadsheet Table to a Document

1. Decide whether you want the table to be a free-floating graphic or an in-line graphic (as described in "Adding Graphics to Word Processing Documents," earlier in this chapter). To create a floating table, click the pointer tool in the Tool panel. For an in-line graphic, position the text insertion point at the spot in the document where you want the table to be placed.

2. Choose ClarisWorks Assistants from the Balloon Help menu or the Help menu.

3. In the Select Assistant dialog box, choose Make Table and click OK. The opening dialog box appears (see Figure 3-40).

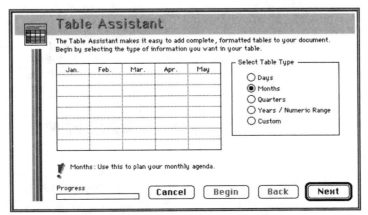

Figure 3-40: Set column headings in this dialog box.

4. Click a radio button to indicate the type of column headings the table will have and then click Next. If none of the numeric options is appropriate, click Custom.

5. Choose additional headings and options from the pull-down menus in the dialog box that appears next (see Figure 3-41) and then click Next to continue. The options and their wording vary depending on the table headings chosen in the preceding dialog box.

   Check the Show Extra Category check box to add a blank column at the start of the table. (If you want to enter row headings manually as well, the extra blank column creates the necessary space for you to do so.)

6. In the final dialog box, set data formatting options. Click Create to generate the table. The table appears in the current document. (If the table is too large to fit within the margins of the document, you may have to adjust either its size or the number of rows or columns.)

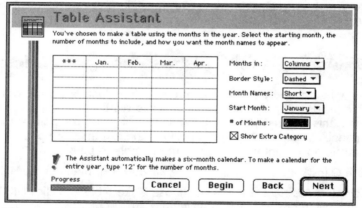

Figure 3-41: Set additional table options.

Note

In addition to helping you create tables in the word processing environment, the Make Table Assistant can also be invoked from a draw document or from Layout mode in a database.

Down to Business: An Improved Fax Form Template

Although ClarisWorks includes a fax form template, you may want to make your own.

I prefer to combine the cover page information with the body of the fax. As you can see in the finished fax form shown in Figure 3-42, the essential To:/From: information takes up less than a third of the page, leaving plenty of room for the fax message. If you use this form rather than a cover page, you can probably reduce most transmissions to a single page.

Figure 3-42: A filled-in fax form template

This exercise illustrates the following ClarisWorks features:

✦ Placing and drawing graphics in a word processing document

✦ Locking graphic elements (so they cannot be moved or inadvertently altered)

✦ Using multiple fonts, styles, and sizes

✦ Paragraph formatting

✦ Creating a footer

✦ Automatic page numbering

✦ Using a spreadsheet frame as a table

✦ Changing spreadsheet column widths

✦ Pasting formulas

✦ Protecting spreadsheet cells

✦ Automatic date stamping

Designing the template

To create the template, begin by creating a new word processing document (choose the New command from the File menu or press ⌘-N). Then choose the Document command from the Format menu. In the Document dialog box that appears, set the Left and Right Margins to *1 in*. This setting ensures you will not lose text from the sides of the document when you send it as a fax.

The key elements of the fax form are numbered in Figure 3-42. The discussion that follows refers to each element by number.

1: Name/Company Name/Return Address

Center your name, company name, and return address on the page. (Click the center-alignment icon in the ruler bar to center text between the margins.) Use 12-point Helvetica Bold for the font.

2: Fax and Voice Phone Numbers

Center these lines as you centered the address information. The phone numbers and the electronic mail account information (America Online) are 10-point Helvetica.

You can replace this e-mail address with your own electronic mail address (if you have one) or with other pertinent information, or you can simply delete it.

Finally, separate the last line of the phone number or electronic mail information from the body text below it. Although you can accomplish this task by pressing Return several times to insert blank lines, inserting them by setting Space After for the final line is preferable. To separate the return address text from the body text, position the text insertion point anywhere in the electronic mail text line. Choose the Paragraph command from the Format menu. The Paragraph dialog box appears. Set Space After to *5 li* and then click OK.

3: Logo or Graphic

I like to use graphics or logos in my faxes. The logos in Figure 3-42 are pasted onto the document as objects rather than as in-line graphics.

Steps: Adding a Graphic to a Template

1. In the Scrapbook, a ClarisWorks library, or a graphics program (the ClarisWorks draw environment, for example), select the image you want to copy.

2. Choose Copy from the Edit menu (or press ⌘-C).

3. Return to the fax form in ClarisWorks and select the pointer tool from the Tool panel.

4. Choose Paste from the Edit menu (or press ⌘-V). The graphic appears on screen, surrounded by handles to show it is selected. (If the handles are not visible, the graphic has been pasted as in-line text rather than as an object. Press Delete to remove the image and return to Step 3.)

Note

If the graphic is in a drag-and-drop-enabled application or desk accessory (such as the Scrapbook), you can drag it onto the fax form, rather than using the copy-and-paste procedure just described.

5. With the image still selected, drag it to the upper-left corner of the fax form. If the image is too large or too small, click its bottom-right handle and, while pressing Shift, drag to resize the image. (Using Shift while resizing a graphic helps to maintain the same proportions.)

6. *Optional:* To make an exact copy of the graphic for use in the upper-right corner of the fax form, select the graphic and choose Copy from the Edit menu (or press ⌘-C).

Choose Paste from the Edit menu (or press ⌘-V). A copy of the graphic is pasted directly on top of the original graphic.

Select the new graphic and, while pressing Shift, drag it horizontally to the right edge of the fax form. (Pressing Shift while dragging an image assures all movements are exactly horizontal or vertical and keeps the two graphics perfectly aligned.)

4: The Spreadsheet Table (Addressee Information)

The addressee information is a spreadsheet frame. Figure 3-43 shows what the spreadsheet frame looks like as you work with it.

	A	B	C	D
1	To:	Jim Abramson	Date:	September 12, 1995
2	Subject:	Article payments	Pages:	1

Figure 3-43: The spreadsheet frame

Steps: Creating the Addressee Table

1. Click the spreadsheet tool in the Tool panel and draw the frame.

2. In cells A1, A2, C1, and C2, enter the following text strings:

Cell	Text
A1	To:
A2	Subject:
C1	Date:
C2	Pages:

Format the four cells with 12-point Helvetica Bold and make them right-aligned. To set the font (Helvetica), style (Bold), and point size (12), select the cells and then choose the appropriate options from the Font, Style, and Size submenus of the Format menu. To set the alignment, choose Right from the Alignment submenu in the Format menu.

3. Use a 12-point font (Helvetica, for example) and the General alignment (the default setting) for the remaining cells (B1, B2, D1, and D2). Set the font and point size for these cells by using the procedure described in Step 2.

4. Add a formula to cell D1 that automatically inserts the current date by selecting the cell and then choosing Paste Function from the Edit menu. The Paste Function dialog box appears, as shown in Figure 3-44.

Figure 3-44: The Paste Function dialog box

5. Select NOW( ) and click OK. The function appears in the entry bar at the top of the spreadsheet.

6. Press Enter to enter the formula in the cell.

7. To display cell D1 as a date, rather than as a numeric string, choose Number from the Format menu. The Format Number, Date, and Time dialog box appears, as shown in Figure 3-45.

Figure 3-45: The Format Number, Date, and Time dialog box enables you to set numeric, date, and time formats for selected cells.

8. Click a radio button for a date format and then click OK. Cell D1 is now formatted as a date.

9. When you first created the spreadsheet frame, the column widths were all uniform. To change them to their final sizes, select a column, choose Column Width from the Format menu, and enter the width. Set the widths as follows (in points):

Column	Width
A	56
B	212
C	46
D	120

10. To get rid of the ugly grid lines and row/column labels, select any cell in the spreadsheet (which cell you select doesn't matter) and then choose Display from the Options menu. The Display dialog box appears.

11. Remove all check marks from the check boxes and then click OK. If any unnecessary rows or columns are visible, drag one of the spreadsheet frame's handles to resize the frame.

12. To prevent the formatting or formula from being changed inadvertently, select cells A1 and A2 and then choose Lock Cells from the Options menu (or press ⌘-H). Repeat this procedure for cells C1, C2, and D1.

13. Drag the spreadsheet frame to its proper position on the fax form. When it is in position, choose Lock from the Arrange menu (or press ⌘-H). This procedure locks the frame into position and displays a gray handle on each corner of the table. (If you later need to change the position of the table, select it and choose Unlock from the Arrange menu.)

5: The Horizontal Lines

A pair of thick horizontal lines separates the addressee information from the rest of the fax form.

Steps: Creating the Lines

1. Select the line tool from the Tool panel.

2. Starting at the left margin, hold down Shift and drag until you reach the right margin. Then release the mouse button.

3. With the newly drawn line still selected, choose *3 pt.* from the Line Width palette in the Tool panel.

4. To make a copy of the line, choose Copy from the Edit menu (or press ⌘-C). Then choose Paste from the Edit menu (or press ⌘-V). A new copy of the line is pasted directly on top of the original copy. (You also could use the Duplicate command to make a copy of the line, but it would be pasted slightly away from the original rather than on top of it.)

5. Select the copy of the line and, while pressing Shift, drag the line down to the bottom of the spreadsheet table.

6. Finally, to keep the two lines from shifting by mistake, select them both (click one and then Shift-click the other) and choose Lock from the Arrange menu.

6: The Body Text

Enter a dummy line of body text, such as *Message goes here*, so you can set the paragraph format and choose a font for the fax text. Move the text insertion point to the end of the electronic mail line in the return address information, press Return, and type the dummy text. Choose a font for the body text from the Font menu and use it to format the dummy text line. Make sure the font you choose is very legible so the recipient's copy will be clear. Times is a good choice.

Every paragraph of the body text uses the same font and paragraph format settings. To set the paragraph format, choose Paragraph from the Format menu. The Paragraph dialog box appears. Set Line Spacing and Space After to *1 li*; all other settings can be left at their defaults.

7: The Footer

The footer repeats on every page of the fax, displaying a standard message and the page number for each page. To create the footer, choose Insert Footer from the Format menu. A blank area at the bottom of the page is now reserved for the footer. Press Return once to add a blank line at the top of the footer (to separate it from the body text). Set the font, style, and size as Helvetica, Bold and Italic, and 10 point, respectively. Type the following message: **Please call immediately if there are problems with this transmission.** Press Tab once and then type **Page**, followed by a space. Drag a right tab — the third tab icon — to the 7-inch mark on the ruler. Doing so causes the page number information to align with the right margin. To complete the footer, insert the automatic page number. With the text insertion point at the end of the footer text, choose Insert Page # from the Edit menu, click the Page Number radio button in the Insert Page Number dialog box, and click OK.

Because you want to have ready access to the template and ensure you do not change it by mistake, save it as a stationery document.

Steps: Saving the Template as a ClarisWorks Stationery Document

1. Choose Document Summary from the File menu. The Document Summary dialog box appears, as shown in Figure 3-46. By filling in the fields in this dialog box, you can make it easier to identify your template.

Of particular importance are the Category and Description fields. The text entered for Category determines the group in which your template is listed when you use the New Document dialog box's Category pop-up menu. General is a good choice for the fax template's category.

Text entered in Description appears beneath the stationery list when the template is highlighted. To remind yourself of what this template is for, enter a short description.

Click OK when you have finished entering the information.

Figure 3-46: The Document Summary dialog box

2. Choose Save As from the File menu. The standard Save file dialog box appears.

3. Click the Stationery radio button. By default, ClarisWorks automatically selects the ClarisWorks Stationery folder. Saving the stationery document in the ClarisWorks Stationery folder will enable you to choose the template easily when creating new files.

4. Enter a name for the document, such as *Fax Form Template*.

5. Click Save.

To open this — or any other — stationery document in ClarisWorks 5.0, choose New Document from the File menu (or press ⌘-N), click the Use Assistant or Stationery radio button, select the correct file list by choosing from the Category pop-up menu, choose a stationery file, and click OK.

Using the template

Now that you have created the fax form template, you need to know how to use it.

Steps: Creating a Fax

1. Choose New from the File menu. The New Document dialog box appears.

2. Click the Use Assistant or Stationery radio button, select the correct file list by choosing from the Category pop-up menu, choose Fax Form Template, and click OK. An untitled copy of the fax form template appears.

3. Fill in the address information. Begin by clicking to the right of the To: field. Enter the name of the fax recipient and press Return. The cursor moves to the cell below, where you can now enter the subject of the fax.

4. Select the line of text that reads *Message goes here*, and type the body of the fax. You'll notice each time you press Return to start a new paragraph, the program automatically inserts a blank line for you.

5. When you've completed the body text, select the spreadsheet cell to the right of the Pages: field and enter the total number of pages for the fax.

6. If you are going to transmit the fax on a standard fax machine, turn on the printer and choose Print from the File menu. The Print dialog box appears. Change settings as necessary (you can usually accept the default settings) and click OK. The fax prints.

— or —

If you are going to transmit the fax via your fax modem, select the Chooser desk accessory from the Apple menu. The Chooser dialog box appears. (The specific procedure for sending a document with your fax modem may differ, depending on the fax software installed on the Mac. See the software manual for exact instructions.)

7. Select the fax modem driver from the left side of the Chooser dialog box and click the close box to make that driver the current driver.

8. In ClarisWorks, choose Page Setup from the File menu and change settings as needed. Click OK to return to the document.

9. Choose Print from the File menu, change settings as necessary, specify a recipient for the fax, and click OK. The document is now translated into fax format and transmitted to the recipient.

Quick Tips

The following quick tips describe how to create glossary terms and suggest ways to improve the quality of your documents by using special papers.

A do-it-yourself glossary

You may have noticed that the ClarisWorks word processor lacks a glossary feature. (A *glossary* enables you to insert frequently used terms and phrases into documents easily by selecting them from lists or by pressing hot keys.) However, with minimal effort, you can create glossary terms. Two approaches work fairly well: using the Find/Change command and using macros.

To use the Find/Change method, you define one or more abbreviations to represent a longer word or phrase, use them in the text, and then issue the Find/Change command to replace each abbreviation with the expanded phrase.

Decide on a term or phrase for which you want to define an abbreviation. The phrase can contain up to 255 characters, including spaces. Pick an abbreviation for the phrase. Ideally, the abbreviation should not be a real word or a portion of a word. For example, you can use three asterisks (***) or a nonsense syllable (cpt). When typing the document, use the abbreviation, rather than the full word or phrase it represents. After you finish typing the document, replace all abbreviations with the full word or phrase. Do so by choosing Find/Change from the Find/Change submenu of the Edit menu (or by pressing ⌘-F), entering the abbreviation in the Find box, entering the expanded word or phrase in the Change box, and clicking Change All.

Alternatively, you can create a macro, as described in the following steps:

Steps: Creating a Glossary Term Macro

1. Open a new or existing word processing document.

2. Choose Record Macro from the Macros submenu of the File menu (or press Shift-⌘-J). The Record Macro dialog box appears, as shown in Figure 3-47.

Figure 3-47: The Record Macro dialog box

3. Enter a name for the macro and specify an Option-⌘ key or function key with which to execute the macro.

4. Choose from the following options:

   • If you don't intend to use the glossary term anywhere other than in the present document, click Document Specific. If you want the macro to be available in other documents, leave that check box blank.

   • If you want to use the glossary term in other environments (in addition to the word processing environment), click their Play In check boxes.

5. Click Record. You are returned to the document, and the macro recorder starts.

6. Type the term or phrase you want to record. In most cases, you will probably want to end the macro term or phrase with a space (that is, you will type "ClarisWorks " rather than "ClarisWorks"). If you include a space at the end of the macro, you don't have to press the spacebar before you type the next word when you execute the macro.

7. Choose Stop Recording from the Macros submenu of the File menu (or press Shift-⌘-J).

Whenever you want to insert the new glossary term, simply press the Option-⌘ key or function key you assigned to the macro.

If you wish, you can also create a custom button for the macro and add it to one or more button bars. (See Chapter 12 for information on creating and using buttons.)

Paper, paper . . . who's got the paper?

Letterhead and fan-fold computer paper do not meet every word processing need. Whether you just want to make a document look its best or you have something different in mind (such as a brochure, an imprinted postcard, or an award certificate), a special paper may be exactly what you need.

Unless you happen to have a heavy-duty stationery shop nearby, one of the best sources of specialty papers is Paper Direct (800-272-7377). Call and ask for a copy of the catalog. If you own a laser printer or a high-quality ink-jet printer, you'll be amazed at the printing capabilities you have but didn't know about.

Summary

✦ Word processing text can contain any combination of fonts, sizes, and styles. You can apply multiple styles to the same text string. If you use certain text styles often, you can add their definitions to the stylesheet.

✦ Paragraph formatting controls the look of a particular paragraph. It includes settings for tabs, indents, line spacing, and text alignment. You can set most paragraph options directly on the ruler or choose the Paragraph command from the Format menu.

✦ ClarisWorks offers four kinds of tab stops: left, centered, right, and character. Character tab stops are frequently used to align a column of numbers on the decimal point. You can also specify a fill or leader character for tab stops.

✦ The four alignment options enable you to create left-, right-, center-, or full-justified paragraphs.

✦ Section commands are used to break a document into logical sections, such as book chapters. Each section can have a different number of columns, a separate title page, and different headers and footers from other sections.

✦ Document commands enable you to see multiple pages of text on screen at the same time, set margins, and choose footnotes or endnotes for the document.

✦ If you want to lay out a newsletter or a magazine article, you can easily change to a multicolumn layout. You can use the Insert Break command to adjust page and column breaks manually and to avoid widows and orphans.

✦ The Find/Change commands enable you to search for words and, optionally, to replace them with other words.

✦ Headers and footers are sections that appear on every page of a document. They are useful for displaying page numbers, a company logo, and so on.

✦ ClarisWorks can automatically number and manage footnotes, or you can mark them with special characters you have selected.

✦ You can insert automatic dates, times, or page numbers into any document. Dates and times automatically update each time you open the document. Page numbers automatically adjust as the pagination for the document changes.

✦ The spelling checker enables you to check the entire document or just text that is currently selected. You can create user dictionaries that contain the spellings of words that are not in the main dictionary. The Word Finder thesaurus helps you find synonyms when you're stuck for a word or phrase.

✦ Use the Word Count command to view summary statistics on an entire document or selected text.

✦ ClarisWorks has an auto-hyphenation feature that can dramatically improve the appearance of documents.

✦ Outlines can be incorporated within a normal ClarisWorks word processing document. There are three general outline formats to choose from, as well as twelve styles of topic labels.

✦ You can add pictures to word processing documents as in-line graphics or as objects. ClarisWorks treats the former as text. The latter are free-floating, and you can position them next to, behind, or in front of text. You can wrap text around free-floating graphics and adjust the vertical alignment of in-line graphics.

✦ ClarisWorks 5.0's new Equation Editor makes it possible to create equations for inclusion in scientific, business, and school reports.

✦ There are four Assistants you can choose from the Balloon Help (System 7.6 and earlier) or Help menu (OS 8) that make it simple to address envelopes, insert footnotes, sort paragraphs, and add tables to word processing documents.

✦   ✦   ✦

The Spreadsheet Environment

Overview

A spreadsheet program is like an electronic version of a bookkeeper's ledger page. A spreadsheet document (or *worksheet*) is a grid composed of numbered rows and lettered columns. You enter data into worksheet *cells* — the intersections of the rows and columns. The default size for a ClarisWorks worksheet is 500 rows by 40 columns. Figure 4-1 shows the components of a worksheet.

Address of active cell

Row
headings   Named Range pop-up menu

                  Cancel button   Entry bar (enter and edit cell contents here)

———————————— Column headings

———————————— Accept button

———————————— Function button

———————————— Active cell

Figure 4-1: The parts of a worksheet

The Function button and the Named Range pop-up menu are new additions to the entry bar. Click the Function button to incorporate a spreadsheet function into the current cell's formula. Use the Named Range pop-up menu to create or modify names of cell ranges.

In This Chapter

Spreadsheet basics (selecting cells, entering and editing data, worksheet navigation)

Formulas and functions

Working with named ranges

Rearranging the worksheet (inserting and deleting cells, rows, and columns; moving cells; sorting; changing the size of the worksheet)

Formatting cell contents and backgrounds

Making charts

Printing worksheets

Other spreadsheet procedures and options, such as locking cells and titles, setting a default font, and choosing display options

The power of the spreadsheet lies in its calculation capabilities. You can mathematically combine the contents of cells by creating *formulas* that add, subtract, divide, or multiply cells by each other or by constants. The ClarisWorks spreadsheet environment also offers a large number of mathematical, statistical, time, text, financial, and logical *functions* that enable you to perform complex calculations, such as determining the average of a group of numbers or computing a modified internal rate of return.

The spreadsheet is the ideal environment for data that requires calculations. As such, it is frequently used for accounting, bookkeeping, and record keeping. You can use the charting capabilities to summarize any portion of your data pictorially. And although the ClarisWorks spreadsheet does not contain the database commands other spreadsheet programs offer, you can still keep simple lists in a worksheet and sort them as needed. You also can use worksheet frames as tables in other ClarisWorks environments.

 Note

A *spreadsheet* is a type of program, or, in ClarisWorks, an environment. A *worksheet* is a spreadsheet document. These terms are sometimes used interchangeably when referring to the document.

Understanding Spreadsheet Basics

Worksheet cells are identified by the letter and number combination of the intersection of the cell's column and row. For example, the cell in the upper-left corner of every worksheet is A1 (column A, row 1). The current cell has a double border and is called the *active cell*. To make a different cell active, you can click it with the mouse, move to it by using the cursor keys, or choose the Go to Cell command (⌘-G) from the Options menu.

The letter and number combination for a cell is called its *cell address*. A cell address uniquely identifies every cell in the worksheet. You can use cell addresses in formulas. For example, to add the contents of cells A1 and B1 and display the result in cell C1, you enter this formula in C1: **=A1+B1**.

 Note

The equal sign (=) informs ClarisWorks that you are entering a formula.

You can use a combination of cell addresses and constants in formulas, as shown in the following formulas: =B3*15 and =(A17/5)+2.37.

You also can work with a rectangular group of cells known as a *range* (see Figure 5-2). You can include ranges in some types of formulas, such as =SUM(A1..A4), where A1..A4 is a range that represents the four cells from A1 to A4 (that is, A1, A2, A3, and A4). This formula adds the contents of the four cells. When you want to apply a format quickly (a font, style, size, or numeric format, for example) to a large number of cells by using a single command, you can select a range prior to issuing a formatting command.

To specify a range in a formula, you separate the upper-left and lower-right cells in the range (called *anchors* or *anchor cells*, as shown in Figure 4-2) with a pair of periods, as in =SUM(A1..A5).

Upper-left anchor cell (D2)

	A	B	C	D	E	F
1	1997 Sales	Qtr. 1	Qtr. 2	Qtr. 3	Qtr. 4	
2	North	2.35	5.35	5.00	4.00	
3	East	2.00	2.31	2.24	2.00	
4	South	3.00	2.28	1.73	1.32	
5	West	4.00	4.59	3.97	3.32	
6						

Sales 1997 (SS)

D2 — 5

Selected range (D2..E5)

Lower-right anchor cell (E5)

Figure 4-2: A range is a rectangular selection of contiguous cells.

New In Version 5 To make it simpler for you to work with ranges, ClarisWorks 5.0 enables you to assign names to ranges (such as Qtr 1, Monthly Sales, or Test Scores). Using *named ranges* often makes it easier to understand the assumptions that underlie a worksheet and communicate what the spreadsheet is about. (For information about using named ranges, see "Working with named ranges," later in this chapter.)

Selecting cells

Many actions in a spreadsheet program require that you preselect one or more cells and then choose the action you want to perform on those cells. After you choose cells, you can apply formats to them, fill them to the right or down, clear them, create a chart based on the selected values, sort them, and so on.

You use the following methods to select cells:

✦ To select a single cell, click it. The cell is surrounded by a double border and becomes the active cell.

✦ To select a cell range, click to select the first cell and then drag the cursor or Shift-click to choose the remaining cells.

✦ To select an entire row or column, click the heading for that row or column or drag through the row or column.

✦ To select the entire worksheet, click the blank box above the 1 heading for row 1 or choose Select All (⌘-A) from the Edit menu.

✦ To select the active area of the worksheet (the cell range that contains entries), press Option as you click the blank box above the 1 heading for row 1.

Cell contents

Every cell can contain a text string, a number, or a formula. Numbers can be positive or negative, and you can type them directly (as in **43** and **-123.654**). You also can type directly any entry that begins with a letter (as in **Sam Jones** and **Social Security #123-45-6789**). As soon as you enter a space or other text character, that cell is treated as text.

To enter a formula, you must precede it with an equal sign (as in **= A5+B4**). If you want to treat a number as text, enter it as if it was a formula; that is, precede the number with an equal sign and enclose it in quotation marks (as in **="1997"**).

ClarisWorks treats cell data and the formatting that has been applied to the data as separate entities. If you delete the contents of a cell, the formatting remains. Understanding this concept is particularly important when you want to print a worksheet. The print range defaults to printing all cells that have data in them — which is interpreted by ClarisWorks to mean all cells that have data *or* formatting. For example, if you use the Select All command to apply a different font or size to all cells when you create the worksheet, every cell in the worksheet will be printed — resulting in pages and pages of blank printout.

Entering and editing data

To enter data into a cell, begin by selecting the cell. The cell is surrounded by a double border, showing that it is the active cell. Type the text, number, or formula you want to enter into the cell. Whatever you type appears in the entry bar at the top of the document window. To accept the entry, press Return, Enter, Tab, or an arrow key, or click the Accept button (the check-mark button) in the entry bar. To cancel the entry, click the Cancel button (the X) in the entry bar or press Esc.

In ClarisWorks 5.0, the way the arrow and Option-arrow keys work is determined by the setting chosen in Spreadsheet Preferences. One set of these key commands moves the cursor in the entry bar (when entering or editing cell data); the other set of key commands moves the cursor from the current cell to an adjacent cell. (See Chapter 11 for details.)

If you press any key other than Enter or Esc to conclude a cell entry, the cursor moves to an adjacent cell and makes that cell the active cell. The direction in which the cursor moves depends on the key you press, as described in Table 4-1.

You can also edit or clear the cell contents. To edit the contents of a cell, click the cell you want to edit. The contents of the active cell appear in the entry bar. In the entry bar, click to position the text insertion point. Use normal editing procedures to add or delete characters and to insert new cell references. (You are always in insertion mode when you are editing or entering text.) To move the cursor within an entry, press the left- or right-arrow key (or the Option-left arrow or Option-right arrow keys — depending on the setting you've chosen for Spreadsheet Preferences). See Chapter 11 for details. To complete the entry, press Return, Enter, Tab, or an arrow key (or Option-arrow key); or click the Accept button.

Table 4-1
Spreadsheet Cursor Movement

Key/Button	Cursor Movement
Esc, Cancel button	Stays in the current cell and cancels the entry
Enter, Accept button	Stays in the current cell and accepts the entry
Return, down arrow (or Option-down arrow)	Moves to the cell below
Right arrow (or Option-right arrow), Tab	Moves to the cell to the right
Left arrow (or Option-left arrow), Shift-Tab	Moves to the cell to the left
Up arrow (or Option-up arrow), Shift-Return	Moves to the cell above

Steps: Clearing the Contents of a Cell or Range of Cells

1. Select the cell or cell range you want to clear.

2. Choose Clear from the Edit menu or press the Clear key (if your keyboard has one). The cell contents, as well as any formats that were applied to the selected cells, are cleared.

— or —

Choose Cut from the Edit menu (or press ⌘-X). The program copies the cell contents to the Clipboard and then clears the cells, as well as any formats that were applied to the selected cells.

— or —

Press Delete. ClarisWorks clears the cell contents, but formats applied to the selected cells remain intact.

Worksheet navigation

The ClarisWorks spreadsheet environment offers a number of ways for you to move about the worksheet:

✦ Use the horizontal or vertical scroll bars.

✦ Press the Page Up or Page Down keys to move up or down one screen.

✦ Press Home or End to move to the top or bottom of the worksheet.

✦ Press Enter to make the worksheet scroll to display the active cell.

None of these commands changes the active cell. They are pure navigational commands. If you want to change your view of the worksheet and also change the active cell, do one of the following:

✦ Choose Go to Cell (⌘-G) from the Options menu to go to a specific cell and make it active.

✦ Press an arrow key, Tab, Return, Shift-Tab, or Shift-Return to move one cell in the appropriate direction (as described previously).

Entering Cell Names and Ranges by Pointing

To prevent inaccuracies when you enter or edit formulas, you can use the cursor to point to cell addresses and ranges instead of typing them. Suppose, for example, you want to add the contents of cells A2 and A3. After selecting the destination cell (A4, for example), you would normally type the following formula: **= A2 + A3**. Or, you can accomplish the same task using the pointing method, as described in the following steps.

Using the pointing method to add two cells:

1. Select cell A4 and press = (the equal sign).

2. Using the pointer, click cell A2, press + (the plus sign), and click cell A3. (Clicking a cell has exactly the same effect as typing its cell address.)

In fact, you can even skip entering the plus sign if you want. If no symbol separates two selected cell addresses or ranges, ClarisWorks assumes you want to add them, and it inserts the plus sign for you.

Pointing is particularly useful for selecting a range. To compute the sum of a particular range (A1 through A6, for example), you can type this formula: **=SUM(A1..A6)**. Or, you can accomplish the same thing using the pointing method, as described in the following steps.

Using the pointing method to add a range of cells:

1. Select the destination cell and press = (the equal sign).

2. Choose Paste Function from the Edit menu, choose SUM, and click OK. The SUM function appears in the entry bar.

3. Highlight the arguments in the SUM function and then use the pointer to highlight the desired range (A1 through A6, for example).

4. Click the Accept button (or press Return, Enter, Tab, or an arrow key) to complete the entry.

Formulas

Formulas are the spreadsheet's raison d'être. A formula can be as simple as adding the contents of two cells (for example, =A1+A2) or so complex it contains several nested spreadsheet functions. As mentioned earlier in this chapter, you need to begin every formula with an equal sign (=).

Table 4-2 lists the numeric operators you can use in formulas.

Table 4-2 Numeric Operators in Formulas		
Symbol	**Meaning**	**Examples**
+	Addition	= A5+3
-	Subtraction or negative number	= B7-6; -15
*	Multiplication	= A2*A3
/	Division	= A7/3
^	Exponentiation (raise to the power of)	= A1^2

The ampersand (&) is the only text operator. You use it to *concatenate* (combine) pairs of text strings. For example, if A1 contains the word *Steve* and B1 contains *Schwartz,* you can place a formula in C1 that creates a full name, as in **=A1 & " " & B1** (that is, *Steve,* a space, and *Schwartz*). Note that you need to surround text constants in formulas — such as the space in the preceding example — with quotation marks.

Precedence in formulas

When a formula contains multiple operators, the precedence of the operators determines the order in which the program performs calculations. Higher-precedence operations are performed before lower-precedence operations. If all operators have the same precedence level, the program evaluates the formula from left to right.

Note

You can use parentheses to change the precedence level. When you use parentheses, ClarisWorks first performs calculations on the innermost set of parentheses.

The precedence levels for different operators are listed in Table 4-3.

Table 4-3
Precedence of Operators

Operator	Precedence Level
% (divide by 100)	7
^ (exponentiation)	6
+, - (sign)	5
*, / (multiplication, division)	4
+, - (addition, subtraction)	3
& (text concatenation)	2
=, >, >=, <, <=, <> (logical comparison)	1

The following examples explain how ClarisWorks evaluates different formulas:

✦ =7+2-5

The result is 4. Because addition and subtraction have the same precedence, the program evaluates the formula from left to right.

✦ =5+4*3

The result is 17. Because multiplication has a higher precedence than addition, the program evaluates 4*3 first and then adds 5 to produce the result.

✦ =(5+4)*3

The result is 27. The parentheses change the calculation order, forcing the program to evaluate 5+4 first and then multiply that result by 3.

✦ =3+(2*(4+5))-5

The result is 16. The program evaluates the contents of the innermost parentheses first, giving a result of 9. Then it evaluates the next set of parentheses, producing 18. Finally, because the formula contains no more parentheses and the remaining operators are the same precedence level, it evaluates the rest of the formula from left to right, giving a result of 16.

Using functions in formulas

ClarisWorks provides more than 100 built-in functions you can use in formulas. Function categories include business and financial, numeric, statistical, text, trigonometric, logical, date/time, and information. For additional information on using the ClarisWorks database and spreadsheet functions, refer to Appendix B or ClarisWorks Help.

Steps: Entering a Formula That Contains a Function

1. Select the cell in which you want to enter the formula.

2. Type = (an equal sign).

3. Choose Paste Function from the Edit menu or click the Function button in the entry bar. The Paste Function dialog box appears, as shown in Figure 4-3.

Figure 4-3: The Paste Function dialog box

Tip

You can move quickly to any function in the list by pressing the letter key for the first letter in the function name.

4. *Optional:* To restrict the displayed functions to a particular type (Text or Numeric, for example), choose a function category from the Category pop-up menu.

5. Choose a function from the scrolling list. (To choose a function, click OK or double-click the function name.) The function and its arguments appear at the text insertion point in the entry bar, as shown in Figure 4-4. The first argument is automatically selected for you.

Figure 4-4: Pasted functions include the arguments to the function (in this case, *number1,number2,...*).

6. Replace the arguments in the function with real numbers and/or cell references.

7. To add more functions to the formula, click in the entry bar to set the text insertion point and repeat Steps 3 through 6.

8. Click the Accept button (or press Return, Enter, Tab, or an arrow key) to complete the entry.

Note

You also can manually enter functions into formulas. Simply type the function and its arguments at the appropriate spot in the formula.

Note

You can nest functions (have one function act on another one). An example is =DAYOFYEAR(NOW( )). The NOW( ) function returns a number from the system clock that represents this moment in time. The DAYOFYEAR function converts the number to the day of the current year. For example, if today was July 26, 1997, the result would be 207. Note that the inner function — NOW( ) — is surrounded by parentheses to set it apart from the outer function, DAYOFYEAR.

Working with named ranges

New In Version 5

In previous versions of ClarisWorks, if you wanted to refer to a range of cells in a formula, you had to write the formula like this: =SUM(B3..B6). The cell address or range had to be entered in this less-than-obvious manner. ClarisWorks 5.0 has now caught up with other spreadsheet programs by supporting *named ranges* (also referred to as *range names*), enabling you to assign a common name to any important cell or range and then use that name in formulas to refer to that cell or range. In the previous example, if B3..B6 represented company sales for the first quarter, you might name it *Qtr 1* and then change the formula to read: =SUM(Qtr 1). Using named ranges rather than cell references makes it simple to understand the cell or range to which the formula refers.

Note

There are some restrictions when naming ranges. Each range name must be unique; the first character must be a letter; it cannot contain operators or punctuation marks; and it cannot resemble a cell reference. It may, on the other hand, contain multiple words, such as *Sales 97*.

You assign names to ranges by choosing options from the Named Range pop-up menu in the entry bar (see Figure 4-5). Menu commands enable you to name ranges manually or automatically; edit or replace range names; replace cell references in formulas with range names and vice versa; and refer to existing range names.

Click to pop up
the Named Range menu

Currently defined
range names

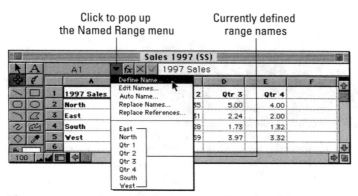

Figure 4-5: Use the Named Range pop-up menu to create or
modify range names.

Autonaming ranges

If a range already has a row or column label, ClarisWorks can automatically use
that label as the range name. To name one or more ranges automatically, select
them in the worksheet — including the row or column labels you want to use to
name the ranges. Click the Named Range pop-up menu in the entry bar and choose
Auto Name. The Auto Define Names dialog box appears (see Figure 4-6). Examine
the list to be sure the names and cell ranges are correct. Remove the check marks
from ranges or names that are incorrect, and then click Define. All names you
accept are inserted alphabetically into the list of range names that appears at the
bottom of the Named Range pop-up menu. (Note that when auto-naming a range,
ClarisWorks does not include the label within the actual range.)

Note

Any labels that violate the previously discussed naming restrictions will not be
listed in the Auto Define Names dialog box.

Manually naming ranges

In those instances where a cell or range is not headed by a row or column label,
you can manually define range names. Highlight the cell or range you want to
name, and choose Define Name from the Named Range pop-up menu. The Defined
Name Range dialog box appears. Enter a name and click Define.

Tip

To see the range to which a particular range name refers, select it in the Named
Range menu. ClarisWorks automatically highlights the matching range.

Figure 4-6: By selecting a worksheet area that contains both row and column labels, you can quickly name a series of ranges.

Using range names in formulas

After defining range names, you can use them in formulas in either of these ways:

✦ Type them by hand. (Letter case is ignored. For example, *Sales* and *sales* are considered to be the same range name.)

✦ Choose them from the Named Range pop-up menu. (Type the formula in the entry bar up to the point where the range name is needed, and then select it from the Named Range pop-up menu.)

Tip

You can also create range names "on the fly." Type a formula using an undefined range name, such as =AVERAGE(Sales), where Sales has yet to be defined as a range name. When you complete the formula, ClarisWorks responds with a #NAME! Error in the cell. Now, define the referenced range name (as explained in "Autonaming ranges" or "Manually naming ranges," previously). The formula will now calculate correctly, using the newly defined range.

Editing range names

You can delete unneeded range names, change range names, or modify the range referred to by any range name by following these steps.

Steps: Modifying Existing Range Names

1. Choose Edit Names from the Named Range pop-up menu. The Edit Names dialog box appears (see Figure 4-7).

Figure 4-7: The Edit Names dialog box

2. From the list of all defined range names for the current worksheet, select the range name you want to modify.

3. If you want to delete (or undefine) the range name, click Remove. Note that range names currently in use in one or more formulas cannot be removed.

4. To change the name of the range, type the new name in the Name box and click Modify.

5. To alter the range to which the range name applies, type the new range — properly formatted — in the Range box and click Modify.

6. Repeat Steps 2 through 5 for any additional range names you want to edit.

7. To accept all changes, click Done. To ignore all changes, click Cancel.

Note

If you insert cells in the middle of a named range, the range automatically adjusts to include the new cells. If you insert cells immediately above, below, to the left, or to the right of an existing named range, however, such cells are not appended to the named range. You must edit the named range if you want to include the new cells.

Replacing names and references in formulas

Although the purpose of using range names is to avoid displaying or having to type range references in formulas, ClarisWorks enables you to replace range names with range references and vice versa.

To replace the use of a range name in a formula with the normal range reference (changing =AVERAGE(Grades) to =AVERAGE(B2..B12), for example), select the cell that contains the formula and choose Replace Names from the Named Range pop-up menu. To replace range references in a formula with defined range names, select the cell that contains the formula and choose Replace References from the Named Range pop-up menu. In either case, a dialog box appears that shows the appropriate range names. If necessary, remove the check mark from any range name you do not want to affect and click Replace.

You can simultaneously replace multiple range names or references. Simply select all cells that contain formulas you want to affect, and then choose the appropriate command from the Named Range pop-up menu. Alternatively, to affect all formulas in the worksheet, choose Select All from the Edit menu prior to choosing the Replace Names or Replace References command.

Filling Cells

ClarisWorks provides two commands for quickly copying a formula into a series of cells: Fill Down and Fill Right. (You also can use Fill Down and Fill Right to copy a single number or text string into a series of cells.) To fill cells down or to the right, select the source cell whose formula you want to copy. Drag the cursor or press Shift to select the additional cells to the right or below that will serve as the destination for the copied formula. Choose Fill Right (⌘-R) or Fill Down (⌘-D) from the Calculate menu, as appropriate. The program copies the formula into every selected cell to the right or below the source cell.

In other spreadsheet programs, you can use Fill Right or Fill Down to number a series of cells conveniently, increasing each one by an increment of your choice. In ClarisWorks 5.0, you can achieve the same effect by using the Fill Special command. Fill Special can fill cells with a repeating pattern, as well as a series of dates or times.

Rather than start with a blank range, you may prefer to enter the initial value in the range before choosing the Fill Special command. If the first cell contains a date, for example, ClarisWorks will try to select the proper sequence for you.

The Fill Special command can also be used to duplicate a pattern. Suppose, for example, you have two column headers labeled Yes and No. If you need to repeat this same set of headers several times, just select the range to which the pattern is to be applied, choose the Fill Special command, click the Pattern radio button, and indicate the number of cells in the pattern (two, in this instance).

Absolute and Relative Cell References

When a formula in a cell refers to another cell or range of cells, it is called a *cell reference*. For example, you may have a formula in cell B1 that multiplies the contents of cell A1 by 0.15, as in =A1*0.15. If you copy cell B1 and then paste it into cell B2, the formula updates to read = A2*0.15. The cell the formula refers to is no longer the original cell. The reason for the change is the initial cell reference is a *relative reference*; that is, the reference is relative to the position of the active cell. ClarisWorks interprets the formula in B1 to mean: "Take the contents of the cell to my immediate left and multiply it by 0.15." No matter which cell you copy this formula to, ClarisWorks interprets it in the same manner.

Normally, a relative cell reference is what you want. When you copy a cell that contains a formula or apply Fill Down or Fill Right to a group of cells that begins with a cell containing a formula, you want the new cells to contain the same formula — but with the appropriate cell references. Occasionally, however, you may want the row or column reference to remain unchanged — pointing to the original row and/or column of the cell. Any reference that does not change when you copy the cell elsewhere is called an *absolute reference*.

Suppose cell A1 contains an estimate of inflation (.15, for example), and the range from A2 to A7 contains various expense figures, as shown in the following figure. In cells B2 through B7, you want to calculate new expense figures after taking inflation into account. If you were using relative cell references, the formula in B2 would read =A2+(A1*A2). However, to keep the reference to cell A1 from changing when you copy or fill the formula in B2 to the remaining cells (B3 through B7), you need to make it into an absolute reference, as in =A2+(A1*A2). The *$* in front of the *A* makes the column reference absolute. The *$* in front of the *1* makes the row reference absolute. When you copy the new formula to cells B3 through B7, every instance refers directly to cell A1. The references to A2, on the other hand, are still relative and are updated to point to the correct relative cell.

Tip: When you enter a formula, you can automatically make a reference absolute by holding down Option and ⌘ when clicking the cell.

You also can create *mixed references*, in which the row reference is absolute and the column reference is relative (or vice versa), as in =B$1+7.

Circular references, on the other hand, are errors, and you should avoid them. They occur when two or more cells depend on the contents of each other. The following formulas contain circular references: A1=B3+7 and B3=A1/5. Because cells A1 and B3 are mutually dependent, the program cannot calculate the results. Cells that contain circular references are indicated by bullets that surround the cell contents, as in •8.75• or •#REF!•.

Steps: Filling Cells with a Special Sequence

1. Drag the pointer to select the cells you want to fill. The selected range must be contained within a single row or column; otherwise, you cannot choose the Fill Special command.

2. Choose Fill Special from the Calculate menu. The Fill Special dialog box appears (see Figure 4-8).

Figure 4-8: The Fill Special dialog box

3. On the left side of the dialog box, click a radio button to indicate the type of data the series will contain: numbers, times, dates, and so on.

4. Depending on the data type selected, either enter a starting number or select a start pattern (Quarter 1, Sunday, and so on).

5. Type or select an increment. (Note that some sequences present additional increment options. Dates, for example, can be incremented by days, weeks, months, or years.)

6. Select additional options, if any are shown.

7. Click OK.

Rearranging the Worksheet

Creating a useful worksheet is an evolving process. The basic structure can change frequently. New rows and columns are inserted, ranges are moved, and columns are sorted as you determine the best way to display the data. ClarisWorks provides all the commands necessary to ensure that rearranging the worksheet is as easy and trouble-free as possible.

Inserting and deleting cells, columns, and rows

Clearing the contents of a cell or range of cells has no other effect on the worksheet (unless formulas in other cells refer to the cleared cells). Sometimes, however, you may want to add one or more new cells, a new row, or a new column to a worksheet; or you may want to delete cells, rows, or columns.

When you add cells, you need to shift other cells below or to the right to make room for the new cells. (The shift is automatic if you insert entire rows or columns.) When you delete cells, you need to close up the hole that is left by the departing cells. (The shift is automatic if you delete entire rows or columns.)

Using the Insert Cells or Delete Cells command (described in the following steps) is much faster than the alternative: cutting, pasting, and otherwise manually rearranging the worksheet. You may find, for example, you haven't left sufficient space at the top of a worksheet for a general label (for example, *Budget Worksheet for Fall 1997*) or other identifying information. You can use the Insert Cells command to insert a row or two easily.

Steps: Inserting New Cells

1. Select the cell or range where you want to add the new cells.

2. Choose Insert Cells from the Calculate menu (or press Shift-⌘-I). The Insert Cells dialog box appears, as shown in Figure 4-9.

Figure 4-9: The Insert Cells dialog box

3. Choose Shift Cells Down if you want the selected cells and all cells directly below the selection to move down.

— or —

Choose Shift Cells Right if you want the selected cells and all cells directly to the right of the selection to move to the right.

4. Click OK. The program inserts the new cell or cells and rearranges the worksheet as requested.

To insert new columns or rows, select the headings for the columns or rows where you want to insert the new columns or rows. Choose Insert Cells from the Calculate menu (or press Shift-⌘-I). New blank columns or rows are inserted in place of the selected columns or rows, and the originally selected columns or rows automatically shift to the right or down to make room.

Steps: Deleting Cells

1. Select the cell or range you want to delete.

2. Choose Delete Cells from the Calculate menu (or press Shift-⌘-K). The Delete Cells dialog box appears.

3. Choose Shift Cells Up if you want the cells below the selection to move up to fill the hole left by the deletion.

— or —

Choose Shift Cells Left if you want the cells to the right of the selection to move left to fill the hole left by the deletion.

4. Click OK. The program deletes the cell or cells and rearranges the worksheet as requested.

To delete entire columns or rows, select one or more columns or rows to be deleted by clicking the column or row headings. Choose Delete Cells from the Calculate menu (or press Shift-⌘-K). The program removes the selected columns or rows, and the columns to the right or rows below automatically move to close the gap.

Copying and pasting cells

One way to duplicate or move cells is to copy or cut the cells and then paste them into a new location. To copy and paste, you select the cells of interest, choose Copy from the Edit menu, select a destination, and then choose Paste from the Edit menu. When you copy a formula, the program reflects the new location by updating the cell references the formula contains.

Note

You cannot paste the copied contents of a single cell into more than one cell at a time. During a paste, the program automatically replicates the shape of the copied cell grouping. Thus, if you copy a single cell and select multiple cells for the paste, the data or formula is copied only to the first cell in the destination range. If you select a string of three cells when copying (A1 through A3, for example), regardless of the area selected for pasting, ClarisWorks fills the first cell of the destination range and the two cells immediately below it.

You also can paste formula results (or *values*), leaving the formulas behind. To paste values, select the cell or cells you want to copy. Choose Copy from the Edit menu (or press ⌘-C). Select a destination. Choose Paste Special from the Edit menu. The Paste Special dialog box appears. Click the Paste Values Only radio button and click OK.

Note

When pasting values only, the cell formatting from the copied cell is ignored. The pasted information is displayed in the worksheet's default font.

You can also move cells from one worksheet location to another by choosing the Move command from the Calculate menu or by using drag-and-drop. See "Moving cells," below.

Moving cells

When you use the cut-and-paste method to move cells from one worksheet location to another, the program updates the relative cell references contained within the moved cells so they refer to the new locations. If you want the cell references to remain unchanged, use the Move command instead.

Suppose, for example, cell A1 contains *10* and cell B1 contains the formula *=A1+5* (which evaluates as 15). If you use the Move command to move cell B1 to D10, the formula remains unchanged (=A1+5). On the other hand, if you simply cut cell B1 and paste it into D10, the formula reads =C10+5 and evaluates incorrectly — assuming you still wanted the cell to reflect the contents of cell A1 plus 5.

In this same example, if you want to move both cells A1 and B1, you can use either the Cut and Paste commands or Move. The result is the same. If a move contains all cells that are referred to by other cells in the move, the program updates the references, just as it does when you cut and paste.

To move the contents of one or more cells, begin by selecting the cell or range you want to move. Then choose Move from the Calculate menu. The Move dialog box appears, as shown in Figure 4-10. Enter a destination cell address (the cell in the upper-left corner of the destination range) for the move, and click OK to move the cell or range to the new location.

Figure 4-10: The Move dialog box

Caution

When executing a move or a paste, be sure there is room at the destination for the moved or pasted cells. Existing data in the destination cells will be overwritten by the moved or pasted data. If you make this mistake, immediately choose Undo Move from the Edit menu.

Tip

You can accomplish a move quickly by pointing or by using drag-and-drop. For either method, begin by selecting the cell or range you want to move. To move the cells by pointing, hold down the ⌘ and Option keys while clicking the destination cell. To move the cells using drag-and-drop, simply drag the cells to the desired destination. (When the spreadsheet cursor changes from the plus symbol to an arrow above a tiny box, it is in drag-and-drop mode.)

Sorting

ClarisWorks has flexible sorting options that enable you to perform one- to three-way ascending or descending sorts on columns (vertical) or rows (horizontal). At the simplest level, a sort can affect a single string of cells in a row or column. To perform this type of sort, you select the cells, issue the Sort command, select an *order key* (a cell within the string), choose ascending or descending order, and specify whether the sort is horizontal or vertical.

More common, however, is sorting a range of cells that consists of several columns and rows, based on the values in one or more of the columns or rows.

Steps: Performing a Sort

1. Select the area of the worksheet you want to sort.

2. Choose Sort from the Calculate menu (or press ⌘-J). The Sort dialog box appears, as shown in Figure 4-11.

Enter from one to three cell addresses to serve as sort keys

```
┌──────────────────── Sort ────────────────────┐
│                                                │
│  Range:  [A1..A10                         ]    │──── Range to be sorted
│                                                │
│  ┌─ Order Keys ──────────┐  ┌─ Direction ──┐   │
│  ┌1st: [A1    ]  ◉ .ıl  ○ lı.  │ ◉ Vertical──┼──── Sort columns
│  │2nd: [      ]  ◉ .ıl  ○ lı.  │ ○ Horizontal─┼──── Sort rows
│  └3rd: [      ]  ◉ .ıl  ○ lı.  └──────────────┘   │──── Each sort can be
│  .ıl = Ascending  lı. = Descending             │      ascending or descending
│     (0-9, A-Z)      (Z-A, 9-0)                 │
│                                                │
│  [?]              ( Cancel )  (  OK  )         │
└────────────────────────────────────────────────┘
```

Figure 4-11: The Sort dialog box

3. If the range selected in Step 1 is incorrect, enter the range in the Range box. Separate the two anchor cells with a pair of periods, as in A1..D7.

4. Click the Vertical radio button to sort columns or the Horizontal radio button to sort rows.

5. In the 1st Order Keys box, enter a cell address from the first column on which you want to base the sort (for a vertical sort) or from the first row on which you want to base the sort (for a horizontal sort).

6. If you want to perform additional sorts, enter a cell address for a second and third column or row on which you want to base the sort.

7. For each order key, click a radio button to indicate whether you want to sort in *ascending order* (from A to Z and lowest to highest number) or *descending order* (from Z to A and highest to lowest number).

8. Click OK. The program performs the requested sort or sorts.

When sorting on a single order key, the program sorts the selected range on the basis of the contents of the key's column (vertical sort) or row (horizontal sort).

When performing a multikey sort, the program sorts the selected range on the basis of the contents of the first key's column (vertical sort) or row (horizontal sort). It then re-sorts on the basis of the second key, where all *ties* (duplicate values) in the first key sort are reordered according to the second key. If you selected a third key, records that are still tied after the program sorts on the second key are reordered according to the third key.

As an example, Figure 4-12 shows a simple address database with fields in columns A through F (First Name, Last Name, Street, City, State, Zip Code). Each row is a record.

To sort the data records by zip code, you would select the data range A2..F7 and choose Sort from the Calculate menu. (You would not include the labels in Row 1 as part of the sort, because you don't want them to change positions.) Enter a key (cell address) from the Zip Code field (F2, for example), click the Ascending radio button, and click OK.

Figure 4-12: The original address worksheet

The result of the sort is shown in Figure 4-13. Because you are simultaneously sorting columns A through F, each entire *record* changes position — not just the zip code. If you set the range as F2..F7, on the other hand, the program reorders only the zip codes — not the accompanying data in columns A through E.

Figure 4-13: The worksheet reordered by zip code

Figure 4-14 shows the settings for and the results of a two-way sort of the same worksheet. The first sort is on State (Column E), and the second sort is on Last Name (Column B). When the program executes the sort instructions, it sorts the entire worksheet (A2..F7) alphabetically based on State. It then re-sorts any duplicate entries (*WA*, in this case) alphabetically according to the person's last name.

Note

When performing a multi-sort, list the sort keys in order of decreasing importance.

Figure 4-14: A two-way sort on the same data

Tip

If you make a mistake during a sort (specify the wrong range, sort in the wrong order, or sort rows instead of columns, for example), you can restore the data to its original condition by immediately choosing the Undo command from the Edit menu (⌘-Z). The Undo command should read *Undo Sort*.

If you've gone a few steps too far, you can choose the Revert command from the File menu to revert to the most recently saved version of the document.

Transposing a range

Another way to rearrange information is to *transpose* it. Transposing a range swaps columns for rows and vice versa. Figure 4-15 shows a range before and after it has been transposed.

	Transpose Example (SS)			
A7	▼	*fx* ✕ ✓		
	A	**B**	**C**	**D**
1		Jan	Feb	Mar
2	Rent	850	850	850
3	Food	827	918	903
4	Entertain.	127	49	98
5				
6				
7		Rent	Food	Entertain.
8	Jan	850	827	127
9	Feb	850	918	49
10	Mar	850	903	98

—Transposed range

Figure 4-15: Range A7..D10 contains transposed information from the range A1..D4.

Steps: Transposing Information

1. Select the area you want to transpose.

2. Choose Copy (⌘-C) or Cut (⌘-X) from the Edit menu to place a copy of the range on the Clipboard.

3. Select a destination cell for the range.

4. Choose Paste Special from the Edit menu. The Paste Special dialog box appears, as shown in Figure 4-16.

Figure 4-16: The Paste Special dialog box

5. Click the Transpose Rows and Columns check box and then click OK.
The range is transposed and pasted into place, starting at the chosen
destination cell.

When you select a destination for the transposed range, be sure to leave enough
room in the cells to the right and below. The transposed range overwrites data in
the cells it covers. If you overwrite important data, immediately choose Undo from
the Edit menu (⌘-Z) and select a different destination.

In some instances, the reason you want to transpose a range is because — after
looking at the original data — it simply makes more sense to display it transposed.
If within the range, the number of rows is the same as the number of columns (a
five-cell by five-cell range, for example), you can safely paste the transposed data
over the *original* range without fear of overwriting other cells in the worksheet.

Changing the size of the worksheet

When you create a new ClarisWorks worksheet, it contains 40 columns and 500
rows. (A new spreadsheet frame in another ClarisWorks environment contains 10
columns and 50 rows.) Although these dimensions are adequate for most
worksheets, you may occasionally find you've run out of room. ClarisWorks
enables you to increase or decrease the number of worksheet rows and/or
columns as your needs change.

To change the size of a worksheet, select Document from the Format menu. The
Document dialog box appears, as shown in Figure 4-17. Specify the number of
columns and rows you want the resized worksheet to contain by entering numbers
in the Size section of the dialog box. Click OK to close the dialog box. The
worksheet is resized according to your specifications. (Keep in mind you can use
this command to reduce or increase the size of a worksheet.)

To reach the Document dialog box from a spreadsheet frame, on the other hand,
you first have to open the frame to full size by choosing Open Frame from the
Window menu. Then choose the Document command from the Format menu.

Figure 4-17: The Document dialog box

Formatting Cells

As recently as a few years ago, worksheets were fairly drab. They were usually restricted to a single font in a single point size. Modern spreadsheet programs, such as the ClarisWorks spreadsheet environment, encourage you to be creative when you format worksheets. For example, you can:

✦ Use multiple fonts, sizes, and styles

✦ Add color to text

✦ Surround cells with border lines

✦ Hide the cell gridlines or row and column headings

✦ Change the width and height of individual columns and rows

✦ Format cells with colors and patterns

Setting cell formats

ClarisWorks provides a host of methods for dressing up the contents of any cell:

✦ Assigning a font, size, and style

✦ Applying a color

✦ Setting an alignment (general, left, right, or center)

✦ Making text wrap in the cell if it is too wide to fit

✦ Assigning a number format for displaying numbers, dates, or times

To assign text formatting attributes to cells, select a cell or range of cells. Choose options from any of the following submenus of the Format menu: Font, Size, Style, Text Color, or Alignment. The program applies the new settings to the entire contents of the selected cells.

Note

The General Alignment option (the default) automatically left-aligns cells that contain text and right-aligns cells that contain numeric data.

If you set a large point size for a cell, ClarisWorks does not automatically adjust the row height to accommodate the largest font in the row. If you do not change the row height, some of the text may be clipped. (Instructions for changing row heights are provided in "Making cell contents fit" later in this chapter.)

Steps: Adding or Removing Cell Borders

1. Select a cell or range of cells.

2. Choose Borders from the Format menu. The Borders dialog box appears, as shown in Figure 4-18.

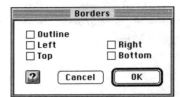

Figure 4-18: The Borders dialog box

3. Place check marks in the check boxes to indicate the sides on which the program should apply border lines. (Each check box works as a toggle.)

   A dash in a check box means that some, but not all, of the selected cells have that particular border option set.

   Removing a check mark clears the border on that side of the selected cell or cells.

4. Click OK. The program applies the selected border options individually to every selected cell. The exception to this rule is the Outline option — if you checked this box in Step 3, an outline border appears around the group of cells you selected, not around every individual cell.

To set a numeric format for one or more cells, select the cell or range of cells and choose Number from the Format menu (or press Shift-⌘-N). The Format Number,

Date, and Time dialog box appears, as shown in Figure 4-19. Set options and click OK to apply the options to the selected cell or cells.

Figure 4-19: Use this dialog box to assign a number, date, or time format to any cell or range of cells.

You can directly summon the Format Number, Date, and Time dialog box by double-clicking any spreadsheet cell.

If you just want to test a numeric format, click the Apply button in the Format Number, Date, and Time dialog box. The selected format is applied to the chosen cells. To accept the new formatting, click OK; otherwise, click Cancel to revert to the original number format for the cell or range.

In ClarisWorks 3.0 and earlier, you could add color to a worksheet in only two ways:

✦ Assign a text color for selected cells.

✦ Add a solid background color (only possible with a spreadsheet frame — not spreadsheet documents).

ClarisWorks 4.0 and 5.0 provide the tools necessary for *spreadsheet publishing* — enabling you to apply colors and/or patterns to selected cells. These features can be used whether the worksheet is a document or a frame.

To assign a cell color or pattern, if the Tool panel is not visible, choose Show Tools from the Window menu, press Shift-⌘-T, or click the Show/Hide Tools control at the bottom of the document window. Select the cell or range of cells you want to format. Choose a fill color and/or fill pattern from the Fill palettes. The color and/or pattern is applied to the selected cells.

Figure 4-20 shows a simple example of a colored, patterned worksheet range.

If you'd like to dress up your worksheets but aren't knowledgeable in design, you can use one of the ClarisWorks predefined table styles in the Stylesheet palette.

		A	B	C	D	E
	1	1997 Sales				Qtr
	2	North	$2.35	$5.35	$5.00	$4.00
	3	East	$2.00	$2.31	$2.24	$2.00
	4	South	$3.00	$2.28	$1.73	$1.32
	5	West	$4.00	$4.59	$3.97	$3.32

Figure 4-20: A section of this worksheet has been embellished with solid and patterned colors.

To format cells with the stylesheet, if the Stylesheet palette is not visible, choose Show Styles from the Window menu (or press Shift-⌘-W). The Stylesheet palette appears, listing the available table styles. Select the range of cells you want to format. (Table styles are meant to be applied to a range.) Click a table style in the Stylesheet palette. The style is applied to the selected range. To see the effect of the table style, click any cell outside of the original range. If you don't like the effect of the current table style, either choose Undo from the Edit menu (it will say *Undo Format*) or select the same range again and choose another table style.

If the button bar is visible above the worksheet, you can also select a spreadsheet style from the Stylesheet pull-down menu on the button bar.

After applying a table style, some tweaking is often required, particularly with number formats, which are often defined as part of the style. For example, you may have to change a column of zip codes from Currency format (as applied by the table style) to the more appropriate General format.

Also, although the Stylesheet palette initially shows seven table styles, ClarisWorks 5.0 contains more than two dozen table styles. To use the others, choose Import Styles from the Stylesheet palette's File menu, open the file named More Table Styles (located in the ClarisWorks Styles folder), and choose the additional styles you want to import. (To learn more about styles and using the Stylesheet palette, see Chapter 15.)

Reusing cell formats

When you are formatting cells, ClarisWorks also provides a pair of commands that enable you to copy an existing cell format and apply it to other cells.

Steps: Copying and Pasting Cell Formats

1. Select a cell that contains the format options you want to duplicate.

2. Choose Copy Format from the Edit menu (or press Shift-⌘-C). All formatting in the cell is copied — including font, size, style, alignment, and color; number format; borders; and cell color and pattern.

3. Select the cell or range to which you want to apply the format options.

4. Choose Paste Format from the Edit menu (or press Shift-⌘-V). The program applies the formats to the target cell(s).

Making cell contents fit

When you make an entry into a cell, sometimes it doesn't fit. If the cell contains text, it overflows into blank cells on the right, left, or both the right and the left — depending on the alignment option you choose for the original cell. If the cell next to the current cell is not empty, only as much of the text string as will fit in the current cell is displayed.

If a number doesn't fit in its cell, the program converts it to scientific notation or displays it as a string of # symbols.

You can make text fit within a cell by applying the Wrap option from the Alignment submenu of the Format menu. Wrap works like the word-wrap feature in a word processing program. You may have to change the row height to see all the wrapped text, however.

In many cases, you may simply prefer to change the width of the column that contains the cell. ClarisWorks enables you to widen or narrow columns selectively. You also can change the height of rows.

Steps: Using the Row Height and Column Width Commands

1. Select a cell or group of cells from the rows or columns whose height or width you want to change.

2. Choose Row Height or Column Width from the Format menu. The Row Height or Column Width dialog box appears, as shown in Figure 4-21.

Figure 4-21: The Row Height and Column Width dialog boxes

3. Type the number of points for the desired height or width. (One inch equals 72 points.) As an alternative, if you click the Use Default check box, ClarisWorks enters the default height (14 points) or width (72 points).

4. Click OK. The program applies the new height or width to the selected rows or columns.

Tip

If you prefer, you can use other units of measurement when entering a new row height or column width. To indicate the unit of measurement, enter one of these abbreviations after the numeric entry: inches (in), millimeters (mm), centimeters (cm), points (pt), or picas (pc).

You can also set row heights and column widths manually. Move the pointer into the heading area at the top or left side of the worksheet. Whenever the pointer is over the dividing line between a pair of rows or a pair of columns, it changes into a special cursor, as shown in Figure 4-22. Click and drag to change the width or height of a column or row.

	Sales 1997 – colored (SS)					—Pointer
E5	▼ *fx* × ✓	=E4+E3				
	A	**B**	**C**	**D**	**E**	
1	**1997 Sales**	Qtr. 1	Qtr. 2	Qtr. 3	Qtr. 4	
2	North	$2.35	$5.35	$5.00	$4.00	
3	East	$2.00	$2.31	$2.24	$2.00	
4	South	$3.00	$2.28	$1.73	$1.32	
5	West	$4.00	$4.59	$3.97	$3.32	
100						

Figure 4-22: This pointer appears when you manually change a column width or row height.

Tip

In many cases, what you really want to do is set a column width so it is just wide enough to accommodate the widest cell in the column or set a row so it can display the highest cell in the row. To accomplish this, double-click the right edge of the column or the bottom edge of the row.

Making Charts

Question of the Day: If a picture is worth a thousand words, how much data is a chart worth?

Charts and graphs provide a pictorial representation of data, making it easy to see significant trends. ClarisWorks has the capability to produce bar, area, line, scatter, pie, pictogram, stacked bar, stacked area, X-Y line, X-Y scatter, hi-low, stacked pictogram, and combination charts.

Note

As long as a chart is attached to a worksheet, changes you make to the data are instantly reflected in the chart. If you copy a chart to another ClarisWorks document, however, the chart loses its link with the data. If the data changes, the chart remains the same. However, the link between the ClarisWorks document and the chart can be maintained by using Publish & Subscribe (as explained in Chapter 18).

Steps: Creating a Chart

1. Select the data range you want to express as a chart.

If you also select the labels above and to the left of the data, they will appear in the chart and be used in the legend. Any text in the upper-left corner of the range becomes the chart title.

2. Choose Make Chart from the Options menu (or press ⌘-M). The Chart Options dialog box appears, as shown in Figure 4-23.

These buttons lead to other dialog boxes

Options for currently selected chart type

Figure 4-23: The Chart Options dialog box

3. Select a chart type from the Gallery section of the dialog box.

4. *Optional:* Choose chart enhancements at the bottom of the dialog box by clicking in check boxes. The enhancements that are listed vary according to the type of chart selected.

5. *Optional:* Set other chart options by clicking the Axes, Series, Labels, or General buttons (these options are discussed in the next section). A different dialog box appears for each button.

6. Click OK. A chart appears with the characteristics you chose.

Figure 4-24 shows the parts of a chart.

Chart options

If a chart doesn't look exactly the way you want it to look, ClarisWorks provides plenty of options for changing it without starting over. The following sections discuss chart options according to the Chart Options dialog box that is displayed.

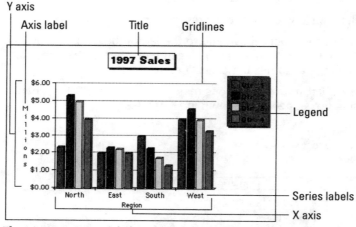

Figure 4-24: Essential chart components

Gallery options

ClarisWorks presents Gallery options (refer to Figure 4-23) whenever you choose the Make Chart command from the Options menu (to create a new chart) or choose Chart Options from the Edit menu (to edit an existing chart). The Gallery options enable you to do the following:

✦ Select an initial chart type.

✦ Change an existing chart to another chart type.

✦ Set basic display options for the chart such as:

  • color versus black and white

  • horizontal versus vertical

  • two-dimensional versus three-dimensional

  • whether shadows appear behind each plotted data series

The display options presented in the Chart dialog box vary according to the chart type chosen.

Axes options

Axes options (see Figure 4-25) enable you to do the following:

✦ Add labels to the X (horizontal) and Y (vertical) axes.

✦ Specify whether grid lines are displayed.

✦ Set minimum, maximum, and/or step values for axis divisions.

✦ Use a log scale.

✦ Specify whether tick marks are shown and, if so, how they appear.

Figure 4-25: Axes options

You have to change the elements of each axis individually. Select an axis by clicking the X axis or Y axis radio button at the top of the Chart Options (Axes) dialog box. All other settings you choose affect that axis only.

Note

The X axis is the horizontal axis, running along the bottom of the chart; the Y axis is the vertical axis, running along the left side of the axis. Pie charts do not have axes.

To change the color, pattern, or line width for an axis and its gridlines, select the axis on the chart and then modify it using the Tool panel palettes. To alter the font attributes for the axis text, select the axis on the chart and then choose the appropriate attributes from the Format menu.

Series options

You use the Series options to specify settings for one or all of the data series included in the current chart. You can label data points with their values and change the type of display for individual data series. The latter option enables you to create combination charts. For example, you can show one data series with bars and the second data series as a line.

Steps: Specifying a Series Option

1. In the Edit Series pop-up menu, choose All or the specific series you want to change.

2. *Optional:* Choose a graph type for the series from the Display pop-up menu.

Some graph types also enable you to pick a symbol to use for data points, as shown in Figure 4-26. To select a symbol for the data points for a particular series, choose a series from the Edit pop-up menu and then click a new symbol. To change a symbol's color, click the box to the right of the Symbol check box and select a color from the pop-up palette. To change the size of a symbol, enter a new number (in points) in the Size text-edit box. (One inch equals 72 points.)

Figure 4-26: You use this dialog box to choose the shape, size, and color of the symbol for data points.

Other graph types, such as pie charts, offer different options, such as the capability to *explode* a slice (pull it away from the body of the pie).

3. *Optional:* To label data points with their values, click the Label Data check box. Click any of the nine radio buttons below the check box to indicate where the data label will appear in relation to each data point.

For some graph types, such as bar and pictogram, an example of a data label is shown in a Sample box.

4. Click OK to put the new options into effect.

To change the color or pattern of any series, select its box in the chart legend and then select another color, pattern, texture, or gradient from the Tool panel. (Textured graph objects is a feature found only in ClarisWorks 5.0.)

Labels options

Use the Labels options (see Figure 4-27) to specify settings for the chart title and legend.

If a title was in the upper-left corner of the selected chart range, it appears in the Title box. You can change it in the spreadsheet or in the Chart Options (Labels) dialog box. If the chart has no title, you can create one in the dialog box. To display the title horizontally, check the Horizontal check box. To display the title vertically, remove the check mark. To add a drop shadow behind the chart title, check the Shadow check box. To specify a different location for the chart title, click one of the eight title placement radio buttons at the right of the Title box. To eliminate the title, delete it from the cell.

Figure 4-27: Labels options

Text characteristics (such as the font and size), the background color, and the pattern for the title come directly from the formatting you apply (or change) in the title's cell in the worksheet. You can also change the title's attributes by selecting it in the chart and then choosing options from the Format menu. You can alter the title's bounding box or background by selecting the title in the chart and then choosing a pattern, gradient, texture, background color, line width, or pen color from the Tool panel.

Labels in the legend are determined by the series labels at the left and top of the worksheet range you specify when you create the chart. To change any of the labels, change the contents of the appropriate cells.

You can alter the legend's background and bounding box by selecting the legend in the chart and then choosing a pattern, texture, gradient, background color, line width, or pen color from the Tool panel. If you don't like the way series names are displayed in the legend, you can select the legend in the chart and then choose new text attributes from the Format menu.

Steps: Modifying the Legend

1. To change from the labels of one series to the labels of another series, click the General button in the Chart Options dialog box. Click the radio button for Series in Rows or Series in Columns to change the series used for the legend. (This action also changes the chart layout.)

2. To change the position of the legend relative to the chart, click one of the eight position radio buttons in the Chart Options (Labels) dialog box.

3. Use the Horizontal check box in the Chart Options (Labels) dialog box to designate whether the legend elements are to be displayed in a vertical or horizontal list.

4. To place a shadow behind the legend box, click the Shadow check box.

5. Some chart types, such as line graphs, use symbols to represent data points. If you want the symbols to be displayed in the legend, click the Use Symbols check box.

6. To hide the legend, remove the check mark from the Legend check box.

General options

Use the General options (see Figure 4-28) to do the following:

◆ Change the data range for the chart.

◆ Use numbers as axis labels.

◆ Indicate whether the data series in the selected range is in rows or in columns.

Figure 4-28: General options

To specify a new chart range, type it into the Chart Range box. Remember to separate the anchor points in the range with a pair of periods, as in A1..D7.

In most cases, you will use text from the worksheet as axis labels. If the first row or first column of the selected chart range contains numbers you want to use as labels, click the (Use numbers as labels in) First Row or First Column check box, as appropriate.

To indicate whether the data series in the selected range is arranged in rows or in columns, click the Series in Rows or Columns radio button, as appropriate. The labels that appear in the Series Names list box represent the data that will be plotted.

Pictograms

Pictograms use pictures, rather than bars, lines, and so on, to represent data. Pictogram images can be a single image or a series of repeating images, one above the other. To use pictogram images in a chart, you must do one of the following:

✦ Select Pictogram or Stacked Pictogram as the chart type.

✦ Set one or more of the series to display as pictograms in the Chart Options (Series) dialog box.

The default pictogram symbol is a large arrow, but you can provide your own symbols, as described below and shown in Figure 4-29.

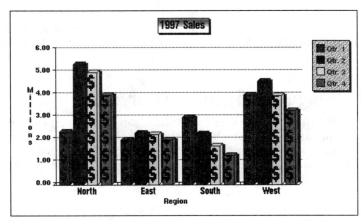

Figure 4-29: A pictogram with a repeating custom symbol (a dollar sign)

Steps: Changing a Pictogram Symbol

1. In the Scrapbook, a graphics program, or a ClarisWorks draw document, select the image you want to use as a pictogram. (Claris recommends using a draw image rather than a paint picture.)

2. Choose Copy from the Edit menu to place a copy of the image on the Mac's Clipboard.

3. In the Chart Options (Series) dialog box, choose All or a specific data series from the Edit Series pop-up menu. (You can use the same image for all series or a different image for each series.) The current pictogram image appears in the Sample box.

4. Click the Sample box. A dark border surrounds the box.

5. Choose Paste from the Edit menu (or press ⌘-V). The image on the Clipboard replaces the one in the Sample box and is used for the selected series or all series, depending on the choice you made in the Edit Series pop-up menu.

6. Click the Repeating check box to make a constant-size symbol repeat in each bar. If you want repeating symbols to overlap each other, enter a number in the % Overlap text-edit box. Leave the Repeating check box blank if you want the symbol to be sized to match the height of the bar.

7. If you want to use the same image for other data series, repeat Steps 3 through 6 as required.

Tip

To display only a pictogram symbol without the usual bounding box, click the box in the legend associated with that data series and then set the line width to None in the Tool panel.

Other chart changes and embellishments

In addition to using the options in the Chart Options dialog boxes, you can use other methods to modify and embellish charts. After you create a chart, it acts like any other ClarisWorks object. When you first click a chart, handles appear at its corners. You can drag it to a new location or resize it by dragging a handle.

You can embellish the chart by adding text (as callouts, for example) and graphics. You can draw attention to an important element in the chart, such as an outstanding quarterly sales figure, by using the drawing tools to add an arrow pointing to the bar or data point. Finish off the effect by selecting the text tool to create a comment (for example, "Best quarter since the company's inception!"), and then surround the comment with a colored box or oval.

Chart-Editing Shortcuts

So you can avoid wading through dialog boxes and buttons, ClarisWorks provides several shortcuts that take you directly to the appropriate Chart Options dialog box:

✦ Double-click an open area of a chart to make the Chart Options (Gallery) dialog box appear. This action is equivalent to choosing Chart Options from the Edit menu. The Chart Options (Gallery) dialog box enables you to change the chart type or to set basic display options.

✦ Double-click the X or Y axis of a chart to make the Chart Options (Axis) dialog box appear.

✦ Double-click a chart symbol in the legend to make the Chart Options (Series) dialog box appear.

✦ Double-click the chart title (if the chart has a title) or the legend to make the Chart Options (Labels) dialog box appear.

You also can add a background color, pattern, texture, or gradient to the chart; color the legend box; and change the line width or color of the box that encloses the chart by choosing options from the palettes in the Tool panel. Because a chart is just another object, to achieve an uncluttered look, you can use the chart to hide the data used to create it. When you copy a chart into a word processing document, you can specify a text wrap for a more professional appearance.

Remember that when a chart is simply pasted into a document, it loses its link with the worksheet in which it was created. You may prefer to add the worksheet to the document as a table and display only the chart portion.

Printing

ClarisWorks has several features that apply only to printing worksheets. These features can be used to do the following:

✦ Add manual page breaks.

✦ Specify a print range.

✦ Decide whether to print or omit the cell grid, as well as the column and row headings.

Adding page breaks

Although ClarisWorks automatically determines where page breaks occur based on full pages, you may want to force a page break at a strategic spot in the worksheet — usually to keep important information from being split across pages.

To insert a page break, select the cell you want to print as the last item on a page and choose Add Page Break from the Options menu. Any cells to the right or below the selected cell will print on succeeding pages.

You can remove a manual page break by selecting the same cell and choosing Remove Page Break from the Options menu. To remove all manual page breaks simultaneously, choose Remove All Breaks from the Options menu.

If you want to see how the worksheet will print (and where the page breaks will occur), choose Page View (Shift-⌘-P) from the Window menu.

Specifying a print range

When the time comes to print the worksheet, ClarisWorks intelligently defaults to printing the entire active portion of the worksheet; that is, it prints all areas of the worksheet (beginning with cell A1) that contain data. You can also specify a different print range. Choose Set Print Range from the Options menu. A Print Range dialog box appears. Click the Print Cell Range radio button and type the specific range you want to print. (Remember that a range consists of the upper-left cell coordinate and the lower-right cell coordinate, separated by a pair of periods.) Click OK to set the new range.

If you preselect a range by dragging and then go directly to the Print command, you do not have to use the Print Range command. The program automatically prints the highlighted range.

Working with a modified Print dialog box

When you choose Print from the File menu (or press ⌘-P), you'll notice that the Print dialog box has been modified slightly, as shown in Figure 4-30. At the bottom of the dialog box is a series of check boxes that appears only when you are printing a worksheet. Depending on the boxes that are checked, you can print or omit column headings, row headings, and the cell grid. Initially, these settings match the options you have chosen in the Display dialog box (which is discussed in "Changing display options" later in this chapter).

Figure 4-30: When you print a worksheet, a modified Print dialog box appears.

Other Procedures and Options

This section explains the remaining commands, procedures, and options available to you in the spreadsheet environment (in short, other stuff). Although you don't have to use any of these features (some you may *never* use), knowing they're available is nice.

Automatic and manual recalculation

Normally, ClarisWorks recalculates the worksheet whenever necessary. If a cell contains a formula that refers to another cell (B17, for example) and you change the contents of that cell (B17), the program automatically recalculates the formula. In very large worksheets or on slow Macs, recalculation can be time-consuming. If you like, you can turn off automatic recalculation by choosing Auto Calc from the Calculate menu and removing its check mark.

When Auto Calc is turned off, ClarisWorks recalculates the worksheet only when you choose Calculate Now from the Calculate menu (or press Shift-⌘-=).

If you check Auto Calc, you *never* have to choose Calculate Now.

Locking cells

Like any other computer document, a worksheet can be a fragile thing. If you make a wrong entry in a critical cell, many of the worksheet's underlying assumptions may become incorrect and lead you to wrong conclusions about the data or its summary figures. If you edit a formula and make a mistake, similar consequences can result. To prevent inadvertent changes of this sort, ClarisWorks enables you to protect selected cells by locking them. To lock a cell or range, select the cell or range you want to protect, and choose Lock Cells from the Options menu (or press ⌘-H).

If you attempt to edit, delete, or move a locked cell, ClarisWorks displays an alert box with the message *Some cells are locked.* If a locked cell contains a formula, on the other hand, the formula will still be recalculated as necessary.

If you need to enter data into any cell that has been locked, you must first unlock that cell. Select the locked cell or range and then choose Unlock Cells from the Options menu (or press Shift-⌘-H).

Locking titles

Depending on the nature of the worksheet, locking row or column titles in place can sometimes be useful. To lock titles, do one of the following:

✦ *To lock a set of row and column titles in place*, select the cell that intersects the row and column titles and choose Lock Title Position from the Options menu.

✦ *To lock a set of column titles in place*, select the entire bottom row of the titles (by clicking the row number heading) and choose Lock Title Position from the Options menu.

✦ *To lock a set of row titles in place*, select the entire right-most column of the titles (by clicking the column number heading) and choose Lock Title Position from the Options menu.

As you scroll the worksheet, the titles remain in view. Figure 4-31 shows a worksheet with Column A and Rows 1 and 2 locked in place.

Figure 4-31: Solid lines, rather than the usual dotted gridlines, surround the cells in the locked rows (1 and 2) and column (A).

To unlock the titles (to choose a different set of locking titles, to edit a cell in the title region, or to remove the locking titles), choose Lock Title Position again.

Setting a default font

Normally, the default font for worksheets is 9-point Geneva. Unless you manually select another font for a cell, the program uses the default font for all formatting. To set a different default font for the current worksheet, choose Default Font from the Options menu. The Default Font dialog box appears. Select a new font from the list box (all fonts installed in the system are displayed in the list) and type a point size in the Size box. Click OK. All cells that have not had a different font or size manually applied to them change to the new default font and size. Cells you have manually set to a specific font or size retain that font or size.

Changing display options

The Display command in the Options menu enables you to exert some control over the way ClarisWorks displays the current worksheet. For example, you may want to alter the display before printing a worksheet or using it as part of a presentation or slide show.

In the Display dialog box (see Figure 4-32), checking or clearing a particular check box has the following effects:

- ✦ *Cell Grid.* When this box is unchecked, ClarisWorks displays the worksheet without a cell grid.

- ✦ *Solid Lines.* When this box is checked, the program displays the cell grid as solid lines. When it is unchecked (the default), a dotted cell grid is displayed.

- ✦ *Formulas.* When this box is checked, ClarisWorks displays formulas in cells, instead of displaying the results of the formulas. This option is useful for checking the accuracy of a worksheet or its underlying assumptions.

- ✦ *Column Headings.* When this box is unchecked, the program does not display column headings (letters).

- ✦ *Row Headings.* When this box is unchecked, the program does not display row headings (numbers).

- ✦ *Mark Circular Refs.* When this box is checked, data in a cell that contains a circular reference is surrounded by bullet characters (•).

Figure 4-32: Use the Display dialog box to set options for viewing and printing the current worksheet.

Down to Business: Creating a Check Register Worksheet

As an illustration of some of the ClarisWorks spreadsheet capabilities, you can create a worksheet that fulfills the reason many new users say they bought their computers: to balance their checkbooks. (Of course, when you think about it, paying several thousand dollars for slightly more power than a hand calculator doesn't make a great deal of sense, does it?)

This worksheet is useful if you don't like to balance your checking account manually or if you want a clean printed copy of your checking activity. But because the worksheet duplicates the check register, you have to enter your checks and deposits twice — once in the check register and once in the worksheet.

In addition to duplicating a standard check register, the worksheet tosses in a few extra features:

✦ Separate Payee and Description columns, so you can record to whom each check was made out as well as what it was for

✦ Automatic calculation of the balance

✦ Automatic calculation of the total of uncleared checks, withdrawals, and deposits (the uncleared total)

Creating the worksheet

Figure 4-33 shows the check register worksheet with a half dozen sample entries. Use the following steps to create a working copy of the worksheet.

					Payment	Deposit			Uncleared
	Number	Date	Payee	Description	or Debit	or Credit	Clr	Balance	Total
		8/21/97		Beginning balance		1,000.00		$1,000.00	$0.00
	127	9/2/97	Ace Hardware	Repair materials	45.77			$954.23	-$45.77
	128	9/3/97	Safeway	Groceries	245.61			$708.62	-$291.38
		9/6/97		Salary		1,478.00		$2,186.62	$1,186.62
		9/8/97		ATM Withdrawal	120.00			$2,066.62	$1,066.62
	129	9/11/97	Federal Express	Package (overnight)	11.00			$2,055.62	$1,055.62

Figure 4-33: The check register worksheet

Steps: Laying Out the Worksheet

Note

1. Create the column labels in Rows 1 and 2.

All label text is 9-point Geneva bold. (All other text is 9-point Geneva.)

2. Set the alignment for each column:

- Set Columns A, B, E, F, H, and I as right-aligned (⌘-]).
- Set Columns C and D as left-aligned (⌘-[).
- Set Column G as center-aligned (⌘-\).

To set the alignment for a column, click a column heading to select the entire column, and then choose an option from the Alignment submenu of the Format menu. If the default button bar is displayed, you may find it faster to click alignment settings in the button bar.

3. Use the Column Width command in the Format menu to set the column widths as follows (all settings are in points):

- A (44)
- B (52)
- C (104)
- D (124)
- E and F (56)
- G (22)
- H and I (64)

4. Add a bottom border to cells A2 through I2 by using the Borders command in the Format menu.

5. Set the number formats for data in the worksheet as follows:

- A (Fixed with a Precision of 0 [zero])
- B (choose the first Date option)

- E and F (Fixed, Commas, Precision 2)
- H and I (Currency, Commas, Precision 2)

To set the number format for a column, click a column heading to select the entire column, choose the Number command in the Format menu (or press Shift-⌘-N), select a format option, and click OK.

6. The record in Row 3 is reserved for the beginning balance. For now, enter the following:
   - Today's date in B3
   - **Beginning balance** in D3
   - **1000** in F3
   - **=F3** in H3
   - **0** in I3

You can change this information later to match your real beginning balance.

7. Enter this formula into cell H4 to calculate the running balance (Balance):

   ```
   =IF(B4<>"",H3-E4+F4,"")
   ```

   After entering the formula, copy it to the remaining cells in Column H by selecting cells H4 through H500 and choosing Fill Down (⌘-D) from the Calculate menu.

8. Enter this formula into cell I4 to calculate the running total of uncleared checks, withdrawals, and deposits (Uncleared Total):

   ```
   =IF(B4="","",IF(G4<>"x",I3-E4+F4,I3))
   ```

   After entering the formula, copy it to the remaining cells in Column I by selecting cells I4 through I500 and choosing Fill Down (⌘-D) from the Calculate menu.

9. To keep the labels in Rows 1 and 2 from scrolling off screen as additional transactions are entered, make them into titles. Select Row 2 by clicking the row heading (the number 2) and choose Lock Title Position from the Options menu.

After you lock the rows, you cannot edit any of the cells in Rows 1 or 2. Later, if you need to make changes in either row, choose Lock Title Position again.

10. *Optional:* Select Columns H and I by clicking their headings and choose Lock Cells from the Options menu (or press ⌘-H) to keep the entries in these columns from being altered accidentally. (The entries in Columns H and I are all calculated automatically, based on your transactions.)

Understanding the formulas

The formulas are fairly complex, so they require further examination. The formula in H4 is as follows:

```
=IF(B4<>"",H3-E4+F4,"")
```

First, the formula checks cell B4 — the date for the current record — to see whether it is empty. If B4 contains something (a date, presumably), the first action is performed. That is, the formula takes the previous balance (H3), subtracts any payment entered for this record (E4), and adds any deposit entered for this record (F4). If, on the other hand, the date field is blank for the record, the second action is taken: the Balance entry is left blank. (You test for the existence of a date because every legitimate record should contain one. If no date is found, you assume the record does not yet exist.)

Note

This formula could have been written as =H3-E4+F4. When filled down to the remaining records, however, transactions that didn't exist yet would all display the current balance. Using this more complex approach to test whether a transaction exists produces a more attractive worksheet.

The formula in I4 is even more complex. It contains an IF function nested within another IF function:

```
=IF(B4="","",IF(G4<>"x",I3-E4+F4,I3))
```

The formula performs two actions. First, if the Date field is blank — (B4="" — it assumes the record does not yet exist and leaves the Uncleared Total entry blank (just as the previous formula left the Balance entry blank). Because the first test has been met, the remainder of the formula is not evaluated.

On the other hand, if the Date field (B4) is not blank, the formula checks the Clr entry (G4) for the current record to see whether it contains an *x*. (You use an *x* to indicate — according to the bank statement — that a check, withdrawal, or deposit has cleared.) If an *x* is not found, the formula takes the previous Uncleared Total (I3), subtracts the current Payment from it (E4), and adds the current Deposit (F4). Thus, if an entry has not cleared, its payment or deposit is reflected in the Uncleared Total. If an *x* is found, on the other hand, the previous Uncleared Total in I3 is simply copied to the cell.

Using the worksheet

The best time to begin using this worksheet is when you open a new account or immediately after you've received a bank statement and balanced your checkbook.

Begin by editing the first record (Row 3). Replace the temporary date (B3) and starting balance (F3) with today's date and your balance. Placing the balance in F3 automatically copies it to the Balance column (H3). Because the beginning balance won't be part of a later reconciliation, type a lowercase *x* in the Clr column (G3) for the entry.

Now go back through your check register and, beginning in Row 4, make an entry for every outstanding check, withdrawal, and deposit. (If you don't want gaps in the register, you can go back to the oldest outstanding check, withdrawal, or deposit, and enter every transaction up to the current date. If you do so, be sure to add an *x* in the Clr field for every item that has cleared.)

When a bank statement arrives, the Checkbook worksheet can help with the reconciliation. Going down G (the Clr column), add an *x* for every item that has cleared. When you are through, the last figure in the Uncleared Total column will represent the total of the outstanding deposits minus the outstanding checks.

Quick Tip: Speeding Data Entry by Preselecting a Range

Although you can tab and click to move from cell to cell when you enter data, you can use a faster method to enter data into a specific section of a worksheet. Start by preselecting the range into which you will be entering data. The range may look like the one in Figure 4-34, for example.

Active cell

Figure 4-34: A preselected range

In a preselected range, the active cell is white, while all other cells are dark. After entering information in the first cell, press Tab. The cell to the right becomes active. If you continue to press Tab after each cell entry, the active cell shifts across each row, one cell at a time. When a row is completed, the cursor drops down to the first cell in the next row. If you press Return (rather than Tab) after each cell entry, the cursor moves down one cell at a time through each selected column.

Moving On Up

Although the ClarisWorks spreadsheet environment is sufficient for many users, as your needs become more complex, you may want to check out a more full-featured spreadsheet program. Features such as a macro language, the capability to define your own functions, additional chart types and functions, and linked and three-dimensional worksheets are all commonplace in commercial spreadsheets. Currently, the leading Mac spreadsheet program is Microsoft Excel (Microsoft Corporation). You might also want to consider Spreadsheet 2000 (Casady & Greene), a distinctly different type of spreadsheet program. If you're looking for additional charting capabilities, check out DeltaGraph (DeltaPoint).

The export capabilities of ClarisWorks make upgrading to other spreadsheets easy. If you save a ClarisWorks worksheet in Excel 3, Excel 4, or SYLK format, most other spreadsheet programs can interpret it correctly. Similarly, if you use a different spreadsheet program at the office and want to continue working on a worksheet at home, you can probably import the spreadsheet into ClarisWorks by using the Open command. Note, however, macros that have been attached to the worksheet (in Excel or 1-2-3, for example) will not function in ClarisWorks.

Summary

✦ A worksheet is a grid composed of numbered rows and lettered columns. A cell is the intersection of a row and a column.

✦ You enter text strings, numbers, and formulas into cells. Formulas can refer to other cells, contain constants, and use any of the 100 built-in ClarisWorks functions.

✦ The cell in which the cursor is positioned is known as the *active cell*. The location of any cell is given by its *cell address*.

✦ A group of cells is known as a range. A *range* is identified by its anchor points — the upper-left and lower-right cells in the range.

✦ Formulas are normally evaluated from left to right. The precedence levels of the operations performed within the formula can change the calculation order, however, as can the use of parentheses to enclose operations.

✦ You can type functions directly into formulas, or you can paste them there (along with dummy arguments) by using the Paste Function command.

✦ To save typing time or make it simpler to understand the assumptions that underlie your worksheet, you can use range names in formulas rather than normal cell references.

✦ You can copy and paste formulas to other cells. You also can paste just the values contained in cells, ignoring the formulas. The Fill Down and Fill Right commands expedite copying a formula to a large range.

✦ The Fill Special command makes it easy to create sequences of numbers and dates. This feature is particularly useful for generating a set of ordered row or column headings.

✦ ClarisWorks provides many commands that make reorganizing a worksheet simple. It has commands that insert and delete cells, columns, and rows; move ranges of cells to new locations; sort data; and transpose a range (swapping the positions of rows and columns).

✦ To make worksheets more attractive, you can selectively apply font, size, style, color, and alignment options to the text in cells. You can also apply colors and patterns to cells (cell shading).

✦ To make the contents of the cell fit inside the cell borders, you can widen column widths, change row heights, or apply a Wrap format.

✦ You can control the way the program displays numbers, dates, and times by choosing options in the Format Number, Date, and Time dialog box.

✦ The Copy Format and Paste Format commands enable you to apply existing cell formats to other cells easily.

✦ ClarisWorks provides a dozen different styles of charts you can use to embellish a worksheet. Because every chart is also an object, you can copy and paste charts into other documents.

✦ When printing a worksheet, ClarisWorks defaults to selecting the entire active area of the worksheet. However, you can specify a particular print range, add manual page breaks, and turn off the printing of some worksheet elements, such as the cell grid and row or column headings.

✦ You can lock important cells to prevent them from being changed inadvertently. You can lock important information (titles, for example) at the top and left sides of the worksheet so it doesn't disappear when you scroll the worksheet.

✦   ✦   ✦

The Database Environment

Overview

A *database* is an organized set of information — usually on one particular topic. One common example of a database is a card file that contains the names, addresses, and phone numbers of business associates, customers, or friends. Other everyday examples of databases you can find around the office or home include employee records, inventory records, a recipe file, and a list of videotapes.

Every database is composed of *records*. In the previous examples, each record contains all the pertinent information about one friend, one employee, one inventory part, one recipe, or one videotape.

Each record is composed of *fields*. A field contains one piece of information about the employee (a social security number, for example), videotape (the name of the star), recipe (cooking time), or friend (date of birth). In an address database, you may have separate fields for each person's first name, last name, street address, city, state, and zip code.

Unlike a word processing document (which is free-form), a computer database has an order that comes from its use of fields. Every field holds one particular type of information (an employee identification number, for example). As you skim through the records of the database, you see that the same type of information is in that field in every record. Figure 5-1 shows the relationship between a database, records, and fields.

Figure 5-1: A computer database contains a series of records; each record is composed of a set of fields.

Although you can keep database information in a word processing document, you lose the data manipulation advantages a database provides, such as the capability to select subsets of records (for example, only employees who make between $20,000 and $30,000 per year), sort records by one or more fields (for example, by last name, years of employment, or cost of ingredients), create fields that perform calculations and computations (for example, totaling all items ordered or combining two text fields), and generate custom reports.

Another great thing about a computerized database, as compared to a paper version, is the ease with which you can modify and reorganize its contents. Early database programs required you to define every field before you started to enter data. If you later decided to add a field, delete a field, or change the type of a particular field (from text to numeric, for example), you had to execute a complex procedure to reorganize the database. Current database programs, such as the ClarisWorks database environment, make reorganizing a database remarkably easy.

If you need a new field, for example, you simply define it and add it to the appropriate layouts.

Using the ClarisWorks database, you can do the following:

✦ Quickly identify records that match simple criteria (for example, Name = Sam Jones) or very complex criteria (for example, Salary <= $40,000 and Age > 45).

✦ Sort the records by the contents of one or more fields (for example, by Last Name within City).

✦ Create multiple layouts for any database (for example, create data entry, phone directory, and label layouts for the same database).

✦ Set data validation criteria for some fields (such as unique data or data within a particular range).

✦ Specify a data type for each field (such as text, number, date, time, multimedia, calculation, or summary).

✦ Automatically enter certain data (today's date or an invoice number).

✦ Perform calculations (totals or averages for each record, a subset of records, or the entire database).

Working with the ClarisWorks Database

You use a ClarisWorks database in four modes: Layout, Browse, Find, and List. In *Layout* mode, you arrange fields and other database objects on a screen page so the program will display and print them the way you want. You use *Browse* or *List* mode to view, edit, add, delete, and sort records. You do all data entry in Browse or List mode. *Find* mode enables you to search for records that meet one or more criteria (Last Name = Smith, for example).

Defining Fields

Every database is composed of fields into which you enter information. In fact, you cannot begin to enter data until you have defined at least one field by specifying its name and the type of data it will contain.

To create new fields, delete fields, or modify the definitions or options for existing fields, choose Define Fields from the Layout menu (or press Shift-⌘-D). The Define Database Fields dialog box appears, as shown in Figure 5-2. Click Done when you are finished.

Figure 5-2: You use the Define Database Fields dialog box to specify a name, field type, and options for every field in the database. You can also use it to modify a field definition or delete a field.

Although the database environment is packed with fancy features, sometimes simplest is best. You can define the necessary fields, accept the default layout, and start entering data. The following example shows the steps for designing a basic address book database. As you progress in this chapter, you will learn how to customize layouts and work with special data types and options.

Steps: Creating a Simple Database

1. Choose New from the File menu (or press ⌘-N). The New Document dialog box appears.

2. Choose Database and click OK. A new database is created, and the Define Database Fields dialog box appears, as previously shown in Figure 5-2.

3. Define the fields you want to use in the database. For the address book database, you'll define the following fields (in order): First Name, Last Name, Address, City, State, Zip, and Birthdate. Birthdate is a date field; all others are text fields.

   For each field, type its name in the Field Name box, choose the appropriate field type from the pop-up menu, and then click Create. The field is added to the list box.

   The name of the field just defined is still in the Field Name box. When you begin typing a name for the next field, the Field Name box automatically clears.

When setting up any database, you should think ahead. By separating first and last name fields, for example, you'll have an easier time doing searches and sorts in the future. Try not to combine important bits of information into a single field.

4. After you have defined all fields, click Done. A database with the default layout (field sizes, placements, fonts, and so on) appears (as shown in Figure 5-3), ready for you to enter the first record.

The current field is indicated by a solid border

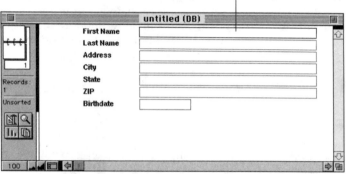

Figure 5-3: After you define the fields, ClarisWorks displays the first blank record.

After completing an entry for a field, you can move to the next field by pressing the Tab key. To create additional records, choose New Record from the Edit menu (or press ⌘-R).

Field types

ClarisWorks 5.0 offers 14 types of fields, each for a different category of data or a specific presentation format: text, number, date, time, name, pop-up menu, radio button, check box, serial number, value list, multimedia, record info, calculation, and summary. By assigning the correct data type to each field, you can let ClarisWorks do some simple validation (for example, making sure only dates are entered in date fields and only numbers are entered in number fields).

Users of earlier versions of ClarisWorks should read this chapter carefully. ClarisWorks 3.0 and earlier provided only six field types. In ClarisWorks 4.0 and 5.0, however, things that were previously considered *formatting options* — pop-up menus, check boxes, and radio buttons — have been defined as separate *field types*. By selecting any of these field types, you can create more attractive databases, while making it easy for users to complete the field — without having to type an entry!

**New In
Version 5**

In addition, ClarisWorks 5.0 adds a new field type: multimedia. You can use multimedia fields to store QuickTime movies and pictures.

Although you can define every field as text, you won't be using ClarisWorks to its full potential if you don't take advantage of the other field types. The following sections describe how each field type works.

Text fields

Although it's called a *text* field, you can enter any type of character into this field. Letters, numbers, punctuation marks, spaces, and so on are all legal characters. Data you enter into a text field will word wrap, just as it does in a word processing document. You can even enter Returns to start new lines. This flexibility makes text fields ideal for notes, as well as for any type of information that contains a mixture of letters and numbers (street addresses, for example).

Options you can set for text fields are shown in Figure 5-4.

```
╔═══════════════════════════════════════╗
║  Options for Text Field "First Name"   ║
╠═══════════════════════════════════════╣
║ ┌ Text Uerification ─┐ ┌ Default Text ─┐ ║
║ │ ☐ Cannot Be Empty  │ │Automatically Fill In:│ ║
║ │ ☐ Must Be Unique   │ │ ┌─────────────┐ │ ║
║ └────────────────────┘ │ └─────────────┘ │ ║
║                        └───────────────┘ ║
║  [?]              [ Cancel ]  [  OK  ]   ║
╚═══════════════════════════════════════╝
```

Figure 5-4: To display this dialog box, select a text field in the Define Database Fields dialog box and click Options.

The left side of the dialog box contains two text verification options:

✦ *Cannot Be Empty*. Click this check box if the field must be filled in for every record. If you attempt to switch to another record, create a new record, change to another mode, or close the database without filling in the field, ClarisWorks presents a warning.

✦ *Must Be Unique*. Click this check box if you don't want to accept duplicate values for a field. (This is a useful option for part numbers in a company catalog or an inventory database, for example.) If you attempt to enter a text string that already exists in this field in another record, ClarisWorks presents a warning.

Note

Either warning can be overridden by clicking Yes in the warning message box.

If there is an entry you use frequently, enter that text string in the Automatically Fill In box. All new records will automatically have that value entered in the field.

As with other fields in a ClarisWorks database, you can apply selective formatting to any portion of the text field's contents. For example, if you create a Comments field that you define as a text field, you can selectively change the font for some words or add a style such as italic to others.

The size of the bounding box for a text field does not restrict the amount of text you can enter in the field. As you type, the bounding box expands vertically as needed to accommodate additional text. When you exit the field (by pressing the Tab key or by clicking in a different field), the bounding box returns to its normal size, obscuring any overflow text. The field expands again whenever you move the text insertion point into it.

Note

If a text field contains overflow text, you should expand the size of the field on the layout before printing the database. Otherwise, the text in the printout will be truncated.

New In Version 5

A ClarisWorks 5.0 text field can hold a maximum of about 1,020 characters — more than twice as much text as allowed in ClarisWorks 4.0 text fields. If you exceed this limit, a message to that effect appears. You will have to edit the contents of the field manually by removing some of the text or style formatting before ClarisWorks will accept the entry.

Number fields

Number fields are for numeric data only, such as prices, quantities, and so on. Legitimate numeric characters can include the digits 0 through 9, parentheses or a minus sign (for negative numbers), the plus sign (+), a percent sign (%), and an *e* (for scientific notation). ClarisWorks automatically flags other characters and requests that you re-enter the number. It ignores commas or dollar signs during data entry. In addition, number fields cannot contain Returns — in every number field, the entire number must be entered as a single, continuous string. The maximum length for a number field is 255 characters.

If you enter a number that exceeds the width of the field, the program converts the number to scientific notation (1.234571+e19, for example). As with overly long text entries, you have to move the text insertion point into the number field to see a number that exceeds the field width.

Like the other field types, there are several verification and default options that can be set for a number field. The Options dialog box for number fields is shown in Figure 5-5.

Figure 5-5: To display this dialog box, select a number field in the Define Database Fields dialog box and click Options.

The left side of the dialog box contains three verification options.

✦ *Cannot Be Empty.* Click this check box if the field must be filled in for every record. If you attempt to change to another record, create a new record, change to another mode, or close the database without filling in the field, ClarisWorks presents a warning.

✦ *Must Be Unique.* Click this check box if you don't want to accept duplicate values for a field. If you attempt to enter a number that already exists in another record for this field, ClarisWorks presents a warning.

✦ *Must Be In Range.* Click this check box and enter a pair of numbers in the From and To boxes if you want to specify a range of allowable numeric entries. If you later enter a number in this field that is outside the range, a warning message appears.

All three warning messages can be overridden by clicking Yes in the warning message box.

You can assign a display format (such as Currency) or a particular number of decimal places to any field. (See "Field formatting" later in this chapter for more information.)

If a particular number is entered more frequently than others in a number field (for example, you might have a default order quantity of 1), you can instruct ClarisWorks to enter that number for you automatically whenever you create a new record. Type the number in the Automatically Enter box in the right side of the Options dialog box. Like the data in other number fields, auto-entered data can be edited, as necessary.

You should define some fields as text fields even though they are composed entirely of numbers. Zip codes are a perfect example. Because number fields cannot display leading zeros, a zip code of 01535 would display as 1535 in a number field. Similarly, numbers that contain parentheses or dashes are not allowed. Thus, Social Security numbers and phone numbers are best defined as text fields, too. In general, if numeric data will not be used in calculations, define it as a text field rather than as a number field.

Date fields

You use date fields, of course, to record calendar dates, such as 7/19/97. Examples include birth dates, the date a product was ordered, the date an employee was hired, or the date a school paper is due. You can enter dates in a number of different ways. All of the following are acceptable:

 ✦ 7/19/97

 ✦ 7-19-97

 ✦ July 19, 1997

 ✦ Jul 19, 97

 ✦ 7/19

 ✦ Jul 19

As you can see, the methods for entering information into a date field are extremely flexible. As long as you enter enough information to identify each portion of the date (the first three letters of the month's name, for example), ClarisWorks will do its best to interpret what you type. If you omit the year, as in the last two examples, ClarisWorks assumes you are referring to the current year and inserts it for you.

Options available for date fields are shown in Figure 5-6. If you choose Must Be In Range as one of the verification options, you must enter valid dates in the From and To boxes. (See "Number fields" earlier in this chapter for more information on verification options and the capability to override verification warnings.)

Figure 5-6: Date field options

In the right side of the Options dialog box, you can enter a default date, if you wish. If there's a particular date that should normally be entered, type it in the Automatically Enter box. If you want to enter the current date when each record is created, click the Current Date radio button. As with other default values, you can edit or replace them in the records, as necessary.

You can display dates within their fields in several ways. For a discussion of formatting options, see "Field formatting" later in this chapter.

Time fields

Time fields enable you to record times in hours, minutes, and seconds. The options for time fields are identical to those for date fields, as described previously in "Date fields." The various time formats (discussed in "Field formatting," later in this chapter) enable you to record times with AM and PM suffixes, as well as in 12- or 24-hour formats.

Name fields

People's names are frequently recorded as two or more fields (First Name and Last Name, for example) because sorting a complete name is difficult. Generally, you sort by the person's last name, but you don't want to enter a full name as Smith Bill, for example, in order to sort correctly. By using ClarisWorks name fields, however, you can gracefully handle complete names as a single field.

By default, entries in name fields are sorted by the last word in the field rather than the first. To force a particular name to be sorted by the first word, enter an @ symbol as the first character (**@John Simms**, for example). To force a particular name to be sorted by the next-to-last word (ignoring the final word), separate the next-to-last and the last word with an Option-space rather than a regular space. This enables a name prefix, such as Jr., to be ignored during the sort.

Name options are shown in Figure 5-7. The two verification options (Cannot Be Empty and Must Be Unique) were explained in earlier sections of this chapter. The default options enable ClarisWorks to enter a specific name (your top salesperson, for instance) or your name (User's Name) automatically, as set in the Sharing Setup control panel.

Figure 5-7: Name field options

Tip

If an incorrect user name appears in the name field, check the name that appears in the Sharing Setup control panel. Change it to reflect the name that *should* be used — your name, in most cases.

Pop-up menu fields

Setting a field type as a pop-up menu adds a menu to the field, as shown in Figure 5-8.

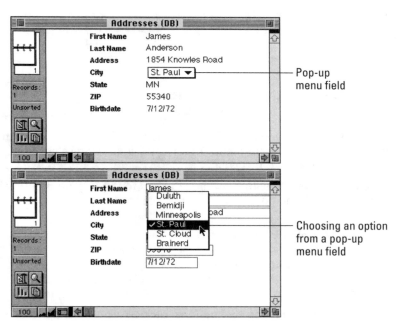

Figure 5-8: A record with a pop-up menu field for City (top), and choosing a city from a pop-up menu field (bottom)

Steps: Creating a Pop-Up Menu Field

1. Choose Define Fields from the Layout menu (or press Shift-⌘-D). The Define Database Fields dialog box appears (refer back to Figure 5-2).

2. Enter a name for the field in the Field Name box, choose Pop-up Menu from the Field Type pop-up menu, and click Create. The Options dialog box appears, as shown in Figure 5-9.

3. To create a choice for the pop-up menu, type a name or value into the Item Label box.

(continued)

Figure 5-9: The Options dialog box for a pop-up menu field

4. Click Create to add the choice to the Items for Control list.

5. Repeat Steps 3 and 4 for all additional menu choices you want to create.

6. In the right side of the Options dialog box, choose a default item from the Automatically Choose pop-up menu. That item will automatically be selected when a new record is created.

7. *Optional:* Enter a new label that will be attached to the pop-up menu field. By default, the field's name is used. You are free to change the label to something else.

   As previously illustrated in Figure 5-8, the normal field label is removed when you display a pop-up menu field, and it is replaced by a label directly tied to the pop-up menu field. Optionally, you can remove the automatic field label as well as the pop-up menu's triangle icon by following the instructions in "Field formatting," later in this chapter.

8. To accept the field's definition and options, click OK; to cancel the changes, click Cancel.

9. Continue defining fields and editing definitions, or click Done to return to the database.

Note

Although entries in the Items for Control list reflect the order in which you created the values, you can change the positions of entries by clicking and dragging items in the list. Items can also be replaced or deleted by selecting the item and then clicking the appropriate button (Modify or Delete).

When you create a new record, the default entry is automatically chosen for any pop-up menu field in the layout. Tabbing into a pop-up menu field does nothing; to change the default entry to a different value, you must deliberately click the pop-up menu and drag to select another value.

Setting a field type as a pop-up menu is an excellent idea when you want to restrict users' choices to a specific set of entries. Note, however, that if you or anyone else wants to enter an unlisted choice, it can't be done. You must choose Define Fields again and add that choice to the Items for Control list.

Radio buttons fields

Radio buttons fields are used to present a specific set of choices to the user, each with its own radio button (as shown in Figure 5-10). As in other programs, the choices are mutually exclusive — only one radio button can be selected. For help creating a radio buttons field, see "Pop-up menu fields" earlier in this chapter. The options and procedures are identical.

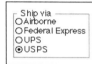

Figure 5-10: A radio buttons field

You can change the size or shape of the radio buttons field by switching to Layout mode and dragging one of the field's handles. You can also alter the appearance of the field by choosing options from the Radio Buttons Style dialog box (described in "Field formatting," later in this chapter).

ClarisWorks provides several interesting keyboard shortcuts for choosing options in a radio buttons field (in addition to simply clicking the button of your choice). You can tab into the field and then:

✦ Press the spacebar repeatedly to cycle through the choices.

✦ Press any of the arrow keys (up, down, right, or left) to cycle through the choices.

✦ Press Tab again to leave the field, or press Enter or choose New Record from the Edit menu to complete the record.

Check box fields

Use a check box field to present a single label preceded by a check box, as shown in Figure 5-11. Check box fields are most appropriate for yes/no, true/false, and on/off types of data. Because they are simple to respond to, check box fields can be extremely useful as parts of data collection forms, such as surveys and business forms.

⊠ Product shipped?

Figure 5-11: A check box field

The check box can be either checked or unchecked, and you can specify either as the default state for the field. The check mark can be toggled between checked and unchecked by clicking it with the mouse, pressing the spacebar, or pressing any of the arrow keys.

Click the Options button in the Define Database Fields dialog box to set a different label for the field and to indicate whether the check box in new records should be initially checked or unchecked. To set formatting options for the field — including whether an *x* or a ✓ will be used as the check mark — change to Layout mode and choose Field Info from the Edit menu.

Serial number fields

Serial number fields are used to assign numbers to records. Each record — including every record already in the database — is automatically given a number that reflects the order in which it was created. Although serial numbers can be edited, deleting records or sorting them does not affect the contents of a serial number field. Serial number fields are often used to number invoices, purchase orders, statements, and checks.

Note

For data entry and editing purposes, an entry in a serial number field is treated like any other number. Only numeric entries are permitted. This means a serial number field cannot be used for part numbers such as 14B73, for example.

After defining a field as a serial number field, you can set options for the field by clicking the Options button in the Define Database Fields dialog box. The Options dialog box appears, as shown in Figure 5-12.

Check Cannot Be Empty if you want ClarisWorks to present a warning if you attempt to leave or close the current record and no serial number is present. If you don't check Cannot Be Empty, you can delete serial numbers. Click Must Be Unique if you want to disallow duplicate numbers. As with the options for other field types, you can override either of these restrictions on a record-by-record basis.

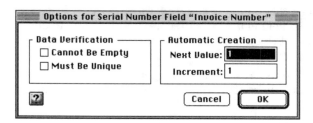

Figure 5-12: The Options dialog box for a serial number field

In the right side of the dialog box, enter numbers for the next value (the serial number to be assigned to the first record in the database) and the increment (how much you want each new serial number to increase over the previous number). When a serial number field is created, ClarisWorks offers 1 as the default next value and 1 as the increment.

Tip

If there are frequent breaks in a serial number field (purchase order numbers that are skipped or checks that are voided, for example), you can go to the Options dialog box for the serial number field and reset the entry in the Next Value box to jump to the next purchase order or check number. Doing this has no effect on the numbers for existing records.

Value list fields

Defining a field as a value list field causes it to present a drop-down list of values from which the user can select. Unlike with pop-up menu fields, the list is automatically presented whenever you tab into the field, you can manually enter unlisted values, and you can set several data validation options. Figure 5-13 shows a record that contains a value list field.

A default value appears here, if one has been specified

Figure 5-13: When a user tabs into the Prefix field of the Address List database, this value list automatically drops down.

The basic steps and options for creating a value list field are identical to those for pop-up menu fields (described earlier in this chapter). In addition to creating the list of values and optionally selecting a default value, you can also set any of the following data verification options:

✦ *Cannot Be Empty*: When this option is selected, ClarisWorks presents a warning if you leave the field empty and then attempt to move to another record, accept the record (by pressing Enter), or create a new record. (This warning can be overridden.)

✦ *Must Be Unique*: ClarisWorks presents a warning if your choice or manual entry for this field is already contained in another record. (This warning can be overridden.)

✦ *Alerts for Unlisted Values*: If you manually enter a value that is not contained in the value list, the warning in Figure 5-14 appears. The buttons enable you to continue editing the field's data (Continue), accept the entry as valid for this record only (Accept), or accept the entry and add it to the field's value list (Add to List). The Add to List option appends the current value to the bottom of the value list and makes the value an acceptable choice for all new and existing records.

Continue editing the contents of the field (that is, try again) — Accept the entry for this record only — Accept the entry for this and every other record in the database

Figure 5-14: This message appears when you manually enter a value into a field for which the Alerts for Unlisted Values option has been selected.

When entering or editing data in a value list field, you can choose a value in several ways:

✦ Double-click the value with the mouse pointer.

✦ Scroll to the value with the up- and down-arrow keys.

✦ Type the first character or two of the value's text.

To complete the selection, you can double-click the value, press Return, or press Enter.

When all of the following circumstances are true, ClarisWorks 5.0 ignores the default value set for a value list field:

✦ You are working in ClarisWorks 5.0 with a converted database (one that was created in an earlier version of the program).

✦ The original database contained a text field that had a value list attached to it.

✦ You have specified a different default value for the field (in the Options dialog box) of ClarisWorks 5.0.

Multimedia fields

 New In Version 5

In previous versions of ClarisWorks, QuickTime movies could only be placed in database layouts as background objects — not stored in fields. This severely limited their usefulness. Now, however, ClarisWorks 5.0's new multimedia fields enable you to store QuickTime movies, sounds, and pictures in any database.

Multimedia fields have no options that can be set in the Define Database Fields dialog box. You can change the size of a multimedia field for all records by changing to Layout mode, selecting the field, and then dragging one of its handles. If you want to maintain the original proportions of the field, press the Shift key as you drag. Field formatting options (such as scaling, cropping, and alignment) can be set for a multimedia field by changing to Layout mode, selecting the field, and choosing Field Info from the Edit menu.

There are several ways to add movies, pictures, or sounds to a multimedia field:

✦ Copy the item from another program or the Scrapbook and then paste it into the field.

✦ Add items from any of the ReadyArt libraries (see Chapter 21).

✦ Use drag-and-drop to move a copy of the item from the Scrapbook, another ClarisWorks document, or a drag-and-drop-enabled program into the field.

✦ Select the field, choose the Insert command from the File menu, and then select the movie, picture, or sound file you want to insert into the field.

 Tip

Sound files must be in QuickTime format to be inserted, copied, or dragged into a multimedia field. To convert a sound file to this format, choose the Insert command from the File menu, select the sound you wish to convert, and click the Convert button.

 Note

To save space, QuickTime movies and sounds are not stored in the database. Instead, ClarisWorks merely records a reference to where they are located (your hard drive, for example). Pictures, on the other hand, *are* stored in the database.

To play a sound or movie that is stored in a multimedia field, double-click the field.

Record info fields

As shown in the Options dialog box in Figure 5-15, record info fields enable you to stamp each record automatically with any of the following:

✦ The date or time the record was created

✦ The date or time the record was last modified

✦ The name of the individual who created or last modified the record

Data in a record info field is entered automatically by ClarisWorks when a record is first created (the Creation and Creator options) or edited (the Modified and Modifier options). Data in a record info field cannot be altered or deleted.

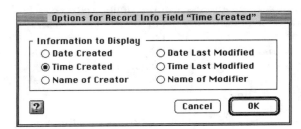

Figure 5-15: Options for a record info field

Calculation fields

The availability of calculation fields sets a ClarisWorks database apart from a paper-based database or one created in a word processor. A calculation field is based on a formula you specify. You can use calculation fields to perform simple math, such as the computation of state sales tax (for example, 'Price'*.07), a product mark-up (for example, 'Cost'*1.5), or the sum of several fields (for example, 'Qty1'+'Qty2'+'Qty3'). Calculation fields can also incorporate any of the ClarisWorks database functions described in Appendix B.

When a database contains a calculation field, a separate result is computed for each record in the database. For example, in a sales database, a calculation field named Total could sum the quarterly sales data for each salesperson, as in: 'Qtr1' + 'Qtr2' + 'Qtr3' + 'Qtr4'.

Steps: Defining a Calculation Field

1. Choose Define Fields from the Layout menu (or press Shift-⌘-D). The Define Database Fields dialog box appears, as shown previously in Figure 5-2.

2. Enter a name for the calculation field in the Field Name box and choose Calculation from the Field Type pop-up menu.

3. Click Create. The Enter Formula dialog box appears, as shown in Figure 5-16.

4. Enter the formula in the Formula box. You can create formulas using any of the following methods:

- Type directly into the box.

- Select fields, operators, and functions from the three scrolling list boxes. (Click an option to insert it into the formula at the text insertion point.)

- Combine the first two approaches (type some parts of the formula and select others).

Choose formula components from these lists

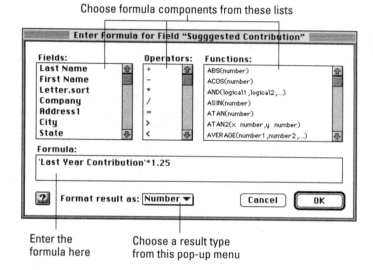

Figure 5-16: The Enter Formula dialog box

Enter the formula here

Choose a result type from this pop-up menu

5. Choose a result type from the Format Result As pop-up menu. The choices are Text, Number, Date, and Time.

6. Click OK to accept the formula. ClarisWorks notifies you if there is an error in the formula. Otherwise, you return to the Define Database Fields dialog box where you can define, modify, delete, or set options for additional fields.

Note

You cannot enter data into a calculation field. The program fills it in automatically, based on the results of the formula for the field. Consequently, during data entry or editing, you cannot move into a calculation field by tabbing or by selecting it with the mouse. To show which fields in a database are user-modifiable and which ones are calculation fields, ClarisWorks surrounds normal fields with a light gray bounding box when you're in Browse or List mode (for data entry and editing). Calculation fields have no bounding box.

Summary fields

Summary fields play an important role in ClarisWorks databases. They can change a database from a static collection of data to something that really works for you — providing information that cannot be gleaned from a simple scan of the records.

A calculation field makes a computation within each record (adding the total of three invoice fields, for example). Summary fields, on the other hand, make calculations across a group of records — either a subset of records (for a sub-summary) or all visible records in the database (for a grand summary).

Every summary field is based on a formula. The built-in database functions in ClarisWorks make it easy to calculate totals, averages, and counts to summarize groups of records or the entire database. Where a summary field is placed in the layout determines whether it summarizes each group of records (the field is in a sub-summary part) or the whole database (the field is in a leading or trailing grand summary part).

When you place a summary field in a sub-summary layout part, you have to specify a sort field for the summary field. The sort field serves to group the records. Suppose, for example, you run a state-wide business and want to track total sales in different cities. You can create a summary field called Sales Total, define its formula as SUM('Sales'), and set the City field as the sort-by field for the summary field. Then after you sort the database by city, the records for each city form a separate group (all customers from Chicago are listed together, for example).

At the end of every city group, the total sales for only that particular city are shown — above or below all the individual records for that city (the location of the summary figure depends on where you place it in the layout). You can also *nest* summary fields. For example, you might use two summary fields to look at total sales within each city within each state.

When you place a summary field in a grand summary layout part, the summary field summarizes all the records in the database (or the found set of records, if you're viewing only a subset of the database). There are two types of grand summaries: leading and trailing. A *leading grand summary* appears above the data it summarizes. A *trailing grand summary* appears below the data.

The Credit Card Charges database described later in this chapter provides additional examples of summary fields — in both sub-summary and grand summary layout parts.

Note

As with calculation fields, you cannot enter information into a summary field. Instead, ClarisWorks automatically calculates results for the field, based on the criteria you set. To see the results for a summary field, you need to either be in Page View or print the database. To have summary fields in a sub-summary part contain the correct information, you need to sort the database by the sort field (the one specified in the Insert Part dialog box when the sub-summary part was created). To be safe, you should always sort the database just before printing a report.

Creating a summary field requires several steps: creating a new field to hold the summary information (similar to the way you create a calculation field), adding a summary part to the layout, placing the summary field in the summary part, and — if the field has been added to a sub-summary part — sorting the records.

Steps: Creating a Summary Field

1. Choose Define Fields from the Layout menu (or press Shift-⌘-D). The Define Database Fields dialog box appears.

2. Type a name for the summary field, choose Summary from the Field Type pop-up menu, and click Create. The Enter Formula dialog box appears (the same dialog box that appears when you create a calculation field).

3. Enter the formula for the summary field in the Formula box. You can create formulas by typing them directly into the box; by selecting fields, operators, and functions from the three scrolling list boxes (click an option to insert it into the formula at the text insertion point); or by combining the two approaches.

4. Choose a result type from the Format Result As pop-up menu. The choices are Text, Number, Date, and Time.

5. Click OK to accept the formula (ClarisWorks notifies you if the formula contains an error), and click Done to exit the dialog box.

6. At the bottom of the Layout menu, choose the layout to which you want to add the summary field.

7. Choose Layout from the Layout menu (or press Shift-⌘-L).

   If an appropriate summary part already exists in the layout, you can skip to Step 11.

8. Choose Insert Part from the Layout menu. The Insert Part dialog box shown in Figure 5-17 appears.

Fields in this list are selectable only when
the Sub-summary radio button is selected

```
┌─────────────────── Insert Part ───────────────────┐
│                                                     │
│  ○ Header                       First Name      ⇧  │
│  ○ Leading grand summary        Last Name          │
│  ● Sub-summary when sorted by   Address            │
│  ○ Trailing grand summary       City               │
│  ○ Footer                       State              │
│                                 Zipcode            │
│  ☐ Page break before part       Phone              │
│  ☐ Page break after part        Company         ⇩  │
│                                                     │
│  [?]                          [ Cancel ]  (  OK  )  │
└─────────────────────────────────────────────────────┘
```

Figure 5-17: The Insert Part dialog box

9. Choose Leading Grand Summary, Sub-summary When Sorted By, or Trailing Grand Summary. (Summary fields cannot be placed in header or footer parts.)

   You use the Leading and Trailing options to provide a summary for the entire database. In a sales database, for example, you can use either of these choices to total or average all sales for the database.

   If you choose the Sub-summary option, you have to choose a sort field from the list on the right side of the dialog box. When you sort the database by the contents of the selected field, the program groups records by the sort field and calculates a subtotal of the found set for each group. If you want to examine sales on a state-by-state basis, for example, you can create a sales sub-summary sorted by state.

10. Click OK to leave the dialog box. (If you selected the sub-summary option, the program asks whether you want the sub-summary part to appear above or below each record group. Choose Above, Below, or Cancel.) The program adds the summary or sub-summary part to the appropriate location in the current layout.

11. Add the summary field to the layout by selecting Insert Field from the Layout menu. The Insert Fields dialog box appears, as shown in Figure 5-18.

12. Select the summary field in the list box and click OK. (You also can double-click the summary field.) In either case, the field and its label appear in the current layout. Drag the summary field and its label into the summary or sub-summary part.

13. Switch to Browse mode by selecting Browse from the Layout menu (or press Shift-⌘-B).

14. If the database is not in Page View, you don't see summary fields. If necessary, choose Page View from the Window menu (or press Shift-⌘-P).

Figure 5-18: The Insert Fields dialog box

15. If the field is a sub-summary field (rather than a grand summary), you need to sort the database by the field specified in the Insert Part dialog box. Choose Sort Records from the Organize menu (or press ⌘-J). The Sort Records dialog box appears, as shown in Figure 5-19.

The icon to the left of each field name indicates whether its sort is ascending or descending

Figure 5-19: The Sort Records dialog box

Use the Move and Clear buttons, as appropriate, to select the sort fields. You can sort each field in ascending or descending order, depending on which radio button you click. Click OK to conduct the sort. The sub-summary information is displayed, grouped according to the contents of the sort-by field.

Tip

If you want to see all the summary data at one time or want to move it into another environment (such as the spreadsheet or word processor), change to Page View (Shift-⌘-P) and choose Copy Summaries from the Edit menu. ClarisWorks transfers the contents of summary fields to the Clipboard, where they are available for pasting into other documents and applications.

The Fine Points of Calculation and Summary Formula Creation

You need to keep the following points in mind when creating formulas:

✦ Only calculation or summary fields can contain formulas. The program computes the results of a calculation field individually for each record in the database. Summary field formulas, on the other hand, summarize information across all or a subset of records. In a product catalog database, for example, you can use a summary field to calculate the total price of every product in the database.

✦ You need to surround field names with single quotes (for example, 'Sales') and text strings with double quotes (for example, "Smithers").

✦ You can add extra space around operators you manually enter (+, - , and so on) to improve readability when you are creating the formula, but ClarisWorks removes extra spaces when it checks and saves the formula.

✦ When evaluating a formula, ClarisWorks examines the elements from left to right. Different mathematical and logical operators (+, >, and so on) have different precedence, however. When you include more than one operator in a formula, the precedence of the operators determines the order in which ClarisWorks performs the calculations.

You can add parentheses to a formula to improve readability or to change the precedence for performing a calculation. If, for example, A=2 and B=3 in a given record, the formula A+B*2 gives a result of 8. Because multiplication has a higher precedence than addition, ClarisWorks evaluates the formula in this order: (B*2) equals 6, to which A is added, giving an answer of 8. By adding parentheses to the formula, as in (A+B)*2, you can change the precedence. Now the program adds A to B first (because elements that are enclosed in parentheses have a higher precedence than elements that are not enclosed in parentheses), giving a result of 5. Next, the program multiplies 5 by 2, giving an answer of 10.

Note: A common error is to have unbalanced parentheses in a formula. The number of left and right parentheses must always be equal.

Precedence levels in database formulas are as follows:

Operator	Meaning
%	percentage (divide by 100)
^	exponentiation (raise to a power, such as 'Length'^2)
+, -	change sign (for example, -'Cost')
*, /	multiplication, division

Operator	Meaning
+, -	addition, subtraction
&	concatenate text strings ("Jim" & " " & "Uris" equals Jim Uris)
=,>,>=,<,<=,<>	comparison operators (equal, greater than, greater than or equal to, less than, less than or equal to, not equal)

✦ Selecting a function from the Function list inserts the function (as well as any appropriate arguments to the function) at the text insertion point. An example of a function is AVERAGE(number1,number2, . . .), where number1, number2, and . . . are the arguments to the function. The *number1,number2, . . .* means you must replace the arguments with numbers or number fields and you can have as many of them as you like.

Arguments are placeholders. You often replace them with field names. The fastest way to replace an argument with a field name is to double-click the argument to select it and then click a field in the Fields list.

An *ellipsis* (. . .) in an argument list means the number of elements of the specified data type you use is up to you. In the Average example, a completed formula may read AVERAGE('Qtr1','Qtr2','Qtr3','Qtr4'), where each of the Qtr fields contains a sales figure or a numeric grade for the quarter.

Note: You can also replace any or all number arguments with real numbers by typing them directly into the formula, as in AVERAGE('Sales',25000).

✦ Although most of the functions are available for use in both spreadsheet and database environments, database functions cannot refer to a range of fields. You must include every individual field name in a database formula, and separate the field names with commas. You can use this formula in a database:

SUM('QTY1','QTY2','QTY3')

But you cannot use this formula:

SUM('QTY1'..'QTY3')

✦ A formula can consist entirely of a single function. You can also embed functions within a larger formula, as well as use one function to modify the result of another function. An example of the latter use is 'Due Date'-TRUNC(NOW()). This formula computes the number of days from the current date until the due date. The decimal portion of today's date and time (NOW()) is eliminated by the TRUNC function, and the result is subtracted from Due Date. (For additional information on using the ClarisWorks database and spreadsheet functions, refer to Appendix B and ClarisWorks Help.)

Modifying field definitions

After you define a field, you can change its type, name, or options. You also can change the formula for a calculation or summary field.

Tip

Changing a field definition from one data type to another sometimes has unfortunate effects, and you cannot use the Undo command to undo such changes. Saving the database before you alter a field definition is a smart idea. If the transformations don't work as you intended, you can simply close the database without saving the changes.

Steps: Changing Field Types

1. Choose Define Fields from the Layout menu (or press Shift-⌘-D). The Define Database Fields dialog box appears, as shown in Figure 5-20.

List of currently defined fields

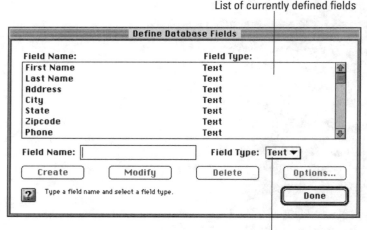

Choose a new field type from this pop-up menu

Figure 5-20: The Define Database Fields dialog box

2. Select the field for which you want to set a new type. The field's name appears in the Field Name box.

3. From the Field Type pop-up menu, choose the new type you want to assign to the field and then click Modify.

The following warning message appears: *When modifying the field type, any data that cannot be converted will be lost.*

4. Click OK to continue or Cancel to leave the original field type unchanged.

5. Click Done to return to the database.

Renaming fields

Once created, field names are not set in stone. To change a field name, choose Define Fields from the Layout menu, select the field name in the field list (in the Define Database Fields dialog box), type a new name, and then click the Modify button. If the field was referenced in any calculation or summary formulas, references to the old field name are automatically changed to reflect the new field name.

Tip

If you want to change a field name to make it more understandable when viewed in the layout, you can simply retype its field label in the layout. The field label has no effect on the actual field, so you can have a field called *tot sls* and label it Total Sales, for example.

Changing field options

As explained in "Field types" earlier in this chapter, most field types have options that can be set, such as setting a default value and choosing data validation measures. Field options can be altered at any time — not just when you first define the field.

To change field options, choose Define Fields from the Layout menu (or press Shift-⌘-D). The Define Database Fields dialog box appears, as shown previously in Figure 5-20. Select the name of the field in the field list, and click the Options button. Change the options, as desired. Then click OK and Done to dismiss the dialog boxes.

Changing a formula for a calculation or summary field

You can also change an existing formula for a calculation or summary field. Choose Define Fields from the Layout menu. The Define Database Fields dialog box appears, as shown previously in Figure 5-20. Select the calculation or summary field in the field list, and then click the Modify button. Change the formula, and then click OK and Done. When the Define Fields dialog box closes, the changed formula is recalculated for all database records.

Deleting fields

Some fields outlive their usefulness, and you can easily delete them. However, deleting a field also deletes all information contained in that field from every record in the database.

Steps: Deleting a Field

1. Choose Define Fields from the Layout menu (or press Shift-⌘-D). The Define Database Fields dialog box appears, as shown previously in Figure 5-20.

2. Highlight the field you want to delete.

3. Click the Delete button. A dialog box appears with the following question: *Permanently delete this field and ALL of its contents?*

4. Click OK to delete the field or Cancel if you change your mind.

5. Repeat Steps 2 through 4 for any additional fields you want to delete.

6. Click Done to exit the Define Database Fields dialog box.

Note

To remove a field from a layout, it is not necessary to use the above procedure. Instead, change to Layout mode, select the field, and press the Delete key. Although the field is now gone from the layout, its data remains available for use in other layouts.

Adding new fields

You can add new fields to the database at any time. Choose Define Fields from the Layout menu (or press Shift-⌘-D). The Define Database Fields dialog box appears, as shown previously in Figure 5-20. Type the name of the new field in the Field Name text box, choose a type for the field from the Field Type pop-up menu, and click Create. The new field is added to the list box.

You can continue to create new fields or click Done to dismiss the Define Database Fields dialog box. When you are finished, ClarisWorks adds the new fields and their labels to the database and to the currently selected layout. Edit the layout to accommodate or omit the new fields, as you prefer (as described in the next section, "Organizing Information with Layouts").

Organizing Information with Layouts

In most database programs, every database has a single screen on which you perform data entry, and you create reports in a separate part of the program. ClarisWorks doesn't force you to make a distinction between data-entry forms and reports. Instead, it uses the concept of layouts.

A *layout* is a particular arrangement of fields you've defined for a database. In each layout, you can use as many or as few of the defined fields as you like. There are no fields you *must* use. And you can have as many layouts for each database as you need. Using an address database as an example, you can create the layouts shown in Figure 5-21.

Figure 5-21: Different layouts provide different views of the same data.

To create a new layout for a database, choose New Layout from the Layout menu or the Layout pop-up menu in the Tool panel (see Figure 5-22). The New Layout dialog box appears, as shown in Figure 5-23.

Layout pop-up ——— ——— Search pop-up
Sort pop-up ———   ——— Report pop-up

Figure 5-22: These four pop-up menus appear in the Tool panel in every mode except Layout mode. Use them to work with layouts, searches, sorting, and reports.

Figure 5-23: The New Layout dialog box

Type a name for the new layout or accept the default name ClarisWorks proposes (Layout #), click a radio button to choose one of the five layout formats, and click OK. Depending on the type of layout chosen, ClarisWorks creates it immediately or asks you to first choose fields and settings, as follows.

✦ If you choose a *Labels* layout, you can pick from any of the predefined label layouts in the pop-up menu or create your own layout by selecting the Custom choice. (See "Working with mailing labels," later in this chapter, for a complete discussion of label options.)

✦ If you choose *Standard*, ClarisWorks creates a default database layout that contains every field you defined for the database. The fields appear one above the other in a vertical list.

✦ If you choose *Duplicate*, ClarisWorks creates an exact copy of the currently selected layout. This option is useful if you want to make a variation of the current layout — perhaps adding a few fields or rearranging the fields. You also can create a duplicate when you want to experiment with the layout. If the experiment doesn't work out, you can simply delete the layout.

✦ If you choose *Blank*, ClarisWorks creates a blank layout. You add all fields by choosing the Insert Field command from the Layout menu. (This option is useful when you want to start from scratch in designing a layout.)

✦ If you choose *Columnar Report* or *Labels* (see the phone directory and label layouts in Figure 5-21 for examples), the Set Field Order dialog box appears, as shown in Figure 5-24.

Figure 5-24:
The Set Field
Order dialog
box

The purpose of the Set Field Order dialog box is to specify the fields you
want to include in the new layout and to designate their order. Choose a field
from the Field List (on the left side of the dialog box) and click Move to add it
to the Field Order list on the right. You can use as many or as few fields in the
layout as you like.

Layout parts

As shown in Figure 5-25, every layout is composed of labeled *parts*.

Figure 5-25: The parts of a database layout

The *body* is the main part of any layout. The body holds the bulk of the data fields,
mainly those into which you enter data.

All other parts of a layout are optional. The optional parts include:

✦ The *header* and *footer* (which hold information that repeats on every page of the layout)

✦ Leading or trailing *grand summaries* (which display summary data at the beginning or end of a report)

✦ One or more *sub-summaries* (which display summary information for groups of records — all records from the same state, for example)

You can change the size of any part by simply clicking the dividing line for the part and dragging to make the part smaller or larger. As long as a part doesn't contain any fields or other objects, you can remove the part by dragging it up into the part immediately above it. (If the part *does* contain fields or other objects, you must delete the fields and objects or move them into other parts before you can remove the part.)

Note

Although you can place any field in the body, header, or footer, you can place only summary fields in a grand summary or sub-summary part.

Arranging fields in a layout

Initially, ClarisWorks arranges fields in the layout according to the layout type you selected when you created the layout (Standard, Duplicate, Blank, Columnar Report, or Labels). Everything you place in a layout — fields, field labels, text, and graphics — is considered a draw object. As such, you can do anything with items in the layout that you can do with an object. Click any object, and you see its handles. You can drag a handle to resize a field (making it larger or smaller); drag fields to different positions; change or delete field labels; align fields with each other or the grid (using the Align commands in the Arrange menu); change the font, size, or style of text in the field or the label; place graphics in the layout; and so on. (See Chapter 6 for additional information on working with objects.)

Adding graphics to a layout

Many layouts can be made more attractive by adding a graphic or two — a logo or some clip art, for example. To add a graphic to a layout, you can do any of the following:

✦ Choose the Insert command from the File menu and open a graphic file.

✦ Copy an image from the Scrapbook, a ClarisWorks paint or draw document, or another graphics program, and then paste it into a layout.

✦ Drag the image from the Scrapbook, a ClarisWorks paint or draw document, or another drag-and-drop-enabled graphics program into a layout.

✦ Select an image from one of the ClarisWorks ReadyArt libraries (see Chapter 21).

✦ Use any of the standard ClarisWorks draw tools to add lines, rectangles, and so on.

Field formatting

The default layouts create serviceable databases, but they aren't particularly attractive. The following instructions describe how to improve a layout by changing the text attributes for field contents and labels; by setting numeric, date, and time formats for fields; and by adding borders around fields.

To set text attributes for fields or labels, begin by choosing the layout in which you want to work from the bottom of the Layout menu. Next, choose Layout from the Layout menu (or press Shift-⌘-L). Click or Shift-click to select the fields and field labels for which you want to set new text attributes. Choose options from the Font, Size, Style, Text Color, and Alignment submenus of the Format menu. The selected fields and labels change to match the new settings.

By selecting a text, name, pop-up menu, radio buttons, check box, value list, or record info field and then choosing Field Info from the Edit menu (or by double-clicking one of these field types), you can summon a special Text Style dialog box in which you can simultaneously set the font, size, and text color for the field (see Figure 5-26). Additional formatting options are also presented for some of these field types.

Figure 5-26: The Text Style dialog box

If a field will contain multiple lines of data (a Comments or Notes field, for example), you can also change the field's line spacing by choosing a setting from the Spacing submenu of the Format menu.

You can change the display format for number, date, time, and serial number fields, as well as for calculation and summary fields that produce a number, date, or time result. To set a number, date, or time format for a field, choose the layout in which you want to work from the bottom of the Layout menu. Next, choose Layout from the Layout menu (or press Shift-⌘-L). Click to select a number, date, time, serial number, calculation, or summary field, and choose Field Info from the Options menu (or double-click the field). Depending on the field type, one of the three dialog boxes in Figure 5-27 appears. Choose options in the dialog box and then click OK. ClarisWorks formats the field according to your selections.

Figure 5-27: Use these dialog boxes to set the display format for number, date, and time fields.

Date format options include slashes, abbreviations, and day names. Time format options include AM/PM, the display of seconds, and normal versus military (24-hour) time. The various number format options produce the following results:

✦ *General.* Displays numbers without commas and shows the number of decimal places entered (or required by a calculation).

✦ *Currency.* Displays a dollar sign and two decimal places, as in $19.81. (You can change the display of commas, negative amounts, and number of decimal places with the Commas, Negatives, and Precision options.)

✦ *Percent.* Adds a percent sign as a suffix and multiplies the field's contents by 100 (for example, 0.1235 × 100 is 12.35%). The Precision setting determines the number of decimal places.

✦ *Scientific.* Uses exponential notation, as in 1.245e+3 (for 1,245), which is useful for displaying very large or small numbers.

✦ *Fixed.* Rounds the results to the number of decimal places shown in the Precision box, as in 21.433 (for a precision setting of 3).

✦ *Commas.* Inserts commas every three digits, as in 18,221.

✦ *Negatives in ().* Surrounds numbers less than zero with parentheses, as in (24), instead of using a minus sign.

✦ *Precision.* Sets the number of decimal places to be shown.

Because they are primarily used to store movies and graphics, the multimedia field options determine how images will be displayed on screen. To set options for a multimedia field, change to Layout mode and either double-click the field or choose Field Info from the Edit menu. The Multimedia Field dialog box appears, as shown in Figure 5-28.

Figure 5-28: Set display options for a multimedia field in the Multimedia Field dialog box.

The following options can be set in the Multimedia Field dialog box:

✦ *Crop Image to Frame.* When this radio button is clicked, images or movies will be trimmed as necessary to fit inside the current frame. When you play a cropped QuickTime movie, the movie is automatically scaled to fit the frame.

✦ *Scale Image to Fit Frame.* Click this option if you want the image to be as large as possible, given the size of the bounding frame. Images smaller than the frame will automatically be enlarged; larger images will be reduced in size to match the size of the frame. To maintain the horizontal and vertical proportions of the image, click the Maintain Original Proportions check box.

✦ *Alignment.* Choose options from the Vertical and Horizontal pop-up menus to specify how images should be aligned within the frame.

You can change the size of any multimedia field by switching to Layout mode, selecting the field, and then dragging one of the four handles. To maintain the field's original proportions, press the Shift key as you drag. (Initially, all multimedia fields are one inch square. A typical QuickTime movie, however, is 2.22 × 1.67 inches. You may want to use those as the starting dimensions for any field designed to hold movies.)

In Browse mode, ClarisWorks database fields are surrounded by thin gray borders. If you like, however, you can change the appearance of any field border by following these steps.

Steps: Creating Field Borders

1. At the bottom of the Layout menu, choose the layout in which you want to work.

2. Choose Layout from the Layout menu (or press Shift-⌘-L).

3. Using the pointer tool, select the fields to which you want to add a border.

4. In the Tool panel, set the pen pattern to opaque. You also can select a different pen color and a line width. After you change to Browse mode (Shift-⌘-B), the fields appear with a border.

You can also set the *background* for any field by switching to Layout mode, selecting the field, and then choosing options from the Fill Color, Pattern, Texture, or Gradient palettes.

Adding and deleting fields from a layout

As mentioned earlier, you can have as many or as few fields in each layout as you like. You can add fields to any layout that doesn't already display every defined field, and you can remove unnecessary fields.

Steps: Adding a Field to a Layout

1. At the bottom of the Layout menu, choose the layout to which you want to add a field.

2. Choose Layout from the Layout menu (or press Shift-⌘-L).

3. Choose Insert Field from the Layout menu. The Insert Fields dialog box appears, as shown in Figure 5-29. Its list box contains only the defined fields that are not already in use in the current layout.

Figure 5-29: The Insert Fields dialog box

4. Select a field and click Insert. ClarisWorks Inserts the field and its label into the layout.

5. If necessary, move and resize the field and its label.

To remove a field from a layout, begin by choosing the appropriate layout from the bottom of the Layout menu. Change to Layout mode by choosing Layout from the Layout menu (or pressing Shift-⌘-L). Use the pointer tool to select the fields you want to remove, and then press Delete or choose Clear or Cut (⌘-X) from the Edit menu. ClarisWorks removes the selected fields from the layout.

Caution

Removing a field from a layout is not the same as deleting the field. Removing a field from a layout does nothing to the data in the field. The field can still appear in other layouts with its data intact. And if you insert the field back into a layout, its data reappears. On the other hand, after you delete a field in the Define Database Fields dialog box (Shift-⌘-D), ClarisWorks removes the field from all layouts and permanently deletes the field's data from the database. Recreating that field will not bring back its data.

Deleting a layout

You can delete any layout you no longer want to use. Choose Edit Layouts from the Layout menu or from the Layout pop-up menu in the Tool panel. The Edit Layouts dialog box appears, as shown in Figure 5-30. Choose the layout by name from the Current Layouts list, and then click Delete. A dialog box appears and asks *Permanently delete this layout?* Click OK to delete the layout, or click Cancel to leave it intact.

Figure 5-30: The Edit Layouts dialog box

A layout can only be deleted if two or more layouts are currently defined. ClarisWorks will not allow you to delete the only layout for a database. Thus, if you want to eliminate the original layout, you first have to create at least one additional layout.

Deleting a layout does not delete the fields you defined for the database or any of the data that appeared in the layout. It merely eliminates one possible view or arrangement of the data. To delete a field, select the field in the Define Database Fields dialog box (Shift-⌘-D) and then click the Delete button. To delete data, remove it from the record or delete the record.

Layout modification options

You can assign a new name to a layout, specify the number of columns that appear in Page View, and close up the space between fields when printing (a particularly useful option for labels).

Steps: Modifying a Layout

1. Choose Edit Layouts from the Layout menu or from the Layout pop-up menu in the Tool panel. Select the name of the layout you want to change and click Modify. The Layout Info dialog box appears, as shown in Figure 5-31.

Figure 5-31: Use the Layout Info dialog box to choose optional settings for the current layout.

2. *Optional*: Enter a new name for the layout by typing it in the Name box.

3. *Optional*: In the Columns section of the dialog box, set the number of columns to be displayed in reports and on screen (in Page View only) by typing a number in the Number Of box. Then click a radio button (Across First or Down First) to indicate the order in which records will be displayed in the columns.

4. *Optional*: Use options in the Slide section of the dialog box to close up space between fields and/or lines when printing. This option is often useful for labels and addressing envelopes. The Slide Objects Left check box closes up space between objects on the same line. For example, the address line

   ```
   Bemidji      , MN  56601
   ```

   would print as

   ```
   Bemidji, MN 56601
   ```

   The Slide Objects Up check box eliminates blank lines in records. For example, when you print an address label layout that contains fields arranged in five lines (1 - name; 2 - company name; 3 - first address line; 4 - second address line; and 5 - city, state, and zip code), labels that contain only one address line or no company name print without blank lines in those spots.

   To make sure objects slide left, they must have the tops of the fields aligned.

5. Click OK to accept the layout options and return to the database.

Setting a tab order

You can use the Tab key to move from field to field when entering data. The Tab Order command enables you to set a new order for navigating between fields when you press Tab.

By default, ClarisWorks sets the tab order for a database to match the order in which you created the fields. If you have altered the default layout by rearranging fields on screen, the tab order may cause the cursor to jump willy-nilly all over the screen. You can change the tab order so the cursor moves more efficiently.

Steps: Setting a New Tab Order

1. At the bottom of the Layout menu, choose the layout for which you want to specify a new tab order.

2. Choose Layout from the Layout menu (or press Shift-⌘-L).

3. Choose Tab Order from the Layout menu. The Tab Order dialog box shown in Figure 5-32 appears. The current (or default) tab order is shown in the Tab Order list box on the right side of the dialog box.

Figure 5-32: The Tab Order dialog box

4. To create a tab order from scratch, click Clear. ClarisWorks clears the Tab Order list box.

5. To specify the new order, choose a field name from the Field List and click Move (or double-click the field name). The program adds the field to the bottom of the Tab Order list. Continue selecting fields, in the order you prefer, until you have copied all the desired fields into the Tab Order list.

You also can Shift-click to choose several contiguous field names simultaneously or ⌘-click to choose several noncontiguous field names.

The tab order for a database layout in List mode matches the order in which the columns are displayed. To set the tab order for a database in List mode, choose List from the Layout menu (or press Shift-⌘-I), and drag columns (by selecting their headings) to new positions in the layout.

If you don't want users to be able to tab into some fields, leave those fields out of the list. When a user is in Browse mode, a press of the Tab key skips right over the fields. Note, however, that users can still enter data in those fields by clicking in them (unless, of course, the fields are calculation, summary, or record info fields). Note, too, that settings in the Tab Order dialog box have no effect on a database when it is in List mode.

Browse and List Modes: Viewing, Entering, and Editing Data

After you have designed a database and created layouts, you will spend most of your time in Browse and List modes — entering, editing, and viewing the data.

List mode displays the database in a spreadsheet-like grid, where each row is a record and each column is a field. Unlike a normal layout viewed in Browse mode — which only displays the fields you have placed in that layout — List mode presents every field that has been defined for the database. Regardless of the layout you were previously viewing, when you change to List mode, the arrangement of data is always the same.

Any database can be viewed in List mode by choosing List from the Layout menu or by pressing Shift-⌘-I. You learn about List mode later in this section.

Browse mode

Whether you need to enter and edit data or just want to flip through records, you can use Browse mode (choose Browse from the Layout menu or press Shift-⌘-B). The advantage of using Browse mode — as opposed to List mode — is you can display your data in any layout you've designed for a database, so you can restrict the set of fields to only those you need at the moment. To select a layout in which to work, choose its name from the bottom of the Layout menu.

Viewing records

When you are working on and viewing records in Browse mode, records can be displayed in any of three ways:

✦ Continuous scrolling list (choose Show Multiple from the Layout menu)

✦ One record per screen (remove the check mark from the Show Multiple command in the Layout menu)

✦ Only as many records as can fit on the current page size as defined in the Page Setup dialog box (choose Page View from the Window menu)

Viewing records in Page View shows exactly how the records will appear when printed. Page View is equivalent to choosing the Print Preview command in many Macintosh programs.

Adding and deleting records

To create a new record for the current database, choose New Record from the Edit menu (or press ⌘-R). The new record appears with the text insertion point in the first field. The database automatically switches to Browse mode.

To delete a record, select the record by clicking any place in the record other than inside a field. (To show the record is selected, ClarisWorks highlights the entire record.) Choose Delete Record, Cut, or Clear from the Edit menu. ClarisWorks removes the record from the database.

Entering and editing data

When a new record appears on screen in Browse mode, the cursor automatically appears in the first field (or in the field which you set as first with the Tab Order command). Complete the field and then press the Tab key to move to the next field. You can also move directly to any field by clicking it with the mouse. Note, however, that you cannot click in or tab to a field that does not allow user input — namely, calculation, summary, and record info fields.

You edit data in exactly the same manner as in any other text-oriented environment. After entering Browse mode (Shift-⌘-B) and tabbing or clicking into a field, you use normal editing techniques to add to, delete, or alter the information in any field.

If a record is substantially similar to an existing record, you can save typing time by creating a duplicate of the existing record and then making the necessary editing changes to the duplicate. To create a duplicate record, select the record and then choose Duplicate Record from the Edit menu (or press ⌘-D).

Navigating among records

You can move among the database records in Browse mode in a number of ways. The following options are available:

✦ *To move to the next or preceding record*, click the bottom or top page of the book icon (see Figure 5-33). In normal view, this action moves to the next or previous record. In Page View, it merely scrolls the records in the appropriate direction.

✦ *To move to the next or previous record while leaving the cursor in the same field*, press ⌘-Return or Shift-⌘-Return, respectively.

✦ *To move to a specific record (by number)*, drag the tab on the right side of the book icon until you see the record number; choose Go to Record from the Organize menu (or press ⌘-G); or click once to select the record number at the bottom of the book icon, type a record number, and press Return or Enter.

✦ *To move up or down through the records*, use the scroll bar at the right side of the database window or press Page Up or Page Down (if you are in Page View and your keyboard has these keys).

✦ *To move to a specific page of the database*, double-click the page number indicator at the bottom of the database window (you must be in Page View). The Go to Page dialog box appears. Type a page number and click OK.

✦ *To move to the beginning or end of the database*, press the Home or End keys (if you are in Page View and your keyboard has these keys), or drag the tab on the right side of the book icon until you reach the top or bottom.

Click to move to the previous record
Drag to any record number
Click to move to the next record
Click and type the record number to which you want to move

Figure 5-33: The book icon

List mode

Everything you can do in Browse mode can also be done in List mode, such as entering and editing data, and adding and deleting records. Working in List mode is a lot like using a spreadsheet — each row represents a single record, while each column is a single field. In normal view, fields are displayed in a continuous list that you can scroll to the right and left. In Page View (choose Page View from the Window menu), columns are separated by page breaks.

As the example in Figure 5-34 shows, all field types are displayed normally in List mode. You can still choose options from pop-up menu fields and value list fields, make checks in check box fields, and play movies in multimedia fields.

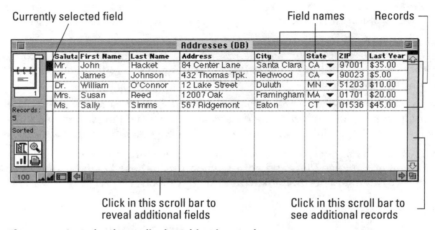

Figure 5-34: A database displayed in List mode

Here are some other things you can do in List mode:

✦ *Change column widths and record heights.* To change the width of a column, move the pointer into the column label area until it is over the right edge of the column whose width you want to change. The pointer changes to a tall double-arrow. Click and drag to change the column's width.

To change the height of any record, move the pointer into the area to the left of the first field for the record. The pointer changes to a tall double-arrow. When the pointer is over the bottom edge of the record of interest, click and drag to change the height of the record.

✦ *Move columns.* To move a column to a new position, move the pointer into the area just above the column of interest. The pointer changes to a short double-arrow. Click and then drag the column to a new position. Release the mouse button to complete the move.

✦ *Change the format of an entire column.* Double-click the column name. Depending on the field type of the column, the Text Style, Number Format, Date Format, Time Format, or Multimedia Field dialog box appears. Set options and click OK. Alternatively, for any field type other than multimedia, you can select the column and then choose options from the Format menu.

You may occasionally find it necessary to select individual or multiple rows or columns. To select an individual row or column, click in the area to the left of the row or in the column label.

To select several records (in order to format, hide, or delete them all at the same time, for example), select one and then Shift-click to select the others. To select multiple, noncontiguous records, hold down the ⌘ key as you click in each record. To select multiple columns (fields), Shift-click as you select the columns. You cannot select noncontiguous columns.

Finding and Selecting Records

Flipping through a database one record at a time is the hard way to find specific information. ClarisWorks has two different commands you can use to find and select records, based on criteria you supply. You use the Find command to restrict displayed records to a particular subset (the program temporarily hides all other records). For example, you may want to look only at records in which State equals Ohio. The Match Records command leaves all records visible and simply selects (highlights) those records that match the criteria.

Note

ClarisWorks 5.0 enables you to save search criteria so you can easily re-execute the search again whenever you like. Saved searches can also be used to create reports in the database report generator. Instructions for saving and reusing search criteria are presented later in this chapter.

Using the Find command

To search for records, you type search criteria on a blank copy of a record that appears when you issue the Find command. To find an exact or partial match, you simply type the text or number you want to search for in the appropriate field. To find all address records for people whose last name contains the string *Sch,* for example, you type **Sch** in the Last Name field. In this type of search, the program considers a record a match if it contains the string *anywhere within the field*, not just at the beginning of the field.

You can also use logical operators to specify search criteria, as described in Table 5-1.

Table 5-1
Logical Search Operators

Operator	Meaning	Examples
=	Find records that exactly match the contents of this field.	(=435; =18 Apple Street)
<	Find records that are numerically or alphabetically less than this value.	(<100; <S)
>	Find records that are numerically or alphabetically greater than this value.	(>180; >Bob)
≤ (Option-<)	Find records that are numerically or alphabetically less than or equal to this value.	(≤2000; ≤D)
≥ (Option->)	Find records that are numerically or alphabetically greater than or equal to this value.	(≥4/19/93; ≥3000)
<>	Find records that are not equal to this value.	(<>10; <>CA; <>11:15)

Note

To search for a blank database field, enter only an equal sign (=) in a field.

Steps: Finding Records

1. At the bottom of the Layout menu, choose the layout you want to use as a search template. (Be sure the fields you intend to use as criteria appear in the layout.)

2. Choose the Find command from the Layout menu (or press Shift-⌘-F). A screen with a blank record appears, as shown in Figure 5-35.

3. Type the search criteria into the appropriate fields.

4. *Optional*: If you want to find all records that do *not* match the search criteria, click the Omit check box.

5. Click the All radio button to search the entire database, or click Visible to search only visible records; that is, those not currently hidden. ClarisWorks conducts the search. It displays matching records and hides all others.

Search controls

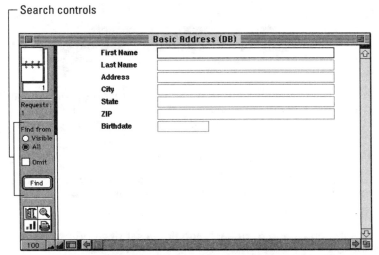

Figure 5-35: You type a search criteria into fields on a blank record.

Note

After you're through examining the records that match the criteria, you can make the entire database visible again by choosing Show All Records (Shift-⌘-A) from the Organize menu.

When you specify multiple criteria in a single Find request, you are conducting an *AND* search. In an AND search, ClarisWorks finds only records that satisfy all the criteria. For example, entering **Santa Clara** for the city and **CA** for the state identifies only the address records for people who come from Santa Clara, California. It does not find records for people from other California cities or from cities named Santa Clara in other states.

Sometimes, you may want to conduct an *OR* search — in which the program finds a record if the record matches any one of several criteria. To conduct this type of search, you have to issue multiple Find requests.

Steps: Conducting an OR Search

1. At the bottom of the Layout menu, choose the layout you want to use as a search template. (Be sure the fields you intend to use as criteria appear in the layout.)

2. Choose the Find command from the Layout menu (or press Shift-⌘-F). A screen with a blank record appears. (Note that even if you were previously in List mode, the Find screen is displayed as it would be in Browse mode for that layout.)

3. Enter a set of search criteria in the record.

4. Before clicking the All or Visible buttons, choose New Request from the Edit menu (or press ⌘-R). Another blank record appears.

5. Enter the next set of search criteria in the new record.

6. Repeat Steps 4 and 5 for each additional set of criteria you want to impose.

7. Click All to search the entire database or click Visible to search only the visible records; that is, the ones not currently hidden.

8. Click Find. The search is conducted. Records that satisfy any of the search requests are displayed and all others are hidden.

Tip

You can issue a Find command from any layout, as long as the fields on which you want to base the search are present. Some layouts, however, are easier to search from than others. A layout that is designed to print mailing labels, for example, makes the task more difficult because the fields are not labeled. Change to a better layout by selecting a layout from the bottom of the Layout menu before initiating the search. After the program finds the records, you can change back to the original layout to view or print the records.

Creating a named search

Although some Find requests are issued once and then never again (when you are searching for a particular record, for example), it's not uncommon to discover you are manually recreating many of the same Find requests over and over. Whether you are selecting important subsets of data to be used in a report or you simply want to look at all sales in a particular region of the country, you can save these Find requests — enabling you to instantly re-execute them whenever you wish.

Steps: Saving a Search Request

1. Choose New Search from the Search pop-up menu (the magnifying glass) in the Tool panel. The dialog box shown in Figure 5-36 appears.

Name for this search:

Search 1

After editing search name, press the enter key to edit search criteria.

Cancel   OK

Figure 5-36: This dialog box appears when you create a new search.

2. Enter a descriptive name for the search, and click OK to continue. A Find request form appears.

3. Enter the search criteria.

4. If you need to use additional Find requests, choose New Request from the Edit menu and enter the search criteria.

5. Click the Store button in the Tool panel or press Enter. The search name is appended to the Search pop-up menu.

After one or more named searches has been created, there are special procedures for using and modifying the searches.

✦ *To execute a named search*, choose its name from the Search pop-up menu.

✦ *To rename a named search*, choose Edit Searches from the Search pop-up menu, choose the named search from the Edit Searches dialog box (shown in Figure 5-37), click Modify, type a new name for the search, and click OK twice to dismiss the two dialog boxes.

✦ *To delete a named search*, choose Edit Searches from the Search pop-up menu, choose the search you wish to eliminate from the Edit Searches dialog box (shown in Figure 5-37), click Delete, and then click OK.

✦ *To edit the Find criteria associated with a named search*, change to Find mode (choose Find from the Layout menu or press Shift-⌘-F), choose the named search from the Search pop-up menu, modify the search criteria, and then click Store or press Enter.

Figure 5-37: The Edit Searches dialog box

There's one general type of named search you may want to add to every database you make — I call it the All search. Instead of trying to remember the command for Show All Records, just create a named search called All or All Records that finds all records in the database. In the Find request form, leave all the fields blank and click the Find from All radio button in the Tool panel.

Using the Match Records command

The Find command is intended for simple searches. If you want to perform a more complex search, you may prefer to use the Match Records feature. A Match Records search selects (highlights) all records that meet the criteria, but it leaves the other records on screen. Because the records are selected (highlighted), using Match Records is an ideal way to identify and delete records you no longer need.

Steps: Selecting Matching Records

1. Choose Match Records from the Organize menu (or press ⌘-M). The Enter Match Records Condition dialog box appears, as shown in Figure 5-38. It is identical to the dialog box you use to define a formula for a calculation field or a summary field.

2. Enter the match formula in the Formula box. You can create formulas by typing them into the box; by selecting fields, operators, and functions from the three scrolling list boxes (click an option to insert it into the formula at the text insertion point); or by combining the two approaches. Field names must be enclosed in single quotes (') and text strings in double quotes ("). The formula shown in Figure 5-38 instructs ClarisWorks to select all records with zip codes that are greater than 80000 and less than 90000.

Figure 5-38: Use this dialog box to specify the search conditions formula.

3. Click OK. ClarisWorks evaluates the formula. If it finds an error, it displays the message *Bad formula.* Otherwise, it highlights the records that match the formula.

After using the Match Records command to select a set of records, you can use two additional commands from the Organize menu to help you focus your attention on the new record subset: Hide Selected (⌘-left parenthesis) and Hide Unselected (⌘-right parenthesis). Hide Unselected has the same effect as the normal Find command. It hides all records that do not match the Match Records formula; that is, the ones that were not selected. Hide Selected has the same effect as a Find command with the Omit check box checked — it displays only those records that were not selected.

You also can use the Hide Selected and Hide Unselected commands after you manually select records. To select a single record, click anywhere in the record except in a field. To select multiple, contiguous records, hold down the Shift key as you select the records. To select noncontiguous records, hold down the ⌘ key as you select the records.

Perhaps the most important reason for using the Match Records command is you want to do something to all members of the selected (or unselected) group. You can view them in context in Browse or List mode (viewing the records of all employees who have not had raises in the last two years, for example).

You can also use Match Records to help purge the database of unwanted records. For instance, you may want to eliminate all invoice records that are more than three years old. After using Match Records to identify the correct records, choose Delete Record from the Edit menu.

In previous versions of ClarisWorks, deleting a record or group of records was difficult to reverse. As long as you had not saved the changes, the best you could do was to restore the database to its state as of the last time it was saved by choosing Revert from the File menu or by closing the database without saving the changes. In ClarisWorks 5.0, however, after deleting one or more records, the Undo command is now changed to read Undo Clear. You can choose this command to restore the deleted records.

Changing the display order of records

You can change the order in which records are displayed by sorting them by the contents of one or several fields. You can do an ascending (A to Z) or descending (Z to A) sort for each sort field. ClarisWorks sorts the database once for each sort field, using the order in which you selected the sort fields. Sorting changes the order of records in the database for all layouts, not just for the one currently displayed.

Steps: Sorting Records

1. Choose Sort Records from the Organize menu (or press ⌘-J). The Sort Records dialog box appears, as shown in Figure 5-39. (If you have previously sorted the database, the program displays the most recent sort instructions.)

Figure 5-39: The Sort Records dialog box

2. Choose the first sort field from the list on the left. To add the field to the Sort Order list, click Move or simply double-click the field name in the Field List. ClarisWorks adds the field to the Sort Order list on the right.

   If you make a mistake (choosing fields in the wrong order, for example), you can start over by clicking Clear, or you can remove individual fields by selecting them in the Sort Order list and clicking Move.

3. To specify an ascending or descending sort for each chosen field, select it in the Sort Order list and then click the Ascending Order or Descending Order radio button.

   Alternatively, you can specify an ascending or descending order sort by clicking the appropriate radio button *before* moving the field into the Sort Order list.

4. Choose additional sort fields by repeating Steps 2 and 3, as required.

5. Click OK to execute the sort instructions. The program displays the records in the new order.

Note

If a layout has sub-summary fields, you have to sort the database by the designated sort field if you want the summary information to be displayed. For example, if you have created a sub-summary when sorted by last name, you must sort by last name. (See "Summary fields" earlier in this chapter for more information.)

New In Version 5

You can also manually reorganize records using drag-and-drop. Simply select the records you want to move and drag them to the desired position in the database. You can accomplish this maneuver in List mode or in Browse mode (when Show Multiple is checked in the Layout menu).

You can save sort criteria so you can easily re-execute a sort whenever you like. Named (saved) sorts can also be used to create reports in the report generator (discussed in "Creating and using named reports," later in this chapter).

Steps: Creating Named Sorts

1. Choose New Sort from the Sort pop-up menu (the three rising bars) in the Tool panel. The Sort Records dialog box appears, as shown in Figure 5-40.

(continued)

The name of the sort appears and
can be changed in this text-edit box

Figure 5-40: This Sort Records dialog box differs from the normal
one only in that it has a box at the bottom in which you can name
the sort.

2. Enter a descriptive name for the sort.

3. Select the sort fields and set ascending or descending order for each one.

4. Click OK. The sort name is appended to the Sort pop-up menu.

After one or more named sorts has been created, there are special procedures for
using and modifying the sorts.

✦ *To execute a named sort*, choose its name from the Sort pop-up menu.

✦ *To rename or edit a named sort*, choose Edit Sorts from the Sort pop-up menu,
choose the sort from the Edit Sorts dialog box, and click Modify. The Sort
Records dialog box appears (previously shown in Figure 5-40). Type a new
name for the sort and/or modify the sort instructions, and then click OK
twice to dismiss the two dialog boxes.

✦ *To delete a named sort*, choose Edit Sorts from the Sort pop-up menu, select
the name of the sort you wish to eliminate from the Edit Sorts dialog box,
click Delete, and then click OK.

Creating Reports

One of the main reasons for building a database is the ease with which you can
create custom reports and mailing labels. Although you can print any layout,
creating special layouts for reports often makes more sense, especially if you
design layouts that show the particular fields and summary information you
require, organized in a manner that makes sense for a report.

To make it easy to recreate a given report, you can select report elements —
including sort instructions, record selection criteria, and the appropriate layout —
and save them as a custom report. Details are provided later in this chapter.

Adding headers and footers

You can add a header and a footer to a database layout. A header or footer
appears in every report page and can be used to show a title or page numbers, for
example. To create a header or footer, switch to the appropriate layout and then
change to Layout mode. Choose Insert Part from the Layout menu. The Insert Part
dialog box appears. Click the Header or Footer radio button and then click OK. A
header or footer area is inserted at the top (header) or bottom (footer) of the
current layout.

You can add graphics or text in the header or footer area. Whatever you insert will
appear in that position at the top or bottom of every page. To see how the header
or footer will look when printed, change to Browse mode (Shift-⌘-B) and choose
Page View (Shift-⌘-P) from the Window menu.

Tip

Headers and footers frequently include a report date and page numbers. To add
automatic page numbering (so page numbers increment by one for each new page)
and date- or time-stamping, select the appropriate layout, change to Layout mode,
select the text tool, click the spot in the header or footer where you want to place
the element, and then choose Insert Page #, Insert Date, or Insert Time from the
Edit menu. You should note, however, that every time you open the database, the
date and time change to match the current date and time. If you want to insert the
current date or time and make sure it does not change, press the Option key when
you choose Insert Date or Insert Time.

Calculating summary and sub-summary information

By creating summary fields and adding them to a layout, you can calculate statistics
that span the entire database or that summarize data based on record groupings
(generating subtotals for each type of household expense, for example). Summary
information can come at the beginning or end of a report or be displayed at the
break between each group of records. And you aren't restricted to just totals. You
can use any formula you like, as well as take advantage of the dozens of database
functions ClarisWorks offers. For instructions on adding summary and sub-summary
fields to a database, see "Summary fields" earlier in this chapter.

Creating and using named reports

Using the Report pop-up menu in the Tool panel, you can save reporting options
and later reuse them to produce complex reports quickly. To create a named
report, choose New Report from the Report pop-up menu in the Tool panel. The
New Report dialog box appears, as shown in Figure 5-41.

Figure 5-41: The New Report dialog box

Enter a name for the report here

Report options

As you can see in Figure 5-41, creating a report consists of the following tasks:

✦ Naming the report (in the Report Name box)

✦ Choosing a layout for the report, search criteria, and sort instructions

✦ Deciding whether or not the report should automatically be printed

Layout choices are restricted to the names of existing layouts, List mode, and None. Search and sort criteria are limited to None or existing named searches and sorts that have been saved for the database. After making your choices, click OK. The name of the new report is added to the Report pop-up menu for the database.

To produce a named report, choose its name from the Report pop-up menu in the Tool panel. The database instantly changes to the selected layout and executes the designated search and sort instructions, if any. If you also clicked the Print the Report check box in the New Report dialog box, a standard Print dialog box appears. Turn on your printer, change options in the Print dialog box (if necessary), and click the Print button.

To modify any of the elements of the report, choose Edit Reports from the Report pop-up menu, select the name of the report in the Named Reports dialog box that appears, click Modify, make the changes, and then click OK twice to dismiss the dialog boxes.

To delete a report, choose Edit Reports from the Report pop-up menu, select the name of the report in the Named Reports dialog box that appears, click Delete, and then click OK.

Working with mailing labels

Although you can design your own layouts for printing labels, ClarisWorks comes with more than 50 predefined layouts for popular Avery labels. And if you don't find a layout to match the size of labels you use, you can easily create a custom layout.

Steps: Using a Predefined Label Layout

1. Choose New Layout from the Layout menu or the Layout pop-up menu in the Tool panel. The New Layout dialog box appears.

2. Click the Labels radio button and then click its pop-up menu. A list of the supported label formats pops up. (If you aren't using an Avery label, measure your label and match it to the equivalent Avery label format or create a custom label layout by following the instructions in "Steps: Creating a Custom Label Layout," later in this chapter.)

3. Choose a label format and click OK. The Set Field Order dialog box appears, as shown in Figure 5-42.

Figure 5-42: The Set Field Order dialog box

4. Select fields in the order in which you want them to appear on the labels and click Move to transfer each field to the Field Order list box.

5. Click OK. The label layout appears.

    In Step 1, if you chose New Layout from the Layout pop-up menu rather than choosing this command from the Layout menu, you will now be in Browse mode. Change to Layout mode by choosing Layout from the Layout menu.

6. Resize and move the fields to correspond with the way they should appear on the labels. Figure 5-43 shows a typical layout after editing.

(continued)

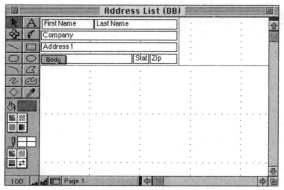

Figure 5-43: A sample label layout

7. If you want an idea of how the labels will look, choose Browse from the Layout menu (or press Shift-⌘-B). Make sure Page View (Shift-⌘-P) is also in effect. (Note that the space between fields, as well as blank lines, will be closed up when you print the labels but not when you view them on screen.)

As an alternative, you can create a new view, tile windows, and have one view in Layout mode and one in Browse mode — giving instant feedback.

Note

To print properly, many of the label layouts require that you set *Larger Print Area* (or *US Letter* rather than *US Letter Small*) in the Page Setup dialog box.

Note

ClarisWorks has unusual requirements you need to adhere to when attempting to close up space during printing. These requirements apply not only to labels but also to any other type of database layout:

✦ *Objects do not slide toward other objects smaller than they are.* In order for a field to slide left, therefore, the field to the left must be exactly the same size or larger than the sliding field. Also, the top edges must be aligned if the fields are on the same line. The left edges must be aligned if fields are stacked one above the other (on different lines).

To check the dimensions of each field, choose Object Size from the Options menu and then click each field. The Size palette lists each field's distance from the margins, as well as its height and width. (See Chapter 6 for information on using the Size palette to set the dimensions of an object.)

✦ Fields will not slide at all if their edges are touching on the layout.

Also, if you are using a laser printer, you should note that the printer cannot print on the entire page. Most laser printers require a minimum margin of 0.2 to 0.25 inches all around the page. To ensure you can print as close to the edges as possible, choose Page Setup from the File menu, click Options, and then click the check box for Larger Print Area (Fewer Downloadable Fonts). Note that if you have the LaserWriter 8.4.3 driver installed (standard with OS 8), you should choose US Letter rather than US Letter Small under Page Attributes.

Finally, because it's difficult to get text to align perfectly on labels, you're well advised to print a test page on standard paper and then place the test printout over a page of labels to see how they align. Continue to adjust the fields and make test printouts until the alignment is correct.

If you don't see a predefined label format that matches the labels you want to use, you can create a custom label layout.

Steps: Creating a Custom Label Layout

1. Choose New Layout from the Layout menu or the Layout pop-up menu in the Tool panel. The New Layout dialog box appears.

2. Click the Labels radio button and be sure the Custom option is selected.

3. Enter a descriptive name for the label layout in the Name box and click OK. The Label Layout dialog box appears, as shown in Figure 5-44.

Figure 5-44: The Label Layout dialog box

(continued)

4. Enter the number of labels across (enter **3** for a page with three labels across it, for example) and the dimensions for a single label, and then click OK. The Set Field Order dialog box appears (refer to Figure 5-42).

You measure the width of a label from the left edge of the first label to the left edge of the next label. Similarly, you measure label height from the top of one label to the top of the label below it. That is, the gaps that follow each label to the right and below are considered part of the label's size.

5. Select the fields you want to appear on the labels, click the Move button to transfer them to the Field Order list, and click OK. The new layout appears.

In Step 1, if you chose New Layout from the Layout pop-up menu rather than choosing this command from the Layout menu, you will now be in Browse mode. Change to Layout mode by choosing Layout from the Layout menu.

6. Resize and move the fields to correspond with the way they should appear on the labels. The initial placement of the body dividing line is correct for the size of label specified. Do not move it, and be sure all fields stay within its boundaries.

7. If you want an idea of how the labels will look, choose Browse from the Layout menu (or press Shift-⌘-B). Make sure Page View (Shift-⌘-P) is also in effect. (Note that the space between fields, as well as blank lines, will be closed up when you print the labels but not when you view them on screen.)

Note

If you want to eliminate some of the fuss of creating mailing labels, you can use the Create Labels Assistant. From any appropriate database, choose ClarisWorks Assistants from the Balloon Help menu or Help menu, and then choose Create Labels. Follow the steps in the series of dialog boxes that are presented. When you are finished, the Assistant generates a new label layout that matches the specifications you just entered.

Creating and Saving Custom Label Definitions

All permanent label layout definitions are stored in a text file named ClarisWorks Labels. By editing this file, you can add your own custom label definitions, as well as change the names of existing layouts (*Diskette Label — 3-up*, rather than *Avery 5096, 5196, 5896*, for example). After you make the changes to the file, you can choose your own label definitions from the Labels pop-up menu in the New Layout dialog box.

To create a new label definition:

1. Locate the ClarisWorks Labels file. It is inside the Claris folder, located inside the System Folder on the start-up hard disk.

2. Select the ClarisWorks Labels icon and choose Duplicate from the Finder's File menu (or press ⌘-D). The file is copied and named ClarisWorks Labels Copy. (Making a duplicate protects the original file.)

3. To protect the original ClarisWorks Labels file, change its name (to ClarisWorks Labels.bak, for example). Keep it as a backup copy in case you have problems with the editing.

4. Load the duplicate copy of the ClarisWorks Labels file into ClarisWorks using the Open command. The file is loaded and converted from plain text to ClarisWorks format. The following figure shows the contents of the ClarisWorks Labels file.

   As you can see in the figure, every label definition consists of eight lines: the label name enclosed in brackets, the number of columns, the horizontal pitch (label width), the vertical pitch (label height), the top margin, the bottom margin, the left margin, and the right margin. (Ignore any information that is preceded by two or more slashes [//]; it is a comment.)

5. Use one of the existing label definitions as a template for designing a new label. Select any eight-line segment, starting with a label name and ending with its right-margin data. Choose Copy from the Edit menu (or press ⌘-C).

6. Select the spot in the label list where you want to insert the new label definition. You may want to keep your own definitions together — at the end of the list, for example.

7. Place the text insertion marker at the spot where you want to insert the definition and choose Paste from the Edit menu (or press ⌘-V). Be sure you do not break up an existing definition when you paste the template.

8. Edit the pasted text by entering your own label name within the brackets and replacing the other lines with the number of columns, width, height, top margin, bottom margin, left margin, and right margin for your label.

9. Save the file by choosing the Save As command from the File menu (or pressing Shift-⌘-S). Choose Text in the Save As pop-up menu, click the Document radio button, and enter **ClarisWorks Labels** as the new filename.

(continued)

(continued)

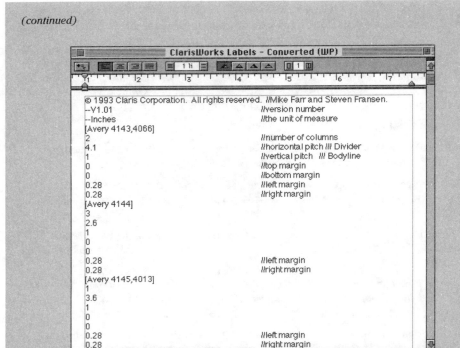

```
┌──────────────────────────────────────────────────────────────┐
│ ≣≣≣≣≣ ClarisWorks Labels - Converted (WP) ≣≣≣≣≣                 │
├──────────────────────────────────────────────────────────────┤
│ © 1993 Claris Corporation. All rights reserved. //Mike Farr and Steven Fransen.│
│ --V1.01                              //version number          │
│ --Inches                             //the unit of measure     │
│ [Avery 4143,4066]                                              │
│ 2                                    //number of columns       │
│ 4.1                                  //horizontal pitch /// Divider│
│ 1                                    //vertical pitch  /// Bodyline│
│ 0                                    //top margin              │
│ 0                                    //bottom margin           │
│ 0.28                                 //left margin             │
│ 0.28                                 //right margin            │
│ [Avery 4144]                                                   │
│ 3                                                              │
│ 2.6                                                            │
│ 1                                                              │
│ 0                                                              │
│ 0                                                              │
│ 0.28                                 //left margin             │
│ 0.28                                 //right margin            │
│ [Avery 4145,4013]                                             │
│ 1                                                              │
│ 3.6                                                            │
│ 1                                                              │
│ 0                                                              │
│ 0                                                              │
│ 0.28                                 //left margin             │
│ 0.28                                 //right margin            │
│ 100   Page 1                                                   │
└──────────────────────────────────────────────────────────────┘
```

10. Quit ClarisWorks. The next time you launch ClarisWorks, the new label layouts will be available.

Changing the name for any of the existing label layouts is even easier. Simply follow the preceding steps, but — instead of adding an entirely new layout — just change the text string between any pair of brackets to something more meaningful, such as [Audio Cassette 2-up] rather than [Avery 5198]. After you change the name for a label layout and save the file, the new name appears in the Labels pop-up menu.

Database printing

To generate a printed database report or other printout from a database, you can just select an appropriate layout and choose Print. However, you can also set other options to make reports and printouts more meaningful. (Every printout can consist of all visible — nonhidden — records or only the currently selected record.)

Steps: Printing from a Database

1. From the bottom of the Layout menu, choose the layout you want to use to generate the printout.

2. Use the Find command (see "Finding and Selecting Records," earlier in this chapter) to select the records you want to include. If you want to use all of the records, choose Show All Records from the Organize menu (or press Shift-⌘-A).

3. If you want the records to display in a particular order, sort the records (as described in "Changing the display order of records," earlier in this chapter).

4. Choose Print from the File menu (or press ⌘-P). The Print dialog box appears, as shown in Figure 5-45.

Click one of these buttons to
determine what will be printed

Figure 5-45: The Print dialog box, as it appears when you are printing a ClarisWorks database. (This Print dialog box is for a LaserWriter; dialog boxes for other printers are different.)

5. Click the Current Record or Visible Records radio button at the bottom of the dialog box, depending on what you want to print.

6. Click Print to send the report to the printer. (Chapter 1 explains other Print and Page Setup options.)

Saving Changes

If you've used FileMaker Pro or any of its earlier incarnations, you've undoubtedly noticed the many features it shares with the ClarisWorks database environment. One of the major differences, however, is the way the two programs handle data and layout storage.

FileMaker Pro automatically saves any database changes, whether they are layout modifications or data additions, deletions, or alterations. In fact, FileMaker Pro doesn't even have a Save command. The plus side of this feature is users never have to worry about whether their changes have been saved. The minus side is the program saves *all* changes — both deliberate changes and unintentional or ill-advised changes. Unless you have a backup of your important FileMaker files, experimentation can be dangerous.

ClarisWorks, on the other hand, does not have an automatic-save feature. You can experiment to your heart's content, secure in the knowledge that you can close the file at any time without saving changes. When you do want to save, on the other hand, choose the Save or Save As command from the File menu.

Importing and Exporting Data

Unless you just bought your Mac, you may already have several databases you designed in other programs. They may be FileMaker Pro or HyperCard databases, or they may be databases you created in an address book program, a word processor, a spreadsheet, or a desk accessory. You can easily import databases into ClarisWorks.

You use the Insert command in the File menu to add information from other databases into a ClarisWorks database. Instead of reorganizing the source database so its fields match those of the target ClarisWorks database, you use the Import Field Order dialog box to match fields between the two databases — regardless of their order and whether the databases have the same number of fields. Thus, importing data is easier than ever.

Steps: Importing Information into a ClarisWorks Database

1. In the source program, save or export the data file as a tab-delimited text file. Some programs, such as spreadsheets, may call this a Text file, ASCII Text file, or Text-Only file. See the program's manual for instructions. (In a tab-delimited text file, each record is a separate paragraph. Every field in a record is separated from the next field by a tab character.)

2. Open or create a ClarisWorks database to receive the imported data. Switch to Browse mode.

3. In ClarisWorks, choose the Insert command from the File menu, choose the tab-delimited text file created in Step 1, and click Insert. The Import Field Order dialog box appears, as shown in Figure 5-46. The fields in the left side of the dialog box are from the file you're importing (the source file). The fields on the right are in the ClarisWorks database (the destination file).

4. Drag to rearrange the fields in the right side of the dialog box so they match the appropriate fields on the left side. Fields with a counterpart you want to import should have a check mark in front of them. Fields with no counterpart are indicated by ellipses (...) and are not imported. You can click a check mark or ellipses to toggle to the opposite state.

Figure 5-46: The Import Field Order dialog box

 Note

Not every field needs to have a counterpart. You may well have more fields in one database than in the other. No restrictions govern how many or how few fields you can import. If you find, however, that the target ClarisWorks database lacks a key field the source file possesses, you may want to cancel the import, add the new field to the ClarisWorks database, and then proceed with the import.

5. Using the Scan Data buttons, check several records of the source file to see whether the fields match correctly. If you're satisfied with the way they match, click OK to import the data. The new records are imported into the database.

As with importing data, when you export data from a ClarisWorks database to use in another program, tab-delimited ASCII text is often the best format to use. Virtually every type of Macintosh program (including word processors) can correctly handle such a file. (A tab-delimited text file contains one record per line, and each field in the record is separated from the next field by a tab character.)

Steps: Exporting a ClarisWorks Database File

1. Open the ClarisWorks database by choosing Open from the File menu (or press ⌘-O).

2. Choose Save As from the File menu (or press Shift-⌘-S).

3. Choose ASCII Text from the Save As pop-up menu, click the Document radio button, and enter a new filename for the export file. (If the receiving program can read other formats, you also can choose a DBF, DIF, or SYLK format for the exported data.)

4. Click Save to save the file.

5. In the destination program, open or import the file. (See the program's manual for instructions on opening or importing foreign files.)

New In
Version 5

In ClarisWorks 5.0, you can also use drag-and-drop to move records between databases. Wherever field names are identical in the two databases (Last Name and Last Name, for example), the data will transfer correctly.

Using a Spreadsheet to Clean Up Import Data

Although you can use the Import Field Order dialog box to match fields as well as possible when you import data into a database, the match between fields isn't always as clean as it could be. When you import address data, for example, two problems are common:

✦ The address, phone number, or name fields in the import file are split into two fields (address line 1 and address line 2, area code and phone number, and first name and last name), but they are in one field in the ClarisWorks database — or vice versa.

✦ Zip codes shorter than five digits are missing the leading zero (1276 rather than 01276).

Instead of importing the data as is and cleaning it up in the database afterward, you can use the ClarisWorks spreadsheet to make the necessary transformations to the data and do it more efficiently. Using the spreadsheet changes the steps in the ClarisWorks database import process.

To use a spreadsheet to import data:

1. Export the data from the database, spreadsheet, or address book program as a tab-delimited ASCII text file.

2. Open the ASCII text file as a ClarisWorks spreadsheet; make the transformations to the data, creating new fields as necessary; and save the revised file as an ASCII text file again.

3. Open the ClarisWorks database and use the Insert command to import the ASCII text file into the database.

The simplest way to make the transformations in the spreadsheet is to create additional columns at the right end of the spreadsheet. Each column will contain a formula that combines or converts one or more columns of the original data. After you create the appropriate formula, use the Fill Down command (⌘-D) to copy it into the remaining cells in the column. The following figures illustrate three typical conversions.

In the first figure, Column A contains first names, and Column B contains last names. The combination formula in the entry bar, =A2&" "&B2, takes the first name in cell A2 (Jim), adds a space to it (" "), and then adds the last name from cell B2 (Abrams) to the end of the text string. The combined fields appear in Column C as one name.

The second figure is an example of combining two address fields into a single address field. Unlike the names in the preceding example, some addresses contain only one part. The equation =IF(B2<>"",A2&", "&B2,A2) checks to see whether the address has a second part (B2<>""). If the second portion is not blank, the formula combines the two portions, separating them with a comma followed by a blank, for example *18 Maple Terrace, Box 432*. If the address does not have a second part, the formula simply copies the first address part (A2) into the cell.

(continued)

(continued)

In the example in the third figure, a leading zero is added to four-digit zip codes. Because zip codes are often treated as numbers, the leading zero may disappear, resulting in an improper four-digit code. The lengthy formula =IF(LEN(A2)=4,"0"&A2, NUMTOTEXT(A2)) checks to see whether the length of the zip code is four digits — LEN(A2)=4. If so, a leading zero is appended to the zip code — "0"&A2, and the zip code is converted to text. If the zip code does not contain four digits, it is converted to text and passed through unaltered — NUMTOTEXT(A2)). Converting zip codes to text is necessary to display leading zeroes and to handle blank zip codes. If the formula simply ended with A2, rather than with NUMTO-TEXT(A2), a blank zip code would translate as a 0 (zero).

	ZIPs converted (SS)			
B2	▼ fx × ✓	=IF(LEN(A2)=4,"0"&A2,NUMTOTEXT(A2))		
	A	**B**	**C**	**D**
1	ZIP	Converted		
2	55067	55067		
3	1759	01759		
4	80096	80096		
5	90057	90057		
6	7097	07097		

Down to Business: Creating a Credit Card Charge Tracker

If all you want to do is keep track of how you're doing on your credit cards, you don't need a dedicated home finance program. You can use a simple ClarisWorks database to record charges and payments, as well as to show how you're doing overall. Figure 5-47 shows what the charge card database you're about to create looks like.

This database enables you to record the following information for every charge: the date of the transaction, the store or business where the charge was made, a description of what was charged, the amount of the charge, and the particular credit card that was used.

Figure 5-47: The Credit Card Charges database

Defining fields for the database

Start by creating a new database and then define the fields listed in Table 5-2.

Table 5-2
Fields for the Credit Card Charges Database

Field Name	Type	Formula/Description
Date	Date	
Store	Text	
Item Description	Text	

(continued)

Table 5-2 *(continued)*		
Field Name	*Type*	*Formula/Description*
Amount	Number	
Charge Card	Value List	American Express, MasterCard, Discover, Visa, and so on
Paid?	Check Box	
Outstanding amount	Calculation	IF('Paid?'=1,0,'Amount')
Charge Total	Summary	SUM('Outstanding amount') (Sub-summary by Charge Card)
Grand Total	Summary	SUM('Outstanding amount') (Trailing grand summary)

The first four fields (*Date, Store, Item Description,* and *Amount*) are self-explanatory. To save typing time and ensure accurate, consistent spelling, *Charge Card* is declared as a value list field and contains a list of the names of all charge cards you intend to track. When you select the Charge Card field in the database (by clicking the field or tabbing into it), the Charge Card field displays a pop-up list of your credit cards.

When you define Charge Card as a value list field, the Options dialog box automatically opens. Create a value list that consists of the names of all the credit cards you intend to track. If you like, you can also specify a default charge card by entering its name in the Default Data section of the dialog box. Finally, click in the Cannot Be Empty and Alerts for Unlisted Values check boxes in the Data Verification section of the dialog box. This ensures that you will receive a warning if you neglect to choose a credit card for a record or if you manually enter an unlisted card. (If you later get a new credit card, you should edit this value list to include that card.) Click OK to dismiss the Options dialog box.

Paid? is a check box field. After defining the Paid? field, select it in the Field Name List, and click Options. In the Options dialog box, delete the text in the Label for Checkbox box, remove the check mark from Initially Checked, and click OK.

Outstanding Amount is a calculation field used to determine whether each charge has already been reconciled (paid). If paid (that is, there is a check in the Paid? check box — which is interpreted as a 1), Outstanding Amount is set to 0 (zero). Otherwise, it is set to whatever number is currently in the Amount field for the record. Unlike the other database fields, Outstanding Amount is not displayed in the layout. It is, however, used to generate the Charge Total for each credit card, as well as the Grand Total (the total amount of all outstanding charges for all cards). Define Outstanding Amount as a calculation field, using the formula shown in Table 5-2.

Charge Total is a summary field that calculates an individual charge total for each credit card when the database is sorted by Charge Card. To create the Charge Total field, enter its name in the Define Database Fields dialog box, choose Summary as the field type, and then click Create. A new dialog box appears in which you can enter the formula shown in Table 5-2. Indicate that you wish the result to be formatted as a number.

Define *Grand Total* using the same technique just used for Charge Total. As Table 5-2 shows, Grand Total uses the same formula as Charge Total.

After creating all the fields and clicking Done, a default layout appears. You won't actually use this temporary layout in the database. The next section describes how to make the real layout.

Making the layout

This database requires only one layout. Not only will it serve for data entry, it will also display on-screen and printed reports.

Steps: Designing the Layout

1. Choose New Layout from the Layout menu or the Layout pop-up menu in the Tool panel.

2. In the dialog box that appears, name the layout *Data Entry*, click the Columnar Report radio button, and then click OK.

3. In the Set Field Order dialog box that appears, select every field except Outstanding Amount and click Move. In order, the fields should be: Date, Store, Item Description, Amount, Charge Card, and Paid? Click OK to create the columnar layout.

4. Change to Layout mode and arrange these fields (in the body) and their respective labels (in the header) so they look like the layout in Figure 5-48.

(continued)

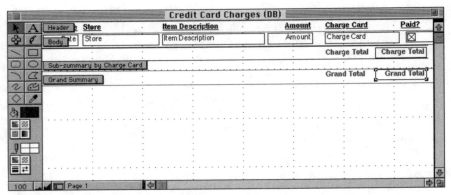

Figure 5-48: The final layout

5. To create the Charge Total sub-summary shown in Figure 5-48, choose Insert Part from the Layout menu. Then choose Sub-summary when sorted by Charge Card and click OK. Click Below in the dialog box that follows. The sub-summary part is added to the layout.

6. To create the Grand Total summary, choose Insert Part from the Layout menu. Then choose Trailing Grand Summary and click OK. The grand summary part is added to the bottom of the layout.

7. To insert the two summary fields into the layout, choose Insert Field from the Layout menu and then double-click Charge Total and Grand Total. After the fields are placed in the layout, drag them to the locations shown in Figure 5-48.

You can add several finishing touches to embellish the database layout:

✦ Set the font and size of all fields to Helvetica 10 point. (Choose Select All from the Edit menu, choose Helvetica from the Font submenu of the Format menu, and choose 10 from the Size submenu of the Format menu.)

✦ Add boldface to the Charge Total and Grand Total fields by selecting the fields and choosing Bold from the Style submenu of the Format menu.

✦ Set right justification as the text alignment for the Date, Amount, Charge Total, and Grand Total fields; set center justification for the Paid? field.

✦ Apply the Currency format to all monetary fields (Amount, Charge Total, Grand Total) by selecting the fields and then choosing Field Format from the Options menu.

✦ Change the height of all the fields in the body of the layout by selecting them, choosing Object Size from the Options menu, and typing **.18** in the Height box of the Size windoid. (The Height box is second from the bottom of the windoid.)

✦ Above and below the Charge Total field, add solid lines that extend the full width of the page.

✦ Drag the Header and Body dividers up to reduce the space they take up in the layout.

Now that the real layout has been created, you can safely discard the original layout. Choose Edit Layouts from the Layout menu, select Layout 1 in the Current Layouts list, and click the Delete button.

Save the database by choosing Save As from the File menu, clicking the Document radio button, entering a name, and clicking Save.

Using the database

Using the database is fairly simple. The basic procedures include starting up, entering new records, establishing a sort order in which to display the records, reconciling the individual charges with payments made to the credit card companies, and deleting records.

Starting up

The first time you use the database, you are likely to have outstanding balances on some of your credit cards. If so, create a Beginning balance record for each charge card, as shown in Figure 5-47. As you pay off (or pay down) the balance, you will reduce it by your payment amounts (as described in "Reconciling the charge statement," later in this chapter).

Entering new charges

Whenever you have a new charge to enter, choose New Record from the Edit menu (or press ⌘-R). A new record appears, and you can enter the charge details. Leave the Paid? field blank (unchecked).

Note

When entering and editing data, you can work in Page view (Page View is checked in the Window menu) or in Normal view (Page View is unchecked in the Window menu). The choice is up to you.

Establishing a sort order

Although you can leave the records in the order in which you enter them, this order complicates reconciliation and makes finding specific records difficult. Furthermore, the Charge Total summaries won't be available to you. You can solve all of these problems by specifying a sort order for the database.

Choose Sort Records from the Organize menu (or press ⌘-J), set ascending sorts for the Charge Card and Date fields (in that order), and then click OK. ClarisWorks sorts the database by charge card and, within each charge card, by date of purchase. If the Charge Totals are still not visible, make sure you have selected Page View from the Window menu.

Each time you finish entering new records, be sure to sort the database again.

Reconciling the charge statement

When a charge statement arrives in the mail, you can reconcile it in one of two ways, depending on whether you pay off the entire balance or pay less than the balance due.

Steps: Reconciling a Statement When You Pay Off the Entire Balance

1. Check each record against the statement to make sure it contains no mistakes.

2. Click in the Paid? check box for each record on the statement (marking them as paid). The Charge Total for that credit card should now show as 0 (zero).

Steps: Reconciling a Statement When You Pay Off Less Than the Entire Balance

1. Check each record against the statement to make sure it contains no mistakes.

2. Subtract the amount you intend to pay on this statement from any of the outstanding charges for that credit card.

For example, suppose you have $500 worth of Visa charges in your database ($300 of it as the beginning balance and two other charges of $100 each). If you are paying $75 today, you can edit any of the original Amount fields for that card by subtracting the $75 payment. Thus, you could reduce the $300 beginning balance to $225, for example.

If you are paying $100, you can simply mark one of the $100 charges as paid (which would instantly remove that amount from the Charge Total for the credit card).

Remember, the object is to show the correct outstanding amount for each card (the Charge Total). What the individual charges show is irrelevant — at least after you've verified that the credit card company has recorded them correctly.

Deleting records

After you've paid off some charges, you can, at your option, delete their records to prevent them from cluttering up the database. (However, you may want to make a printout of the database for your permanent records first.) The simplest way to remove all the paid records is to use the Match Records command.

Steps: Selecting and Deleting the Paid Records

1. Choose Match Records from the Organize menu (or press ⌘-M). The Match Records dialog box appears.

2. Enter the formula shown below and then click OK. The records that have been paid are selected.

   ```
   'Paid?'=1
   ```

   Instead of trying to remember this formula, you can create a ClarisWorks macro to type it for you and delete the paid records. (See Chapter 13 for instructions.)

3. Choose Clear from the Edit menu. The paid records are removed from the database.

Quick Tips

The following quick tips suggest some simple ways to empty a database field for an entire database; perform date calculations; and use the spelling checker, thesaurus, and stylesheet in databases.

In addition, a final tip lists several programs to consider when you're ready for a more powerful database.

Emptying a database field for an entire database

Suppose you want to erase the contents of a single field within every record in a database. The database environment does not provide an easy way to perform this task, but you can do it if you enlist the spreadsheet to help.

Steps: Emptying a Database Field

1. Open the database in ClarisWorks and choose the Save As command from the File menu (or press Shift-⌘-S).

2. Save the file in ASCII text format (choose this option from the Save As pop-up menu) and enter a new filename.

3. Choose Open from the File menu (or press ⌘-O), and choose Spreadsheet from the Document Type pop-up menu. The ASCII text file appears in the file list.

4. Choose the ASCII text file and click Open. The text file is converted to a spreadsheet that has one database field in each column.

5. Select the column of data that corresponds to the database field you want to empty — *Phone* in this example. (Click the letter at the top of a column to select the column.)

6. Choose Clear from the Edit menu. The cells are cleared.

7. Save the file as text again by choosing Save As from the File menu, choosing ASCII Text in the Save As pop-up menu, and changing the filename back to the one you used in Step 2. This step replaces the original ASCII text file with the modified version you just created in the spreadsheet.

8. Switch to the database screen. Choose Show All Records from the Organize menu (Shift-⌘-A), followed by Select All from the Edit menu (⌘-A). All records in the database are highlighted/selected.

9. Choose Clear from the Edit menu to remove all records simultaneously.

10. Choose Insert from the File menu, and choose the ASCII text version of the spreadsheet you saved in Step 7. Click Insert. The Import Field Order dialog box appears, as shown in Figure 5-49. This box shows you, one record at a

time, how the imported data will be entered into the database fields. The match should be perfect. (Of course, the field you just emptied — Phone, in this example — should be blank.)

Figure 5-49: The Import Field Order dialog box

11. After using the Scan Data buttons to check several records, click OK. The procedure is now complete. Figure 5-50 shows the results of clearing the Phone field for all records.

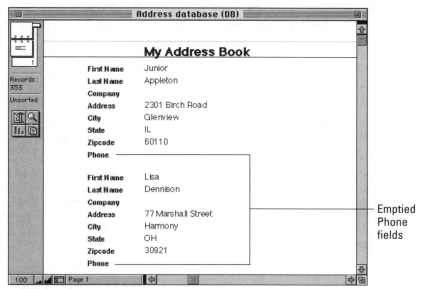

Figure 5-50: The revised database records

Date calculations

Because the ClarisWorks database environment also enables you to create calculation fields, you may sometimes want to record two dates and then determine the number of days between them. You can calculate the number of days that completing a project required or the number of days until a special event will occur (days until your mother's birthday or payday, for example). The following steps show how to accomplish these tasks in your own databases.

Steps: Calculating the Number of Days Between Two Dates

1. Choose Define Fields from the Layout menu (or press Shift-⌘-D). The Define Database Fields dialog box appears.

2. Create a pair of date fields (Start Date and End Date, for example).

3. Create a calculation field to compute the difference between the dates (Total Days, for example). The formula for the field is 'End Date'-'Start Date'. Set Number as the result type in the Format Result As pop-up menu.

Steps: Calculating the Number of Days Until an Upcoming Event

1. Choose Define Fields from the Layout menu (or press Shift-⌘-D). The Define Database Fields dialog box appears.

2. Create a date field (such as Due Date) in which to record the target date.

3. Create a calculation field to compute the number of days between today and the target date. The formula for the field would be 'Due Date'-TRUNC(NOW()). In the Format Result As pop-up menu, choose Number as the result type.

   The NOW( ) function takes the current date and time from the Mac's internal clock. When you truncate the date and time with the TRUNC function, the program discards the fractional portion of the day. Because you want to know only how many full days remain until the event, this formula produces a whole number as the result (7 days, rather than 7.1852 days, for example).

Note If the due date has already occurred, the result of this formula is a negative number. A result of -5 indicates the event occurred five days ago.

Formatting with style

Although the default stylesheet doesn't contain any useful styles that can be applied to fields, labels, or static text in a database, there's nothing stopping you from creating your own field styles.

Steps: Creating Styles for Fields

1. Select a field and format it as desired. Formatting settings can include font, size, style, alignment, text color, pen color and line width (for a border), fill color, fill pattern, texture, gradient, and so on.

2. If the Stylesheet palette isn't open, choose Show Stylesheet from the Window menu (or press Shift-⌘-W).

3. Click the New button at the bottom of the Stylesheet palette. The New Style dialog box appears, as shown in Figure 5-51.

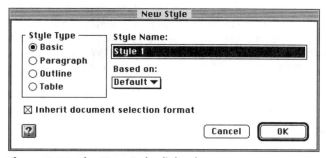

Figure 5-51: The New Style dialog box

4. Be sure the Basic radio button is selected and the Inherit Document Selection Format check box is checked, and then enter a name for the style.

5. Click OK to close the dialog box. The new style is added to the document's stylesheet.

To format other fields, labels, or static text using this new style definition, select the items in the layout and then click the style's name in the stylesheet. Note that the modified stylesheet is automatically saved when you save the database. (For more information on using stylesheets, see Chapter 15.)

Don't forget the spelling checker and thesaurus!

The name of this section says it all. Although you normally think of the spelling checker and thesaurus in connection with word processing documents, you also can use them in other ClarisWorks environments, such as the database. You may even want to create special user dictionaries for some databases. A dictionary that contains the spellings for company and customer names would be useful for a contacts or client database, for example, and would help to ensure the accuracy of the data you enter.

If your database includes large text fields, such as fields for notes or comments, you may want to turn on the auto-hyphenation feature. To do so, select Auto Hyphenate from the Writing Tools submenu of the Edit menu.

Moving On Up

If you're lusting for more database power, you'll find the transition to Claris's FileMaker Pro an easy one. The features in the ClarisWorks database environment are a subset of the features in FileMaker Pro. FileMaker Pro enables you to create powerful database scripts with a simple-to-use scripting system, add script buttons to layouts, and exercise greater control over the way layouts display on screen. FileMaker Pro also has relational database capabilities.

Summary

✦ A database is an organized set of information on one particular topic. Every database is composed of records, and the records are made up of fields.

✦ The ClarisWorks database has four essential modes: Layout, Browse, List, and Find. Both Browse and List modes can be used to edit, enter, and view data. List mode is layout-independent; instead of just showing the fields present in a single layout, List mode simultaneously shows all fields that have been defined for the database.

✦ ClarisWorks offers 14 types of database fields: text, number, date, time, name, pop-up menu, radio buttons, check box, serial number, value list, multimedia, record info, calculation, and summary. You use different field types to allow only certain types of data to be entered into the fields and to present the data in special ways (as check boxes, radio buttons, or pop-up lists or menus, for example). The new multimedia fields in ClarisWorks 5.0 enable you to store QuickTime movies, pictures, and sounds in your databases.

✦ Entries in calculation and summary fields are always the result of a formula you have specified. You cannot manually enter data into a calculation or summary field. ClarisWorks also automatically fills in the data in record info fields. Like calculation and summary fields, you cannot enter or modify data in a record info field.

✦ The ClarisWorks database environment includes several data validation and auto-entry options you can set for fields. These options can help ensure the accuracy of the data you enter and speed up the data-entry process.

✦ For each database, you can create as many *layouts* (arrangements of data fields and other objects) as you need. Each layout can offer a different view of the data and use different subsets of fields.

✦ In addition to the body part of each layout (where most of the fields are placed), you can create header and footer parts (for information you want to appear on every page of the database), as well as summary and sub-summary parts (where you can calculate statistics or formulas for the entire database or selected record groupings).

✦ By sorting the database on the contents of one or more fields, you can change the order in which the records are displayed and the way in which they are grouped.

✦ You can search for records by using two commands: Find and Match Records. The Find command displays the subset of records that match the search criteria, while hiding all other records. Match Records merely selects the subset without hiding the other records.

✦ Entering multiple criteria in a single Find request results in an AND search (finding records that match this criterion and that criterion). You also can issue multiple Find requests to execute an OR search (finding records that match this criterion or that criterion).

✦ ClarisWorks provides more than 50 layouts for Avery labels. You also can create custom label layouts.

✦ As with the other environments, the database can import and export records in a number of different formats. Importing enables you to merge records from other data files with an existing ClarisWorks database. Exporting data is useful when you want to examine or use the database data in another program (a spreadsheet or desktop publishing program, for example).

✦ You can click the pop-up menus in the Tool panel to create and switch to layouts, as well as save and execute complex searches, sorts, and reports.

✦   ✦   ✦

Graphics: The Draw and Paint Environments

Overview

ClarisWorks has two graphics environments: draw and paint. Using the draw tools, you create *objects* — graphics you can move, resize, and place in layers over each other. Because the graphics are objects, they maintain a separate identity from everything else on the page. You can select any draw object separately from other images. However, editing affects the entire object. You cannot, for example, remove a few dots from an object or cut a section away. But changing the color, pattern, or line width for an object is simple.

In paint documents or frames, on the other hand, images are composed entirely of dots (or *pixels*), and you can edit them at the dot level. This capability makes the paint environment excellent for creating detailed images, such as illustrations.

Here are the major differences between the two environments:

- ◆ Draw tools are always available (except in the communications environment). The paint tools remain hidden until you select the paintbrush tool (to work in or create a paint frame) or open a paint document or frame.

- ◆ Draw objects are solid; you can edit them only as a whole. Paint images are composed of dots; you can edit them at the dot level.

- ◆ Selecting and manipulating draw objects is easy. Working with portions of paint images can be more difficult because they do not maintain a separate identity. (A paint image is just a mass of dots.)

✦ You can place draw objects in layers, with some objects obscuring portions of other objects. The objects retain their independence, enabling you to change their attributes and their position in the layers. In the paint environment, after you cover part of an image with another image, the obscured portion is gone forever (unless you immediately choose the Undo command).

✦ There is no such thing as a draw frame. You can place draw objects directly onto the pages of most ClarisWorks documents. Paint images, however, must be in a paint document or in a paint frame. If you copy and paste a portion of a paint image into another document, ClarisWorks automatically embeds it in a rectangular paint frame.

✦ You can align draw objects to each other or to the grid.

✦ You can rotate either type of image, flip them horizontally or vertically, and scale them to a different size.

✦ The paint environment enables you to apply a variety of special effects to selections. Some of the effects are invert, blend, tint, shear, distort, and perspective.

✦ You can alter the resolution and depth of paint documents.

Because the two environments share similar purposes and capabilities, this chapter discusses both of them.

The Draw Environment

The draw environment enables you to create graphics objects you can easily move, resize, and combine. You can place these objects on any document page, copy them to other applications, and store them in the Scrapbook desk accessory.

The draw tools are available in every environment other than communications. Because everything on a draw page is treated as an object (including frames from other environments), the draw environment is excellent for laying out newsletters and ad copy.

Creating objects with the draw tools

ClarisWorks provides draw tools for the following objects:

✦ *Lines.* A line has two endpoints. You can draw lines at any angle or restrict them to multiples of the Shift constraint angle (as set in Preferences). You can apply only pen attributes (pen color, pen pattern, line width, and arrows) to a line.

✦ *Rectangles.* A rectangle is an object with four sides, and every corner angle is 90 degrees. In addition to normal rectangles and squares, ClarisWorks also supports *rounded rectangles* (rectangles with rounded corners).

✦ *Ovals.* An oval is a closed object shaped as an ellipse or a circle.

✦ *Arcs.* An arc is a curved line. Although arcs are typically drawn as open objects, you can assign fill colors, patterns, or gradients to them.

✦ *Polygons.* A polygon is any figure with a fixed number of sides. Polygons can be closed or open, contain uneven sides, or have sides of equal length (*regular polygons*).

To create any of these draw objects, you select the appropriate drawing tool from the Tool panel (see Figure 6-1) and then click and drag in the current document. When you release the mouse button, the object is surrounded by tiny dark squares called *handles* (see Figure 6-2). By dragging the handles, you can change the object's size.

Figure 6-1: The draw tools

Figure 6-2: A simple draw object

After you create an object, ClarisWorks normally selects the pointer tool from the Tool panel. To keep the original drawing tool selected, double-click it when you select it, instead of single-clicking it. When you select a tool by double-clicking it, the tool's symbol in the Tool panel becomes black, instead of merely darkening, and you can draw multiple objects of the same type without selecting the tool each time.

Note

Pressing Shift as you create an object constrains the effects of the following drawing tools:

✦ *Rectangle* or *rounded rectangle tool*. A square or rounded square is drawn.

✦ *Oval tool*. A circle is drawn.

✦ *Arc tool*. A quarter circle is drawn.

✦ *Line tool*. A straight line is drawn. Only lines that are a multiple of the Shift constraint angle (as set in the Graphics section of the Preferences dialog box) can be drawn. (To find out how to change the Shift constraint, refer to Chapter 11.)

Creating or adjusting round corners on a rectangle

You can adjust the roundness of corners or add round corners to a standard rectangle.

Begin by selecting an existing rectangle or a rounded rectangle. Choose the Corner Info command from the Edit menu or double-click the rectangle. The Corner Info dialog box appears, as shown in Figure 6-3. To create a rectangle with semicircles at the corners, click the Round Ends radio button and then click OK. If you prefer to specify a different curve, on the other hand, click the Radius radio button, enter a new radius (in the text-edit box) for the circle that forms the curve, and click OK.

Figure 6-3: The Corner Info dialog box

Reshaping an arc

The direction in which you drag when creating an arc determines the arc's curve.

Normal drawing results in a quarter ellipse. To increase or decrease an arc angle, you must modify it. You can reshape an arc in three different ways:

✦ Select a handle and drag. This changes the size (diameter) of an arc.

✦ Use the Reshape command. This enables manual resizing of the arc angle.

✦ Use the Modify Arc command. This enables precise angle adjustment and framed edges.

To reshape an arc, select the arc with the pointer tool. Choose Reshape from the Arrange menu (or press ⌘-R). A special reshape cursor appears. Click one of the arc's handles and drag to reshape the arc. The cursor is constrained to the arc's diameter. To complete the editing, select another tool or choose the Reshape command again.

To modify an arc, select the arc with the pointer tool. Choose Arc Info from the Edit menu or double-click the arc. The Arc Info dialog box appears, as shown in Figure 6-4. Choose Normal for a normal arc or choose Frame Edges to create a *pie wedge* (closing the arc). Enter numbers in the Start Angle and Arc Angle fields. Click OK to execute the instructions and close the dialog box.

Figure 6-4: The Arc Info dialog box

Drawing and reshaping polygons

The tool you use to draw a polygon depends on whether the polygon will have sides of equal length.

To draw a polygon with uneven sides, select the polygon tool in the Tool panel. Click the document page once to select the starting point and then move the mouse to create the first line of the polygon. (If you press Shift as you move the mouse, the angle of the line will be restricted to an increment of the Shift constraint set in the Graphics preferences.) Click once to set the endpoint for the line. Move the mouse again and click to complete the next line. Repeat this step as many times as necessary to complete the polygon. To finish the polygon, click the starting point (to create a closed polygon), double-click, or press Enter.

Note

To make polygons close automatically (the equivalent of clicking the starting point), choose the Graphics preferences option for Automatic Polygon Closing. (For information on setting preferences, see Chapter 11.)

To draw a polygon that has equal sides, use the regular polygon tool. A regular polygon has three or more sides, and all sides are equal in length. The default setting is for a six-sided polygon (a hexagon).

To draw a regular polygon, select the regular polygon tool in the Tool panel. To set the number of sides for the polygon, choose Polygon Sides from the Edit menu. (The Polygon Sides command is available only when the Regular Polygon tool is selected.) In the dialog box that appears, enter the number of sides desired and click OK. Click the document page once to select the starting point and then drag to create the polygon. You can rotate the polygon as you drag. When you release the mouse button, the polygon is completed.

If you press Shift as you draw the regular polygon, its angle of placement on the page is restricted to the Shift constraint that is set for the mouse in the Graphics section of the Preferences dialog box. By default, the angle is set to 45-degree increments.

You can use the Reshape command to change the angles between polygon sides, add anchor points, or change a straight line into a curve.

Steps: Reshaping a Polygon

1. Select the polygon with the pointer tool.

2. Choose Reshape from the Arrange menu (or press ⌘-R). The reshape pointer appears.

3. Drag a handle to reshape the polygon.

— or —

Click an anchor point and, while pressing the Option key, drag to create a curve.

— or —

Click between any pair of anchor points to add a new anchor point. The new anchor point can now be dragged or Option-dragged, as described previously.

4. To complete the editing, select another tool or choose the Reshape command again.

Drawing other shapes

You can use the freehand tool to create free-form objects. Unlike other objects, which are set to have a white fill, freehand objects have a transparent fill. They can, however, be made solid by assigning a fill color, pattern, texture, or gradient to them.

By default, ClarisWorks automatically smoothes freehand shapes (removes some of the irregularities in the lines and curves). To avoid smoothing, uncheck the Automatically Smooth Freehand check box in the Graphics preferences options. (For information on setting preferences, see Chapter 11.)

The bezigon tool enables you to draw complex shapes composed of curves and straight lines.

Steps: Drawing with the Bezigon Tool

1. Select the bezigon tool in the Tool panel.
2. Click to select the starting point and then move to select the endpoint for the first line or curve.
3. Click to set the endpoint. To create an angular point, press Option as you click. To create a more dramatic curve, click and drag.
4. Repeat Steps 2 and 3 as required.
5. Double-click to close the shape.

To reshape any of the curves in a bezigon shape, choose Reshape from the Arrange menu (or press ⌘-R) and click the object. Select any of the hollow handles that appear and drag to reshape. To add a new anchor point, click anywhere on a line. To delete an anchor point, select it and press the Delete or Backspace key. When you've finished reshaping the object, choose the Reshape command again or select another tool.

Note that there are two types of hollow handles: circles for curved points and squares for sharp points. Pressing Option while clicking a square handle enables you to change it to a curve. Click on the handle and then drag right and/or left. Option-clicking a *Bézier handle* (one of the tiny dots that appear when creating or modifying a curve) resets the curve to a sharp point.

The bezigon editing procedures can also be applied to freehand shapes.

Editing objects

Drawing an object is often only the first step. You can use the different commands, procedures, and palettes to change an object's size, shape, color, pattern, and so on.

Selecting and deselecting objects

In order to do anything with an object (change its size, position, or attributes, for example), you must first select it. To select an object, choose the pointer tool from the Tool panel and click the object. Handles appear around the object's border to show it is selected. (Normally, four handles appear, but you can increase the number of handles by changing the Graphics preferences. See Chapter 11 for details.)

To select a transparent object, you have to click its border.

You can also select *multiple* objects. This capability is useful when you want to apply the same command or formatting to a number of objects. To select more than one object, do one of the following:

✦ Select the pointer tool and press Shift as you click objects.

✦ Select the pointer tool and drag a selection rectangle around the objects.

✦ Select the pointer tool and press ⌘ as you drag through the objects.

✦ Choose Select All from the Edit menu (or press ⌘-A) to select all objects on the current document page.

✦ Click an object type in the Tool panel and then choose Select All from the Edit menu to select all objects of that type.

The last technique works differently with bezigons, polygons, regular polygons, and freehand shapes. If you select one of these objects from the Tool panel and issue the Select All command, objects of all of these types are selected.

To deselect an object, click anywhere outside the object. To deselect individual objects when several have been selected, Shift-click them.

Changing the size of an object

You can change the size of a selected object in three ways:

✦ Dragging one of its handles

✦ Using the Scale By Percent command

✦ Using the Object Size command

When dragging one of an object's handles to change the size of the object, you can constrain the angle of movement by pressing Shift as you drag. You can change the Shift constraint in the Graphics preferences. By default, the angle is set to increments of 45 degrees.

Steps: Changing an Object's Size Using the Scale By Percent Command

1. Select the object or objects whose size you want to change.

2. Choose Scale By Percent from the Arrange menu. The Scale By Percent dialog box appears (see Figure 6-5).

Figure 6-5: The Scale By Percent dialog box

3. Enter new figures for the vertical or horizontal dimensions of the selected object. (To change the dimensions proportionately, enter the same percentage for both dimensions.)

4. Click OK.

You can easily change an object's size or rotation with the Object Size command. Select the object whose size you want to change, and choose Object Size from the Options menu. The Size *floating windoid* appears (see Figure 6-6). To change the horizontal or vertical dimensions (width or height) of the selected object, type new figures in the Width and/or Height text-edit boxes. To change an object's orientation (rotation), type a new figure in the bottom text-edit box.

Distance from edges
Width
Height
Rotation angle

Figure 6-6: The numbers in the Size floating windoid refer to the currently selected object.

Smoothing and unsmoothing objects

You can smooth or unsmooth polygons, regular polygons, bezigons, and freehand shapes. *Smoothing* an object converts all angles into curves. *Unsmoothing* an object changes curves into angles. To smooth an object, select it and choose Smooth from the Edit menu or press ⌘-(. To unsmooth an object, choose Unsmooth from the Edit menu or press ⌘-).

When you are working with a bezigon, smoothing and unsmoothing are not necessarily opposites. You may prefer to use the Undo command in the Edit menu to return to the original shape after you use the Smooth or Unsmooth command for a bezigon.

Setting object attributes

You can set the following object attributes to draw objects:

✦ Fill color

✦ Fill pattern

✦ Fill texture

✦ Gradient

✦ Pen color

✦ Pen pattern

✦ Line width

✦ Arrowheads for lines

You can set these attributes before or after you create an object. To set attributes beforehand, select them from the Tool panel pop-up palettes (see Figure 6-7) and then draw the object. The object will automatically use the current attributes.

Figure 6-7: Tool panel pop-up palettes

To assign or change attributes for an existing object, select the pointer tool, select the object, and then select the new attributes from the various Fill and Pen palettes in the Tool panel.

Although lines are normally solid, you can apply a pen pattern to a line to achieve interesting effects. For example, try different dot pen patterns to create dotted lines.

Transparent and opaque objects

Every object can be either transparent or opaque. An *opaque* object has a fill pattern, color, and/or gradient, and it obscures anything on the page that it covers. A *transparent* object, on the other hand, has no fill color, pattern, or gradient, and you can see anything on the page that it covers.

To make an object transparent, select the first fill pattern in the palette (the two linked blank squares). Any fill color, pattern, or gradient is temporarily removed. If you set the default fill pattern to transparent, the transparent icon is displayed as a reminder in the pattern indicator in the Tool panel (see Figure 6-8).

 —Transparent icon   **Figure 6-8:** The default fill pattern is now transparent.

To make an object opaque (the default for all objects other than freehand shapes), select the second fill pattern in the palette (the linked blank and black squares). Any fill color, pattern, texture, or gradient that was previously applied to the object is restored.

You can tear off any attribute palette and drag it onto the page as a floating windoid. After you expose the palette in this manner, you can quickly set a particular attribute for many objects without having to pop up the attribute palette again. You can manipulate floating attribute palettes in the following ways:

✦ To move a palette, drag it by its title bar.

✦ To close a palette, click its close box (in the upper-left corner).

✦ To shrink or expand a palette, click the box in the palette's upper-right corner.

Copying object attributes with the eyedropper tool

After setting attributes for an object, you can copy those attributes to other objects by using the eyedropper tool. To use the eyedropper tool, select the eyedropper tool from the Tool panel. Click the object whose attributes you want to copy. Select the eyedropper tool again and ⌘-click the objects to which you want to apply the attributes.

Like other draw tools, you can use the eyedropper repeatedly by double-clicking its icon in the Tool panel.

If a destination object has a transparent fill, you need to ⌘-click its border with the eyedropper to apply the attributes.

Arranging objects

The Arrange menu contains commands for moving, aligning, and reorienting objects. You can also move objects manually by dragging them.

Moving objects

To reposition an object manually, select it with the pointer tool and drag the object to a new location. When you move a line, arc, rectangle, or oval, an outline of the object is visible as you drag. When you move other objects, only the bounding box is displayed as you drag.

To see the actual outline of a polygon, bezigon, or freehand shape as you drag it (rather than a rectangular bounding box), press ⌘ as you drag. To restrict movements to the current Shift constraint angle (set in the Graphics preferences), press Shift as you drag. (The Shift technique is particularly useful when you want to keep objects aligned with each other.)

You can also move a selected object by pressing any of the arrow keys. When Autogrid is turned off, the object moves one pixel in the direction of the arrow key. When Autogrid is turned on, the object moves one grid division (determined by the ruler type currently set). To turn Autogrid on or off, press ⌘-Y or choose the appropriate command from the Options menu (Turn Autogrid On or Turn Autogrid Off).

One other way to move an object is to use the Size palette (previously shown in Figure 6-6), which is displayed when you choose Object Size from the Options menu. To change the position of a selected object, simply type new numbers in the Size palette to set the object's distance from the left edge, top, right edge, or bottom of the page.

About the graphics grid

The dotted lines you see on a new draw document are called the *graphics grid*. The ruler type in effect and the number of divisions specified for that ruler govern the spacing of the dots. (By default, the unit of measurement is inches, and each inch has eight divisions.) When you use the Rulers command in the Format menu to change the ruler or the number of divisions, you change the grid.

The grid can be shown or hidden. To hide the grid, choose Hide Graphics Grid from the Options menu. To make it visible again, choose Show Graphics Grid from the Options menu.

Only a portion of the grid is visible. You may want to think of the visible portion (grid points) as being grid border markers. As Figure 6-9 illustrates, many additional grid points are inside each rectangular grid section.

Figure 6-9: This single grid section is magnified 200 percent. The small dots inside the grid represent the grid points you cannot see.

Aligning objects

The Autogrid feature causes objects to align with the nearest point on the grid. When Autogrid is off, you can place objects without being constrained to a grid point. Choose Turn Autogrid On or Turn Autogrid Off from the Options menu (or press ⌘-Y) to change the state of the grid.

When Autogrid is off, you can still make objects align with the grid by using the Align to Grid (⌘-K) command.

In many cases, having a set of objects align perfectly with one another is more important than having them align with the grid.

Steps: Aligning Objects to Each Other

1. Select the objects you want to align to one another. (Drag or Shift-click to select multiple objects.)

2. Choose Align Objects from the Arrange menu (or press Shift-⌘-K). The Align Objects dialog box appears, as shown in Figure 6-10.

(continued)

Figure 6-10: The Align Objects dialog box

3. Click the radio buttons for the desired alignment options.
4. Click OK to perform the alignment.

If the result is not what you intended, immediately choose Undo from the Edit menu and perform the steps again.

Object layers

You can place draw objects over one another, creating *layers*. Using the appropriate menu command, you can move an object to the top or bottom layer of a drawing or one step up or down in the layer hierarchy. Figure 6-11 shows two different stacking orders for the same set of objects.

Figure 6-11: Bring the box in back to the top or front layer by choosing the Move to Front command.

To change an object's layer, start by selecting the object. To move one layer toward the front or back, choose Move Forward (Shift-⌘-+) or Move Backward (Shift-⌘- – [minus sign]) from the Arrange menu. To move the object directly to the top or bottom layer, choose Move to Front or Move to Back from the Arrange menu.

Flipping and rotating objects

The Transform submenu of the Arrange menu has commands you can use to change the orientation of selected objects:

✦ *Flip Horizontally* creates a mirror image of an object, reversing the left and right sides.

✦ *Flip Vertically* creates a reflection of the object (as though it was sitting on the edge of a lake), reversing the top and bottom.

Figure 6-12 shows the result of applying these commands to an object.

Original object

Figure 6-12: The original object and the object after the Flip Horizontally and Flip Vertically commands are applied to it

Flip horizontally   Flip vertically

Draw objects also can be rotated — either manually or by typing a specific angle of rotation.

To rotate an object manually, click to select the object. Choose Free Rotate from the Arrange menu (or press Shift-⌘-R). The cursor changes to an *x*. Click one of the object's handles, and drag to rotate the object. When the object is correctly rotated, release the mouse button.

To rotate an object to a specific angle, click to select the object. Choose Rotate from the Arrange menu. The Rotate dialog box appears. Enter the angle to which the object should be rotated (counterclockwise) and then click OK.

You can also rotate an object to a specific angle using the Size windoid (as previously shown in Figure 6-6). Choose Object Size from the Options menu. In the Size windoid, type a rotation angle in the bottom text-edit box. Type a positive number to rotate the object counterclockwise or a negative number to rotate it clockwise.

Duplicating objects

In addition to the normal copy-and-paste routine, you can use the Duplicate command to make a copy of an object and simultaneously paste it. To duplicate an object, select it and choose Duplicate from the Edit menu (or press ⌘-D). A copy of the object appears. If you immediately move the duplicate to its new position and then choose the Duplicate command again, the new duplicate will be offset the same distance and direction as the preceding one. Duplicate is extremely useful for quickly creating a series of parallel, equidistant lines or other objects.

Note

Here's a fun tip: The duplicate changes direction if placing it would otherwise force it over a page margin. With this in mind, if you use the Duplicate command repeatedly with the same object, you can create interesting graphic effects — such as the 3D tube shown in Figure 6-13.

Figure 6-13: Dozens of repetitions of the Duplicate command can have surprising results.

Deleting objects

To delete an object, select it and use one of the following methods:

✦ Press Delete, Backspace, or Clear.

✦ Choose Clear from the Edit menu.

✦ Choose Cut from the Edit menu (or press ⌘-X).

The Cut command places a copy of the object on the Clipboard. The other procedures delete the object without copying it to the Clipboard.

Note

You also can use any of these procedures to delete *several* selected objects at the same time.

Combining objects

Sometimes, combining objects is useful. ClarisWorks provides two methods of combining objects: *grouping* (which enables you to treat several objects as a single object) and *reshaping* (which links objects end to end).

Combining objects with the Group command

After you painstakingly create a complex series of interrelated objects, dealing with the objects as a whole is often easier and safer than dealing with the individual objects. After you select all the components of the image, you can create a single object with a single set of handles by choosing the Group command from the Arrange menu (or pressing ⌘-G). You can then, for example, move all the objects at the same time without fear of leaving a piece or two behind. You also can apply other Arrange commands to the new object group to flip or rotate it, or you can choose a new color, gradient, texture, or pattern.

If you ever need to work with the component parts, simply select the grouped object and choose Ungroup from the Arrange menu (or press Shift-⌘-G). The components reappear, and you can work with them individually again.

Combining objects with the Reshape command

The Group command enables you to treat several distinct objects as a united group. The Reshape command, on the other hand, enables you to link two or more freehand shapes, polygons, or bezigons end to end. This technique can be useful when you are designing repeating patterns, such as those often used in picture borders.

Steps: Linking Freehand Shapes, Polygons, or Bezigons

1. Choose Reshape from the Arrange menu (or press ⌘-R). The reshape cursor appears.

2. Select the freehand shape, polygon, or bezigon you want to attach to another object. Hollow handles appear around the selected object.

3. Choose Copy from the Edit menu (or press ⌘-C). A copy of the object is placed on the Clipboard.

(continued)

4. Select the second object (the one to which you want to attach the first object).

5. If you want to attach the object to the second object's starting point, select the starting point. Otherwise, the object will be attached to the endpoint.

6. Choose Paste from the Edit menu (or press ⌘-V). A copy of the first object is connected to the second object.

7. If required, repeat Step 6 to attach additional copies end to end.

8. Choose Reshape from the Arrange menu or select another drawing tool to complete the process.

If you press Option while choosing the Paste command in Step 6, the last point (rather than the first point) of the copied object will be attached to the second object.

Locking and unlocking objects

If the position or attributes of a particular object are critical to a document, you can lock the object in place and keep it from being altered by selecting the object and choosing Lock from the Arrange menu (or pressing ⌘-H). If you later want to modify, delete, or move the object, choose Unlock from the Arrange menu (or press Shift-⌘-H).

Creating custom colors, patterns, textures, and gradients

If you want to use special colors, patterns, textures, or *gradients* (fills that blend from one color to another) that are not already in the palettes, you can create new ones.

Custom colors, patterns, textures, and gradients are automatically saved with the document in which they are created. You can also save the palette separately for use with other documents. To create a reusable color palette, you have to use the Editable 256 Color Palette (in the Palettes section of the Preferences dialog box) and then save the palette as a color palette document.

Note

You can also edit colors, patterns, textures, and gradients in the paint environment.

Steps: Creating a Custom Color for the Current Document

1. Choose Preferences from the Edit menu.

2. Choose Palettes from the Topic pull down-menu, click the Editable 256 Color Palette radio button, and click OK.

3. Click the Fill Color or Pen Color palette and tear it off by dragging the palette onto the screen.

4. Double-click the color you want to replace. A color picker dialog box appears, as shown in Figure 6-14.

Figure 6-14: Select a new color from the color picker in System 7.5/7.6 (top) or OS 8 (bottom).

5. To select a replacement color, you can do any of the following (or use a combination of these approaches). The options depend on the color picker in use.

   • Click a different color on the wheel or other color picker.

   • Drag the scroll bar to change the lightness (brightness) of the colors.

   • Enter new numbers for Hue Angle, Saturation, or Lightness.

6. Click OK to save the change. The new color replaces the original one in both the Fill Color and Pen Color palettes. (To revert to the original color, click Cancel.)

Note

If you want to be able to reuse the revised color palette in other documents, you can save it. To save the current color palette, choose Preferences from the Edit menu, choose Palettes from the Topic pull down-menu, click the Editable 256 Color Palette radio button, and click Save. A standard file dialog box appears. Enter a name for the palette and click Save. When the Preferences dialog box reappears, click OK.

You can also load any of the color palettes included with ClarisWorks, as well as ones you've saved. Choose Preferences from the Edit menu, choose Palettes from the Topic pull-down menu, click the Editable 256 Color Palette radio button, and click Load. A list of all color palettes appears. Select a palette, click Open, and then click OK.

Steps: Creating a Custom Pattern for the Current Document

1. Choose Patterns from the Options menu. The Fill Pattern palette and the Pattern Editor appear (see Figure 6-15). Select the pattern to be edited by clicking it in the Fill Pattern palette.

   — or —

   Tear off the Fill Pattern or Pen Pattern palette and double-click the pattern you want to replace. The Pattern Editor appears (see Figure 6-15), set for the chosen pattern.

2. In the box on the left side of the Pattern Editor, click or drag to change the pattern. White spots that are clicked turn black; black spots turn white. To reverse the pattern (swapping whites for blacks and vice versa), click Invert.

3. Click OK to accept the new pattern or Cancel to revert to the previous pattern. The edited pattern appears in both the Fill Pattern and Pen Pattern palettes.

Edit the pattern in this box

Sample box

Selected pattern

Figure 6-15: The Fill Pattern palette and the Pattern Editor

New In
Version 5

ClarisWorks 5.0 includes a new Fill Texture palette in the Tool panel, which you can use to fill draw objects and selected areas in paint documents and frames. The palette includes 20 colorful textures you can use as-is or replace with others of your own design. Additional textures can be loaded from or saved to disk in the Palettes section of the Preferences dialog box (see Chapter 11).

Steps: Creating a Custom Texture for the Current Document

1. Choose Textures from the Options menu. The Fill Texture palette and the Texture Editor appear (see Figure 6-16). Select the texture to be edited or replaced by clicking it in the Fill Texture palette.

   — or —

   Tear off the Fill Texture palette and double-click the texture you want to replace. The Texture Editor appears (see Figure 6-16), set for the chosen texture.

2. Select a height and width for the texture from the pop-up menus in the left side of the Texture Editor. To choose an editing color, click the Color pop-up palette. To fill the entire texture with the current color (to serve as a background, for example), click the Fill button.

3. In the box on the right side of the Texture Editor, click or drag to change the current texture. As you edit, the changes are shown in the sample in the upper-left corner of the Texture Editor dialog box.

(continued)

Preview of the texture   Edit the texture in this box

Selected
texture

Figure 6-16: The Fill Texture palette and the Texture Editor

4. Click OK to save the new texture, Cancel to ignore the changes, or Revert
to change the texture back to its ClarisWorks default. The new texture
appears in the Fill Texture palette.

Although you can create new textures by hand, you can also paste an existing
texture or graphic image into the Texture Editor. Simply copy an image from
ClarisWorks, the Scrapbook, or another graphics program and then — with the
Texture Editor on screen — choose Paste from the Edit menu (or press ⌘-V).

Every gradient is a sweep from one color to another and can contain two to four
colors. ClarisWorks supports three types of sweeps: *directional, circular,* and *shape
burst*. Every sweep has a *focus* (shown as a hollow circle or hollow square in the
Focus section of the Gradient Editor). In a directional sweep, the focus is the spot
at which the final color appears. In a circular sweep, the focus is the point around
which the gradient sweeps. A shape burst sweep is based on the shape of the
object around which the gradient sweeps, and the focus is the bottom-right corner
of the rectangle.

The following steps explain how to create your own gradients. When working in
the Gradient Editor, you can immediately see the effects of your changes by
watching the Sample box.

Steps: Creating a Custom Gradient for the Current Document

1. Choose Gradients from the Options menu. The Gradient palette and the Gradient Editor appear (see Figure 6-17). Select the gradient to be edited by clicking it in the Gradient palette.

— or —

Tear off the Gradient palette and double-click the gradient you want to replace. The Gradient Editor appears (see Figure 6-17), set for the chosen gradient.

Figure 6-17: The Gradient palette and the Gradient Editor

2. Choose a sweep type from the Sweep pop-up menu.

3. Make the changes you want. The options are as follows:

   • *Directional sweep.* You can set the number of colors by choosing a number from the Colors pop-up menu. Select the specific colors for the sweep from the pop-up color palettes. To change the focus, drag the hollow circle in the Angle section of the Gradient Editor. You can set a new angle for the sweep by dragging the line or by typing an angle in the Angle text-edit box.

(continued)

- *Circular sweep.* You can set the number of colors by choosing a number from the Colors pop-up menu. Select the specific colors for the sweep from the pop-up color palettes. To change the focus, drag the hollow circle in the Angle section of the Gradient Editor. You can set a new angle for the sweep by dragging the filled circle or by typing an angle in the Angle text-edit box.

- *Shape burst sweep.* You can set the number of colors by choosing a number from the Colors pop-up menu. Select the individual colors for the sweep from the pop-up color palettes. To change the size of the shape burst focus, press the Option key and drag the black handle of the focus box in the Focus section of the Gradient Editor. You can set the location of the focus by dragging the focus box to a new spot.

4. Click OK to save the new gradient, Cancel to ignore the changes, or Revert to change the gradient back to its ClarisWorks default.

Note   Like custom color palettes, pattern, texture, and gradient palettes can also be saved on disk and loaded for use in other documents. To save a custom pattern, texture, or gradient palette, choose Preferences from the Edit menu; choose Palettes from the Topic pull-down menu in the Preferences dialog box; click the Patterns, Textures, or Gradients radio button (as appropriate); and click Save. Enter a name for the new palette, click Save, and then click OK. To load a saved palette so it can be used with the current document, follow the same procedure, but click the Load button. Select a palette file to load, click Open, and then click OK.

Adding pages to a draw document

By default, a draw document contains only a single page. Adding more pages can be useful (when you are creating a slide show, for example). To add pages to a draw document, choose Document from the Format menu. The Document dialog box appears. Increase the number of pages across and/or pages down in the Size section of the dialog box. Click OK. The pages you specified are added to the document.

Down to business: creating border designs

Whether you're getting ready for a presentation or just want to add some pizzazz to your document, a border frame is often a nice touch. For example, adding a border to a master page can lend consistency to slide show presentations. The following steps show you how to create a simple but attractive border that is composed of overlapping diamonds.

Steps: Creating a Simple Border

1. Launch ClarisWorks and create a new draw document.

2. Make sure Autogrid is on. (The command in the Options menu should read Turn Autogrid Off.) Having Autogrid turned on makes aligning the shapes easy.

3. Select the regular-polygon tool from the Tool panel. (It's shaped like a diamond.)

4. Choose Polygon Sides from the Edit menu, type **4** in the dialog box that appears, and click OK.

5. Select a fill color, texture, or gradient from the relevant pop-up palette in the Tool panel.

6. Drag to create a small diamond shape and place the shape in the upper-left corner of the page.

7. With the shape still selected, choose Duplicate from the Edit menu (or press ⌘-D).

8. Press the up-arrow key once. The second diamond overlaps the first one and is slightly offset to the right.

9. Press ⌘-D repeatedly to create additional diamonds for the top border. Each one should overlap the previous diamond in exactly the same way as the first duplicate did. Stop when the top border is the desired width.

10. Using the pointer, drag a selection rectangle around the row of diamonds.

11. Choose Group from the Arrange menu (or press ⌘-G). The row of diamonds is now treated as a single object.

12. With the row still selected, choose Copy from the Edit menu (or press ⌘-C).

13. Choose Paste from the Edit menu (or press ⌘-V). A copy of the row is pasted over the original row.

14. Choose Rotate from the Arrange menu, enter **90** in the dialog box that appears, and click OK. A vertical column of diamonds appears.

15. Drag the column to the left side of the page and place it so it overlaps with the left end of the original row of diamonds.

16. With the column still selected, choose Copy and then Paste from the Edit menu. A copy of the column is pasted over the original column.

17. Drag the column to the right side of the page and place it so it overlaps with the right end of the original row of diamonds. If you press Shift as you drag, the column moves in a perfectly straight line.

18. Click to select the top row of diamonds and choose Copy and then Paste from the Edit menu. A copy of the row is pasted over the original row.

19. Drag the copy down until it overlaps with the bottom ends of the two columns. The resulting border should look like the one shown in Figure 6-18.

Figure 6-18: The finished diamond border

20. After the border is satisfactory, you can lock the rows and columns in place. Shift-click to select the four elements (or choose Select All from the Edit menu) and then choose Lock from the Arrange menu (or press ⌘-H).

If you plan to use this border frequently, you can save it as a ClarisWorks stationery document rather than as a normal document. (For instructions on working with stationery documents, see Chapter 10.)

The Paint Environment

The paint environment enables you to create and edit *bitmapped images*, which are graphics composed entirely of dots. Unlike draw objects, paint images can be edited at the dot level. The precise control this capability provides is what makes the paint environment so useful in creating complex illustrations.

Creating a new paint document or frame

Although you can create draw objects in almost any document type, you must either design paint images in a paint document or place them in a paint frame in another ClarisWorks environment. To create a new paint document, choose New from the File menu (or press ⌘-N). When the New Document dialog box appears, choose Painting and then click OK.

Note

If there is not sufficient memory available, you may be notified that the document size will be reduced. For instructions on increasing the available memory (and, in turn, the size of your paint documents), see "Quick Tips" at the end of this chapter.

To create a paint frame in another ClarisWorks environment, click the paintbrush tool in the Tool panel and drag to draw the paint frame.

Paint frames and paint documents can contain only bitmapped graphics. Although you can place draw objects and frames from other environments into a paint frame or document, the object or frame from the other environment loses its environmental identity the instant you deselect it — by clicking outside the frame, choosing another tool, or so on. At that moment, the frame is converted to a paint image, which you can edit only by using the paint tools. The same is also true for text you type or paste into a paint document or frame.

Tip

Like other frames, a paint frame is surrounded by a rectangular border. To make the border invisible (so the paint image will blend with the rest of the document), set the pen color to white, the line width to none, or set the pen pattern to transparent.

While you are working in a paint frame or in a paint document, the normally hidden paint tools are displayed and available for use (see Figure 6-19).

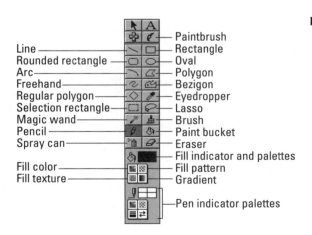

Figure 6-19: The paint tools

The upper nine tools, which, in ordinary circumstances, produce draw objects, are now paint tools. When you use them in a paint frame or a paint document, these tools create bitmapped graphics — not objects. For instructions on using these tools in a paint frame or paint document, see "Creating objects with the draw tools," earlier in this chapter. The information in that section concerning the Shift constraint also applies.

Many of the object modification commands are no longer available as menu commands when you are working in the paint environment. However, you can make the following dialog boxes appear:

✦ *Round Corners*. Double-click the rounded rectangle tool in the Tool panel.

✦ *Modify Arc*. Double-click the arc tool in the Tool panel.

✦ *Number of sides*. Double-click the regular polygon tool in the Tool panel.

You may also want to experiment by double-clicking other tools while working in a paint document or frame. For example, double-clicking the eraser erases the entire frame or paint document, double-clicking the spray can presents a dialog box in which you can edit the spray pattern, and double-clicking the selection marquee selects the entire frame or paint document.

Paint modes

ClarisWorks supports three paint modes:

✦ *Opaque*. Any color, pattern, or gradient placed on another image completely covers the image beneath.

✦ *Transparent pattern*. Any pattern that contains white areas or dots enables the image beneath to show through. A gradient or solid color placed over another image, however, is still treated as opaque (completely covering the image beneath).

✦ *Tint*. A color, pattern, or gradient placed on another image results in a blending of the colors. Depending on the colors chosen, the overlap may not show change. For best results, use colors with greater contrast.

Figure 6-20 shows examples of the three paint modes.

Transparent pattern mode

Tint mode

Opaque mode

Figure 6-20: The three paint modes

To set the paint mode, choose Paint Mode from the Options menu. The Painting Mode dialog box appears. Click the radio button for Opaque, Transparent Pattern, or Tint, and then click OK.

Using the paint tools

When you create draw objects, you can set attributes before or after you create the object. When you work in the paint environment, on the other hand, you should generally select fill and pen attributes before you use each tool. Except for filling closed images, assigning attributes after you create an image can be very difficult.

Note

When you select a paint tool from the Tool panel, it automatically remains selected until you choose a different tool. You do not have to double-click the tool to keep it selected, as you do in the draw environment.

Using the pencil

You use the pencil tool to create and edit single dots, make freehand drawings (much as you do with the freehand tool), and draw thin lines. When you first open a paint document or paint frame, the pencil is automatically selected.

Only the fill color setting affects the pencil. Other settings from the Fill and Pen palettes have no effect.

You can click to create single dots or click and drag to create lines. If you press Shift as you draw with the pencil, you can make straight vertical or horizontal lines.

When you click a blank or colored pixel on the screen with the pencil, a dot of the current fill color is produced. If you click a pixel that is the same color as the current fill color, on the other hand, the pixel changes to white.

Double-clicking the pencil tool icon zooms the document window to 800 percent, making it easy to do fine editing. To return to the 100-percent view, double-click the pencil tool again or click the Zoom Percentage box in the lower-left corner of the document window and select 100%.

Using the brush

Use the brush tool to paint in the current fill color and pattern. (You cannot use a gradient fill with the brush, but you can use a fill texture.) To change to a different brush shape, double-click the brush icon in the Tool panel or choose Brush Shape from the Options menu. The Brush Shape dialog box appears.

To choose a different brush, select it and click OK. To create a new brush (by editing one of the existing brush shapes), select a brush shape and click Edit. The Brush Editor appears.

Alter the brush shape by clicking and dragging in the box. When you click a white spot, it becomes black. When you click a black spot, it becomes white. Click OK to accept the new brush shape (for this document only), and then click OK again to close the Brush Shape dialog box.

The Brush Shape dialog box now sports a new Effects pop-up menu, which enables you to change the effect the brush has on existing pixels it touches. Normal simply paints over them, but you can also choose Blend, Lighter, Darker, or Tint.

You can cut brush patterns out of images by setting the fill color to white or the fill pattern to transparent before you use the brush. Be sure the brush shape is set to Normal.

Using the paint bucket

The paint bucket tool's sole function is to fill a closed area with a color, pattern, texture, or gradient. The tip of the bucket (the tiny stream of paint pouring over its side) is the active area of the paint bucket cursor (see Figure 6-21). It shows where the paint will be applied.

Figure 6-21: The paint bucket is poised to fill the pimento in this olive.

If the paint bucket is applied to an area that is currently filled with a pattern or gradient, a solid color fill will seldom be successful. The procedure for refilling an area that contains a pattern or gradient is to select it and then choose Fill from the Transform menu. (If the area is filled with a solid color, on the other hand, you can use the paint bucket to fill the area with a color, pattern, texture, or gradient.)

If the area you're attempting to fill is not completely closed, the fill color, pattern, texture, or gradient may be applied to many unintended areas in the document or frame. Choose Undo immediately to remove the fill. Before filling again, zoom the screen to locate and fill in the pixels needed to close the area. If you deliberately apply the paint bucket to a blank area in the background, on the other hand, you can quickly add a color, pattern, texture, or gradient to the entire background for a picture or paint frame.

Using the spray can

The spray can tool works like an artist's airbrush. You can change both the dot size and the flow rate to achieve different effects.

To use the spray can, select a fill color, select the spray can in the Tool panel, and either click the mouse to spray or press the mouse button and drag. To spray in a straight vertical or horizontal line, press Shift as you click and drag.

Steps: Changing the Spray Can Settings

1. Double-click the spray can icon in the Tool panel or choose Spray Can from the Options menu. The Edit Spray Can dialog box appears, as shown in Figure 6-22.

Sample area

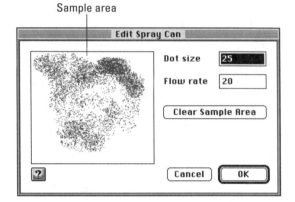

Figure 6-22: The Edit Spray Can dialog box

2. Enter new figures for Dot Size (1 to 72) and Flow Rate (1 to 100).

   Dot size is in pixels, and there are 72 pixels in an inch. (Dot size doesn't really vary the size of the dots; it changes the size or spread of the dot pattern.)

   Flow rate governs how fast the paint flows. At the highest setting, you get splotches of color everywhere the spray pattern touches.

3. To test different combinations of dot size and flow rate with the current fill color, click and drag in the sample area of the dialog box. (If you want to test different combinations in a clean sample area, you can click Clear Sample Area at any time.)

4. Click OK when the settings are to your liking.

Editing paint images

As in most other graphics programs, you usually spend as much time editing an image as you do creating it. Editing tools include the eraser, the selection rectangle, the lasso, and the magic wand.

Using the eraser

You use the eraser tool to erase portions of a paint image. Click to erase the part of the image that is beneath the eraser. You can click and drag to erase larger portions of the image. If you press Shift as you erase, you can drag the eraser in a straight horizontal or vertical line. (The first move you make as you drag determines the direction.)

If you double-click the eraser icon in the Tool panel, you erase the entire paint document or frame.

You cannot resize the eraser. If it's too big to erase a small section of a painting, zoom the screen to a greater magnification.

Selecting images and portions of images

When you want to work with a portion of a picture — to cut, copy, or move it; change the fill; or add a special effect to it — you first have to select the specific portion of the picture you want to edit. With draw objects, this task is simple. You just click the particular object you're interested in. In a paint document or frame, on the other hand, everything is just dots. Three tools are available for selecting a portion of a picture:

✦ The *selection rectangle tool* enables you to make rectangular selections. Click to position one corner of the selection rectangle and then drag. When you release the mouse button, the selection is defined by the area enclosed in the flashing rectangle.

You can also use a selection rectangle in the following ways:

- Press ⌘ while you drag a selection rectangle around an image to make the selection snap around the image, just as the lasso tool does (described below).

- Double-click the selection rectangle icon in the Tool panel to select the entire paint document or frame.

- Press ⌘ while you double-click the selection rectangle icon to select only the images within the paint document or frame (ignoring blank spaces).

- Press Option while you drag a selection to make a copy of it. (For example, you can use this feature to take a picture of one car and change it into a traffic jam.)

✦ The *lasso tool* enables you to make irregular selections in a paint document or frame. Click and then drag around the area you want to select. When you release the mouse button, the lasso snaps around the images you have selected, ignoring blank background areas.

You can double-click the lasso icon in the Tool panel to select only the images within the paint document or frame. You also can press Option while you drag a selection to make a copy of it.

✦ The *magic wand tool* enables you to make selections based on color. When you position the head of the magic wand over the desired color or pattern and click the mouse button, all adjacent pixels that are the same color or pattern are selected.

Tip

When you are attempting to select a pattern, dragging the magic wand through a small area of the pattern may be easier than just clicking. As you drag, a freehand-style line is displayed. When you release the mouse button, the selection is made.

To deselect an image, click outside of the selection, click any tool icon, choose Undo Select from the Edit menu, or press ⌘-Z.

Moving, cutting, copying, or duplicating a selection

When you move the cursor over a selection you have made, the cursor changes to a pointer. If you click while the pointer is visible, you can drag the selection to a new location. If you press Shift as you drag, you drag straight horizontally or straight vertically.

You can also use the arrow keys to move the selection one pixel at a time. (If Autogrid is on, the selection moves one grid-point at a time.)

Commands in the Edit menu become available after you select an image or a portion of an image. You can cut (⌘-X) or copy (⌘-C) the image to the Clipboard, clear the image, or duplicate it (⌘-D).

Applying special effects to a selection

Special effects in the Transform menu also become available after you make a selection. These effects include Shear, Distort, and Perspective. *Shear* adds a vertical or horizontal slant to an image. *Distort* enables you to stretch an image in any direction. *Perspective* makes the image appear as if you are viewing it from an angle.

Steps: Shearing, Distorting, or Adding Perspective to a Selection

1. Select a portion of the image by using one of the selection tools (selection rectangle, lasso, or magic wand).

2. Select Shear, Distort, or Perspective from the Transform menu. Blank handles appear around the selection.

3. Drag a handle to achieve the desired effect.

4. Click away from the selection to remove the handles.

Figure 6-23 shows the effects of applying Shear, Distort, and Perspective to an image.

Figure 6-23: Special effects

Original image

Shear   Distort   Perspective

Tip

You lose resolution when you modify an object by using these commands. Because you're in a 72-dpi mode and are in a bitmapped document, the pixels are modified during the transformation. Some pixels become larger, some smaller. This change is normal. If there are too many jagged edges for you, clean up by zooming in and using the tools to smooth out the image. Another trick is to use the Blend option. This option makes the edges less noticeable.

Changing the size of a selection

Two commands in the Transform menu enable you to change the size of a selection: Resize and Scale By Percent. To change the size manually, use the Resize command. To change the size by specifying scaling proportions, use Scale By Percent.

Steps: Using the Resize Command

1. Select a portion of the image by using one of the selection tools (the selection rectangle, lasso, or magic wand).

2. Choose Resize from the Transform menu. Blank handles appear around the selection, as shown in Figure 6-24.

Figure 6-24: The Resize command adds handles to the selection.

3. Drag a handle to change the size of the selection. When you release the mouse button, the selection is redrawn to the specified size.

4. Click away from the image to eliminate the Resize handles.

Note

If you press Shift as you drag a handle, the original proportions of the selection rectangle are maintained.

Steps: Using the Scale By Percent Command

1. Select a portion of the image by using one of the selection tools (the selection rectangle, lasso, or magic wand).

2. Choose Scale By Percent from the Transform menu. The Scale By Percent dialog box appears, as shown in Figure 6-25.

Figure 6-25: The Scale By Percent dialog box

(continued)

3. Type percentages for enlargement (greater than 100%) or reduction (smaller than 100%). If you want to maintain proportions, enter the same percentage for both the horizontal and vertical dimensions.

4. Click OK. The selection is resized.

Orientation transformations

The same commands available in the draw environment for changing an object's orientation are also available in the paint environment. To change the orientation of a selection, select a portion of the image and choose Flip Horizontally, Flip Vertically, Free Rotate, or Rotate. The first three commands — Flip Horizontally, Flip Vertically, and Free Rotate — work exactly the same way they do in the draw environment. (For additional information, see the description of these commands in "Flipping and rotating objects," earlier in this chapter.)

Like the Object Size command in the draw environment, the paint environment's Rotate command enables you to enter a rotation angle for a selection directly. To use the Rotate command, select a portion of the image by using one of the selection tools (the selection rectangle, lasso, or magic wand). Choose Rotate from the Transform menu. The Rotate dialog box appears. Enter a number (in degrees) for the counterclockwise rotation you desire. Click OK. The selection is rotated.

ClarisWorks 4.0 had a Rotate 90° command that is no longer available in ClarisWorks 5.0. However, if the Default button bar is displayed, you'll see a Rotate 90° button, which performs the same action on any selected image in a paint document or frame.

Color transformations

At the bottom of the Transform menu are a number of useful color-related transformation commands. Here is what they do:

✦ *Fill*. This command duplicates the function of the paint bucket tool, enabling you to fill any selection with a color, pattern, texture, or gradient. The difference is that the fill is applied only to the selected area, so it does not matter whether an image is closed or open; nor does it matter whether the selected area contains a solid color, a gradient, a texture, or a pattern.

✦ *Pick Up*. This command enables you to transfer the design and attributes of one image to another image. To use the command, select an image, drag it over another image, and choose Pick Up from the Transform menu.

Creating patterned text is one interesting application of Pick Up. Type the text, select it by pressing ⌘ as you drag the selection rectangle tool around it, move it over an interesting pattern, and choose the Pick Up command. Figure 6-26 shows some text with a gradient pattern that was created in this manner.

Original text

Text with a gradient that was picked up from the box below

Figure 6-26: Gradient text created with the Pick Up command

✦ *Invert*. Use this command to make a negative image of a selection. Colors in the image are reversed, but not necessarily as you might expect them to be. An inverted grayscale gradient, for example, may show shades of yellow, green, and blue.

✦ *Blend*. Use Blend to provide a smooth transition between colors by adding intermediate shades.

✦ *Tint*. Choose Tint to tint a selection with the current fill color.

✦ *Lighter* and *Darker*. Use these commands to add white or black to a selection, making it lighter or darker.

Tip

When you use any of the color transformation commands, make sure you select only the outline of an object and not part of the background, too. Each command applies to everything within the selection. To select only an object without the surrounding background, use the lasso or press ⌘ while you drag the selection rectangle.

Creating custom colors, patterns, textures, and gradients

As in the draw environment, you can replace colors, patterns, textures, and gradients in the palettes with ones of your own choosing. Follow the instructions presented earlier in this chapter (in "Creating custom colors, patterns, textures, and gradients" for the draw environment).

Other paint settings

Other menu commands that appear in the paint environment enable you to change the document size, the depth and resolution of the image, and the grid size (in conjunction with the Autogrid feature).

To change the size of a paint document, choose Document from the Format menu. The Document dialog box appears, as shown in Figure 6-27. In the Size section of the dialog box, enter new numbers for pixels across and pixels down. As with points, there are 72 pixels per inch. The maximum for either dimension is 2,000 pixels; the minimum is 36 pixels. Click OK to resize the document to the new dimensions.

The *resolution* of a paint document is initially set to match the resolution of a typical Macintosh screen — 72 dots per inch (dpi). If you are printing on a high-resolution printer, you can change the resolution to match that of the printer.

Figure 6-27: The Document dialog box

As you increase the resolution, however, the document and its contents shrink accordingly. At 300 dpi, for example, a standard paint document reduces to about 1.5 × 2.25 inches. If you have enough free memory, you can increase the size of the document by following the preceding steps. You should note, however, that the higher the resolution and the larger the document size, the more memory is required. For this reason, many users will prefer to use the default 72 dpi setting for resolution.

Depth refers to the number of colors available for displaying the document. Depth is initially set to match the setting in the Monitors control panel.

Steps: Changing the Depth and Resolution of a Paint Document or Frame

1. Choose Resolution & Depth from the Format menu. The Resolution and Depth dialog box appears, as shown in Figure 6-28.

Figure 6-28: The Resolution and Depth dialog box

2. Choose a resolution by clicking its radio button. Follow these guidelines:
   - Use 72 dpi for a document you intend to display only on screen or print on an ImageWriter printer. You can also use higher multiples of 72 (144 and 288) to maintain proportions when you print to an ImageWriter or equivalent printer.
   - Use 300 dpi to match the resolution of many laser printers.
   - Use 360 dpi to match the resolution of many ink-jet printers.

3. Choose a depth by clicking its radio button. The amount of memory the new Depth setting requires is shown at the bottom of the dialog box.

4. Click OK to accept the new settings or Cancel to ignore any changes.

If you are working in a paint frame, rather than in a paint document, select the frame and then choose Frame Info from the Edit menu. A similar dialog box appears, which enables you to set the resolution, depth, and the *origin* (starting point) for displaying the contents of the frame. Enter values (in pixels) for the horizontal and vertical coordinates. (See Chapter 14 for additional information.)

When importing a PICT file into a paint frame or document, ClarisWorks automatically matches the resolution of the image and uses the document's original color table.

When the Autogrid option is on (in the Options menu), the grid size determines where you can place objects and how far they will move at each step when you drag or nudge them with an arrow key. The larger the setting for grid size, the farther apart the grid locations are. You can set the grid size to 2 pixels for fine control over image placement.

To change the grid size, choose Grid Size from the Options menu. The Painting Grid Size dialog box appears. Click the radio button for the desired grid size and click OK.

Down to business: editing a screen capture

If you're new to the Mac or haven't read your system software manual, you may not be aware that the Mac has a built-in screen-capture utility. By pressing Shift-⌘-3, you instruct the Mac to *capture* (make a copy of) the current screen image. Commercial screen-capture utilities add other functions, such as the capability to capture a selected portion of the screen, capture pull-down menus, hide or display the cursor in the capture, and more.

If you have OS 8 and press Shift-⌘-4, you can capture a selected area of the screen rather than the full screen. For purposes of this discussion, however, I will assume you are making a full-screen capture.

After you capture the screen, you'll often want to edit the capture. In the following steps, you learn to capture a screen that displays one of the Paint dialog boxes, edit the capture so only the dialog box remains, and then change the image into a draw object so you can place and resize it in any type of document.

The steps demonstrate the following paint activities:

✦ Editing a full-screen capture at a high zoom magnification

✦ Using the eraser

✦ Using the selection rectangle

✦ Using the Scrapbook to change a paint image into a resizable PICT object

Steps: Cleaning Up a Screen Capture

1. In ClarisWorks, create a new paint document and add some shapes to it.

2. Choose Spray Can from the Options menu. The Edit Spray Can dialog box appears.

3. Test the current spray pattern by clicking and dragging in the sample box.

4. If you do not have a separate capture utility, press Shift-⌘-3. A copy of the screen is saved on disk as a new file with the name Picture *x*.

   — or —

   If you have a separate screen-capture utility, you may be able to capture a specific portion of the screen, determine whether the cursor will be included in the screen shot, and set other useful options. Issue the utility's capture command to capture the full screen or a selection that includes the dialog box.

5. Close the paint document by clicking its close box. Do not save the document.

6. Choose Open from the File menu (or press ⌘-O). A file dialog box appears.

7. Choose Painting from the Document Type pop-up menu at the bottom of the dialog box. (Choosing Painting restricts the file list to documents you can open in the paint environment.)

8. Navigate to the drive and folder where the screen capture is stored, select the file, and click Open. The screen capture opens as a paint document. Figure 6-29 shows what the screen may look like.

   If you have performed a full-screen capture, the program may inform you that the document will be opened at a reduced size. If the entire dialog box is not visible in the document window, quit ClarisWorks and increase the memory available to the program. (See "Quick Tips" at the end of this chapter for instructions.) Then restart ClarisWorks and return to Step 6.

9. Choose the selection rectangle from the Tool panel and drag to select the dialog box.

10. Choose Cut from the Edit menu (or press ⌘-X). A copy of the dialog box is transferred to the Clipboard.

11. Double-click the eraser tool. The entire painting is erased.

12. Choose Paste from the Edit menu (or press ⌘-V). A copy of the dialog box is pasted onto the blank document page.

13. Click the Zoom Percentage box in the lower-left corner of the document window and select 200%. This setting makes editing the image easier. (With practice and a steady hand, you can also do this kind of editing at 100%.)

Figure 6-29: The screen capture opened as a ClarisWorks paint file

14. If the eraser isn't still selected, choose it now. To remove the stray patterns and colors from around the border of the dialog box, position the eraser so its edge is touching — but not covering — one of the sides of the dialog box. Press Shift, click the mouse button, and drag to erase the stray material along that side of the dialog box. Repeat for the other three sides.

15. Click the Zoom Percentage box in the lower-left corner of the document window and select 100%. The image returns to its normal size.

16. Save the edited picture of the dialog box. (In case anything goes wrong in the remaining steps, you can reopen the edited file and proceed from this step.)

17. Choose the selection rectangle tool from the Tool panel. While pressing the ⌘ key, drag a selection rectangle around the dialog box. When you release the mouse button, the selection rectangle snaps around the dialog box.

18. Choose Copy from the Edit menu (or press ⌘-C). A copy of the edited dialog box is transferred to the Clipboard.

19. Close the paint document. If you are asked whether you want to save the document, click Don't Save.

20. Open the Scrapbook desk accessory by selecting it from the Apple menu. (Using the Scrapbook to change images from painting to PICT format is discussed in the next section.)

21. Press ⌘-V. A copy of the dialog box picture is added to the Scrapbook, as shown in Figure 6-30.

Figure 6-30: The dialog box pasted into the Scrapbook

22. Press ⌘-X. The copy of the dialog box picture is removed from the Scrapbook and changed into a PICT image (an object).

23. Click the close box on the Scrapbook to put it away.

24. In ClarisWorks, create a new drawing or word processing document.

25. Choose Paste from the Edit menu (or press C-V). A copy of the dialog box is pasted into the document.

The dialog box is now an object. You can manipulate this dialog box object as you can any other object. You can, for example, change the size of the dialog box or add a border color around it.

Quick Tips

The following quick tips describe how to:

  ✦ Edit draw objects in the paint environment

  ✦ Change an edited paint image into a draw object

  ✦ Increase the memory available to ClarisWorks

✦ Create and work with a second copy of a paint document

✦ Preview images before opening them

✦ Insert graphics from the ClarisWorks ReadyArt libraries

Editing draw objects in the paint environment

Occasionally, being able to edit draw objects at the dot level is useful. To perform this task, you simply copy the object, paste it into a paint document, edit, copy again, and then paste it back into the original document.

Although this procedure works, it has an unfortunate side effect: When you paste the image back into the original document, it is a paint frame — a bitmap. It is enclosed by a border, and you can no longer resize it the way you can resize an object. Here's a better method.

Steps: Changing a Paint Image into a Draw Object

1. After you finish editing in the paint document, select and copy the image.

2. Pull down the Apple menu and choose the Scrapbook desk accessory.

3. Press ⌘-V. The image is pasted into the Scrapbook.

4. Press ⌘-X. The image is removed from the Scrapbook and copied to the Clipboard as an object.

5. Open the target document (a draw or word processing document, for example) and choose Paste from the Edit menu (or press ⌘-V). The image is pasted into the document as an object.

Paint memory requirements

If you plan on working in the paint environment regularly — particularly with full-screen images — increasing the memory available to ClarisWorks is a good idea. Otherwise, you'll frequently see the following message: *The document size has been reduced to fit available memory.*

Steps: Increasing the Memory Available to ClarisWorks

1. Quit ClarisWorks (if it is running), go to the desktop, and select the ClarisWorks program icon.

2. Choose Get Info from the File menu (or press ⌘-I). The Info window for ClarisWorks appears, as shown in Figure 6-31.

ClarisWorks Info

ClarisWorks
ClarisWorks 5.0

Kind: application program
Size: 2.9 MB on disk (3,031,203 bytes used)
Where: Databases : ClarisWorks 5.0 Folder :

Created: Tue, Jun 24, 1997, 1:00 PM
Modified: Thu, Jul 17, 1997, 11:35 PM
Version: ClarisWorks 5.0d68
Tuesday, June 24, 1997
Comments:

---**Memory Requirements**---
Suggested size: 4329   K
Minimum size: 4129   K
☐ **Locked**   Preferred size: 4329   K

Note: Memory requirements will decrease by 2,329K if virtual memory is turned on in the Memory control panel.

Type a number here to increase the memory available to the program

Figure 6-31: The ClarisWorks Info window

The Info window enables you to change the program's memory allocation (the amount of memory the system will give you to run ClarisWorks and work with ClarisWorks documents).

3. Type a larger number in the Preferred Size text-edit box.

4. Click the Info window's close box.

You can change the memory allocation as often as necessary. To track how much memory you're using in ClarisWorks, go to the desktop and select About This Macintosh (System 7.x) or About This Computer (OS 8) from the Apple menu. A window appears that shows how much memory the system and any open programs (ClarisWorks, for example) are currently using (see Figure 6-32).

Figure 6-32: The About This Macintosh window in System 7.x (top) and the About This Computer window in OS 8 (bottom) show how much memory the system and any open programs are currently using and how much memory is free.

You can also see the amount of memory that is still free for use by other programs, desk accessories, and so on. A bar for each program shows the total memory allocated to that program. The dark area of each bar represents memory currently in use. The light area is memory you can use to open additional documents or expand the size of current documents.

Painting in two views

When you edit a paint image at a high magnification, seeing a normal view of the image at the same time is sometimes helpful. To create a second copy of a paint document, choose New View from the Window menu. To help you see both copies at the same time, choose Tile Windows from the Window menu. The two copies are displayed together, one above the other. Set the magnification for one of the copies to a higher level (between 200% and 800%, for example) by clicking the Zoom Percentage box in the lower-left corner of the document.

Changes made in one copy of the document are simultaneously reflected in the other copy. However, scrolling is not synchronized between the two documents. You have to scroll the copies manually to make sure the same portions of the document are displayed in both copies.

Previewing documents

If you load Apple's QuickTime extension at the start of your computing session, you can preview graphics files before you open them in ClarisWorks 5.0. In the Open dialog box, ClarisWorks can present a thumbnail image of every graphics file. If you have a large number of files, using the Preview feature can help you avoid opening the wrong document. (For information on creating previews, see Chapter 1.)

Inserting art from the ReadyArt libraries

ClarisWorks 5.0 includes dozens of clip-art images you can use in your own documents. These images are stored in *libraries* (image collections organized around a theme, such as world maps, hands, and computers).

Steps: Adding a Library Image to a Draw or Paint Document

1. Choose the library of interest from the Library submenu of the File menu. The selected library appears in its own windoid.

2. Scroll to the image you want to use.

3. To add the image to the current document, do one of the following:

   • Drag the name of the image onto the document.

   • Drag the thumbnail picture of the image onto the document.

   • Choose the image or its name, and click the windoid's Use button.

   The image is inserted into the document. When added to a draw document, the graphic is inserted as a draw object; when added to a paint document or frame, the graphic is a paint (bitmapped) image.

Note When adding a library image to a paint frame, be sure you are in paint mode. (When in paint mode, the paint tools are visible in the Tool panel.) If you are not in paint mode, the chosen image is added as a free-floating draw object rather than as a paint graphic.

You can also add your own graphics to existing libraries or create new libraries. (To learn more about working with libraries, see Chapter 21.)

Moving On Up

When — or if — your image creation and editing needs expand, you can choose from dozens of commercial graphics programs. These programs can be classified roughly according to their capabilities:

✦ *Draw programs.* If objects are your thing, you may prefer a capable draw program, such as ClarisDraw.

✦ *PostScript drawing programs.* These programs are capable of creating extremely complex and detailed PostScript images — the natural choice of illustrators and designers. The most popular of these programs are Adobe Illustrator and FreeHand (Macromedia). PostScript drawing programs tend to have a very steep learning curve, however. They're not for casual artists or users with simple graphics needs.

✦ *Image editors/high-end paint programs.* These programs extend paint capabilities by enabling you to create or edit 8-, 16-, 24-, or 32-bit color or grayscale images. If you need to edit scanned images or video captures, a program such as Adobe Photoshop or Canvas is a godsend.

✦ *QuickTime editors.* If you want to make your own QuickTime movies, you need software tools that make it possible. Adobe Premiere is a popular choice.

✦ *Special-purpose graphics programs.* A wide variety of graphics niche programs are also available. Some specialize in 3D images (Specular Infini-D, Strata StudioPro, and Adobe Dimensions, for example); some enable you to switch freely between paint and PICT modes or combine them in the same document (Adobe SuperPaint, for example); and some imitate an artist's brush strokes (Fractal Design Painter, for example).

Depending on your graphics needs, you may find that you require *several* programs — each for a different purpose. (You may also need more memory.)

Summary

✦ ClarisWorks includes a pair of graphics environments. You use the draw environment to create objects and the paint environment for bitmapped images.

✦ Draw objects are solid; you can edit them only as a whole. Paint images are composed of dots; you can edit them at the dot level.

✦ The first step in editing a draw object is to select it. After you have made a selection, you can move the object, apply different fill and pen attributes to it, or choose editing commands. You can also select several objects at the same time.

✦ When you want to edit a paint image, three tools enable you to select a portion of a picture: the selection rectangle, the lasso, and the magic wand. After you make a selection, you can move it, resize it, or alter its attributes.

✦ Unlike draw objects (which you can place in almost any environment), you can use paint images only in paint documents and paint frames.

✦ Although you can easily add to or change the attributes of a draw object at any time, setting paint attributes is easier before you create each portion of an image than it is afterward.

✦ Paint documents can be memory hogs. You may have to increase the memory available to ClarisWorks if you regularly work with large paint documents.

✦ ClarisWorks 5.0 includes dozens of ReadyArt libraries of clip art that you can insert into your documents.

✦   ✦   ✦

The Communications Environment

Overview

Communications (also called *telecommunications*) is the process of exchanging information between computers. This chapter discusses communications by means of a device called a modem or a direct-connect cable. Computers can also exchange information on a network (which I will not discuss here).

A *modem* is a hardware device connected to a computer, either internally in an available NuBus slot, PDS (processor-direct slot), or a PCI slot; or externally to one of the computer's serial ports. The job of the modem is to translate outgoing data from its original digital form (ones and zeros) to an analog form (sounds) telephone lines can carry. The modem attached to the receiving computer translates these sounds back into a digital form the computer can understand.

The name *modem* comes from the description of what the device does. It *mod*ulates and *dem*odulates computer data. Because modems exchange data over phone lines, you can use a modem to communicate with a computer down the street or across the country.

Modems can do the following:

◆ Connect your computer to information services, such as CompuServe, Prodigy, GEnie, and America Online

◆ Connect your computer to bulletin board systems (BBSs)

◆ Communicate directly with computers used by your colleagues and friends

✦ Connect to networks and larger computers (mainframes)

✦ Connect your computer to the Internet

Information services charge you according to the amount of time you spend *online* (connected) each month. Others charge a flat monthly fee that provides unlimited use of basic services, and charge separately for using other parts of the system (for downloading programs and other files from its computer to your Mac, accessing financial services, and so on). Also common is single-fee pricing that enables you to use all available services for an unlimited number of hours each month. The larger information services provide local phone numbers (*access nodes*) you dial to connect with their systems. Thus, if you live in a metropolitan area, you can frequently connect to the service without incurring long-distance phone charges. When you buy a modem, sign-up information for several information services is often included in the box. Most major information services (such as America Online and CompuServe) now provide access to the Internet as part of their service package.

A *BBS* is like a miniature information service and is often run by just one person. Users can typically download files and send messages to other subscribers. A BBS can be as small as a single modem and phone line, or it can contain a bank of phone lines to handle multiple subscribers simultaneously — much the same as information services do. Fees for becoming a subscriber, if any, are usually quite reasonable.

One-to-one communication is also very popular. You can exchange documents and programs with any other person who has a modem — even if you are using different types of computers (a Mac and a PC, for example). Overnight delivery services take a full day to deliver a document, but a pair of high-speed modems can deliver an important document in a few minutes, and often at a fraction of the cost of using a delivery service.

The ClarisWorks communications environment cannot be used to connect your computer to the *Internet*. To accomplish this, you will need a suite of other applications, such as a Web browser to view pages on the World Wide Web (Netscape Navigator or Internet Explorer, for example), an electronic mail (e-mail) program, and a newsgroup reader. In addition, you must obtain access to the Internet. For most users, this means opening an account with an information service or an *ISP* (Internet service provider). Note that ClarisWorks Office includes the basic Internet software you need (Netscape Navigator), as well as sign-up information for several ISPs. (To learn more about how ClarisWorks supports Internet activities, see Chapters 22 and 23.)

Note

Mac OS 8 includes several applications to help make the Macintosh Internet-ready.

Unlike most of the chapters in this book, this chapter is primarily oriented to teaching by example. It contains several "Down to business" sections that show you, step by step, how to use the ClarisWorks communications environment to perform the following tasks:

✦ Connect with an information service or BBS by using a modem

✦ Connect with another Mac by using a modem

✦ Transfer files between a pair of Macs by using a direct-connect cable

✦ Transfer files between a Mac and a PC by using a direct-connect cable

Choosing a Modem or Fax Modem

If your Mac didn't come with an internal or external modem (most don't), several factors can help you decide which modem is best for you.

Speed
Different modems support different maximum data transmission speeds. Speed is stated in terms of *baud* or *bps (bits per second)*. When a modem is advertised as a 33600 bps unit (or — more commonly — as simply 33.6 or 33.6K), for example, the ad is stating the modem's top transmission speed. Most modems can also perform at lower speeds for compatibility with older or less capable modems.

At this time, most advertised modems are 33600 (33.6K) or 56000 (56K) bps units. For communicating with information services (such as CompuServe, GEnie, America Online, and Prodigy), either modem type will serve you well. (Note, however, that currently, the international standards for 56K modems are still being set. Any 56K modem purchased today may not be compatible with those produced after the standards have been set. In addition, many ISPs and information services do not currently support speeds above 33.6Kbps.)

If much of your communicating will be with friends or colleagues, on the other hand, the faster the modems, the better. And if this two-way communication has to occur at long-distance phone rates, the faster the transmissions occur, the lower the charges will be.

Note: Because graphics are frequently found on Web pages and can take a long time to transmit, having a fast modem is particularly important if you intend to use the Internet.

You can increase *throughput* (the data transfer rate) in a file transfer if both modems have data compression routines in their ROMs (Read-Only Memory). Data compression squeezes information into a smaller package, reducing the time required to transmit files. Because it is handled entirely by the modems rather than in software, the compression occurs very quickly. One standard called MNP5 (Microcom Networking Protocol) offers compression of approximately two to one. Another standard, V.42 bis, which was developed by CCITT (the Consultative Committee for International Telephone and Telegraph), offers four-to-one compression. The amount of compression varies, depending on the type of data you are transferring. Graphics and text tend to compress very well. Computer programs compress very little. To use compression at all during a communications session, however, both modems must support the same compression features.

(continued)

(continued)

If two modems cannot perform compression, you can use one of the many Mac compression programs to compress files prior to going online. The most popular compression program for the Mac is StuffIt Deluxe (Aladdin Systems). If the files are precompressed in this manner, however, make sure you are not also using modem-provided compression. This causes the files to be compressed a second time, which — in most cases — will not improve the compression and can result in the files taking *longer* to transmit.

Although 33.6K and 56K modems are now common, the technology is still relatively new. If you're outfitting different branches of your company with high-speed modems and want to be assured of reliable connections, your best bet is to buy the same brand and model of modems for each branch. Also, because the manufacturers may tweak the instructions and algorithms in the ROMs of these modems over the next year (to improve compatibility, reliability, and performance), you may prefer modems that have *flash ROMs*. Flash ROMs can be updated by downloading new instructions to them, in much the same way you download files from information services.

Data Modems Versus Fax Modems
As its name implies, you use a *data modem* strictly to exchange computer data — documents, graphics, programs, and so on. A *fax modem* is a data modem that can also send and receive faxes. Most fax modems now offer the same feature set as advanced data modems, as well as providing the capability to fax documents that reside on a Mac's hard disk and to display incoming faxes on the Mac's screen.

Essentially, a fax modem is a paperless fax machine. Using a special print driver that comes with the fax software, you can issue the Print command from within almost any program. The current document is then translated into fax format and sent through the modem to the destination fax machine or fax modem. Documents you send or receive with a fax modem are indistinguishable from documents you send or receive with a standard fax machine. If anything, documents you send with a fax modem tend to be a little clearer because the original document isn't scanned — it is simply converted into fax format by software. Most fax modems can send and receive faxes at speeds up to 14,400 bps. For compatibility with older fax modems and fax machines, however, they can also send and receive at 9,600 and 4,800 bps.

One important drawback of fax modems is you cannot fax an external document, such as a lease or a photograph, unless you also have a scanner. All documents have to be resident in the Mac in order for you to fax them.

Special Features
The many useful and esoteric features you can add to a modem are like the add-ons a dealer offers when you buy a new car. The following features are among the available options:

♦ Advanced error correction and data compression protocols, which, because they are coded into the modem's ROM, work much faster than the same features in a communications program

♦ Voice capabilities for modems that also work as answering machines

♦ Voice/fax switching for modems that can sense what type of information is conveyed in an incoming call and automatically switch it to the appropriate device — either ringing the phone or sending a fax answer tone

Communications Terminology

Like most areas of computing, communications has its own language. Following are some communications terms you need to understand:

♦ *Access number, access node.* A phone number you can dial to reach an information service or BBS. Larger services frequently provide local access numbers for major cities. When you dial an access number, it automatically connects you with the system, and you avoid long-distance charges.

♦ *Baud, bps (bits per second).* The operating speed of a modem. Although the terms have different meanings, they're often used interchangeably. Whether the advertising says a modem is 28800 baud or 28800 bps, it simply means the modem's top speed (without compression) is 28,800 bits per second.

Note

In many advertisements and catalogs, the baud/bps figure is abbreviated. If you see an ad for a "33.6 modem," it is referring to a modem with a top speed of 33,600 bps — the thousands are assumed.

♦ *Download, downloading.* Retrieving a file or program for your own use from an information service, BBS, or another user's computer.

♦ *E-mail (electronic mail).* Private messages you leave for another user or another user leaves for you.

♦ *Log on, logging on.* Connecting with an information service or BBS. Often you have to provide a user ID and password to complete the connection and gain access to the service or BBS.

♦ *Log off, logging off.* Ending a session with an information service or BBS. Most systems have a command (such as Bye, Off, Logoff, End, or Quit) you must type or choose to end the session.

✦ *Protocol, protocol transfer.* The computer algorithm you've selected for assuring error-free data transfers between your computer and the other system when you are uploading or downloading files. Each protocol has its own method of making sure each block of data is received correctly. In most cases, when an error occurs, the protocol instructs the system to resend the block. Examples of protocols include XMODEM, 1K XMODEM, Kermit, YMODEM, ZMODEM, and CompuServe B. Different information services, BBSs, and communications programs support different protocols.

✦ *Session.* The period during which you are connected to another computer, information service, or BBS.

✦ *SIG (special interest group).* A section of an information service devoted to a particular topic (such as legal issues, writing, Macintosh users, game playing, or hang gliding). Information services often have many SIGs. Within each SIG, you may be able to participate in interactive discussions, read and post messages, and download files that interest you.

✦ *Upload, uploading.* Transmitting a file or program from your Mac to an information service, BBS, or another user's computer.

Communication Essentials

Whether you are connecting by modem to an information service, a BBS, or another computer, or transferring files between two computers by using a direct-connect cable, the two communications programs need to have matching parameters. Both modems have to transmit data at the same speed, use the same file transfer protocols, and so on. If any of the essential communication parameters do not match, you may see garbage characters on screen, have difficulty transferring data, lose the connection inadvertently, or not be able to connect at all. Having mismatched parameters is like trying to converse with someone when each of you is speaking a different language.

After you create a standard communications document for a modem, you can use it as the starting point for any new communications session you undertake.

Figure 7-1 shows the components of a communications document window.

Phone
Book   Connection   Connection   Scroll back panel (data that has
control   clock   status   scrolled off screen appears here)

Cursor   Terminal status   Terminal pane (incoming and
            indicators (optional) outgoing text is displayed here)

Figure 7-1: A communications document window

Steps: Creating a General Communications Document for Use with a Modem

1. Choose New from the File menu (or press ⌘-N), select Communications from the scrolling list, and click OK. An untitled communications document appears, as previously shown in Figure 7-1.

2. Choose Connection from the Settings menu. The Connection Settings dialog box appears, as shown in Figure 7-2. You use this dialog box to set up the current communications document for a modem connection (Apple Modem Tool) or a direct cable connection (Serial Tool).

3. Choose Apple Modem Tool from the Method pop-up menu. The default settings in the Port Settings section of the dialog box are 2400 bps (bits per second), no parity, 8 data bits, 1 stop bit, and no handshake. Generally, these settings are correct for a Mac with a 2400 bps modem that will be communicating with an online information service, a BBS, or a friend with a similar modem.

(continued)

Select a connection tool from this pop-up menu

Connection Settings   (**OK**)

Method: [Apple Mode... ▼]   (Cancel)

┌ When dialing ─────────────────┐ ┌ Port Settings ──────────────────┐
│ Dial Phone Number [   ] ▼ │ │ Baud Rate : [2400 ▼]   (Cabling...) │
│   │ │ Parity :   [None ▼]   │
│ Dialing Method : [Touch-Tone™ ▼]│ │ Data Bits : [8 ▼]   │
│ ☒ Redial [3] times every [10] seconds │ │ Stop Bits : [1   ▼]   │
│   │ │ Handshake : [None   ▼]   1.5.5 │
├ When answering ───────────────┤ │   │
│ Answer phone after [2] rings   │ │   │
├ Modem options ────────────────┤ │   [Modem Port]   [Printer Port] │
│ Modem : [Hayes-Compatible Modem ▼] │ │   │
│ Error Correction : [None   ▼] │ │   │
│ Correction Type : [Software MNP ▼] │ │ ◁   ▷   │
│ ☐ Display Modem Monitor Window │ └─────────────────────────────────┘

Figure 7-2: The Connection Settings dialog box

If you have a 9600 bps or faster modem, however, you need a special cable
wired for a *hardware handshake.* The computer uses one line of the cable
to tell the modem that data is being sent to the Mac faster than the Mac can
handle it and that the modem needs to pause until the Mac catches up. If
you have such a cable, choose the appropriate setting from the Handshake
pop-up menu.

4. In the Modem Options section of the dialog box, choose your modem
from the Modem pop-up menu.

If your specific brand or model isn't listed, the Hayes-Compatible Modem
choice will work for most modems. Check your modem user's guide for
more details about your modem.

To choose options from the pop-up menus for Error Correction and
Correction Type, you must select a modem that supports error correction. If
you have a non-Apple modem, choose Custom from the Modem pop-up
menu and enter the appropriate settings for your modem in the Custom
Modem Definition dialog box that appears (see Figure 7-3). To fill in the
settings, you will need to have your modem manual in hand. Turning on
Balloon Help also helps.

If you have a non-Apple modem and need additional assistance in
entering the proper strings for a Custom Modem Definition, call the
modem manufacturer or contact Claris Technical Support.

Figure 7-3: Use the Custom Modem Definition dialog box to enter settings for non-Apple modems.

5. In the When Dialing section, enter the telephone number of the other computer system, BBS, or information service; the type of phone service you are using (touch-tone, pulse, or mixed); the number of times you want the modem to redial the number if it detects a busy signal; and the number of seconds between redials. (If you don't want it to redial, remove the check from the Redial check box.)

When you type the phone number, include all digits that must be dialed. For example, if the call is long-distance, the number is usually preceded by 1. If your phone system requires you to dial 9 to get an outside line, the first digit of the phone number you enter should be 9. You can include hyphens in the number to improve readability, although they are not required.

You can also add pauses by inserting one or more commas between numbers. Each comma normally represents a two-second pause. If you need to reach an outside line before you dial the phone number, for example, the entry may look similar to the following:

```
9,,555-8812
```

In this example, the modem dials 9, waits four seconds, and then dials the rest of the number.

6. In the When Answering section, set the number of rings the modem must detect before it answers an incoming call.

The minimum allowable number of rings is 1. If you never want the modem to answer incoming calls, you can set this item to a very high number, such as 255.

(continued)

7. *Optional:* If you want to see the modem commands as they occur during the session, check Display Modem Monitor Window at the bottom-left corner of the Connection Settings dialog box. A Modem Monitor window appears at the bottom of your screen.

8. In the bottom-right section of the dialog box, click the icon of the port to which the modem cable is connected.

9. Click OK to retain the new connection settings.

10. Choose Terminal from the Settings menu. The Terminal Settings dialog box appears (see Figure 7-4).

Figure 7-4: The Terminal Settings dialog box (VT102 options shown)

When a Mac is connected with another computer by modem or by cable, the Mac can *emulate* (pretend to be) a number of different computer terminals. Different emulation choices provide varying degrees of control over how text and graphics are displayed on the Mac's screen. There are two general types of emulation provided: the VT102 Tool and the TTY tool. *VT102* provides emulation support for several varieties of intelligent terminals from Digital Equipment Corporation; *TTY* (Teletype) is for dumb terminals.

11. Select the emulation type and terminal settings appropriate for your communications setup.

Table 7-1, presented after these steps, describes the VT102 terminal settings you are most likely to use. For an explanation of the other settings, refer to ClarisWorks Help.

Click the screen icons to select Screen settings. The effects of your choices are shown in the text box on the right side of the dialog box. If you choose the TTY Tool, rather than the VT102 Tool, a single screen appears (see Figure 7-5). The screen contains options that are a subset of the options available for the VT102.

Figure 7-5: TTY Tool options

12. Click OK to record the terminal settings.

13. Choose File Transfer from the Settings menu to choose a default method for conducting file transfers. The File Transfer Settings dialog box appears. If you prefer, however, you can wait until you're online to make a selection. (File transfer options are discussed later in this chapter. Refer to the "Down to business" sections for suggested protocols.)

14. Save the communications document.

If you want to use the document as the basis for most communication documents, refer to the section in Chapter 10 on using stationery documents to set new defaults for an environment.

Note

When you save a communications document, text in the terminal and scrollback panes is also saved. If you want to use the document as a communications template, you may want to clear both panes by choosing the Clear Screen and Clear Saved Lines commands from the Session menu.

Table 7-1	
VT102 Tool Settings	
General	
Setting	*Description*
Terminal mode	Terminal choices include ANSI/VT102 and VT52 (two varieties of terminals from Digital Equipment Corporation), and TTY (Teletype).
	Begin by trying the ANSI/VT102 choice, particularly if you are connecting to a PC rather than a Mac. If the information service or BBS does not respond properly to the ANSI/VT102 setting (or if you don't need the features and special keys defined for the VT102), use the TTY Tool setting.
On Line	When this box is checked, you can connect and communicate with the other computer system. Leaving it unchecked means you want to work offline. Normally, you should check the On Line box.
Local Echo	When this box is checked, everything you type is automatically displayed in the terminal window. When this box is unchecked, you are relying on the other computer to echo back to your screen whatever you just typed. After you connect with the other computer, check this box if nothing you type appears on your screen. Remove the check mark if you see double characters for everything you type (HHeelllloo, for example).
Show Status Bar	When this box is checked, informative status indicators are added to the top of the communications window (refer back to Figure 7-1). This setting does not affect communications.
Show Tab Ruler	When this box is checked, a ruler bar is added to the top of the communications window. This setting does not affect communications.
Text Cursor	The cursor can be shown as either a flashing underline or a flashing block. Choose the one you prefer.
Answerback Message	If you want, you can enter a brief text string ("Connected with Steve's Mac," for example) that will automatically be transmitted when another computer connects with yours.

Screen

Setting	Description
Width	The text width. Terminal width options are 80 or 132 characters per line.
Size	The text size. Characters can be displayed in 9- or 12-point type.
Auto Wrap to Next Line	When this box is checked, if a line contains more characters than the line number specified for the terminal width, it will automatically wrap to the next line.
Insert Characters	When this box is checked, you can insert characters in the middle of a text string you are typing. When unchecked, characters will replace existing text.
Scroll Text	Select Jump or Smooth to determine how incoming text will scroll.
Inverse Video	Checking this box displays white text on a black background, rather than black text on a white background.

Keyboard

Setting	Description
Keyclick Sound	When this box is checked, you hear a click whenever a key is pressed.
New Line on a Return	Click this check box if the cursor does not automatically move to a new line when you press the Return key to end a paragraph.

Making the connection

When you are ready to connect with another computer, turn on the modem and follow one of the following procedures (depending on whether you or the other computer will initiate the connection).

Steps: Initiating a Call to Another Computer

1. Open the ClarisWorks communications document.
2. Check the Connection, Terminal, and File Transfer settings.
3. To initiate the call, choose Open Connection from the Session menu (or press Shift-⌘-O).

(continued)

The program dials the number you entered in the Dial Phone Number text-edit box in the Connection Settings dialog box. If the text-edit box is blank (that is, you haven't entered a number), ClarisWorks prompts for the number to dial.

As an alternative, if you have created a Phone Book entry for the service, BBS, or computer (as discussed later in this chapter in "Using the Phone Book feature"), you can initiate the connection by choosing Phone Book from the Settings menu; pressing ⌘-B; or clicking the phone-book control (the dial icon), choosing the name of the system with which you want to connect, and clicking Connect (see Figure 7-6). If you can't find the name of the system you want to call or you change your mind, click Done.

Figure 7-6: You can dial the number for the system you want to connect with by choosing its name from the Phone Book.

Note

Normally, you can turn on the modem just before you initiate a connection or before the other computer calls you. You don't have to leave the modem on when you don't need it. However, you need to turn on some modems, particularly some fax modems, prior to starting up the Mac. Otherwise, the software that controls the modem may not be in effect for that computing session. Check your manual to see whether your modem has any special on/off requirements.

Steps: Waiting for a Call from Another Computer

1. Open the ClarisWorks communications document.
2. Check the Connection, Terminal, and File Transfer settings.

3. Choose Wait for Connection from the Session menu (or press Shift-⌘-W). A Modem Status window appears, as shown in Figure 7-7, and the modem is instructed to wait for and automatically answer calls. You can click Cancel at any time to reset the modem so it will not continue to wait for an incoming call.

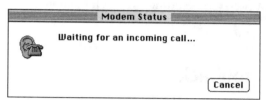

Figure 7-7: The Modem Status window when the modem is waiting for a call

The first time you attempt to connect with another person's computer, an information service, or a BBS, you should agree on the communication parameters beforehand. At a minimum, you need to agree on the following parameters:

✦ Baud rate

✦ Parity

✦ Data bits

✦ Stop bits

✦ A protocol for file transfers (if you intend to exchange files during the session)

During the initial few seconds of the connection, many modems can negotiate some of the more important settings, such as speed and protocols for error correction and compression. Unfortunately, many other modems can't negotiate these settings. If one of the users attempts to correct a mismatch by changing the settings while online, the connection may be lost. You can avoid potential aggravation by agreeing on settings before you try to connect.

Setting Communication preferences

The Preferences command in the Edit menu enables you to do the following:

✦ Set defaults for how the scrollback pane operates.

✦ Choose the method for capturing incoming data.

✦ Determine what to do — if anything — when a communications document is opened.

✦ Select a folder in which downloads will automatically be stored.

✦ Choose tools for the connection, terminal emulation, and the file transfer protocol.

You can establish different preference settings for each communications document. You can also set global defaults to be used with every new communications document (see Chapter 11 for details).

Controlling the scrollback

Most communications programs automatically track all data that is sent or received during a session. As you type new text and as information is transmitted to you, the session data scrolls off the screen. If you want to see what someone said to you earlier in the session, or find the ID number of a file that has scrolled off screen, you simply drag the scroll bar back until the information reappears.

ClarisWorks, on the other hand, takes a different approach to recording session data in order to accommodate Macs that have little memory to spare. First, instead of being automatic, recording the data is an optional part of a communications session. Second, you can use the Preferences dialog box to specify how the program should handle scrollback data. Third, ClarisWorks displays the information in a separate pane at the top of the communications window.

There are two ways of looking at the ClarisWorks scrollback options:

✦ The ClarisWorks scrollback options offer extensive control over how much old data is retained in memory and whether it is saved to disk when an information service or BBS sends a command to clear your screen.

✦ The ClarisWorks scrollback options introduce an unnecessary set of procedures for handling something that is normally transparent to communications users.

Whichever way you choose to look at it, you're stuck with the scrollback options. The following sections describe how they work.

Viewing the scrollback

As the terminal window fills with data, old information scrolls off the top of the window. As long as the Save Lines Off Top command (⌘-T) in the Session menu is preceded by a check mark, the old data is recorded rather than discarded. Whether the scrollback pane is displayed or hidden, the data is still being recorded.

When you first open a communications document, the scrollback pane is hidden. To view the scrollback, you can use either of the following methods:

✦ Choose Show Scrollback from the Settings menu (or press ⌘-L).

✦ Drag down the scrollback pane divider, as shown in Figure 7-8.

As soon as the system has received a screenful of data, the data begins to appear in the scrollback pane.

To hide the scrollback pane, press ⌘-L again, choose Hide Scrollback from the Settings menu, or drag the scrollback pane divider up until it disappears.

Figure 7-8: You can manually open or resize the scrollback pane.

Setting scrollback preferences

You set scrollback defaults in the Preferences dialog box. Choose Preferences from the Edit menu and choose Communications from the Topics pop-up menu in the Preferences dialog box that appears (see Figure 7-9).

You set scrollback settings in the upper-left section of the Preferences dialog box; Unlimited scrollback is the default setting. You can limit scrollback to a specific number of data lines, screens, or kilobytes (groups of 1,024 characters) by using the pop-up menu and text-edit box.

Set scrollback options here

Figure 7-9: You set communications defaults in the Preferences dialog box.

Note

Some information services and BBSs send information one screen at a time and send a command to clear the current screen before transmitting the next one. To avoid losing the previous screen, click the Save Screen Before Clearing check box. (For more information about setting Communications preferences, see Chapter 11.)

Working with the scrollback pane

When the scrollback pane is open, you can do several things:

✦ Scroll backward and forward by using the scroll bar.

✦ Copy the current screen in the terminal window into the scrollback pane by choosing Save Current Screen from the Session menu.

✦ Eliminate all data in the scrollback pane by choosing Clear Saved Lines from the Session menu.

✦ Copy selected data from the scrollback pane and paste it into the terminal window. The system sends information you paste into the terminal window to the other computer or information service, just as if you had typed it manually.

Tip

Copying information from the scrollback pane and then pasting it into the terminal window can be handy. For example, you can use this method to download files from a BBS. In order to download a file, you often have to identify it by its ID number. You can request a directory of new files and then, after you receive the directory, go back into the scrollback. Next, select and copy (⌘-C) the ID number for the first file you want to download. When the program prompts you for the file to download, use the Paste command (⌘-V) to enter the ID number.

Capturing text

In most cases, you will want to use one of the more advanced file transfer protocols, such as XMODEM or Kermit, to transfer files from one computer to another. Regardless of whether the file is a formatted word processing document, a Macintosh program, or a simple ASCII text file, you can still use a file transfer protocol.

Occasionally, however, you may want to make a record of incoming text, such as a lengthy help message from an information service or an author's description of a program he or she has uploaded. Because such information is normally just displayed on the screen (it doesn't have to be downloaded), a different procedure is used to capture the text. No file transfer protocol is needed.

Just before the information you want to capture appears on screen, choose Capture to File from the Session menu. A standard file dialog box appears. Type the filename under which the text will be saved and click Save. All incoming data is saved to the file. When you want to stop capturing incoming text, choose Stop Capture from the Session menu.

You can capture data in two different formats: Port or Screen. You select the format in the Preferences dialog box that appears when you choose Preferences from the Edit menu (refer to Figure 7-9 and see Chapter 11 for instructions).

Port format captures data exactly as it is sent, along with any tabs, line feeds, or form feeds that have been embedded in the text. *Screen* format, on the other hand, is straight ASCII text.

Working with tables

You can convert some tables you get from information services into a table format suitable for manipulating in a spreadsheet. Stock information is a common example.

To copy data in a tabular format, select the table in the terminal window, and choose Copy Table from the Edit menu. If the table is in the middle of the terminal window, you can copy just the contents of the table and ignore information in the left and right margins by pressing the ⌘ key as you drag to highlight the table. Paste the table into a spreadsheet by clicking a destination cell and choosing Paste from the Edit menu (or pressing ⌘-V).

Using the Phone Book feature

The Phone Book is an optional directory you can use to record and dial the phone numbers of information services, BBSs, and other computers with which you want to connect. Every communications document can have its own Phone Book. If you use the same communication parameters for several information services or BBSs, you can create a generic communications document and add all the appropriate phone numbers to the document's Phone Book.

Steps: Creating a Phone Book

1. Open the communications document to which you want to attach a Phone Book.

2. Choose Phone Book from the Settings menu, press ⌘-B, or click the Phone Book control (previously shown in Figure 7-1) and choose Edit Phone Book. The Phone Book Entry dialog box appears, ready for you to create a new listing (see Figure 7-10).

Figure 7-10: A blank page for a new Phone Book entry

3. In the appropriate boxes, enter a name for the service or computer and a complete phone number (including any required prefixes).

4. For a modem connection, leave PhoneNumber in the Type box.

5. Click OK to accept the new entry.

Steps: Dialing with the Phone Book

1. Turn on the modem.

2. Open the communications document to which the Phone Book is attached.

3. Choose Phone Book from the Settings menu (or press ⌘-B). The Phone Book for the current document appears (illustrated previously in Figure 7-6), listing all the entries you have created.

4. Select the entry you want to dial and click Connect. The number is dialed and a connection is attempted, using the current communication parameters for the document.

— or —

1. Turn on the modem.

2. Open the communications document to which the Phone Book is attached.

3. Click the Phone Book control (the telephone dial icon at the top-left of the communications document window). A pop-up menu that lists all services, BBSs, and other computers in the current document's Phone Book appears below the control. Drag down until the correct service is selected and release the mouse button. The number for the service is dialed and a connection is attempted using the current communication parameters for the document.

You can edit Phone Books to add new numbers, delete unwanted numbers, and edit existing numbers. To edit the Phone Book, choose Phone Book from the Settings menu, press ⌘-B, or click the Phone Book control and choose Edit Phone Book. You can make any of the following changes:

✦ Click New to create a new entry.

✦ Select an entry and click Delete to remove it from the Phone Book.

✦ Select an entry and click Edit to change the name or number for an entry.

Click Done when you finish making changes.

Connecting via Modems

The most common uses for the ClarisWorks communications environment are connecting with an information service, a BBS, or another user's computer by using a modem. After you have determined the correct numbers and settings, you can save the communications document as a stationery document to eliminate the setup time for future sessions.

Down to business: connecting with an online information service

Many of the larger information services, such as America Online, have their own communications software you need to use in order to connect with their service. These services either include the cost of the software in their sign-up fee or provide it at no cost.

You can access text-based information services and BBSs with any standard communications program, including the ClarisWorks communications environment.

Steps: Accessing an Online Information Service or BBS by Using ClarisWorks

1. Obtain an access number and a list of connection parameters from the service.

   Information service access numbers are often restricted to particular modem speeds. Be sure to select one that corresponds with your modem's capabilities.

2. Choose Connection and Terminal from the Settings menu, and set parameters to match the parameters the service requires. Be sure to enter the access number for the service in the Connection Settings dialog box.

   As a starting point, you can use the communications document you created in the section "Communication Essentials," earlier in this chapter. You may also want to select a file transfer protocol at this time, or you can select it while online, prior to initiating the first transfer.

3. Choose Open Connection from the Session menu (or press Shift-⌘-O). The number you entered in the Connection Settings dialog box is dialed.

4. When the information service or BBS responds (you may see a message saying *CONNECT,* for example), enter any information requested. Entering this information is essential to the logon process.

For example, the service may ask you to enter a user name, an ID, or your full name, address, and so on. Many services also expect you to enter a password you've selected or that has been assigned to you.

5. When you want to end the session, type or choose the command that the information service or BBS requires (Off, Bye, Quit, and Logoff are common examples). After the system responds, choose Close Connection (Shift-⌘-W) from the Session menu. The modem disconnects and releases the phone line.

Tip

If the information service doesn't have a local access number in your city or town, don't choose one for the nearest city. Instead, pick one in a neighboring state. Depending on your agreement with your chosen long-distance company, out-of-state long-distance calls may be much cheaper than in-state long-distance calls. Some information services also have an 800 number you can use to connect with them. Although such numbers are normally provided at an extra cost to you, they may be cheaper than a long-distance call.

Down to business: connecting with a Mac or a PC

From a communications standpoint, connecting with another PC or Mac differs little from connecting with a BBS or an information service. The main differences are:

✦ *Speed.* Because you do not have to pay surcharges for high-speed connections, you can use the fastest speed both modems support.

✦ *Modem features used.* If both modems offer advanced error correction or data compression protocols in ROM, you can use those features to ensure error-free, speedy file transfers.

Steps: Connecting with a Mac or a PC

1. Agree on a set of communication parameters to use. In particular, the parameters should include baud rate, parity, data bits, and stop bits. When you set the baud rate, select the highest speed both modems support. When one is a 28800-baud modem and the other is a 9600-baud modem, for example, set the baud rate at 9600 for both modems.

(continued)

2. In ClarisWorks, choose Connection and Terminal from the Settings menu and set parameters to match the parameters the other computer requires. Be sure to enter the phone number for the other computer in the Connection Settings dialog box. You may also want to select a file transfer protocol at this time, or you can select it while you are online, prior to initiating the first transfer.

   The other computer user should open his or her communications program and set the initial communications parameters.

3. If you are going to initiate the call, the other computer user should set the communications program to wait for your incoming call. In ClarisWorks, you then choose Open Connection from the Session menu (or press Shift-⌘-O). The number you entered in the Connection Settings dialog box is dialed.

   — or —

   If you are going to receive the call, choose Wait for Connection from the Session menu (or press Shift-⌘-W). The other computer user then instructs the communications program to dial your computer's phone number.

The communications program on the receiving computer automatically answers the phone after the predetermined number of rings. During the first few seconds of the connection, the two modems negotiate about which special features — such as data compression and error correction — to use. They may also agree on an optimal baud rate for the session.

If the connection is successful, you should now be able to type in the terminal window and have your text appear on the other user's screen (and vice versa).

Transferring files while online

Transferring data and program files between two computers is a bit different from transferring them with an information service or BBS. No menus appear to help you through each step or help you choose a file transfer protocol. Setting matching protocols on the two systems is your responsibility, as is initiating the Send File and Receive File commands.

To transmit a file, begin by selecting a mutually agreeable file transfer protocol. Both programs should be set to use the same protocol. Type a message to the receiving system, telling it you are about to begin sending. The other computer should choose the appropriate command to receive a file. (In ClarisWorks, choose Receive File from the Session menu.) To begin transmitting, choose Send File from the Session menu, and choose the file to send.

To receive a file, begin by selecting a mutually agreeable file transfer protocol. Both programs should be set to use the same protocol. When the other user instructs you to prepare for the transmission, choose Receive File from the Session menu. In the sending program, the other user should choose the command to send a file and choose the file to send.

Note

You can set some protocols, such as Kermit, to receive files automatically without using a Receive File command.

Ending the session

When you are ready to end the session, type your intent to the other user and choose Close Connection from the Session menu (or press Shift-⌘-O).

The Direct Connection

You can transfer files between any two computers — including computers of different types, such as Macs and PCs — by connecting their serial ports with a *null-modem cable*. (You don't need modems.) To connect a pair of Macs that are Mac Pluses or newer, you can use a mini DIN-8 to mini DIN-8 ImageWriter cable.

After you make the connection, all you need to do is launch a communications program on each machine, set matching communication parameters, and then use any communications protocol they have in common — XMODEM, for example — to perform file transfers in either direction. Because you are using a cable and the Serial Tool, rather than communicating over a phone line with modems, file transfers can occur at much higher speeds.

Down to business: transferring files between a pair of Macs

Here are some common examples of instances when you may want to transfer files between a pair of Macs that are connected by a cable:

✦ You have two Macs — a desktop Mac and one you use outside the office, such as a PowerBook. You can use a direct hookup to transfer files you've edited or created outside the office to your desktop system.

✦ You've prepared some important files for a presentation you plan to give to a client. Use the direct-connect method to transfer copies of the files to your PowerBook before you hit the road.

✦ You have purchased a new Mac and want to copy some important data files to it quickly.

✦ One or more of the files you need to move between machines is too large to fit on a floppy disk.

Tip

Another way to connect a pair of Macs without dealing with a communications program is to connect them with a standard AppleTalk network cable, creating a two-person network. After turning on file sharing with the appropriate system software control panels, you can easily exchange files between the two Macs.

Connecting the cable

You can use a standard ImageWriter II printer cable to connect any pair of Macs that are Mac Pluses or newer. Each end of the cable has a round 8-pin connector called a *mini DIN-8*. Attach the cable to the modem or printer port on the back of each Mac. Before you connect or disconnect the cable, turn off both machines.

Configuring the communications document

In this section, you will create a communications document you can use to transfer data between a pair of Macs. After you create and save the document, make a copy of it on a floppy disk, install it on the second Mac, and perform a typical file transfer. The first step is to configure the communications document.

Steps: Creating a Mac-to-Mac Communications Document

1. Create a new communications document by choosing New from the File menu (or pressing ⌘-N).

2. When the document opens, choose Connection from the Settings menu. The Connection Settings dialog box appears. Use the following settings:

   Method: Serial Tool

   Baud Rate: 57600

   Parity: None

   Data Bits: 8

   Stop Bits: 1

   Handshake: None

3. Be sure the port to which the communications cable is connected is selected in the Current Port box.

4. Click OK to accept the new settings.

If another person is going to be involved in the file transfers, you can configure the Terminal settings so you can type back and forth to each other between transfers (Step 5). If not, skip to Step 6.

5. Choose Terminal from the Settings menu. The Terminal Settings dialog box appears (illustrated previously in Figure 7-4 and described in Table 7-1). Choose the VT102 Tool from the Emulation pop-up menu and set the following options (you can leave all other settings as they were initially):

General: On Line, Local Echo

Screen: Auto Wrap to Next Line

Keyboard: New Line on a Return

After making the changes, click OK to accept the new settings.

6. Choose File Transfer from the Settings menu. The File Transfer Settings dialog box appears, as shown in Figure 7-11.

Figure 7-11: The File Transfer Settings dialog box

7. Choose the following settings from the pop-up menus:

Protocol: XMODEM Tool

Method: MacBinary

Transfer Options: 1K Blocks or CleanLink

8. Check the boxes for Use Filename Sent by Remote Computer and Enable Auto Receive. Click OK to accept the new settings.

Files will be received in the folder you specified in the Communications section of the Preferences dialog box. (For information on setting preferences, see Chapter 11.)

(continued)

9. Save the communications document (you might name it *Mac-to-Mac,* for example).

10. Make a copy of the communications document on a floppy disk and copy it to the other Mac.

Next, test the file transfer process.

Steps: Transferring Files

1. Launch ClarisWorks on both Macs and open the Mac-to-Mac communications document.

2. On both machines, choose Open Connection from the Session menu (or press Shift-⌘-O).

3. To test the connection, type some text on one of the Mac keyboards. It should appear simultaneously in the terminal window on both Macs.

4. Choose Send File from the Session menu on one of the Macs. A standard file dialog box appears.

5. Select a file to send and click the Send Button. The file transfer occurs automatically.

Because you selected Enable Auto Receive, file transfers can occur without requiring the receiving computer to choose Receive File from the Session menu. You can use this configuration to send files in either direction. When you are through transferring files, choose Close Connection from the Session menu on both Macs (or press Shift-⌘-O).

The 1K XMODEM protocol is sufficiently speedy and error-free for most file transfers. If you want to send a large number of files, however, you may prefer to use the Kermit protocol. Of the protocols supported by ClarisWorks, Kermit is the only one that permits unattended transfers of *batches* of files. (For more information on using Kermit, see "The Kermit File Transfer Protocol" later in this chapter.)

Caution

If you use the Kermit protocol's Overwrite Existing Files option, and you transfer a file with the same name as one that already exists in the destination folder on the receiving machine, the existing file will be replaced by the new one.

Down to business: transferring files between a Mac and a PC

With Apple's continued penetration into the business market, finding both Macs and PCs in the same office is becoming more common. In the past, sharing files between the two platforms was difficult. Disks were formatted differently, and file formats varied widely between the systems.

The inclusion of an Apple SuperDrive (the 1.4MB, 3.5-inch floppy disk drive) in all Macs that are Mac Pluses or newer has helped minimize the differences between Mac and PC data. With PC Exchange (included with all recent versions of the Macintosh system software) and several other commercial programs from third-party software companies, Macs equipped with a SuperDrive can both read from and write to 3.5-inch PC floppies. Similar software is also available for the PC.

There are several translation software programs designed to handle the differences in file formats. Many programs, such as ClarisWorks, can import and export data by using file formats that are compatible with formats of other programs, so moving data between Macs and PCs is relatively easy.

This section explains how to use a direct-connect cable to shuttle files between the two systems. This approach is particularly useful in the following circumstances:

✦ When some files are too large to fit on a single floppy disk

✦ When you need to move many files

✦ When you frequently need to move files between the systems

Although you also can use a pair of modems (one for each computer) that are connected over a telephone line to accomplish the same thing, a direct-connect cable has one huge advantage — speed. You can move data easily and reliably across a serial cable at 57,600 baud.

The biggest problem with the direct-connect approach to data transfer between Macs and PCs is the difficulty in locating an off-the-shelf cable designed to do the job. Unless you are up to the task of building your own cable, you will probably need to have one built for you. Figure 7-12 shows the appropriate cable pin-outs, depending on whether the PC has a 25-pin or 9-pin serial port.

Figure 7-12: Cable pin-outs

Connecting the cable

Attach the circular 8-pin end of the cable (the mini DIN-8 connector) to the modem or printer port on the back of the Mac. Connect the other end (either 9-pin or 25-pin) to any free serial port on the back of the PC. On some PCs, the ports will be labeled (Serial 1 and Serial 2 or COM1 and COM2). The number of serial ports varies from one manufacturer to another, but PCs usually have one or more such ports. Do not use the port to which the PC's modem is connected or assigned.

Configuring the communications programs

On the Mac side, use a ClarisWorks communications document as the communications software. For the PC, almost any communications program will do. The following steps explain how to configure the two programs so the machines can communicate with each other.

Steps: Configuring ClarisWorks for Mac-to-PC Communications

1. Open a new communications document by choosing New from the File menu (or pressing ⌘-N).

2. Choose Connection from the Settings menu. The Connection Settings dialog box appears (shown previously in Figure 7-2). Choose the following settings:

   Method: Serial Tool

   Baud Rate: 57600

Parity: None

Data Bits: 8

Stop Bits: 1

Handshake: None

3. Be sure the port to which the communications cable is connected is selected in the Current Port box.

4. Click OK to accept the new settings.

Because you are only transferring files from one computer to the other, the Terminal settings are irrelevant. They control what appears on the two screens when text is typed on either keyboard; they don't affect file transfers.

5. Choose File Transfer from the Settings menu. The File Transfer Settings dialog box appears. Choose the following settings from the pop-up menus:

Protocol: XMODEM Tool

Method: Straight XMODEM

Transfer Options: 1K Blocks or CleanLink

You can ignore the other settings.

6. Click OK to accept the new settings.

7. Choose Terminal from the Settings menu.

8. With the General icon selected in the left window, click the On Line and Local Echo check boxes, and then click OK.

9. Choose Open Connection from the Session menu (or press Shift-⌘-O).

Now set up the PC communications program.

Steps: Configuring the PC Communications Program

1. Run the DOS or Windows communications program, such as HyperTerminal (Windows 95).

2. Configure the program to match the settings in ClarisWorks:

Baud Rate: 57600

(continued)

Parity: None

Data Bits: 8

Stop Bits: 1

Handshake: None

3. Be sure the port to which the communications cable is connected is selected in the program. In most cases, the port is COM1 or COM2.

4. Set Local Echo (sometimes called *Half Duplex*) to On.

5. If the program enables you to set a default for the file transfer protocol, choose 1K XMODEM.

6. If the program does not automatically connect to the Mac, issue the command to put the PC program online.

Windows 95 and Direct-to-Mac Connections

If the PC is running Windows 95, you can use HyperTerminal as the PC communications program. (HyperTerminal is included with Windows 95.) To set up a direct connection to a Mac with HyperTerminal, first make sure HyperTerminal has been installed. It is normally found in the C:\Program Files\Accessories\HyperTerminal directory. If it is not found, you can install it from your Windows 95 setup disk or CD.

Once you launch HyperTerminal (Hypertrm), a Connection Description dialog box appears. Name the connection, select an icon to represent the connection, and click OK. The Phone Number dialog box appears. Click the Connect Using pop-up menu, choose the communications port to which the direct-connect cable is attached (*Direct to Com 2,* for example), and click OK. In the COM Properties dialog box that appears, set Bits per Second to *57600* (the highest rate supported by the Apple Communications Toolbox), Flow Control to *None,* and click OK.

After testing the connection by transferring files (as described in this section), save the connection setup to disk so it can be reused for additional PC-to-Mac file transfers.

Note   When transferring files from PC to Mac, be sure you choose an appropriate file transfer protocol from the Protocol pop-up menu in HyperTerminal's Send File dialog box.

Testing the connection

When both programs are running, you can test the connection by typing a string of text on the Mac's keyboard. As you type, the characters should appear on the PC's screen.

Now perform the test again by typing something on the PC's keyboard. The characters should appear on the Mac's screen.

In the tests, you don't need to be concerned if text overlaps on the same line or you see extra blank lines between lines of text when you press Return. What's important is that the exact letters you type on one machine appear on the screen of the other machine. If nothing appears on the other machine's screen, you can probably trace the problem to one of the following causes:

✦ The wrong serial port is selected in either the Mac or the PC communications program.

✦ The cable is incorrectly wired.

If you see garbled characters on the other screen, the communication parameters between the two programs are probably mismatched. Check to make sure you have set all of the parameters correctly. If they are correct, reduce the baud rate setting in the two programs and try again.

Transferring files

You can move document files of almost any type (word processing, spreadsheet, and graphics, for example) from one machine to the other. There is usually little point in moving programs, however. Mac programs cannot normally be run on a PC, and vice versa.

Steps: Transferring Files from the Mac to the PC

1. If necessary, save or export the Macintosh documents to a format the destination program on the PC can read.

   If you use Microsoft Word for Windows, for example, you can save ClarisWorks word processing documents as Microsoft WinWord files. Be sure to check the import capabilities of the destination program on the PC. You may find it can read some Macintosh files directly without any conversion.

2. In ClarisWorks, choose Send File from the Session menu. A standard file dialog box appears.

3. Select the file you want to transmit and click Send.

4. On the PC, issue the communication program's command to receive a file. If you are prompted for a file transfer protocol, select 1K XMODEM. You may also be asked to name the file and choose the directory in which the file should be saved.

(continued)

During file transfers, ClarisWorks displays a window in which you can keep an eye on the progress (see Figure 7-13). Most PC communication programs display similar information.

Figure 7-13: ClarisWorks displays this window during file transfers.

Note

Even though you have selected 1K XMODEM as the transfer protocol in both programs, don't be surprised if a different XMODEM protocol is used (as shown in Figure 7-13).

Steps: Transferring Files from the PC to the Mac

1. If necessary, save or export the PC documents to a format the software on the Mac can read.

   If you are transferring documents from a program for which ClarisWorks does not have translators, check the export capabilities of the PC program. It may offer an export or save option that ClarisWorks (or another destination program on the Mac) understands, such as Microsoft's Rich Text Format (RTF).

Note

   Alternatively, System 7.5 and higher include the Macintosh Easy Open control panel and DataViz translators that can translate many common PC files to formats that can be read by the Mac. ClarisWorks 5.0 also includes a version of these translators, control panel, and extensions that — when enabled — give ClarisWorks the same translation capabilities.

2. On the PC, issue the communication program's command to send a file. You are asked to type the name of the file or select it from a file list. Be sure to specify the correct drive and directory in which the file is located. If you are prompted for a file transfer protocol, select 1K XMODEM.

3. In ClarisWorks, choose Receive File from the Session menu. The transfer begins. After the file is received, a standard file dialog box appears.

4. Select the destination drive and folder, type a filename, and then click Save.

For occasional file transfers between two Macs, or a Mac and a PC, the direct-connect approach works fine. If you regularly make these types of transfers, however, you should check out some products that are dedicated to performing this task. Both MacLinkPlus/PC (DataViz) and LapLink Mac III (Traveling Software), for example, enable you to move files between computers effortlessly, as well as translate them between a number of Mac and PC formats. Each product also includes an appropriate cable for connecting a Mac with another Mac or a PC.

The Kermit File Transfer Protocol

Although XMODEM will readily handle transfers of any file type from one machine to another, it has a couple of disadvantages:

✦ You can transfer only one file at a time.

✦ Because the filename is not transmitted with the file, you must name each file manually as it is received.

If you're willing to put up with Kermit's slower performance, you can use the Kermit protocol to transfer batches of files with a single command. When the files are received, they can also be named automatically.

Steps: Using Kermit to Transfer Batches of Files

1. In ClarisWorks, choose File Transfer from the Settings menu. The File Transfer Settings dialog box appears.

2. Set options in the dialog box to match the settings shown in Figure 7-14.

   When you are connecting a Mac and a non-Mac (such as a PC), select Binary as the method. The Binary option enables you to transfer ordinary text files or formatted documents. When you are connecting two Macs, use MacBinary as the method. MacBinary can transfer any type of Mac document, including programs.

(continued)

Figure 7-14: Settings for a batch file transfer

Tip

Selecting a larger packet size (Extra Long Packets, in this example) can improve the speed of the transfer if both programs can use the larger packet size.

3. On the PC, set Kermit as the new file transfer protocol. Depending on the communications program, you may be able to set a file transfer protocol as a default, or you may have to select the protocol immediately prior to issuing the send or receive command.

4. On the PC or Mac, choose the command to send a file or send a group of files. (In ClarisWorks, choose Send File or Send Batch from the Session menu. If you choose Send Batch, you can specify several files to transmit together.)

5. Set the other machine to receive a file. (If the PC is the receiving machine, you may have to specify the Kermit protocol at this time.) The file transfer commences.

Note

When you are using the Kermit protocol to transfer PC files to the Mac, ClarisWorks may not recognize that the final transfer has been completed. If the transfer status window does not close by itself, click the Cancel Transfer button.

Note

When you use Kermit, the transfer speed can be moderately or considerably slower than when you use XMODEM. But if you aren't in a rush, you can use Kermit to transfer a batch of files to either machine, automatically, while you occupy yourself with something more productive.

Quick Tips

The following quick tips tell you how to deal with a common file transfer problem, create an auto logon macro and macros to automate routine communications tasks, quickly check basic communications settings, and issue AT commands.

Choosing the correct file transfer method

Whether you're connected to an online service or are simply downloading files from another computer, pay close attention to the file transfer method. *MacBinary* is the default and can only be used with Mac files. If you download files from a service (GEnie or CompuServe, for example), the files may not be true Mac files — they may be generic for multiple platforms — and an *Out of Memory* error message may appear, even if you have plenty of memory allocated. Switch to XMODEM if this problem occurs.

Creating an auto logon macro

Although ClarisWorks includes Phone Books for recording the numbers of the colleagues, friends, and information services with which you regularly connect, the Phone Book feature does not enable you to save a logon sequence along with the phone number. For most of us, memorizing IDs and passwords is a pointless exercise. With a little bit of work, you can use the ClarisWorks macro feature to create auto logon sequences that respond to a series of prompts on your favorite BBS or information service and, optionally, take you to the first area of the service you normally visit.

Steps: Recording an Auto Logon Macro

1. Open the communications document you have created for the information service or BBS, and choose Open Connection from the Session menu (or press Shift-⌘-O). ClarisWorks dials the number for the service.

2. After the connection has been established, choose Record Macro from the Macros submenu of the File menu. The Record Macro dialog box appears.

3. Name the macro, choose an Option-⌘-key combination or function key with which you will execute the macro, and click the Document Specific check box.

4. Click Record to begin recording.

5. Press whatever keys are necessary (if any) to complete the connection. (Some systems, for example, expect you to press Return immediately upon making the connection.)

(continued)

6. When the first system prompt appears (requesting a user ID, password, or both, for example), choose Macro Wait from the Macros submenu of the File menu (or press Shift-⌘-J). The Macro Wait dialog box appears, as shown in Figure 7-15.

Figure 7-15: The Macro Wait dialog box offers two options: Wait for a text string, or wait for a specific number of seconds of line inactivity.

7. Click the first radio button, type the system prompt (or enough of it to uniquely identify the text string for which you are waiting), and click OK.

8. After the dialog box disappears, type your normal response to the system prompt and then press Return.

9. If additional actions are required to complete the logon or to move to a particular part of the information service or BBS, record them now.

10. When the logon is completed, choose Stop Recording from the Macros submenu of the File menu (or press Shift-⌘-J).

11. Continue with the online session or issue the command to log off the system.

As an example, to log onto an information service and move to the Macintosh software library, you might use a macro that contains the following steps:

1. Macro Wait for text string: *U#=*

2. In the terminal window, type your user identification number, a comma, and your password, and then press Return.

3. Macro Wait for text string: *continue?*

4. Press Return in the terminal window.

5. Macro Wait for text string: *<H>elp?*

6. Type **Mac** in the terminal window and press Return.

7. Macro Wait for text string: *<H>elp?*

8. Type **3** in the terminal window and press Return.

To test or use your macro, choose Open Connection from the Session menu (or press Shift-⌘-O). As soon as the connection is established and before the first prompt from the service or BBS appears, execute the macro by pressing the Option-⌘-key or function key you defined for it. In the logon example, to avoid timing problems, you may want to eliminate Step 1 (Macro Wait for text string: *U#=*) and begin with Step 2. Then you can execute the macro after the ID prompt appears, instead of trying to sneak it in within the few seconds between the connection and the appearance of the ID prompt.

You have to observe a few precautions when you are working with communications macros. First, as the preceding example shows, macros are highly dependent on an unchanging information service or BBS structure and prompt sequences. If the service alters its logon sequence, reorganizes the names or locations of SIGs you regularly visit, or changes the wording of its prompts, the macro will fail. Then you have to re-record each macro that is affected — you cannot edit ClarisWorks macros.

Second, although auto logon macros are convenient, anyone can use them to log onto your account with the information service or BBS. If security is a problem in your office or home, you may want to assign a password to the communications document, as explained earlier in Chapter 1.

Third, you don't need to type the entire text string in the Macro Wait dialog box. However, you need to be careful to type a sufficient amount of text so the string is unique. In the auto logon example, Steps 5 and 7 wait for the text string *<H>elp?*. If the macro had been instructed to simply wait for *elp,* the next step could have been mistakenly triggered by any sentence or text string that contained *elp,* such as *helpful.* If the macro responds too early, it may fail.

Fourth, think twice before you check Play Pauses in a communications macro. Although recording the amount of time between each command you issue (rather than using Macro Wait commands) may seem logical and easier, times can vary significantly from one session to the next. The line conditions, the number of other users accessing the BBS or information service at the same time, and so on, affect the amount of time required for prompts to appear. If your responses are sent before they are requested, the information service or BBS may ignore them and ruin the macro in the process.

Note

If this or any other macro doesn't work, you can halt its execution at any time by pressing ⌘-period.

Automating a communications session with macros

Just as you can create auto logon macros, you can create macros to perform other common communication actions, such as:

✦ Going to specific SIGs and the electronic mail section of the service

✦ Selecting a file transfer protocol for downloads

✦ Logging off the system

For complex activities that require decision capabilities (such as checking for new mail and, if found, capturing the letters to a text file), you may want to investigate a more powerful commercial macro program, such as QuicKeys (CE Software).

Checking your communications settings

ClarisWorks provides an extremely handy command that enables you to examine basic communications settings quickly — without having to open all those Settings dialog boxes. Choose Info from the Settings menu (or press ⌘-I). The dialog box in Figure 7-16 appears.

Figure 7-16: Among other things, the Info command tells you the connection tool, terminal tool, and file transfer protocol currently in use, as well as the number of lines that are stored in the scrollback pane.

Those ubiquitous AT commands

Your communications software — in this case, the ClarisWorks communications environment in combination with Apple's Communications Toolbox — controls the modem attached to your Mac. The software controls the modem by sending instructions called *AT commands* (*AT* stands for *Attention*) to the modem.

If you are adventurous and want to learn more about your modem's capabilities, you can send AT commands to it. Grab your modem manual, turn to the listing of its commands, and follow the steps below for issuing AT commands.

Caution

Before you modify any of the modem's default commands, be sure the modem has a command you can use to reset it to its factory settings. (Often, this command is *AT&F.*) If you change a setting that shouldn't be changed, resetting the modem to its defaults will get you out of trouble.

Steps: Issuing AT Commands

1. Create or open a new communications document.

2. Choose Connection from the Settings menu. The Connection Settings dialog box appears.

3. Select Serial Tool as the method and choose a baud rate supported by the modem. Leave the other settings alone.

4. Click OK to accept the new connection settings.

5. Choose Terminal from the Settings menu. The Terminal Settings dialog box appears.

6. With the General icon selected (on the left side of the dialog box), enter check marks in the On Line and Local Echo check boxes. Leave the other settings alone.

7. Click OK to accept the new terminal settings.

8. Choose Open Connection from the Session menu (or press Shift-⌘-O). The modem will now respond to commands you type in the communications document.

9. Because some commands will eventually scroll off the screen, choose Show Scrollback from the Settings menu (or press ⌘-L).

As the example shows, type **AT** and press Return. (You have to end every instruction you send to the modem by pressing Return.) The modem should respond by displaying *OK* below your command.

Note

If you see double letters when you type commands (as in *AATT*), repeat Steps 5 through 7, but remove the check mark from the Local Echo check box.

The normal format for an AT command is *AT,* the command, an optional parameter number, and Return. An ampersand (&) or backslash (\) symbol precedes some commands. You select an option in other commands by ending them with a number (ATM0 or ATM1, for example).

You can issue multiple AT commands on the same line, as in the following:

```
AT M1L0
```

As the example shows, you can add spaces between commands to improve readability. As usual, you have to end the command string by pressing Return.

You can do the following useful things with AT commands (although not all modems offer these features):

✦ Change the volume of the modem's speaker or turn off the speaker entirely.

✦ Dial a phone number through the modem, using a pulse or touch-tone phone line (ATDT*phone number*, as in ATDT555-1212).

✦ Store frequently dialed numbers in the modem's memory.

✦ Store multiple communication setups, view them, and switch between them as needed.

✦ Switch between data and voice modes so you can speak to the person on the other end of the line without having to hang up and call back.

You can also use AT commands to modify the initialization string by selecting Custom from the Modem pop-up menu in the Modem Settings section of the Connection Settings dialog box. The default commands are listed, which you can then change (to turn off the modem's speaker, for example).

If you want to learn more about the commands your modem supports and how to issue them, refer to your modem manual. Remember, however, that unless you know what you're doing, you need to reset the modem to its factory defaults when you finish experimenting. Modern modems often include some special memory chips that retain your changes even after you turn off the modem.

Moving On Up

For basic communications, ClarisWorks serves most users very well. However, several major features are missing that you may eventually want to have, such as:

✦ *More-advanced file transfer protocols.* In particular, the YMODEM, YMODEM-G, and ZMODEM protocols provide faster data transfers and batch transfers. When the connection is broken during a file transfer, ZMODEM can pick up automatically where the transfer left off — instead of restarting the download from the beginning. These protocols are often available in inexpensive shareware communications programs, such as ZTerm. And other programs that rely on the Communications Toolbox may provide a ZMODEM tool that is compatible with the ClarisWorks communications environment. SITComm (Aladdin Systems) is one such program.

✦ *Faster direct-connect file transfers.* As long as your Mac communications program relies on the Communications Toolbox for serial transfers (as ClarisWorks does), file transfer speed is limited to 57600 bps. If you use ZTerm, for example, you can double the speed of file transfers and simultaneously obtain support for the ZMODEM protocol.

✦ *A more powerful macro or scripting language.* The ClarisWorks macro facility is crude when compared to that of stand-alone macro programs, such as QuicKeys. In particular, the inability to perform branching limits the usefulness of ClarisWorks macros.

For example, you may want to create a macro or script that checks for new mail and, if it finds any, automatically downloads the mail or captures it to a text file for you. If new mail is not found, on the other hand, the macro or script could simply log off the system. You cannot use a ClarisWorks macro to perform this task.

Summary

✦ A communications document can connect your Mac to information services, BBSs, or other computers via a modem. With the proper Communication Toolbox settings, you can also link a pair of computers with a special direct-connect cable.

✦ To assure a trouble-free connection, you must set matching communication parameters in both the sending and receiving communications programs.

✦ The Connection Settings dialog box enables you to specify whether you want to make a modem connection (Apple Modem Tool) or a direct link (Serial Tool). It also enables you to select a communications port (modem or printer) and specify the port settings.

✦ You use the Terminal Settings dialog box to specify a terminal emulation and set characteristics for how text will be displayed in the terminal pane, as well as how it will be transmitted to the other computer.

✦ In the File Transfer Settings dialog box, you select a protocol to use when sending or receiving files. The purpose of a file transfer protocol is to assure error-free data transfers. The protocol you choose must be supported by both the sending and receiving computers.

✦ You can store phone numbers for systems you want to call in the Connection Settings dialog box or in the communication document's Phone Book. Every communications document can have its own Phone Book for dialing one or more information services, BBSs, or other computers.

✦ With the proper settings, you can initiate a modem call or instruct ClarisWorks to wait for and answer an incoming modem call.

✦ Rather than storing old data in the terminal window, ClarisWorks provides a scrollback pane at the top of the window. As data is cleared from the terminal window, it is automatically transferred into the scrollback pane. You can scroll through the information in the scrollback pane, copy the information and paste it into the terminal window (or into other documents), force the current screen to be copied into the pane, and clear the contents of the pane.

✦ You can transfer files between a Mac and a non-Mac, as well as between Macs.

✦ No modems are necessary if you want to connect a pair of computers over a direct-connect cable. You must, however, have the proper cable and a communications program running on both systems. Because direct-connect file transfers between systems are not limited by modem capabilities, they can occur at very high speeds.

✦ You can use the ClarisWorks macro recorder to create auto logon macros, as well as to automate many routine communications tasks.

✦ The communications program sends commands to the modem. You can issue the same commands manually by selecting the Serial Tool and typing the commands in the terminal window.

✦   ✦   ✦

Integrating the ClarisWorks Environments

Generating a Mail Merge

Overview

A *merge* combines information from a database with a word processing document. In the most common use of a merge, a *mail merge,* you personalize form letters by inserting names from a database into a word processing document. The merged letters read "Dear Mickey" or "Dear Mrs. Samuels," rather than "Dear Friend" or "Dear Customer."

Every merge has two components: a database and a merge form. The *database* contains the information you want to insert into the merge form (names and addresses of friends, sales commission figures, or descriptions of catalog items, for example). The *merge form* is a text document, such as a form letter. You insert placeholders in the merge form, and each placeholder specifies the name of a database field (Last Name, for example). During the merge, data from the fields of each visible database record is inserted into the placeholders in the merge form. One copy of the merge document is printed for each visible (selected) database record.

Although a merge form is usually a word processing document, you can create it within a text frame in any ClarisWorks environment. For example, you can design a party invitation in a draw document and personalize it with information you place in a text frame. Also, even though merge forms are traditionally restricted to word processing documents, ClarisWorks can merge data into a spreadsheet document or frame, too.

Creating the Merge Database

You create a merge database as you do any other type of ClarisWorks database — by defining fields and creating records. (Refer to Chapter 5 for detailed information on ClarisWorks databases.)

You can also use the Address List Assistant to create an address database. Choose New from the File menu. The New Document dialog box appears. Click the Use Assistant or Stationery radio button in the New Document dialog box, choose All Assistants from the Category pop-up menu, choose the Address List Assistant, and click OK. Save your new address database before continuing.

The Elements of a Merge Form

As discussed previously, the merge form contains placeholders for data from database fields. Each placeholder contains the name of a database field, surrounded by special bracket symbols (as in «») that are added automatically when you select field names from the Mail Merge windoid (see Figure 8-1). To enter a field name and its surrounding brackets, you must select the field in the Mail Merge windoid, as explained in the step-by-step instructions for creating a merge form later in this chapter.

As with any other text in a word processing document or frame, you can apply different fonts, styles, colors, or other formatting options to the placeholders. You simply double-click to select the entire field name, including the brackets, and then apply formatting options.

You can use punctuation and spaces to separate merge fields from each other and from surrounding text. If the merge form contains two placeholders for the components of a name, as in «First»«Last», when the merge is performed, the result is the first name followed immediately by the last name (with no space in between), as in *TomJohnson*. To separate the two fields in the merge, add a space between the fields, as in «First» «Last».

You also can combine merge fields with normal text. For example, you can embed a merge field in a sentence:

✦ Just imagine your surprise when our prize van pulls up to the doorstep of the «Last Name» household.

✦ Because your sales were so extraordinary this quarter, «First Name», please find enclosed a commission check for «Commission» and a 15 percent bonus of «Bonus Amount».

Creating a Merge Form

To create a merge form, you type the basic text for the letter or document (that is, all the text that will be identical for each letter or document) and then, using the Mail Merge windoid, insert field placeholders at the appropriate spots in the text.

Steps: Inserting Fields into a Merge Form

1. Open the merge document or create a new one. (Remember that the merge form can be a word processing document, a non-word processing document that contains a text frame, a spreadsheet document, or a spreadsheet frame.)

2. Choose Mail Merge from the File menu. A standard Open file dialog box appears.

3. Choose a merge database, and click Open. If the database is not already open, it now opens. The Mail Merge windoid appears, as shown in Figure 8-1.

Figure 8-1: The Mail Merge windoid

If you discover you've opened the wrong database for the merge, click Switch Database in the Mail Merge windoid, and choose another database from the file list that appears.

4. In the merge document, set the text insertion point where you want to insert the first field placeholder.

5. In the Field Names list box of the Mail Merge windoid, select the field you want to insert.

6. Click Insert Field to add the field name and its surrounding brackets at the current text insertion point.

7. Repeat Steps 4 through 6 for additional field placeholders you want to add to the merge form.

8. Save the merge document. Saving the merge form associates the merge database with it. The next time you open the merge form and choose the Mail Merge command, the associated database automatically opens.

Figure 8-2 shows a completed merge form.

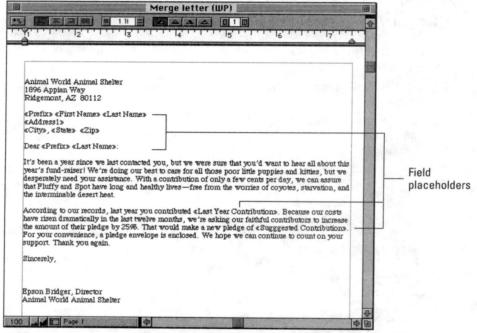

Figure 8-2: A typical merge form. All words in brackets are merge fields.

Viewing Data in a Merge Form

When working in a ClarisWorks merge form, you can look at either field names or actual data from the merge database. To view data, click the Show Field Data check box in the Mail Merge windoid (see Figure 8-3). The field placeholders disappear and are replaced by information from the first record of the merge database. To view other records, click the up- or down-arrow icons beside the Record text-edit box or type a specific record number in the Record text-edit box.

Click to flip through database records

Actual data is shown   Current record

Figure 8-3: Click Show Field Data to show information from database records in the merge form rather than field name placeholders.

Performing a Merge

After the merge form is ready, the mechanics of performing the merge are straightforward.

Steps: Performing a Merge

1. Open the merge database, if it is not already open.

2. To merge the entire database with the merge form, choose Show All Records from the Organize menu (or press Shift-⌘-A) and go to Step 3.

— or —

To merge selected records with the merge form, choose the Find command from the Layout menu (or press Shift-⌘-F). When the blank find request appears, specify criteria to find the record or records you want to print. Click Visible to search only the visible records or All to search the entire database. Click Find to execute the search.

3. *Optional:* If you want the merge documents to print in a specific order (alphabetically by last name or in zip code order, for example), sort the records by choosing the Sort Records command from the Organize menu (or press ⌘-J).

4. Open the merge document.

5. Choose Mail Merge from the File menu. The Mail Merge windoid appears.

6. Click the Print Merge button in the Mail Merge windoid. The Print dialog box appears.

7. Click Print, and the merge commences. One copy of the merge document is produced for each visible database record.

Before committing yourself to a massive merge, examine a few records on screen by clicking the Show Field Data check box in the Mail Merge windoid and then flipping through the records. This procedure (described in "Viewing Data in a Merge Form," earlier in this chapter) can save an enormous amount of paper if you have, for example, selected a wrong database field, forgotten to restrict the records to a particular subset, or incorrectly set the spacing between fields.

Down to Business: An Envelope Merge

After you understand the mechanics of a merge, the process becomes routine. Rather than step you through another typical mail merge, the following instructions explain how to perform a type of merge you may not have considered — an envelope merge. With a little experimentation, you can not only format and print envelopes from ClarisWorks, but also use a merge to automate the process by grabbing the mailing addresses from a database (an essential technique for mass mailings).

If you just want to print a single envelope, you can use ClarisWorks's Envelope or Address Envelope Assistant. (See Chapter 3 for details.)

Designing the merge form

This section explains how to create an envelope merge form as a document in the word processing environment. Figure 8-4 shows one such form that was designed for a center-feeding Apple LaserWriter IINT. The graphic rulers are displayed, rather than the normal word processing ruler, to show the approximate placement of the mailing address and return address sections.

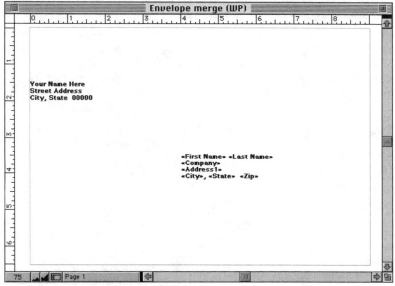

Figure 8-4: An envelope merge form

Steps: Creating the Envelope Merge Form

1. Create a new word processing document by choosing New from the File menu (or pressing ⌘-N). Choose Word Processing and then click OK.

2. Choose Page Setup from the File menu. The Page Setup dialog box appears.

3. Click the icon for landscape mode printing (the sideways icon) and select the paper option that corresponds to a #10 business envelope. Then click OK.

4. Choose Rulers from the Format menu. The Rulers dialog box appears.

5. Click the Graphics and Inches radio buttons and then click OK. The graphics rulers appear at the top and left sides of the blank word processing document (as previously shown in Figure 8-4). The outline of the document page should correspond to that of a #10 business envelope — 6.5 × 9 inches.

6. Type the return address in the position shown in Figure 8-4 or, if your envelopes are already imprinted with a return address, leave this part of the envelope blank.

Note

These instructions assume you are using a center-feed printer. If the printer is a right- or left-feed printer, enter the mailing address and return address at the top or near the bottom of the form, respectively.

7. For the mailing address section, press Return several times until you reach the 3.5- to 4-inch mark on the vertical ruler.

8. To align the lines of the address, choose the Tab command from the Format menu. The Tab dialog box appears (see Figure 8-5). Set a left tab at the 4-inch position by matching the settings shown in the figure, and then click OK. Press the Tab key once. The text insertion point is now correct for the first field of the mailing address.

Figure 8-5: To create a left tab at the 4-inch mark, match these settings.

9. Choose Open from the File menu and open the database that contains the mailing addresses.

(The remainder of this example uses the field names from Address List. If you are using your own database, substitute field names as appropriate.)

10. Select the envelope word processing document from the Window menu.

11. Choose Mail Merge from the File menu. A standard Open file dialog box appears. Choose an address database, and click Open. If the database is not already open, it opens now. The Mail Merge windoid appears (refer to Figure 8-1).

12. In the Mail Merge windoid, select the name of the first field you want to insert and click Insert Field. For this example, insert a First Name field.

13. Press the spacebar once to add a space after the field and insert the next field (in this case, Last Name).

14. Press Return to start a new line, followed by a tab to align the text with the line above it. Then insert the Address1 field.

15. Press Return to start another new line, followed by a tab to align the text with the line above it. Then insert the City field.

16. Type a comma and a space, and then insert the State field.

17. Type one or two spaces and insert the Zip field.

18. If you want to apply different fonts, sizes, or styles to the text, do so now.

19. Save the merge form as a normal ClarisWorks document.

As mentioned in Step 6, if your envelopes have a return address printed on them, leave the return address section of the template blank. If you routinely use both kinds of envelopes — blank envelopes and envelopes with a preprinted return address — you can create two envelope merge forms.

Testing the merge form

Now comes the fun part — making sure the mailing and return addresses print correctly. Before even thinking of printing on an envelope, however, you should do a few test printouts on standard letter paper. You do test printouts for a more important reason than to avoid wasting envelopes. If you insert an envelope into the printer and it prints outside the area of the envelope, it is printing onto the printer drum rather than onto the envelope. You won't have that problem with letter paper.

Before printing, place a small pencil mark on the paper in the upper-right corner of the page. When you issue the Print command (don't do a merge at this point), you may see a message saying some of the printing may be clipped. Ignore it. When the printout appears, the pencil mark tells you the following:

✦ The side of the paper on which the printer prints (so you know whether to insert the envelopes right side up or upside down)

✦ Which edge of the envelope to insert into the printer (left or right)

✦ Whether the printing is being clipped

Now check the positions of the mailing and return addresses on the test printout. (You may want to lay the printout over an envelope to see how well they match up.) If necessary, adjust the positions of the mailing and return addresses and do another test. When you hold the printout sideways (so you can read it), the printing should be centered from top to bottom on a center-feed printer, near the top of the page on a right-feed printer, or near the bottom of the page on a left-feed printer. When the alignment looks correct, repeat the test with an envelope. After you print an envelope correctly, you can do the merge, as described in the next section.

Envelope Feed Methods and Page Setup Dialog Boxes

Unfortunately, no one method for printing envelopes is universal to all printers. Some printers, such as the original ImageWriter, weren't designed to handle envelopes. You can use the instructions in this chapter with such printers, but I don't recommend doing so.

In general, laser and ink-jet printers are best for printing envelopes. They have trays that assure the envelopes are correctly aligned and the envelopes' paper path (the route paper takes after you feed it into the printer) is straight. The ImageWriters use a standard platen (roller bar) to feed paper. Although the platen is excellent for tractor-feed paper (paper with tiny holes on both sides) and reasonably good for letter paper, it's so-so for envelopes. Envelopes tend to slide around too much and can jam.

The method for feeding envelopes varies considerably among Macintosh-compatible ink-jet and laser printers. Some printers, such as the LaserWriter II series, expect you to *center-feed* envelopes (center them on the manual feed tray or in an envelope tray) and insert them facing up with the left edge of the envelope forward. Other printers require that you feed envelopes from the left or right side of the feed tray. Some printers are designed so you have to feed paper upside down.

If you aren't sure of the printer's envelope feeding requirements, check its manual. The envelope template shown in this chapter is designed for a center-feed printer. You need to adjust the placement of the text to make it work properly with a right- or left-feed printer.

To make things more complicated, every printer also has its own version of the Page Setup dialog box. Luckily, the dialog boxes contain options that make formatting a standard #10 business envelope simple. The figure shows the settings for LaserWriter printers. (Note the envelope paper choice, as well as the Landscape Orientation option.)

Performing the envelope merge

Because different people have different merge needs, this section contains instructions for two types of envelope merges: printing a single envelope and printing a series of envelopes.

Steps: Printing a Single Envelope

1. Open the merge database.

2. Choose the Find command from the Layout menu (or press Shift-⌘-F). A blank find request appears.

3. Specify criteria to find the record you want to print. Click Visible to search only the visible records or All to search the entire database.

4. If more than one record is found, use the mouse to select the specific record you want to print. (To select a record, click anywhere in the record other than inside a field.) Then choose Hide Unselected from the Organize menu. All records other than the one you selected are hidden.

5. Open the envelope document.

6. Choose Mail Merge from the File menu. The Mail Merge windoid appears.

7. Click the Print Merge button. The Print dialog box appears.

8. Insert an envelope into the manual feed tray of the printer and click Print to print the envelope.

Occasionally, you may want to use the merge form to do a mass mailing — perhaps to send holiday greetings to all your friends or a business message to your clients or coworkers.

Steps: Printing a Set of Envelopes

1. Open the merge database.

2. *Optional:* If you want to merge only a subset of records from the database, select the records you want to use. To select the records, use the Find command or the Match Records and Hide Unselected commands. (Remember, the merge prints an envelope for every visible database document, so you have to hide all the records you do not want to print.) For instructions on using the Find and Match Records commands, refer to Chapter 5.

3. *Optional:* If you want the envelopes to print in a specific order (alphabetically by last name or in zip code order), sort the records by choosing the Sort Records command from the Organize menu.

4. Open the envelope document.

5. Choose Mail Merge from the File menu. The Mail Merge windoid appears.

6. Click the Print Merge button. The Print dialog box appears.

7. Insert an envelope into the manual feed tray or paper tray for the printer, turn on the printer, and click Print to print the envelopes. As each envelope feeds into the printer, insert the next one. Continue until all the envelopes have been printed.

Tip

If you have an envelope tray for your printer, you can print 15 to 20 envelopes at a time without having to stand and watch the process.

Quick Tips

The following quick tips explain how to:

✦ Use a calculation field to perform a conditional merge

✦ Use a merge to address a form letter when you don't know the names of all of the customers

✦ Insert one of two different amounts in a merge

✦ Use a spreadsheet frame as a merge form

✦ Update merge forms created in older versions of the program so they work with ClarisWorks 5.0

Conditional merges

If you're searching for the conditional merge capabilities many of the popular stand-alone word processing programs offer, you can stop looking — ClarisWorks doesn't have them. An example of a conditional merge is: *If database field X contains information that matches these criteria, do this; otherwise, do something else.*

Although ClarisWorks isn't equipped for sophisticated merges, you can jury-rig a conditional test by creating a calculation field that uses the IF database function. The following examples illustrate this application. (Refer to Appendix B for more information on database functions.)

Example 1

You have a customer database that contains a title, first name, last name, and address for each customer. Now you want to mail a form letter to everyone, telling them about your annual fall sale. Unfortunately, through sloppy record keeping, you didn't always record the customers' names. How do you address the letters?

Steps: Addressing a Form Letter When You Don't Know Some Customers' Names

1. In the address database, choose Define Fields from the Layout menu (or press Shift-⌘-D). The Define Fields dialog box appears.

2. Define a new calculation field called *Name Present?* using this formula:

```
IF('Last Name'="","Customer",'Prefix'&" "&'Last Name')
```

The formula checks to see whether the Last Name field is blank. If it is, the word *Customer* is entered in the Name Present? field. If the Last Name field is not blank, the prefix (Mr., Dr., and so on), a blank space, and the last name are combined and copied into the Name Present? field (Ms. Smith, for example).

The field names in the formula are ones from the Address List database created with the ClarisWorks Assistant. If you are using a different database, substitute the names of your fields for Last Name and Prefix.

3. In the Format Result As pop-up menu, choose Text.

4. Use the following line as the salutation line of the form letter:

```
Dear «Name Present?»:
```

When the merge is performed, the Name Present? placeholder is evaluated separately for each record included in the merge. If a last name has been recorded for a given customer, it is combined with a prefix, producing *Dear Mrs. Johnson*, for example. If no last name is found for a record, the line becomes *Dear Customer*.

Note

As this example illustrates, you can use any properly defined field in a database as a placeholder in a merge form. The field does not need to be visible in the layout.

Example 2

You've volunteered as a fund-raiser for a local nonprofit organization. The amount each patron contributed last year is recorded in a ClarisWorks database. You've decided that to increase contributions this year, you will ask patrons who gave $50 or more last year to consider increasing their donation by 25 percent. If they gave less than $50, you will ask them for the same amount. How can you accomplish this task?

Steps: Inserting One of Two Different Amounts in a Merge

1. In the address database, choose Define Fields from the Layout menu (or press Shift-⌘-D). The Define Fields dialog box appears.

2. Define a new calculation field called *Suggested Contribution*. Use the following formula for the field:

   ```
   IF('Last Year Contribution'>=50,'Last Year
   Contribution'*1.25,'Last Year Contribution')
   ```

   The formula checks the amount in the field named Last Year Contribution. If it is greater than $50, the amount is multiplied by 1.25 to increase the amount by 25 percent. Otherwise, the Last Year Contribution field is copied directly into the Suggested Contribution field.

3. In the Format Result As pop-up menu, choose Number.

4. In the form letter, insert the Suggested Contribution field in the line of text where you suggest a donation amount, as in the following example:

   ```
   Based on your generous contribution last year, we
   suggest a donation of «Suggested Contribution».
   ```

Note

You do not need to place the calculation field in a database layout. As long as you have properly defined a field, you can use it in the database as a placeholder in a merge form — whether or not it is visible in a layout.

Using a spreadsheet frame as a merge form

At the beginning of this chapter, I mentioned that a spreadsheet or spreadsheet frame also can serve as a merge form. You may ask, "Why would you want to use a spreadsheet in this manner?" I thought for a long time and came up with an instance where this might be useful: for filling in spreadsheet tables.

As an example, suppose you've designed a letter you want to send to all members of your company's sales force. In the word processing document, you can embed a spreadsheet table that shows each salesperson's quarterly or monthly sales and commissions earned. Because the information is merged into a spreadsheet frame rather than a text frame or document, you can also use the power of the spreadsheet to create formulas that further manipulate the merged data. Formulas could calculate each person's total annual sales or average monthly sales, for example.

Updating old merge forms for ClarisWorks 5

In versions of ClarisWorks prior to 4.0, there were two ways to insert fields into a merge form:

✦ Choosing field names from the Mail Merge windoid

✦ Typing the brackets and field names directly into the merge form

In ClarisWorks 4 and 5, however, you *must* select all fields from the Mail Merge windoid — typed fields and brackets are not recognized as merge fields.

If you have merge forms created in earlier versions of ClarisWorks, you can update them so they will work with ClarisWorks 5 by replacing each field with one listed in the Mail Merge dialog windoid. To do this, select the field in the merge form (including its surrounding brackets), choose a field name in the Field Names pane of the Mail Merge windoid, and click Insert Field.

Tip

Not sure which fields are old ones and which fields have already been updated or replaced? On the merge form, double-click anywhere in a field name. If it is a ClarisWorks 4.0 or 5.0 field name, the entire field — including the surrounding brackets — will be selected. If the field was inserted or typed in a previous version of ClarisWorks, only a portion of the field name will be selected (one word of a multiword field name, or the field name but not its surrounding brackets, for example). The important point to remember is ClarisWorks 4.0 and 5.0 treat an inserted field name as a single entity, starting with the left bracket and ending with the right bracket.

Summary

✦ A merge requires two components: a database and a merge form (a word processing document, text frame, spreadsheet document, or spreadsheet frame). Information from the database fields is inserted into field place-holders in the merge document.

✦ Every merge field name is surrounded by special brackets («»). The brackets are added automatically when you select the field names from the Mail Merge windoid.

✦ Punctuation and spaces can separate merge fields from each other, as well as from surrounding text. You also can apply formatting, such as different fonts and styles, to the merge fields.

✦ In a merge, every visible database record produces its own merge document. You can restrict the number of records by using the Find or Match Records commands. You can also arrange the records in a particular order by using the Sort Records command.

✦ Merge forms designed in versions of ClarisWorks prior to 4.0 must be updated before you can use them with ClarisWorks 5. Field names must be reinserted by choosing them from the Mail Merge windoid.

✦   ✦   ✦

Adding Spreadsheet Charts and Tables to Reports

Overview

Only a few high-end word processing programs include a special feature for laying out tables. When you use a word processor without such a feature, your only recourse is to set a series of tabs and use them to format a table. Although you can use tabs to create tables in the ClarisWorks word processor, a better way to make a table is to use a spreadsheet frame. This method enables you to reap the benefits of working in an environment in which you can manipulate numbers as well as format text. (For information on the spreadsheet environment's features and functions, refer to Chapter 4.)

This chapter explains how to add a spreadsheet table or chart to a word processing document. Because of the tight integration of ClarisWorks environments, however, you can apply the techniques described in this chapter in the other environments as well — in paint or draw documents, for example.

Note

ClarisWorks 5 also includes a Make Table Assistant that you can use to create simple tables. (See Chapter 3 for instructions.)

Spreadsheet Tables

Although you can design a spreadsheet table in the spreadsheet environment, creating a spreadsheet frame in a word processing document is simpler. This method also enables you to tell whether the table is the correct size for the document.

Steps: Creating a Spreadsheet Table

1. Open an existing word processing document or create a new one by choosing the appropriate command from the File menu (Open or New).

2. If the Tool panel isn't visible, click the Show/Hide Tools control at the bottom of the document window.

3. Select the spreadsheet tool (the large plus symbol near the top of the Tool panel).

4. To create the table, click where you want the upper-left corner to start and then drag down and to the right. When you release the mouse button, a new spreadsheet frame appears, as shown in Figure 9-1.

Figure 9-1: A new spreadsheet frame in a word processing document

Don't be overly concerned about the initial appearance or dimensions of the table. You can change its size, the number of columns and rows, column widths, and row heights as needed.

Entering Data

To enter text and data into the spreadsheet table, click the table once to select it and then click any cell in the table. The selected cell has a dark border around it. You can now enter data in that cell or anywhere else in the spreadsheet, as shown in Figure 9-2.

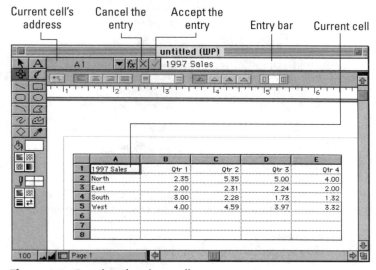

Figure 9-2: Entering data in a cell

As you type an entry for a cell, text or numbers appear in the *entry bar,* which is shown in Figure 9-2. (Note that as you work in the spreadsheet frame, the word processing ruler is still visible but not active.) To accept the entry, do any of the following:

✦ Click the check mark (which is the Accept button).

✦ Press Enter or Return.

✦ Press an arrow key (or an Option-arrow key).

✦ Press Tab or Shift-Tab.

To cancel a cell entry, click the *x* button in the entry bar.

In ClarisWorks 5.0, the functions of the arrow and Option-arrow keys are defined in Spreadsheet Preferences (see Chapter 11). To accept a cell entry or move to another cell, you can use either the unmodified arrow keys or the Option-arrow keys — depending on how you set these preferences.

Clicking the check mark or pressing Enter accepts the entry but leaves the cursor in the current cell. The other options (Return, arrow key or Option-arrow key, Tab, and Shift-Tab) accept the entry as well, but they move the cursor to a new cell, as described in Table 9-1.

Table 9-1 Cell Navigation	
Key	*Movement*
Return	To the cell immediately below
Right arrow (or Option-right arrow) or Tab	To the cell immediately to the right
Left arrow (or Option-left arrow) or Shift-Tab	To the cell immediately to the left
Down arrow (or Option-down arrow)	To the cell immediately below
Up arrow (or Option-up arrow)	To the cell immediately above
Enter	No movement

You can also use the keys in Table 9-1 for pure cursor movements. If you are not entering data, pressing these keys simply moves the cursor in the direction stated.

You can move directly to any cell by clicking it with the mouse. In many cases, this method is the quickest way to get to any cell in the table that is not adjacent to the current cell.

Note

You can also choose the Go to Cell command from the Options menu (or press ⌘-G) and specify the coordinates of the desired cell (A7, for example) in the dialog box that appears. Because most tables are rather small, however, clicking a cell to select it is usually quicker.

Tip

For fast data entry in contiguous cells, you can select a cell range by Shift-clicking. The current cell (which is white) is in the upper-left corner of the selected range, as shown in Figure 9-3. If you press Return after you enter the data for each cell, the current cell automatically shifts on a column-by-column basis, as shown in the table at the top of the figure. If you press Enter or Tab as you complete each cell entry, the current cell automatically shifts on a row-by-row basis, as shown in the table at the bottom of the figure.

Press Return after each entry to move the cursor in this pattern

Press Enter or Tab to move the cursor in this pattern

Figure 9-3: Entering data into a selection of cells

Changing the appearance of the table

By using the mouse and menu commands, you can make any of the following changes to the appearance of the table:

✦ Change the number of columns or rows displayed

✦ Change row heights and column widths

✦ Make text wrap within selected cells

✦ Add shading to selected cells

✦ Display or hide the cell gridlines, column letters, and row numbers

Changing the number of displayed columns or rows

Although a spreadsheet frame is simply a window into a larger worksheet, you can increase or reduce the number of visible columns and rows. To change the number of displayed columns or rows, click the spreadsheet table once to select it. Then click one of the table's handles and drag. When you release the mouse button, the table reforms and displays only the columns and rows you have indicated.

Note

Many finished tables look better if you hide the column and row headings (as described later in this chapter). If hiding the headings leaves an extra blank row at the bottom or a blank column at the right end of the table, you may need to resize the table again.

Changing row heights and column widths

ClarisWorks enables you to include varying sizes of text in a worksheet. You can adjust the heights and widths of individual rows and columns to accommodate large headings (formatted as 24-point text, for example) or long text strings that spill over into adjacent cells.

Steps: Changing Row Heights and Column Widths

1. Click the spreadsheet table once to select it. Handles appear at its four corners, and the cursor changes to a pointer.

2. Click any cell in the column or row whose width or height you want to change.

   To change the width or height of several columns or rows simultaneously, Shift-click to select a series of contiguous columns or rows.

3. From the Format menu, choose Column Width or Row Height, as appropriate. The Column Width or Row Height dialog box appears. Figure 9-4 shows the Column Width dialog box.

Figure 9-4: The Column Width dialog box

4. Enter a new number for the width or height.

   Height and width numbers are shown in points rather than in characters. Points are often used for measuring type. (An inch contains 72 points.)

5. Click OK. The new column width or row height is put into effect. If multiple rows or columns were selected, they will all now have the same height or width, respectively.

Tip

Although the default unit of measurement for entering row heights and column widths is points, you can use other units by typing the appropriate abbreviation after the numeric portion of the entry. You can use inches (in), millimeters (mm), centimeters (cm), points (pt), or picas (pc).

Changing column widths or row heights manually by using the mouse — as described in the following steps — is sometimes easier.

Steps: Changing Row Heights and Column Widths Manually

1. Click the spreadsheet table once to select it. Handles appear at the four corners, and the cursor changes to a pointer.

2. Move the pointer into the heading area for the column or row whose width or height you want to change. As the cursor moves over the right edge of the column or the bottom edge of the row, a two-headed pointer appears.

To change the width or height of several columns or rows simultaneously, Shift-click to select a series of contiguous columns or rows.

3. While pressing the mouse button, drag to change the column width or row height.

4. When the width or height is correct, release the mouse button.

ClarisWorks 5.0 provides a third way to adjust rows and columns that you'll find handy. Using the following technique, you can automatically resize rows or columns so they are the minimum height or width necessary to accommodate the largest cell in the range:

✦ To autosize a row, move the pointer into the row headings area of the worksheet (on the far left) and double-click the bottom of the row you want to resize. The row height adjusts to fit the tallest text in the row.

✦ To autosize a column, move the pointer into the column headings area of the worksheet (at the top) and double-click the right side of the column you want to resize. The column width adjusts to fit the longest text string in the column.

This technique can also be used to autosize a series of rows or columns simultaneously. Select the rows or columns, and then double-click the bottom of any of the selected rows or the right side of any of the selected columns. ClarisWorks determines the minimum height or width necessary to accommodate the largest or longest text in the selected range. All selected rows or columns are resized to match that height or width.

Although there are no menu commands you can choose to perform row and column autosizing, there are two shortcuts you can add to the button bar that will accomplish the same trick: Autosize Row and Autosize Column. (See Chapter 12 for information on modifying button bars.)

Setting text wrap for a cell

When a text string is too long to fit in a cell, it spills into adjacent empty cells. (The direction in which it spills depends on the original cell's Alignment setting.) To keep the entire string in its original cell, you can either widen the column (as described previously) or format the text to wrap within the cell.

To make text wrap within selected cells, click the spreadsheet table once to select it. Select the cell or cells to which you want to apply the Wrap format. Then choose Wrap from the Alignment submenu in the Format menu. If the text no longer fits in the cell (some of it may be clipped at the bottom of the cell), you can change the row height by using any of the methods described previously.

Shading cells

To highlight important data or simply dress up your worksheet, ClarisWorks 5 enables you to apply shading to individual cells. Begin by selecting the cell or cells to which you want to apply the shading. Then select a fill color and/or pattern from the Tool panel. (If the Tool panel isn't visible, click the Show/Hide Tools control at the bottom of the document window.) The color and pattern are applied to the selected cells.

Note

You cannot apply fill gradients, textures, pen colors, or pen patterns to cells. Although you can select these options, ClarisWorks ignores them.

Applying styles

The ClarisWorks 5 stylesheet contains several predefined spreadsheet styles you may find helpful in creating attractive tables. To see the stylesheet, choose Show Stylesheet from the Window menu.

To apply a table style to a worksheet frame, click to select the worksheet frame or the specific range you want to format. Then choose any of the predefined styles in the stylesheet. Figure 9-5 shows a table formatted with the 3D Table 2 style with a few minor modifications. (See Chapter 15 for more information on using stylesheets.)

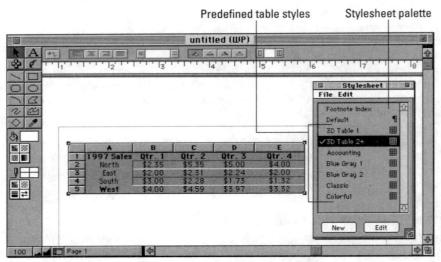

Figure 9-5: A table formatted using one of ClarisWorks's predefined styles

Setting display options

By setting options in the Display dialog box, you can change the on-screen and printed look of any worksheet or table.

Steps: Displaying or Hiding the Cell Gridlines, Column Letters, and Row Numbers

1. Click the spreadsheet table once to select it. Handles appear at the four corners, and the cursor changes to a pointer.

2. Click in any cell of the spreadsheet. The spreadsheet menus appear in the menu bar.

3. Choose Display from the Options menu. The Display dialog box appears, as shown in Figure 9-6.

Figure 9-6: The Display dialog box

Note

You can also open the Display dialog box by selecting the spreadsheet frame and choosing Frame Info from the Edit menu.

4. Select or deselect display options by clicking the check boxes. To change the table's appearance, consider these important options:

- *Cell Grid.* When this option is checked, the cell separators are dotted grid lines. When it is unchecked, lines do not appear.

- *Solid Lines.* When this option is checked, the cell separators are solid grid lines.

- *Column Headings and Row Headings.* If these options are unchecked, you do not see the letters and numbers normally used to label columns and rows.

5. Click OK. The changes in appearance are made.

Note

If you have applied shading to all cells in the table, the display settings for Cell Grid and Solid Lines are irrelevant. Cell separators are not visible through cell shading.

Positioning the table

After you finish entering data and formatting the table, you may want to change the table's position on the page. Up to this point, the spreadsheet frame has been just another object floating on the document page. You can leave it that way and, optionally, specify a text wrap for it (remember, it's an object — just like a draw graphic), or you can move it into the text as an in-line graphic. Because ClarisWorks treats in-line graphics as text, you can apply paragraph formatting commands to center the table on the page and separate it from the surrounding paragraphs. Figures 9-7 and 9-8 show the two table treatments.

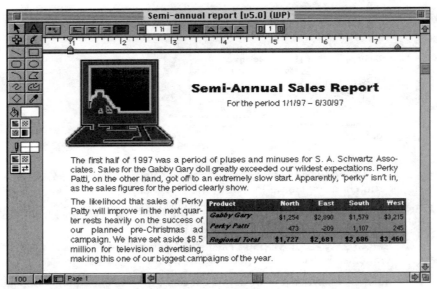

Figure 9-7: A spreadsheet table as an object

To treat a spreadsheet table as an object, click the spreadsheet table once to select it. Drag the table to its new position, and choose Text Wrap from the Options menu. The Text Wrap dialog box appears. Click the Regular or Irregular icon and then click OK. Nearby text wraps around the table. Continue to drag the spreadsheet until the text wraps exactly as you want. You can fine-tune the position of the table by pressing the arrow keys.

You can specify a distance (in points) between the object and the surrounding text by entering a number in the Gutter box of the Text Wrap dialog box.

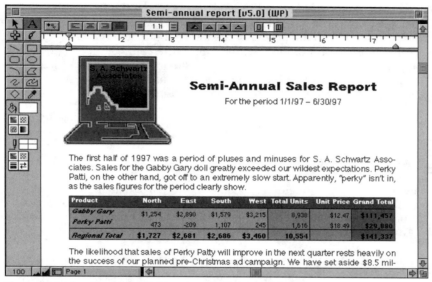

Figure 9-8: A spreadsheet table as an in-line graphic

Steps: Treating a Spreadsheet Table as an In-Line Graphic

1. Click the spreadsheet table once to select it. Handles appear at the corners.

2. Choose Cut from the Edit menu (or press ⌘-X). The worksheet is removed, and a copy of it is placed on the Clipboard.

3. Click the text tool (the capital A) and move the text insertion point to where you want to place the table. (Because formatting is much simpler when the table is in a paragraph by itself, you may want to press Return to create a blank paragraph to receive the table.)

4. Choose Paste from the Edit menu (or press ⌘-V). The table is inserted at the text insertion point.

5. *Optional:* If you want to center the table in its line, place the text insertion point at the beginning or end of the paragraph that contains the table and then click the Centered Alignment control in the ruler bar (see Figure 9-9).

Centered alignment control

Figure 9-9: Use the Centered Alignment control to center the table.

6. *Optional:* If you want to add some space between the table and the paragraphs that lie immediately above and below it, place the text insertion point at the beginning or end of the paragraph that contains the table and choose Paragraph from the Format menu. The Paragraph dialog box appears. Enter new figures for Space Before and Space After (1 li, for example) and click OK. The table is now separated from the surrounding paragraphs by the amount of space you entered.

Deleting a table

At some point, you may decide you don't need a particular table after all. To delete a table, click the table once to select it and then press Delete. If the table is an in-line graphic rather than a floating object, place the text insertion point at the end of the table and then press Delete.

If you want to use the table on a different page or in a different document, select the table and then press ⌘-X or choose Cut from the Edit menu. You can then use the Paste command to move the table to its new location.

You can also drag the table to another open ClarisWorks document — taking advantage of ClarisWorks 5.0's support for drag-and-drop.

Spreadsheet Charts

You can also place spreadsheet charts in word processing reports. The easiest way to create a chart is to do so in a spreadsheet document (rather than in a spreadsheet frame in the word processing document).

Steps: Adding a Chart to a Word Processing Document

1. Open an existing spreadsheet or create a new one by choosing Open or New from the File menu.

2. Select the cell range from which the chart will be created.

3. Choose Make Chart from the Options menu. The Chart Options dialog box appears, as shown in Figure 9-10. (See Chapter 4 for details on creating and modifying charts.)

4. Select a chart style and click OK. The chart appears on the current document page and is automatically selected, as shown in Figure 9-11 (note the handles).

Figure 9-10: To design a chart, select options from the Chart Options dialog box.

5. Choose Copy from the Edit menu (or press ⌘-C). A copy of the chart is placed on the Mac Clipboard.

6. Switch to the word processing document by selecting its name from the list at the bottom of the Window menu. (If it isn't already open, choose Open from the File menu.)

7. Choose Paste from the Edit menu (or press ⌘-V). The chart appears in the word processing document.

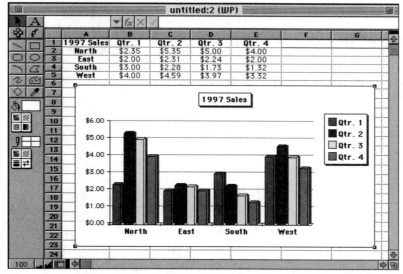

Figure 9-11: A new chart created in the spreadsheet environment simply floats on the page.

You can change the chart's position and size — as well as treat it as an object or an in-line graphic — by following the directions given previously for spreadsheet tables. And as stated previously, you can move the chart via drag-and-drop (rather than cut-and-paste), if you prefer.

Tip   Any chart pasted into a document in this manner is a static entity. If you later change the chart's worksheet, the pasted chart will not reflect the changes. If you want to maintain a link between the worksheet and the chart, you can use Publish & Subscribe, as described in Chapter 18.

Quick Tip: Other Table Formatting Options

As you design the table, keep in mind that you are working in a spreadsheet that just happens to be embedded in a word processing document. All the power of the spreadsheet environment can be brought to bear on the table. Not only can you enter calculations and formulas, you can also choose from additional formatting options, such as the following:

✦ Choosing different fonts, styles, sizes, and colors for the text in selected cells

✦ Changing the alignment of text and numbers within cells

✦ Applying special formats for displaying numbers and dates

✦ Sorting cells

✦ Adding borders to cells

✦ Embellishing the table with graphics

As an example, Figure 9-12 shows a fully dressed spreadsheet table with multiple font styles, sizes, and alignments; cell shading; selective cell borders; and graphics embellishments (an oval around a number, an arrow, and a callout that contains text). (Refer to the instructions in Chapter 4 for help in formatting spreadsheet tables.)

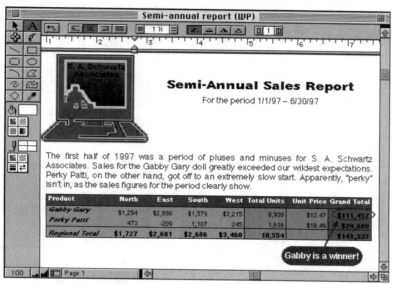

Figure 9-12: An example of a formatted spreadsheet table

Summary

✦ Using a spreadsheet frame to create a table in a word processing environment enables you to reap the benefits of working in an environment where you can manipulate numbers as well as format text.

✦ Some of the changes you can make to spreadsheet tables include modifying row heights and column widths (to properly display text), changing the table's size, adding text wrap for some cells, applying cell shading, and hiding row and column headings.

✦ You can change column widths and row heights manually, or you can change them by entering numbers in a dialog box. Changing them manually is often the most accurate method.

✦ Like spreadsheet tables, charts can also be used to dress up a text-based report or memo.

✦ You can position tables and charts as floating objects (with text wrap) or as in-line graphics (which are subject to regular paragraph formatting commands). Both approaches work well.

✦   ✦   ✦

Mastering
ClarisWorks

Using Stationery Documents and Assistants

Overview

When you have a document you work with frequently but usually need to modify somewhat, the best way to save it is as a *stationery document* rather than as a normal ClarisWorks file. A stationery document is a template. It can include static text and graphics, as well as placeholders for other text elements you intend to change each time you use the document. A letterhead template is an example of a document that would make a good stationery file. In the template, you can include your return address, a standard salutation, and a closing. Then, whenever you want to write a new letter, you just open the stationery file, enter the addressee's name and address, and fill in the body of the text. Figure 10-1 shows a typical stationery document.

Assistants are intelligent helpers that make performing complex tasks in ClarisWorks a snap. Because you choose all stationery documents and many of the Assistants from the New Document dialog box, they are discussed together in this chapter.

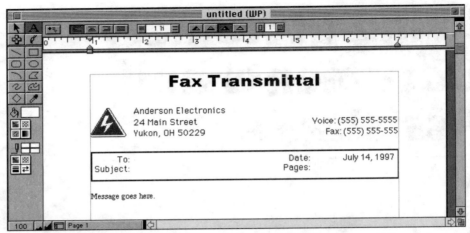

Figure 10-1: A fax template saved as a stationery document

Stationery Documents Versus Normal ClarisWorks Documents

Of course, you don't have to save a template as a stationery file. You can save it as a normal ClarisWorks document. However, if you accidentally issue the Save command while you are working with a template that is not a stationery file, you will replace the template with a filled-in copy of the letterhead, fax, or whatever type of document you are working on. Bye-bye, template.

Saving the template as a stationery document protects you from this kind of mistake. When you open a ClarisWorks stationery file, you're opening a copy of the file, rather than the original. In fact, ClarisWorks treats the document that appears on screen just as it treats a file you create with the New command. It even names the file *Untitled* to remind you it's not the original.

Creating Stationery Documents

You can easily create a stationery document from any ClarisWorks file. To save a document as stationery, choose Save As from the File menu. The standard Save As dialog box appears (see Figure 10-2). Click the Stationery radio button. Enter a name for the document, and save the stationery document to the desired folder.

If you want to be able to choose the stationery document from the New Document dialog box, save it in the ClarisWorks Stationery folder (located inside the ClarisWorks 5.0 program folder). This folder is automatically chosen when you click the Stationery radio button in the Save As dialog box.

Figure 10-2: Any document can be saved as a
normal ClarisWorks file or a stationery file.

Any ClarisWorks stationery file you save or move into the ClarisWorks Stationery folder is available in the file list when you issue the New command, click the Use Assistant or Stationery radio button, and then choose All Stationery or an appropriate category from the Category pop-up menu.

In versions of ClarisWorks prior to 4.0, the ClarisWorks Stationery folder was located inside the Claris folder within the System Folder of the startup hard disk or within the program folder. If you have stationery documents created with ClarisWorks 4 that you also want to use with ClarisWorks 5, simply copy or move the files into the ClarisWorks Stationery folder (located in the ClarisWorks 5.0 folder).

Of course, as with any other documents, you can save stationery files anywhere you choose. If you save them in a different location, they still function as stationery documents, but you have to load them by using the Open command from the File menu, rather than the New command.

There's another way to create stationery documents that you can do from the desktop rather than from within ClarisWorks. You can change any ClarisWorks document into a stationery document by selecting the file's icon in the Finder, choosing Get Info from the File menu, clicking the Stationery Pad check box, and then closing the Info window. In the future, double-clicking the file icon automatically launches ClarisWorks and presents a fresh, untitled copy of the stationery document.

ClarisWorks enables you to set preferences (such as the date format and palette options) that you can save with the current document. When you open the document, its preference settings override the normal ClarisWorks preferences. If you set preferences for a document and then save it as stationery, this rule still applies. Whenever you open a copy of the stationery document, any preferences you have set for the document take precedence over the ClarisWorks preferences. (For additional information on preferences, see Chapter 11.)

Special Considerations When Saving Stationery Documents

When you save a ClarisWorks 5.0 document as a stationery file, it is presented in the New Document dialog box according to the information (or lack of it) you provided for the file in the Document Summary dialog box (see Figure 10-3). To ensure that you can easily find and promptly identify your stationery document, choose Document Summary from the File menu prior to saving the file. Be sure to fill in the following items:

✦ *Category.* Whatever text you enter here is used as the category in which the document is listed. To include the stationery document in an existing category (General, Internet, or Business, for example), type that category name. You can also create a new category (Personal, for instance), or you can simply lump the file in with all other unclassified stationery documents by not entering a category.

✦ *Description.* This descriptive text appears whenever the stationery file is highlighted in the file list.

Figure 10-3: The Document Summary dialog box

Other items in the Document Summary dialog box are optional. They do not affect the presentation of stationery files in the New Document dialog box. (For additional information about the Document Summary dialog box, see "Saving New Files" in Chapter 1.)

Opening a Stationery Document

You can open a stationery document in precisely the same way you open any other document:

✦ Select it from the file list ClarisWorks presents when you choose Open from the File menu (or press ⌘-O).

✦ Double-click the document icon on the desktop to launch ClarisWorks and open the document simultaneously.

In addition to these methods, the New Document dialog box contains a Use Assistant or Stationery radio button you can click to see the categories of stationery documents you can open (see Figure 10-4). If the template is one that came with ClarisWorks 5.0 or one you saved in the ClarisWorks Stationery folder, you can choose it when creating a new document or when launching the program. (The latter option assumes the General Preferences setting for *On startup, show* is set to *New Document,* as described in Chapter 11.)

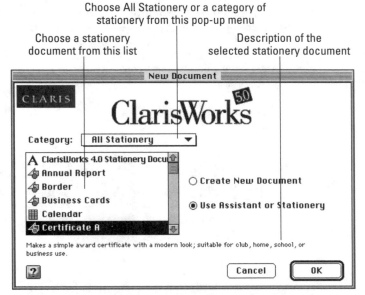

Figure 10-4: You can open many stationery documents from the New Document dialog box.

Making a New Version of a Stationery Document

After you open a copy of a stationery document, you can edit the document and then save it under a new name, or you can simply close the file without saving it if you don't need a copy on disk. If, on the other hand, you've modified the stationery file with the intent of making a new, improved template, you can save the new file over the old one by typing the original stationery filename and clicking the Stationery radio button in the Save As dialog box. Click Replace when the program asks whether you want to replace the original file.

Note

If you aren't using the ClarisWorks Stationery folder for your stationery documents, be sure to save the revised stationery document in the same folder as the original. Otherwise, you could end up with multiple versions of the same file.

Using Stationery to Set New Environment Defaults

Although the Preferences command in the Edit menu enables you to set a handful of default options for several environments (see Chapter 11), you can add many more settings as defaults so they are automatically in effect whenever you create a new document. To add settings as defaults, simply create a document that contains the new default settings and then save it as a specially named stationery document in the ClarisWorks Stationery folder. Claris refers to these special documents as *default stationery documents*.

To save documents as default stationery documents, you need to name the files as shown in Table 10-1.

Table 10-1 Default Stationery File-Naming Conventions	
Environment	***Name of Default Stationery Document***
Word Processing	ClarisWorks WP Options
Drawing	ClarisWorks DR Options
Painting	ClarisWorks PT Options
Spreadsheet	ClarisWorks SS Options
Database	ClarisWorks DB Options
Communications	ClarisWorks CM Options

For example, to make the word processing environment open new documents with my defaults, I created a blank stationery document, set the starting font to Times, defined four frequently used text styles, and added the styles to the stylesheet for the document. Now every new word processing document defaults to the Times font, and the four text styles are always available.

You can create your own default stationery documents with the options you prefer. Note, however, that you can have only one default stationery document for each environment. If you want to change an existing default stationery document, you need to save the new one over the old one — in other words, replace it.

Steps: Creating an Environment Default Stationery Document

1. Choose New from the Edit menu.

2. Highlight the environment of your choice and click OK. A blank document appears.

3. Set options for the document (and, if you want to, set preferences by using the Preferences command from the Edit menu).

4. Choose Save As from the File menu. The normal file dialog box appears.

5. Click the Stationery radio button. The ClarisWorks Stationery folder is automatically selected for you.

6. Name the file according to the conventions listed in Table 10-1, and click Save.

After you save a default stationery document, ClarisWorks adds it to the list of environments in the New Document dialog box. The default stationery document you save replaces the original ClarisWorks default document as the one that will be automatically used for that environment. The original default document is retained as the "Standard" document for the environment.

For example, if you create a ClarisWorks WP Options file, it will be shown in the New Document dialog box as Word Processing. If, at any time, you'd like to use the original ClarisWorks default for the environment, choose Standard Word Processing.

If you already have some default stationery files you designed for ClarisWorks 4, you can also use them with ClarisWorks 5, if you like. Just copy or move the files into the ClarisWorks Stationery folder inside the ClarisWorks 5.0 folder.

Using the ClarisWorks Assistants

ClarisWorks 5.0 includes a variety of Assistants, each designed to perform a specific task for you. You choose the majority of the Assistants in the New Document dialog box. Most of them create new documents. You need to invoke the other Assistants from within an existing document.

Each Assistant is self-explanatory. When you invoke an Assistant, you see a list on screen of any preparatory steps you need to perform, such as selecting a text insertion point or highlighting an address. Each Assistant is presented as a dialog box or a series of dialog boxes. You move forward (Next) and backward (Back) through the dialog boxes by clicking buttons. After you make selections from the pop-up menus, set necessary options, and type text entries, you click Create, Done, or Start (as appropriate) to make the Assistant execute.

New Document Assistants

You can choose ten Assistants from the New Document dialog box. Each of these Assistants produces a new document, created according to your specifications.

After you click the Use Assistant or Stationery radio button and choose All Assistants or a particular class of Assistants from the Category pop-up menu, you see the new document Assistants (see Figure 10-5). They include the following:

New In Version 5

- ✦ *Address List.* Creates a personal, business, or student name and address database.

- ✦ *Business Cards.* Designs a business card for business or personal use.

- ✦ *Calendar.* Creates a single-month or multiple-month calendar. Each month is a separate ClarisWorks spreadsheet.

- ✦ *Certificate.* Creates decorative certificates, awards, and diplomas.

- ✦ *Envelope.* Creates a word processing document formatted as a business envelope (with an addressee and a return address).

- ✦ *Find ClarisWorks Documents.* Locates ClarisWorks documents on the current disk. (See Chapter 1 for a more detailed discussion of this Assistant.)

- ✦ *Home Finance.* Creates worksheets that help you compute the answers to common financial questions.

- ✦ *Newsletter.* Designs a newsletter or informational booklet in a variety of styles. Placeholders are reserved for your copy.

- ✦ *Presentation.* Generates elaborate, multipage presentation templates that can be displayed on screen, shown on an overhead projector, or printed.

- ✦ *Register ClarisWorks.* Creates a form you can use to register your copy of ClarisWorks 5.0.

Choose All Assistants or a category of Assistants
from this pop-up menu

Choose an Assistant
from this list

Description of the
selected Assistant

Figure 10-5: Selecting a new document Assistant

Other Assistants

You invoke the following Assistants from within open ClarisWorks documents
rather than from the New Document dialog box:

New In
Version 5

✦ *Insert Footnote.* Adds a footnote to a word processing document, correctly
formatted in the chosen style. (See Chapter 3 for instructions.)

✦ *Make Table.* Adds a spreadsheet table to a word processing document, a
draw document, or a database (in Layout mode only). (See Chapter 3 for
more information.)

✦ *Address Envelope.* Copies the highlighted address from a word processing
document and creates a new document that is formatted as a business
envelope. You do not need to type the address information manually, as you
do for the Envelope Assistant. Instead, the Address Envelope Assistant uses
information already present in the document. (See "Using the Word
Processing Assistants," in Chapter 3 for instructions.)

✦ *Paragraph Sorter.* Arranges selected document paragraphs in alphabetical
order, random order, or according to leading numbers. (See "Using the Word
Processing Assistants," in Chapter 3 for instructions.)

✦ *Create Labels*. Helps you design Avery or custom label layouts to be used with the current database. (See "Working with Mailing Labels," in Chapter 5 for instructions.)

You select these Assistants by choosing ClarisWorks Assistants from the Balloon Help menu or the Help menu.

Quick Tips

Any file you intend to reuse can be a stationery document. Keep in mind, however, that if you never intend to alter the base document, saving it as a stationery file is pointless. For example, if you have a letter you always send without changes, you can save it as a normal ClarisWorks file and simply reprint it as often as you like.

Here are some ideas for stationery documents:

✦ *Fax form or cover sheet*. Remove everything but the static information (the logo, return address, and phone number as well as the reserved areas for the date, subject, number of pages, recipient's name, and fax number) from your normal fax form or cover sheet (which is probably a word processing or draw document). Then use the Insert Date command in the Edit menu to enter the send date, so whenever you open a copy of the stationery document, the current date is filled in automatically.

✦ *Letterhead*. If you have a laser or ink-jet printer, you can save money by printing your own letterhead.

✦ *Weekly, monthly, quarterly, or annual worksheets*. Many worksheets are reusable. (I keep my personal financial records in several of them, for example.) Open the worksheet and remove all the data, making sure to leave cells that contain labels or formulas intact. Then save the worksheet under a new name as a stationery document. Whenever the new week, month, quarter, or year begins, you can open a copy of the template and plug in the new numbers. You can use the same tactic for record-keeping database templates.

✦ *Business forms*. Templates are perfect for standard business forms, such as invoices, statements, petty cash vouchers, and the like.

✦ *Contracts*. Most legal documents, whether they are wills, leases, or terms of work-for-hire, consist largely of standard language. By saving them as stationery, you can dramatically reduce writing time on subsequent contracts.

✦ *Common communications settings*. You can create a general-purpose communications stationery document that contains the options you most frequently use for the baud rate, transfer protocol, and so on. Most online sessions will require only slight modifications to the settings in the template.

Summary

✦ Save files as stationery documents when you want to use them as templates.

✦ When you open a stationery document, your template is opened as a new untitled document — protecting the original from unintentional modifications.

✦ When you launch ClarisWorks or create a new file, you can select any stationery document in the ClarisWorks Stationery folder by clicking the Use Assistant or Stationery radio button, and then choosing All Stationery or a particular class of stationery from the Category pop-up menu.

✦ You can set defaults for any environment by designing a ClarisWorks default stationery document and following a special convention for naming the document when you save it in the ClarisWorks Stationery folder.

✦ ClarisWorks includes Assistants that walk you through common business and home computing tasks.

✦   ✦   ✦

Setting Preferences

Overview

By setting preferences, you can customize ClarisWorks to fit the way you work. To view the current preferences settings or change them, choose Preferences from the Edit menu. The Preferences dialog box appears (see Figure 11-1). At the top of the Preferences dialog box is a Topic pull-down menu, which lists the different parts of ClarisWorks you can customize. The areas for which you can set preferences in ClarisWorks 5.0 are General, Text, Graphics, Spreadsheet, Palettes, and Communications.

Topic pull-down menu

Figure 11-1: The Preferences dialog box (General preferences shown)

Default and Document-Specific Preferences

In ClarisWorks, you can set preferences in two ways:

✦ You can create a group of *default preferences* to be used automatically for all new documents in the current session and in future sessions.

✦ You can set *document-specific preferences* that apply to one document and are saved with that document.

Steps: Setting New Default Preferences

1. Choose Preferences from the Edit menu.

2. Choose a preference category from the Topic pull-down menu at the top of the Preferences dialog box to select the type of preference settings you want to modify.

3. Change the settings in the dialog box as desired.

4. Repeat Steps 2 and 3 for any other preferences you want to change.

5. Click Make Default.

The new preferences become the default settings for all new documents you create in this session and in future sessions.

Tip

If you ever decide you'd like to revert to the original preference settings for ClarisWorks 5.0, delete the file named ClarisWorks 5 Preferences (located in the Preferences folder inside your System Folder).

Steps: Setting Document-Specific Preferences

1. Select the document whose preferences you want to set, making it the active document (bringing it to the front if you have two or more open documents). You can use a document you have just created or one you have loaded from disk.

2. Choose Preferences from the Edit menu.

3. Choose a preference category from the Topic pull-down menu at the top of the Preferences dialog box to select the type of preference settings you want to modify.

4. Change the settings in the dialog box as desired.

5. Repeat Steps 3 and 4 for any other preferences you want to change.

6. Click OK.

The new settings apply only to the current document. Other new documents you create in the session will still use the default settings, unless you also set preferences for them. Because preference settings are saved with each document, the next time you run ClarisWorks and open the document, the preferences will be intact.

Preferences are also stored with files you save as stationery documents.

General Preferences

You use General preferences to customize many of the basic options in ClarisWorks (refer to Figure 11-1), such as whether warnings are displayed and how graphics files are shown in Open dialog boxes and on the desktop. You can also use General preferences to set the startup action for ClarisWorks.

Although you normally use the Make Default and OK buttons to modify the ClarisWorks default and document-specific preferences settings, the OK button has a different function when you use it in conjunction with General preferences. Clicking OK puts the changed settings into effect for the entire session (until you quit the program), rather than just for the current document. For example, if you click the Create Custom Icon check box and then click OK, a custom icon is automatically created for every draw or paint document you save during the session. In the next ClarisWorks session, however, you'll find that the Create Custom Icon setting has been turned off again. To set new General preferences as permanent defaults, click the Make Default button.

General preferences settings include the following:

✦ *On Startup, Show.* Determines what you see first each time you launch ClarisWorks. The default choice is to display the New Document dialog box. Alternatively, you can have the program display the Open dialog box (to open an existing document) or no dialog box at all. If you normally begin each session by starting a new document or opening an existing one, you can click the New Document or Open Document radio button. If your initial action varies from one session to the next, you are better off clicking the Nothing button, which enables you to select an appropriate startup action for each session.

✦ *Saved Documents.* Click Create Custom Icon to instruct ClarisWorks to create file icons that are miniature representations of paint and draw images. A special icon is automatically created whenever a graphics file is saved.

Click Create Preview to tell ClarisWorks to save a thumbnail preview of each text, paint, or draw document. The preview will be shown in the dialog box that appears when you choose Open from the File menu.

Click Remember Translator to assist you in saving translated documents in their native formats. With this option chosen, whenever you edit a translated document and then save it, the Save As pop-up menu is automatically set for the program in which the translated document was created (Microsoft Word, for example). Of course, you can still select ClarisWorks or any other file type as the Save As format.

✦ *Show Fonts in Font Menu.* Shows font names in their respective typefaces in the Font submenu of the Format menu.

✦ *Old Version Alert.* Displays a warning message whenever you open a file created in an earlier version of the program.

✦ *Locked File Warning.* Displays a warning whenever a locked file is opened. (Locked files can be read but not altered.) To unlock a file, quit ClarisWorks, select the file's icon on the desktop, press ⌘-I, remove the check mark from the Locked check box, and click the close box.

✦ *Paint Reduction Warning.* Warns when there is insufficient memory to create a full-page paint document. The document will be created at a reduced size. (See "Quick Tips" at the end of Chapter 6 for instructions on avoiding this situation by increasing the memory allocation for ClarisWorks.)

✦ *[v5.0] Suffix.* Appends this suffix to the name of any file you open that was created with an earlier version of ClarisWorks. Because adding the suffix changes the filename, this option protects the original file from being overwritten by mistake.

Tip

The option to *Show Fonts in Font Menu* can be very slow on some machines. If you already know what your fonts look like or find that the Font menu displays very slowly, you may want to turn off this option.

Text Preferences

Text preferences apply to any text you type in a ClarisWorks document, regardless of the environment you're in. Figure 11-2 shows the options for Text preferences.

Figure 11-2: Text preferences

Text preferences options include the following:

✦ *Date Format.* The format you select is used whenever you insert the current date into a document by choosing the Insert Date command from the Edit menu.

✦ *Smart Quotes.* With Smart Quotes enabled, ClarisWorks automatically translates your presses of the ' or " keys into curly quotes (" and "), as shown in Figure 11-3. Smart Quotes are applied intelligently. In most cases, the program can correctly determine when a right-facing or left-facing quotation mark is appropriate.

Smart Quotes off

This text sample shows some text with and without "Smart Quotes." You'd think that most people would prefer the way that quotation marks ("") and apostrophes (") look when using Smart Quotes.

This text sample shows some text with and without "Smart Quotes." You'd think that most people would prefer the way that quotation marks ("") and apostrophes (') look when using Smart Quotes.

Smart Quotes on

Figure 11-3: Examples of Smart Quotes settings

Note

Curly quotes are preferred in modern correspondence and publications. Correct uses for straight quotes include displaying feet (') and inches (") in measurements.

Tip

To type curly quote characters manually (when Smart Quotes is off), use the keys listed in Table 11-1.

Table 11-1 Curly Quote Keys	
Character	*Key*
"	Option-[
"	Shift-Option-[
'	Option-]
'	Shift-Option-]

✦ *Show Invisibles.* When this option is checked, you can see characters that are normally invisible, such as tabs, spaces, and end-of-paragraph markers (see Figure 11-4). Turning this option on after you finish a report or letter makes clean-up editing simpler. For example, it enables you to find extra spaces between words. You also can toggle this option off and on in the button bar.

Show Invisibles off

This text sample is used to illustrate the difference when Show Invisibles is checked and when it is unchecked.

In particular, Show Invisibles helps you see extra spaces between words and sentences. It also clearly shows the end of each paragraph with a special symbol.

This·text·sample·is·used·to·illustrate·the·difference·when·Show· Invisibles·is·checked·and·when·it·is·unchecked.↵

In·particular,·Show·Invisibles·helps·you·see·extra·spaces· between·words·and·sentences.·It·also·clearly·shows·the·end·of· each·paragraph·with·a·special·symbol.↵

Show Invisibles on

Figure 11-4: Examples of the Show Invisibles settings

✦ *Fractional Character Widths.* Choose this option to tighten spacing between characters (when printing to a laser printer, for example). Do not check this option if you are printing to an ImageWriter printer — unless you also have the ATM control panel from Adobe Systems installed.

✦ *Word Services.* Clicking this check box adds an Edit Word Services command to the Writing Tools submenu of the Edit menu. This command enables you to use certain add-on programs with ClarisWorks 5.0.

✦ *Default Font.* Select a starting font to be used for all new documents. All fonts currently installed on your computer are listed in the drop-down menu.

In ClarisWorks 3.0 and earlier versions, the Text preferences also included settings for footnotes. Those settings are now document-specific rather than preferences. To set footnote options, choose Document from the Format menu.

Graphics Preferences

The Graphics preferences (shown in Figure 11-5) affect both draw and paint graphics, as the following explanations indicate.

Figure 11-5: Graphics preferences

Note

✦ *Polygon Closing.* Polygon closing can be Manual or Automatic. When you choose the Automatic setting, you don't have to complete the final side of a draw or paint figure. You simply double-click the last point of the polygon. In Manual mode, if you want a closed polygon, you have to finish the figure by clicking its starting point. (If most of your polygons will be closed, selecting Automatic can save considerable time compared to manually clicking an object's starting point.)

The Polygon Closing preference setting also affects bezigons.

✦ *Object Selection (draw).* When you select draw objects with the pointer, they can be displayed with four or eight handles. Note that the extra handles do not provide additional object manipulation capabilities.

✦ *Gradient.* Choosing the Fast Gradient Display option speeds up the display of gradients by temporarily showing them as rough approximations (frequently with banding lines), rather than as smooth transformations from one color to another.

✦ *Automatically Smooth Freehand.* When this option is checked, shapes that are drawn freehand are automatically transformed into relatively smooth curves.

✦ *Mouse Shift Constraint.* You use this setting to specify an angular constraint for drawing with the mouse while the Shift key is pressed. The default setting enables you to draw in increments of 45 degrees, as shown in Figure 11-6.

Figure 11-6: Lines drawn with a mouse Shift constraint of 45 degrees

Spreadsheet Preferences

The Spreadsheet preferences (see Figure 11-7) enable you to customize the way the arrow keys and Enter key are used when you are working in a spreadsheet document or frame.

Depending on which Pressing Arrow Keys preference you choose, pressing an arrow key does one of the following:

✦ *Always Selects Another Cell.* Selects the cell to the immediate right, left, above, or below the current cell when you press the right, left, up, or down arrow key, respectively.

✦ *Moves the Insertion Point in the Entry Bar.* Used only for entering and editing data.

Figure 11-7: Spreadsheet preferences

Regardless of which setting you choose, you can achieve the opposite function by pressing Option in combination with an arrow key. Thus, if you elect to use the arrow keys for cell selection, you can still move to the right or left when you enter or edit data by pressing Option-right arrow or Option-left arrow.

The Press Enter to Confirm Entry And preference setting enables you to set the action that occurs when you complete a cell entry by pressing the Enter key. If you've used other spreadsheet programs, you may prefer to use the default setting: Stay in the Current Cell. Other options enable the Enter key to duplicate the function of the Return key (Move Down One Cell) or the Tab key (Move Right One Cell).

Remember that, as with other preferences, you can set Spreadsheet preferences for one document or globally. Most users prefer to choose one way of doing things and then click Make Default to set preferences for all future ClarisWorks worksheets.

Palettes Preferences

The Palettes preferences enable you to use the standard 81-color Drawing and Text Colors palette (which you cannot modify) or load a color palette of your choice (Editable 256 Color Palette). ClarisWorks 5.0 installs a Palettes folder (stored in the Claris folder within the System Folder), which contains predefined palettes you can use. Figure 11-8 shows the Palettes preferences options.

Figure 11-8: Palettes preferences

In addition to color palettes, ClarisWorks 5.0 enables you to save and load pattern, texture, and gradient palettes.

Loading palettes

As with many other preferences, loading a color palette affects only the active document. Thus, every document can have its own special color palette. Note that unless one or more ClarisWorks documents is open, the Palettes preferences do not appear in the Topic pull-down menu.

The number of colors available in the drawing and text colors palettes depends on the capabilities of your monitor and video card, as well as the settings in the Monitors control panel. For example, if your system is currently set to display 16 colors, the color palettes will only show those 16 colors. To see the complete palette of 81 different colors, your Mac must be set for (and capable of displaying) 256 or more colors.

To load a color palette, click the Colors radio button, followed by the Editable 256 Color Palette radio button. Click the Load button, and select a palette from the Palettes folder. To load a stored pattern, texture, or gradient palette to use with the current document, click the Patterns, Textures, or Gradients radio button, click

Load, and then select the desired palette. The loaded palette is now available for use in the current document.

Editing palettes

To edit a color palette, tear off the Fill Color or Pen Color palette from its location in the Tool panel. Double-click the color you want to change. A color selector appears. (The style of color selector shown depends on the version of system software installed on your Mac.) You can switch directly to a different color by clicking the color in the wheel. Alternatively, you can enter different numerical settings in the boxes on the left or use the scroll bar (or bars) to change the wheel's color scheme. Make the desired changes and then click OK. Repeat this procedure for any other colors you wish to replace. To revert to the normal 256 color palette, click the Use Standard button in the Palettes section of the Preferences dialog box.

To edit a pattern, texture, or gradient palette, begin by tearing off the appropriate palette from the Tool panel, and then double-click the pattern, texture, or gradient you wish to replace. An appropriate editor dialog box appears, such as the one shown in Figure 11-9. Make the necessary changes and click OK. (For details on using these editors, see "Creating Custom Colors, Patterns, Textures, and Gradients" in Chapter 6.)

Figure 11-9: The Texture Editor

Saving palettes

If you think you may want to reuse a palette you've customized, you can save it by clicking the Save button in the Palettes Preferences dialog box. To use the palette as the default for all new documents, click the Make Default button.

Communications Preferences

At a minimum, changing the default Communications preferences is useful for selecting a folder to receive electronically transmitted files and for establishing other generic communications settings. You may also want to create several different communications documents, each with its own preference settings.

For example, you can create a document for communicating with a friend that starts by automatically instructing the modem and software to wait for the friend's call. And for logging onto a communications service, you can create a document that attempts to connect the moment you open the document. Figure 11-10 shows the Communications preferences options.

Figure 11-10:
Communications preferences

The following descriptions explain what the Communications preferences do and how they affect activity during a session:

✦ *Scrollback.* Incoming text often arrives faster than you can read it, particularly if you are using a fast modem. The Scrollback setting determines how many lines or screens of text are available for you to scroll back through. You can choose a specific number of lines, *kilobytes* (sets of 1024 characters), or screens; or you can choose Unlimited. Unless you find yourself running out of memory, the best choice is Unlimited.

If you choose anything other than Unlimited, ClarisWorks discards the oldest lines, kilobytes, or screens when the limit is reached. Similarly, some information services clear each screen before sending a new one. Check the Save Screen Before Clearing check box if you want the program to store the old information in memory rather than discarding it.

✦ *Paste Delay.* This setting instructs ClarisWorks to pause between the characters or lines of text it transmits. This feature enables a slower computer on the other end of the line to keep up. Numbers entered in either box are in $1/60$ second. (An entry of 5, for example, represents a $5/60$ second delay.) Normally, this option can be left as is (0, for no delays).

✦ *On Open.* This setting determines the action taken, if any, when you open a communications document. The choices are Do Nothing, Automatically Connect, and Wait for Connection. In general, you rarely need to change the default setting of Do Nothing.

However, you may want to set an option for some communications documents. For example, the Automatically Connect setting is a good choice for a communications document you use with a bulletin board service (BBS) or with an information service such as GEnie. Do Nothing is the best choice for documents when you initiate the connection sometimes, and a friend or colleague initiates it at other times.

✦ *Connection.* ClarisWorks ships with two connection tools: the Apple Modem Tool (for Apple and Hayes-compatible modems) and the Serial Tool (for direct communications between a pair of computers over a serial cable). Other programs may add their own connection tools that also appear in this pop-up menu.

✦ *Terminal.* This option enables your Mac to work like a Teletype (TTY) or a DEC VT-102 terminal. A TTY is a very basic scrolling terminal. Text is sent as a continuous stream of characters and lines. The VT-102 terminal is more advanced and enables the other computer to send special commands, such as one that clears your screen. Most information and bulletin board services support at least one of these terminal types.

✦ *File Transfer.* ClarisWorks supports three file transfer protocols: Text, Kermit, and XMODEM. XMODEM is the most widely used and supported protocol — especially for transferring standard Mac files. For example, you can use XMODEM to transfer ClarisWorks word processing files between two Macs. The receiving Mac will be able to open the file in ClarisWorks.

The Text option is useful for transferring text-only files between computers that don't have the same programs, as well as between different types of computers (Macs and PCs, for example).

Although slow, Kermit enables you to transfer batches of files with a single command. It is a poor substitute for ZMODEM (which ClarisWorks has consistently failed to support), but it is better than nothing.

✦ *Capture from [Screen or Port].* This setting determines whether incoming text that is captured with the Capture to File command from the Session menu is formatted or unformatted. To save the formatting (such as tabs, linefeeds, and formfeeds), choose Port. To ignore these formatting characters, choose Screen. In general, you should choose Port when you intend to use the information in a spreadsheet or database document. Choose Screen when you want to use the captured data in a word processing document that you plan to reformat anyway.

New In
Version 5

✦ *Speak Text.* When checked, this option enables your Macintosh to speak the text of communication messages. You must have the PlainTalk system software installed.

✦ *Receiving Folder.* This setting identifies the folder that will be used to save captured text and protocol transfers (when you download files from an information service, for example). Click the button to select a folder.

Summary

✦ ClarisWorks has two kinds of preferences settings: default and document-specific. Changing a default preference affects all new documents. Setting a document-specific preference affects only that particular document.

✦ Program areas for which preferences can be set include General, Text, Graphics, Spreadsheet, Palettes, and Communications.

✦ Curly quotes, which are automatic with the Smart Quotes text preferences option, help create more professional-looking documents.

✦ The Show Invisibles text setting is useful when you perform a clean-up edit on documents.

✦ The Spreadsheet preferences specify the actions that occur when you press arrow keys or the Enter key during data entry and editing.

✦ The Palettes preferences enable you to load and save custom color, pattern, gradient, and texture palettes that you can reuse with new documents.

✦ The On Open item in the Communications preferences can make a communications document automatically wait for an incoming call from another modem or connect with a particular information service, computer, or BBS.

✦   ✦   ✦

Using the Button Bars

Overview

New In
Version 5

In previous versions of ClarisWorks, you could open the
Shortcuts palette — a tiny floating window covered with
buttons — and click buttons to execute common commands,
such as printing the current document or changing the style
of selected text to italic. In ClarisWorks 5.0, the Shortcuts
palette no longer exists. In its place are *button bars*;
customizable rows and/or columns of buttons that perform
commands similar to the buttons in the former Shortcuts
palette. Although you will see many similarities between the
button bars and the Shortcuts palette, you will also quickly
discover that button bars are a more elegant and efficient way
of accomplishing ClarisWorks tasks.

In addition to buttons, a button bar can contain any or all of
the following items (see Figure 12-1):

+ Pop-up menus that enable you to set attributes for
  selected text (font, size, style, and color)

+ The Stylesheet pop-up menu

+ An information line that provides a brief description of
  each button

+ Button bar balloons that pop up (similar to Balloon
  Help) when the cursor rests over a button

Figure 12-1: The default button bar for a word processing document

The buttons on the button bar automatically change to match the environment of the document or frame in which you are working. Spreadsheet-related buttons are presented only when you are working with a spreadsheet document or frame, for example.

ClarisWorks provides more than 200 predefined buttons you can add to a button bar. You also can add custom buttons for executing macros you've created. Other customization options include the following:

✦ Determining whether the button bar appears automatically when ClarisWorks is launched or appears only when you choose Show Button Bar from the Window menu

✦ Picking a location for the button bar (top, left, right, bottom, or floating) and resizing the bar

✦ Specifying the number of rows and columns of buttons to be shown

✦ Changing the arrangement of buttons on any bar

✦ Removing unwanted buttons from button bars

To get you started, ClarisWorks provides three standard button bars: *Default* (the button bar that appears when you create a new document), *Internet* (Internet-related commands), and *Assistant* (a button bar that provides access to a dozen ClarisWorks Assistants). Although you can freely modify these button bars (as you can any other bar), they cannot be deleted. You can also design your own custom button bars with only the commands you need, as well as share button bars with friends and colleagues.

Setting Button Bar Options

Click the pop-up menu at the left side of the button bar (refer to Figure 12-1) to set options for all button bars, display a different bar, create and edit buttons, and customize a particular button bar. When you click the downward-pointing triangle, the menu in Figure 12-2 appears. The top section of the menu lists the standard button bars, as well as those you have created; the middle section presents button bar creation and editing options; and the bottom section contains general configuration options, as described below.

Defined button bars

Button bar creation and editing options

General setup options

Figure 12-2: The button bar pop-up menu

Visible at Startup

By default, the Visible at Startup command is checked. Whenever ClarisWorks is launched and you open a document, the button bar automatically appears. If you prefer to display the bar only on your command, choose Visible at Startup to remove the check mark. If you later decide to use a button bar, you can choose Show Button Bar (Shift-⌘-X) from the Window menu. To eliminate the button bar, choose Hide Button Bar from the Window menu.

Button Bar Setup

To set display options for all button bars, choose the Button Bar Setup command. The Button Bar Setup dialog box appears, as shown in Figure 12-3.

Figure 12-3: The Button Bar Setup dialog box

To specify a default screen position for displaying the button bar, choose an option from the Position pop-up menu (Top, Left, Right, Bottom, or Free Floating). When you choose Free Floating, the button bar becomes a floating palette. It can be collapsed, expanded, resized, and closed, as well as freely moved to any convenient location.

You can specify the pop-up text formatting menus that appear on the button bar by clicking the Text Font, Text Size, Text Style, or Text Color check boxes. To add the Stylesheet pop-up menu to the button bar, check the Styles check box.

You can also specify two types of information that will appear whenever the cursor rests over a button. Click the Info Line check box if you want explanatory text to appear in the button bar. Click the Button Bar Balloons check box to make balloon-style descriptions appear over the buttons.

Help information displayed in the Info Line and in Button Bar Balloons is identical. There is little point in selecting both forms of help.

Unless you resize it, the button bar normally displays only one row or column of buttons. The number of buttons shown is restricted by the size of your monitor. To display additional rows or columns, change the number in the Columns and/or Rows boxes. (Note that — depending on the number of button rows and columns in the button bar — the Button Bar Setup dialog box may contain a Rows box, a Columns box, or both boxes.)

Manually setting the button bar's appearance

You can also manually set the location and size of the button bar, as well as the positions of buttons. To move the button bar, click in any blank area of the bar and drag it to a new location. As you drag the bar, an outline shows where it will appear when you release the mouse button (on the top, left, right, or bottom of the screen). Drag toward the center of the screen to make the bar free floating.

To change the shape of the button bar, move the pointer over the inner edge of the bar, causing it to change to a double-headed arrow cursor. Click and drag to change the size of the button bar. (The free-floating button bar can also be resized by clicking in the Grow box and dragging.) To change a button's position in the button bar, press ⌘-Option and drag the button to a new location.

Unless you have a very large monitor, it is unlikely you will be able to see all the buttons that have been assigned to the bar, as is the case with the Default button bar for most environments. To display all the buttons, drag the inner edge of the button bar to increase the number of rows or columns.

Hiding and showing the button bar

If the button bar is not on screen, you can make it appear by choosing Show Button Bar (Shift-⌘-X) from the Window menu.

To hide the button bar from view, take any of the following actions:

✦ Choose Hide Button Bar from the Window menu.

✦ Press Shift-⌘-X.

✦ If the button bar is free floating, click the close box in the upper-left corner of the bar.

Like other ClarisWorks windoids, such as the tear-off fill and pattern palettes, the free-floating button bar has a control box in its upper-right corner called the *collapse/expand box* (see Figure 12-4). If you click the collapse/expand box when the button bar is displayed, the bar shrinks to show only its title and moves out of the way (similar to the way the WindowShade box works in OS 8). If you click the box a second time, the bar expands to its normal size and returns to its original location. The free-floating button bar also has a grow box in the lower-right corner. Click and drag in the grow box to resize the button bar.

Collapse/Expand box

Grow box

Figure 12-4: The button bar as a floating palette

Choosing a Button Bar to Display

Only one button bar can be used at a time. If you have not chosen a specific button bar to display (Internet, Assistant, or one you have created), ClarisWorks displays the Default button bar that matches the current document's environment. To display a different button bar, choose its name from the pop-up menu at the end of the button bar (refer to Figure 12-2). To display a document-specific button bar you created for use with this document, choose Document from the pop-up menu.

Note

ClarisWorks remembers the last button bar you used — even between sessions — and automatically displays it in subsequent sessions.

Executing Buttons

Buttons in the button bar work just like buttons in other Macintosh programs. If the button bar is not visible, choose Show Button Bar (Shift-⌘-X) from the Window menu. Position the cursor in your document, select the item to be modified or perform whatever action is necessary — if any — to set up the conditions for the button, and click the button. For example, if a button is designed to act on a graphic object, you must first select an object.

Customizing the Button Bar

Although the Default button bar offers a nice selection of commands, the fact that you can customize the bar in so many ways — as well as create your own button bars — adds appreciably to its power. If you don't like the commands a given bar includes, you can remove them and, optionally, replace them with commands that are more useful to you. You can even add buttons that execute macros you've created.

Adding buttons to a bar

The Default button bar contains the buttons that Claris thinks are most useful in the various ClarisWorks environments. However, you can choose from many other predefined icons to add to the bar, as well as add buttons to any other button bars that have been created. And, as explained in Chapter 13, you can create ClarisWorks *macros* (sequences of steps and commands), make buttons for them, and add the macros to button bars. (Designing icons to represent macros and attaching the macros to buttons is described in "Creating and Editing Custom Buttons" later in this chapter.)

Note

Whether or not you think the Default button bar could stand some modification, you'll still want to check out the other predefined buttons. Just choose Edit Button Bars from the pop-up menu at the end of the button bar, choose Default, and click the Modify button. Each button is accompanied by a description in the box to the right of the buttons. Click a few buttons to see what you're missing.

Steps: Adding Buttons to a Button Bar

1. Choose Edit Button Bars from the pop-up menu at the end of the button bar, choose the name of the button bar you want to alter, and click the Modify button. The Edit Button Bar dialog box appears, as shown in Figure 12-5. (Note that the name of the button bar being edited is part of the window's title.)

Choose a button
category to view

Choose buttons
to add or remove

Figure 12-5: The Edit Button Bar dialog box

2. Choose a category from the Button Category pop-up menu.

3. Click any button to select it. A brief description of the selected button's function appears in the Description box.

4. To add the button to the button bar, click Add.

5. Repeat Steps 2 through 4 for additional buttons you want to add to the button bar.

6. Click OK to save your changes or Cancel to leave the button bar unchanged.

Removing buttons from a bar

There's nothing sacred about the set of buttons ClarisWorks initially includes in the predefined button bars. For example, many of the buttons merely correspond to menu commands that have Command-key equivalents, such as Cut, Copy, Paste, Open, Save, and Print. Similarly, some buttons you previously added may no longer be necessary. By eliminating some of these buttons, you can keep the button bar manageable.

Note

Removing a macro-based button from a button bar does not delete it. It merely eliminates the button from that button bar. (It can still exist in or be added to other button bars.) To *delete* the button and its associated macro, choose the Macros command from the File menu and then choose Edit Macros (as explained in Chapter 13).

Steps: Removing Buttons from a Button Bar

1. Choose Edit Button Bars from the pop-up menu at the end of the button bar, choose the name of the button bar you want to alter, and click the Modify button. The Edit Button Bar dialog box appears, as shown previously in Figure 12-5. (Note that the name of the button bar being edited is part of the window's title.)

2. Choose a category from the Button Category pop-up menu.

3. Buttons that are presently assigned to the button bar are shown with a gray background. Click to select one of these buttons.

4. To remove the button from the button bar, click Remove.

5. Repeat Steps 2 through 4 for any additional buttons you want to remove from the button bar.

6. Click OK to save your changes or Cancel to leave the button bar unchanged.

Rearranging buttons

Another way you can customize a button bar is by changing the order in which the icons are displayed. For example, if you constantly use a few buttons, you can group them together to make them easily accessible.

To move a button to another position on the bar, hold down the Option and ⌘ keys as you click and drag the button. When the button is where you'd like it to be, release the mouse button.

Creating and Editing Custom Buttons

New In
Version 5

In previous versions of ClarisWorks, new buttons were defined and their icons created as part of the macro recording process. In ClarisWorks 5.0, button icons are designed separately from the macro recording process by choosing the New Button command from the pop-up menu at the end of the button bar. New functions can also be assigned to buttons, such as launching a program, opening a document in ClarisWorks or another program, opening a URL on the Internet, or running an AppleScript.

Steps: Creating a New Button

1. Choose New Button from the pop-up menu at the end of the button bar. The New Button dialog box appears (see Figure 12-6).

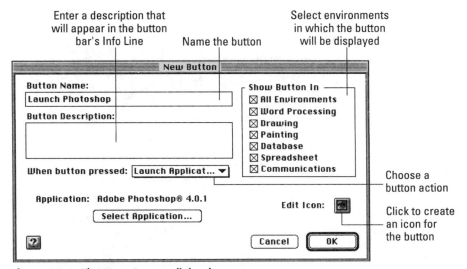

Figure 12-6: The New Button dialog box

2. Enter a name for the button in the Name box.

3. Enter a description for the button in the Description box.

   Text entered in the Description box is displayed in the Info Line of the button bar when the cursor rests over the button. If no description is entered, the button's name is displayed in the Info Line.

4. Choose an action for the button from the When Button Pressed pop-up menu. Complete the action specification by selecting a macro to play, a URL to open, a document to open, an application to run, or an AppleScript to execute.

5. If the action is anything other than playing a macro, choose the environments in which the button will be available by clicking check boxes in the Show Button In section of the dialog box.

6. To create or edit an icon for the button, click the icon to the right of Edit Icon. The Edit Button Icon dialog box appears (see Figure 12-7).

7. Create the icon by selecting colors from the palette and then drawing in the icon area. An actual-size representation of the icon is shown in the top-right section of the dialog box. When you are done, click OK.

Figure 12-7: The Edit Button Icon dialog box

When launching a program is the button action, the program's file icon is automatically used as the button icon. When opening a document is the button action, the program's document icon is used as the button icon. Like user-created icons, you are free to modify these icons as you wish.

8. Click OK to save your changes.

Although you cannot change the definitions or icons for Claris-provided buttons, you can freely modify custom buttons you or another user created. The following steps explain how to modify user-created buttons.

Steps: Modifying a Custom Button

1. Choose Edit Buttons from the pop-up menu at the end of the button bar. (If no custom buttons have been created using the New Button command, the Edit Buttons command cannot be chosen.) The Edit Buttons dialog box appears, as shown in Figure 12-8.

Figure 12-8: The Edit Buttons dialog box

2. Choose a button to modify from the Defined Buttons list.

3. Click Modify to change the chosen button.

   (If you want to permanently remove the button, click Delete.)

4. Make the desired changes to the button's name, definition, or icon, as previously described in "Creating a New Button."

5. Repeat Steps 2 through 4 for any additional buttons you want to alter or delete.

6. Click OK and then Done to save your changes or Cancel to leave the button definitions unchanged.

A Secret Shortcut for Designing Buttons

Designing icons for buttons is fine if you have some artistic skills and can work within the confines of the icon drawing area. If you consider yourself the reigning king or queen of ugly buttons, though, there's a much simpler way to create attractive ones.

Open your Scrapbook desk accessory, a ClarisWorks draw document, or a paint document, and then use the Copy command to copy an image you like (press ⌘-C or choose Copy from the Edit menu). Go to the Edit Buttons dialog box in ClarisWorks and paste the image (press ⌘-V or choose Paste from the Edit menu). ClarisWorks automatically reduces the image so it fits on a button and remaps its colors to those of the standard 16-color icon palette. Simple images give the best results.

Creating New Button Bars

In addition to modifying the button bars that come with ClarisWorks, you can also create new button bars. New button bars can contain Claris-provided buttons, as well as buttons you have created. New button bars can be saved as a part of ClarisWorks (and available for use with any ClarisWorks document) or they can be document-specific (available only with one particular ClarisWorks document).

Steps: Creating a New Button Bar

1. Choose New Button Bar from the pop-up menu at the end of the button bar. The New Button Bar dialog box appears (see Figure 12-9).

   The button bar is cleared to show that it contains no buttons.

Figure 12-9: The New Button Bar dialog box

2. Enter a name for the button bar in the Name box.

3. Choose a category from the Button Category pop-up menu. (To add buttons for macros you have created, choose the User Defined category.)

4. To add a button from the current category, click to select the button, and click Add. The button is now colored gray to indicate it has been added to the button bar. It is also displayed in the button bar.

5. Repeat Steps 3 and 4 for additional buttons you want to add to the button bar.

6. Click OK to save your changes or Cancel to leave the button bar unchanged.

Any ClarisWorks document can have its own document-specific button bar. In the pop-up menu at the end of the button bar, the document-specific button bar is named Document. To design a Document button bar for a document, choose Edit Button Bars from the pop-up menu, select the Document button bar, click Modify, and then add (or remove) buttons as you see fit. When you save the document, the document-specific button bar is automatically saved with the document.

To display the Document button bar for any document, choose Document from the pop-up menu at the end of the button bar. If a Document button bar has not been created for the document, the bar will be empty.

Sharing Buttons and Button Bars with Others

If you want to share buttons or a button bar with another person, edit the Document button bar for that document and then give a copy of the file to the person. For all buttons to function correctly on the person's computer, the following restrictions must be noted:

✦ If the button plays a macro, the macro must be saved as part of the document rather than as a general ClarisWorks macro (see Chapter 13).

✦ If the button plays an AppleScript, you must provide the AppleScript to the user.

✦ If the button opens a document, provide the document to the user. The appropriate application must also be installed.

✦ If the button launches a particular program, the user must have that program installed on his or her computer.

✦ If the button launches the user's browser or displays a Web page, the user must configure ClarisWorks to work with a browser (see Chapter 22).

Summary

✦ ClarisWorks includes several predefined button bars you can use to execute common commands and user-defined macros quickly.

✦ Buttons in the Default button bar automatically change to reflect the environment or frame in which you're working.

✦ You can show or hide the button bar, change the number of button rows and/or columns displayed, and move it wherever you like. If the button bar is free floating, you can also collapse, expand, and resize it.

✦ You can add and remove buttons from any button bar. By holding down Option-⌘, you can click and drag a button to a new location on the button bar.

✦ In addition to using dozens of predefined buttons, you can create your own macros, design custom icons for them, and add them to button bars. You can also create buttons that launch programs, open documents, open your Web browser to a given page on the World Wide Web, or run an AppleScript.

✦ You can design your own button bars, including just the buttons necessary for a particular task, such as working on the Internet.

✦ If you want to share your custom buttons or button bars with other users, edit the Document button bar for the document and then save the file. The Document button bar is automatically saved as part of each ClarisWorks document.

✦   ✦   ✦

CHAPTER

Using Macros

Overview

Although the ClarisWorks macro recorder doesn't have many
of the capabilities that stand-alone macro utilities have (such
as repeating a macro; linking to other macros; and branching
to different parts of a macro, based on certain conditions), it
does provide an easy way to perform many repetitive, well-
defined tasks in ClarisWorks.

The macro recorder works like a tape recorder. It simply
watches the actions you perform when you click the mouse
button (such as making choices in dialog boxes and choosing
commands from menus) and keeps track of the characters
you type. It does not record mouse movements, however. You
cannot, for example, use the recorder to capture figures you
create with the freehand drawing tool.

To make it easy to execute some of your macros, you can
assign keyboard shortcuts to them or add them to any of the
new ClarisWorks 5 button bars (making them available at the
click of a button). For help adding macros to button bars, see
Chapter 12.

Recording a Macro

ClarisWorks makes recording a macro easy.

Steps: Recording a Macro

1. To start the macro recorder, choose Macros from the File
menu and then choose Record Macro (or press Shift-⌘-J).
The Record Macro dialog box shown in Figure 13-1
appears.

In This Chapter

Recording and
setting options for
ClarisWorks macros

Playing macros

Deleting macros

Creating macros that
execute automatically

Transferring your
macros to other users

Click to set options

Enter name for macro

Enter the key that will be used to play the macro

Select environments where the macro can be employed

Click to begin recording the macro

Figure 13-1: The Record Macro dialog box

2. Name the macro and, optionally, specify a function key or Option-⌘-key combination that can be used to invoke the macro.

The Function Key radio button is grayed out (unselectable) if you do not have an Extended keyboard.

3. Set options for the macro as follows:

- Choose Play Pauses if you want the macro to record the amount of time it takes you to perform each step. Otherwise, the macro plays back at the fastest speed possible. This option is particularly useful when you're using ClarisWorks for step-by-step demonstrations or slide shows.

- Choose Document Specific if you want the macro to be available only in this particular document, rather than in any ClarisWorks document of the appropriate type.

4. Choose the desired Play In environments on the right side of the Record Macro dialog box. By default, ClarisWorks automatically chooses the environment you are currently using. Check all environments in which you want to be able to use the macro.

5. To begin recording the macro, click Record. You return to the document. To remind you that you are recording, a flashing cassette replaces the apple at the top of the Apple menu. (If you decide not to record the macro, click Cancel in the dialog box.)

6. Perform the steps of the macro.

7. To end the macro, choose Macros from the File menu and then choose Stop Recording (or press Shift-⌘-J).

Playing a Macro

Depending on the options you chose when you created the macro, you can invoke the macro in the following ways:

✦ Press the Option-⌘-key combination or the function key you assigned to the macro.

✦ Choose Macros from the File menu and then choose Play Macro. When the Play Macro dialog box appears (see Figure 13-2), choose the name of the macro and click Play.

✦ Click a button in the button bar that you created for the macro. (By following the instructions in Chapter 12, you can create custom icons for your favorite macros and add them to any button bar so they are readily accessible.)

Figure 13-2: The Play Macro dialog box

Note

Remember to set up the conditions that are needed for the macro before you execute it. For example, if you need to select some text before you can use a word processing macro, the macro will not work properly if you have not selected the text. If the macro does not execute when you press its keyboard shortcut or click its button in the button bar, or if it is not on the list in the Play Macro dialog box, you are in the wrong environment, or you clicked the Document Specific check box when you designed the macro and that particular document is not the active one.

Editing Macro Options

You cannot edit the steps of a macro. If you are dissatisfied with any step or need to make a change such as adding a step, you have to re-record the macro.

Note

You cannot use the same name or key combination for two macros. If you want to reuse either component, you must delete the original macro first, as described in "Deleting a Macro" later in this chapter.

On the other hand, if you want to change some of the *options* for a macro, you can alter as many of them as you like at any time. You can even create or edit a button bar icon if you wish.

Steps: Editing Macro Options

1. Choose Macros from the File menu and then choose Edit Macros. The Edit Macros dialog box appears, as shown in Figure 13-3.

Figure 13-3: The Edit Macros dialog box

2. Select the macro you want to edit from the scrolling list, and then click Modify.

3. Change whatever options you like, and click OK.

4. Repeat Steps 2 and 3 for other macros you want to change.

5. To record the changes and return to ClarisWorks, click OK. Or, to ignore all changes and leave your macros unaltered, click Cancel.

Deleting a Macro

If you no longer need a particular macro, you can remove it from the document in which it was saved or from ClarisWorks (depending on whether or not you chose the Document Specific option). You can also delete a macro if you made a mistake in it or if it doesn't play back correctly. (Remember, you can't reuse a macro name or key combination unless you first delete the old macro.)

To delete a macro, choose Macros from the File menu and then choose Edit Macros. The Edit Macros dialog box appears, as shown previously in Figure 13-3.

Select the macro you want to remove, and click Delete. If there are other macros you want to delete, you can do so now. To complete the deletions, click OK. If you change your mind and decide to leave the macro list unaltered, click Cancel.

Using the Macro Wait Command

In the communications environment, timing is everything. If you send your password to an information service before the service requests it, chances are excellent that the service won't receive it and you won't be able to *log on* (connect with the service) successfully.

Although you can record and play pauses in macros, often this capability isn't sufficient to ensure correct timing. Information services sometimes slow down (when they are handling large numbers of users, for example), so pauses between commands can vary dramatically from one session to the next. However, you can use a special ClarisWorks macro command — Macro Wait — to remedy this situation in macros you create for the communications environment. The Macro Wait command has two options:

✦ Wait for a specific text string to be received from the other computer.

✦ Wait for a specific number of seconds of line inactivity.

When the condition is met, the macro continues to play. For example, in a logon macro that automatically logs you onto an information service, you can use the Macro Wait command to wait for a specific prompt (such as *Password?*) before transmitting your password.

Steps: Creating a Communications Macro That Uses Macro Wait

1. Create a new communications document or open an existing document.

2. At the proper point in the communications session, start the macro recorder by choosing Macros from the File menu and then choosing Record Macro (or by pressing Shift-⌘-J). The Record Macro dialog box appears.

Note

Depending on what you want the macro to do, you may want to start the recorder (to record a logon sequence) just before you choose Open Connection from the Session menu, or you may want to start the recorder during the actual session.

3. Name the macro and, optionally, specify a function key or Option-⌘-key combination that can be used to invoke the macro.

4. Choose options for the macro.

5. Choose Communications as the Play In environment. (Normally, this option is already selected.)

6. To begin recording the macro, click Record. You return to the communications document. To remind you that you are recording, a flashing cassette replaces the apple at the top of the Apple menu.

7. Perform the steps of the macro. At the appropriate times, you can specify a wait period or a text string by choosing Macros from the File menu and then choosing Macro Wait. The Macro Wait dialog box appears, as shown in Figure 13-4.

Figure 13-4: In the Macro Wait dialog box, type a text string or the number of seconds to wait.

8. Choose a Macro Wait option by clicking the appropriate radio button. If you choose the first option, enter the text string for which you want to wait. The text string has to be exact — with the correct spelling, capitalization, punctuation, and spaces. If you choose the second option (Wait for *x* Seconds of Line Inactivity), enter the number of seconds.

9. When you're ready to end the macro, choose Macros from the File menu and then choose Stop Recording (or press Shift-⌘-J).

Tip

If you want to avoid the Macro Wait command or are having difficulty getting it to work reliably, you can create a normal macro and use it at the point in the session when you might otherwise use a Macro Wait command.

Designing Automatic Macros

ClarisWorks provides a special type of macro capability: *automatic macros*. You can create automatic macros that play whenever:

✦ ClarisWorks is launched

✦ A new document is created in a particular environment (a new spreadsheet, for example)

✦ Any document from a selected environment is opened (a word processing file, for example)

To create an automatic macro, in the Record Macro dialog box (see Figure 13-1), enter one of the special names shown in Table 13-1 (spelling, capitalization, and hyphenation must be exact). Set options and select the appropriate Play In environment (or deselect all environments). Finally, record the macro steps (as described in "Recording a Macro" earlier in this chapter).

Table 13-1	
Automatic Macro Names and Definitions	
Macro Name	*Executes When...*
Auto-Startup	ClarisWorks is launched
Auto-Open WP	A word processing document is opened
Auto-Open DR	A draw document is opened
Auto-Open PT	A paint document is opened
Auto-Open SS	A spreadsheet document is opened
Auto-Open DB	A database document is opened
Auto-Open CM	A communications document is opened
Auto-New WP	A new word processing document is created
Auto-New DR	A new draw document is created
Auto-New PT	A new paint document is created
Auto-New SS	A new spreadsheet document is created
Auto-New DB	A new database document is created
Auto-New CM	A new communications document is created

As you can see in the table, an automatic macro executes when one of three actions occurs: ClarisWorks launches, a particular document type is opened, or a particular document type is created. You can have only one ClarisWorks macro for each of the macro names listed in Table 13-1.

If you want to delete an automatic macro, choose Edit Macros from the Macros submenu of the File menu, select the macro from the scrolling list, and then click Delete.

The Auto-Open macro

Although the Auto-Open macros normally run whenever you open any document in the chosen environment, you can restrict an Auto-Open macro to a particular document by clicking the Document Specific check box when you define the macro. By linking the Auto-Open DB macro to one particular database file, for example, you can automatically sort that database and display the last record each time the file is opened. If any other database is opened, the macro will not play. If you use the Auto-Open DB macro in this manner, however, you cannot also create a similar macro for any other database; nor can you design a macro that will run when *any* database is opened. Remember, only one macro can be defined for each macro name.

Automatic macros versus stationery documents

You can easily create stationery documents or choose certain preference settings to accomplish many of the tasks that environment-specific automatic macros perform. For example, you can use a stationery or default stationery document (see Chapter 10), rather than an Auto-New WP macro, to set a particular font, display the current date, and include a Memo heading. To be truly useful, automatic macros should accomplish tasks that stationery documents and preferences cannot perform. For example, you can use an automatic macro to customize an environment by hiding or showing rulers, setting a zoom level, choosing a given tool in the Tool panel, or switching to a specific database layout.

Getting Down to Business: Creating a Small Caps Macro

Although ClarisWorks has many of the text formatting options other word processing programs offer, it does not provide a *small caps* feature. (A phrase or text string formatted with small caps is completely capitalized, but the letters are slightly smaller than the surrounding text.) However, by typing text in all capital letters and choosing a smaller point size, you can create the effect of small caps in ClarisWorks.

Steps: Manually Creating Small Caps

1. Type the text in all caps. Alternatively, you can add the Uppercase button to the button bar, select the text, and then click the button to change the text's case (see Figure 13-5).

   Figure 13-5: The Uppercase button

2. Select the part of the text you normally would have typed in lowercase letters. Ignore letters you normally capitalize (the first letter in a proper noun or the first letter of the word at the beginning of a sentence, for example).

3. In the Size menu, choose the next smaller point size. As an alternative, you can click the Decrement Font Size button in the button bar a few times to change the font size.

Now that you know how to generate small caps, you can design a macro that will perform the small caps conversion for you.

Steps: Creating the Small Caps Macro

1. Create a new word processing document or open an existing document.

2. Add the Uppercase button to the button bar as follows:

   • If the button bar is currently hidden, choose Show Button Bar from the Window menu (or press Shift-⌘-X).

   • Choose Edit Button Bars from the button bar pop-up menu (the downward-pointing triangle at the left end of the button bar).

   • In the Edit Button Bars dialog box, select the button bar where you want the macro to be available and click Modify. (To restrict the button to the current document, select Document.)

   • Select Word Processing from the Button Category pop-up menu, click the Uppercase button's icon (refer to Figure 13-5), and click Add.

3. Type a single word (**macros**, for example).

4. Position the cursor so it's directly in front of the *m* in *macros*.

5. To start the macro recorder, choose Macros from the File menu and then choose Record Macro (or press Shift-⌘-J).

6. Name the macro (*Small Caps*, for example) and set other options for it, such as the Option-⌘-key combination you'll use to invoke the macro.

   Because you'll want to be able to use the macro in other word processing documents, be sure you do not check the Document Specific check box.

7. Click Record to begin recording the steps of the macro.

8. Press Shift-Option-right arrow. The entire word (*macros*) is selected.

9. Click the Uppercase button in the button bar. The word is changed entirely to uppercase (capital letters). Letters already in uppercase are unchanged.

10. Click the Decrement Font Size button in the button bar twice (shown in Figure 13-6). The point size of the word is reduced by two points.

 Figure 13-6: The Decrement Font Size button

11. To complete the process, choose Macros from the File menu and then choose Stop Recording (or press Shift-⌘-J). The macro is saved in the document or in ClarisWorks, depending on whether you checked Document Specific when you named the macro.

Steps: Playing the Small Caps Macro

1. Position the cursor immediately in front of the first letter of the word you want to change to small caps.

2. Press the ⌘-Option keystroke or function key you assigned to the macro.

— or —

If you didn't assign a special keystroke to the macro, choose Macros from the File menu, choose Play Macro, and then choose the macro from the list that appears.

The macro automatically converts any word to an all-caps version of the word, two points smaller than the surrounding text.

There are several advantages to the manner in which you have constructed this small caps macro:

✦ Because the macro works on selected text, you can use it to convert an entire word (by positioning the insertion point just before the first letter of the word) or everything except the first letter of the word (by positioning the insertion point just after the first letter of the word).

Any word that is entirely composed of lowercase letters should be completely converted. If a word begins with a normal capital letter, on the other hand, the macro should be applied to everything but the first letter of the word.

✦ Clicking the Uppercase button relieves you from typing the original text in uppercase. ClarisWorks has no comparable menu command to change the case of text.

✦ Clicking the Decrement Font Size button is a more flexible approach than selecting a specific font size from the Size menu.

The macro always reduces the size by two points, regardless of whether the original text size was 10, 12, or 14 points, for example.

Note

If you had simply instructed the macro to set the selected text size to 10 points, the macro would not have worked with 10-point or smaller text, and it would have looked ridiculous when applied to large text, such as 24-point or bigger. (Admittedly, though, a 2-point reduction applied to a large text size will not have the intended effect.)

✦ Although you can run macro commands by clicking buttons on the button bar, the macro runs correctly whether or not the button bar is on screen. (Hide the button bar and play the macro to prove to yourself it still works.)

Quick Tips

The following quick tips discuss one-time macros, ideas for macros, how to avoid keystroke conflicts, and transferring macros to other users.

Sometimes once is enough

Most people normally think of using macros when they have a task they will need to repeat, perhaps frequently. Sometimes, however, you have a task that may never come up again, but you need to perform it 25 times in the current document (changing every occurrence of "Ace Auto Parts" to Helvetica italic, for example).

Just because you won't use a particular macro again after today doesn't mean you shouldn't make the macro. Create the macro and make it specific to the document in which you use it, or just delete it when you're done.

Macro ideas

Having trouble coming up with reasons to create macros? Here are a few suggestions that may start those neurons firing:

✦ Create keyboard shortcuts for menu commands that don't have shortcuts.

In the word processor, for example, you can create a macro that inserts the current date, one that pops up the Paragraph dialog box from the Format menu, and another that chooses a particular font and applies it to the currently selected text.

✦ Create a series of macros that perform online communications activities for you.

For example, you can create macros that take you directly to forums or special interest groups (SIGs), such as the Mac forum, a writers' forum, or a financial forum. You can also create one macro that automatically chooses the XMODEM file transfer protocol from an information service's menus and another macro that performs a *logoff* for you (quitting from a communications session and closing the connection).

✦ Try to think in terms of many steps.

You'll get the greatest gains in productivity by automating complex, multistep procedures. For example, you can create a macro that conducts an entire online communications session — connecting ClarisWorks with a BBS, changing to the Macintosh forum, capturing a list of all new files, and then logging off. After you have the list of files, you can read it at your leisure and check off the ones you're interested in. Then log back on and download the files you want.

✦ Think about ClarisWorks activities you routinely perform.

Not every macro needs to have a grandiose purpose. If you use a macro regularly for even small tasks, you will save a considerable amount of time.

Note Remember, you can also create separate custom buttons for macros so you don't have to memorize any additional commands.

Avoiding keystroke conflicts

You can assign ClarisWorks macros to function keys (if you have an extended keyboard) or to Option-⌘-key combinations. Because ClarisWorks uses neither of these approaches for invoking its menu commands and keyboard shortcuts, the particular key combinations you choose should be of little consequence, right? Well, maybe.

Many desk accessories and control panels have key combinations you can use to pop them up or to make them perform particular functions. This can cause conflicts with your ClarisWorks macros. The usual symptom of a conflict is the ClarisWorks macro does not function and is overridden by the desk accessory or control panel (or vice versa). The solution is to choose another key combination for the ClarisWorks macro or choose another key combination for the desk accessory or control panel, if you can.

Transferring macros to other users

You can share macros with friends and colleagues. You simply save the macros in a document file, rather than in ClarisWorks itself. All your friend has to do is open the file and change each macro from a document-specific macro to a ClarisWorks macro.

Steps: Transferring Macros

1. Create a new document (choose New from the File menu) and record the macros.
2. When saving the macros, click the Document Specific check box.
3. Save the document and give a copy of it to the other user.
4. The other user launches ClarisWorks and opens the document in which you saved the macros.
5. The user chooses Macros from the File menu and then chooses Edit Macros. The Edit Macros dialog box appears.
6. The user selects a macro to add to ClarisWorks and clicks Modify.
7. The user removes the check mark from the Document Specific check box by clicking once in the check box, changes other options (such as the key combination used to invoke the macro) as desired, and then clicks OK.

To add other macros to ClarisWorks, the user repeats Steps 6 and 7.

8. The user clicks OK to save the changes.

Moving On Up

The ClarisWorks macros are fine for simple tasks, but you may want to investigate one of the more powerful commercial macro programs for your more complex tasks. In addition to working with ClarisWorks, these macro programs also work in other programs and with the Finder.

QuicKeys (CE Software) and Tempo (Affinity Microsystems) are general-purpose macro utilities that are intended for the "typical" Macintosh user. Both programs provide a recorder function you can use to record most macros, as well as the capability to edit macros without re-recording them.

Summary

✦ Macros enable you to automate ClarisWorks tasks and perform them by clicking a button or pressing an Option-⌘-key combination.

✦ Every macro can be a general ClarisWorks macro (available in any new document of the correct type) or document-specific (available only when a particular document is active).

✦ You can assign a macro to a button bar and display a custom icon on the macro's button.

✦ Although you cannot edit the steps of a macro, you can edit the options for a macro.

✦ You can delete macros when you no longer need them.

✦ The communications environment has a special macro option called Macro Wait, which causes the macro to wait a specific number of seconds or for a particular incoming text string before it continues.

✦ You can create automatic macros that automatically run when you launch ClarisWorks, open a particular document type, or create a new file in a specific environment.

✦ You can share macros with another user by creating several macros in the same document and making them document-specific. The recipient then opens the file and changes the macros to general ClarisWorks macros.

✦   ✦   ✦

Working with Frames

Overview

The concept of *frames* is what puts the integration into
ClarisWorks. You can create a document in one environment
and embed other environments in the document by adding
frames. For example, in a word processing document, you can
embed paint frames that contain illustrations and spreadsheet
frames that contain tables and charts (see Figure 14-1).

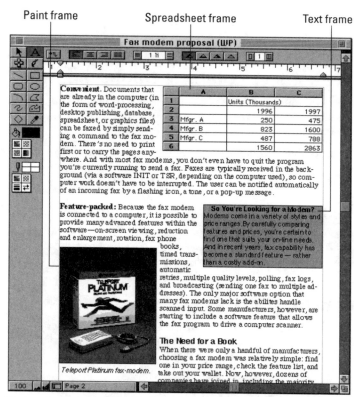

Figure 14-1: Frames embedded in a word processing document

Only the spreadsheet, word processing, and paint environments can be frames. When you work in a frame, it acts the same as a regular document created in its original environment — the same menu commands and tools are available.

Unfortunately, the types of documents that enable you to use frames, the methods with which you create frames, the modes in which you can access the frames, and so on are not consistent across environments. The next section lists the most important frame exceptions and "gotchas."

Frame Exceptions

You should be aware of the following rules and exceptions when creating and working with frames. Many of them are obvious and are based on common sense (for example, there are no communications frames, nor are frames allowed in communications documents). Others are simply Claris design decisions — as in, that's the way it is.

Read the rules once and then go about your normal ClarisWorks business. If you don't remember whether a certain frame procedure works in a particular environment, just try it. Refer to this section only when you have problems. If you try to memorize any rules other than the most critical ones, you'll needlessly confuse yourself.

No communications or database frames allowed

✦ Communications documents cannot contain frames, nor can you embed a communications frame in any other type of document. (There are no communications frames.)

✦ Although you can embed frames within database documents (in Layout view only), you cannot create database frames in other kinds of documents.

Draw objects, not frames

✦ There are no draw frames. Draw objects are always drawn directly onto a document or within a frame. Draw objects can be added to the word processing, spreadsheet, database, and draw environments.

Same-environment frames

✦ You can place word processing frames into word processing documents and spreadsheet frames into spreadsheet documents. To do so, press the Option key while you draw the frame.

Adding frames to database documents

✦ Frames can be placed and edited in database documents, but only when you're in Layout view.

Adding frames to paint documents

✦ The moment you stop working in a frame that has been placed in a paint document, the contents of the frame become a regular paint image. In other words, you can no longer edit or manipulate the frame contents with its original environment tools — you can only use paint tools.

✦ You cannot add draw objects to paint documents, but draw documents can contain paint frames.

Creating text frames

You do not have to draw an outline to place a text frame in a document (as you do with spreadsheet and paint frames). You can simply click to position the cursor and begin typing.

Opening frames

✦ You can open spreadsheet or paint frames to display them separately in a full-sized window, but you cannot open text frames in this manner.

✦ You cannot open spreadsheet frames that are embedded in paint documents (because once placed in a paint document, *all* frames become graphics).

Linking frames

✦ You cannot link a pair of existing frames.

✦ You cannot link frames from different environments.

✦ You cannot link frames in a paint document.

See "Linking Frames" later in this chapter for more information on linking.

Creating Frames

To create a spreadsheet, paint, or text frame within a document, select the appropriate tool from the Tool panel (see Figure 14-2), click to position one corner of the frame, and, while pressing the mouse button, drag to complete the frame. After you release the mouse button, the frame appears. Figure 14-3 shows the creation of a spreadsheet frame within a word processing document.

Select to create a text frame
Select to create a paint frame
Select to create a spreadsheet frame

Figure 14-2: To create a frame, first select one of these tools from the Tool panel.

To: Jim Smith	Date:	April 27, 1995
Subject: Quarterly Report	Pages:	1

The following table shows sales for your division as compared to the other divisions in Acme, Inc. Congratulations on a job well done.

Figure 14-3: Drag the pointer to create a frame.

If Autogrid (from the Options menu) is on, the frame aligns with the grid. (When Autogrid is on, the menu command reads Turn Autogrid Off; when it is off, the menu command reads Turn Autogrid On.)

If frame links have not been set for the frame, a text frame will shrink to fit the text it contains. To retain a full word processing frame (as you drew it), turn on frame links.

When you are creating frames, keep the following points in mind:

✦ Although there is no such thing as a draw frame, you can place a draw object into word processing, spreadsheet, draw, or database documents (in Layout mode only) by choosing a draw tool and drawing.

✦ Spreadsheets and word processing documents can contain frames of their own type; that is, a spreadsheet can contain spreadsheet frames and a word processing document can contain text frames. To create such a frame, start by selecting the text or spreadsheet tool, as appropriate. While pressing the Option key, click the mouse button and drag to make the frame. Figure 14-4 shows a text frame in a word processing document.

✦ You can select the text tool and drag to create a text frame, but you don't have to go to that trouble. As long as you're not in a text environment, you can click once to create a small text frame and immediately begin typing. You can later resize the frame as required (see "Resizing and Positioning Frames" later in this chapter).

Text frame

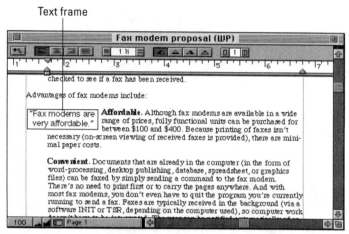

Figure 14-4: A text frame in a word processing document

Working in Frames

To work inside a frame, double-click it. The first click selects the frame; the second click moves you into the frame's environment and changes the pointer, tools, and menus to those of the new environment.

To stop working in a frame and return to the document's main environment, double-click anywhere outside the frame. If you happen to click within another frame (rather than in the main environment), the clicked frame is selected.

Resizing and Positioning Frames

After you place a frame in a document, you can treat its bounding rectangle just as you treat any other object — you can reposition it or use the handles to resize it.

Steps: Changing the Size of a Frame

1. Click the frame once to select it. Handles appear at the corners of the frame.

2. Select any handle, press the mouse button, and drag to change the size of the frame.

A frame pasted into a word processing paragraph as an in-line object has only a single handle (in the lower-right corner). To resize such a frame, drag the handle.

3. Release the mouse button to set the new size. Note that this procedure changes only the size of the frame, not the size of the image or data within the frame.

Note

If you want to make precise changes to the size of a frame, you can use the Size windoid to enter new dimensions (choose Object Size from the Options menu), or you can use the Scale By Percent command (found in the Arrange menu) to increase or decrease the horizontal and vertical dimensions by specific percentages.

Steps: Changing the Location of a Frame

1. Click the frame once to select it. Handles appear at its corners.

2. Click anywhere inside the frame and, while pressing the mouse button, drag the frame to its new location.

3. Release the mouse button to set the new position.

Keep in mind the following points about resizing and positioning frames:

✦ Although you can change the size of a text frame, the moment you leave the frame, it is adjusted to the smallest height that can still contain the text. Only the new width is retained. (Note, however, if Frame Links is turned on, the height is retained.)

✦ You can drag spreadsheet frames to any size, but when you release the mouse button, the frame resizes itself to show only complete rows and columns.

✦ After you place a frame in a paint document, it ceases to be a frame. It becomes a paint image. The entire contents — text and objects — are changed to patterns of dots. Text can no longer be edited and there is no longer a front-to-back layering of objects. To move the contents of a former frame, select its contents with the marquee tool and drag it to a different location. To change the size of the contents of a former frame, select it with the marquee tool and choose the Resize command from the Transform menu.

Opening and Closing Frames

Because spreadsheet and paint frames are merely windows on what may be much larger documents, you can open these frames in separate document windows. Changes you make while the frame is open are automatically carried to the frame in the document.

When you resize either a paint or spreadsheet frame by making it smaller, the rest of the image or cells don't disappear. They're simply outside the frame window — temporarily out of sight.

To open a spreadsheet or paint frame, click the frame once to select it and choose Open Frame from the Window menu. If a spreadsheet frame was selected, a full-screen copy of the frame opens in a new document window. If a paint frame was selected, a same-size copy of the frame opens in a new document window.

You can also open a spreadsheet or paint frame by selecting the frame and then pressing Option while double-clicking it.

To close an opened frame, click the close box in the upper-left corner of the window. The frame disappears, and you return to your original document.

Changing the Display of Spreadsheet and Paint Frames

ClarisWorks has a Frame Info command you can use with spreadsheet or paint frames:

✦ When you use Frame Info with a spreadsheet frame, you can decide whether the cell grid, row headings, and column headings should be visible or hidden and whether data or formulas are displayed. You can also set a different *origin* (the upper-left corner of the worksheet frame) to display.

✦ When you use Frame Info with a paint frame, you can set a different resolution and depth for the frame's contents, as well as specify a different origin.

Steps: Modifying a Spreadsheet or Paint Frame

1. Select the frame. Handles appear around the border of the frame.

2. Choose Frame Info from the Edit menu. One of two dialog boxes appears, depending on whether a spreadsheet or paint frame is currently selected (see Figure 14-5).

Figure 14-5: Dialog boxes for modifying spreadsheet and paint frames

3. If a spreadsheet frame is selected, set options by clicking check boxes. To set a different cell origin (the cell that appears in the upper-left corner of the frame), type the new cell coordinates (**B14,** for example) in the Origin text-edit box.

— or —

If a paint frame is selected, you can set a different *resolution* (the number of dots per inch) and *depth* (number of colors/data bits) for the images in the frame. As you click different radio buttons, the amount of memory required is shown.

If desired, specify a different origin for displaying the paint image within its frame. The two Origin text-edit boxes are used to set the horizontal and vertical coordinates (in pixels). An inch contains 72 pixels. For example, to specify starting coordinates of 1 inch to the right and 1.5 inches down, you enter **72** and **108.**

4. Click OK to accept the changes.

Note

When importing a PICT file into a paint frame or document, ClarisWorks automatically matches the resolution of the image and uses the document's original color table.

Changing the color depth of a paint frame can alter the colors in the painting. Such a change cannot be reversed with the Undo command. Thus, it's a good idea to save a copy of the document before changing the color depth.

Linking Frames

Although you can easily create multicolumn text in the word processor, ClarisWorks provides a more flexible method for creating complex layouts. You can link text frames to one another — in much the same way as you can in desktop publishing programs. A document can contain a series of linked text frames that are placed wherever you like. When text exceeds the available space in one text frame, it automatically flows into the next frame (as shown in Figure 14-6). If the linked frames do not have enough room to contain the total text, an overflow indicator (a small box with an x in it) appears in the lower-right corner of the final frame. A document can also contain combinations of linked and unlinked frames.

Figure 14-6: Linked text frames with indicator symbols

Steps: Creating Linked Text Frames

1. Select the pointer tool in the Tool panel.

2. Choose Frame Links from the Options menu (or press ⌘-L).

3. Select the text tool from the Tool panel and draw a text frame. (If the Tool panel isn't visible, choose Show Tools from the Window menu or press Shift-⌘-T.)

4. Click outside the text frame. An empty text frame with top-of-frame and continue indicators appears, as shown in Figure 14-7.

Figure 14-7: An empty linked text frame

5. Click the continue indicator (the black triangle at the bottom of the frame) and draw a box for the next text frame.

6. Repeat Steps 4 and 5 for any additional continuation frames you want to create.

7. Add text to the first frame by typing, pasting, or inserting. When the frame fills, additional text automatically flows into the other frames linked to it.

8. If additional frames are required, click the continue indicator of the last linked frame and draw another frame. Repeat this step as necessary.

You can also start with a single frame that already contains text and then link new text frames to the first frame. Simply use the pointer tool to select the first frame, choose Frame Links from the Options menu, and go to Step 5 in the preceding instructions.

Tip

You can insert a linked frame in the middle of several links — not just at the end. Simply use the pointer tool to click the link indicator on any linked frame and then draw the new frame.

Note

Draw documents can have multiple pages, and you can link frames across pages (linking an article that starts on Page 1 to a continuation on Page 5, for example). To add pages to a draw document, first choose Document from the Format menu. In the Size section of the dialog box that appears, indicate the number of pages you want. To see the breaks between pages, choose Page View from the Window menu (or press Shift-⌘-P).

You can also create linked spreadsheet frames and linked paint frames. Unlike linked text frames, any linked spreadsheet or paint frame is merely a window into the complete spreadsheet or paint document. The purpose of creating linked spreadsheet or paint frames is to provide multiple views into the same document. You can, for example, show some pertinent raw data from a worksheet in one frame and display summary figures from the same worksheet in another frame.

Why Use Linked Frames?

In a word, freedom. Unlike in a word processing document — even a multicolumn one — you can place linked text frames anywhere you like. You can also have some text frames that are linked and other text frames that stand alone. By using linked text frames, you can create layouts that are as complex as layouts designed with some desktop publishing programs. The following figure shows a simple newsletter layout in a draw document that incorporates linked text frames, stand-alone text frames, and draw objects.

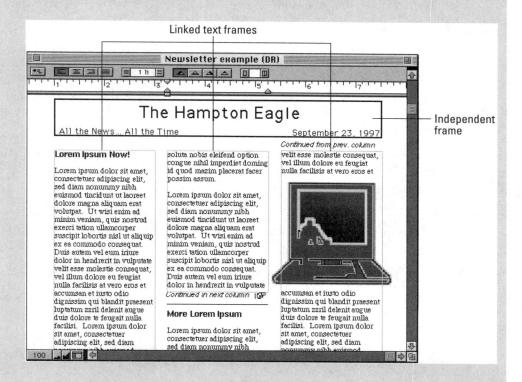

To help align the different objects and frames, you can turn on the Autogrid. After you have placed objects in position, you can select the frames and then choose the Lock command from the Arrange menu (⌘-H) to lock the frames in position. Locking the frames keeps them from moving but enables you to edit the text within.

To create linked spreadsheet or paint frames, start by using the pointer tool to select the frame. Choose Frame Links from the Options menu (or press ⌘-L). Click the continue indicator at the bottom of the frame and draw a box for the continuation frame. Repeat this process for any additional continuation frames you want to create.

Note   You can open a spreadsheet to full-screen size for editing or open a second view of a paint frame. You can also change the origin used to display any spreadsheet or paint frame. For details, refer to "Opening and Closing Frames" and "Changing the Display of Spreadsheet and Paint Frames," earlier in this chapter.

Quick Tips

The following quick tips give some examples of things you can do to frames and provide instructions for creating spreadsheet charts (within a frame or as free-floating objects).

Frames are objects

If it isn't apparent from the preceding discussion, I'll tell you now: *Other than in the paint environment, all frames are objects.* Anything you can do to an object, you can do to a frame. Examples include the following:

✦ Changing the pen color, line width, and pattern for the border (or making the border transparent)

✦ Adding a background color, pattern, or texture

✦ Resizing the frame

✦ Placing one frame over another and sending frames forward or backward

Using spreadsheet charts in frames

You can embed spreadsheet charts in a spreadsheet frame or create them as free-floating objects.

Steps: Making a Free-Floating Chart

1. Enter the spreadsheet frame by double-clicking a cell.

2. Select the data you want to use for the chart.

3. Choose Make Chart from the Options menu (or press ⌘-M). The Chart Options dialog box appears.

4. Choose a chart type, choose options, and click OK. The chart appears, separate from the worksheet.

Steps: Making a Chart Within a Spreadsheet Frame

1. Enter the spreadsheet frame by double-clicking a cell.

2. Choose Open Frame from the Window menu. The worksheet expands to a full-screen view.

3. Select the data you want to use for the chart.

4. Choose Make Chart from the Options menu (or press ⌘-M). The Chart Options dialog box appears.

5. Choose a chart type, choose options, and click OK. The chart appears, embedded as an object in the worksheet.

6. Click the close box in the spreadsheet window to return to the original document.

Other objects — such as paint frames, text frames, and draw graphics — can also be embedded in a worksheet. The objects can be created or pasted when you're in the Open Frame view, or you can create them by drawing with the appropriate tool (the text tool, spreadsheet tool, paint tool, or any of the draw tools).

Summary

✦ Any ClarisWorks document other than a communications document can contain frames from other environments.

✦ When you work in a frame, the menu commands, button bar, and tools change to match the environment of the frame. When you leave the frame, they change back to match the base document's environment.

✦ Frames are objects, and, except for frames you create in paint documents, you can resize or move them. You can apply any attribute to a frame that you can apply to an object.

✦ Spreadsheet and paint frames are merely windows into larger documents, and you can expand them to full-screen size.

✦ You can link text, spreadsheet, and paint frames to other frames. When you link text frames, text can flow automatically from one frame to another. Linking spreadsheet or paint frames enables you to display multiple views of the same underlying spreadsheet or paint document.

✦   ✦   ✦

Working with Styles

Overview

ClarisWorks's *Stylesheet* feature enables you to create your own reusable text, paragraph, outline, and worksheet table styles, and apply them to any text or worksheet areas you like. You can also design styles for objects — making it a snap to apply the same line settings, pen and fill colors, patterns, and gradients to objects. (You no longer have to guess what shade of blue you chose for text or a cell border, for example.)

By using styles instead of manually formatting text and objects, you can ensure that the appearance of elements will be consistent not only in the current document, but across an entire set of documents as well.

In addition to reusability, the real power of styles becomes apparent when you change a style that's already in use in a document. For example, if you have a paragraph style called Main Head that is defined as centered, 18-point, Times, bold, italic text and then change the definition so it is left-aligned, 14-point, Helvetica, and bold, all headings to which that style has been applied are immediately reformatted to match the new definition!

To see the Stylesheet palette, choose Show Stylesheet from the Window menu or press Shift-⌘-W. To hide the palette, click its close box, choose Hide Stylesheet from the Window menu, or press Shift-⌘-W. The Stylesheet palette is shown in Figure 15-1.

New In Version 5

The same styles can also be selected from the Stylesheet menu in the button bar. If the button bar is hidden, you can display it by choosing Show Button Bar from the Window menu (or pressing Shift-⌘-X).

Stylesheet pop-up menu

Figure caption labels:
- Currently selected style
- Stylesheet palette

Figure 15-1: Styles can be selected from the Stylesheet palette or the Stylesheet pop-up menu.

Note

You can also show or hide the stylesheet by clicking the Stylesheet button in the button bar (see Figure 15-2).

  Figure 15-2: The Stylesheet button

About the Stylesheet

Each document has its own stylesheet. When you save a document, you are simultaneously saving the current state of the stylesheet, too. Any changes you have made to the stylesheet — whether you have edited any of the standard styles, deleted some styles, or created your own styles — are stored with the document. When you change from one document to another, the stylesheet changes to display the styles of the second document. Similarly, when you switch to a different environment within the same document, the *classes* of styles presented also change. Table styles are shown only when a spreadsheet document or frame is currently selected, for example.

There are four classes of styles. Each class corresponds to a particular type of ClarisWorks element to which it can be applied:

✦ *Basic*. Basic styles are for formatting text selections (applying font, size, style, and color options) and objects, such as draw graphics, spreadsheet cells, and database fields.

✦ *Paragraph*. Paragraph styles are applied to entire paragraphs and include indents, tabs, alignment, line spacing, and before and after spacing. Paragraph styles can also include text formatting commands (setting a font, size, style, and color for the text in the paragraph, for example).

✦ *Outline*. Outline styles are used to apply outline formats to paragraphs.

✦ *Table*. Table styles enable you to apply cell shading, borders, and other formatting options to selected worksheet ranges.

To make it simple to identify the different classes of styles in the stylesheet, each has a distinctive icon that appears to the right of the style name, as shown in Table 15-1.

Table 15-1 Style Icons	
Icon	**Type of Style**
No icon (blank)	Basic style
¶	Paragraph style
☰	Outline style
⊞	Table style

Applying Styles

To apply a style, select the text, paragraph, outline topic, object, or so on to which you want to apply the style, and then choose a style from the stylesheet by clicking its name (as previously shown in Figure 15-1). Alternatively, you can choose the same styles from the Stylesheet pop-up menu in the button bar. If nothing is selected in the document when you choose a style from the stylesheet or stylesheet menu, it is applied to the next text you type or object you create.

The current style — the one with the check mark in the stylesheet — is sometimes followed by a plus sign (+). This means you have modified the selected item (text, object, or paragraph, for example) by adding formatting that is different from the style definition. For example, suppose you have defined a basic style named TB 24 that is Times, bold, 24-point text, and you have applied it to a heading. If you then reformat the heading by changing its font, size, or style, the style name is shown as TB 24+. If you edit the style by clicking the Edit button in the stylesheet, you'll note that some properties are shown in italic at the top of the Properties list. These are the properties you have manually changed for the selected item.

When working in a paint document or frame, you cannot apply basic styles to selected portions of a painting. Instead, any basic style chosen from the stylesheet or Stylesheet pop-up menu is applied to the next text you type or image you paint.

In ClarisWorks 4.0, styles could only be applied individually to selected text, objects, cells, and so on. If you applied one style from the stylesheet and then applied another, the second style replaced the initial style. ClarisWorks 5.0, on the other hand, enables you to combine styles. To allow multiple styles to be applied to selected text and objects in the current document, choose Compound Styles from the stylesheet's Edit menu. With Compound Styles checked, you might apply a basic style that sets the font and size to 24-point Times, for example, and then apply another basic style that adds italic.

Removing Applied Styles

Styles that have been applied to text, a paragraph, an object, a spreadsheet range, and so on can be removed with the Unapply Style command.

Unapply Style is like an Undo command with an extremely long memory. You can use Unapply Style to remove any applied style whenever you like — even after hours of editing. As long as the original formatting was added by choosing options from the stylesheet or the Stylesheet pop-up menu, the formatting can be removed with Unapply Style.

The following points explain how to remove the four classes of styles:

✦ *Removing a basic style from some text*. Reselect the text in the word processing document or frame, spreadsheet cell, or database field. A check mark appears beside the name of the basic style that was previously applied to the text. Choose Unapply *style name* from the stylesheet's Edit menu (Unapply Times Bold 12, for example).

✦ *Removing a basic style from an object* (a draw graphic or a database field in Layout or List mode). Reselect the object. A check mark appears beside the name of the basic style that was previously applied to the object. Choose Unapply *style name* from the stylesheet's Edit menu.

✦ *Removing a paragraph or outline style from a paragraph.* Reselect the paragraph or outline topic. (It is not necessary to select an entire paragraph. As long as the text insertion point is somewhere within the paragraph, it is considered selected.) A check mark appears beside the name of the paragraph style that was previously applied to the paragraph. Choose Unapply *style name* from the stylesheet's Edit menu.

You can also use the Unapply Style command on a series of contiguous paragraphs, as long as they were all formatted with the same paragraph style. If you select two or more paragraphs that were assigned different paragraph styles, the Unapply Style command is not available.

✦ *Removing a table style from a spreadsheet table.* Reselect the entire range of the table that was previously formatted with a table style. Choose Unapply *style name* from the stylesheet's Edit menu.

There are other procedures you can also use to remove applied styles:

✦ Reselect the style in the stylesheet with which the text, object, or cell was previously formatted. Doing so removes the selected style.

✦ To remove manually applied text styles, choose the same commands again from the Style menu or choose the Plain Text style (⌘-T).

✦ To remove manually applied text styles that have been applied in addition to styles from the stylesheet (such styles are marked with a plus symbol), select the style in the stylesheet and click the Edit button. The manually applied styles are shown in italic at the top of the Properties section of the window. Select the property you want to remove, and choose Clear Properties from the stylesheet's Edit menu.

Creating Styles

The process of creating a new style always includes the same series of initial steps.

Steps: Creating a New Style

1. Click the New button in the stylesheet. The New Style dialog box appears, as shown in Figure 15-3.

Figure 15-3: The New Style dialog box

2. Select a class of styles by clicking one of the Style Type radio buttons.

3. Decide whether or not the style should be based on an existing style. If so, select the style's name from the Based On pop-up menu. Choose None if you do not want to base the new style on an existing style.

4. Decide whether or not the new style should inherit format settings from the currently selected text, paragraph, cell, or object. To inherit settings, click the Inherit Document Selection Format check box.

5. Type a name for the style in the Style Name text-edit box, and click OK. The new style's name is added to the stylesheet.

This ends the initial style definition process. However, the definition may not be complete, particularly if you chose not to base the style on an existing style or on a currently selected item (text, a paragraph, an object, and so on). To refine the definition, click the Edit button at the bottom of the stylesheet. The stylesheet expands and its title changes to Edit Style. The pointer changes to the stylesheet edit pointer (a hollow S).

Select the style by clicking its name (in the left side of the stylesheet). The current *properties* for the style (the formatting options that make up the style definition) appear in the stylesheet's Properties list, as shown in Figure 15-4. You can modify the properties by choosing formatting commands from the normal ClarisWorks menus (such as Font, Size, and Style), from the button bar, from the ruler bar (if you're working in a word processing document or frame), and from the fill, pen, and line palettes in the Tool panel. When you are finished making changes, click Done.

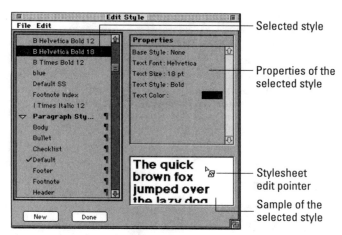

Figure 15-4: The Edit Style dialog box

Style definitions are not universal. Each new style is only available in the document in which the style was created. If you create a new document or open another document, you'll see the styles you've defined have disappeared from the stylesheet. They only return when you switch back to the document in which the styles were defined. If you want a given set of styles to be available for all new documents in an environment (word processing, for example), you should create a default stationery document that contains the new styles (see Chapter 10).

Editing Styles

As mentioned earlier, editing can be a necessary part of the initial style definition process. On the other hand, editing styles that are already in use may also be necessary. By changing a paragraph style you previously defined for hanging indents, body text, or headings, for example, you can instantly change the formatting of those paragraphs throughout your document. Editing options for styles include renaming the style, changing the style on which the current style is based, and changing the style's properties.

When editing styles, it is often helpful to see the cumulative effects of your edits. Choose Show Sample from the Edit menu to display style samples in the lower-right corner of the stylesheet. (Samples are visible only when you are editing styles; that is, when the stylesheet is expanded.) Repeatedly click the sample box to see how the current style affects paragraph, selected text, spreadsheet, and object formatting. To turn off the display of samples, choose Hide Sample from the stylesheet's Edit menu.

You can rename a style or change the style on which a style is based by using the Modify Style command. Select the style's name in the stylesheet and choose Modify Style from the stylesheet's Edit menu. The Modify Style dialog box appears, as shown in Figure 15-5. Enter a new name for the style and/or choose a different style on which to base the style from the Based On pop-up menu. Click OK to accept the changes.

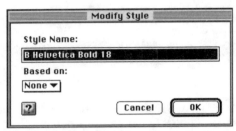

Figure 15-5: The Modify Style dialog box

Modifying style properties

Styles consist of *properties* (formatting options). To change a style, you change the properties of that style. After clicking the Edit button in the stylesheet and selecting a style to edit, you can use any of the following procedures to modify the properties of a style:

✦ *Choose new properties* from ClarisWorks menus, the ruler bar, the button bar, and the fill, pen, and line palettes. As you select them, the new properties are added to the style definition or replace components of the definition.

✦ *Remove properties* by selecting them in the Properties section of the stylesheet and then choosing Clear Properties or Cut Properties from the stylesheet's Edit menu.

✦ *Transfer properties* from one style to another. Select a property in the Properties section of the stylesheet and choose Copy Properties from the stylesheet's Edit menu. Select the style you want to modify, click in the Properties section, and choose Paste Properties from the stylesheet's Edit menu.

You can copy and paste several properties simultaneously, if you like. Before copying the properties, Shift-click to select several contiguous properties or ⌘-click to select noncontiguous properties.

When you are through editing styles, click the Done button. The new style definitions are immediately available for use.

There is no Cancel button in the stylesheet when styles are being edited — nor can changes you make while editing a style be corrected with an Undo command. If you don't like the effects of your editing, you must either redo the editing, close the document without saving the changes, or use the Revert command to restore the document to its state as of the last save.

If certain styles become unnecessary (or you just want to eliminate the clutter in a crowded stylesheet), you can delete selected styles (unless the style is currently in use somewhere in the document, in which case, you will not be allowed to remove it).

Steps: Deleting a Style

1. If the Stylesheet palette is not visible, choose Show Stylesheet from the Window menu (or press Shift-⌘-W).

2. Click the Edit button at the bottom of the Stylesheet palette. The palette window expands.

3. In the left side of the palette, click the name of the style you want to delete. A check mark appears beside the style name, indicating it is now the selected style.

4. From the palette's Edit menu, choose either Cut Style or Clear Style.

   Cut Style places a copy of the style definition on the Clipboard, enabling you to paste the style definition back into this stylesheet or the stylesheet for another document. Clear Style simply deletes the style definition without placing a copy of it on the Clipboard.

Transferring Styles to and from Documents

If you've defined a style you'd like to reuse in another document (or in *many* other documents), you can do any of the following:

✦ Save the document as a stationery file. (Each copy of the file you open will contain the new styles you have defined.) See Chapter 10 for help creating stationery documents.

✦ Save the document as a default stationery document for an environment, such as word processing. (Every new document created in that environment will share the same initial stylesheet.) See Chapter 10 for help creating default stationery documents.

✦ Copy the styles from the original document's stylesheet and paste them into the stylesheets of the other documents (described in the following steps).

✦ Use the stylesheet's Import and Export commands (described later in this section).

Steps: Transferring a Style to Another Document via Cut-and-Paste

1. If the Stylesheet palette is not visible, choose Show Stylesheet from the Window menu (or press Shift-⌘-W).

2. Click the name of the style you want to transfer. A check mark appears, indicating this is now the selected style.

3. From the stylesheet's Edit menu, choose Copy Style.

4. Open or change to the ClarisWorks document that is to receive the style.

5. From the stylesheet Edit menu, choose Paste Style. The new style is added to the document's stylesheet. Repeat Steps 2 through 5 for any additional styles you wish to copy.

Note

The stylesheet maintains its own equivalent of the Mac's Clipboard. Any style that is copied or cut (with the Copy Style or Cut Style command) remains available for pasting — in as many documents as you like — until you replace the Clipboard's contents by choosing Copy Style or Cut Style again.

The stylesheet's Export command enables you to save a selected set of styles to a disk file. Then, by using the Import command and choosing the new style file, you can quickly merge those styles with the current styles of as many documents as you like. The Export/Import procedure is the best means of moving many styles between documents, as well as the primary way of sharing your styles with other users.

Steps: Exporting Styles

1. Open the document whose styles you wish to export.

2. If the Stylesheet palette is not visible, choose Show Stylesheet from the Window menu (or press Shift-⌘-W).

3. Choose Export from the stylesheet's File menu. The Select Styles to Export dialog box appears, as shown in Figure 15-6.

Figure 15-6: The Select Styles to Export dialog box

4. Click the names of the styles you want to export. You can use the Check All or Check None buttons to speed the style selection process.

5. In the standard file dialog box that appears, enter a filename for the exported styles. (By default, the ClarisWorks Styles folder is selected. You can save the styles there or navigate to a different drive and/or folder.)

6. Click the Save button. The styles file is created.

Steps: Importing Styles

1. Open the ClarisWorks document into which you want to import the styles.

2. If the Stylesheet palette is not visible, choose Show Stylesheet from the Window menu (or press Shift-⌘-W).

3. Choose Import from the stylesheet's File menu. A standard file dialog appears and shows the names of the stylesheets that are stored in the ClarisWorks Styles folder.

4. Choose the name of one of the style files or navigate to a different drive and/or folder and choose another file. The Select Styles to Import dialog box appears, as shown in Figure 15-7.

Figure 15-7: The Select Styles to Import dialog box

ClarisWorks 5.0 includes a style file called More Table Styles that provides additional spreadsheet table styles.

5. Click the names of the styles you want to import. You can use the Check All or Check None buttons to speed the style selection process.

6. If you check the Replace All Styles With Same Name check box, imported styles with names that match those of existing styles in the document automatically replace those styles.

   If you remove the check mark, ClarisWorks asks you how to handle each duplicate style name. You can either replace the old style with the imported style or rename the imported style.

7. Click OK to import the selected styles. The imported styles appear in the document's stylesheet and can now be used.

Be careful when importing styles with names that duplicate those in the current stylesheet. If you check the Replace All Styles with Same Name check box, and both stylesheets have a style named Body, for example, any text in the document that is already formatted as Body instantly changes to match the imported style's definition. Of course, in many cases, this is exactly what you want (for example, you may want to make the document's formatting consistent with a company-wide stylesheet).

Summary

✦ By using styles instead of manually formatting text, paragraphs, worksheet cells, and objects, you can improve consistency in your documents. You can also save considerable time.

✦ Styles are document-specific; that is, they are only available in the document in which they were created. Saving a document also saves the styles that have been defined for that document.

✦ There are four classes of styles: basic (for selected text and objects), paragraph, outline, and table (spreadsheet tables).

✦ You can choose styles from the stylesheet or from the Stylesheet pop-up menu in the button bar. If Compound Styles has been chosen from the stylesheet's Edit menu, you can apply multiple styles to text, objects, spreadsheet cells, and so on.

✦ Any style that has been applied by using the stylesheet or the Stylesheet pop-up menu can be removed by choosing Unapply *style name* from the stylesheet's Edit menu.

✦ When you create a style, it can be based on any existing style in the current document; on the currently selected text, paragraph, object, and so forth; or it can be designed from scratch.

✦ When modifying a style, you can add new or replacement properties by choosing ClarisWorks menu commands, clicking icons in the ruler bar, or choosing settings from the palettes in the Tool panel.

✦ Styles can be moved between documents by using copy-and-paste or the Export and Import commands.

✦   ✦   ✦

Creating a
Slide Show

Overview

You don't need fancy software to create and display most
presentations. All you need is a program with a slide show
feature — the capability to present a series of text charts,
graphs, and other images on screen. ClarisWorks has such a
feature. You can use it from any environment except
communications, and it is surprisingly flexible.

Slide Show Fundamentals

Every slide show is based on a single ClarisWorks document,
and each page of the document is treated as a separate slide.
Within the slide show document, you can

   ✦ Rearrange pages to display them in a different order

   ✦ Make pages opaque, transparent, or hidden

   ✦ Specify special effects for the presentation, such as
     fading out between slides and looping (for continuous,
     self-running demonstrations)

   ✦ Place QuickTime movies on slides

After you create a slide show document, you choose Slide
Show from the Window menu, set options, and then run the
slide show. Creating an effective slide show tends to be an
iterative process that consists of refining the slides, trying out
different backgrounds, and experimenting with effects until
you have the presentation you want.

Preparing for a Slide Show

Although you can take any document and instantly transform it into a serviceable slide show, a polished presentation requires that you spend some time examining different options and determining which options are best for the presentation. This chapter examines the slide show features and explains how each feature affects the presentation.

Setting the number of slides

In every environment except word processing, you have to set the number of slides that will appear in the slide show. Word processing is an exception because its documents are designed to accommodate multiple pages automatically. In most of the other environments, you have to add pages beyond the first one.

Note

Regardless of the environment you use, be sure that ClarisWorks is set for Page View in the Window menu (or press Shift-⌘-P) so you can see where the page breaks occur. Also, unless Page View is selected, the Display options in the Document dialog box are grayed out.

The instructions that follow explain how to set the number of slides in different environments.

Draw documents

To set the number of slides for a draw document, choose Document from the Format menu. The Document dialog box appears, as shown in Figure 16-1. In the Size section of the dialog box, enter the number of pages across and pages down. (When presented as a slide show, draw pages are shown across and then down.)

```
╔══════════════ Document ══════════════╗
┌─ Margins ────────────┐  ┌─ Page Display ──────────┐
  Top:     [0.43 in]       ☒ Show margins
  Bottom:  [0.43 in]       ☒ Show page guides
  Left:    [0.43 in]     └─────────────────────────┘
  Right:   [0.40 in]     ┌─ Size ──────────────────┐
  ☐ Mirror Facing Pages    Pages Across:  [1]  ──── Enter dimensions here
└──────────────────────┘   Pages Down:    [1]  ────
┌─ Page Numbering ─────┐  └─────────────────────────┘
  Start at Page: [1]
└──────────────────────┘
  [?]              [ Cancel ]  [  OK  ]
```

Figure 16-1: The Document dialog box for a draw document

Note

A draw document can also have a *master page*. You use a master page to display a logo or other static objects on each slide. (See Chapter 17 for more information.)

Paint documents

To set the number of slides for a paint document, choose Document from the Format menu. The Document dialog box appears, as shown in Figure 16-2. In the Size section of the dialog box, enter the number of pixels across and pixels down. (An inch contains 72 pixels.)

Figure 16-2: The Document dialog box for a paint document

Note

Large paint documents use a lot of memory, so they are not well suited for slides.

Spreadsheet documents

To set the number of slides for a worksheet, choose Document from the Format menu. The Document dialog box appears, as shown in Figure 16-3. In the Size section of the dialog box, enter the number of columns across and rows down. Using the default column width and row height, a standard slide page is 7 columns wide and 50 rows high (or 9 columns wide and 37 rows high in landscape mode).

Figure 16-3: The Document dialog box for a spreadsheet document

Database documents

Follow these steps to set the number of slides for a ClarisWorks database.

Steps: Setting the Number of Slides for a Database Document

1. Create a layout that displays a single record per page.

2. Choose Browse (Shift-⌘-B) from the Layout menu.

3. Choose Slide Show from the Window menu. The Slide Show dialog box appears, as shown in Figure 16-4.

4. Set options and click Start.

5. If more than one record appears on each slide or if the record isn't properly positioned on the slide screen, choose the Document command from the Format menu. Change the margins and then repeat Steps 3 and 4 until only a single record is displayed on each slide. (As an alternative, you can change the record layout so it fills the screen by choosing Layout — Shift-⌘-L — from the Layout menu and dragging the body part downward.)

Figure 16-4: The Slide Show dialog box

Tip

To determine quickly whether the database will show a single record on each slide, check the page numbers listed in the Order section of the Slide Show dialog box (previously shown in Figure 16-4). The number of pages listed should match the number of records you are including in the slide show.

When creating a database slide show, you can use the Find command in the Layout menu (or press Shift-⌘-F) to choose the records you want to display as slides. If you want to display all records, choose Show All Records from the Organize menu (or press Shift-⌘-A).

Changing the order of slides

The slide order is displayed in the left side of the Slide Show dialog box. To alter the order, you simply select a page with the mouse and then drag it to a new position in the Order list.

Setting layering options

Each slide can be opaque, transparent, or omitted (hidden) from the presentation. An opaque slide is solid and completely obscures any slides you have already shown. A transparent slide, on the other hand, lets the slide beneath it show through. You can place several transparent slides on top of one another to create special effects. One common use for a series of transparent slides is to present a text chart that adds one new bullet point per slide.

To change a slide's layering in the Order list, click the icon to the left of the page number. As you click, the layering cycles through its three options: opaque, transparent, and hidden. Figure 16-5 shows examples of icons for pages that are opaque, transparent, and hidden.

Figure 16-5: Slide layering options

If you are using a master page as a background for a draw document, it will show through on all slides, regardless of whether they are opaque or transparent. (See Chapter 17 for more information on master pages.)

Slide display options

You can also use the Slide Show dialog box to set slide display options.

Steps: Setting Slide Display Options

1. Open the document you want to use for the presentation.

2. Choose Slide Show from the Window menu. The Slide Show dialog box appears (refer to Figure 16-4).

3. Set the Slide and QuickTime options you want to use in the presentation (as described in the "Slide options" and "QuickTime options" sections later in this chapter).

4. Click Start to see the slide show.

5. Press Q to exit the slide show (or press ⌘-period, Clear, or Esc).

6. Click Done to save the settings and return to the document, or click Cancel to ignore the new settings and revert to the previous ones.

You can repeat Steps 3 through 5 as many times as necessary. If you want to record the slide show settings permanently, save the document with the Save or Save As command from the File menu.

Options in the Order section of the Slide Show dialog box are discussed earlier in this chapter. The next two sections describe how the Slide options and QuickTime options affect a slide show.

Slide options

The upper-right section of the Slide Show dialog box contains the Slide options that govern the display of the slides and the manner in which they are presented. Slide options include the following:

✦ *Fit to Screen*. This option resizes each slide to make it fit on the current screen. The slides maintain the proportions of the original document pages.

✦ *Center*. This option centers the slides on the screen.

✦ *Show Cursor*. With Show Cursor checked, the cursor remains on screen as a pointer throughout the presentation. This feature is useful if you want to point at objects or text during the presentation. Leave Show Cursor unchecked if the presentation is a self-running (looping) demonstration.

✦ *Fade*. When checked, Fade causes the screen to fade out and then fade back in between each pair of slides.

✦ *Loop*. Check Loop if you want the slide show to run continuously. After completing a cycle through the slides, the show starts over again from the beginning. Normally, you use Loop in conjunction with the auto-advance feature (the Advance Every *x* Seconds option). You stop a looping presentation in the same manner you stop a normal presentation — by pressing Q, ⌘-period, Clear, or Esc.

✦ *Advance Every x Seconds*. When this option is checked, slides automatically advance at the rate set in the text-edit box. When it is unchecked, you have to advance pages manually by clicking the mouse or by pressing special keys (see "Running a Slide Show" later in this chapter). Note that even when the auto-advance feature is set, you can still advance any slide manually.

✦ *Background*. Choose from these pop-up palettes to add a color or fill texture to the background of a slide. The background is used for the entire slide show. The default background is white.

✦ *Border*. Choose from these pop-up palettes to add a color or fill texture to the border of a slide (the area around the outside edges of the slide page). The border is used for the entire slide show. The default border is black.

If a slide fills the screen, the border may be very thin. In this case, you may want to set the background and border to the same color.

QuickTime options

The QuickTime options are selectable only if the QuickTime extension is loaded when your Mac starts up. You can set the following QuickTime options in the Slide Show dialog box:

✦ *Auto Play.* When this option is checked, a QuickTime movie automatically runs when the slide in which it is embedded appears on screen.

✦ *Simultaneous.* If you have more than one QuickTime movie on a slide, checking this option enables them to play at the same time. When this option is unchecked, the movies play in sequence from back to front according to the draw layer in which they are embedded.

✦ *Complete Play Before Advancing.* This option forces the slide show to wait until the QuickTime movie has finished before moving to the next slide — even if you have set the Advance Every *x* Seconds option.

For more information about incorporating QuickTime movies into your ClarisWorks documents, see Chapter 20.

In ClarisWorks 3.0 and earlier versions, a QuickTime movie in a slide show always played from the point at which it was last stopped. You had to make sure the movie was set to its beginning before starting the presentation. In ClarisWorks 5.0, however, a movie is automatically reset to its beginning whenever you display the slide in which it is embedded. Thus, whether you are presenting a slide show to a new audience or are simply returning to a slide that contains a QuickTime movie, the movie will play from the beginning.

There is one exception to this rule: If you have been playing a movie manually — outside of the slide show — the movie will start from the point at which you stopped it. You must manually reset the movie to its beginning before starting the slide show. Otherwise, it will continue to start from the point at which it was manually stopped.

Running a Slide Show

To run a slide show, choose Slide Show from the Window menu, set options, and then click Start. You can also start a show without displaying the Slide Show dialog box by pressing the Option key while choosing Slide Show from the Window menu.

While a slide show is running, you can use the keyboard commands and mouse actions shown in Table 16-1 to control the presentation.

Table 16-1
Slide Show Keyboard Commands and Mouse Actions

Command	Key or Action
Show next slide	Mouse click, right-arrow key, down-arrow key, Page Down, Return, Tab, or spacebar
Show previous slide	Left-arrow key, up-arrow key, Page Up, Shift-Return, Shift-Tab, or Shift-spacebar
Show final slide	End (extended keyboards only)
Show first slide	Home (extended keyboards only)
Play a QuickTime movie	Click in the movie frame
Pause or resume a movie	⌘-click or Option-click in the movie frame
Halt a QuickTime movie	Click in the playing movie's frame
End the slide show	Q, ⌘-period, Esc, or Clear

Quick Tips

The following quick tips tell you how to use Page Setup to make slides fit on the screen, how to create overlays and animate objects, how to create appealing bullet characters, and how to run a remote slide show.

Using Page Setup for correct slide display

In most cases, monitors are considerably wider than they are tall. If you find that portions of the slides are clipped at the edges, choose Page Setup from the File menu and set the document for landscape mode by clicking the sideways icon in the Page Setup dialog box (see Figure 16-6). ClarisWorks uses the Page Setup settings when displaying documents on screen and when printing them.

Figure 16-6: The Page Setup dialog box for an Apple LaserWriter

Note   The dialog box will be different depending on the printer you have and the version of system software you are running.

Movement in presentations

By making several consecutive transparent slides, you can create overlays. One example is a bulleted list that adds a new bullet on each slide — enabling you to build on points as you move through the presentation.

Better bullets for text charts

Items in text charts are frequently preceded by a bullet character (•). Everyone recognizes the standard bullet (Option-8), and it's available for every font. Unfortunately, it's dull. If you have the Zapf Dingbats font, on the other hand, there are dozens of interesting characters to choose from. Table 16-2 lists some Zapf Dingbats characters you may prefer to use as bullets, adding visual appeal to your slides.

Tip   The Symbol font — available on every Mac — also has characters you can use as bullets. You can also paste a draw object (a circle with a gradient, for example) as an in-line graphic for a really unique and interesting bullet character.

Table 16-2 Zapf Dingbats Characters	
Zapf Character	**Keystroke**
✓	3
✔	4
☞	Shift-8
☆	Shift-p
●	l
○	m
■	n
❑	o
❒	p

Zapf Character	Keystroke
❑	q
❐	r
▲	s
◆	u
➠	Shift-Option-7
➣	Shift-Option-0
➢	Shift-Option-W

Running a remote slide show

ClarisWorks 5.0 includes an AppleScript called Remote Slide Show, which enables you to use one computer on your network to remotely control a ClarisWorks slide show running on another computer. For information on using this AppleScript, read the document named "About the AppleScripts" (found in the ClarisWorks Scripts folder).

Summary

✦ You can use documents from any environment except communications as the basis for a slide show.

✦ In environments other than the word processing environment, you need to use a special procedure to create a multipage document (if you want to include more than one slide in a presentation).

✦ You can change the order in which slides are presented without affecting the contents of the underlying document. You can also specify which slides are shown as opaque, transparent, or hidden.

✦ If you base a slide show on a draw document, you can create a master page and use it to display static information on every slide (a company logo, for example).

✦ You use the Slide Show dialog box to set most options for the presentation, including the placement of the slides on screen, background and border colors, special effects, and play settings for QuickTime movies.

✦   ✦   ✦

Designing Master Pages

In This Chapter

Creating master
pages for draw
documents

Changing the
layering position of a
master page

Overview

Although you can use headers and footers to add graphics and other items you want to appear at the top and bottom of every page of a document, things get a bit sticky when you want an item to appear somewhere else on every page. To handle this situation, ClarisWorks provides a feature called the *master page*.

Think of a master page as an extra layer or special page that appears on screen (and is printed) behind every page of the document. A master page lends consistency to the background elements in a document without forcing you to paste and realign the objects on every new page. Master pages are commonly used to create backgrounds for ClarisWorks slide shows (see Chapter 16), but are also useful for adding static information to letterhead templates and corporate forms. Objects you may want to place on a master page include *rules* (solid lines that appear at the top of each page or that separate columns of text), page borders, a solid background or gradient, company logos, and presentation instructions (for example, "Press Tab to advance to next slide; press Shift-Tab to view previous slide").

You can create master pages only in draw documents. However, because you can place word processing, paint, and spreadsheet frames on draw documents, you should consider this a minor limitation, rather than a major inconvenience.

Creating Master Pages for Your Documents

You can easily create master pages to add the same background elements to all pages in a document.

Steps: Creating a Master Page

1. Open an existing draw document by pressing ⌘-O, or create a new one by pressing ⌘-N. (Alternatively, you can choose the Open or New command from the File menu.)

2. Choose Edit Master Page from the Options menu. A blank master page is displayed, as shown in Figure 17-1. To remind you that you are editing a master page rather than working in the normal layer of the draw document, a check mark appears next to the Edit Master Page command in the Options menu and the page number indicator at the bottom of the document window is replaced with the text *Master Page.*

— Master page indicator

Figure 17-1: The Master Page indicator enables you to distinguish a master page from other pages of the document.

3. Add the master page elements to the page.

4. Choose Edit Master Page from the Options menu. The check mark next to the Edit Master Page command in the menu disappears, and the regular document is displayed.

5. If you are not in Page view, choose Page View from the Window menu (or press Shift-⌘-P). Master page elements can only be seen when the document is in Page view.

You can edit master page elements, just as you can edit any other object, image, or text string that appears in a regular ClarisWorks document. Simply choose Edit Master Page from the Options menu and make whatever changes are necessary.

Layering Objects in Relation to a Master Page

A master page is normally assumed to be the lowest layer of a draw document; that is, its elements appear behind everything else in the document. However, by applying the Move to Back command to objects in the normal draw layer, you can effectively change the layering position of the master page elements — elevating them to the top layer, for example.

> ## Steps: Altering the Layer in Which Master Page Elements Appear
>
> 1. If you are working on the master page, switch to the draw layers of the document by choosing Edit Master Page from the Options menu. The Edit Master Page command should no longer be preceded by a check mark.
>
> 2. If you are not in Page view, choose Page View from the View menu.
>
> 3. Use the pointer tool to select the objects that are to appear behind the master page elements.
>
> 4. Choose Move to Back from the Arrange menu. All selected objects now appear behind the master page elements.

Quick Tips

The following quick tips tell you how to add a rotated *rubber stamp* to a master page and how to hide master page elements.

Adding a rotated rubber stamp to a master page

Rubber stamps, such as "Confidential," "Draft," or "Paid," are excellent objects to include on a master page. Text placed over a Confidential or Draft rubber stamp, for example, is still perfectly legible, but the stamp clearly shows that the document is not intended for general distribution.

To achieve a rubber stamp effect in versions of ClarisWorks prior to 4.0, you had to create the text in a paint document or frame, rotate the text, copy it, and then paste the text into the master page of the draw document. Free rotation was only available for paint images. Objects — such as text strings — could also be rotated, but only in 90-degree increments.

ClarisWorks 5.0 has powerful rotation commands. Now objects of any sort — including text — can be directly rotated to any angle, not just in 90-degree increments.

Steps: Creating Rotated Text

1. Open or create the draw document to which rotated text will be added.

2. Choose Edit Master Page from the Options menu.

3. Choose a font, size, and style from the Font, Size, and Style submenus of the Format menu.

4. Choose Text Color from the Format menu, and select a color for the text. Because you normally want to be able to read the text in the overlying document, a light color or shade of gray is best for rubber stamp text. (A black rubber stamp would make the other text unreadable.)

5. Select the text tool (the A) from the Tool panel. Click and drag to create a text frame that is large enough to hold the rubber stamp text.

6. Type the text string for the stamp.

7. Select the pointer tool, and click the text string to select it. Handles appear around the text object to show it is selected.

8. Choose Free Rotate from the Arrange menu (or press Shift-⌘-R). The cursor changes to a thin X. To rotate the text, click any of the text frame's handles and drag. When you are finished, choose the Free Rotate command again to turn off the feature.

— or —

Choose Rotate from the Arrange menu. In the dialog box that appears, enter an angle of rotation. (Positive numbers rotate counterclockwise; negative numbers rotate clockwise.)

— or —

Choose Object Size from the Options menu. The Size palette appears (see Figure 17-2). Type an angle of rotation in the bottom box of the Size palette. Press Return, Enter, or Tab to apply the new rotation angle to the text. Figure 17-2 also shows the completed rubber stamp.

Rubber stamp text   Size palette   Enter a rotation angle here

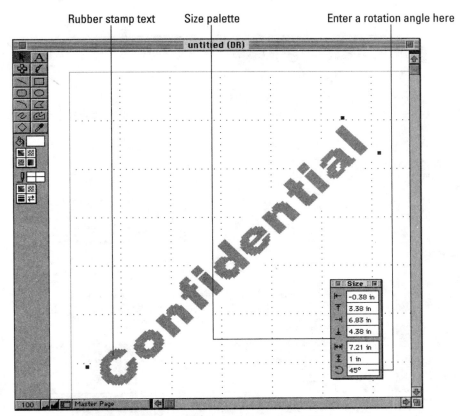

Figure 17-2: An example of rotated text on a master page

Obscuring elements on the master page

Occasionally, you may want to obscure some of the elements on the master page. For example, you may want all elements to show through on every page except the first page of the document. (Perhaps you intend to use the first page as a title page.) A simple way to hide a master page element without altering the master page itself is to cover the element with an opaque white square, which you place on the regular document page. The following instructions describe how to hide the Draft rubber stamp shown in Figure 17-3.

Master page elements

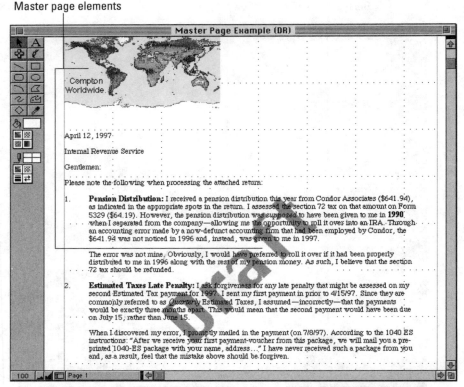

Figure 17-3: The original document with two master page elements: a logo and a Draft rubber stamp

Steps: Hiding a Master Page Element

1. Open the draw document that contains the master page.

2. Pull down the Options menu and make sure Edit Master Page does not have a check mark beside it. If it does, choose it again. (This action ensures that you are editing the regular document page, not the master page.)

3. If you cannot see the master page elements, choose Page View from the Window menu (or press Shift-⌘-P).

4. Select the rectangle tool from the Tool panel.

5. Draw a rectangle that completely covers the master page element you want to hide.

6. With the rectangle still selected, set the fill and pen color to white, and set the fill and pen pattern to opaque. The document should look like the one shown in Figure 17-4.

Opaque rectangle

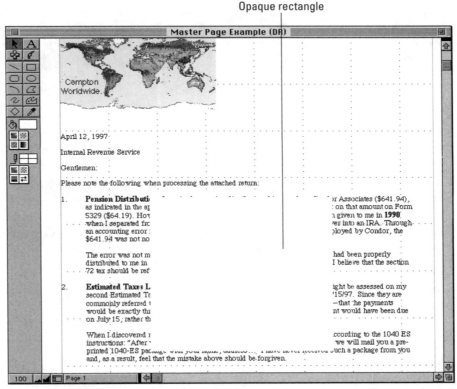

Figure 17-4: The opaque white rectangle obscures the master page Draft element.

Notice in addition to obscuring the master page Draft element, the white rectangle obscures much of the body text of the document. To correct this problem, you need to move the rectangle into the proper document layer.

7. Choose Move Backward from the Arrange menu or press Shift-⌘- - (minus sign). The rectangle moves into the layer between the master page and the body text.

Dummying Up Your Document

Why would you want master page elements to obscure the normal objects and text on a page? One example is when you are designing a new layout that contains dummy or draft text. By placing a Draft or Sample rubber stamp on a master page and then forcing the master page to the top layer (causing the rubber stamp to overwrite the normal text), you can show what the layout will look like without fear that the text will be critiqued or reproduced. This is similar to adding dummy graphics to a layout and overprinting them with *For Position Only*.

Summary

✦ Elements you place on a master page automatically appear in the same position on every page of the document.

✦ Although you can create a master page only in a draw document, you can get around this limitation by placing word processing, paint, and spreadsheet frames on draw documents.

✦ You can edit master page elements as often as you like. However, you can only see master page elements when you are editing the master page or have chosen Page View from the Window menu.

✦   ✦   ✦

Publish & Subscribe

Overview

Publish & Subscribe is a major connectivity advance introduced in System 7. This feature provides a simple way to integrate and share data among multiple programs, documents, and users without resorting to the normal Macintosh copy-and-paste procedure. Publish & Subscribe maintains an active link between elements from two or more documents. If the published material (text or an object such as a spreadsheet chart, for example) is changed in the original document, the revised text or object can be automatically or manually updated in any document that is subscribing to the material. This feature makes Publish & Subscribe an ideal tool for coordinating the work of several individuals, as well as for linking frequently changing data and objects from different programs.

Some of the ways you can use Publish & Subscribe include the following:

✦ Incorporating the work of several individuals on a network in a single master document (a departmental report composed of budget data from every department head, for example)

✦ Combining data from several different programs (adding ClarisWorks charts and Adobe Illustrator drawings to a shareholders' report created in Adobe PageMaker, for example)

✦ Maintaining live links between elements created in different ClarisWorks environments

Every Publish & Subscribe transaction has three components:

✦ The *publisher* is the portion of the document that is the source data — the text or object you want to make available for use by others or in other documents.

✦ The *subscriber* is the area in a second document in which you see the published information or object.

✦ The *edition* is a special file that serves as the link between the publisher and the subscriber. It contains a copy of the publisher's contents. This intermediate file transparently notifies the subscriber whenever the publisher's data has changed and then executes whatever updates are required.

Figure 18-1 shows the relationship among these components.

Publisher document   Edition   Subscriber document

Figure 18-1: An example of Publish & Subscribe

Note

You can only publish database elements from Layout mode, and you cannot publish or subscribe to information from the ClarisWorks communications or paint environments. Otherwise, documents from all other environments and elements, such as word processing text, worksheet sections, charts, and draw objects, are eligible for Publish & Subscribe.

At a minimum, every Publish & Subscribe transaction has a single publisher, a single subscriber, and an edition file. However, you can have multiple publishers and subscribers in any document. You can also have multiple subscribers — in different documents — to any published material.

Using Publish & Subscribe

Two steps create the link between the publisher and the subscriber: publishing the item and subscribing to the item's edition.

Steps: Publishing an Item

1. Open the document that contains the item you want to *publish* (make available to other users or use in other documents).

2. Select the item to be published, such as a text segment, a spreadsheet chart, a range of cells, or a draw object.

3. Choose Create Publisher from the Publishing submenu of the Edit menu. The dialog box shown in Figure 18-2 appears.

Figure 18-2: The publishing file dialog box shows a preview of the object or data that will be published.

4. Navigate to the drive and folder where you want to store the edition file, type a name for the new edition, and click Publish. The edition file is created, and the selected text or object is surrounded by a border (to show and remind you it is now a publisher).

Steps: Subscribing to an Edition

1. Open the document in which the published item will be placed.

2. Select the location in the document where you want the edition to be placed (a text insertion point in a word processing document or frame, a location in a draw document, or a range of spreadsheet cells, for example).

If the edition contains an object you intend to place in a word processing document, you can make it a free-floating object by choosing the pointer tool. Otherwise, the object will be placed as an in-line graphic at the text insertion point.

If the edition is to be placed in a spreadsheet, be sure to choose a range large enough to hold the data. If the range is too small, the new data will spill over into additional cells — overwriting any data they contain.

3. Choose Subscribe To from the Publishing submenu of the Edit menu. A dialog box similar to the one in Figure 18-2 appears.

4. Navigate to the drive and folder where the edition file is stored, select the edition's filename from the list, and click Subscribe. A copy of the edition is placed in the document.

Publish & Subscribe: An Example

The easiest way to learn more about Publish & Subscribe is to work through a simple example — one you can do entirely within ClarisWorks. Using Publish & Subscribe, you'll create a ClarisWorks worksheet with a chart in it, publish the chart, and then subscribe to it in a report created in the ClarisWorks word processor.

When a chart is simply pasted into another document, it loses all connection with the worksheet in which it was created. By using Publish & Subscribe, however, you maintain the link between the chart and the worksheet in which it was created. If you later modify the chart or the data on which it is based, the chart in the word processing report can be updated automatically.

As you read and work through this example, keep in mind the following steps can also be done by two people on a network — one person publishing the chart and another person (the author of the report) subscribing to it. Similarly, two different programs can be used. For example, the chart can be created in and published from the ClarisWorks spreadsheet and subscribed to by a desktop publishing program or by a different word processing program.

To keep things simple, you'll use Mortgage Analyzer and Résumé 1 — two stationery files (a spreadsheet and a word processing document) that come with ClarisWorks 5.0.

Follow these steps to see how Publish & Subscribe works:

1. Choose New from the File menu (or press ⌘-N). In the New Document dialog box that appears, click the Use Assistant or Stationery radio button and choose All Stationery from the Category pop-up menu. Choose Mortgage Analyzer from the file list, and then click OK.

2. The capability to update a subscribed-to object requires that the original be saved on disk. Because stationery files open as untitled temporary documents, save the Mortgage Analyzer spreadsheet by choosing Save from the File menu, naming the file (*Test*, for example), and then clicking the Save button.

3. Using the mouse, click to select the chart on the right side of the page (it begins near cell K19). Handles appear at the corners of the chart to show it is selected. (You may want to scroll down and over in order to get a better view of the chart.)

4. Select Create Publisher from the Publishing submenu of the Edit menu. A file dialog box appears, as previously shown in Figure 18-2.

5. Type a filename for the new edition or accept the one presented. ClarisWorks uses the convention previously shown in Figure 18-2 to name all edition files (*ClarisWorks Edition x*). Click Publish to create the edition.

6. Choose New from the File menu (or press ⌘-N). In the New Document dialog box that appears, click the Use Assistant or Stationery radio button and

choose All Stationery from the Category pop-up menu. Choose the Résumé 1 word processing stationery document, and then click OK. The document opens in a new window.

7. In this example, you'll place the chart in the résumé as an in-line graphic rather than as a floating object. Click the line immediately below Highlights of Qualifications and press Return.

8. Select Subscribe To from the Publishing submenu of the Edit menu. A file dialog box appears similar to the one in Figure 18-2. Select the name of the edition file created in Steps 4 and 5, and then click Subscribe. A copy of the chart appears in the word processing document.

The chart is surrounded by a gray border to show it is a subscriber object. If you like, you can turn the border off by choosing Hide Borders from the Publishing submenu of the Edit menu.

9. With the chart selected, drag the chart's handle (in its bottom-right corner) to reduce the size of the chart. Make it approximately 2 inches wide and 1.5 inches high.

10. To center the chart on the page, click the centered alignment control on the ruler bar. Figure 18-3 shows what the finished document looks like in ClarisWorks.

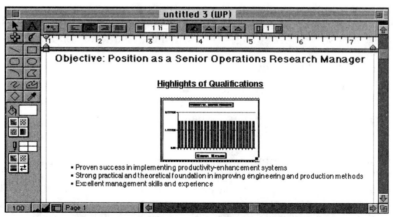

Figure 18-3: The word processing document now includes a chart to which it subscribes.

11. To see how updating works, make a change to the chart. In the worksheet, select the chart and choose Modify Chart from the Options menu. In the Chart Options dialog box, click a new chart type, such as Stacked Area, and then click OK to close the dialog box.

12. Because the published chart is updated in the edition only when its document is saved, choose the Save command from the File menu. (If you like, you can use the Save As command to save the document under a new name.)

13. Return to the word processing document. Notice the original chart has been replaced with the revised chart. When you are done experimenting with Publish & Subscribe, close both documents.

This example demonstrates two important points. First, when you save a file that contains published material, the edition can track the file even if it has been renamed. The edition also knows when the file has been moved to a new location, and, of course, it tracks normal Saves, too. Second, the updated chart is the same size as the original rather than the size to which you previously reduced it in the word processing document. You will have to resize the chart.

Note

While the preceding example shows how to place an object (a chart, in this instance) as an in-line graphic, you can also place an object as a free-floating graphic and then wrap surrounding text around it. While a programming error in ClarisWorks 4.0 prevented text from wrapping around a subscribed-to object, this feature works correctly in ClarisWorks 5.0. (For information on wrapping text around objects, see "Adding Graphics to Word Processing Documents" in Chapter 3.)

Updating an Edition

Until their edition is updated, subscribed-to elements remain unchanged (unless, of course, you edit them in the subscribing program). Although you can continue to edit the text or object in the original document from which they were published, the subscriber will reflect changes only when the following conditions are met:

✦ The original document is saved again.

✦ The edition is manually or automatically updated.

After the edition has been updated, changes in published material are made available to all subscribing documents.

By default, editions are automatically updated whenever a published document is saved. (It doesn't matter whether the subscribing document is open at the time the update occurs. The next time you open the subscribing document, you'll see the updated material.) However, automatic updating may not always be what you want. To control when updates occur, the person publishing the material or the one subscribing to it can set updates to occur manually, or they can force updates.

Steps: Updating an Edition Manually

1. Select the published material in the publishing or the subscribing document. (If the material is an object, be sure its outer border is selected.)

2. If you're working in the publishing document, choose Publisher Options from the Publishing submenu of the Edit menu. The Publisher To dialog box appears, as shown in Figure 18-4.

Publisher to: ☐ ClarisWorks Edition 2 ▼

Send Editions:
◉ On Save
○ Manually   [Send Edition Now]

Latest Edition: Friday, July 25, 1997 12:12:16 PM

[Cancel Publisher]

[Cancel] [OK]

Figure 18-4: The Publisher To dialog box

3. Click the Send Edition Now button. The most recently saved copy of the published material is sent from the edition to the subscribing document.

$-$ or $-$

If you're working in the subscribing document, choose Subscriber Options from the Publishing submenu of the Edit menu. The Subscriber To dialog box appears, as shown in Figure 18-5.

Subscriber to: ☐ ClarisWorks Edition 2 ▼

Get Editions:
◉ Automatically
○ Manually   [Get Edition Now]

Latest Edition: Friday, July 25, 1997 12:12:16 PM

[Cancel Subscriber]

[Open Publisher]

[Cancel] [OK]

Figure 18-5: The Subscriber To dialog box

4. Click the Get Edition Now button. The most recently saved copy of the published material is sent from the edition to the subscribing document.

Note

When you are performing a manual update, it doesn't matter whether the Send Editions setting in the Publisher To dialog box (Figure 18-4) or the Get Editions setting in the Subscriber To dialog box (Figure 18-5) is set to be done automatically or manually. Clicking the Send Edition Now button or the Get Edition Now button forces an update to occur based on the most recently saved copy of the published material.

Caution

To ensure only manual updates can occur (if you want to exercise total control over the update process), select the Manually option in either the Publisher To dialog box or Subscriber To dialog box. When you select Automatically or On Save, on the other hand, an update occurs every time the document containing the published material is saved.

Setting Subscriber Options

In addition to specifying an edition update method (automatic or manual), you can use the Subscriber Options command to find and open the publisher file, break the Publish & Subscribe link for any subscribed-to edition, and allow modification of the subscriber.

Opening a publisher

When you are using Publish & Subscribe, you don't need to have the documents that contain the publisher and the subscriber open at the same time. If, on the other hand, the subscriber document is open and you need to view or work with the publisher, ClarisWorks provides a command to locate and open the publisher file quickly.

Steps: Opening the Document That Contains the Publisher

1. Select the subscriber. If the subscriber is an object, select its border. If the subscriber is text or a portion of a worksheet, click anywhere inside the subscribed material.

2. Choose Subscriber Options from the Publishing submenu of the Edit menu. The Subscriber To dialog box appears, as previously shown in Figure 18-5.

3. Click the Open Publisher button. ClarisWorks locates and opens the document that contains the publisher in a new window.

Open Publisher is a very powerful feature. You can use it to open published documents from other programs! For example, you can design and publish an illustration in a high-end graphics program and then subscribe to it in a ClarisWorks document. If you later find you need to edit the graphic (to set a different background color, for example), click Open Publisher to launch the graphics program and load the document for editing.

Note

Open Publisher cannot be used to open a ClarisWorks publisher. If you try to do this, an error message appears (*Could not open the publisher document*). If you're working in a ClarisWorks document that subscribes to an object or text from another ClarisWorks document, you must use the Open command in the File menu to open the publisher.

Canceling a subscriber

To break the link to a subscriber (so you can prevent further updates), you cancel the subscriber.

Steps: Canceling a Subscriber

1. Select the subscriber. If the subscriber is an object, select its border. If the subscriber is text or a portion of a worksheet, click anywhere inside the subscribed material.
2. Choose Subscriber Options from the Publishing submenu of the Edit menu. The Subscriber To dialog box appears (as previously shown in Figure 18-5).
3. Click Cancel Subscriber.

Modifying a subscriber

Rather than just maintaining a link to the publisher, you may also want to make your own alterations to a subscriber. However, if the subscriber is an object (such as a draw image), changes to the object are limited to its size, placement, and text wrap. To make other modifications, return to the document from which the object was published, make the changes, and then update the edition to transfer the changes to the subscriber.

Modifying a subscriber that is placed as text, on the other hand, is a simple procedure.

Steps: Modifying a Text Subscriber

1. Select the subscriber text by clicking anywhere within it.
2. Choose Subscriber Options from the Publishing submenu of the Edit menu. The Subscriber To dialog box appears.
3. Click the Allow Modification check box. (If the box is not present, the text has probably been placed as an object rather than as text.)
4. Click OK. You can now edit the text subscriber and add formatting to it. However, if the published text is later updated, it will replace any edits you have made to the subscriber.

The Allow Modification check box is only guaranteed to be present if the subscribed-to text originated in a ClarisWorks document. If the text originated in another word processing program, you may have to open it in the original program, make your changes, and then perform the update.

Setting Publisher Options

Other than specifying whether a publisher will be automatically or manually updated, there is only one publisher option: canceling the publisher. Canceling a publisher has no effect on the edition or its subscribers. It merely cuts the link between publisher and subscribers. Any additional changes that are made to the published material are not sent as updates to the subscribers.

Steps: Canceling a Publisher

1. Select the publisher. If the publisher is an object, select its border. If the publisher is text or a portion of a worksheet, click anywhere inside the published material.

2. Choose Publisher Options from the Publishing submenu of the Edit menu. The Publisher To dialog box appears (as previously shown in Figure 18-4).

3. Click Cancel Publisher.

Canceling a publisher does not eliminate its edition file (*ClarisWorks Edition 5* or whatever you named it). After you cancel a publisher, you may want to drag its edition to the trash.

Quick Tips

The following tips explain how to deal with subscribed-to objects that are larger than the document page in which they are placed and give suggestions for using Publish & Subscribe with other programs.

Handling large subscribers

Finding that a subscriber in a ClarisWorks document is too wide to display completely is not unusual. And because many subscribers are objects, the resize handle (the black dot in the lower-right corner) may be off screen. Here are two ways you can deal with this situation:

✦ If the object is free floating, click anywhere inside the object and drag to the left until the resize handle appears. You can then resize the object as needed.

✦ If the object has been placed as an in-line graphic (embedded in a sentence or paragraph as a "graphic character" of sorts), you can't drag it. Instead, select the object and use the Scale By Percent command from the Format menu to shrink the object to the proper size.

Note

You can also apply the Scale By Percent command to free-floating objects. In this case, the command is located in the Arrange menu.

Program differences in the implementation of Publish & Subscribe

If you examine different programs that support Publish & Subscribe, you will find that implementations of this feature vary considerably. For example, Adobe PageMaker (a desktop publishing program) has only Subscribe features. To determine the differences in Publish & Subscribe capabilities, options, and procedures, you need to check the manuals of the programs involved carefully. And don't be afraid to experiment. Sometimes it's the quickest way to find out how a feature works.

Summary

✦ Publish & Subscribe enables data to be shared by multiple users (over a network) and among multiple programs. For example, a non-Claris desktop publishing program can subscribe to a chart that was created in a ClarisWorks worksheet.

✦ The three components in every Publish & Subscribe transaction are a publisher, an edition, and a subscriber. If necessary, you can have multiple publishers and/or subscribers.

✦ Editions can be updated automatically (whenever the published material is saved) or manually (on request by either the individual who published the material or by the one who subscribed to it).

✦ Additional Publish & Subscribe options enable you to break the link between the publisher and the subscriber (so future changes in the published material will not be reflected in the subscribed-to material), find and open the document that contains the published material, and modify a subscriber.

✦ Other programs may handle the Publish & Subscribe process differently — offering and supporting different options, for example.

✦   ✦   ✦

Working with Document Links

Overview

New In Version 5

One of the most interesting and potentially useful features introduced in ClarisWorks 5.0 is *links*. After embedding links in a ClarisWorks document, you can click them to jump to a particular spot in the same document, open another ClarisWorks document, or launch a browser to view a Web page on the Internet.

There are three kinds of links you can define: book marks, document links, and URL links. *Book marks* are used to mark places you want to be able to access quickly in a document. *Document links* are clickable links in a document that display a book mark in the current document, open a different ClarisWorks document, or go to a book mark in another ClarisWorks document. *URL links* are links in a document that — when clicked — instruct ClarisWorks to open a connection to the Internet, launch your default Web browser (Internet Explorer, Netscape Navigator, or CyberDog, for example), and display a specific page on the World Wide Web. URL links can also instruct your Mac to launch its default e-mail program or connect to a file download site on the Internet. URL links can be embedded in a normal ClarisWorks document or in a Web page you've designed in ClarisWorks (see Chapter 22).

To help you create and manage links, ClarisWorks 5.0 provides the new Links palette (see Figure 19-1).

Choose a type of link
to view and manage
from this menu

List of defined links
(book marks, in this case)

Click to enable or
disable live links

Figure 19-1: The Links palette

You can use the Links palette to create new links, jump to any defined link, edit or delete links, and change the way links are arranged in the palette. To display (or close) the Links palette, choose Show (or Hide) Links Palette from the Window menu (or press Shift-⌘-M).

General Information About Links

Regardless of the types of links you are creating or modifying, there are several basic rules and procedures you should understand, as described below.

Creating and saving links

✦ Links are created by selecting text, items, frames, or spreadsheet cells to define the link; choosing the link type from the pop-up menu in the Links palette; and then choosing the New command from the Links menu.

✦ Regardless of whether you are creating, editing, or managing links, you can only work with one link type at a time. Click the pop-up menu near the top of the Links palette to choose a link type.

✦ If you add or enable the links-related buttons in the button bar (New Book Mark, New Document Link, New URL Link, and Live Links On/Off), you can create links by clicking buttons, rather than by choosing commands from the Links palette.

✦ A given book mark can be associated with multiple document links. If you are creating a series of related Web pages, you might place a Home icon on each page, which displays the main Web page when clicked, for example.

✦ Links are always document-specific. When you create links of any type, they are automatically saved as part of the document.

Viewing and testing links

✦ Text links are shown by default as blue underlined text (unless you edit the link styles). The appearance of other types of links (objects, frames, images, and spreadsheet cells) is unchanged.

✦ If the live links feature is enabled, you can test document and URL links by clicking them. When the cursor moves over a text link, it changes to a pointing hand to show a link is present. To activate a non-text document link or URL link (or to check if the item is a link), you must often click it two or three times. The number of clicks depends on the mode you are currently in and whether the link is an object, frame, or an item/selection within a frame.

✦ It's often helpful to turn off live links when editing link items.

✦ The live links feature is document-specific. It must be turned on or off for each document.

✦ You can specify the order in which links are listed in the Links palette by choosing a Sort command from the Special menu: *Sort by Position* (arrange the links according to their position in the document) or *Sort by Name* (arrange the links alphabetically).

Moving and deleting links

✦ If an item that defines a link is deleted, the associated link is automatically removed from the Links palette as well.

✦ When an item that defines a link is moved within the current document (using cut-and-paste or drag-and-drop), the link continues to work normally.

✦ Links can also be moved *between* ClarisWorks documents via cut-and-paste or drag-and-drop. URL links and book marks moved in this fashion function correctly. Document links, on the other hand, are a special case. If a document link and its book mark were originally in the same document, the object of the document link is treated as undefined; you must create or choose a new book mark with which to associate the document link. On the other hand, if the object of the document link was another ClarisWorks document or a specific book mark in another document, the document link functions properly in the new document.

Book Marks

Book marks are special, non-clickable place holders in a ClarisWorks document. You can attach a book mark to almost any item in a ClarisWorks document, such as a text string, paint image or selection, draw object, frame, spreadsheet cell, or a cell range. You can instantly go to a given book mark by double-clicking its name in the Links palette, by selecting its name in the Links palette and choosing Go to Book Mark from the Links menu, or by clicking a document link that has been associated with that book mark (in the current document or a different ClarisWorks document).

Although book marks are often associated with document links, they don't have to be. Such stand-alone book marks, however, can only be reached by double-clicking their names in the Links palette or by choosing the Go to Book Mark command.

Creating book marks

Whether you just want to mark important spots in a document so you can immediately find them or intend to create clickable document links that transfer the reader to a particular section in this or another ClarisWorks document, you must create the necessary book marks.

Steps: Creating a New Book Mark

1. If the Links palette isn't open, choose Show Links Palette from the Window menu (or press Shift-⌘-M).

2. In the ClarisWorks document, select the text string, object, image, frame, or spreadsheet cells that will serve as the book mark.

3. Choose Book Marks from the Links palette's pull-down menu.

4. In the Links palette, choose New Book Mark from the Links menu. The New Book Mark dialog box appears, as shown in Figure 19-2.

Figure 19-2: The New Book Mark dialog box

5. Enter a name to identify the book mark. (If a text string is currently selected in the ClarisWorks document, the selected text will automatically be proposed as the book mark's name.)

6. *Optional:* If book marks for the document are organized within folders, you can choose a folder in which to store the book mark from the Folder drop-down list. Choose None if you do not want the current book mark placed in a folder.

7. Click OK to create the book mark.

Note

Book marks are attached to a particular text, object, image, frame, or so forth — not to a location in the document (Page 12, for example). If you delete or cut the book mark item, the book mark ceases to exist and its name is automatically removed from the Links palette. If you move the book mark item to a new location in the document — either by dragging or using cut-and-paste — the book mark moves to the new location, too.

Editing book marks

Existing book marks can be deleted, renamed, and moved into or out of folders. To delete a book mark, select its name in the Links palette and choose Delete Book Mark from the Links menu.

Caution

When you elect to delete a book mark (or any other type of link), the command is carried out immediately and cannot be undone.

To rename a book mark or change the folder in which it is stored, select the book mark's name in the Links palette and choose Edit Book Mark from the Links menu. The Edit Book Mark dialog box — identical to the New Book Mark dialog box — appears. To change the book mark's name, edit or replace the text in the Name box. To change the folder in which the book mark is stored, choose a folder name from the Folder pop-up menu. You can choose None to store the book mark at the main (top) level. Click OK to save your changes. For more information about creating and using book mark folders, see "Organizing book marks" below.

Organizing book marks

ClarisWorks helps you organize book marks in two ways. First, you can specify the order in which they are listed in the Links palette by choosing a Sort command from the Special menu: *Sort by Position* (arrange the book marks according to their position in the document) or *Sort by Name* (arrange them alphabetically).

Second, if the document contains many book marks or you simply want to impart additional order on them (perhaps breaking them up according to key document sections), you can create folders in which to store the book marks. Book mark folders serve the same function as the folders on your hard disk in which you organize files and programs. If you like, you can even create folders nested within other folders.

Steps: Creating a New Book Mark Folder

1. Choose Book Marks from the Links palette's pull-down menu.

2. Choose New Folder from the Special menu. The New Folder dialog box appears (see Figure 19-3).

Figure 19-3: The New Folder dialog box

3. Enter a name for the folder in the Name box.

4. *Optional:* To create the folder within an existing book marks folder, choose the folder name from the drop-down menu.

5. Click OK to create the folder, or click Cancel if you change your mind.

Document Links

Every document link is associated with a book mark in the current document, with another ClarisWorks document, or with a specific book mark in another ClarisWorks document. When you click a document link, ClarisWorks automatically displays the associated book mark or ClarisWorks document. For example, you can use document links to create a live table of contents. When the user clicks an entry in it, the associated chapter document will open or ClarisWorks will scroll the current document to the appropriate heading. You can also embed document links in Web pages you've created in ClarisWorks, enabling the user to navigate to particular sections of the document by just clicking. Such document links are automatically converted to appropriate HTML instructions when you save the page as an HTML document (that is, a Web page).

Steps: Creating a Document Link

1. If the Links palette isn't open, choose Show Links Palette from the Window menu (or press Shift-⌘-M).

2. In the ClarisWorks document, select the text string, object, image, frame, or spreadsheet cells that will serve as the document link.

3. Choose Document Links from the Links palette's pull-down menu.

4. In the Links palette, choose New Document Link from the Links menu. The New Document Link dialog box appears, as shown in Figure 19-4.

Figure 19-4: The New Document Link dialog box

5. Enter a name to identify the document link. (If a text string is currently selected in the ClarisWorks document, the string will automatically be proposed as the document link's name.)

6. To associate the document with a book mark in the current document, choose one from the Book Mark drop-down list.

— or —

To cause the document link to open a specific ClarisWorks document to its first page, click Choose Document, and select the desired ClarisWorks file.

— or —

To cause the document link to open a specific ClarisWorks document to a particular book mark, click Choose Document, and select the desired ClarisWorks file. Then choose a book mark from the Book Mark drop-down list.

7. Click OK to create the document link.

Although document links cannot open documents created in other programs, you can create buttons for a button bar that can do this. (For information, see Chapter 12.)

To test a document link, turn on live links by clicking the Live Links check box in the Links palette or by clicking the Live Links On/Off button in the button bar (if the button is displayed). Then click the document link. (Note that you can go directly to any document link in the current document by selecting its name in the Links palette and choosing Go to Document Link from the Links menu. This command selects the link without executing it.)

To modify a document link, select the link in the Links palette and choose Edit Document Link from the Links menu. The Edit Document Link dialog box appears. You can change the link's name, associated book mark, and/or the destination document to display. Click OK to save the changes.

Document links can be deleted by highlighting the link in the Links palette and choosing Delete Document Link from the Links menu. Note that when deleting a Document link, the command is carried out immediately and cannot be undone.

URL Links

When a URL link is clicked, the user's Web browser opens and displays a particular page from the World Wide Web, addresses an e-mail message to a specified user or company, or performs some similar action. (See "Creating non-HTTP URL links" at the end of this chapter for additional information.) The document in which the URL link is embedded can be an ordinary ClarisWorks document (an inter-office memo that has related information stored on the Internet or the company's intranet, for example) or it can be a Web page that was created in ClarisWorks (as explained in Chapter 22).

For URL links to function properly, several conditions must be met. The user must have a way to connect to the Internet or a corporate intranet (typically over a modem, network, or dedicated line), a Web browser must be installed and designated as the default browser in Internet Config, and the URL address must be correct. (For more information about connecting to the Internet, see Chapters 22 and 23.)

Steps: Creating a New URL Link

1. If the Links palette isn't open, choose Show Links Palette from the Window menu (or press Shift-⌘-M).

2. In the ClarisWorks document, select the text string, object, image, frame, or spreadsheet cells that will serve as the URL link.

3. Choose URL Links from the Links palette's pull-down menu.

4. Choose New URL Link from the Links menu. The New URL Link dialog box appears, as shown in Figure 19-5.

            — Name the URL link

            — Specify the address of the destination Web page

Figure 19-5: The New URL Link dialog box

5. Enter a name to identify the URL link. (If a text string is currently selected in the ClarisWorks document, the string will automatically be proposed as the URL link's name.)

6. Enter a complete Web page address, mailto command, ftp command, newsgroup name, or newsgroup message ID in the URL box. (See "Creating non-HTTP URL links" at the end of this chapter for help typing URLs.)

7. Click OK to create the URL link.

Note

Although a hypertext URL link can be the Web page's address (such as http://www.abbott.com), it can just as easily be any text string (such as *Click here to visit my home page*).

Tip

It's easy to mistype a URL; many Web page addresses are long and complex. To avoid mistyping the URL, open your Web browser, go to the desired Web page, copy the URL from the browser's Address box, and then paste it into the New URL dialog box.

To test a URL link, turn on live links by clicking the Live Links check box in the Links palette or by clicking the Live Links On/Off button in the button bar (if the button is displayed). Then click the URL link. (Note that you can go directly to any URL link in the current document by selecting its name in the Links palette and choosing Go to URL Link from the Links menu. This command selects the link without executing it.)

To modify a URL link, select the link in the Links palette and choose Edit URL Link from the Links menu. The Edit URL Link dialog box appears and displays the current name and URL for the chosen link. You can change the link's name, destination address, or both. Click OK to save the changes.

URL links can be deleted by highlighting the link in the Links palette and choosing Delete URL Link from the Links menu. Note that when deleting a URL link, the command is carried out immediately and cannot be undone.

Quick Tips

The following quick tips show how to create links using the button bar rather than the Links palette, how to use links to create Help files for complex ClarisWorks documents, and how to launch your browser to view a Web URL represented by a text string in a ClarisWorks document.

Using the button bar to create links

While it is simple to designate new links by choosing the New command from the Links menu in the Links palette, it's also the slow way. If you want to create new links quickly, consider creating a Links button bar, which contains the three links buttons and the enable/disable live links button (see Figure 19-6). These buttons are all available in the Internet button bar and are automatically displayed when creating a Web page with any of the Web templates included in ClarisWorks 5. (For details on creating button bars or adding these buttons to an existing button bar, see Chapter 12.)

Figure 19-6: A Links button bar

Creating Help links

If you ever wished you could create Help files for some of your more complex documents, you can now use a document link for that purpose. Figure 19-7 shows one such paired document and Help file.

	Spreadsheet with Help (SS)

Figure 19-7: All cells in Column A are a document link to a Help file. To view the associated Help document, the user only has to click a cell in the column. Displaying the Help file can be avoided by using the cursor keys for between-cell movements or by turning off live links.

Treating a text selection as a URL

When the Internet button bar is displayed or the Open URL button (see Figure 19-8) has been added to the current button bar, ClarisWorks can treat a selected text string as a URL, launch your browser, and attempt to display the URL's page from the World Wide Web. You can create a spreadsheet or database of technical support, shareware, or financial news URLs, for instance. To view a Web page, select the text for the URL in the ClarisWorks document, and then click the Open URL button.

Figure 19-8: The Open URL button

Creating non-HTTP URL links

While URL links are most commonly used to display particular Web pages, you can also create URL links with any of the functions shown in Table 19-1.

Table 19-1
URL Links

URL Prefix	Function(s)	Example(s)
http://	Display a Web page or a particular location on a page; download a file to user's computer	http://www.Korinna.com/index.html (display a Web page); http://www.kemco.com/update.sit.hqx (download a compressed file saved in BinHex format)
ftp://	Enable user to download a file from an ftp (file transfer protocol) server	ftp://ftp.smartsoft.com/pub/avatar.hqx
mailto:	Launch user's e-mail program and create a message for a specific e-mail address	mailto:mjones@aol.com
news:	Display a given message from a newsgroup or a list of all messages in a newsgroup	news:340BF126.2208@acenet.com (specific message i.d.); news:comp.sys.mac.databases (list of all messages from a newsgroup)

Summary

✦ To provide improved connectivity within and between documents, ClarisWorks 5.0 introduces three kinds of links: *book marks* (a marked location in a document), *document links* (a link to a book mark in the same document or to another document), and *URL links* (links to pages on the World Wide Web, newsgroup messages, downloadable files, and so on). Links are created and managed in the Links palette.

✦ Many items in ClarisWorks documents can be designated as links — including text strings, paint images or selections, draw objects, frames, and spreadsheet cells.

✦ The Internet button bar contains buttons you can click to create new links quickly. The buttons duplicate commands found in the Links palette.

✦ With live links enabled, you can test document and URL links by clicking them.

✦ When clicked, a document link can bring you to a selected book mark in the current document, open another ClarisWorks document to its first page, or open another ClarisWorks document to a particular book mark.

✦ A document link or URL link can also be executed by double-clicking the link name in the Links palette.

✦   ✦   ✦

QuickTime Movies

Overview

QuickTime is an Apple-provided system extension that
enables you to add movie clips, music, and sounds to
Macintosh documents. You can insert QuickTime clips into
most ClarisWorks documents (and documents of other
programs that support QuickTime), just as you now add
static images such as logos. Anyone else who has the
QuickTime extension and the program in which you created
the document can play the movie.

Note If you are successfully running ClarisWorks 5.0, you already
have the necessary hardware and system software to use
QuickTime. (ClarisWorks 5 has more stringent hardware and
system software requirements than QuickTime.)

Note If you have yet to install ClarisWorks 5.0, you can determine
which version of system software you're using by returning
to the desktop, pulling down the Apple menu, and choosing
About This Macintosh (System 7) or About This Computer
(Mac OS 8). The window that appears shows the system
software version, along with the total memory installed in
the Macintosh (see Figure 20-1).

Figure 20-1: The system software version and the total installed memory are shown in the About This Macintosh window (System 7).

Obtaining and Installing QuickTime

You can obtain QuickTime in a number of ways. QuickTime is included when you buy a new Macintosh or purchase a system software update. You can also download it from most major information services (such as CompuServe, America Online, and GEnie) or purchase it as part of the QuickTime Starter Kit from Apple Computer. The current version of QuickTime is 2.5 — although new versions are released on a regular basis.

Current versions of QuickTime include an Installer program, similar to the Installer for ClarisWorks. To install QuickTime, double-click the Installer's icon and follow the installation instructions provided.

Inserting a QuickTime Movie into a Document

You can incorporate QuickTime movies in a ClarisWorks document in several ways:

✦ Open them by choosing Open (⌘-O) from the File menu and choosing Drawing from the Document Type pop-up menu in the file dialog box.

✦ Insert them into a word processing, spreadsheet, draw, or database document by choosing Insert from the File menu.

✦ Copy and paste them into a word processing, spreadsheet, draw, or database document by selecting the movie in the Scrapbook or another program and then choosing Copy (⌘-C) and Paste (⌘-V) from the Edit menu. You can also use drag-and-drop to move QuickTime movies between applications and documents.

As with other ClarisWorks objects, you can add QuickTime movies as in-line graphics or as objects (refer to Chapter 6 for a discussion of in-line graphics and objects). In-line graphics become part of the paragraph into which you paste them, enabling you to format them with standard paragraph commands. To add a movie as an in-line graphic, set the text-insertion point within a word processing paragraph before choosing the Insert or Paste command.

Objects, on the other hand, are free floating, and you can move them anywhere on the page. You can also specify a text wrap style if you place the object in a word processing document or frame. To add a movie as a floating object, select the pointer tool from the Tool panel before choosing the Insert or Paste command.

Note

A QuickTime movie you add to a paint document or frame appears as a static picture. You cannot play it.

Playing Movies

Figure 20-2 shows a word processing document with a QuickTime movie. The control badge (the film-strip icon) identifies the graphic as a QuickTime movie.

You can play a movie that is an object by double-clicking it or by using the special pop-up movie control bar. The only way to play movies that are in-line graphics is to double-click them. (They have no control bar.)

Figure 20-2: A document that includes the QuickTime movie Liftoff from the QuickTime Starter Kit (Apple Computer Inc.)

Using the double-click method

Double-clicking a movie causes it to play automatically with any options that are set for the movie. Normally, the movie plays from beginning to end with the default volume setting for audio that accompanies the clip. You can pause or stop the playback by clicking once anywhere on the screen. Double-click again to resume play from the point at which you halted the movie.

Using the movie control bar

For movies that are objects, clicking the film-strip icon exposes a movie control bar at the bottom of the movie, as shown in Figure 20-3.

Play/Stop   Step Forward
Volume control   Step Backward
Forward/Reverse slider

Figure 20-3: The movie control bar

The control bar contains the following buttons:

✦ *Volume control.* Click this button to expose a slider control for playback volume. Move the slider higher for louder volume and lower for less volume.

✦ *Play/Stop button.* When the movie is not playing, this button appears as a right-facing triangle. Click it once to begin playing the movie. When the movie begins to play, the button changes to a Stop button with a pair of vertical lines on it. Click the Stop button to stop or pause the movie.

✦ *Forward/Reverse slider.* You can use the mouse to drag this slider forward or backward in the movie to any point you want. As you drag the slider, the movie plays (without sound) either forward or backward until you release the mouse button.

✦ *Step Backward and Step Forward buttons.* The last two buttons enable you to step backward or forward through the movie one frame at a time — again, without audio.

Changing the Size of a Movie Frame

ClarisWorks enables you to change the size of any movie frame, regardless of whether the movie is an in-line graphic or an object.

Steps: Resizing a Movie

1. Click once on the movie to select it. If the movie is an in-line graphic, a single handle appears at the lower-right corner of the movie frame. If it is an object, handles appear at all corners of the movie frame.

2. Select a handle with the mouse and then drag to resize the movie frame. (To maintain the original proportions of the frame, press Shift as you drag diagonally.)

3. Release the mouse button when the frame is the desired shape and size.

In addition to using the mouse, you can also control playback directly from the keyboard. Table 20-1 shows the keyboard shortcuts I've discovered.

Table 20-1
Keyboard Shortcuts for Playback Control

Key	Effect
Return or spacebar	Start/Stop playback
Period (.)	Stop playback
Up-arrow key	Increase volume
Down-arrow key	Decrease volume
Right-arrow key	Step forward a frame at a time (hold the key down to step forward quickly)
Left-arrow key	Step backward a frame at a time (hold the key down to step backward quickly)

Setting Playback Options

You can set a variety of playback options for a movie you have added to a ClarisWorks document as an object. (On the other hand, you can only play, pause, and restart in-line movies.) To see the different options, select the movie (the handles should appear) and then choose Movie Info from the Edit menu. The Movie Info dialog box shown in Figure 20-4 appears.

Figure 20-4: The Movie Info dialog box

Playback options in the Movie Info dialog box include the following:

✦ *Use Movie Bounds.* If you have changed the size of the movie window, clicking this check box restores the movie frame to its original size. If you have not resized the movie, this option is *grayed out* (unselectable).

If you have a QuickTime version prior to 2.0, the Use Movie Bounds check box is labeled Normal Size. However, it serves exactly the same function as Use Movie Bounds.

✦ *Selection Only.* If you have selected only a portion of the movie, checking this option restricts playback to the selection, rather than to the entire movie. (See "Working with Movie Selections," later in this chapter.)

✦ *Speed.* By typing a number in the Speed box, you can change the playback speed, as well as make the movie play backward. The default setting is 1. Table 20-2 shows how different settings affect playback.

Table 20-2
Effects of Different Speed Settings

	Slower Speed	*Normal*	*Faster Speed*
Play forward	Decimal between 0 and 1	1	Positive integer larger than 1
Play backward	Decimal between 0 and -1	-1	Negative integer smaller than -1

Tip

You can also change the playback speed by pressing the Control key while you click either the Step Forward or Step Backward button on the control bar. A slider appears, which you can use to select a new playback speed. The white area in the middle of the slider represents the normal speed setting. Moving the slider to the left of the white area sets backward playback speed, and moving it to the right of the white area sets forward playback speed.

✦ *Loop*. When this option is checked, the movie plays in a continuous loop. The radio button you click (Forward Only or Forward & Backward) determines the direction of playback. When Loop is set for a clip, you click once to halt the playback.

After setting options, click OK to put them into effect, or click Cancel if you change your mind.

Working with Movie Selections

As the discussion on setting playback options states, you can also work with *selections* (or portions) of any movie that is an object. This capability enables you to do some rudimentary movie editing, such as cutting and pasting selections into the same or another QuickTime movie.

Steps: Making a Selection Within a Movie

1. Use the Step Backward and Step Forward buttons or the Forward/Reverse slider in the movie control bar to find the starting frame of the selection.

2. Press Shift while you use the Step Backward and Step Forward buttons, the Forward/Reverse slider, or the left and right arrow keys to move to the

(continued)

end of the intended selection. The selected portion of the clip is shown as a dark area on the Play bar (see Figure 20-5).

Figure 20-5: The Play bar shows what portion of the movie is selected.

Play bar
Movie selection

3. Release the Shift key and the mouse button when the selection is correct.

You can extend a selection or reduce its size in the same way you extend or reduce a text selection in a word processing document. Simply press Shift while dragging to the left or right. To clear a selection quickly, click the control bar once.

After you make a selection, you can perform either of the following tasks:

✦ Copy the selection by pressing ⌘-C.

✦ Delete the selection by pressing ⌘-X, or the Delete, Del, or Clear key.

After you copy (⌘-C) or cut (⌘-X) a selection from a movie, the selection is transferred to the Macintosh Clipboard where it is available for pasting. You can paste the selection into a different spot in the same movie or into a different movie.

Steps: Pasting a Movie Selection

1. Click the control badge (the film-strip icon) on the destination movie to expose the control bar.

2. Use the Step Backward and Step Forward buttons or the Forward/Reverse slider to move to the spot in the movie where you want to make the insertion.

3. Press ⌘-V. The selection is pasted into the movie.

Quick Tips

The following quick tips tell you how to store QuickTime movies in the Scrapbook, how to find missing movies, how to share QuickTime movies with other users, and how to eliminate choppiness when you play movies.

Using the Scrapbook to store movies

If you install the new version of the Scrapbook desk accessory that comes with QuickTime or with System 7.5 or higher, you can use it to store and play movies. Like movies pasted into documents, however, the movie does not actually reside in the Scrapbook. Instead, the Scrapbook merely maintains a pointer to the movie's actual location on disk.

Steps: Inserting a Movie into the Scrapbook

1. Open the movie in any application that can read it. (You can insert it into a ClarisWorks document, for example.)

2. Select the movie (its handles appear) and then choose Copy from the Edit menu (or press ⌘-C).

3. Choose the Scrapbook desk accessory from the Apple menu. The Scrapbook opens.

4. Using the scroll bar at the bottom of the Scrapbook window, move to the spot in the Scrapbook where you want to insert the movie.

5. Choose Paste from the Edit menu (or press ⌘-V). The movie appears in the Scrapbook, as shown in Figure 20-6.

Figure 20-6: A movie in the Scrapbook (System 7.5.5)

Locating missing movies

When you attempt to display a movie file — embedded in a document or on a page in the Scrapbook — QuickTime immediately searches for the disk on which the movie file is stored. If the original disk is not mounted on the desktop, the program asks you to insert it. Insert the requested disk. If the disk isn't available, click Cancel.

If you click Cancel, QuickTime automatically searches all mounted disks for a copy of the missing movie file. If it finds the movie file, it makes a record of the file's location and uses that file for all future requests. If it doesn't find the file, you get one last chance to find it, as Figure 20-7 shows.

Figure 20-7: Last chance to find the movie file

If you click Cancel in the new dialog box and the movie is not found, the movie is automatically changed to a static picture. If you think you can still find it (you have it on a different disk that is not currently mounted, for example), click Search. The file dialog box shown in Figure 20-8 appears.

Figure 20-8: Insert the disk that contains the movie file or use this dialog box to search for it manually.

With OS 8, the process of locating a missing QuickTime movie is a little different. A dialog box appears that presents two options: Search and Don't Search. If you click Don't Search, the movie image is immediately changed to a static picture. If you click Search, you are given an opportunity to locate the file. If you fail to find it (indicated by clicking the Cancel button in the Open dialog box), the movie is then changed to a static picture.

Sharing QuickTime movies with others

Again, because QuickTime movies aren't actually stored in the documents in which they're embedded, if you give someone a ClarisWorks document or another type of document that contains a QuickTime movie, you need to give them a copy of the movie, too.

The first time the other person attempts to view the movie, a dialog box appears, explaining that the original disk cannot be found and it should be inserted. Clicking Cancel forces QuickTime to search for the file, and it will locate the file if your friend or colleague has copied the movie to a hard disk or has the document distribution disk inserted in a drive.

Improving QuickTime playback

If you want to play a movie with minimal choppiness, you can improve playback by storing the movie on the fastest disk drive you own. CD-ROM and floppy drives, for example, are extremely slow. SyQuest, Bernoulli, ZIP disks, and optical disk cartridges are faster. A hard disk is better still.

If you intend to use QuickTime movies in a presentation, are running System 7 or higher, and have the memory to spare, consider copying the movie to a *RAM disk*. A *RAM disk* is a temporary disk that is created from your Mac's memory. Because files and programs that are run from a RAM disk are accessed almost instantly (unlike a hard disk, a RAM disk has no moving parts), movie playback from a RAM disk is exceptional.

Depending on the amount of RAM installed in your Mac and the size of the movie file(s), using a RAM disk may not be a workable solution. (If you don't have at least 8MB of RAM, for example, a RAM disk for use with QuickTime isn't practical.) Any memory that is allocated for a RAM disk is not available for programs or desk accessories.

Steps: Creating and Using a RAM Disk

1. Choose Control Panels from the Apple menu. The Control Panels folder opens.

2. Double-click the Memory control panel. If your model of Mac supports it, the bottom section of the Memory control panel contains a RAM Disk section (see Figure 20-9).

Figure 20-9: The System 7 Memory control panel

3. Click the On radio button in the RAM Disk section and move the slider to set the size of the RAM disk. (Try setting it to the total size of the ClarisWorks document plus the movie file.)

4. Click the Memory control panel's close box to save the changes.

5. Restart the Macintosh. A RAM disk appears on the right side of the desktop.

6. Copy the ClarisWorks document and movie files to the RAM disk.

7. Make a backup copy of the movie file on a floppy disk or removable hard disk and then delete the original.

8. Double-click the ClarisWorks document that is on the RAM disk to launch ClarisWorks and load the document.

9. Because the QuickTime movie is no longer in its original location, a dialog box may appear to inform you of that fact. If the dialog box appears, click Cancel. QuickTime will locate the file on the RAM disk and use that copy to play the movie.

Later, to regain the memory that has been allocated to the RAM disk, open the Memory control panel again, click the Off button in the RAM Disk section, close the control panel, and restart your Mac.

Moving On Up

ClarisWorks wasn't designed for heavy-duty QuickTime editing. Also, you can only use it to play movies that have been provided to you (in the QuickTime Starter Kit, for example). If you want more control over the content of movies, want to add your own sound track, or want to make your own movies, you need to invest in some additional hardware and software.

If you want to capture video from an external source, such as a TV, videotape, or video camera, you need a way to change the video signals into a form that's compatible with the Macintosh. In most cases, you can use a video capture board or desktop video camera, such as the Connectix QuickCam, to accomplish this. With many of the newer PowerMacs, you can use the Apple Video Player software to control a TV Tuner Card or a VCR that is connected to the Mac's video input ports. Even if you only want improved editing capabilities, you may want to invest in a video editing program such as Adobe Premiere.

Summary

✦ You can add QuickTime movies to most ClarisWorks documents. However, the word processing, draw, spreadsheet, and database environments are preferable for movie clips.

✦ As with static graphic images, you can paste or insert movies into documents as objects or as in-line graphics. If you want access to the movie control bar, however, you have to add the movies as objects.

✦ Movies you add as objects contain a pop-up movie control bar with which you can vary the playback direction and speed and do minor editing of the movie. You can only play, pause, and restart movies that are in-line graphics.

✦ You can change the size of any movie embedded in a ClarisWorks document by dragging a handle on the movie frame.

✦ In the Movie Info dialog box, you can change playback settings for movies that are objects.

✦ In addition to working with the entire movie, you can select a portion of the movie (for selective playback or editing).

✦   ✦   ✦

Working with Libraries

Overview

ClarisWorks 3.0 included an impressive collection of clip art
for embellishing your documents. ClarisWorks 4.0 also
included clip art, but made it easier to use because the clip
art was in *libraries* — collections organized around a theme.
ClarisWorks 5.0 expands your choices further by providing
many new clip-art libraries. Using any image from a ReadyArt
library is as simple as dragging the image of choice into your
document or frame.

Libraries can also be used to hold things other than draw and
paint images. You can store boiler-plate text, spreadsheet cells,
QuickTime movies, and frames of any type, for example. Thus,
in addition to using the provided clip art, you can add your
own material to the Claris libraries or create new libraries.

When you open a library — regardless of whether it is a
ClarisWorks-provided library or one you created — the
library appears in a palette. Like other palettes, every library
palette has a title bar, a close box, and a shrink/expand box,
as shown in Figure 21-1.

Library palettes are different from Tool panel palettes in three
ways:

- ✦ Library palettes can be expanded to show additional
  options (by clicking the tiny arrow at the bottom-left
  corner of the palette).
- ✦ A library palette contains its own menu bar.
- ✦ You can customize the way information in each library
  palette is presented (by choosing options in the
  palette's View menu).

Figure 21-1: Standard and expanded library palettes

> You must open a document or create a new document before opening a library. If no documents are open, the Library submenu cannot be selected.

Think of a library as a special kind of ClarisWorks document. Although you can add and remove items, rename items, and change the viewing preferences for a library, all changes are lost unless you also save the library. To remind you of this, if you close a library that has been changed without choosing Save or Save As from the library's File menu, ClarisWorks presents the same dialog box used when you try to close a changed document without saving, as shown in Figure 21-2.

Figure 21-2: This dialog box appears if you close a library palette before saving your changes.

Opening and Closing Libraries

Libraries stored in the ClarisWorks Libraries folder (found inside the ClarisWorks 5.0 folder) are automatically listed in the Library submenu of the File menu. These libraries can be opened by selecting their names from the Library submenu. Libraries saved in other folders or on different disks, on the other hand, can only be opened by choosing Open from the Library submenu, navigating to the appropriate disk and folder, and then clicking the Open button.

When you close all active ClarisWorks documents, any libraries that are still open automatically close. You can also close libraries manually by doing either of the following:

✦ Click the library palette's close box.

✦ Choose Close from the library palette's File menu.

If you have made changes to the library, ClarisWorks presents a dialog box asking if you want to save the changes (previously shown in Figure 21-2). Click Save to save the changes, Don't Save to close the library without saving changes, or Cancel if you change your mind and decide to keep the library open.

Tip

You can simultaneously close all open library palettes by holding down the Option key as you click any library's close box.

Note

There is no command to delete a library. If you want to delete an existing library, go to the desktop, open the ClarisWorks Libraries folder inside the ClarisWorks 5.0 folder (or wherever you saved the library), click to select the library, and drag it to the trash.

Creating New Libraries

Although you may be satisfied with using the ClarisWorks libraries as is — by simply dragging the provided clip art into your documents — you may also want to create your own libraries to store logos, scanned signatures, spreadsheet formulas, and important text.

To create a new library, you must first open or create a ClarisWorks document. Then from the Library submenu of the File menu, choose the New command. A new, empty library palette appears, as shown in Figure 21-3. The library is given a temporary name of *Library x*, where *x* is a number.

Figure 21-3: A new, empty library

Every new library is considered temporary until it has been saved. At any point before you close the library, you can choose the Save As or Save command from the library's File menu to save the library and — optionally — give it a more descriptive name. The library is saved and, if saved in the ClarisWorks Libraries folder, its name is automatically added to the Library submenu of the File menu.

Remember that if a library is saved in a folder other than the ClarisWorks Libraries folder or on a different disk, its name is not added to the Library submenu. To later open such a library, you must choose the Open command from the Library submenu of the File menu, and then locate the library file in the file dialog box that appears.

It's not really a library until you add something. To learn how to add items to a library, see "Editing Libraries" later in this chapter.

Inserting Library Objects into Documents

There are two ways to insert a library object into the current document:

✦ Drag the object or its name from the library palette into the document, and then release the mouse button.

✦ Select the object or its name in the library palette, and then click Use.

Depending on the type of document or frame into which the object is being inserted, it will either appear as a floating object or an in-line object (see "Adding Graphics to Word Processing Documents" in Chapter 3).

✦ *Draw documents:* All objects are inserted as floating objects. You can specify the approximate spot where the object is placed by clicking it with the pointer tool before you click Use.

✦ *Paint documents or frames:* Library objects — regardless of whether they are graphics or text — are inserted as bitmapped graphics. They are surrounded by a selection rectangle, enabling you to move or delete the graphic.

✦ *Word processing documents or frames:* If a text-insertion point is currently set in the document or frame and you click Use, a graphic object is added at the insertion point as an in-line object. If the insertion point is not currently set and you click Use, a graphic object is added as a floating object. You can also insert text library items into word processing documents by dragging them or clicking Use, as described later in this chapter in "Text as library items."

✦ *Databases:* Library objects can only be inserted when you are in Layout mode. All objects are placed as floating objects.

New In
Version 5

The sole exception to this rule is you can insert library objects into a ClarisWorks database's multimedia field when you are in Browse mode.

✦ *Spreadsheet documents or frames:* All graphics and text strings are added as objects that float on the spreadsheet. Worksheet cell data stored in a library, on the other hand, is inserted as normal data beginning at the selected cell.

✦ *Communications documents:* No library objects can be inserted into communications documents. To emphasize this fact, when a communications document is active, the Library submenu is grayed out and all open libraries are temporarily hidden.

Note

As you're dragging an object into a document, you may notice it's either the wrong object or the wrong document. To cancel a drag in progress, move the hand cursor back over the original library palette and release the mouse button.

Editing Libraries

The contents of any library can be altered in several ways. You can:

✦ Add items to a library

✦ Remove items from a library

✦ Reorganize the contents of a library

Adding items to libraries

The way in which an item is added to a library depends on whether the item is currently selected in a ClarisWorks document or has been copied (using the Copy command) from another program.

Steps: Adding a ClarisWorks Object or Selection to a Library

1. Open the library to which you want to add the item.

2. In the ClarisWorks document or frame, select the object, text, spreadsheet cells, frame, paint selection, or database data of interest.

3. Click the library's Add button.

— or —

Drag the item onto the library palette.

— or —

Copy the item by choosing Copy from the Edit menu in ClarisWorks (or pressing ⌘-C). Then choose Paste from the library's Edit menu.

4. The material is added as a new item named *Object x*, where *x* is the number of the next object in the library.

Steps: Adding an Object or Selection from Another Program to a ClarisWorks Library

1. In the other program, select the object, image, or text of interest, and choose the Copy command (⌘-C) from the Edit menu. A copy of the object or text is transferred to the Mac's Clipboard.

2. Launch ClarisWorks 5.0 (if it isn't already running), open an existing document or create a new one, and then choose the appropriate library from the Library submenu of the File menu.

Note

Unless at least one ClarisWorks document is open, the Library command cannot be selected. Because libraries are not linked to particular documents, however, it doesn't matter *which* ClarisWorks document is open; any one will do (with the exception of communications documents).

3. Choose Paste from the library's Edit menu. The object or text is added as a new item named *Object x*, where *x* is the number of the next object in the library.

You can also use drag-and-drop to transfer items into ClarisWorks libraries from drag-and-drop-enabled programs, such as the Scrapbook desk accessory. Similarly, you can drag text or picture clippings from the desktop into a library.

There's a simple procedure for copying an object in one library and inserting it into another library. For the sake of convenience, you might want your company logo to appear in several libraries, for example. Just select the object in any open library and then drag it into the palette of any other open library. Note that the object's original name is also transferred to the receiving library.

Adding other types of items to libraries

Because the supplied ClarisWorks libraries contain only clip art, many users assume this is all a library can hold. As the previous discussion attests, however, this assumption is incorrect. Libraries can also store text, spreadsheet cells, and database records. However, there are some special considerations when adding and using such material as library items.

Spreadsheet cells as library items

You may find it helpful to store complex spreadsheet formulas in a library so they can be easily reused. When selecting a formula to add to a library, you must be sure to select all cells that are referenced by the formula. Otherwise, when you drag the formula into another worksheet, the references will be incorrect. For example, a formula in C1 that reads =A1+B1 will only be stored correctly if you select all three cells (A1, B1, and C1) before clicking the library's Add button.

You should also note that libraries can only store a limited amount of spreadsheet data. If the selected cells contain more than 50 rows or 10 columns (Columns A through J, for example), additional rows or columns are truncated from the library copy, and the dialog box in Figure 21-4 appears.

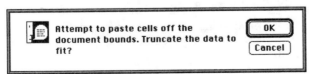

Figure 21-4: Click OK to truncate the cells to fit or Cancel to abort the library addition.

Note

When dragged into a worksheet, any library item that contains something other than worksheet cells (a graphic or text string, for instance) will simply float on the worksheet; it will not be entered into the selected cell or cells.

Database records as library items

In general, database fields or records cannot be selected and then added to a library by clicking the Add button. Nor can you insert data into a database by dragging it from a library. (All library buttons are grayed out when you're working in a database in Browse mode.)

New In Version 5

ClarisWorks's new multimedia fields are an exception to these rules, however. The contents of multimedia fields *can* be added to libraries, and such fields can also receive images from libraries.

To store data from any field type other than a multimedia field, use the copy-and-paste procedure described earlier in this chapter in "Steps: Adding a ClarisWorks Object or Selection to a Library." To store a database record in a library, select the entire record, choose Copy from ClarisWorks Edit menu (or press ⌘-C), and then choose the library's Paste command.

Note

When you click Use or drag a database record object into a word processing document, the object is inserted as tab-delimited text; that is, fields are separated by tab characters.

Text as library items

As mentioned earlier in this chapter, it's easy to add text to a library. If the text is in a ClarisWorks document, just select the text and click the library's Add button. If the text is from a non-ClarisWorks document, select it, use the program's Copy command to copy it to the Clipboard, switch to ClarisWorks, and then choose the library's Paste command.

Inserting text from a library into word processing documents and frames is also simple. There are two ways to do this:

✦ Position the text insertion point at the spot in the word processing document where you want to add the text, select the text in the library palette, and click Use. The text is added at the insertion point.

✦ Drag the text into the word processing document. As you drag, a thick text-insertion bar moves to show where the insertion will appear. Release the mouse button to insert the text.

To insert library text into a draw document, paint document, or paint frame, drag the text into position or click the Use button. Text inserted into a paint document or frame becomes a bitmapped graphic. Text inserted into a draw document is treated as an object (unless you drag the text into a word processing frame inside the draw document).

Saving an edited library

To save an existing library to which you've made changes, choose the Save command from the library's File menu. If you want to save the library using a new name or in a new location, choose the Save As command from the library's File menu.

Removing items from libraries

A library's Edit menu contains the following two commands for removing items from the library:

✦ *Delete*. To remove an item without transferring a copy of it to the Clipboard, select the item in the library palette and choose Delete from the library's Edit menu.

✦ *Cut*. To remove an item and simultaneously transfer a copy of it to the Clipboard, select the item in the library palette and choose Cut from the library's Edit menu.

The Cut command is useful for removing an item you also intend to paste somewhere else — into a ClarisWorks document, another library, or a document in another program. Much of the time, however, you only really care that the item is removed from the library. In those cases, you can use either command.

Renaming library items

When you add a new item to a library, ClarisWorks assigns a generic name to the item in the form *Object x*. Because *Object 12* isn't a very descriptive name — it's like naming a document *Untitled 7* — you can use the library palette's Rename button to assign a better name.

To rename a library object, select the object or its name (depending on the View options currently set for the palette) in the library palette. If the bottom portion of the palette is not exposed, click the tiny triangle beside the Add button. Delete the text in the Name box, type a new name, and click Rename. The new name appears in the palette's list of objects.

Reorganizing a library

By default, library items are listed in the order in which they were added to the library. Renaming items does not change that order. If you prefer items listed alphabetically by their names, choose Alphabetize from the library's View menu. If you later add new objects to the library and still want the list to be alphabetical, you must choose Alphabetize again.

Setting Palette Viewing Preferences

Viewing preferences must be individually set for each library palette. There is no Preferences command you can use to affect the display of all library palettes simultaneously. Viewing preferences enable you to do the following:

✦ Show or hide the bottom part of the palette.

✦ Display all objects simultaneously or one at a time.

✦ Determine the number of rows, columns, and size of thumbnails in the palette.

The first decision you have to make is whether to display a palette of thumbnail icons (similar to the way the button bar is usually shown) or list the objects by name and display only one thumbnail at a time. To show a palette of thumbnails, choose By Object from the library's View menu. To show a list of names, choose By Name from the library's View menu. Figure 21-5 shows examples of both viewing settings.

Figure 21-5: A library palette set for viewing by object (left) and by name (right)

The objects or names in a library can be listed in the order in which they were added to the palette or sorted alphabetically. To sort the objects, choose Alphabetize from the library's View menu.

You can also change the number of rows and columns in a palette, as well as the size of the thumbnails. Choose View Options from the library's View menu. In the View Options dialog box that appears (see Figure 21-6), you can make whatever changes you like.

Figure 21-6: The View Options dialog box

Viewing preferences are saved separately with each library. To record your new viewing preferences, you must choose the library's Save command.

Other Library Commands

Libraries have two other commands you'll probably never use. You can make an exact copy of an object and add it to the current palette (select an object and choose Duplicate from the Edit menu), and you can search for objects within a library (type any part of an object name in the library's Name box and click Find).

I can't think of a good reason to duplicate an object in a library — unless you want to have multiple copies of an object with different names. The Find command is useful only with a library that contains many images and when you can remember part of the object's name (any part will do).

You should note, however, that because searching always begins at the top of the library, Find will locate only the first matching object name in the library. Thus, if a library has three objects with Office in their names, only the first one will be found — regardless of how many times you click Find.

Quick Tip: Organizing Personal Libraries

Rather than just tossing your new libraries in the middle of the extensive list of Claris-provided libraries, you can create one or more new folders in which to organize them. When you save your first new library, click the New folder button in the Save dialog box, as shown in Figure 21-7. Name the new folder (Personal Libraries, for example), and then save the newly created library in the new folder.

The next time you open the Library submenu of the File menu, your new folder will be displayed as a submenu item.

Figure 21-7: Creating a new folder in which to store personal libraries

When creating additional personal libraries, be sure to store them in the new folder inside the ClarisWorks Libraries folder (rather than within the ClarisWorks Libraries folder itself).

Summary

✦ ClarisWorks 5.0 includes an assortment of clip art stored in libraries. You can also create your own libraries.

✦ Before you can work with a library, you must have at least one ClarisWorks document open.

✦ To save changes made to a library — including newly added objects, renamed objects, deletions, and viewing preferences — you must save the library.

✦ Libraries you save in the ClarisWorks Libraries folder (the default location) are automatically listed in the Library submenu of the File menu.

✦ To store a ClarisWorks object, text string, or set of spreadsheet cells in a library, select the object, text, or cells in the ClarisWorks document and click the library's Add button. To store non-ClarisWorks items in a library, copy them and then choose the library's Paste command.

✦ To insert an item stored in a library into the current document, click Use or drag the item onto the document.

✦ You can customize the appearance and object presentation order for each library.

✦   ✦   ✦

Creating Web Pages for the Internet

Overview

The *World Wide Web* — a network of computers providing
information and resources on the Internet — grew out of a
hypertext project started at CERN, the European Laboratory
for Particle Physics. As a resource for finding information and
services ranging from ancient Mayan archeological digs to
pizza deliveries, the World Wide Web (WWW) — or Web, for
short — has become a centerpiece of the information
superhighway. To access information on the Web, you use a
hypertext-based browser application that leads you to the
desired documents and then displays that information on
your computer screen.

At the heart of the Web is a platform-independent page
description language called *Hypertext Markup Language*
(HTML). Based on the *Standard Generalized Markup Language*
(SGML), HTML is used to prepare documents (referred to as
Web pages) for the Web that contain embedded control codes.
Different codes (commonly referred to as *tags*) are used to
designate titles, headings, text formatting, and hypertext
links. Figure 22-1 shows a typical Web page.

The HTML code

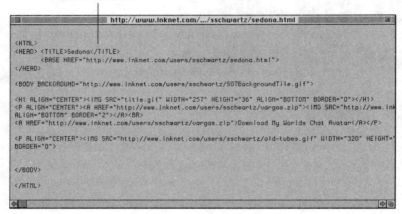

```
<HTML>
<HEAD> <TITLE>Sedona</TITLE>
        <BASE HREF="http://www.lnknet.com/users/sschwartz/sedona.html">
</HEAD>

<BODY BACKGROUND="http://www.lnknet.com/users/sschwartz/S07BackgroundTile.gif">

<H1 ALIGN="CENTER"><IMG SRC="title.gif" WIDTH="257" HEIGHT="36" ALIGN="BOTTOM" BORDER="0"></H1>
<P ALIGN="CENTER"><A HREF="http://www.lnknet.com/users/sschwartz/vargas.zip"><IMG SRC="http://www.lnk
ALIGN="BOTTOM" BORDER="2"></A><BR>
<A HREF="http://www.lnknet.com/users/sschwartz/vargas.zip">Download My Worlds Chat Avatar</A></P>

<P ALIGN="CENTER"><IMG SRC="http://www.lnknet.com/users/sschwartz/old-tubes.gif" WIDTH="320" HEIGHT="
BORDER="0">

</BODY>

</HTML>
```

The Web page the code produces
(when viewed in a Web browser)

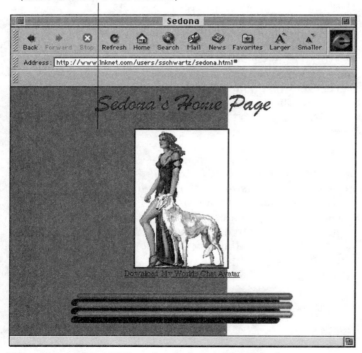

Figure 22-1: This HTML code produces this Web page.

To access the WWW and display Web pages on your computer, you must have access to the Internet — either through an information service (such as CompuServe, Prodigy, or America Online) or from an Internet service provider. You must also have an application called a *Web browser*, such as Netscape Navigator, Netscape Communicator, Internet Explorer, or CyberDog. A Web browser translates the HTML code into formatted text and graphics.

If you're not content to just look at other people's Web pages, you can use ClarisWorks's HTML translator to design your own Web pages in the word processor. With ClarisWorks's capability to launch your preferred browser, you can quickly see how your page will look when viewed on the Internet by others.

If you previously used the WWW [HTML] stationery document to design Web pages with ClarisWorks 4.0, you should consider this chapter essential reading. The procedures and features for creating Web pages in ClarisWorks 5.0 have changed dramatically.

If you have the full version of ClarisWorks Office (rather than the ClarisWorks 5.0 upgrade), you can use the included copy of Claris Home Page Lite to make short work of most page-creation tasks. And if you want to work directly with the HTML code, you can edit the pages produced by Claris Home Page Lite within ClarisWorks.

What Is HTML?

If you can remember the early days of personal computing (way back in the late 1970s) and the first word processing programs, you're already familiar with the way HTML works. Back then, if you wanted to print some selected text in bold or italic, you had to embed control codes in the document — one to turn on boldface (at the beginning of the text string) and a second code to turn off boldface (at the end of the text string).

HTML works in much the same way. Most tags work in pairs; the first tag turns on the feature and a second copy of the tag that is preceded by a slash (/) turns off the feature. For instance, to mark a level-one head, the text is surrounded by a pair of tags like this:

```
<H1>HTML for Fun and Profit</H1>
```

When a browser sees this tagged text, it interprets the tags and then formats the text according to the conventions set for the browser — typically, a level-one head is displayed in a large, bold font.

Note There is little standardization among Web browsers. Unlike PostScript (a device-independent printing language that provides the same results on a wide variety of printers), conventions set in the user's browser application determine the way HTML text is displayed. Thus, while a particular head may appear as 20-point Times in one browser, it may appear in a small font in all capital letters when viewed with a different browser.

Using the ClarisWorks HTML Translator and Web Page Templates

New In Version 5
When you use ClarisWorks 5.0 to design Web pages, the program simultaneously functions as a word processor and a crude browser. There's no need to apply HTML tags as you did in ClarisWorks 4.0. Instead of manually typing tags or choosing them from an HTML stylesheet, you simply format the page as you would any other ClarisWorks document or use one of the 12 stationery files included for this purpose (Web Page Templates). Using the new Links palette, you can add hyperlinks to the documents, which can be used to navigate within the page or to a different site on the World Wide Web.

Instead of displaying the tags as part of the text (as most text editors, word processors, and HTML editors do), ClarisWorks presents the document as an approximation of what it might look like in a browser. As a result, you don't see the tags at all — unless you later open the document as a text file rather than as a ClarisWorks file. When you save the document as an HTML file, ClarisWorks does the necessary conversions for you — adding HTML tags as necessary and changing all images on the page to *GIF* (Graphic Interchange Format) or *JPEG* (Joint Photographic Experts Group) files.

Prerequisites and caveats

Consider the following information when deciding whether to use ClarisWorks to create HTML documents:

✦ You should know how to use the ClarisWorks word processing environment, as well as the button bars, Stylesheet palette, and Stylesheet pop-up menu in the button bar. (For more information on these topics, refer to Chapters 3, 12, and 15.)

✦ You should have Internet access (through an information service or Internet service provider) and a Web browser, as discussed previously in this chapter.

Although you can create and view your Web pages exclusively in ClarisWorks, you create HTML documents to prepare pages that will be displayed on the World Wide Web and viewed in browsers.

✦ Although HTML is not essential, a basic understanding of HTML is helpful — particularly if you want to tweak the HTML files generated by ClarisWorks or understand the techniques used by others to create their Web pages. Similarly, there is HTML style to consider. The correct use of HTML only assures your document will display properly — not that it will be attractive or make efficient use of space, for example. If you are new to HTML, see "Quick Tips" at the end of this chapter for useful reference material concerning HTML definitions, coding practices, and style.

✦ You should understand that ClarisWorks's HTML support is very basic. Although you can certainly use ClarisWorks to create attractive Web pages (complete with graphics and hyperlinks to other pages), you will find it difficult to design the eye-popping pages you've seen in magazines or on corporate Web sites — unless you're willing to work in text mode and enter and modify the necessary HTML tags by hand. A better approach is to use one of the many Web page design programs or editors, such as Claris Home Page Lite (which is a part of ClarisWorks Office).

Configuring ClarisWorks to work with a Web browser

Although you can do all your work in ClarisWorks 5.0, you should have an installed Web browser so you can see your creations as they will look to others viewing them on the Web. By clicking the Open Document in Browser button on the button bar, you can instruct ClarisWorks to convert the current document to HTML format and then display it in your chosen browser. Because creating Web pages is an iterative process, this is the best way to design pages in ClarisWorks 5.0.

Steps: Specifying a Web Browser to Use with ClarisWorks

1. If the button bar is currently hidden, choose Show Button Bar from the Window menu (or press Shift-⌘-X).

2. Choose Internet from the drop-down menu at the left end of the button bar. The Internet button bar appears.

3. Click the Configure Internet button, as shown in Figure 22-2. Internet Config — a program used to configure a Mac for using the Internet — launches, as shown in Figure 22-3.

Figure 22-2: The Configure Internet button (in the Internet button bar)

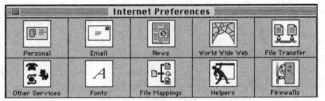

Figure 22-3: Configure your Macintosh for the Internet by clicking buttons in the Internet Preferences window.

4. Click the Helpers button. The Helpers dialog box appears.

5. Scroll down and locate the HTTP item, and click change. The Add Helper dialog box appears. Click the Choose Helper button.

6. In the file dialog box that appears, locate and select your Web browser (such as Internet Explorer or Netscape Navigator), and click Open.

7. To save your changes, click OK, close the Helpers dialog box, and choose Save from the File menu. Exit Internet Config by choosing Quit from the File menu.

Note

When you choose a browser in Internet Config, that browser becomes the default browser for all Internet-related programs — not just ClarisWorks. If you have another browser installed on your Macintosh that you occasionally want to use, you can still launch it by double-clicking its icon on the desktop.

Creating Web pages

You can use any of the Web Page Template stationery documents to design Web pages in ClarisWorks 5.0, or you can create pages from scratch using ordinary word processing documents. Regardless of the approach you use, ClarisWorks attempts to match your paragraph formatting, text formatting, and graphic placement as closely as possible when converting the document to HTML.

Steps: Opening a Web Page Template Stationery Document

1. In ClarisWorks, choose New from the File menu (or press ⌘-N). The New Document dialog box appears.

2. Click the Use Assistant or Stationery radio button, choose Web Page Templates from the pop-up Category menu, select the page style of your choosing (as shown in Figure 22-4), and then click OK.

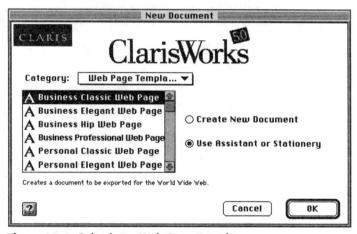

Figure 22-4: Selecting a Web Page Template

The selected stationery document appears.

— or —

Click the Use Assistant or Stationery radio button, choose All Stationery from the pop-up Category menu, select Web Page Template Index, and then click OK. The Web Page Template Index is displayed (see Figure 22-5).

Click any of the template descriptions to open that template as a new ClarisWorks document.

Figure 22-5: The Web Page Template Index is a visual guide to the templates.

3. If the button bar is currently hidden, choose Show Button Bar from the Window menu (or press Shift-⌘-X). Then choose Internet from the pop-up menu at the left end of the button bar. The Internet button bar appears, as well as the Stylesheet pop-up menu shown in Figure 22-6.

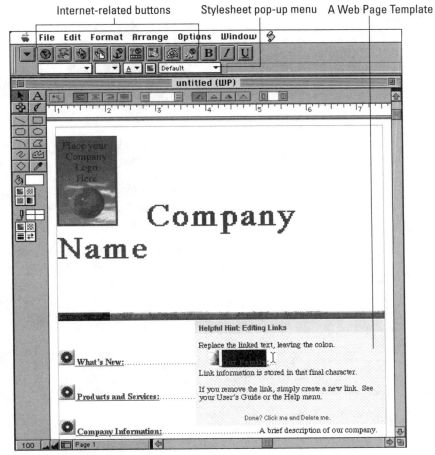

Figure 22-6: The Internet button bar

Now that you have a copy of the stationery document on screen and have displayed the Internet button bar, you are ready to begin entering the text for your Web page.

As you type, you can press Return to end a paragraph or Shift-Return to create a line break. Most browsers display paragraphs by adding white space after each one. A break, on the other hand, merely starts a new line without adding white space after it. You can also make text boldface or italic by selecting it and then choosing the appropriate option from the Style menu.

Considerations when creating pages

When creating your pages, be aware of the following suggestions and limitations that affect the way pages are translated:

✦ Do not bother using multiple fonts when formatting text. Only the default font for your computer is used when generating the HTML file. On the other hand, you can vary the size, style, and color of text, and ClarisWorks will attempt to match it. (Note, however, that the Outline, Shadow, Condense, and Extend styles are converted to plain text.)

Do not format text with the underline style. Underlined text in a Web page normally denotes a hypertext link and may confuse people who are viewing the page.

✦ Do not use tabs to format text. When the HTML file is generated by the translator, tabs are converted into single spaces.

✦ Soft hyphens are ignored.

✦ You can use the alignment controls on the ruler bar to set left-, right-, or center-aligned text. Text formatted as justified is interpreted the same as left-aligned text.

✦ You can specify a single header and/or a footer that will appear at the top and bottom of the page, respectively. A header is automatically followed by a horizontal rule and a footer is preceded by one.

✦ Footnotes and endnotes are all treated as endnotes (and placed at the bottom of the Web page). Footnote or endnote numbers in the body of the page are shown as superscript numbers surrounded by parentheses and become clickable links to their respective notes at the bottom of the Web page.

✦ Do not use the Insert Page Number command to generate page numbers. Such page numbers are shown as the number sign (#).

✦ To create bulleted lists, format the items using the Diamond, Bullet, or Checklist outline style.

✦ To create numbered lists, format the items using the Harvard, Legal, or Number outline style.

✦ In ClarisWorks 4.0, rules were created by clicking a button on the Shortcuts palette. This button no longer exists in ClarisWorks 5.0. To add a horizontal rule to a page (useful for breaking a page into sections), position the cursor and choose Insert Page Break or Insert Section Break from the Format menu. (ClarisWorks ignores automatic page breaks when creating HTML files.)

✦ To create tables in Web pages, use a spreadsheet frame. The table will be aligned with the left or right margin, depending on its position in the original document.

✦ Pages can include in-line and floating graphics and frames. An in-line graphic or frame appears in its original position. A floating object or frame is placed at the left or right margin, depending on its location in the original document. All graphics are automatically converted to GIF or JPEG files, depending on the option chosen in the HTML Configuration dialog box. (See "Adding graphics and a page background," later in this chapter.)

✦ Floating text frames are ignored.

Working with links

A *hyperlink* is a text string or graphic that — when clicked — typically displays another Web page or scrolls to a different spot in the current page. ClarisWorks 5.0 supports three types of links: Book Marks, Document Links, and URL Links. *Book marks* are placeholders in the document; a book mark is the object of a document link. When a *document link* is clicked, the browser scrolls to display the book mark in the same Web page associated with that document link. A *URL link* is used to link to a different Web page — either within the current Web site or a completely different site. (For information about other types of URL links you can embed in Web pages, see "Creating non-HTTP URL links" in Chapter 19.)

Note

Book marks and document links can be attached to text strings, objects, graphics, paint frames, or spreadsheet frames.

Links can be created by clicking buttons on the Internet button bar or by using the Links palette (choose Show Links Palette from the Window menu or press Shift-⌘-M). Because the button bar approach is extremely simple, I describe it here. For information about using the Links palette, refer to Chapter 19.

Creating document links and book marks

To let the user easily navigate within a given Web page, you only need to pair a document link (a clickable text string or graphic) with a book mark (another text string or graphic) in the same Web page. When the user clicks the document link, the browser automatically scrolls to the specified book mark. You can pair document links with book marks to implement a live table of contents or create clickable buttons at the bottom of each Web page to carry the user forward or backward one page, for example.

Steps: Creating a Paired Document Link and Book mark

1. Select the text string or graphic that will serve as the book mark (the spot in the Web page that will be displayed when the associated document link is clicked).

2. Click the New Book Mark button (see Figure 22-7) in the Internet button bar. The New Book Mark dialog box appears.

  Figure 22-7: New Book Mark button (left) and New Document Link button (right)

3. Name the book mark and click OK.

4. Select the text string or graphic that will serve as the clickable document link.

5. Click the New Document Link button (see Figure 22-7) in the Internet button bar. The New Document Link dialog box appears (see Figure 22-8).

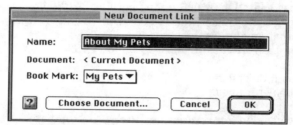

Figure 22-8: The New Document Link dialog box

6. Name the document link, choose a book mark to associate with the link from the Book Mark drop-down list, and click OK.

If ClarisWorks's live links feature is enabled, you can test document links within the ClarisWorks document. (Otherwise, links can only be tested in a Web browser.) To enable or disable live links, click the Live Links On/Off button in the Internet button bar (see Figure 22-9). Repeatedly clicking this button switches live links on and off. (You can also enable or disable live links in the Links palette.)

 Figure 22-9: The Live Links On/Off button

Creating URL links

When clicked, a URL link carries the user to a different page on your or another person's Web site, according to the address or *URL* (Uniform Resource Locator) you specify when you create the link. A URL link is clickable and can be a text string, graphic, object, text frame, paint frame, spreadsheet frame, spreadsheet cells or range, or a selection in a paint image. Some examples of URLs are:

http://www.apple.com
(This URL points to Apple Computer's home page on the World Wide Web.)

http://www.claris.com
(This URL points to Claris Corporation's home page.)

http://www.macworld.com/buyers/hotdeals/
(This URL points to a particular page within Macworld's Web site.)

Note

URL links can also be used to download a file from an *ftp* (file transfer protocol) site, open the user's e-mail program to send a message, or display a message from a newsgroup. (For information about these types of URL links, see "Creating non-HTTP URL links" in Chapter 19.)

Steps: Creating a URL Link

1. Select the text string, object, graphic, or other item that will serve as the URL link (the spot in the Web page that the user will click).

2. Click the New URL Link button (see Figure 22-10) in the Internet button bar. The New URL Link dialog box appears (see Figure 22-11).

Figure 22-10: The New URL Link button

Figure 22-11: The New URL Link dialog box

3. Enter a name for the URL link in the Name box.

The link's name is merely an identifier to enable you to distinguish one link from another. The specific name chosen is entirely up to you.

4. Type the destination address of the link in the URL box and click OK. The link is added to the Links palette for the current document.

If live links are currently enabled for the document, you can test the link by clicking it. Your Mac will attempt to connect to the Internet (if you are not already online), your browser launches, and an attempt is made to find the Web page specified by the link's URL.

Text links are normally seen by the user as underlined text (such as <u>Current Catalog</u> or <u>Resumé of Robert Jones</u>). Objects, such as buttons or pictures, are also frequently used to denote URL links. Modern browsers typically have one or more ways of showing that a graphic is actually a link, rather than just another picture. In Internet Explorer, for example, when the user moves the cursor over any URL link, the link address is shown in the browser's status bar and the cursor changes to a hand pointer.

By default, text URL links are formatted as blue underlined text. If you like, you can choose another color for them (such as purple) or a different style (such as bold, underlined text). You can also change the formatting for book marks and document links. Simply open the stylesheet and modify the Hot Text (book marks), Document Links, or URL Links styles. (See the instructions for editing styles in Chapter 15.) Note that these styles are only displayed in the stylesheet when working with the Web Page Templates stationery files.

Modifying links

To change or delete book marks, document links, or URL links, open the Links palette for the document (choose Show Links Palette from the Window menu or press Shift-⌘-M). From the pop-up menu in the palette, choose the class of link you want to modify. Select the appropriate link from the displayed list and then choose the Edit or Delete command from the Links menu, as appropriate.

Adding graphics and a page background

Graphics can be added to your Web page document as floating or in-line images. (Refer to "Adding Graphics to Word Processing Documents" in Chapter 3.) The images can be pasted or dragged onto the page from a document in another graphics program, imported by choosing the Insert command from the File menu, designed in ClarisWorks, or added from the ReadyArt libraries (refer to Chapter 21).

GIF and JPEG images are the only types of viewable graphics that can be embedded in Web pages. ClarisWorks 5.0 now supports both formats. When you save a Web page as an HTML file, ClarisWorks automatically converts all embedded images to the GIF or JPEG format, as specified in the HTML Configuration dialog box (see Figure 22-12). The following steps explain how to set a preferred export format for embedded images and how to select a background color or graphic for Web pages.

Set a background color or image

Select an output image format

Figure 22-12: In the Export Preferences (Basic) section of the HTML Configuration dialog box, you can set graphic-handling options and specify a background color or image for Web pages you create in ClarisWorks.

Steps: Setting Basic Export Preferences

1. If the button bar is currently hidden, choose Show Button Bar from the Window menu (or press Shift-⌘-X).

2. Choose Internet from the pop-up menu at the left end of the button bar. The Internet button bar appears.

3. Click the Configure HTML button, as shown in Figure 22-13. The HTML Configuration dialog box appears, as shown previously in Figure 22-12.

Figure 22-13: The Configure HTML button

4. To specify a background color to appear behind the Web page, choose it from the drop-down Color menu.

5. To choose a background image to appear behind the Web page, click Set Background Image and select a graphic file from the file dialog box that appears. (If you do not want a background image for the current Web page and one is currently set, click Remove Background Image.)

Although you can specify both a background image and a color, it is more common to choose only one or the other.

6. Select an export format for converting embedded graphics from the Image Export Format pop-up menu.

7. To accept the new settings, click OK.

The options you choose in the HTML Configuration dialog box affect all future Web pages you design in ClarisWorks — not just the current page. If you wish to use a different background image or color for a new page, you must change the settings in the HTML Configuration dialog box.

Viewing the Web page in a browser

Although ClarisWorks can show you an approximation of what your Web page will look like in a Web browser, you must view the page through a real Web browser, such as Netscape Navigator or Internet Explorer, to see what it will really look like. If you click the Open Document in Browser button on the Internet button bar (see Figure 22-14), an HTML file is automatically created from the current ClarisWorks document and displayed in your designated browser (see Figure 22-15).

Figure 22-14: Click this button to convert the current document to HTML format and display it in your browser.

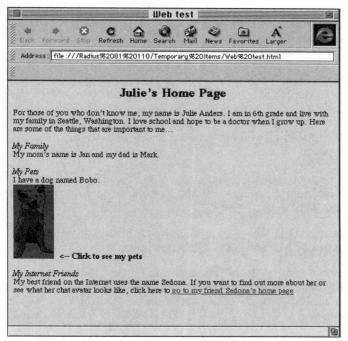

Figure 22-15: Here is a simple ClarisWorks-generated Web page as it appears when viewed in Internet Explorer.

Tip

You also can manually load any saved HTML file by choosing the browser's Open, Open File, or Open Local command. As you make changes to the HTML document in ClarisWorks, you can view the modifications in your browser by clicking the Open Document in Browser button. (Click the browser's Reload or Refresh button to make sure you are viewing the most recently saved copy of the HTML document.)

Saving an HTML document

Because of the way the ClarisWorks HTML translator operates, you need to save *two* files for every Web page you create. First, save the page as an ordinary ClarisWorks document. You will make any additional, necessary changes in this file. Second, you must use the Save As command in combination with the HTML translator to save the page in HTML format. You will post this file on the World Wide Web.

To create the HTML file, choose Save As from the File menu. In the Save As pop-up menu, select HTML as the format. Navigate to the drive and folder in which you want to save the file, type a filename ending with .htm or .html (such as *Index.htm* or *Index.html*), and click Save.

When you save the document as an HTML file, the translator automatically converts all graphics in the file to either GIF or JPEG format (as specified in the HTML Configuration dialog box). All graphics are saved in the same folder as the one specified for the HTML file. Because it is easier to maintain a Web page if you keep all necessary files together, you may want to create a separate folder for your Web page and its graphics.

When you are ready to post your Web pages for others to view, contact your Internet provider or information service for instructions concerning uploading the page elements to their Web server.

Opening an existing HTML document

If you later need to make changes to a Web page you created in ClarisWorks, you should open and edit the original ClarisWorks document, rather than the exported HTML file. This will enable you to continue working with the Web page as a normal document — shielding you from the embedded HTML codes. ClarisWorks can also open and convert HTML code created outside of ClarisWorks so you can work with it as you do a normal ClarisWorks file.

On the other hand, you may sometimes prefer to work directly with the actual HTML code. The following steps explain how to open existing HTML documents as ClarisWorks documents and as HTML documents.

HTML documents you pull off the Web may be littered with HTML tags that are not supported by the ClarisWorks translator. They will appear in the file as embedded tags and formatting codes.

Steps: Opening an HTML File in ClarisWorks

1. In ClarisWorks, choose Open from the File menu, and then navigate to the drive and folder that contains the HTML document you want to open.

2. To open a ClarisWorks document you created from scratch or from a Web Page Template stationery document, simply select the original document — not the converted HTML file — from the file list and click Open.

— or —

To open a foreign HTML file as a ClarisWorks document (similar to what appears when designing pages in ClarisWorks), choose HTML from the File Type pop-up menu, select the HTML file you want to open, and click Open. ClarisWorks attempts to convert the file to ClarisWorks format prior to opening it.

— or —

To work directly with the embedded HTML code in a ClarisWorks-created or foreign HTML file, select the HTML file, and click Open.

Summary of File Procedures

Even if you have some HTML experience or have already read the suggested reading material at the end of this chapter, if you keep the following points and procedures in mind, you'll have a much easier time using ClarisWorks to create and edit Web pages.

✦ *Creating a new HTML document:* Choose New from the File menu, click Use Assistant or Stationery, choose Internet from the pop-up Category menu, select one of the Web Page Template documents, and then click OK. Choose Internet from the pop-up menu on the left side of the button bar. (You can also create HTML files in a normal ClarisWorks word processing document. In either case, ClarisWorks makes the necessary conversions when you save the document as an HTML file.)

✦ *Saving an HTML document:* Choose Save As from the File menu, choose HTML from the Save As pop-up menu, add **.htm** or **.html** to the end of the filename, and click Save. The document is converted to HTML format. If you think you may need to make further modifications to the document, save it as a normal ClarisWorks document, too (after removing the .htm or .html extension).

✦ *Opening an HTML file:* If you want to make changes to a ClarisWorks-generated Web page, open the original ClarisWorks document — not the HTML file. To convert non-ClarisWorks HTML files so they can be worked with in ClarisWorks, choose HTML as the file type in the Open dialog box. (The only reason to use the normal Open procedure is if you want to view the actual HTML tags in the file rather than the formatted text.) To use the Internet-related buttons when working with the document, choose Internet from the pop-up menu on the left side of the button bar.

Quick Tips

The following quick tips offer methods for gaining a better understanding of HTML, as well as ways to work more productively and efficiently with HTML.

Learn from others

Perhaps the fastest way to learn about HTML conventions and how to create pages that have class is by examining other people's Web pages. Most browsers have a Save, Save Page, Save Source, Source, or View Source command that enables you to examine and save the HTML code of any page you're currently viewing. Grab some good examples from the Web in this manner and check out the tags they used by opening the document in ClarisWorks.

More powerful HTML editors

If you want to move beyond the tags supported by the ClarisWorks HTML translator, you may want to check out one of the many Web page layout programs, such as Claris Home Page, Visual Page (Symantec Corporation), and PageMill (Adobe Systems). More advanced designers may prefer to work in a text or an HTML editor, such as BBEdit (Bare Bones Software).

Help with HTML

If your appetite for HTML has been whetted, there are several excellent sources of in-depth HTML information — in print and on the Web itself. One of my favorite HTML books is *Teach Yourself Web Publishing with HTML in a Week* by Laura Lemay (SAMS Publishing). Several titles from IDG Books Worldwide also explain how to work with HTML:

✦ *Macworld Creating Cool Web Pages with HTML*

✦ *HTML for Dummies*

✦ *HTML Publishing Bible*

✦ *HTML & Web Publishing Secrets*

In addition, some useful documents you can find on the Web include:

✦ A Beginner's Guide to HTML

   `http://www.ncsa.uiuc.edu/General/Internet/WWW/HTMLPrimer.html`

✦ HTML Quick Reference

   `http://kuhttp.cc.ukans.edu/lynx_help/HTML_quick.html`

✦ Composing Good HTML

`http://www.cs.smu.edu/~tilt/cgh/`

Note Unlike books, the content of Web sites changes constantly. Occasionally, the particular site that contains an item of interest — like these documents about HTML — also changes. (Don't blame me if they've moved.)

Summary

✦ ClarisWorks 5.0 includes a dozen new Web Page Templates you can use to design a simple Web page. As an alternative, you can create Web pages from scratch in a ClarisWorks word processing document.

✦ ClarisWorks 5.0 provides a translator that enables you to create, edit, and save documents in HTML format — the language used to display pages on the World Wide Web. The translator attempts to match the formatting you have applied to the document as closely as possible.

✦ The Internet button bar contains buttons that enable you to configure ClarisWorks for use with a Web browser, set conversion preferences, add document and URL links to the page, and display the current document in the browser as a finished Web page.

✦ All graphics in a document are automatically changed to Web-compatible GIF or JPEG files when you save a document as an HTML file.

✦   ✦   ✦

Using the ClarisWorks Office Add-Ons

P A R T

V

In This Part

Chapter 23
The ClarisWorks
Office Add-Ons

The ClarisWorks Office Add-Ons

CHAPTER

23

◆ ◆ ◆ ◆

In This Chapter

Using the JIAN
Business Templates

Using Netscape
Navigator to browse
Web pages, send
and receive e-mail,
and read and post
messages to
newsgroups

Creating Web pages
with Claris Home
Page Lite

◆ ◆ ◆ ◆

Overview

ClarisWorks Office includes several add-on programs and
templates that are not provided with ClarisWorks 5.0.
Specifically, the primary add-ons in ClarisWorks Office
include:

✦ *JIAN Business Templates.* These 64 ClarisWorks
templates help you handle various business and
financial functions.

✦ *Netscape Navigator.* This is a combination Web browser,
e-mail program, and newsgroup reader for users who
have — or intend to get — Internet access. Navigator is
included as a component of the two Internet service
providers' software on the ClarisWorks Office CD.
(NETCOM's installer also adds Telnet, e-mail, and chat
programs; EarthLink's software includes Eudora, an
e-mail program.)

✦ *Claris Home Page Lite 2.0.* This program enables you to
create personal, business, and educational pages for
posting on the World Wide Web.

✦ *Third-party applications.* There are also a variety of
demos, shareware, trialware (time-limited programs),
and fully functioning applications on the CD, such as
SurfWatch, Internet Phone, and Adobe Acrobat Reader.
Refer to the programs' documentation and Help files for
assistance.

Note

None of the add-ons are installed when you run the
ClarisWorks 5 installer. To install the add-ons, open the
ClarisWorks Office folder. Inside you will find folders for the
add-ons, separate installation programs, documentation, and
important notes.

JIAN Business Templates

ClarisWorks Office includes 64 stationery documents you can use to create press releases, financial worksheets, telemarketing scripts, and the like. Because they are stationery documents rather than normal ClarisWorks files, you can use them over and over without fear of inadvertently altering the originals.

There are two ways to open a JIAN template. Choose New from the File menu (or press ⌘-N), click the Use Assistant or Stationery radio button, and then do one of the following:

✦ Choose JIAN Finance and Accounting, JIAN Management and Operations, or JIAN Sales and Marketing from the Category pop-up menu, and then select the specific template you want to use.

— or —

✦ Choose All Stationery from the Category pop-up menu, and select JIAN Business Basics Index from the scrolling list. The Business Basics Index opens (see Figure 23-1). Click any of the underlined links to create a fresh copy of the template you want to use.

The template opens as a new, untitled document. Instructions for using the template are in the document. Be sure to save the document before quitting.

The templates vary in their usefulness, complexity, and completeness. For example, the invoice template (a ClarisWorks spreadsheet) calculates line-item totals but not a grand total. You are free to modify the templates for your own use as necessary.

Netscape Navigator 3

If you're thinking about connecting to the Internet, Netscape Navigator is an all-in-one program that provides three essential Internet components:

✦ *Browser*. This is the main component of Netscape Navigator — the part of the program most users first see when they launch Navigator. The browser enables you to view the graphically rich pages of the World Wide Web.

✦ *Netscape Mail*. This is an electronic mail (*e-mail*) program with which you can send messages to and receive messages from anyone on the Internet.

✦ *Netscape News*. This is a newsgroup reader. You use it to view and post messages to any of the thousands of USENET newsgroups. Every newsgroup has a theme (using Macintosh database programs, breast cancer, or raising pets, for example).

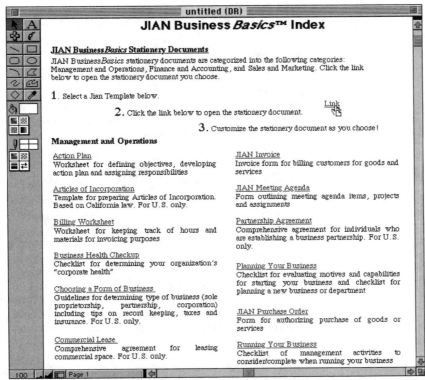

Figure 23-1: Click the underlined text in the Business Basics Index to choose a document to open.

Navigator is included as a component of the Internet access software for both EarthLink and NETCOM (two Internet service providers represented on the ClarisWorks Office CD). If you do not currently have an Internet account, you may want to check out what they have to offer.

To run their installers (and install Navigator in the process), open the ClarisWorks Office folder, the Internet Access folder, and then either the EarthLink or NETCOM folder. Note that if you elect to install Navigator on a Mac with less than 12MB of memory, you should first read the instructions in the folder named "If you have LESS than 12 MB RAM." To check your installed memory, go to the desktop, click the Apple menu, and choose About This Macintosh (System 7.x) or About This Computer (Mac OS 8).

Note that there are three different versions of Netscape Navigator on the CD: NETCOM installs version 3.0.1, EarthLink installs version 2.0.2, and the "If you have LESS than 12 MB RAM" folder contains version 2.0.

If you have installed Mac OS 8, the installed version of Netscape (3.0.1) is the same one installed by NETCOM. However, the Directory menu in the OS 8 version is customized for Apple Web sites. (Because of time constraints, the screen shots of Navigator in this chapter were from version 3.0.1 provided with OS 8.)

Configuring your Mac for the Internet

Each time you launch Netscape Navigator, the program automatically sends instructions to your Internet dialer program (PPP or FreePPP, for example) telling it to connect to the Internet — assuming you aren't already connected. Thus, before running Navigator for the first time, you must obtain Internet access — by opening an account with an Internet service provider (*ISP*); by joining an information service that provides Internet access (such as America Online, for example); or by obtaining a connection through your company's network. If you won't be connecting through a network, you will also need your own *modem* — a hardware device that enables your Mac to send and receive data over a telephone line. Finally, your Mac's system software must be configured to connect with your Internet service provider, information service, or company network.

If you are running OS 8, you can use the included Internet Setup Assistant to make your Mac ready for the Internet. Regardless of the version of system software you are running, you can use a utility called Internet Config to create a single set of configuration information that can be used by all Internet programs (so you don't have to configure each one separately).

Whether you use the Internet Setup Assistant or manually configure your Mac, you will need the following information: the dial-up phone number for your provider, the ID numbers of the primary and secondary domain name servers (such as 208.225.43.1), the domain name of your provider (such as linknet.com), the names of the incoming and outgoing mail servers (such as mail.linknet.com and/or pop.linknet.com), the name of the news server (such as news.linknet.com), your user name (such as rainbow), your account password, and your e-mail name (such as rainbow@linknet.com).

Using the browser

You use a browser to view pages on the part of the Internet known as the World Wide Web. The parts of the browser window are shown in Figure 23-2.

Status Bar

Address of the current Web page
or name of the current disk file

Toolbar

Directory
buttons

Figure 23-2: The browser window

The toolbar has buttons that duplicate common menu commands, as follows:

✦ *Back*. Redisplays the most recent page viewed during the current session. (The Back button is grayed out if this is the only page viewed so far.)

✦ *Forward*. If you have clicked Back to step back through pages viewed in the current session, you can click Forward to step forward through the viewed pages.

✦ *Home*. Click Home to view the startup (*home*) page you have set for Netscape Navigator. You can change your home page in the Appearance section of the General Preferences dialog box, as explained later in this chapter.

✦ *Reload*. Click Reload to reload the current page from disk (if its contents are in Navigator's cache) or from the Web.

✦ *Images*. Instructs Navigator to download all images that are part of the current Web page immediately.

✦ *Open*. Open a particular address from the Web or a file on your hard disk.

✦ *Print*. Print the current page.

✦ *Find*. Search for a text string on the current Web page.

✦ *Stop*. Click Stop to keep additional material for the current page from downloading. This command is very useful when it is apparent that a Web page does not contain the information you seek.

You can go to any Web page by typing or pasting its address (also called a URL or Uniform Resource Locator) into the Location box. The address of the current page is always displayed in this box. (Note that the name of this box changes. It may also be called Go To or Netsite, for example.)

The buttons beneath the Location box correspond to important Web sites listed in the Directory menu. Click any of them to go to the chosen site.

The current Web page is displayed in the main area of the browser window. To see information that is off screen, use the vertical and horizontal scroll bars, as you would in any other program.

The status bar at the bottom of the window provides important information when you use Navigator. When you load a Web page, the status bar shows the names and sizes of items that are loading, such as graphic images. If you move the cursor over a text or graphic link embedded in a Web page, the address of the link is shown in the status bar. (When clicked, a link may take you to a different spot on the current Web page, display a different Web page, or download a file to your hard disk, for example.)

Visiting Web pages

The primary use of any Web browser is to display pages from the World Wide Web. Millions of companies and individuals such as you have sites on the Web, where they offer products for sale, describe their services, or talk about their families, hobbies, and pets. There are several ways you can visit pages on the Web:

✦ *Type the page address in the Location/Go To/Netsite box and press Return*. An address uniquely identifies every page on the World Wide Web. A typical address might look like this: http://www.macworld.com/index.html

It isn't necessary to type the prefix for many addresses. If you leave off the http:// or even the http://www., Netscape completes the address for you. You can also leave off the .com portion of addresses, if you like.

✦ *Choose Open Location from the File menu, click the Open button on the toolbar, or press ⌘-L*. A dialog box appears in which you can type or paste a Web page address. This is equivalent to typing an address in the Location/Go To box.

✦ *Click a link on the current page.* Links are text or graphics that — when clicked — instruct Navigator to load the specified page. Text links are typically shown as underlined text. The destination page may be in the current Web site or at an entirely different location. The author of the Web page specifies where each link will take you. Other types of links enable you to download files (programs, documentation, or graphics, for example), send e-mail to the Webmaster or Webmistress (the person responsible for the Web site), or display newsgroup messages. When you move the cursor over a link, it changes to a pointing hand (see Figure 23-3). The link destination is simultaneously shown in the status bar at the bottom of the window.

✦ *Choose an entry in the Bookmarks menu.* Bookmarks are addresses of favorite Web sites you've asked Navigator to remember. (You can view this list in its own window by choosing Bookmarks from the Window menu or by pressing ⌘-B. Double-click any entry in the Bookmarks window to visit that page.) See "Creating and managing bookmarks" later in this chapter for more information about working with bookmarks.

✦ *Click the Home button.* This button displays the page that normally appears when you launch Navigator. You can set or change your home page by choosing General Preferences from the Options menu, clicking the Appearance tab, and typing the page address in the Home Page Location box.

✦ *Click the Back or Forward button.* These buttons take you back to the last page visited during the current session or forward to the next page (if you have previously clicked Back).

✦ *Choose an entry from the History list (displayed at the bottom of the Go menu).* The History list shows the Web pages you have recently visited. You can also view this list and visit any of its pages by choosing History from the Window menu.

✦ *Click any of the buttons beneath the Location/Go To/Netsite box.* Each button takes you to a particular Web page (indicated by the button's label).

✦ *Choose a Web site from the Directory or Help menu.* These are special page addresses that provide important information about Netscape Navigator, the Macintosh, and the Internet. Choose Handbook from the Help menu, for example, to get general instructions for configuring and using Navigator.

Note

The length of a Web page need not correspond to the size of the screen or to a normal piece of paper. A Web page can consist of a single screen or even hundreds of screens. In lengthy Web pages, it is not uncommon to provide a series of links that serve as a table of contents. When clicked, these links take you to different spots in the page or in the Web site. Similarly, many pages contain Previous and Next (or Back and Forward) buttons you can click to navigate through the site.

The object or destination of the current link   Text link

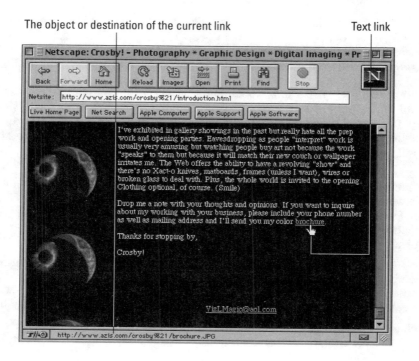

The object or destination of the current link   Graphic link

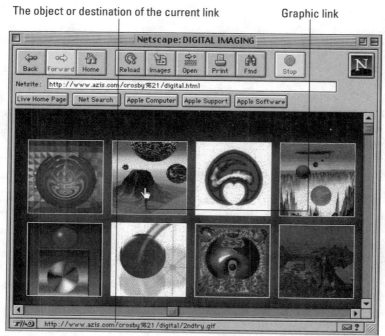

Figure 23-3: Links can be text (top) or graphics (bottom).

Tip

In most cases, each new Web page replaces the previous one in the browser window. You can open additional browser windows whenever you like by choosing New Browser Window from the File menu. New browser windows work independently from other windows. When a given page is loading very slowly, for example, you can use a second window to view a different page as the slow one loads. You can also instruct Navigator to open a particular link as a new window by holding down the mouse button as you click and then choosing New Window with This Link from the pop-up menu that appears.

Creating and managing bookmarks

Bookmarks are stored addresses of pages on the Web that you want to revisit. Because the content of some Web pages changes frequently, there are many you will want to visit regularly. Navigator has commands and procedures for creating, deleting, editing, and organizing your bookmarks.

To create a new bookmark, go to the Web page you want to save as a bookmark. Choose Add Bookmark from Bookmarks menu or press ⌘-D. The title of the Web page is added to the bottom of the Bookmarks menu.

To go to a Web page that has been saved as a bookmark, choose the page from the Bookmarks menu. Alternatively, if the Bookmarks window is open (choose Bookmarks from the Window menu), you can double-click the bookmark's title.

Bookmarks can be renamed, reordered, deleted, or stored in folders. To perform any of these tasks, choose Bookmarks from the Window menu or press ⌘-B. The Bookmarks window appears (see Figure 23-4).

Figure 23-4: You can organize, edit, and go to bookmarks in the Bookmarks window.

✦ To change a bookmark's name, URL, or description, select its name in the Bookmarks window and choose Edit Bookmark from the Item menu. The Edit Bookmark dialog box appears (see Figure 23-5). Make the necessary changes and click OK. (Note that a description is optional — although you can conduct searches for text contained in the description.)

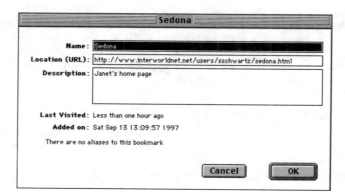

Figure 23-5: The Edit Bookmark dialog box

✦ To change a bookmark or folder's location in the list, click and drag it to a new position.

✦ You can also change the organization of your bookmarks by creating folders and subfolders in which to store them. You might create a Shareware folder, for example, in which to record the addresses of major shareware sites. Choose Insert Folder from the Item menu to create a new bookmark folder. The New Folder dialog box appears. Name the folder, enter an optional description, and click OK.

✦ To delete a bookmark, select its name in the Bookmarks window and press Delete or ⌘-Delete; choose Cut (⌘-X) or Clear from the Edit menu; or choose Delete Bookmark from the Item menu.

✦ If you can't remember the name or location of a bookmark, you can search for it by choosing Find from the Edit menu or pressing ⌘-F. The Find Bookmark dialog box appears. Enter a search string, set options, and click Find. The first matching bookmark — if any — is highlighted. To search for additional matches, choose Find Again from the Edit menu or press ⌘-G.

You can create a clickable shortcut for any bookmark by dragging its icon from the Bookmarks window onto the desktop.

To find out if pages in your bookmark list have changed since your last visit, choose What's New? from the File menu. After Navigator checks all the selected Web pages, ones that have changed are marked with a special icon in the Bookmarks window.

Tip

You can share bookmarks with friends and colleagues. Create an *HTML* page (HyperText Markup Language, the page-creation language for the World Wide Web) from your bookmark list, and choose Save As from the File menu (see Figure 23-6). To append your bookmarks to theirs, they need only choose Import Bookmarks from the File menu and then open your bookmark file.

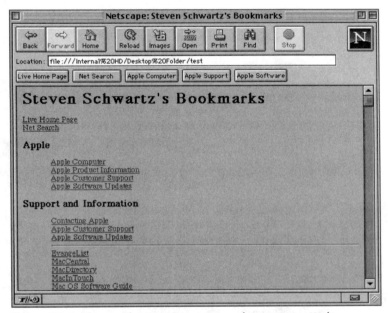

Figure 23-6: Choose the Save As command to create a Web page document from your bookmark list. If this file is opened on another computer, clicking a link will instruct the user's browser to load the chosen page.

Downloading files

The Internet is the supreme source for files of all kinds. You can download commercial programs (for a fee), updates, documentation, demos, *shareware* (software you can try before buying), *freeware* (free programs), and graphic images of all kinds.

The process of downloading files is very simple. In most cases, you just click a text or graphic link to begin the download. When all the data has been received by your computer, you use a normal Save dialog box to specify the location on your hard disk where you want to save the file.

Tip   Many files you can download are encoded in some fashion. They may be compressed archives in .sit (StuffIt) or .zip (WinZip) format; they may be BinHex encoded; or they may be compressed *and* BinHex encoded. Names of files that are intended to be used on a Mac will usually end with an .hqx (BinHex) or .bin (MacBinary) extension. To extract the contents of such files and make them usable, you need a conversion program. One of the best is StuffIt Expander. It is installed as part of NETCOM's installation program or can be downloaded from Aladdin Systems's Web site at:

    http://www.aladdinsys.com

Note   StuffIt Expander is included with OS 8, as is a copy of the Aladdin Systems shareware product DropStuff with Expander Enhancer. (This product enables Expander to handle many additional formats.)

In addition to downloading files, you can save copies of any graphic images you see on Web pages. To save a graphic, move the pointer over it, and then click and hold down the mouse button. A pop-up menu appears, as shown in Figure 23-7. Choose Save This Image As, and then specify a disk location in which to save the graphic.

Figure 23-7: Click and hold the mouse button over a graphic to display this pop-up menu.

Searching the Web

As you'll quickly learn, the Web is not an organized collection of data. Imagine instead that you have strolled into the largest library in the world, only to discover all the books are strewn in a heap in the center of the floor. Although the information you seek may well be there, locating it can be extremely difficult.

And so it is with the Web. Luckily, many enterprising companies have created *search engines* that enable you to search the Web for material. From their search sites, you type one or more keywords in a text box and then click a button to begin the search. The site then provides you with a list of Web pages (*hits*) that contain one or more of your search terms. To go to a prospective hit, you simply click the page's link.

Netscape Navigator offers easy access to Excite, one of these general search sites. Click the Net Search button or choose Net Search from the Bookmarks menu. Table 23-1 provides addresses of some other search sites you may want to try. Because no single search site lists all the pages on the Web, if you don't find what you are looking for at one site, you are well-advised to try another.

Table 23-1 Web Search Sites	
Site Name	*Address*
General Web Search Sites	
AltaVista	http://www.altavista.digital.com/
HotBot	http://www.hotbot.com/
Lycos	http://www.lycos.com/
Yahoo!	http://www.yahoo.com/
Address, Phone Number, E-mail Address Search Sites	
Four11 Directory Services	http://www.four11.com/
WhoWhere	http://www.whowhere.com/

Note   Some of the general Web search sites (such as Yahoo! and Lycos) can also help you search for addresses, phone numbers, and e-mail information.

Finding text on the current page

After using a search site to find potential hits, you can use Navigator's Find command to go to the part of the page where the keyword was found. Click the Find button on the toolbar, choose Find from the Edit menu, or press ⌘-F. The Find On Page dialog box appears (see Figure 23-8).

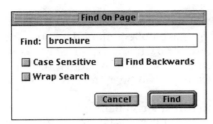

Figure 23-8: Use the Find On Page dialog box to search for text on the current Web page.

In the Find box, type the word or text string you want to find. Click the Find button to begin the search. Each search starts at your current position within the Web page. If the search string is found, Navigator highlights the matching text. To search for other occurrences of the string, choose Find Again from the Edit menu or press ⌘-G. If no additional occurrences of the string are found, Navigator beeps.

Note that the Find On Page dialog box also has options to make the search case-sensitive, search backwards from the current position on the page (toward the top rather than the bottom), or make the search wrap around the entire page (regardless of the current position).

Setting browser preferences

Although the standard Navigator preferences are fine for most users, there are a few preferences you may want to examine and change. All preferences are set by choosing commands from the Options menu.

Appearance preferences

Many basic Navigator preferences are set in the Appearance options. Choose General Preferences from the Options menu. Click the Appearance tab, if it is not already selected (see Figure 23-9).

✦ To specify whether the browser, mail, or news window appears each time you run Navigator, click the appropriate radio button in the On Startup Launch section of this screen.

✦ Whenever you click a link on a Web page, it is temporarily recorded in Navigator's History folder. Specify the number of days to store links by typing a number in the After *x* Days box. To clear the current contents of the History folder immediately, click the Expire Now button.

✦ To change your *home page* (the page that normally appears when you launch Navigator or when you click the Home button in the toolbar), enter the page's address in the Home Page Location box. If you prefer to start without loading a particular Web page, click the Blank Page radio button.

Figure 23-9: You set Appearance options in the General Preferences dialog box.

Downloads directory

Downloaded files are stored on your hard disk. To specify the drive and folder in which new downloads are stored, choose General Preferences from the Options menu, click the Applications tab, and click the Browse button to the right of the Downloads Directory option.

Cache preferences

To speed up subsequent visits to the same Web pages, Navigator automatically creates a *cache* (a location on your hard disk where page elements, such as graphics, are stored). If you later revisit the Web page, Netscape can pull these elements from your hard disk, rather than downloading them a second time. You can control how the cache works by choosing Network Preferences from the Options menu. The Network Preferences dialog box appears. Click the Cache tab (see Figure 23-10).

By default, the cache is stored in a special folder within the System Folder of your start-up hard disk. If you want to change the location of the cache folder (perhaps placing it on a different hard disk that has more free space), click the Browse button and select a disk and folder for the cache.

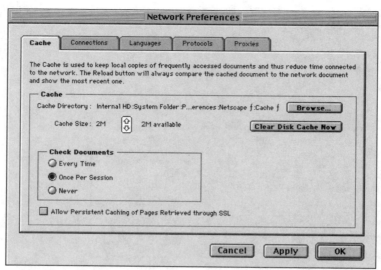

Figure 23-10: Setting cache preferences

As the cache fills, Navigator automatically empties it to make room for new Web materials. The larger the cache, the more Internet materials can be recorded in it and the less frequently Netscape will need to empty it. You can set the size of the cache by clicking the up and down arrows beside the Cache Size preference. Note that whatever size you choose, the space will be reserved for the cache; you will not be able to use it to store other programs or documents.

You don't have to wait for the cache to fill before clearing it. You can click the Clear Disk Cache Now button to empty the cache whenever you like.

The Check Documents setting determines how frequently Navigator checks each Web page against items in the cache. For most users, the default choice (Once Per Session) works best. It tells Navigator to check each page when you first visit it during an online session. If the page contains new material, the material is downloaded to the cache. On subsequent visits to the page in the same session, Navigator automatically pulls the entire page's contents from the cache and assumes the page has not changed.

If you suspect a page has changed and you are viewing outdated material, you can force the material to be downloaded again by clicking the Reload button on the toolbar, choosing Reload from the View menu, or pressing ⌘-R.

Using Netscape Mail

Netscape Mail enables you to send and receive electronic messages called *e-mail*. These text messages can also contain enclosures (known as *attachments*), such as formatted ClarisWorks or Microsoft Word documents, graphics, and even programs. Many people routinely use e-mail to transmit important documents and files to one another.

Netscape Mail has several advanced mail functions not found in lesser e-mail programs, such as the capability to send and display complete Web pages. To display the Mail window, choose Netscape Mail from the Window menu.

Setting Mail preferences

Before you can use Netscape Mail to send or receive e-mail, there are several essential pieces of information you must enter in the Mail & News Preferences dialog box. From the browser or Mail window, choose Mail & News Preferences from the Options menu and do the following (at a minimum):

✦ If you want a record of all your outgoing messages, click the Composition tab in the Mail & News Preferences dialog box. In the *By default, copy outgoing messages to a file* section of the window, check the Mail File box. This creates a Sent folder in which a copy of every e-mail message you send is stored.

✦ Click the Servers tab in the Mail & News Preferences dialog box (see Figure 23-11). Enter the information requested in the first three lines of the Mail section. The names of the outgoing and incoming mail servers can be obtained from your Internet service provider or network administrator. If you want Netscape to regularly check for and retrieve new mail, click the *Check for mail every...* radio button and enter a frequency (in minutes).

✦ Click the Identity tab in the Mail & News Preferences dialog box. Complete the first two boxes by entering your name and e-mail address. This information is used to identify you in the header section of outgoing e-mail messages and posts to newsgroups.

✦ Click the Organization tab in the Mail & News Preferences dialog box. To avoid manually typing your password each time you connect to the mail servers, click the check box for Remember Mail Password. (If you work in an open environment, however, you may prefer the safety afforded by manually typing your password each time.)

Note

If you use Internet Config to record important Internet information, such as your e-mail address and server names, you may prefer to click the check box for Use Internet Configuration System. This option tells Netscape to take your e-mail and newsgroup configuration data from Internet Config rather than from these dialog boxes.

Figure 23-11: You can identify your primary mail and news servers in the Servers section of the Mail & News Preferences dialog box.

Using the Address Book

Every Internet user with an active e-mail account is identified by a unique address, composed of a user name, the @ symbol, and the domain name of the person's Internet service provider. Some examples of e-mail addresses are johnboy@aol.com and ksamuels@linkworld.net. Because such names can be lengthy and difficult to remember, Netscape Mail provides an address book in which you can record e-mail addresses to use to address outgoing messages. To open the Address Book (see Figure 23-12), choose Address Book from the Window menu. The Address Book must be open when adding or editing individual users or *lists* (groups of related addresses).

Icons represent individual entries in the Address Book

An Address Book list

Figure 23-12: The Address Book

To create a new Address Book entry, open the Address Book and choose Add User from the Item menu. An untitled address dialog box appears (see Figure 23-13). At a minimum, you must enter a name and a complete e-mail address. If you wish, you can also enter a nickname and a description. Click OK to add the person or company to the Address Book.

Figure 23-13: Creating an Address Book entry

Names in the Address Book are automatically sorted according to their first word. You may find it easier to locate names in the Address Book if you create them in last name, first name format (such as Jones, Sarah).

To edit an existing address, select it in the Address Book and choose Edit Address Book Entry from the Item menu (or press ⌘-I). To delete an address, select it in the Address Book and choose Delete Address from the Edit menu, press ⌘-Delete, or press Delete.

If you want to categorize the friends, colleagues, and business associates in your Address Book, you can create *lists*. A list is a named folder inside the Address Book, such as Relatives or The Gordon Project. To create a list, choose Add List from the Item menu. A dialog box appears, similar to the one used when creating a new address. It contains three lines: Nickname, Name, and Description. Only the Name box must be completed.

To add individuals to any list, open the Address Book and drag their icons onto the appropriate list folder or folders. An individual can be added to as many lists as you like.

Like most Internet users, you will receive e-mail from many people you will want to include in your Address Book. Although you can copy the address from a message and then paste it into the Address Book, a faster way is to select the message header and choose Add to Address Book from the Message menu.

Creating and sending e-mail

You can compose and send messages from within Navigator, Mail, or News. In any of the three, you can choose New Mail Message from the File menu (or press ⌘-M). In Mail or News, clicking the To: Mail button in the toolbar has the same effect. A new Message Composition window appears (see Figure 23-14).

Figure 23-14: A new e-mail message

Fill in the sections of the message as follows:

✦ *Subject.* Enter a subject/title for the message. Choose it carefully; it identifies the contents of the message to the recipients.

✦ *Mail To.* Enter the address of the intended recipient(s). You can drag addresses from the Address Book, type complete e-mail addresses (multiple addresses must be separated by commas), or type each person's name or nickname (indicating you want Netscape Mail to find the address for you in the Address Book).

To view and use the Address Book, click the Address Book button at the top of the Message Composition window or choose Address Book from the Window menu.

✦ *Cc.* Enter the addresses of individuals (if any) to whom a copy of this message should be sent. Use the same procedures as described above for completing the Mail To box.

✦ *Body.* Type the body of the message in the large box at the bottom of the Message Composition window. Note that the window works like a word processor, automatically wrapping text to the next line as needed.

✦ *Attachments.* All files and URLs (Web page addresses) attached to the message are listed in this box. You can add attachments by dragging them into the Attachments box, clicking the Attach button, or choosing Attach from the File menu. If either of the latter options is chosen, the Attachments dialog box appears (see Figure 23-15). To send a URL as an attachment, click Attach Location (URL) and then type or paste the URL into the dialog box that appears. To send a file, click Attach File and then select the file to send.

Figure 23-15: The Attachments dialog box

You can also create a new letter by double-clicking a recipient's name in the Address Book. Doing so simultaneously addresses the message for you. To send a message to a list, double-click the list name or drag it onto the Mail To line.

In Navigator, you can send the current Web page to a user — as an HTML file rather than the page's URL — by choosing Mail Document from the File menu. Assuming the recipient's mail program is capable of displaying Web pages, he or she will see something similar to the screen shown in Figure 23-16. However, many e-mail programs cannot interpret HTML files. If the recipient wants to see the Web page, he or she will have to open it in a browser.

New messages can be sent immediately or stored in Netscape Mail's Outbox to be sent as a batch at a later time. To send a message as soon as it is written, choose Immediate Delivery from the Options menu. If you'd rather store the message in the Outbox for later delivery, choose Deferred Delivery. When you are done composing the message, click the Send Now (or Send Later) button. All messages in the Outbox can be transmitted by choosing Send Messages in Outbox from the File menu.

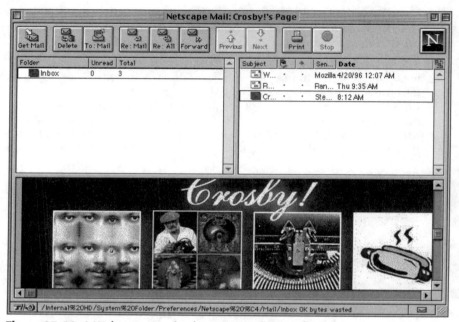

Figure 23-16: A Web page received as an e-mail message

There are other fields you can include in the address section of outgoing mail by choosing commands from the View menu. *Mail Bcc* (blind carbon copy) is sometimes useful, for example, because it enables you to send a copy of the current message to a person without informing the recipients listed in the Mail To and Cc lines. When sending important messages to coworkers, you might want to send a blind carbon copy to your supervisor, for instance.

Reading and replying to mail

There are several ways to check for incoming mail. You can click the Get Mail button in the toolbar, click the envelope icon in the bottom-right corner of the Mail window, choose Get New Mail from the File menu, or press ⌘-T. If new messages are found, they are downloaded to your computer and listed in the Inbox. Select any message header to read the message.

If a message contains attachments, they are listed as links at the bottom of the message window. Click the link (shown as underlined text) to open or save the attachment. If the attachment is a GIF or JPEG graphic image (or any other file type supported by Netscape Navigator), the file opens and is displayed in a new browser window (see Figure 23-17). Otherwise, you will see a standard Save dialog box, enabling you to save the attachment to disk.

As an alternative, you can click and hold down the mouse button over the attachment link. A pop-up menu appears (see Figure 23-18), enabling you to open or save the attachment.

Figure 23-17: Some graphic attachments, such as this JPEG file, can be displayed by Navigator.

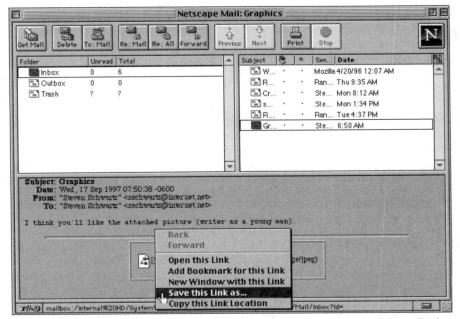

Figure 23-18: Click and hold the mouse button over an attachment link to display a menu of options.

If people occasionally send you Web pages as attachments, the attachments can be viewed in the Mail window by choosing Attachments Inline from the View menu.

Replying to messages

Incoming messages often require a response. To ensure the sender knows the specific message to which you are responding, Netscape Mail provides two reply commands. To reply to a message from an individual, select the message header and choose Reply from the Message menu, press ⌘-R, or click the Re: Mail button. To reply to a message from a group, select the message header and choose Reply to All from the Message menu, press Shift-⌘-R, or click the Re: All button. Responses sent using either command automatically use the original Subject line, preceded by Re:, as in Re: Good News.

You can also quote text from the original message when writing your reply. Choose Mail & News Preferences from the Options menu to specify how and when quoted text is displayed in replies. If you typically quote the original message in replies, click the Composition tab and check *Automatically quote original message when replying*. Click the Appearance tab to specify the style, size, and color of quoted text.

Like other text in the message, you can edit quoted text. For example, it is a common practice to delete extraneous quoted text, leaving only the pertinent parts.

If automatic quoting is not set, you can still quote the original message by clicking the Quote button or by choosing Include Original Text from the File menu.

Forwarding mail to others

If you like, you can forward received messages to others. To forward a message, select it in the right side of the Mail window and click the Forward button in the toolbar, choose Forward from the Message menu, or press ⌘-L. A new message window opens with the original message enclosed as an attachment. Fill in the address information, type any additional message text you want, and click Send Now (or Send Later).

If you prefer, you can forward the message as quoted text (each line is preceded by the > symbol). Choose Forward as Quoted Text from the Message menu or press Shift-⌘-D.

Managing your mail

Netscape Mail stores messages in folders: *Inbox* (received messages), *Outbox* (messages to be sent using deferred delivery), and *Trash* (messages marked for deletion). If you indicate in the Composition preferences that you want Mail to keep a copy of all sent messages (as described earlier in this chapter), you will also have a *Sent* folder.

You can create additional folders to group related messages together. While working on this book, for example, I created a ClarisWorks folder to store originals or copies of all messages related to this book. To create a new folder, choose New Folder from the File menu, name the folder, and click OK.

You can move messages from one folder to another by dragging them. As an alternative, you can select the message, choose Move or Copy from the Message menu, and then choose the folder to which the message should be moved or copied.

Not all messages are worth saving. To eliminate a message, select it and click the Delete button, choose Delete Message from the Edit menu, or press ⌘-Delete. All deleted messages are stored in the Trash folder. To remove the messages permanently, you must periodically choose Empty Trash Folder from the File menu. Similarly, to recover wasted disk space, you should occasionally select each folder and choose Compress Folder from the File menu.

Using Netscape News

At present, there are thousands of newsgroups in existence, covering subjects such as hobbies, computer programs, used and new items for sale, class assignments at particular universities, movie stars, and virtually anything else you can imagine. The easiest way to understand newsgroups is to think of them as repositories for e-mail messages relevant to that subject. Messages posted to a newsgroup may contain comments, questions to which a person seeks answers, or responses to the messages of others. To display the News window, choose Netscape News from the Window menu.

Setting News preferences

Before you begin working with Netscape News, there are some setup issues to which you must attend. Begin by choosing Mail & News Preferences from the Options menu, and click the Servers tab. At the bottom of the Mail & News Preferences dialog box (refer to Figure 23-11), enter the name of your primary news server (usually in the form *news.service provider*, such as *news.robonet.com*). If you didn't already enter your name and e-mail address in the Identity section when configuring Netscape Mail, do so now.

Note

News servers are responsible for collecting the messages for all newsgroups they host or follow. It's not unusual for an Internet service provider to follow 30,000 or more newsgroups. And many companies, such as Microsoft and Symantec, have their own news servers from which you can read company news, messages about software testing, and the like.

In Netscape News, you can have multiple news servers — not just your default one. To add additional news servers, choose Open News Host from the File menu and enter the name of the news server.

Once you have designated at least one news server, the next task is to download a list of the newsgroups the server carries. To do so, select the server's name in the News Server window and choose Show All Newsgroups from the Options menu. If you have added other news servers, repeat this procedure for them, too.

Reading News Posts

Once you have reviewed the names of the newsgroups (listed beneath each server's name in the News Server pane, as shown in Figure 23-19), it's a simple matter to retrieve and read the messages within the newsgroups. Click once to select a newsgroup that interests you. Netscape News automatically downloads the most recent message headers for the newsgroup and lists them in the top-right pane of the News window.

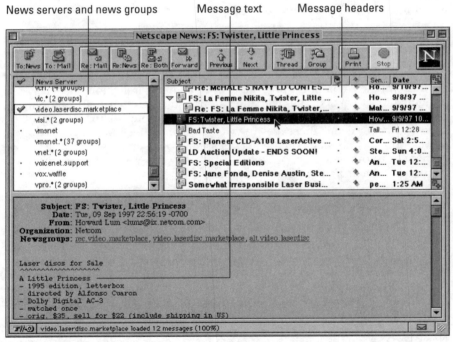

Figure 23-19: The News window is divided into three panes.

To read a message, click its header. As you click headers, the messages are downloaded to your Mac and displayed in the bottom of the News window (refer to Figure 23-19). Headers for previously read messages are shown in plain type; new and unread messages have boldface headers. In addition to clicking messages that interest you, you can move from one message to the next by pressing the up- and down-arrow keys. Note, however, that this downloads each message to your computer, whether you are interested in reading it or not.

You'll note that some messages are indented under others. This is referred to as a *thread* (a group of related messages).

After reviewing messages in several newsgroups, you will probably find newsgroups you want to follow. To make it easy to find these newsgroups in later sessions, you can *subscribe* to them. Unlike magazine subscriptions, there is no fee associated with subscribing to newsgroups. Subscribing merely instructs Navigator to remember the groups for you.

To subscribe to a newsgroup, click in the column to the left of the newsgroup's name. A check mark should appear, indicating you are now subscribed to the newsgroup. In subsequent sessions, you can quickly view your subscribed newsgroups by choosing Show Subscribed Newsgroups from the Options menu. If you want to see just the subscribed newsgroups that contain new messages, choose Show Active Newsgroups from the Options menu.

Netscape News has many commands to help you read newsgroup messages. Here are a few of the most useful ones:

✦ *Options ⇨ Show All Messages; Options ⇨ Show Only Unread Messages.* Choose one of these commands to indicate whether you want to view only new/unread messages or all messages. Most users prefer to see only the unread messages.

✦ *Message ⇨ Mark As Read.* Messages are automatically marked as read when you select them. In many cases, however, there will be messages you simply want to ignore. The best way to do this is to mark them as read without downloading them to your Mac. To mark a series of messages as read, ⌘-click or Shift-click the messages and then choose the Mark As Read command. You can mark an entire message thread as read by selecting a message in the thread and either choosing Mark Thread Read or clicking the Thread button. You can mark an entire newsgroup as read by choosing the Mark Newsgroup Read command or clicking the Group button.

✦ *File ⇨ Get More Messages.* Choose this command to check the server for any additional messages that can be downloaded for the current newsgroup.

Posting messages to newsgroups

Although reading messages can be fun and informative, you can also participate in newsgroups by posting your own comments and questions. To create a new message (unrelated to a thread), click the To: News button in the toolbar or choose New News Message from the File menu. A new message window appears with the current newsgroup designated as the recipient. Type your message and click the Send Now (or Send Later) button to post it to the newsgroup.

On occasion, you may also want to respond to the messages of others, offering your comments or attempting to answer questions that have been posed. You can send your response to the newsgroup, directly to the individual (as e-mail), or both. Click Re: News to send your response to the newsgroup and automatically become part of the selected message thread; click Re: Mail to send a response directly to the individual's e-mail address; or click Re: Both to post your response to the newsgroup and mail a copy to the individual.

Note

When answering a question, consider whether others would also profit by your answer. If so, respond both to the newsgroup and the individual. If not, respond directly to the person.

In any event, it is often good form to use e-mail to communicate directly with the individual. Finding responses in a constantly changing newsgroup can be challenging; opening one's e-mail, on the other hand, is not!

Claris Home Page Lite 2

As explained in Chapter 22, Web pages are constructed from text and embedded HTML tags (control codes that designate titles, headings, text formatting, and hypertext links). While you could create a Web page in a text editor or word processor by typing the necessary HTML tags, Claris Home Page Lite provides an easier way for you to construct pages. Think of Home Page as a visual Web page construction kit. You choose text formatting options from menus — just as you might in a word processing program. And you can insert graphics, rules, tables, and links by clicking buttons. There is no need to type HTML tags; Home Page handles it for you. A simple text-only Web page such as the one in Figure 23-20 (as viewed in Claris Home Page) is based on a more complex HTML file.

Note

Some features available in the full version of Claris Home Page 2 are not included in Claris Home Page Lite. Specifically, there is no support for frames, using the spelling checker, server-side image maps, creating forms, viewing/editing the source code (the HTML tags), or downloading files from a remote server. If you need these features and like what you've seen in this limited version of the program, you may want to consider upgrading to the full version of Claris Home Page. See the Claris Web site at http://www.claris.com/chplite-upgrade or call Claris at 800-544-8554 for details.

Web page

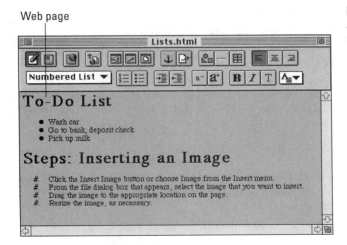

Figure 23-20: A Web page (top) and the underlying HTML file (bottom)

HTML code

```
file:///.../Incoming/Preview.html

<!--This file created 9/21/97 5:56 AM by Claris Home Page Lite-->
<HTML>
<HEAD>
   <TITLE>Lists</TITLE>
   <META NAME=GENERATOR CONTENT="Claris Home Page Lite">
   <X-SAS-WINDOW TOP=41 BOTTOM=620 LEFT=3 RIGHT=533>
</HEAD>
<BODY>

<H1>To-Do List</H1>

<UL>
   <LI>Wash car

   <LI>Go to bank; deposit check

   <LI>Pick up milk
</UL>

<H1>Steps: Inserting an Image</H1>

<OL>
   <LI>Click the Insert Image button or choose Image from the Insert
   menu.

   <LI>From the file dialog box that appears, select the image that
   you want to insert.

   <LI>Drag the image to the appropriate location on the page.

   <LI>Resize the image, as necessary.
</OL>
</BODY>
</HTML>
```

Setting preferences

As with most major applications, you can customize the way Claris Home Page Lite works. You can set preferences in these categories: General, Images, Browser Preview, Fonts, and HTML Output.

To view, set, or change your preferences, choose Preferences from the Edit menu. The following are a few preferences you may want to set immediately. Refer to Claris Home Page Help for an explanation of the other preference items.

General preferences

> ✦ *Auto-save Documents*. Computers occasionally crash. If you are lazy about saving your pages, you may want to check this option and specify the number of minutes between saves.

> ✦ *Remember FTP Passwords*. If you use Claris Home Page Lite to upload your Web pages and supporting material to a Web server, this option relieves you of memorizing your user password.

Browser preview preferences

> ✦ *Preview Browser*. By default, Home Page assumes you are using Netscape Navigator as your browser. If you are using a different browser, click the Set button and navigate to the folder in which your browser is stored.

> ✦ *Auto-save Before Previewing in Browser*. When you click the button or choose the menu option to preview the current Web page in your browser, the most recently saved version is retrieved from disk. Clicking this check box assures the preview you see is up to date.

The basics of creating a Web page

In many ways, Claris Home Page works like a word processing program. Choose New Page (or press ⌘-N) to open a new, blank page. Click to position the cursor and then type your text, pressing Return only when you want to start a new paragraph. The text automatically wraps to the width of the document window. You can format text by choosing menu options or clicking buttons — setting the paragraph format or the style of selected text within the paragraph. You can also insert graphic images (JPEG or GIF files) and QuickTime movies, if you like.

Because Home Page is drag-and-drop enabled, you can drag text or graphics from the desktop or other drag-and-drop-enabled programs and add them to your Web page. And, of course, you can copy and paste within and between documents. (You can also drag text and images *within* the document. This has the same effect as cutting the material and then pasting it into the new location.) All additions and changes to the page are made in Edit mode, represented by the first icon in the toolbar (see Figure 23-21).

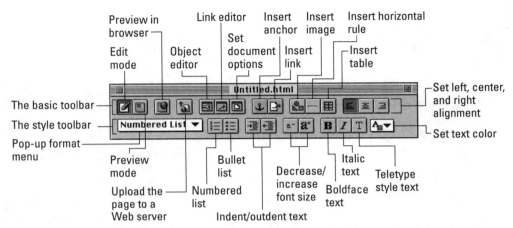

Figure 23-21: The toolbar contains two sections: the basic toolbar (top) and the style toolbar (bottom) for formatting text.

There are some important differences between Home Page and a word processing program. There is no ruler bar, for example, because you cannot set margins or tabs. When displayed in a Web page, paragraphs automatically flow to fit the width of the user's browser window — just as they do when you view a document in a text editor such as SimpleText. If the browser window is resized, the text wrap changes. And although you can type multiple spaces to try to change the position of text on the page, most browsers substitute a single space for every string of spaces found.

Web pages can also contain links that — when clicked — take you to a different spot in the current page, open a different Web page, send instructions to download a file, or open the user's e-mail program, for example.

To test links and get an idea of what the page might look like when viewed in a typical browser, you can switch to Preview mode by clicking the second button on the toolbar. To see exactly what the page will look like in a browser, click the third button in the toolbar. Home Page launches your default browser and opens the page for viewing.

The first time you save a Web page on which you are working (by choosing Save from the File menu or pressing ⌘-S), you actually accomplish two things. First, you give the document a title. In most browsers, this title appears at the top of the browser window. Second, you name the file, adding an .htm extension to indicate it is a Macintosh HTML file. If you later want to change the title of the page, choose Document Options from the Edit menu (or press ⌘-J) and type a new title in the Document Title box.

Note

In subsequent Home Page sessions, you can open the HTML files with the Open command or select the filename from the bottom of the File menu.

Preparing Pages for the Web

The ultimate purpose of creating Web pages is to display them on the World Wide Web where others can see them. When you design Web pages on your Mac, all links and graphics on the page refer to the locations of these items on your hard disk. When you upload your materials to a Web server, however, you want the locations to refer to the Web server — not to your hard disk.

When Claris Home Page Lite uploads files to the server, it makes the appropriate changes so all references point to the server. It does so by using what are called *relative references*. To make sure this process is handled correctly, however, you should follow these steps:

1. On your hard disk, create a new folder in which your HTML file and the site definition file will be stored. Inside that folder, create a folder called Images. Move all images that will be used on the Web page (including the background image, if any) into the Images folder.

2. In Home Page, choose New Page from the File menu to create a new HTML file. Save it in the directory you created in Step 1. (You can save the HTML file whenever and as often as you like.)

3. Choose Preferences from the Edit menu and then choose HTML Output from the pop-up menu at the top of the Preferences dialog box. Be sure the check box for Use Absolute Pathnames is not checked. (This establishes relative references for the current Web page.)

4. Create a site definition file. You can do this by choosing New Site from the File menu, or by clicking the Publish button on the toolbar and indicating you want to create a new site definition file. When asked to name and save the site definition file, save it in the folder created in Step 1 (the same folder that contains the HTML file).

Formatting text

In an HTML document — as in a word processing document — you can apply paragraph formatting (creating headings, body text, or numbered lists, for example) as well as format selected text within any paragraph (making it italic or changing its size, for example).

Paragraph formatting

Every paragraph in an HTML document has its own format. It may be a heading of a particular size, normal text, or a bullet point, for example. Both the Format menu and the Format pop-up menu in the toolbar contain basic HTML paragraph formatting tags, as described below. To apply any HTML style to a paragraph, change to Edit mode, position the cursor in the paragraph to which the style will be applied, and choose a command from the Format pop-up menu in the toolbar or from the Format menu.

✦ *Heading 1 - Heading 6.* As when writing an outline or a report, you organize material in your Web pages via headings. The larger the heading, the more important the material. A Heading 1 tag is used to indicate a level-1 heading (a main point).

When you use Heading tags in a page, it is considered good style to use them in order (as you would in an outline). Don't start with Heading 3 because you prefer the way it looks on screen, for example.

✦ *Normal.* Use this style to format body paragraphs.

✦ *Preformatted.* Use this style to format text you want to appear exactly as typed. Browsers display preformatted text in a monospaced font.

Browsers strip out additional spaces between words in normal text, replacing them with a single space. Spaces added to preformatted text, on the other hand, *are* displayed.

✦ *Bullet List; Numbered List.* HTML supports two types of lists: unordered (bullet-style) and ordered (numbered). Items in a bullet list are preceded by the bullet character (•); numbered lists are preceded by numbers — in sequential order.

✦ *Address.* You can use this tag to format the address section of your Web page, if there is one. You might include your name and e-mail address in such a section, for instance.

✦ *Term; Definition.* If you want to add a glossary of terms to a Web page, this tag pair makes it simple. Type the glossary term, choose the Term tag, and press Return. Home Page automatically applies the Definition tag to the following line (on which you will type the definition).

✦ *Blockquote.* Choose this command from the Format menu (or press ⌘-]) to format the paragraph as a block quotation, indented from both the left and right margins.

Alignment settings (left, right, or centered) can be applied to any paragraph or table cell — whether the paragraph or cell contains text or graphics. Click in the paragraph or cell of interest, and then click the appropriate button on the toolbar or choose a command from the Alignment submenu of the Format menu.

Formatting selected text

In addition to formatting entire paragraphs, you can apply formatting options to selected text within any paragraph. When you apply a font, style, size, or color to text by choosing commands from the Style menu or by clicking style buttons in the toolbar, Home Page inserts the appropriate HTML codes. To remove a style, reselect the text and choose Plain from the Style menu.

Although you can set a particular font for selected text, there is no guarantee that the people who view your page will have the same font installed on their computers. The font they see may be very different from the one specified. If a particular font is critical for some text, you may want to consider typing and formatting the text in a graphics program and then saving it as a JPEG or GIF graphics file.

The Raw HTML style is used to enter special characters, such as trademark, copyright, and currency symbols. To enter a special symbol, type the code for the symbol, and then format it as Raw HTML. For example, to enter the registered trademark symbol (®), you would type:

```
&#174;
```

For a list of supported special characters and their codes, see "Raw HTML Character Style" in the Claris Home Page Help Index.

Working with images

As you browse the Web, you'll note that many pages are embellished with graphics. Images can be used to illustrate a point or serve as clickable links to other parts of the Web site, for instance. To be added to a Web page, images must be in one of two formats: GIF (Graphics Interchange Format) or JPEG (Joint Photographic Experts Group). If the image you want to add is in PICT format, Claris Home Page can convert it for you. If the image is in an unsupported format (TIFF, for example), you must use another program to convert it to JPEG or GIF. You can use ClarisWorks 5 or Adobe Photoshop to resave most images in JPEG or GIF format.

Placing and resizing images

To add an image to a page, choose Image from the Insert menu, click the Insert Image button on the toolbar, or drag the image onto the page from the desktop (dragging the file icon) or a drag-enabled program (dragging the actual image). Once the image is placed, you can change the location of the image by dragging it to a new position. You can resize an image by clicking to select it and then dragging the right button to change the width or dragging the bottom button to change the height. To change the image size proportionately, press the Shift key as you drag the button in the image's bottom-right corner.

Home Page also includes a variety of clip-art buttons, icons, and horizontal rules you can add to your pages. To view these images, choose Open Library from the File menu and then select Clip Art Library. Click an icon at the top of the page to view a particular part of the library (see Figure 23-22). If you see an image you like, you can drag it onto your Web page.

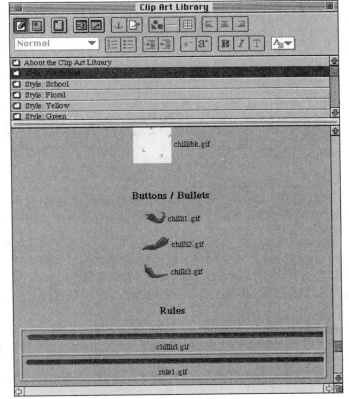

Figure 23-22: The Southwest Style clip-art library

Setting image attributes

To set the attributes for an image, double-click the image, or select it and do one of the following: click the Object Editor icon in the toolbar, choose Show Object Editor from the Window menu, or press ⌘-E. An Image windoid opens, showing the current attributes of the selected image (see Figure 23-23).

Figure 23-23: The Image windoid displays attributes of the currently selected object.

Changes you make in the windoid are automatically made to the image. There is no need to close the windoid.

You can set the following attributes in the Image windoid:

✦ *Alt Label.* This text label appears in place of the image if the user's browser cannot display images or the user has turned off this feature. Thus, an alternate label serves to identify important graphics the user may not be able to see.

✦ *Border.* If you like, you can set a border (in pixels) around any image. By default, all borders are initially set to 0 (none).

✦ *Alignment.* You can specify how surrounding text will align itself with the graphic by choosing an option from the Alignment pop-up menu. (If the image is in its own paragraph and there is no surrounding text, this setting is irrelevant. In that case, you can specify a page alignment for the image itself by clicking an alignment icon in the toolbar.)

✦ *Width/Height.* Alter the size of the image in pixels or by a percentage. (If these settings are not visible, click the tiny triangle at the bottom of the windoid to reveal them.)

✦ *Transparency and Interlace.* By clicking the Set button beside this option, you can specify whether the image is to be treated as transparent on its Web page and whether it will be interlaced (downloaded in window-pane fashion rather than from top to bottom). The image opens in the Transparency and Interlace Image Editor (see Figure 23-24).

To make the background transparent, move the cursor over the image. The cursor changes to an eyedropper. Click an area that contains the color you want to make transparent. You can toggle the transparency status of the image by clicking the appropriate button.

Normally, each graphic on your page loads from top to bottom. Interlacing the image causes it to load in waves, enabling the person viewing the page to determine quickly if this is something he or she wants to see. Thus, interlacing can be particularly useful for displaying large graphics. To specify an interlace setting, click the Interlace or Don't Interlace button.

Turn on
transparency

Turn off
transparency

Eyedropper

Figure 23-24: This graphic title will blend into the Web page better if the background is transparent.

✦ *Client-Side Image Map.* You'll note that in some Web pages you can click different spots on a graphic to go to different pages within the site. In Web parlance, the graphic is a *client-side image map.* You can specify the hot spots and the URLs to which they link by drawing selection rectangles or circles on the image (see Figure 23-25).

Rectangle
selection tool

Circle
selection tool

Enter a URL

Figure 23-25: Choose a selection tool, select an area on the image, and then enter a URL for the selected area.

Tip You can set the transparency or interlacing for *any* image — not just ones you have placed on the current Web page. Choose the Open command (⌘-O) from the File menu to open any image in the Transparency and Interlace Image Editor.

Note An entire image can also serve as a link to another spot on the current page, a different page, or a different Web site. For example, you might show a thumbnail graphic that — when clicked — displays a full-size version of the same image on a new Web page. Similarly, some graphics can serve as buttons that carry the user to the previous, next, and home pages. (See "Creating links" later in this chapter for instructions on creating links from graphics.)

Choosing a background image or color

Every Web page can have a background image, color, or neither. (In the latter instance, the page background will be the default color set by each user in his or her browser.) To specify a background for the current page, choose Document Options from the Edit menu or press ⌘-J. An Options dialog box appears (see Figure 23-26).

✦ To choose a background color for the page, click the Background box and select a color from the color picker that appears.

✦ To choose a background image for the page, click the Set button and select an image file.

To remove a background image, click None. To remove a background image and reset the background color to its default, click the Use Defaults button.

Choose a background color   Choose a background image

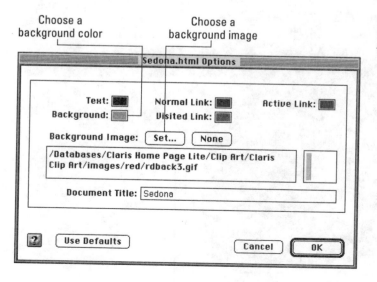

Figure 23-26: Selecting a background color or image for the current Web page

Note

If you're looking for additional backgrounds for your Web pages, you'll find 36 of them in the HTML Background Images folder.

Note

Although you can use virtually any image as a background, you will quickly discover that some work better than others. When tiled to cover the Web page, many images make it extremely difficult to see your links and read the text. Buried several layers within the Clip Art folder, there is a Borders folder, which contains many excellent background borders as well as several color-specific border folders (Blue, for example).

Making lists

HTML supports two types of lists: bullet lists (unordered) and numbered lists (ordered). List items formatted as bullet lists are indented and preceded by the bullet character (•). Numbered list items are preceded by numbers and are also indented. In Edit mode, the numbers are shown as the pound character (#). The actual numbers only appear when viewing the page in Preview mode or in your browser.

Figure 23-27 shows an example of the two list types. To create a bullet or numbered list item, click the appropriate icon in the toolbar, or choose Bullet List or Numbered List from the Format menu or the pop-up Format menu on the toolbar.

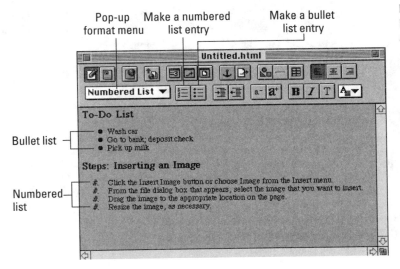

Figure 23-27:
Examples of bullet and numbered lists

Working with tables

Like worksheets, a table is a rectangular array of cells. You can specify the number of rows and columns, place whatever you wish in each cell (text or an image, for example), and set an alignment for each cell. Many formatting nightmares can easily be resolved by using a table — placing text descriptions beside graphics, for instance, as shown in Figure 23-28. To create a new table, choose Table from the Insert menu or click the Insert Table button in the toolbar. A 2 × 2 table is inserted into the Web page.

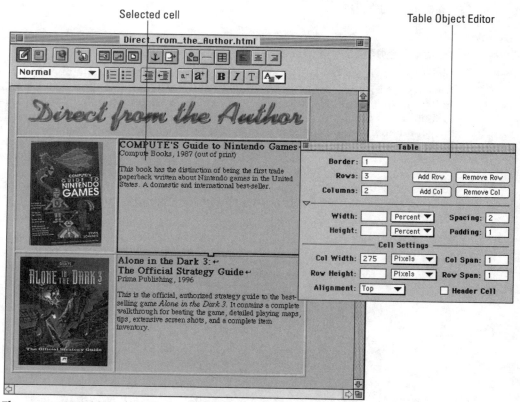

Figure 23-28: Tables can contain text and graphics. You can resize rows and columns as well as make a single row span multiple columns.

Tip

You can also create tables from spreadsheet or tab-delimited text files by copying and pasting or by using drag-and-drop.

Once the table has been created, you can begin typing the necessary text and inserting images, movies, and the like. You can visually resize the entire table, column widths, or row heights by clicking a border and dragging. To make other modifications or make ones with greater precision, open the Table Object Editor (shown previously in Figure 23-28) by double-clicking the table's border, clicking the Object Editor button in the toolbar, choosing Show Object Editor from the Window menu, or pressing ⌘-E.

You can set the following table attributes in the Table Object Editor:

✦ *Borders*. Specify the thickness (in pixels) of the table border.

✦ *Rows; Columns*. Set the number of rows or columns for the table by typing numbers or clicking the Add/Remove buttons. Columns are added and removed from the right side; rows are added and removed from the bottom.

✦ *Width; Height*. Change the width or height of the entire table.

✦ *Spacing; Padding*. Set the between-cell spacing and the amount of blank space around cell contents (measured in pixels).

You can also set attributes for individual cells in the table. When a cell is selected, the Table Object Editor expands to show the following cell settings:

✦ *Col Width; Row Height*. Set the width or height of the current column or row.

✦ *Col Span; Row Span*. Set the number of columns or rows the current row or column will span. The default is 1. (As shown at the top of Figure 23-28, you can use this feature to create a title row that spans the entire width of a table.)

✦ *Alignment*. Specify the vertical alignment of the text or object in the cell.

✦ *Header Cell*. Instruct Home Page to treat the current cell as a row or column header. The characteristics of header text may vary from browser to browser.

Creating links

Much of the power of Web pages comes from the implementation of the *hypertext* concept. When the user clicks a hypertext or graphic link, the browser carries out the instructions that were specified for the link. Clicking a link can cause the user's browser to display a different spot on the current Web page, display a different page in your site, display a different Web site, or download a file. A *mailto* link can open the user's e-mail program so he or she can create and send a message to you. You can also link to an *FTP* (file transfer protocol) site from which the user can download files.

Linking to a Web page

This is unquestionably the most common type of link you will encounter while Web surfing. When clicked, such a link carries you to the top of a given Web page in your site or to a particular page in another site.

Steps: Creating a Link to a Web Page in Your Site

1. Select the text string or object that will serve as the link.

2. Click the Insert Link to File button in the toolbar or choose Link to File from the Insert menu. A standard file dialog box appears.

3. Select the HTML document to which you want to link.

Note

If you prefer, you can specify a URL for a page in your own Web site by following the directions in the next set of steps.

Steps: Creating a Link to a Web Page in Another Site

1. Select the text string or object that will serve as the link.

2. Click the Link Editor button in the toolbar or choose the Link to URL command from the Insert menu. The Link Editor window appears (see Figure 23-29).

Enter URL   Break the link

Click to hide
or show examples

Figure 23-29: The Link Editor window

3. In the URL box, type or paste the address of the Web page to which you want to link.

If you have created a client-side image map (with multiple links specified in a single image), you can specify the action taken by each link region by double-clicking the image and then clicking the Edit button beside the Client-Side Image Map label. Then you can set or change the URL for a region by double-clicking the region or selecting the region and clicking the Link Editor button in the toolbar.

Linking to an anchor

Although linking to the top of a Web page is easy, it isn't always what you want. For instance, if you have created a set of links that serves as a table of contents for the current Web page, you will want to go to a specific section of the page rather than the top of the page. To go to a particular spot in a page, you must create *anchors* (text strings or graphics within the page that serve as link destinations).

Note

In ClarisWorks 5.0 or Office, anchors are called *bookmarks*. (See Chapter 19 for more information about creating and using bookmarks.)

To create an anchor, select the text or object to which you want to scroll. Then choose Anchor from the Insert menu or click the Insert Anchor button on the toolbar. An Anchor Name dialog box appears in which you name the anchor. If a text string is currently selected, it is proposed as the anchor name. However, you can name the anchor anything you like. When viewed in Edit mode, a tiny anchor icon is shown beside each defined anchor.

To link to an anchor, select the text string or object that will serve as the link (do not select the anchor), and click the Link Editor button or choose Link to URL from the Insert menu. Then follow the conventions in Table 23-2 when specifying the anchor.

Table 23-2 Specifying an Anchor Location	
Anchor Location	**Format**
Current Web page	#anchorname
Different page in current site	file.html#anchorname
Page in a different site	http://.../file.html#anchorname

Creating an e-mail link

E-mail or *mailto* links can be very useful. When the user clicks such a link, the browser attempts to launch the person's default e-mail program and opens a blank message already addressed to the e-mail address specified in the link. It is a common practice to provide an e-mail link, so viewers can send comments to you about your Web site, for example.

To create an e-mail link, select the text string or object that will serve as the link, and click the Link Editor button or choose Link to URL from the Insert menu. Type the link address using the following format:

```
mailto:e-mail address
```

For instance, if your e-mail address was roadwarrior@jobnet.com, you would type: **mailto:roadwarrior@jobnet.com**.

Linking to an FTP site

Rather than store large programs and demos on your ISP's Web server, you may simply want to provide links to an FTP site from which the user can download the files. To define a link that — when clicked — downloads a file from an FTP site, select the text string or object that will serve as the link, and click the Link Editor button, or choose Link to URL from the Insert menu. Then enter a URL in this format:

```
ftp://servername/dir/filename
```

This only works for FTP sites that allow anonymous connections. If the site requires the user to enter a password, the link will not function properly.

Changing and removing links

You can modify the object of a link (an HTML filename, URL, page anchor, e-mail address, or FTP site) by selecting the link and clicking the Link Editor button on the toolbar (refer to Figure 23-29). To change the link, type or paste it in the URL box, choose it from the pop-up menu to the right of the URL box, or click Browse (to link to a file or HTML document on disk). To break the link, click the Remove Link button in the Link Editor window.

You can also change the names of anchors. Double-click the tiny anchor icon beside the anchor and then type a new name. Note, however, that any existing links to the anchor must also be changed.

Publishing your pages on the Web

When you create Web pages, the real payoff is not in previewing them in your browser, it's viewing them on the Internet! In order to do this, however, you must upload your pages, graphics, and linked material to a Web server, such as one maintained by your ISP or an information service such as America Online.

Prior to uploading your site, you will need to know the server name, your user name, and the password necessary to transfer files to the server. (Contact your service provider for this information.) In addition, your service provider may need to create your main directory on the server.

Note

If your Web pages will be published on America Online, see the Read Me file inside the Claris Home Page Lite folder for detailed instructions on how to upload your pages.

Claris Home Page uses FTP to upload your Web site to a server; Home Page refers to this process as *publishing* a site. To publish your Web site, you must first create a site definition file by choosing New Site from the File menu or by clicking the Publish button on the toolbar. During the consolidation process, all materials for your site are copied into two folders. The main folder contains the HTML file and the site definition file created in Home Page. Within that folder is another folder called Images in which your image files are stored. By organizing your materials in this manner, you can use relative paths to identify the locations of each file and image. Doing so enables the materials to be referenced correctly once they are uploaded to the Web server.

Steps: Publishing a Web Site

1. Save any changes made to your HTML file.
2. Click the Publish button in the toolbar. The Publish dialog box appears.
3. Click the radio button that indicates you want to create a new site definition file.
4. Name the site definition file, saving it in the same folder that contains the HTML file.
5. In the dialog box that appears (see Figure 23-30), choose or enter the following:

Figure 23-30: The Site Definition dialog box

Service Provider: Choose ISP/LAN or America Online, as appropriate.

Server Name: Enter the name of the server, as directed by your service provider.

User Name: Enter your user name. In most cases, this will be the same name you use when logging onto your Internet account, such as *bhamilton* or *roadrunner12*.

Remote Directory: Enter the name of the directory on the server in which the HTML file will be stored. Generally, this is the same name as the directory on your hard disk in which the HTML file is currently located. (If the directory does not exist on the server, Home Page creates it for you.)

Before Upload: Consolidation makes sure your files are accounted for and in the correct directories before the upload commences. Choose whichever option is most appropriate for you. (Note that you can consolidate the files at any time by clicking the Consolidate button.)

Only upload files that have changed...: To avoid uploading files that are already on the Web server and have not changed, check this box.

6. Be sure your modem is on, and click Upload Site. The files are uploaded to the Web server. New directories are created during the upload process, if necessary.

Tip

If you later need to make changes to your Web site, you can quickly do so by choosing Open from the File menu and then opening the site definition file.

Quick Tips

The following quick tips explain the importance of previewing your Web pages in multiple browsers, tell how to work directly with the HTML code, enable you to check the time it takes to display each page, and offer help with managing files on your Web site.

Browser differences

As you construct your Web pages, keep in mind that different browsers have different capabilities. Although those from Netscape and Microsoft can easily display tables, for example, less capable browsers may show something quite different from what you see in Preview mode or when viewing the page in your browser.

Before finalizing and posting your pages, it is a good idea to first open them in several different browsers. You may also want to consider making two versions of your pages; one that uses advanced features and one that only uses basic HTML features.

Working directly with HTML

Although Home Page Lite does not provide an option for you to view the HTML code on which your Web page is based, you can view and work directly with the code by opening the HTML file in any text editor or word processor. (HTML files are ordinary text files.) If you make changes, be sure to save the file as Text-Only.

Checking download times

Although people love to browse the Web, their patience may be limited. Web pages that contain huge graphics can take a long time to download with a slow modem. If your Web page loads slowly, many people will leave without bothering to wait for it.

To give you an idea of how long it will take people to download the current page, choose Document Statistics from the Edit menu. A statistics window appears (see Figure 23-31) that shows approximately how long — at a minimum — a 14.4K and 28.8K modem might take to download the page. If you want to check just part of a page (a large graphic, for example), select it prior to choosing the Document Statistics command.

Figure 23-31: The Document Statistics window shows approximate download times for the current Web page and/or a selected portion of the page.

Managing your Web site

Unless you are lucky enough to have your own Web server, there is usually a limit to the amount of space you are allotted for storing your Web pages. While 2–5MB, for example, may seem like a lot of space, it can quickly be eaten up by files that are no longer needed. Unfortunately, Claris Home Page Lite is not a general FTP program; you cannot use it to delete old files and folders on the server.

One such FTP program is Fetch, a shareware application by Jim Matthews (Dartmouth College). Using Fetch, you can upload files to and download files from your site (or any other FTP site), delete individual files, and create and delete directories. To set up Fetch so you can connect to your Web site directory, choose New Bookmark from the Customize menu. In the Bookmark Editor dialog box that appears (see Figure 23-32), enter essentially the same information that was required when you created the site definition file.

Figure 23-32: In the Bookmark Editor dialog box, enter log-in information for the Web server.

About frames

Displaying frames is a feature handled by the more advanced browsers, such as Netscape Navigator, Netscape Communicator, and Internet Explorer. Frames enable you to display two or more Web pages within a single page, with each frame containing a different page. One common use of frames is to display a clickable table of contents or index in one frame and the linked documents in a second frame. When links in the contents frame are clicked, the appropriate Web page is displayed in the second frame. Note that Claris Home Page Lite does not support frames, but the full version of the program does.

Summary

✦ ClarisWorks Office has all the features of ClarisWorks 5.0, plus several add-on programs: JIAN Business Templates, Claris Home Page Lite, and sign-up information and software for some Internet service providers.

✦ All 64 JIAN templates are ClarisWorks stationery documents, so they can be used repeatedly while protecting the original files.

✦ Three versions of Netscape Navigator are provided on the ClarisWorks Office CD: 2.0, 2.0.1, and 3.0.1. (The latter is discussed in this chapter.) Navigator includes three essential Internet components: a browser, an e-mail program, and a newsgroup reader.

✦ The browser portion of Netscape Navigator is used to view the part of the Internet known as the World Wide Web. You can move from page to page and site to site by clicking text and graphic links on Web pages. You can also go to a Web page by typing its address (URL) or by choosing the page from a list of your favorite sites (bookmarks).

✦ You can download files such as documentation, program updates, demos, and shareware from some Web sites.

✦ To make it possible for you to find particular information on the World Wide Web (such as references to *chameleons* or *Mark Twain*), there are dedicated search sites you can use.

✦ With an e-mail account and Netscape Mail, you can exchange messages and files with anyone on the Internet. To make it easy to address messages, Mail includes the Address Book in which you can store the addresses of friends, relatives, and colleagues.

✦ E-mail messages can contain *attachments* (files transmitted along with the text message). You can send and receive formatted desktop publishing documents, spreadsheets, or even programs as attachments.

✦ You can use Netscape News to read and post messages to any of the thousands of newsgroups throughout the world. By subscribing to newsgroups, you can keep up with ongoing discussions about your hobbies, business, and other interests.

✦ Using Claris Home Page Lite, you can create professional-looking Web pages and post them to the World Wide Web. The program shields you from dealing with HTML (the language used to format Web pages). Instead, you can design pages in a manner similar to working in a word processing program.

✦ To add elements to a Web page, you can choose commands from the Insert menu, use cut-and-paste, or use drag-and-drop.

✦ You can test a Web page by changing to Preview mode or by viewing the page in your default browser, such as Netscape Navigator, Internet Explorer, or CyberDog.

✦ Paragraphs are formatted by choosing commands from the Format menu or the Format pop-up menu in the toolbar. Text strings within a paragraph are formatted by choosing commands from the Style menu or by clicking style buttons on the toolbar.

✦ Any graphic placed on a Web page must be in JPEG or GIF format. ClarisWorks Office can readily convert many types of images to either of these formats.

✦ Optionally, you can specify a background image or color to be used for each Web page you create.

✦ You can make two types of lists to be displayed on a Web page: bullet lists and numbered lists.

✦ Although you can create spreadsheet-like grids called tables in Home Page Lite, you cannot create frames (enabling you to show multiple Web pages within a single page).

✦ You can add text and graphic links to your Web pages that — when clicked — display another section of the same Web page, display a different Web page, enable the user to download files, or open a new message window in the user's e-mail program.

✦   ✦   ✦

Appendixes

Keyboard Shortcuts

Tables A-1 through A-17 list ClarisWorks keyboard shortcuts that will increase your productivity and make you feel at ease if you're not used to using a mouse or you don't like taking your hands off the keyboard.

Table A-1
General Menu Commands (Available in Most Environments)

Command	Key Sequence	Menu
Bold	⌘-B	Style or Format⇨Style
Center	⌘-\	Format⇨Alignment
Check Document Spelling	C-=	Edit⇨Writing Tools
Check Selection Spelling	Shift-⌘-Y	Edit⇨Writing Tools
Clear	Clear (extended keyboard)	Edit
Close	⌘-W	File
Copy	⌘-C, F3 (extended keyboard)	Edit
Cut	⌘-X, F2 (extended keyboard)	Edit
Find/Change	⌘-F	Edit⇨Find⇨Change
Find Again	⌘-E	Edit⇨Find⇨Change
Find Selection	Shift-⌘-E	Edit⇨Find⇨Change

(continued)

Table A-1 *(continued)*

Command	Key Sequence	Menu
Frame Links	⌘-L	Options
Help Contents	⌘-?, Help (extended keyboard)	Balloon Help or Help
Italic	⌘-I	Style or Format⇨Style
Justify	Shift-⌘-\	Format⇨Alignment
Larger	Shift-⌘->	Size or Format⇨Size
Left	⌘-[	Format⇨Alignment
New	⌘-N	File
Open	⌘-O	File
Other	Shift-⌘-O	Size or Format⇨Size
Page View	Shift-⌘-P	Window
Paste	⌘-V, F4 (extended keyboard)	Edit
Plain Text	⌘-T	Style or Format⇨Style
Print	⌘-P	File
Quit	⌘-Q	File
Record Macro/ Stop Recording	Shift-⌘-J	Format⇨Macros
Right	⌘-]	Format⇨Alignment
Save	⌘-S	File
Save As	Shift-⌘-S	File
Select All	⌘-A	Edit
Show/Hide Button Bar	Shift-⌘-X	Window
Show/Hide Links Palette	Shift-⌘-M	Window
Show/Hide Rulers	Shift-⌘-U	Window
Show/Hide Stylesheet	Shift-⌘-W	Window
Show/Hide Tools	Shift-⌘-T	Window
Smaller	Shift-⌘-<	Size or Format⇨Size

Command	Key Sequence	Menu
Thesaurus	Shift-⌘-Z	Edit⇨Writing Tools
Underline	⌘-U	Style or Format⇨Style
Undo/Redo	⌘-Z, F1 (extended keyboard)	Edit

Table A-2
General Navigation Commands

Command	Key Sequence
Go to beginning of document	Home (extended keyboard)
Go to end of document	End (extended keyboard)
Scroll down one screen	Page Down (extended keyboard)
Scroll up one screen	Page Up (extended keyboard)

Table A-3
Other General Commands

Command	Key Sequence
Cancel printing and most dialog boxes	⌘-.
Delete character to left of cursor	Delete
Delete character to right of cursor	Del (extended keyboard)
Discretionary hyphen	⌘-hyphen
End slide show	q, ⌘-., Esc, Clear
First slide	Home (extended keyboard)
Last slide	End (extended keyboard)
Next slide	Right arrow, down arrow, Page Down, Return, Tab, Spacebar
Previous slide	Left arrow, up arrow, Page Up, Shift-Return, Shift-Tab, Shift-Spacebar

Table A-4
Communications Menu Commands

Command	Key Sequence	Menu
Info	⌘-I	Settings
Open/Close Connection	Shift-⌘-O	Session
Phone Book	⌘-B	Settings
Save Lines Off Top	⌘-T	Session
Show/Hide Scrollback	⌘-L	Settings
Wait for Connection	Shift-⌘-W	Session

Table A-5
Database Menu Commands

Command	Key Sequence	Menu
Browse	Shift-⌘-B	Layout
Define Fields	Shift-⌘-D	Layout
Duplicate Record	⌘-D	Edit
Find	Shift-⌘-F	Layout
Go To Record	⌘-G	Organize
Hide Selected	⌘-(	Organize
Hide Unselected	⌘-)	Organize
Layout	Shift-⌘-L	Layout
List	Shift-⌘-I	Layout
Match Records	⌘-M	Organize
New Record	⌘-R	Edit
Show All Records	Shift-⌘-A	Organize
Sort Records	⌘-J	Organize

Table A-6
Database Navigation Commands

Command	Key Sequence
Move to beginning of field	⌘-left arrow
Move to end of field	⌘-right arrow
Move to next field	Tab
Move to previous field	Shift-Tab
Move to next record (same field)	⌘-Return
Move to previous record (same field)	Shift-⌘-Return

Table A-7
Other Database Commands

Command	Key Sequence
Deselect records	Enter
Insert a tab in a text field	⌘-Tab
Paste current date, time, or record number	⌘-- (hyphen)[1]

[1]You must be in a field of the correct type (that is, a date, time, or number field).

Table A-8
Draw Menu Commands

Command	Key Sequence	Menu
Align Objects	Shift-⌘-K	Arrange
Align to Grid	⌘-K	Arrange
Duplicate	⌘-D	Edit
Free Rotate	Shift-⌘-R	Arrange
Group	⌘-G	Arrange

(continued)

Table A-8 (continued)

Command	Key Sequence	Menu
Lock	⌘-H	Arrange
Move Backward	Shift-⌘-- (hyphen)	Arrange
Move Forward	Shift-⌘-+	Arrange
Reshape	⌘-R	Arrange
Smooth	⌘-(	Edit
Turn Autogrid On/Off	⌘-Y	Options
Ungroup	Shift-⌘-G	Arrange
Unlock	Shift-⌘-H	Arrange
Unsmooth	⌘-)	Edit

Note

Many of the commands for the Arrange and Options menus in Tables A-8 and A-9 are also available to you when creating or modifying database layouts (in Layout mode).

Table A-9
Other Draw Commands

Command	Key Sequence
Complete open or closed polygon or bezigon	Enter
Move selected image one pixel or gridpoint	Any arrow key
Select eyedropper tool	Tab

Table A-10
Paint Menu Commands

Command	Key Sequence	Menu
Duplicate	⌘-D	Edit
Free Rotate	Shift-⌘-R	Transform
Turn Autogrid On/Off	⌘-Y	Options

Table A-11
Other Paint Commands

Command	Key Sequence
Complete open or closed polygon or bezigon	Enter
Move selected image one pixel or gridpoint	Any arrow key
Select eyedropper tool	Tab

Table A-12
Spreadsheet Menu Commands

Command	Key Sequence	Menu
Calculate Now	Shift-⌘-=	Calculate
Copy Format	Shift-⌘-C	Edit
Delete Cells	Shift-⌘-K	Calculate
Fill Down	⌘-D	Calculate
Fill Right	⌘-R	Calculate
Go to Cell	⌘-G	Options
Insert Cells	Shift-⌘-I	Calculate
Lock Cells	⌘-H	Options
Make Chart	⌘-M	Options
Number	Shift-⌘-N	Format
Paste Format	Shift-⌘-V	Edit
Sort	⌘-J	Calculate
Unlock Cells	Shift-⌘-H	Options

Table A-13
Spreadsheet Navigation Commands

Command	Key Sequence
Move one cell down	Return, down arrow (or Option-down arrow)[1]
Move one cell up	Shift-Return, up arrow (or Option-up arrow)[1]
Move one cell right	Tab, right arrow (or Option-right arrow)[1]
Move one cell left	Shift-Tab, left arrow (or Option-left arrow)[1]
Move one character right (in entry bar)	Option-right arrow (or right arrow)[1]
Move one character left (in entry bar)	Option-left arrow (or left arrow)[1]
Stay in current cell	Enter

[1]Whether you use an arrow key or an Option-arrow combination depends on how the spreadsheet preferences are set.

Note

You can also use each of the commands in Table A-13 to complete a cell entry. The functions of these keys are determined by the settings in Spreadsheet Preferences.

Table A-14
Other Spreadsheet Commands

Command	Key Sequence
Cancel entry	Esc
Clear cell contents and format	Clear (extended keyboard)
Delete character to left (in entry bar)	Delete
Delete character to right (in entry bar)	Del (extended keyboard)

Table A-15
Word Processing Menu Commands

Command	Key Sequence	Menu
Apply Ruler	Shift-⌘-V	Format
Copy Ruler	Shift-⌘-C	Format
Insert Column Break	Enter	Format
Insert Footnote	Shift-⌘-F	Format
Insert Page Break	Shift-Enter	Format
Insert Section Break	⌘-Enter	Format
Move Above	Control-up arrow	Outline
Move Below	Control-down arrow	Outline
Move Left	Shift-⌘-L/Control-left arrow	Outline
Move Right	Shift-⌘-R/Control-right arrow	Outline
New Topic Left	⌘-L	Outline
New Topic Right	⌘-R	Outline
Subscript	Shift-⌘-- (hyphen)	Style
Superscript	Shift-⌘-+	Style

Table A-16
Word Processing Navigation Commands

Command	Key Sequence
Move up one line	Up arrow
Move down one line	Down arrow
Move left one character	Left arrow
Move right one character	Right arrow
Move to beginning of document	⌘-up arrow
Move to end of document	⌘-down arrow
Move to beginning of line	⌘-left arrow

(continued)

Table A-16 *(continued)*

Command	Key Sequence
Move to end of line	⌘-right arrow
Move to beginning of paragraph	Option-up arrow
Move to end of paragraph	Option-down arrow
Move to beginning of word	Option-left arrow
Move to end of word	Option-right arrow

Table A-17
Other Word Processing Commands

Command	Key Sequence
Accept footnote entry and return to main body of document	Enter
New outline topic at same level	⌘-Return
New outline topic with same format as previous topic	Return
Select outline topic and its subtopics	Shift-Control-Spacebar
Select text from insertion point to beginning of document	Shift-⌘-up arrow
Select text from insertion point to end of document	Shift-⌘-down arrow
Select text from insertion point to beginning of paragraph	Shift-Option-up arrow
Select text from insertion point to end of paragraph	Shift-Option-down arrow
Show/Hide invisible characters	⌘-;

Shortcuts for Dialog Box Buttons

With the exception of the *default button* in dialog boxes (a button surrounded by a double line that you can select by pressing Enter or Return), you normally have to use the mouse to click buttons. But some people are lazy. Dragging the mouse to the correct position just so you can click a button sometimes seems like more work than it's worth. Recognizing this fact, Claris built keyboard shortcuts into ClarisWorks dialog boxes so you can click buttons from the keyboard.

To click a dialog box button using the keyboard, press the ⌘ key while the dialog box is on screen. Any button that has a ⌘-key equivalent will change to display the proper keystrokes inside the button (see Figure A-1).

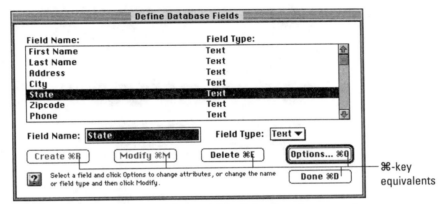

Figure A-1: In the Define Database Fields dialog box, for example, the Create, Modify, Delete, Options, and Done buttons have ⌘-key equivalents.

Spreadsheet and Database Function Definitions

Appendix B is a complete reference to the spreadsheet and database functions of ClarisWorks 5.0. The functions are listed alphabetically. Each section includes the format for the function (that is, how it is entered in a worksheet or database formula, along with the types of arguments required), a description of how the function works, and one or more examples for the spreadsheet and database environments.

Note

Some functions are available in the spreadsheet environment only; they cannot be used in a database. These functions are listed with the following text: *This is a spreadsheet-only function.* Note also that some functions have optional arguments. Such arguments are surrounded by bracket symbols ({}).

ABS (Absolute Value)

Format: ABS (number)

ABS is used to calculate the absolute value of a worksheet cell address, a number, or a database field, ignoring the result's sign. The result is either a positive number or zero. ABS is used when you are interested in the magnitude of a number or a difference, irrespective of the sign. Note that the absolute value of an empty cell or field returns a value of zero (0).

Spreadsheet examples: The formula =ABS(-17.35) returns 17.35; =ABS(18-A3) returns 5, where cell A3 evaluates as 23; =ABS(C7) returns 18.5, where cell C7 evaluates as either 18.5 or -18.5; =ABS(B4) returns 0, where cell B4 contains the number zero, evaluates as zero (as in the formula =5-5), or is blank.

Database examples: The formula ABS('GRADE 1'-'Grade 2') can be used to evaluate the difference between two Grade fields. The result, however, shows only the magnitude of the difference between the two grades; that is, it is a measure of change, not the direction of the change (whether the grade improved or became worse).

ACOS (Arc Cosine)

Format: ACOS (number)

ACOS calculates the arc cosine (inverse of a cosine), returning an angle in radians between 0 and π. Taking the cosine of the result produces the argument to the function.

The argument to ACOS must be a number between -1.0 and 1.0 or an operation that yields a value within that range. (**Note:** If a blank cell or blank field is used as an argument, ACOS treats the blank as though it contains a zero.)

Spreadsheet examples: =ACOS(3/4) returns 0.7227 radians; =ACOS(0) returns 1.5708; =ACOS(1) returns 0; =ACOS(-2/3) returns 2.3005 radians; =ACOS(-1) returns 3.14159 or π.

Database examples: ACOS('Field 1') returns the arc cosine of the field.

ALERT

Format: ALERT (message {, type})

ALERT displays a dialog box with a message of your choosing (message). If the Type number (discussed below) is omitted, the alert box includes only an OK button that the user must click to dismiss the alert. When the alert is triggered, the contents of the ALERT message are entered into the current cell.

New In
Version 5

By including an optional Type number, you can specify the buttons that appear in the alert box, as shown in the following table. Depending on the button clicked, either a 0 or 1 is returned in the current cell. You can then create other formulas that take different actions based on the returned value.

Type Number	Buttons	Default Choice	Values Returned
1	OK; Cancel	OK	OK = 1; Cancel = 0
2	Yes; No	Yes	Yes = 1; No = 0
3	OK; Cancel	Cancel	OK = 1; Cancel =0

Because a text message is part of an ALERT, this function may be preferred to that of BEEP, which only plays the current system sound. *This is a spreadsheet-only function.*

Spreadsheet examples: =IF(C12<0,ALERT("Accept a score less than zero?",2),"") asks how you wish to handle a negative number that was entered in cell C12. The 2 at the end of the formula instructs ClarisWorks to present Yes and No buttons in the alert box. An alternate formula =IF(C12<0,ALERT("This score is less than zero"),"") simply notifies you that a negative number was entered in the same cell, and returns only the alert message.

AND

Format: AND (logical1, logical2, ...)

AND enables you to evaluate one or more arguments or conditions, and returns TRUE if all arguments or conditions are true; otherwise, it returns FALSE.

Spreadsheet examples: The formula =AND(A1>50000,B1<35) could be used to identify individuals with salaries of more than $50,000 who are less than 35 years old. =AND(D3) returns true if D3 contains any number other than zero.

Database examples: To determine if a customer is eligible for a special discount, you could use a formula such as: AND('Product Total'>250,'MemberTime'>3). This equation yields a 1 (TRUE) only if the current order is for more than $250 of goods and the individual has been a member of the club or service for more than three years.

ASIN (Arc Sine)

Format: ASIN (number)

The ASIN function is used to calculate the inverse of a sine (the arc sine). The result is an angle in radians in the range $-\pi/2$ to $\pi/2$. The argument to ASIN must be a sine value (a number between -1.0 and 1.0) or a simple operation that yields a sine.

Spreadsheet examples: =ASIN(1) returns 1.570796; =ASIN(-1) returns -1.570796; =ASIN(0) returns 0; =ASIN(0.75) returns 0.848062.

ATAN (Arc Tangent)

Format: ATAN (number)

The ATAN function calculates the inverse of a tangent (the arc tangent). The result is an angle in radians in the range $-\pi/2$ to $\pi/2$.

Spreadsheet example: The formula =ATAN(1) returns 0.7854.

ATAN2 (Arc Tangent 2)

Format: ATAN2 (x number, y number)

The ATAN2 function calculates the angle in radians between the positive X axis and a line that starts at the origin (coordinates 0, 0) and passes through the specified X and Y coordinates. The result is an angle in radians, in the range $-\pi$ to π (or -3.14159 to 3.14159).

Spreadsheet examples: The formula =DEGREES(ATAN2(5,5)) returns 45, indicating that a straight diagonal line (passing through coordinate 0,0 and 5,5) is a 45-degree angle.

AVERAGE

Format: AVERAGE (number1, number2, ...)

AVERAGE calculates the arithmetic average of a set of numbers expressed as numbers, cell references, a range, or field names. The formula for an AVERAGE is the sum of the numbers divided by the number of numbers in the set.

Spreadsheet examples: =AVERAGE(7,12,5) returns 8 (that is, 24/3); =AVERAGE(A1...A5) returns 10, where cells A1, A2, A3, A4, and A5 contain 12, 4, 8, 16, and 10, respectively (that is, 50/5).

Database example: You could use AVERAGE('SCORE 1','SCORE 2') to determine the average of the two scores for each record.

BASETONUM

Format: BASETONUM (text, base)

BASETONUM examines a text string and interprets it as a number in the specified base (between 1 and 36). The text string must be less than 256 characters long.

Spreadsheet example: The formula =BASETONUM(10110,2) returns 22; that is, the base 2 number 10110 is 22.

BEEP

Format: BEEP ()

BEEP plays the alert sound that is currently set in the Sound control panel. You can use BEEP to notify you of an unusual or important situation, such as a data entry error.

Spreadsheet example: =IF(C12<0,BEEP(),IF(C12>4,BEEP(),"")) could be used to notify you of a numeric grade in cell C12 that was out of range; that is, less than 0 or greater than 4.

Database example: IF('Due Date'< NOW( ),BEEP(),"Due in "&'Due Date'-TRUNC(NOW())&" days.") could be used to let you know when a project is overdue. If the due date for a record has passed ('Due Date'< NOW()), a beep is sounded. If the due date still lies ahead, on the other hand, a message is displayed in the field, as in: "Due in 10 days."

CHAR (Character)

Format: CHAR (number)

The CHAR function returns the ASCII (American Standard Code for Information Interchange) character that corresponds to the number in the specified cell or database field. If the number contains a fractional part, the fraction is discarded when the number is evaluated.

Note that ASCII codes can vary between 0 and 255. Numbers outside of that range return an error. Also, depending on the font selected, not all codes have an associated character, and codes less than 32 are control characters. In general, codes between 32 and 127 correspond to the normal typewriter letters, numbers, and symbols, while codes above 127 correspond to the foreign language characters and special symbols. Non-Roman fonts (such as Zapf Dingbats) may display decidedly different characters from Roman fonts (such as Times).

Spreadsheet examples: =CHAR(68) returns a D; =CHAR(154) returns an ö.

Database example: CHAR('ITEMNO')

CHOOSE

Format: CHOOSE (index, value1, value2,...)

The CHOOSE function is used to select a value from an array of values. The value of the index argument (a number or numeric expression) determines which value in the array is chosen. The values in the array can contain text or numeric expressions.

Spreadsheet examples: The formula =CHOOSE(2,15,"Apple",7,"Medium",15) returns Apple; the formula =CHOOSE(B6,"Sunday","Monday","Tuesday","Wednesday", "Thursday","Friday","Saturday") returns a day of the week, assuming that cell B6 contains an index value between 1 and 7; and the formula =CHOOSE(4, B1, B2, B3, B4, B5) returns the contents of cell B4.

CODE (ASCII Code)

Format: CODE (text)
CODE returns the ASCII code (American Standard Code for Information Interchange) of the first character in the text string of a selected cell or field.
Spreadsheet examples: =CODE("a") returns 97; =CODE("Schwartz") returns 83, which corresponds to the code for a capital S; the formula =IF(OR(CODE(A1)<65, CODE(A1)>90),"Not a capital letter","Okay") could be used to check if a cell's text begins with a capital letter. Any character outside of the range A–Z results in the message: *Not a capital letter.*
Database example: A similar formula to the error-checking formula above can be used to check that each last name begins with a capital letter, as in: IF(OR(CODE('Last Name')<65,CODE('Last Name')>90),"Error in Last Name","OK")

COLUMN

Format: COLUMN ({cell})
Returns the number of the column referenced by cell or the column in which the current cell is contained. *This is a spreadsheet-only function.*
Spreadsheet examples: =COLUMN(C12) returns 3, since Column C is the third column; =COLUMN() returns the column in which the formula is located.

Tip

If you want to number a group of columns beginning with Column A quickly, enter the formula =COLUMN() in Column A, highlight that cell as well as the appropriate cells to the right, and then choose Fill Right from the Calculate menu (or press ⌘-R).

CONCAT (Concatenation)

Format: CONCAT (text1, text2,…)
CONCAT is used to join text strings, producing a single text string as a result.
Spreadsheet examples: =CONCAT(A1," ",B1) returns *Steve Schwartz* when A1 contains "Steve" and B1 contains "Schwartz". Note that text strings also can be concatenated with the & symbol, as in: =A1 & " " & B1.
Database examples: CONCAT can be used to create a new field that combines First Name and Last Name fields into a single Name field, as in: CONCAT('First Name'," ", 'Last Name'). To generate a sentence in a merge form, you could use CONCAT in the following manner: CONCAT("Your commission is $",'Commission',".").

COS (Cosine)

Format: COS (number)
COS calculates the cosine of a number, where the number is an angle in radians.
Spreadsheet example: =COS(1) returns 0.5403.

COUNT

Format: COUNT (value1, value2,...)

Count is used to display the number of values (numbers, text, cell or range references, or formulas) in a list. Empty worksheet cells or database fields are not counted.

Spreadsheet examples: The formula =COUNT(B1, B2*3, 5) returns 2 or 3, depending on whether cell B1 is blank. Note that even if B2 is blank, the formula B2*3 still adds one to the count.

One typical use of COUNT is to determine the number of non-empty cells in a range, such as =COUNT(C1..C10). To display the number of blank cells, the previous formula could be changed to read: =10-(COUNT(C1..C10)).

Database example: Suppose you want to calculate an average of four numeric fields, but some of the fields may be empty. If you use the AVERAGE function, the results would be erroneous because AVERAGE treats the missing fields as though they each contain zero (0) and then divides by four. To calculate a true average, you can use the COUNT function, as follows:

```
('q1'+'q2'+'q3'+'q4')/COUNT('q1','q2','q3','q4')
```

COUNT2

Format: COUNT2 (search value, value1, value2,...)

Use COUNT2 to show the number of values in a list that match the specified search value. The values can be numbers, text, cells, or fields.

Note that when COUNT2 is used in a database formula, a separate value is returned for each record. COUNT2 does not summarize a search across all records. Note, too, that COUNT2 does not count instances in which the search value is embedded in a text string or sentence. For example, in a database, COUNT2("Macintosh",'Comments') only counts instances in which the Comments field contains only the word *Macintosh*.

Spreadsheet examples: The formula =COUNT2(4,3,7,4,-1) yields 1, since there is only a single instance of the search value (that is, 4) in the list. The formula =COUNT2(0,A1..A20) returns the number of cells in the range that contain 0. In an address book worksheet, the formula =COUNT2("CA",G2..G400) could be used to count the number of cells in the range for which CA was entered as the state (assuming that Column G was used to enter state information).

Database example: COUNT2(100,'Score1','Score2','Score3') counts the number of times 100 was achieved as a score in the three fields.

DATE

Format: DATE (year, month, day)

Use the DATE function to convert a date to a serial number that represents the number of days since January 1, 1904.

Spreadsheet examples: =DATE(1995,9,21) yields 33501. If you have spread the components of a date across cells A1 through C1 in month, day, year order, the formula =DATE(C1,A1,B1) could be used to combine them.

Database examples: If a date has been entered as three separate components, each in its own field, you could use the following formula to combine it into a single field: DATETOTEXT(DATE('Ship Year','Ship Month','Ship Day')). The DATE portion of the formula creates a serial number from the three date components; the DATETOTEXT function changes the serial number into a normal date, such as 9/21/95.

DATETOTEXT

Format: DATETOTEXT (serial number {, format number})

The DATETOTEXT function changes a serial number (the number of days that have passed since January 1, 1904) to a normal date in a particular format. Format options are as follows:

0 = 10/15/95 (the default format)

1 = Oct 15, 1995

2 = October 15, 1995

3 = Sun, Oct 15, 1995

4 = Sunday, October 15, 1995

Spreadsheet examples: =DATETOTEXT(33525,1) yields Oct 15, 1995; =DATETOTEXT(33525) yields 10/15/95, the default date format; =DATETOTEXT(A7,1) yields Nov 5, 1995 when cell A7 contains a date or serial number that represents 11/5/95.

The latter example illustrates a way to convert one date format to another — just change the format number in the formula. Of course, you could also use the spreadsheet's Format Number command to select a different date format.

DAY

Format: DAY (serial number)

For any serial number, DAY returns the day of the month.

Spreadsheet examples: =DAY(33525) yields 15, since the serial number 33525 represents October 15, 1995.

You can also use the DAY function to extract the day number from a formatted date. The formula =DAY(A9) yields 7 when A9 contains a date, regardless of how it is formatted (for example, 12/7/95 or Thu, Dec 7, 1995).

Database example: DAY('DATE')

DAYNAME

Format: DAYNAME (number)
DAYNAME converts a number between 1 and 7 into the appropriate day name, as follows:

Number	Day Name
1	Sunday
2	Monday
3	Tuesday
4	Wednesday
5	Thursday
6	Friday
7	Saturday

Note that the argument to the DAYNAME function must always be, or evaluate to, a number between 1 and 7. Anything else, such as a complete date or a serial number, will result in an error.

Spreadsheet examples: =DAYNAME(5) yields Thursday.

Tip

One use for the DAYNAME function is to create worksheet headings that list the days of the week. To create them as column headings, enter the formula =DAYNAME(COLUMN()) into Column A, and then use the Fill Right command (⌘-R) to add the formula to the cells in Columns B through G. To create day name row headings, enter the formula =DAYNAME(ROW()) into Row 1, and then use the Fill Down command (⌘-D) to add the formula to the cells in Rows 2 through 7.

DAYOFYEAR

Format: DAYOFYEAR (serial number)
DAYOFYEAR extracts the day of the year from a serial number. Note that this function also works on formatted dates.
Spreadsheet examples: =DAYOFYEAR(33525) yields 288, where 33525 is the serial number for October 15, 1995; =DAYOFYEAR(33247) yields 10, where 33247 is the serial number for January 10, 1995.
Database example: DAYOFYEAR('DATE')

DEGREES

Format: DEGREES (radians number)
The DEGREES function converts radians to the corresponding number of degrees.
Spreadsheet examples: =DEGREES(1.58) returns 90.5273; =DEGREES(1) returns 57.29578; =DEGREES(-3) returns -171.8873; =DEGREES(π()) returns 180; =DEGREES(-(π())) returns -180.

ERROR

Format: ERROR ()
The ERROR function returns *#ERROR!* It has no arguments.
Spreadsheet examples: The formula =IF(C2>2,ERROR(),"OK") returns *#ERROR!* if the value in cell C2 is greater than 2; otherwise, it returns *OK*. If you only want the erroneous condition to return a text string, the formula could be changed to read: =IF(C2>2,ERROR(),"").
Database example: You can use the ERROR() function to report the result of a test on a field, as in: IF('Hours'<0,ERROR(),"OK!").

EXACT

Format: EXACT (text1, text2)
EXACT compares two text strings, and returns TRUE when the two strings are identical — including case. Otherwise, it returns FALSE.
Spreadsheet examples: =EXACT(A1,A2) returns true only when the contents of cells A1 and A2 are identical. The formula =EXACT("Minnesota",B5) returns FALSE if cell B5 contains anything other than the string *Minnesota*. If B5 held MINNESOTA, the formula would still return FALSE, since the case of the two strings is different.
Database example: EXACT('Last Name','First Name') returns 1 (True) when the contents of the Last Name field matches that of the First Name field; otherwise, it returns 0 (False).

EXP (Exponent)

Format: EXP (number)
EXP calculates e to the power of the argument.
Spreadsheet examples: =EXP(1) yields 2.718281; =EXP(2) yields 7.389 (or e^2).

FACT (Factorial)

Format: FACT (number)
FACT calculates the factorial of any positive whole number. Factorials of negative numbers or real numbers produce errors. Note that the factorials of 0 and 1 are both 1.
Spreadsheet examples: =FACT(3) returns 6 (or 3*2*1); =FACT(4) returns 24 (or 4*3*2*1); =FACT(B7) returns 120 when cell B7 contains, or evaluates as, 5.

FIND

Format: FIND (find-text, in-text {, start-offset})
The FIND function searches the text specified in in-text and attempts to locate an occurrence of the search string (find-text). It returns the position of the first instance that it finds, if any. (0 is returned if the find-text is not found.)
Optionally, you can specify a character starting position by adding the start-offset; that is, the number of characters from the beginning of the text string. Each search is case-sensitive and blanks are counted.

Spreadsheet examples: The formula =FIND("Beth","Where is Beth?") returns 10; =FIND("BETH","Where is Beth?") returns 0 because the case of the find-text does not match that of the text within the string that was searched.

Adding a start-offset, such as =FIND("Beth","Where is Beth?",5) makes the formula begin its search with the fifth character in in-text. The result is still 10, since Beth is found starting at the tenth character of in-text. On the other hand, if a start-offset of 11 was used, Beth would not be found and a result of 0 (zero) would be presented.

FRAC (Fraction)

Format: FRAC (number)

The FRAC function calculates the fractional part of a real number. The result is always a positive number.

Spreadsheet examples: The formula =FRAC(17.237) returns 0.237, the part of the number to the right of the decimal point; the formula =FRAC(-123.7) returns 0.7; and the formula =FRAC(10) returns 0 (zero).

Database example: FRAC('Hours') returns the fractional portion of the number in the Hours field.

FV (Future Value)

Format: FV (rate, nper, pmt {, pv} {, type})

FV calculates the future value of an investment, given a particular interest rate per period (*rate*) and number of periods (*nper*). Specifying the present value of the investment (pv) and the payment type (*type*) are optional. The default type is 0, indicating that the payment is made at the end of the first period. A type of 1 means that the payment is made at the beginning of each period.

The rate can be entered as a percentage (9.5%) or a decimal (.095). Payment amounts and the present value should be entered as negative numbers, since they represent money paid out.

Spreadsheet examples: The formula =FV(10%,10,-500) returns $7968.71, the future value of an annual investment of $500 for 10 years at an interest rate of 10%. Because the type was not indicated, it is assumed that each yearly investment is made on the last day of the year. On the other hand, if the annual investment was made on the first day of each year, as shown in the revised formula =FV(10%,10,-500,0,1), the result is $8765.58 — a gain of almost $800. To calculate the future value of an initial investment of $10,000 with annual additions of $1,000 at an interest rate of 5.5% over a five-year period (with each addition made at the beginning of the year), you would use this formula:

```
=FV(5.5%,5,-1000,-10000,1)
```

returning an answer of $18,957.65.

Note

If the interest is compounded more frequently than the investments are made, you should enter the *APR* (annualized percentage rate) rather than the purported rate.

HLOOKUP (Horizontal Lookup)

Format: HLOOKUP (lookup value, compare range, offset {, method})
HLOOKUP checks the top row of the compare range for the lookup value. If the search condition is met, the row number of the found cell is increased by the amount of the offset and the function returns the contents of the new cell. If the search condition is not met, an error is returned.

Specifying a method is optional. When the values in the first row are arranged in increasing order, use a method of 1 to find the largest value that is less than or equal to the lookup value. When the values in the first row are arranged in decreasing order, use a method of -1 to find the smallest value that is greater than or equal to the lookup value. Use a method of 0 to accept only an exact match. *This is a spreadsheet-only function.*

Spreadsheet example: In the grading spreadsheet shown in Figure B-1, the formula =HLOOKUP(A5,A1..F2,1,1) in cell B5 examines the numeric score that has been entered in cell A5 and then returns the letter grade to be assigned. The compare range (A1..F2) contains the possible scores in the top row (the row that the function searches), and the corresponding letter grades are listed in the second row. Note that the scores in Row 1 represent the minimum score required to achieve a particular grade.

Figure B-1: A grading worksheet that uses the HLOOKUP function

HOUR

Format: HOUR (serial number)
The Macintosh represents the current date and time as a single serial number, such as 34202.346644, for August 22, 1997 at 8:19AM. The date portion of the number is to the left of the decimal; the time is to the right of the decimal. The HOUR function extracts the hour from the time portion of a serial number (the numbers to the right of the decimal point). The return value is a whole number between 0 and 23.

Spreadsheet examples: The formula =HOUR(33370.80478) returns 19 (for 7 PM); =HOUR(33370.402) returns 9 (for 9 AM).

To calculate the current hour, you can use the formula =HOUR(NOW()).

Database example: HOUR('TIME')

IF

Format: IF (logical, true value, false value)
Use IF to perform a conditional test. If the test condition is fulfilled, the true value is displayed or performed. If the test condition is not fulfilled, the false value is displayed or performed.
Spreadsheet examples: The formula =IF(A10=1053,"You're rich! You picked today's number!","Too bad. Try again.") could be used to check cell A10 for the winning number for today's lottery. If the number found is 1053, the first message (the true value) is displayed. If any other number is found, the second message (the false value) is displayed.
The formula =IF(B7,2,4) displays 2 if B7 contains any value at all, but shows 4 if the cell is blank.
Database example: IF('Result'>0,"Positive trend","Negative trend or no change").

INDEX

Format: INDEX (range, row, column)
The INDEX function is used to reference the contents of a cell that is *x* number of rows and *y* number of columns away from the first cell in the range. The referenced cell must be within the specified range. *This is a spreadsheet-only function.*
Spreadsheet examples: =INDEX(A55..C63,7,2) returns the contents of cell B61, seven cells down in the range and in the second column of the range.

New In
Version 5

Because the first argument to the Index function is a range, you can also use a named range. For example, a column might contain the names of the months of the year for which you have created a named range called Months. The formula =INDEX(Months,5,1) would return May.

INT (Integer)

Format: INT (number)
The INT function returns the integer (whole number) closest to the value of the argument number. For any positive number, INT simply returns the integer portion of that number (the same as the TRUNC function). For negative numbers, the argument number is rounded down to the next lowest whole number.
Spreadsheet examples: =INT(4.53) returns 4; =INT(-2.33) returns -3; =INT(0.321) returns 0; =INT(-0.321) returns -1.
Database example: INT('Item 1'+'Item 2').

IRR (Internal Rate of Return)

Format: IRR (range {, guess})

IRR is an approximate interest rate returned on an investment consisting of a series of payments (negative values) and income (positive values). If an optional initial guess for the internal rate of return is not entered, a default rate of 10% is used. If a result is not obtained within 20 iterations, the function returns a #NUM! error.

The range contains future cash flow amounts in the order that they are paid out or received. The first amount is the amount of the initial investment and is entered as a negative number. *This is a spreadsheet-only function.*

Spreadsheet example: When formatted as a percent, the formula =IRR(B1..B5) returns 6.65% when B1..B5 contains -10000, 2000, 2500, 2500, 5000.

ISBLANK

Format: ISBLANK (value)

The ISBLANK function enables you to distinguish between blank cells or fields and those that contain an entry. If the cell is empty, ISBLANK returns TRUE. If the cell contains text or a number, ISBLANK returns FALSE. When ISBLANK is used in a ClarisWorks database, the return values are 1 and 0 rather than TRUE and FALSE, respectively.

Spreadsheet examples: =ISBLANK(5.45), =ISBLANK(0), and =ISBLANK("IDG") return FALSE. The formula =ISBLANK(B6) returns TRUE only if cell B6 is empty; otherwise, it returns FALSE.

Database example: =ISBLANK('Last Name') returns 1 if the contents of the Last Name field is empty; otherwise, it returns 0 (zero).

ISERROR

Format: ISERROR (value {, error type})

The ISERROR function is used to check for errors in expressions. Optionally, ISERROR can check for a specific type of error, rather than errors of any type. ISERROR returns TRUE or FALSE in a worksheet, and 1 or 0 in a database. Error types that can optionally be included are:

Error Type	Explanation
#ARG!	Incorrect number of arguments or argument type
#DATE!	Incorrect date
#DIV/0!	Divide by zero
#ERROR!	Not a true error
#N/A!	Not available
#NUM!	Incorrect number
#REF!	Reference to incorrect cell
#TIME!	Incorrect time
#USER!	User-defined error
#VALUE!	Incorrect value

Spreadsheet examples: The formula =ISERROR(F5) examines the contents of cell F5 and returns FALSE (if there is no error in cell F5) or TRUE (if there is an error in cell F5). The formula =ISERROR(F5,#DIV/0!) examines cell F5 and returns TRUE if it contains a divide by zero error. If it contains no error or an error of another type, it returns FALSE.

Database example: The formula ISERROR('Division Result',#DIV/0!) checks the field called Division Result and displays a 1 (TRUE) if a divide by zero error is detected. Other errors or no error result in a returned value of 0 (FALSE).

ISLOGICAL

Format: ISLOGICAL (value)

The ISLOGICAL function determines whether the argument contains a Boolean expression; that is, one which can be evaluated as either TRUE or FALSE. If so, ISLOGICAL returns TRUE; otherwise, it returns FALSE.

Spreadsheet examples: The formula =ISLOGICAL(1.5>4) returns TRUE because the argument is a Boolean expression. As this example shows, it doesn't matter whether the expression is true or false; only that it is a Boolean expression. The formula =ISLOGICAL(C1) checks to see if cell C1 contains a Boolean expression.

ISNA (Is Not Available)

Format: ISNA (value)

ISNA checks for the presence of the #N/A! (Not Available) error. If that specific error is found, TRUE is returned. If no error (or an error of another type) is found, FALSE is returned. Because the MATCH, LOOKUP, VLOOKUP, and HLOOKUP functions may return an #N/A! error, ISNA can be used to check the results of formulas that include these functions. *This is a spreadsheet-only function.*

Spreadsheet examples: The formula =ISNA("Happy!") returns FALSE, since "Happy!" is a text expression and not the #N/A! error. The formula =ISNA(C3) returns TRUE only if cell C3 contains the #N/A! error. The formula =ISNA(NA()) returns TRUE because NA() is the Not Available error.

ISNUMBER

Format: ISNUMBER (value)

The ISNUMBER function enables you to check the contents of a cell or database field for the presence of a number. If the cell contains a number, ISNUMBER returns TRUE. If the cell contains text or is blank, FALSE is returned.

When ISNUMBER is used in a ClarisWorks database, the return values are 1 and 0 (rather than TRUE and FALSE, respectively). Note, however, that ISNUMBER is seldom used in ClarisWorks databases because:

✦ Number fields can only contain numbers, so there's no reason to check them further.

✦ A number found in a Text field is treated as text, so ISNUMBER always returns 0 (false).

✦ When importing data, text in Number fields is ignored (so there's no reason to use ISNUMBER to check for import errors).

On the other hand, ISNUMBER can be used to check for blank Number fields, much as the ISBLANK function is used. For blank fields, ISNUMBER returns 0 (false), while ISBLANK returns 1 (true).

Spreadsheet examples: The formula =ISNUMBER(17.235) returns TRUE; =ISNUMBER(Apple) returns FALSE; =ISNUMBER(D5) returns TRUE if cell D5 contains a number or a formula that results in a number, or returns FALSE if the cell contains text or is empty.

Database example: ISNUMBER('Amount') returns 0 (false) if the Amount number field is empty; otherwise, it returns 1 (true).

ISTEXT

Format: ISTEXT (value)

The ISTEXT function is used to determine whether an expression is text, or a cell reference, function, or number that evaluates as text. ISTEXT always returns either TRUE or FALSE.

Applying the ISTEXT function to cells that contain dates or times can give confusing results. If a date or time is entered directly (as 1/12/96 or 4:43, for example), it is a number; ISTEXT returns FALSE. However, if a date or time is entered as text (="1/12/95"), ISTEXT returns TRUE. Finally, if a slash- or dash-delimited date is entered with a century (as in 12/14/1996), it is treated as text by ISTEXT and returns TRUE.

Spreadsheet examples: The formula =ISTEXT(D2) returns TRUE if the cell contains text, or a cell reference, function, or number that evaluates as text; =ISTEXT(Snakes) and =ISTEXT("24 Sapperstein Way") both return TRUE; =ISTEXT(147) and =ISTEXT(PI()) both return FALSE. The complex formula =ISTEXT(123/5 &" is the answer") returns TRUE. Although the formula contains numeric data, the result of the calculation is text (that is, *24.6 is the answer*).

LEFT

Format: LEFT (text, number of characters)

The LEFT function returns a text string that contains the number of characters specified, counting from the leftmost character in the target text string. Note that if the target text string contains fewer characters than the number specified in the LEFT function, those characters that are present are returned. Also, the LEFT function can be applied to numbers, but the returned value is text.

Spreadsheet examples: =LEFT("123 Williams Avenue",3) returns 123; =LEFT(Samuel Smith,3) returns Sam; =LEFT(47259,4) returns 4725; =LEFT(Apple,12) returns Apple, since there are fewer than 12 characters in the string.

Database example: LEFT('ID',5) returns the leftmost five characters of the contents of the ID field.

If you have a worksheet or database that contains nine-digit zip codes, you can convert them to five-digit codes by using the LEFT function, as follows:

In a worksheet: =LEFT(C1,5)

In a database: LEFT('ZIP Code',5)

Similarly, if you have a worksheet or database that holds phone numbers that are formatted as 303-772-0054, you can extract the area code with the following formulas:

In a worksheet: =LEFT(F1,3)

In a database: LEFT('Phone Number',3)

LEN (Length)

Format: LEN (text)

LEN counts the number of characters in a text string. Spaces, numbers, and special characters also count toward the total.

Spreadsheet examples: =LEN(A1) returns 16, where A1 contains the string "Washington, D.C." The formula =IF(LEN(A1)>5,BEEP(),) checks the length of the text string in cell A1, and beeps if it contains more than five characters. Otherwise, it does nothing.

Database examples: The formula LEN('Last Name') returns the number of characters in the Last Name field.

LN (Natural Log)

Format: LN (number)

LN calculates the natural logarithm of a positive number.

Spreadsheet example: The formula =LN(5) returns 1.6094.

LOG

Format: LOG (number {, base})

The LOG function calculates the logarithm of a positive number to a base. If no base is specified, it is assumed to be base 10.

Spreadsheet examples: The formula =LOG(5) returns 0.69897; =LOG(5,2) returns 2.3219.

LOG10 (Log to Base 10)

Format: LOG10 (number)

LOG10 calculates the logarithm of a number to base 10; it is the inverse of the number *e* in scientific notation.

Spreadsheet examples: The formula =LOG10(1000) returns 3; =LOG10(10000) returns 4.

LOOKUP

Format: LOOKUP (lookup value, compare range, result range {, method})

The LOOKUP function searches for the lookup value row-by-row within the compare range and then returns the value of the corresponding cell in the result range. It is assumed that the values in the compare range are organized in ascending order — going from left to right and top to bottom. If they are arranged in descending order, enter -1 for the optional method.

When the search is conducted, ClarisWorks seeks the largest number that is less than or equal to the lookup value. If no cell satisfies the search criteria, an error is returned. *This is a spreadsheet-only function.*

Spreadsheet example: Figure B-2 contains a worksheet that can be used to calculate the amount of postage required for a specific weight of letter. The exact weight is entered in cell A2; the lookup weights and corresponding postage amounts are listed in C2..C11 and D2..D11. The LOOKUP formula presents the answer in cell B2, using the formula:

```
=LOOKUP(IF(TRUNC(A2)=A2,A2,A2+1), C2..C11,D2..D11)
```

The IF function checks the contents of cell A2. If the value in A2 is equal to the truncated value of the same number (i.e., A2 contains a whole number), A2 is used as the lookup value. If A2 contains a fractional portion, an additional ounce (1) is added to it, so A2 +1 is used as the lookup value. (The post office requires that all fractional weights be increased to the next full ounce).

The formula then compares the lookup value to the values in Column C of the worksheet and locates the largest weight value that is less than or equal to the lookup value. It then returns the appropriate postage amount from Column D.

Figure B-2: This small worksheet uses the LOOKUP function to determine the correct postage for a letter of a particular weight.

LOWER

Format: LOWER (text)

The LOWER function converts uppercase letters in text to lowercase letters.

Spreadsheet examples: =LOWER("FuNnY") returns *funny*; =LOWER("Bob lives in DC.") returns *bob lives in dc.*

Database example: The formula LOWER('Comments') converts the entire contents of a Comments field to lowercase letters.

MACRO

Format for macros and buttons: MACRO (name {,type})
Format for AppleScripts: MACRO (name {,type} {, subroutine} {, ...})
Use the MACRO function to execute a named macro, click a button on the button bar, or run an AppleScript. The macro name must be enclosed in quotation marks, spelled correctly, and have the proper capitalization. Refer to ClarisWorks Help for additional details.
Spreadsheet example: The formula =IF(A1,MACRO("Chart"),0) checks cell A1 for the presence of any non-zero number and, if it finds one, the macro named Chart is played.

MATCH

Format: MATCH (lookup value, compare range {, type})
The MATCH function checks a specified range for a matching value and, if it finds one, reports the element number (the position) of that cell within the range. The compare range can contain text or numeric expressions. It is assumed that the values in the compare range are arranged in ascending or descending order, moving from left to right and top to bottom of the range. Optionally, you can enter 1 for the type to indicate an ascending range, -1 to indicate a descending range, or 0 for an exact match (range order is unimportant). *This is a spreadsheet-only function.*
Spreadsheet example: In Figure B-3, the compare range (C1..D7) contains the numbers from 1 to 14 and is shown in light gray. The formula =MATCH(5,C1..D7,1) in cell A1 instructs ClarisWorks to locate the first 5 in the compare range and specifies that the array is arranged in ascending order. The equation reports a match position at the fifth cell in the range (5).

Lookup value   Compare range

Figure B-3: An example of the MATCH function

MAX (Maximum)

Format: MAX (number1, number2,...)
The MAX function returns the largest number in a list of values. This function is often used to identify the largest number in a worksheet column or row. Note that blank cells are ignored when calculating the MAX value for a worksheet range.

Spreadsheet examples: The formula =MAX(17,23,4,19,-111) returns 23; =MAX(5,3,6.27) returns 6.27; =MAX(C2..C25) returns the largest number in the range from cell C2 to C25.

Database example: The formula MAX('Sale 1','Sale 2','Sale 3') identifies the largest of the three sales for each record.

MERGEFIELD

Format: MERGEFIELD (text)

As explained in Chapter 9, a worksheet can also be used as a merge form. Use the MERGEFIELD function to create merge fields in a worksheet. *This is a spreadsheet-only function.*

Spreadsheet example: The formula =MERGEFIELD("First Name") results in <<First Name>> being entered in the cell. When a merge is performed with this worksheet, data from the First Name field will replace the <<First Name>> placeholder.

MID (Middle)

Format: MID (text, start position, number of characters)

MID examines a target text string and returns a string of a specific number of characters, based on the starting position indicated in the formula. Note that when counting character positions, a blank is also considered a character, as are all letters, numbers, and punctuation marks.

Spreadsheet example: =MID("Steven Alan Schwartz",8,2) returns *Al*, since the starting position is the eighth character and the desired string is two characters long.

Database example: Assuming that you have a database with a phone number field and every number is formatted as ### - ### - ####, the formula MID('Phone',5,3) could be used to extract the phone number's exchange.

MIN (Minimum)

Format: MIN (number1, number2,…)

The MIN function returns the smallest number in a list of values. The MIN function is often used to identify the smallest number in a worksheet column or row. Note that blank cells are ignored when calculating the MIN for a worksheet range.

Spreadsheet examples: The formula =MIN(17,23,4,19,-5) returns -5; =MIN(5,3,6.27) returns 3; =MIN(C2..C25) returns the smallest number in the range from cell C2 to C25.

Database example: The formula MIN('Sale 1','Sale 2','Sale 3') identifies the smallest of the three sales for each record.

MINUTE

Format: MINUTE (serial number)

The MINUTE function calculates the minutes for a serial time or date number. Note that in a serial date, the numbers to the right of the decimal represent the time.

Spreadsheet examples: =MINUTE(33374.41288) and =MINUTE(0.41288) both return 54, since the time represented is 9:54 a.m.

MIRR (Modified Internal Rate of Return)

Format: MIRR (safe, risk, values...)

The MIRR function calculates the modified internal rate of return of a series of cash flows, given particular safe and risk investment rates. *Safe* is the rate returned by the investment that finances the negative cash flows; *risk* is the rate at which positive cash flows can be reinvested; and the *values* are the future cash flows. Ranges can also be specified for the values.

Spreadsheet example: The formula =MIRR(5%,15%,C12..C16) returns 18.65% when cells C12..C16 contain the values -5000, 2000, 4000, -2000, and 5000.

MOD (Modulo)

Format: MOD (number, divisor number)

The MOD function returns the remainder when one number is divided by another. The sign of the remainder matches that of the dividend.

Spreadsheet examples: The formula =MOD(5,2) returns 1; =MOD(-5,2) returns -1; and =MOD(5,-2) returns 1. The formula =MOD(5.75,3) returns 2.75. The formula =MOD(16,2) returns 0 because there is no remainder; that is, 2 divides evenly into 16.

MONTH

Format: MONTH (serial number)

The MONTH function converts a date serial number into the number of the corresponding month (1 through 12). MONTH also can be used to extract the month from a numeric date referenced in another cell.

Tip

To calculate the current month, use the formula =MONTH(NOW()).

Spreadsheet examples: The formula =MONTH(23140) returns 5, since this is the serial number for May 10, 1967; =MONTH(B5) returns 4 when cell B5 contains 4-15-85 or April 15, 1985, for example.

Database example: The formula MONTH('Start Date') can be used to extract the month number from a date in the Start Date field.

MONTHNAME

Format: MONTHNAME (number)

The MONTHNAME calculates the text name of a month. Acceptable arguments are the numbers from 1 to 12. Real numbers and numbers that are out of range (less than 1 or greater than 12) return errors.

Spreadsheet examples: The formula =MONTHNAME(5) returns May; =MONTHNAME(12) returns December; =MONTHNAME(B10) returns January, when B10 contains 1 or evaluates as 1.

Database example: The formula MONTHNAME(MONTH('Start Date')) extracts the name of the month from the date in the Start Date field. (**Note:** The nested MONTH function is required in order to reduce the date in Start Date to a month number between 1 and 12 that MONTHNAME can act on.)

NA (Not Available)

Format: NA ()

The NA() function takes no arguments and returns the error value #N/A!

Spreadsheet examples: An IF formula can use the NA() function to force an error for one condition, such as =IF(ISBLANK(E1),NA(),"Okay"). In this instance, if cell E1 is blank, it generates the #N/A! error.

NOT

Format: NOT (logical)

NOT returns the opposite result of a logical expression, in the form TRUE or FALSE. The argument must evaluate as a Boolean expression.

Spreadsheet examples: The formula =NOT(C1) returns TRUE only if C1 evaluates as 0; in all other cases, the formula returns FALSE. The formula =NOT(C1>D1) returns TRUE if C1 is less than or equal to D1; otherwise, it returns FALSE.

You can use a formula in the form =NOT(ISBLANK(D4)) to test for the presence of any value in a cell. If cell D4 contains anything (text, a number, or a formula), the formula returns TRUE; if D4 is empty, it returns FALSE.

NOW

Format: NOW ()

The NOW function returns the current date and time (according to the Macintosh clock), expressed as a serial number (representing the number of days since January 1, 1904). NOW takes no arguments and is written as NOW(). You can update a =NOW() formula to the current date and time by choosing Calculate Now (Shift-⌘-=) from the Calculate menu.

The result of NOW() is shown by default as a serial number. In most cases, however, you'll probably want to show it as a date. NOW() can be displayed in any of several date formats, such as 5/12/95 or May 12, 1995, for example, by assigning a date format to the cell or field.

To set a date format in a worksheet, highlight the cell and select the Number command from the Format menu. To display NOW() as a date in a database field, specify Date as the result type for the calculation. Then choose a date format by changing to Layout mode (Shift-⌘-L), selecting the field, and then choosing Field Format from the Options menu.

Note that you also can express =NOW() as a time rather than a date by setting a time format for the cell or Time as the result type for the database field. The desired time format can be set as discussed above for setting a date format.

Spreadsheet example: The formula =NOW() could return 33369.876875, 5/12/95, May 12, 1995, or Friday, May 12, 1995, depending on how the field was formatted. Note that the fraction in the serial number represents the fractional portion of the day at the moment NOW() was calculated (that is, the number of hours, minutes, and seconds that have elapsed since midnight).

Database example: NOW()

NPER (Number of Periods)

Format: NPER (rate, pmt, pv {, fv} {, type})
NPER is used to calculate the number of periods required for an investment involving constant cash flows. *Rate* is the interest rate per period; *pmt* is the payment to be made each period; *pv* is the present value of the investment; *fv* is the future value of the investment after the last payment is made (fv is optional — if not included, it is assumed to be 0); and *type* represents the payment scheme (type is optional — if included, enter **0** if payments are due at the end of each period or **1** if payments are due at the beginning of each period; 0 is the default).
Spreadsheet example: The formula =NPER(8.75%/12,-250,10000) returns 47.46 as the number of periods (payments) required to pay off a $10,000 loan at an annual rate of 8.75%, assuming that each payment is $250.

NPV (Net Present Value)

Format: NPV (interest rate, payment1, payment2,...)
Use NPV to calculate the net present value of an investment based on a series of future payments or income, assuming a fixed interest rate. *Payments* can be replaced with a range, rather than listing the individual values within the formula.
Spreadsheet example: The formula =NPV (8%, -10000, 0, 12000, 12000, 12000) returns $17,254.08, and represents an initial investment of $10,000 with annual income of $0, $12,000, $12,000, and $12,000.

NUMTOBASE

Format: NUMTOBASE (number, base {, minimum digits})
The NUMTOBASE function converts a number in base 10 to another base and returns a string representing the converted number. *Base* can be any number between 1 and 36. *Minimum* digits is optional and represents the minimum number of digits that will be returned in the result. If the result requires fewer digits, leading zeroes will be added to the result.
Spreadsheet example: The formula =NUMTOBASE(200,2) converts the number 200 to base 2, returning 11001000.

NUMTOTEXT

Format: NUMTOTEXT (number)
NUMTOTEXT changes a number into a text string.
Spreadsheet example: To retain leading zeroes in a set of imported numeric zip codes (for example, 07146), you can change the contents of the cells from numbers to text. (Numbers cannot have leading zeroes.) To add a leading zero to any four-digit codes that are found, you could use this formula:

```
=IF(LEN(D11)<5,"0" & NUMTOTEXT(D11),NUMTOTEXT(D11))
```

This formula examines the contents of a cell (D11, in this instance), and checks to see if it contains fewer than five characters. If there are fewer than five characters, it creates a new zip code by converting the numeric zip code to a text string and appending a zero to the string (as in 04331). If the zip code already contains at least five characters, it also is converted to a text string but passed through unchanged (as in 34412 or 12203-3802).

OR

Format: OR (logical1, logical2,...)
The OR function tests the logical arguments specified and returns TRUE if any argument is true; otherwise, it returns FALSE.
Spreadsheet example: The formula =OR(A1, B1, C1) returns TRUE if any of cells A1, B1, or C1 evaluates as true.
Database example: The formula OR('QTR 1','QTR 2') returns 1 (True) if either of the fields QTR 1 or QTR 2 contains a value.

PI

Format: PI ( )
PI produces the value of π (that is, 3.141592653...). Note that PI has no arguments.
Spreadsheet example: Use =PI()*(A9^2) to calculate the area of a circle, where cell A9 contains the radius.
Database example: PI()*('RADIUS'^2).

PMT (Payment)

Format: PMT (rate, nper, pv {, fv} {, type})
The PMT function is used to calculate payments given a specific interest rate, number of periods, present value, future value, and type of payment. The last two arguments are optional. The *future value* (fv) represents the value of the investment or cash value remaining after the final payment. The default value is 0. Type determines whether payments are due at the beginning (1) or end (0) of each period; 0 is the default.
Spreadsheet example: To calculate monthly payments on a car loan, you could enter =PMT(8.75%/12,36,19000,-9000,1). This indicates an annual percentage rate of 8.75%, a 3-year loan (36 months), a cost (pv) of $19,000, a future value of -$9,000 (the down payment), and that payments are made at the beginning of each period.

PRODUCT

Format: PRODUCT (number1, number2,...)
Product calculates the product of the numbers in the argument list; that is, it multiplies them together.
Spreadsheet examples: The formula =PRODUCT(1.5, 4.5) returns 6.75; =PRODUCT(A1..A3) multiplies the contents of cell A1 times cell A2 times cell A3 (or A1*A2*A3).
Database example: PRODUCT('HEIGHT','WIDTH')

PROPER

Format: PROPER (text)
Use the PROPER function to capitalize the first letter of every word in a cell or field.
Spreadsheet example: =PROPER("Steve's great adventure") returns *Steve's Great Adventure.*
Database example: PROPER('Book Title').

PV (Present Value)

Format: PV (rate, nper, pmt, {, fv} {, type})
PV calculates the present value of an investment; that is, the amount of money you'd have to invest now — in addition to making fixed payments at specific periods getting a fixed interest rate — in order to have *fv* dollars at the end. *Type* is optional; the default of 0 means that payments/investments are made at the end of each period; 1 indicates that payments/investments are made at the beginning of each period.
Spreadsheet example: The formula =PV(8%,36,-250,10000) indicates that to have $10,000 after three years (36 payments) of investing $250 per month at 8% annual return, an initial investment of $2,303.05 is required.

RADIANS

Format: RADIANS (degrees number)
Use RADIANS to convert a number of degrees to radians (standard units for trigonometric functions).
Spreadsheet examples: The formula =RADIANS(45) returns 0.785; =RADIANS(120) returns 2.094.

RAND (Random)

Format: RAND ({number})
Use the RAND function to generate random numbers. If no argument is given, as in RAND(), the returned value is a fraction between 0 and 1. If an argument is given, an integer is returned between 1 and the argument.
Negative arguments are also allowed. For the formula =RAND(-20), an integer between -1 and -20 is returned.

Because the RAND function gives a different answer each time it is calculated, you can instantly generate a new set of random numbers by choosing Calculate Now from the Calculate menu (or pressing Shift-⌘-=).

If you're a lottery fan, you can use the RAND function to generate picks. For example, if your lottery is based on the numbers between 1 and 40 and you must choose six, enter the formula =RAND(40) in a cell, select the cell and the five beneath it, and then choose Fill Down from the Calculate menu (or press ⌘-D). Each time you press Shift-⌘-=, a new set of six random numbers appears. (Note, however, that you may get some duplicate numbers in a set. They are random, after all.)

Spreadsheet examples: =RAND( ) can return any fraction between 0 and 1, such as 0.49774; =RAND(10) returns a whole number between 1 and 10, such as 7; the range and type of random number returned for =RAND(B2) depends on the contents of cell B2.

RATE

Format: RATE (fv, pv, term)
The RATE function is used to determine the interest rate needed for a present value to grow to a given future value over a particular term, where *fv* is the future value of the investment; *pv* is the present value of the investment; and *term* is the number of payments.
Spreadsheet example: The formula =RATE(10000,6000,5) returns 10.76%. It means that if you currently have $6,000 to invest and need it to be worth $10,000 in five years, you must find an investment paying an annual yield of 10.76% to reach your goal.

REPLACE

Format: REPLACE (old text, start number, number of characters, new text)
The REPLACE function is used to replace one text string with another string, starting from the indicated character position and continuing for *x* characters.
Spreadsheet example: The formula =REPLACE(D32,8,4,"Yahoo!") takes the text string in cell D32, counts eight characters into the string, removes four characters (characters 8-11), and inserts the string Yahoo! at that position. Assuming that cell D32 contained *Steven Alan Schwartz*, the cell with the formula specified above would contain *Steven Yahoo! Schwartz*.

REPT (Repeat)

Format: REPT (text, number of times)
The REPT function repeats a given text string the specified number of times.
Spreadsheet examples: The formula =REPT("Hello! ",5) returns Hello! Hello! Hello! Hello! Hello!; =REPT("•",10) returns ••••••••••.

RIGHT

Format: RIGHT (text, number of characters)
The RIGHT function returns a text string that contains the number of characters specified, counting from the last character in the target text string. Note that if the target text string contains fewer characters than the number specified in the RIGHT function, those characters that are present are returned. Note, too, that the RIGHT function can be applied to numbers, but the returned value is text.
Spreadsheet examples: =RIGHT("123 Williams Avenue",6) returns Avenue; =RIGHT(Samuel Smith,5) returns Smith; =RIGHT(47259,4) returns 7259; =RIGHT(Apple,12) returns Apple, since there are fewer than twelve characters in the string.
Database example: You could create a customer identification number by taking the final four digits of his/her phone number or Social Security number, as in RIGHT('Phone',4) or RIGHT('Soc. Sec. #',4).

ROUND

Format: ROUND (number, number of digits)
Use ROUND to specify the number of digits from the decimal point to which a number should be rounded. Note that the number of digits can be positive (to the right of the decimal) or negative (to the left of the decimal).

Spreadsheet examples: =ROUND(A3,2) rounds the contents of cell A3 to two decimal places. If A3 contains 14.33632, the result is 14.34; if A3 contains 14.333, the result is 14.33. The formula =ROUND(4235,-3) produces a result of 4000, while =ROUND(4512,-3) produces a result of 5000.

Database example: ROUND('Grand Total',0) could be used to round a total figure to a whole dollar amount.

ROW

Format: ROW ({cell})

Returns the number of the row referenced by cell or the row in which the current cell is contained (when no argument is included). *This is a spreadsheet-only function.*

Spreadsheet examples: =ROW(C12) returns 12, since cell C12 is in the twelfth row; =ROW() returns the row in which this formula is located.

Tip

If you want to number a group of rows beginning with Row 1 quickly, enter the formula =ROW() in Row 1, highlight that cell as well as the appropriate cells below, and then choose Fill Down from the Calculate menu (or press ⌘-D).

SECOND

Format: SECOND (serial number)

The SECOND function calculates the seconds for a given serial number. It can also return the number of seconds from a normal time.

Spreadsheet examples: The formula =SECOND(NOW()) returns the number of seconds for the current time (press Shift-⌘-= and watch the seconds change); =SECOND(D7) returns 27 when cell D7 contains 1:43:27; =SECOND(0.5003) returns 26.

Database example: SECOND('End Time'-'Start Time').

SIGN

Format: SIGN (number)

SIGN returns the sign of a numeric value. It displays 1 for a positive number, -1 for a negative number, and 0 for zero (or for a blank cell or field).

Spreadsheet examples: =SIGN(-423.75) yields -1; =SIGN(12) yields 1; =SIGN(0) yields 0; =SIGN(A2-3) yields 0, when the contents of cell A2 evaluates as 3. A formula such as the following can use the SIGN function to test cell contents:

```
=IF(SIGN(B5),"OK","Empty or zero")
```

If the sign of the cell is non-zero (either 1 or -1), *OK* is returned. If the cell is blank or evaluates as zero, *Empty or zero* is returned.

SIN (Sine)

Format: SIN (number)

The SIN function calculates the sine of a number, where that number is an angle in radians.

Spreadsheet examples: =SIN(RADIANS(15)) yields 0.25881; =SIN(RADIANS(90)) yields 1.0.

SQRT (Square Root)

Format: SQRT (number)

SQRT calculates the square root of a number. Note that square roots can only be calculated for positive numbers.

Spreadsheet examples: =SQRT(2); =SQRT(5.73); =SQRT(A1); =SQRT(A1+(B7/5))

Database example: SQRT('LENGTH').

STDEV (Standard Deviation)

Format: STDEV (number1, number2,...)

The standard deviation is a measure of how values are spread around the *mean* (average). The larger the standard deviation, the greater the spread. The STDEV function calculates the standard deviation of a population from the list of sample arguments provided. (Note that the standard deviation is simply the square root of the *variance*, another statistical measure of spread; see VAR.)

The formula used to calculate the standard deviation is:

$$\sqrt{\sum_{i=1}^{N} \frac{(X_i - \overline{X})^2}{N-1}}$$

Spreadsheet examples: The formula =STDEV(12,3,15,7.2,8) returns 4.616; =STDEV(125,100,110,115) returns 10.408.

SUM

Format: SUM (number1, number2,...)

SUM adds the numbers in the argument list. The arguments can be numbers, cell references, or database field names. The SUM function is particularly useful for totaling worksheet columns or rows.

Spreadsheet examples: =SUM(A1..A4) adds the contents of cells A1, A2, A3, and A4; =SUM(A1,B5,17.4) adds the contents of cells A1 and B5, and then adds 17.4 to the total; =SUM(B1..B3,5.7,C5) totals the contents of the cells in the range B1..B3, and then adds 5.7 plus the contents of cell C5.

Database examples: SUM('Product Total',5,'Product Total'*.06) could be used to add a fixed shipping charge of $5 and a sales tax of 6% to a customer's order total. This same formula also could be created without using the SUM function, as in: 'Product Total'+5+('Product Total'*.06).

TAN (Tangent)

Format: TAN (number)

The TAN function calculates the tangent of a number, where the argument is an angle in radians.

Spreadsheet example: The formula =TAN(RADIANS(0)) returns 0.

TEXTTODATE

Format: TEXTTODATE (date text)

The TEXTTODATE function is used to convert a date in text form to a date serial number. The date text can be in any acceptable date format.

Although TEXTTODATE normally expects quoted date text as the argument, it also works with cell references that contain date text. The following date styles are treated as text by ClarisWorks and can be used with the TEXTTODATE function:

✦ Any date entered as a formula, such as ="3/5/95", ="5/25/1915", ="7/19/45" or ="Mar 4, 1943"

✦ Any slash- or dash-delimited date that includes the century as part of the year, such as 3/4/1927 and 4-5-1996

✦ Any date with a two-digit year between 00 and 09, such as 5/12/06, 12/18/02, and April 4, 02 (representing dates between the year 2000 and 2009)

Spreadsheet examples: The formula =TEXTTODATE("12/5/96") returns 33942; =TEXTTODATE("Jan 5, 1960") returns 20458; =TEXTTODATE(C1) returns 33942, when C1 contains an acceptable date such as 12/5/1996, ="12/5/96", ="12/5/1996", or ="Dec 5, 1996".

TEXTTONUM

Format: TEXTTONUM (text)

TEXTTONUM converts a text string to its numeric equivalent. Non-numeric characters are ignored when converting the string to a number. (Note that when applied to a number rather than a text string, TEXTTONUM passes the number through unaltered.)

Spreadsheet examples: The formula =TEXTTONUM("$12,453.47") returns 12453.47; =TEXTTONUM("123 Apple Way, Apt. 4") returns 1234 (the numbers are extracted and combined); =TEXTTONUM("(602) 555-1295") returns 6025551295; =TEXTTONUM(B2) returns 477401122, when B2 contains the Social Security number 477-40-1122; =TEXTTONUM(45.67) returns 45.67 (numbers are passed through unaltered).

TEXTTOTIME

Format: TEXTTOTIME (time text)

The TEXTTOTIME function converts a time text string into a time serial number. The text time is expressed in hours, minutes, and seconds order. The seconds and an AM/PM suffix are optional.

Spreadsheet examples: The formula =TEXTTOTIME("1:15 PM") returns 0.5521; =TEXTTOTIME("1:15") returns 0.0521 (times without at AM/PM suffix are assumed to be in 24-hour format); =TEXTTOTIME("10:20:23 PM") returns 0.9308.

TIME

Format: TIME (hour, minute, second)

The TIME function converts a time (based on a 24-hour clock) into a serial number between 0 and 1, representing the fractional portion of the day from midnight. Note that all arguments must be present; those that are not normally needed are represented by zeroes. For example, 7AM would be shown as =TIME(7,0,0); that is, 7 hours, 0 minutes, 0 seconds.

Spreadsheet examples: The formula =TIME(7,45,30) returns 0.3233 (for 7:45:30AM); =TIME(17,30,0) returns 0.7292 (for 5:30PM); =TIME(12,0,0) returns 0.5 (for noon).

Database example: TIME('Hours','Minutes','Seconds') returns a fraction based on the contents of three fields named Hours, Minutes, and Seconds.

TIMETOTEXT

Format: TIMETOTEXT (serial number {, format number})

Use TIMETOTEXT to convert a time serial number to text. (Note that the time portion of a serial number is found to the right of the decimal point. This function also works with a complete serial number, and simply ignores the digits to the left of the decimal point.)

Add an optional format number if you want to specify a format for the time text. If a format number is not entered, ClarisWorks uses format 0. If you mistakenly enter a format number that is out of range (such as -3 or 4), ClarisWorks also treats it as though you requested format 0.

Format Number	Format Applied
0	Hours:Minutes AM/PM (12-hour clock)
1	Hours:Minutes:Seconds AM/PM (12-hour clock)
2	Hours:Minutes (24-hour clock)
3	Hours:Minutes:Seconds (24-hour clock)

Spreadsheet examples: The formulas =TIMETOTEXT(33373.6009375) and =TIMETOTEXT(0.6009375) both return 2:25 PM. Since a format number was not entered, format 0 is used. The formula =TIMETOTEXT(0.653,0) returns 3:40 PM; =TIMETOTEXT(0.653,1) returns 3:40:19 PM; =TIMETOTEXT(0.653,2) returns 15:40; and =TIMETOTEXT(0.653,2) returns 15:40:19.

Note

Applying the TIMETOTEXT function to a serial number has the same effect as selecting a time formatting option from the Number command in the Format menu.

Tip

To display the current time, use the formula =TIMETOTEXT(NOW()).

TRIM

Format: TRIM (text)

The TRIM function removes extra spaces from text strings. Each group of spaces is reduced to a single space. TRIM can be very useful in cleaning up text.

Spreadsheet examples: =TRIM("Woodsbridge, MD   30919") returns Woodsbridge, MD 30919.

Database examples: TRIM('Comments') can be used to remove extraneous spaces in a text field named Comments.

TRUNC (Truncate)

Format: TRUNC (number)

TRUNC discards the decimal portion of the argument number, returning only the whole number that remains.

Spreadsheet examples: =TRUNC(12.365) returns 12; =TRUNC(0.12) returns 0; =TRUNC(-5.67) returns -5.

Database example: Assuming that Total Hours is a calculation field that sums the number of hours worked, the formula TRUNC('Total Hours') returns the number hours worked during the period, ignoring any fractional part of an hour.

TYPE

Format: TYPE (value)

The TYPE function evaluates the contents of the argument and determines its data type. Possible return values are as follows:

Data Type	Returned Value
Blank	1
Logical	2
Number	3
Text	4

Spreadsheet examples: The formula =TYPE(C7) returns 1 if cell C7 is empty; =TYPE(FALSE) and =TYPE(ISBLANK(D3)) both return 2; =TYPE(0.56) and =TYPE(-147) both return 3; =TYPE(Kenneth) and =TYPE("Empire State") both return 4.

UPPER

Format: UPPER (text)

UPPER converts lowercase text to uppercase text. Non-text characters, such as numbers and punctuation marks, are passed through unaltered.

Spreadsheet examples: =UPPER("Steve") returns STEVE; =UPPER("January 5, 1996") returns JANUARY 5, 1996.

Database example: In a field intended for state abbreviations, UPPER('State') could be used to change all entries to uppercase, such as MN, AZ, and NY.

VAR (Variance)

Format: VAR (number1, number2,...)

Variance is a statistic that shows the distribution of values. The VAR function calculates the population variance from the sample that you provide as arguments. Arguments can include numbers, cell references, or ranges. The square root of the variance is the *standard deviation* (see STDEV).

The formula used to calculate variance is:

$$\sum_{i=1}^{N} \frac{(X_i - \overline{X})^2}{N - 1}$$

Spreadsheet examples: The formula =VAR(12,3,15,7.2,8) returns 21.308; =VAR(125,100,110,115) returns 108.333.

VLOOKUP (Vertical Lookup)

Format: VLOOKUP (lookup value, compare range, offset {, method})

A vertical lookup (VLOOKUP) conducts a lookup based on columns. It searches the leftmost column of the compare range for the specified lookup value. If the lookup condition is met, the column number of the found cell is offset by the amount specified in the offset and the function returns the contents of that cell. An error is returned if the search condition is not satisfied.

Method is optional. Enter **1** to locate the largest value which is less than or equal to the lookup value; enter **-1** to find the smallest value which is greater than or equal to the lookup value; or enter **0** to return only an exact method. If no method is specified, a match of 1 is used. *This is a spreadsheet-only function.*

Spreadsheet example: The worksheet shown in Figure B-4 uses VLOOKUP to choose the proper postage for any weight entered in cell A2. The formula in B2 (where the result is returned) is:

```
=VLOOKUP(IF(TRUNC(A2)=A2,A2,A2+1), C2..D11,1,1)
```

Enter a lookup value here (cell A2)

Result appears here (cell B2)

Compare range

Figure B-4: A VLOOKUP example

The IF function checks the contents of cell A2. If the value in A2 is equal to the truncated value of the same number (i.e., A2 contains a whole number), A2 is used as the lookup value. If A2 contains a fractional portion, an additional ounce (1) is added to it, so A2 +1 is used as the lookup value. (The post office requires that all fractional weights be increased to the next full ounce).

The formula then compares the lookup value to the values in Column C of the worksheet and locates the largest weight value which is less than or equal to the lookup value (as specified by the method entry of 1). It then uses the offset value (the first 1) to return the postage amount from Column D.

WEEKDAY

Format: WEEKDAY (serial number)

The WEEKDAY function extracts the day of the week from any serial number (the number of days since January 1, 1904). WEEKDAY returns a value between 1 and 7, representing the days from Sunday (1) to Saturday (7).

The WEEKDAY function can also be used to return the day of the week from a date in month/day/year format, such as =WEEKDAY(C1), where C1 contains 3/18/96.

Spreadsheet example: The formula =WEEKDAY(33369) returns 6, since 33369 is the serial number for May 12, 1995 (a Friday).

Database examples: The formula DAYNAME(WEEKDAY('Important Date')) returns the name of the day of the week that corresponds with the date entered in the Important Date field. (If the DAYNAME section of this formula is removed, the number of the day of the week is returned rather than the day's name.

WEEKOFYEAR

Format: WEEKOFYEAR (serial number)

The WEEKOFYEAR function calculates the week of the year from a serial number (the number of days since January 1, 1904).

The WEEKOFYEAR function can also be used to extract the week of the year from a date in month/day/year format, such as =WEEKOFYEAR(C1), where C1 contains 3/18/96, for example.

Spreadsheet example: The formula =WEEKOFYEAR(20776) returns 47. (The serial number 20776 represents November 18, 1960, and November 18th fell within the 47th week of the year.)

YEAR

Format: YEAR (serial number)

The YEAR function calculates the year from a serial number (the number of days since January 1, 1904).

The YEAR function can also be used to extract the year from a date in month/day/year format, such as =YEAR(C1), where C1 contains 3/18/96, for example.

Spreadsheet example: The formula =YEAR(20776) returns 1960. (20776 is the serial number for November 18, 1960.)

Index

(continued)

(continued)

Pick Up command, 304
pictograms, 173–174
pictures
    adding to word processing documents, 111–116
    See also graphics; image selections
pie wedge, 273
Play Macro dialog box, 441
playing
    macros, 441
    QuickTime movies, 527–528
    slide shows, 488–489
polygon tool, 273–274
polygons
    drawing and reshaping, 273–274
    preference settings, 417
pop-up menu fields, 197–199
Port format, 337
positioning
    frames, 458
    spreadsheet tables in documents, 390–392
posting newsgroup messages, 601–602
PostScript drawing programs, 316
precedence levels of operators
    in database formulas, 210–211
    in spreadsheet formulas, 143–144
predefined mailing labels, 243–245
preferences, 411–423
    Claris Home Page Lite, 604
    communications, 335–336, 421–423
    default, 412
    document-specific, 412–413
    general, 413–414
    graphics, 416–417
    Netscape Navigator
        browser, 588–590
        Netscape Mail, 591–592
        Netscape News, 599–600
    overview, 411
    palettes, 419–420
    spreadsheet, 418
    text, 414–416
preselected ranges, 184
Presentation Assistant, 406
Print dialog box, 30–31
    spreadsheet modifications, 176–177
printing, 30–32
    database reports, 248–249
    from the desktop, 42–43
    envelopes, 374, 375–376
    mailing labels, 248–249
    specialty papers for, 135
    spreadsheets, 175–176
properties, 472, 474–475
protocols, file transfer, 324
    Kermit, 353–354
    XMODEM, 346, 352, 353
Publish & Subscribe feature, 501–511
    editions, 502
        subscribing to, 503
        updating, 506–507
    example of using, 504–506
    program differences in implementing, 511
    publishers, 501
        canceling, 510
        opening, 508
    publishing an item, 502–503
    subscribers, 502

canceling, 509
    handling large, 510–511
    modifying, 509–510
    setting options, 508–510
Publisher To dialog box, 507
publishers, 501
    canceling, 510
    opening, 508
    See also Publish & Subscribe feature
publishing a Web site, 619–620

Q

QuicKeys utility, 361, 451
QuickHelp, 32–37
QuickTime editors, 316
QuickTime movies, 525–538
    improving playback quality of, 535–537
    inserting into a document, 526–527
    locating missing, 534–535
    obtaining and installing QuickTime, 526
    overview, 525–526
    playback options, 530–531
    playing, 527–528
    resizing movie frames, 529
    selections from, 531–532
    sharing, 535
    slide show options, 488
    storing in the Scrapbook, 533
    upgrading movie capability, 537
quitting
    ClarisWorks program, 38–40
    See also closing
quotes, curly, 415

R

radio buttons fields, 199
RAM disk, 535–537
RAM (Random Access Memory)
    changing the allocation of, 40–41, 313
    disk space vs., 7
    paint environment requirements, 312
ranges, 138–139
    clearing the contents of, 141
    locking, 177–178
    named, 139, 146–150
    preselecting, 184
    transposing, 159–160
    See also cells; spreadsheet
reading e-mail messages, 596, 598
ReadyArt libraries. *See* libraries
recalculating worksheets, 177
reconciling statements, 260–261
record info fields, 204
Record Macro dialog box, 134, 440
recording macros, 439–440
records, 187
    adding, 228
    deleting, 228, 261
    editing data, 228
    entering data, 228
    finding, 231–236

(continued)

my2cents.idgbooks.com

Register This Book — And Win!

Visit **http://my2cents.idgbooks.com** to register this book and we'll automatically enter you in our monthly prize giveaway. It's also your opportunity to give us feedback: let us know what you thought of this book and how you would like to see other topics covered.

Discover IDG Books Online!

The IDG Books Online Web site is your online resource for tackling technology — at home and at the office.

Ten Productive and Career-Enhancing Things You Can Do at www.idgbooks.com

1. Nab source code for your own programming projects.

2. Download software.

3. Read Web exclusives: special articles and book excerpts by IDG Books Worldwide authors.

4. Take advantage of resources to help you advance your career as a Novell or Microsoft professional.

5. Buy IDG Books Worldwide titles or find a convenient bookstore that carries them.

6. Register your book and win a prize.

7. Chat live online with authors.

8. Sign up for regular e-mail updates about our latest books.

9. Suggest a book you'd like to read or write.

10. Give us your 2¢ about our books and about our Web site.

Not on the Web yet? It's easy to get started with *Discover the Internet,* at local retailers everywhere.

Free Gift!